THE *Jane Austen* FILES

THE *Jane Austen* FILES

A Complete Anthology of Letters & Family Recollections

HELEN AMY

AMBERLEY

All images taken from the author's collection.

First published 2015

Amberley Publishing
The Hill, Stroud
Gloucestershire, GL5 4EP

www.amberley-books.com

British Library Cataloguing in Publication Data.
A catalogue record for this book is available from the British Library.

ISBN 978-1-4456-2139-5 (hardback)
ISBN 978-1-4456-2144-9 (ebook)

Typesetting and Origination by Amberley Publishing.
Printed in the UK.

Contents

Chronology of Jane Austen's Life

1764

26 April – Marriage of George Austen and Cassandra Leigh.

1765

13 February – Birth of James Austen.

1766

26 August – Birth of George Austen (the younger).

1767

7 October – Birth of Edward Austen.

1768

July/August – The Austen family moved to Steventon Rectory.

1771

8 June – Birth of Henry Austen.

1773

9 January – Birth of Cassandra Austen (the younger).

2 March – George Austen became the rector of Deane as well as Steventon.

1774

23 April – Birth of Francis Austen.

1775

16 December – Birth of Jane Austen.

1779

23 June – Birth of Charles Austen.

3 July – James Austen matriculated at St John's College, Oxford.

1783

Edward Austen was adopted by Thomas and Catherine Knight.

Spring – Jane, Cassandra and their cousin Jane Cooper went to Oxford to be tutored by Mrs Cawley.

Summer – Mrs Cawley relocated to Southampton where Jane nearly died of putrid fever.

1785

Spring – Jane, Cassandra and Jane Cooper went to Abbey School, Reading.

1786

December – Jane and Cassandra returned home from school. Their father began to tutor them.

1787

Jane began to write her Juvenilia.

1788

1 July – Henry Austen matriculated at St John's College, Oxford.
December – Francis Austen began his naval career.

1790

Spring – James Austen began his clerical career.

1791

27 December – Marriage of Edward Austen and Elizabeth Bridges.

1792

March – Marriage of James Austen and Anne Mathew.
Winter(?) – Engagement of Cassandra Austen and Tom Fowle.

1793

23rd January – Birth of Edward Austen's first child Fanny.
15 April – Birth of James Austen's first child Anna.
Spring – Henry Austen became Lieutenant in Oxfordshire Militia.
3 June – Jane wrote the last item of her Juvenilia.

1794

September – Charles Austen began his naval career.
23 October – Death of Thomas Knight.

1795

Jane probably wrote *Elinor and Marianne* this year.
3 May – Death of James Austen's wife Anne.

1796

October – Jane began to write *First Impressions*.

1797

17 January – Marriage of James Austen and Mary Lloyd.
February – Death of Cassandra's fiancé Tom Fowle in the West Indies.
August – Jane finished *First Impressions*.
November – *First Impressions* was rejected by the publisher Thomas Cadell.
November – Jane began to change *Elinor and Marianne* into *Sense and Sensibility*.
November – Mrs Knight handed over the Knight estates to Edward Austen who moved with his family into Godmersham House.
31 December – Marriage of Henry Austen and Eliza de Feuillide.

1798

August – Jane began the first draft of her novel *Susan* (later *Northanger Abbey*).

9 August – Death of Jane Williams (nee Cooper) in carriage accident.

17 November – Birth of James Austen's son James Edward Austen.

1799

Summer – Jane probably finished the novel *Susan* (*Northanger Abbey*).

14 August – Mrs Leigh Perrot was charged with theft and jailed pending trial.

1800

29 March – Acquittal of Mrs Leigh Perrot.

December – Revd George Austen decided to retire and move to Bath.

1801

January – Henry Austen resigned his commission and set himself up as a banker and Army agent in London.

May – The Austen family left Steventon. James Austen became Rector of Steventon.

End of May – Revd and Mrs Austen, Cassandra and Jane moved into 4 Sydney Place, Bath.

1802

2 December – Jane rejected a proposal of marriage from Harris Bigg-Wither.

Winter – Jane revised *Susan* (*Northanger Abbey*).

1803

Spring – *Susan* (*Northanger Abbey)* was sold to the publisher Richard Crosby of London.

1804

The Watsons was probably written this year.

25 October – Austens moved to 3 Green Park Buildings, Bath

16 December – Death of Mrs Lefroy in a riding accident.

1805

21 January – Death of Revd George Austen.

25 March – Mrs Austen and her daughters moved to 25 Gay Street, Bath.

16 April – Death of Mrs Lloyd, Martha Lloyd joined the Austen household.

18 June – Birth of James Austen's daughter Caroline.

1806

29 January – Mrs Austen, her daughters and Martha Lloyd moved to Trim Street, Bath.

2nd July – Mrs Austen, her daughters and Martha Lloyd left Bath.

24th July – Marriage of Francis Austen and Mary Gibson.

1807

March – Mrs Austen, Cassandra, Jane and Martha Lloyd moved to Southampton and joined households with Francis and Mary Austen.

19 May – Marriage of Charles Austen and Fanny Palmer.

1808

10 October – Death of Edward Austen's wife Elizabeth.

1809

5 April – Jane attempted to get *Susan* (*Northanger Abbey*) published by Richard Crosby, who had bought the manuscript from her in 1803.

7 July – Mrs Austen, Cassandra, Jane and Martha Lloyd moved to Chawton Cottage in Hampshire.

August – Jane began writing again.

1810

Winter – *Sense and Sensibility* was accepted for publication by Thomas Egerton of London.

1811

February – Jane began planning *Mansfield Park*.

30 October – *Sense and Sensibility* was published.

Winter – Jane began to revise *First Impressions* which became *Pride and Prejudice*.

1812

14 October – Death of Mrs Knight. Edward Austen adopted the name of Knight.

Autumn – The copyright of *Pride and Prejudice* was sold to Thomas Egerton.

1813

28 January – *Pride and Prejudice* was published.

25 April – Death of Henry Austen's wife Eliza.

July – Jane finished *Mansfield Park*.

November – *Mansfield Park* was probably accepted for publication.

1814

January – Jane began writing *Emma*.

9 May – *Mansfield Park* was published.

6 September – Death of Charles Austen's wife Fanny.

8 November – Marriage of Anna Austen to Ben Lefroy.

1815

29 March – *Emma* was finished.

8 August – Jane started writing *Persuasion*.

13 November – Jane visited Carlton House, the Prince Regent's residence.

End of December – *Emma* was published.

1816

Spring – Jane's illness began.

Spring – Henry Austen bought back the manuscript of *Susan* (*Northanger Abbey*) which Jane revised.

15 March – Henry Austen's bank failed.

6 August – *Persuasion* was finished.

December – Henry Austen was ordained and became curate of Chawton.

1817

27 January – Jane began to write *Sanditon*.

18 March – Jane ceased writing.

28 March – Death of James Leigh Perrot.

27 April – Jane wrote her Will.

24 May – Cassandra took Jane to Winchester to be near her doctor.

18 July – Death of Jane Austen.

24 July – Jane was buried in Winchester Cathedral.

End of December – *Northanger Abbey* and *Persuasion* were published with the addition of Henry Austen's *Biographical Notice*.

Introduction

Jane Austen, a parson's daughter, who grew up in rural Hampshire in the late eighteenth century, became one of England's greatest novelists. Although her novels sold steadily during her lifetime, she did not stand out among the many novelists of her day. The growth of Austen's literary reputation was a gradual process following her death. In the words of her nephew James Edward Austen-Leigh,

Seldom has any literary reputation been of such slow growth as that of Jane Austen ... To the multitude her works appeared tame and commonplace, poor in colouring, and sadly deficient in incident and interest. It is true that we were sometimes cheered by hearing that a different verdict had been pronounced by more competent judges; we were told how some great statesman or distinguished poet held these works in high estimation; we had the satisfaction of believing that they were most admired by the best judges...But though such golden opinions were now and then gathered in, yet the wide field of public taste yielded no adequate return either in praise or profit. Her reward was not to be the quick return of the cornfield, but the slow growth of the tree which is to endure to another generation.

Among the great poets referred to by Austen-Leigh were Robert Southey, S. T. Coleridge and Walter Scott. The last-named lamented the loss caused by Jane Austen's early death with the words, 'What a pity such a gifted creature died so early.'

The first biographical material on Jane Austen was published by her brother Henry, her literary executor. In 1818 Henry Austen published his sister's two unpublished novels, which he named Northanger Abbey *and* Persuasion, *and included a 'Biographical Notice of the Author'. In 1833 a revised and extended version of this was included in a new edition of the six novels.*

In the early Victorian period Austen's novels were not as popular as the passionate works of Charlotte Brontë, or the social novels of Mrs Gaskell and Charles Dickens. Her works were seen by many as superficial, and Jane herself was regarded as rather prim and prudish. However, in time, her reputation and fame grew to such an extent that, by the 1850s, countless people were flocking to Winchester Cathedral to visit her grave. As there was no indication on the tablet marking Jane Austen's grave that she was a famous author a puzzled verger enquired 'Was there anything particular about that lady?'

Jane Austen's popularity also increased rapidly in other parts of the world. In 1852 Francis Austen, her last surviving sibling, received a letter from a Miss Quincey of Boston, Massachusetts who informed him that Jane's genius was 'extensively recognized' in America. She requested more information on Jane's life than had been published by Henry Austen and also asked for an autograph or a few lines of one of her manuscripts. Francis sent the lucky Miss Quincey one of his sister's letters.

The death of Francis Austen in 1865 prompted the next generation to consider recording their memories of Jane. Her niece Caroline Austen wrote:

The generation who knew her is passing away – but those who are succeeding us must feel an interest in the personal character of their Great Aunt, who has made the family name in some small degree, illustrious.

By this time Jane Austen had been recognised as a great novelist and the public demand for more information about her was growing all the time. Her family recognised the necessity of satisfying this curiosity and Jane's nephew James Edward Austen-Leigh (known as Edward) decided to write a biography of her. His decision was also driven by the fear that someone less qualified may attempt the task and he wanted to have some control over what was published about his aunt.

Austen-Leigh sought the help of his sister, half-sister and cousins in gathering material. Unfortunately, one cousin, Fanny Knatchbull, was not willing to contribute to the biography and could not remember the location of a large number of Jane's letters which were in her possession. Edward set to work with the limited material available to him. A Memoir of Jane Austen *was published in 1869 and, much to the surprise and delight of the author, was well received by both his family and the reading public. This led to a demand for further information on Jane Austen and the unpublished manuscripts which had been mentioned in the biography. A second, extended edition of the Memoir, was therefore published in 1871.*

In 1884 further information about Jane Austen's life and work was published. Two years earlier, when Jane's niece Fanny Knatchbull died, her eldest son Lord Brabourne had discovered the box containing the large number of Jane's letters which had been left to her. As this important source of information had not been available to Edward Austen-Leigh, Lord Brabourne decided to publish these letters with some additional biographical material to fill in the gaps in the Memoir and produce a more complete picture of Jane Austen's life.

Around the turn of the twentieth century a few biographies were written by authors outside Jane's family. These included Jane Austen, Her Homes and Her Friends *by Constance Hill which was published in 1901. Miss Hill visited all the places connected with Jane Austen in order 'to find out all that could be known of her life and its surroundings'. Her artist sister went with her to draw illustrations. The Austen family gave Miss Hill access to various papers and lent her family portraits, pictures and contemporary sketches. The resulting illustrated biography made an excellent addition to the already published material.*

Not long afterwards the next generation of Jane's family published further books on her life. In 1911 a memoir of James Edward Austen-Leigh, which contained information about life in Steventon and Chawton in Jane Austen's day, was published privately by his daughter Mary Augusta Austen-Leigh. She also assisted her brother and her nephew to update the family record using new material including a few unpublished letters. The Life and Letters of Jane Austen, *by William and Richard Arthur Austen-Leigh, was published in 1913 and came to be regarded as the definitive biography. Another book was published in 1920 by Mary Augusta Austen-Leigh.* Personal Aspects of Jane Austen *was written largely to dispel various myths and misconceptions about Jane Austen which the family records had failed to put to rest, and some mistaken new ideas which had emerged.*

These family records and Jane Austen's surviving letters are brought together in this book. It also contains extracts from the diary of her niece Fanny Knight, to whom Jane was particularly close. As well as providing a fascinating insight into the life, works and character of Jane Austen, this book opens a window onto life in late Georgian and Regency England, the England in which she lived and set her novels.

This book is lightly annotated for the general reader who does not need the impediment of heavy academic notes. The editor's notes are added in square brackets within the texts – some are repeated in each text for the benefit of readers who wish to dip into the book rather than read it through.

Incorrect spellings and unconventional use of capital letters in the original texts have not been changed.

1

A Biographical Notice

The first biographical information about Jane Austen was written by her brother Henry, who was said to have been her 'favourite brother'.

Henry had always supported Jane in her writing. He particularly liked her third published novel Mansfield Park, *which he first read in proof form on a long journey from Hampshire to London in March 1814. He acted as his sister's literary representative and negotiated with publishers on her behalf. Henry was so proud of Jane's talent and achievements that he inadvertently revealed the long-kept secret of her authorship.*

Soon after her death in 1817 Henry, as his sister's literary executor, began to prepare her two unpublished novels for the press. These novels, her first and last written works, he named Northanger Abbey *and* Persuasion. *They were published in 1818 by John Murray of Albemarle Street, London and included the following* Biographical Notice of the Author *by Henry Austen. It was in this* Notice *that Jane Austen was revealed as the author of her six novels, which were all published without giving her name on the title page.*

Henry depicted Jane's life as quiet, happy and uneventful, a view not shared by some later biographers. Henry's portrayal of his sister seems too good to be true. According to him, not only was she physically attractive, of cheerful and benevolent disposition, and 'faultless', but she was also said to have been a modest 'genius' who became an author through 'taste and inclination' rather than for fame or profit. Henry stated that Jane's 'most important trait' was her devout and sincere Christianity.

BIOGRAPHICAL NOTICE OF THE AUTHOR HENRY AUSTEN (1818)

The following pages are the production of a pen which has already contributed in no small degree to the entertainment of the public. And when the public, which has not been insensible to the merits of *Sense and Sensibility, Pride and Prejudice, Mansfield Park,* and *Emma,* shall be informed that the hand which guided that pen is now mouldering in the grave, perhaps a brief account of Jane Austen will be read with a kindlier sentiment than simple curiosity.

Short and easy will be the task of the mere biographer. A life of usefulness, literature, and religion, was not by any means a life of event. To those who lament their irreparable loss, it is consolatory to think that, as she never deserved disapprobation, so, in the circle of her family and friends, she never met reproof, that her wishes were not only reasonable, but gratified; and that to the little disappointments incidental to human life was never added, even for a moment, an abatement of good-will from any who knew her.

Jane Austen was born on the 16th December, 1775, at Steventon, in the county of Hants. Her father was Rector of that parish upwards of forty years. There he resided, in the conscientious and unassisted discharge of his ministerial duties, until he was turned of seventy years. Then he retired with his wife, our authoress, and her sister, to Bath, for the remainder of his life, a period of about four years. Being not only a profound scholar, but possessing a most exquisite taste in every species of literature, it is not wonderful that his daughter Jane should, at a very early age, have become sensible to the charms of style, and enthusiastic in the cultivation of her own language. On the death of her father she removed, with her mother and sister, for a short time, to Southampton, and finally, in 1809, to the pleasant village of Chawton, in the same county. From this place she sent forth into the world those novels, which by many have been placed on the same shelf as the works of a D'Arblay [Fanny Burney] and an Edgeworth [Maria Edgeworth]. Some of these novels had been the gradual performances of her previous life. For though in composition she was equally rapid and correct, yet an invincible distrust of her own judgement induced her to withhold her works from the public, till time and many perusals had satisfied her that the charm of recent composition was dissolved. The natural constitution, the regular habits, the quiet and happy occupations of our authoress, seemed to promise a long succession of amusement to the public, and a gradual increase of reputation to herself. But the symptoms of a decay, deep and incurable, began to shew themselves in the commencement of 1816. Her decline was at first deceitfully slow; and until the spring of this present year, those who knew their happiness to be involved in her existence could not endure to despair. But in the month of May, 1817, it was found advisable that she should be removed to Winchester for the benefit of constant medical aid, which none even then dared to hope would be permanently beneficial. She supported, during two months, all the varying pain, irksomeness, and tedium, attendant on decaying nature, with more than resignation, with a truly elastic cheerfulness. She retained her faculties, her memory, her fancy, her temper, and her affections, warm, clear, and unimpaired, to the last. Neither her love of God, nor of her fellow creatures flagged for a moment. She made a point of receiving the sacrament before excessive bodily weakness might have rendered her perception unequal to her wishes. She wrote whilst she could hold a pen, and with a pencil when a pen became too laborious. The day preceding her death she composed some stanzas replete with fancy and vigour. Her last voluntary speech conveyed thanks to her medical attendant; and to the final question asked of her, purporting to know her wants, she replied, "I want nothing but death."

She expired shortly after, on Friday the 18th July, 1817, in the arms of her sister, who, as well as the relator of these events, feels too surely that they shall never look upon her like again.

Jane Austen was buried on the 24th July, 1817, in the cathedral church of Winchester, which, in the whole catalogue of its mighty dead, does not contain the ashes of a brighter genius or a sincerer Christian.

Of personal attractions she possessed a considerable share. Her stature was that of true elegance. It could not have been increased without exceeding the middle height. Her carriage and deportment were quiet, yet graceful. Her features were separately good. Their assemblage produced an unrivalled expression of that cheerfulness, sensibility, and benevolence, which were her real characteristics. Her complexion was of the finest texture. It might with truth be said, that her eloquent blood spoke through her modest cheek. Her voice was extremely sweet. She delivered herself with fluency and precision. Indeed she was formed for elegant and rational society, excelling in conversation as much as in composition. In the present age it is hazardous to mention accomplishments. Our authoress would, probably, have been inferior to few in such acquirements, had she not been so superior to most in higher things. She had not only an excellent taste for drawing, but, in her earlier days, evinced great power of hand in the management of the pencil. Her own musical attainments she held very cheap. Twenty years ago they would have been thought more of, and twenty years hence many a parent will expect their daughters to be applauded for meaner performances. She was fond of dancing, and excelled in it. It remains now to add a few observations on that which her friends deemed more important, on those endowments which sweetened every hour of their lives.

If there be an opinion current in the world, that perfect placidity of temper is not reconcileable [*sic*] to the most lively imagination, and the keenest relish for wit, such an opinion will be rejected for ever by those who have had the happiness of knowing the authoress of the following works. Though the frailties, foibles, and follies of others could not escape her immediate detection, yet even on their vices did she never trust herself to comment with unkindness. The affectation of candour is not uncommon; but she had no affectation. Faultless herself, as nearly as human nature can be, she always sought, in the faults of others, sometimes to excuse, to forgive or forget. Where extenuation was impossible, she had sure refuge in silence. She never uttered either a hasty, a silly, or a severe expression. In short, her temper was as polished as her wit. Nor were her manners inferior to her temper. They were of the happiest kind. No one could be often in her company without feeling a strong desire of obtaining her friendship, and cherishing a hope of having obtained it. She was tranquil without reserve or stiffness; and communicative without intrusion or self-sufficiency. She became an authoress entirely from taste and inclination. Neither the hope of fame nor profit mixed with her early motives. Most of her works, as before observed, were composed many years previous to their publication. It was with extreme difficulty that her friends, whose partiality she suspected whilst she honoured their judgement, could prevail on her to publish her first work. Nay, so persuaded was she that its sale would not repay the cost of publication, that she actually made a reserve from her very modest income to meet the expected loss. She could scarcely believe what she termed her great good fortune when 'Sense and Sensibility' produced a clear profit of £150. Few so gifted were so truly unpretending. She regarded the above sum as a prodigious recompense for that which had cost her nothing. Her readers, perhaps, will wonder that such a work produced so little at a time when some authors have received more guineas than they have written lines. The works of our authoress, however, may live as long as those which have burst on the world with more éclat. But the public has not been unjust; and our authoress was far from thinking it so. Most gratifying to her was the applause which from time to time reached her ears from those who were competent to discriminate. Still, in spite of such applause, so much did she shrink from notoriety, that no accumulation of fame would have induced her, had she lived, to affix her name to any productions of her pen. In the bosom of her own family she talked of them freely, thankful for praise, open to remark, and submissive to criticism. But in public she turned away from any allusion to the character of an authoress. She read aloud with very great taste and effect. Her own works, probably, were never heard to so much advantage as from her own mouth; for she partook largely in all the best gifts of the comic muse. She was a warm and judicious admirer of landscape, both in nature and on canvass [*sic*]. At a very early age she was enamoured of Gilpin [William Gilpin, artist and one of the originators of the idea of the 'picturesque'] on the Picturesque; and she seldom changed her opinions either on books or men.

Her reading was very extensive in history and belles lettres; and her memory extremely tenacious. Her favourite moral writers were [Samuel] Johnson in prose, and [William] Cowper in verse. It is difficult to say at what age she was not intimately acquainted with the merits and defects of the best essays and novels in the English language. [Samuel] Richardson's power of creating, and preserving the consistency of his characters, as particularly exemplified in 'Sir Charles Grandison', gratified the natural discrimination of her mind, whilst her taste secured her from the errors of his prolix style and tedious narrative. She did not rank any work of [Henry] Fielding quite so high. Without the slightest affectation she recoiled from anything gross. Neither nature, wit, nor humour, could make her amends for so very low a scale of morals.

Her power of inventing characters seems to have been intuitive, and almost unlimited. She drew from nature; but, whatever may have been surmised to the contrary, never from individuals.

The style of her familiar correspondence was in all respects the same as that of her novels. Every thing came finished from her pen; for on all subjects she had ideas as clear as her expressions were well chosen. It is not hazarding too much to say that she never dispatched a note or letter unworthy of publication.

One trait only remains to be touched on. It makes all others unimportant. She was thoroughly religious and devout; fearful of giving offence to God; and incapable of feeling it towards any fellow creature. On serious subjects she was well instructed, both by reading and meditation, and her opinions accorded strictly with those of our Established Church.
London, Dec. 13, 1817

Postscript

Since concluding the above remarks, the writer of them has been put in possession of some extracts from the private correspondence of the authoress. They are few and short; but are submitted to the public without apology, as being more truly descriptive of her temper, taste, feelings and principles than anything which the pen of a biographer can produce.

The first extract is a playful defence of herself from a mock charge of having pilfered the manuscripts of a young relation.

'What should I do, my dearest E. with your manly, vigorous sketches, so full of life and spirit? How could I possibly join them on to a little bit of ivory, two inches wide, on which I work with a brush so fine as to produce little effect after much labour?'

The remaining extracts are from various parts of a letter written a few weeks before her death.

'My attendant is encouraging, and talks of making me quite well. I live chiefly on the sofa, but am allowed to walk from one room to the other. I have been out once in a sedan-chair, and am to repeat it, and be promoted to a wheel-chair as the weather serves. On this subject I will only say further that my dearest sister, my tender, watchful, indefatigable nurse, has not been made ill by her exertions. As to what I owe her, and to the anxious affection of all my beloved family on this occasion, I can only cry over it, and pray to God to bless them more and more.'

She next touches with just and gentle animadversion on a subject of domestic disappointment. Of this the particulars do not concern the public. Yet in justice to her characteristic sweetness and resignation, the concluding observation of our authoress must not be suppressed.

'But I am getting too near complaint. It has been the appointment of God, however secondary causes may have operated.'

The following and final extract will prove the facility with which she could correct every impatient thought, and turn from complaint to cheerfulness.

'You will find Captain ______ a very respectable, well-meaning man, without much manner, his wife and sister all good humour and obligingness, and I hope (since the fashion allows it) with rather longer petticoats than last year.'

London, Dec. 20, 1817

2

A Memoir of Miss Austen

In 1833 Richard Bentley of New Burlington Street, London published all six of Jane Austen's novels in his series of one volume 'Standard Novels'. His edition of Sense and Sensibility *included the following* Memoir of Miss Austen, *a revised and extended version of Henry Austen's* Biographical Notice of the Author *published in1818. This was included by Bentley in further editions of* Sense and Sensibility *up until 1869, when he published the first biography of Jane Austen.*

The first part of this Memoir *was substantially the same as the earlier* Notice, *except for some changes to the wording and a few additional anecdotes. To make up for the absence of material for a more detailed account of Jane's life, Henry added excerpts from articles on her novels published by two critical journals. The first of these articles drew attention to Jane Austen's mastery in depicting human character and the second emphasised the unobtrusive Christianity which underpinned her writing. By including these articles in his* Memoir *Henry Austen influenced the way the novels were viewed in the Victorian period.*

A MEMOIR OF MISS AUSTEN
HENRY AUSTEN
(1833)

Jane Austen was born on the 16th December, 1775, at Steventon, in the county of Hants. Her father was rector of that parish upward of forty years. There he resided in the conscientious and unassisted discharge of his ministerial duties until he was turned of seventy years. Then he retired with his wife, our authoress, and her sister, to Bath, for the remainder of his life, a period of about four years. Being not only a profound scholar, but possessing a most exquisite taste in every species of literature, it is not wonderful that his daughter Jane should, at a very early age, have become sensible to the charms of style, and enthusiastic in the cultivation of her own language. On the death of her father, she removed, with her mother and sister for a short time, to Southampton; and finally, in 1809, to the pleasant village of Chawton in the same county. From this place she sent her novels into the world. Some of them had been the gradual performances of her previous life; for though in composition she was equally rapid and correct, yet an invincible distrust of her own judgement induced her to withhold her works from the public, till time and many perusals had satisfied her that the charm of recent composition was dissolved. The natural constitution, the regular habits, the quiet and happy occupations of our authoress, seemed to promise a long succession of amusement to the public, and a gradual increase of reputation to herself. But the symptoms of a decay, deep and incurable, began to show themselves in the commencement of 1816. Her decline was at first deceitfully slow; but in the month of May,1817, it was found advisable that she should be removed to Winchester for the benefit of constant medical aid, which none, even then, dared to hope would be permanently beneficial. She supported, during two months, all the varying pain, irksomeness, and tedium, attendant on decaying nature, with more than resignation – with a truly elastic cheerfulness. She retained her faculties, her memory, her fancy, her temper, and her affections, warm, clear, and unimpaired, to the last. Her last voluntary speech conveyed thanks to her medical attendant; and to the final question asked of her, purporting to know her wants, she replied, 'I want nothing but death.' She expired shortly after, on Friday, the 18th July, 1817, in the arms of her sister; and was buried, on the 24th of the same month, in the cathedral church of Winchester.

Of personal attractions she possessed a considerable share; her stature rather exceeded the middle height; her carriage and deportment were quiet, but graceful; her features were separately good; their assemblage produced an unrivalled expression of that cheerfulness, sensibility, and benevolence, which were her real characteristics; her complexion was of the finest texture – it might with truth be said, that her eloquent blood spoke through her modest cheek; her voice was sweet; she delivered herself with fluency and precision; indeed, she was formed for elegant and rational society, excelling in conversation as much as in composition. In the present age it is hazardous to mention accomplishments; our authoress would probably have been inferior to few in such acquirements, had she not been so superior to most, in higher things.

It remains to make a few observations on that which her friends deemed more important, on those endowments which sweetened every hour of their lives. If there be an opinion current in the world that a perfectly amiable temper is not reconcilable to a lively imagination, and a keen relish for wit, such an opinion will be rejected for ever by those who had the happiness of knowing the authoress of the following work. Though the frailties, foibles and follies of others, could not escape her immediate detection, yet even on their vices did she never trust herself to comment with unkindness. The affectation of candour is not uncommon, but she had no affectation. Faultless herself, as nearly as human nature can be, she always sought, in the faults of others, something to excuse, to forgive, or forget. Where extenuation was impossible, she had a sure refuge in silence. She never uttered either a hasty, a silly, or a severe expression. In short, her temper was as polished as her wit; and no one could be often in her company without feeling a strong desire of obtaining her friendship, and cherishing a hope of having obtained it. She became an authoress entirely from taste and inclination. Neither the hope of fame nor profit mixed with her early motives. It was with extreme difficulty that her friends, whose partiality she suspected, whilst she honoured their judgment, could persuade her to publish her first work. Nay, so persuaded was she that the sale would not repay the expense of publication, that she actually made a reserve from her moderate income to meet the expected loss. She could scarcely believe what she termed her great good fortune, when 'Sense and Sensibility' produced a clear profit of about £150. Few so gifted were so truly unpretending. She regarded the above sum as a prodigious recompense for that which had cost her nothing. Her readers, perhaps, will wonder that such a work produced so little, at a time when some authors have received more guineas than they have written lines. But the public has not been unjust; and our authoress was far from thinking it so. Most gratifying to her was the applause which from time to time reached her ears from those who were competent to discriminate. When 'Pride and Prejudice' made its appearance, a gentleman, celebrated for his literary attainments, advised a friend of the authoress to read it, adding, with more point than gallantry, 'I should like to know who is the author, for it is much too clever to have been written by a woman.' Still, in spite of such applause, so much did she shrink from notoriety, that no increase of fame would have induced her, had she lived, to affix her name to any productions of her pen. In the bosom of her family she talked of them freely; thankful for praise, open to remark, and submissive to criticism. But in public she turned away from any allusion to the character of an authoress. In proof of this, the following circumstance, otherwise unimportant, is stated. Miss Austen was on a visit to London shortly after the publication of 'Mansfield Park': a nobleman, personally unknown to her, but who had good reasons to consider her the authoress of that work, was desirous of her joining a literary circle at his house. He communicated his wish in the politest manner, through a mutual friend, adding, what his Lordship doubtless thought would be an irresistible inducement, that the celebrated Madame de Stael [French woman of letters] would be of the party. Miss Austen immediately declined the invitation. To her truly delicate mind such a display would have given pain instead of pleasure.

Her power of inventing characters seems to have been intuitive, and almost unlimited. She drew from nature, but, whatever may have been surmised to the contrary, never from individuals. The style of her familiar correspondence was in all respects the same as that of her novels. Everything came finished from her pen; for on all subjects she had ideas as clear as her expressions were well chosen. It is not too much to say that she never dispatched a note or letter unworthy of publication. The following few short extracts from her private correspondence are submitted to the public without apology, as being more truly descriptive of her temper, taste and feelings, than anything which the pen of a biographer can produce. The first is a playful defence of herself from a mock charge of having pilfered the manuscripts of a young relation. 'What should I do, my dearest E., with your manly, vigorous sketches, so full of life and spirit? How could I possibly join them on to a little bit of ivory, two inches wide, on which I work with a brush so fine, as to produce little effect after much labour?' The remaining extracts are from a letter written a few weeks before her death. 'My medical attendant is encouraging, and talks of making me quite well. I live chiefly on the sofa, but am allowed to walk from one room to the other. I have been out in a sedan chair, and am to repeat it, and be promoted to a wheel-chair as the weather serves. On this subject I will only say farther, that my dearest sister, my tender, watchful, indefatigable nurse, has not been made ill by her exertions. As to what I owe her, and to the anxious affection of all my beloved family on this occasion, I can only cry over it, and pray to God to bless them more and more.' She next touches with just and gentle animadversion on a subject of domestic disappointment. Of this, the particulars do not concern the public. Yet, in justice to her characteristic sweetness and resignation, the concluding observation of our authoress thereon must not be suppressed. 'But I am getting too near complaint. It has been the appointment of God, however secondary causes may have operated.'

The above brief biographical sketch has been, in substance, already published with Miss Austen's posthumous novels. It is a matter of deep regret to the writer, that materials for a more detailed account of so talented a woman cannot be obtained; therefore as a tribute to her memory, he subjoins the following extracts from a critical journal of the highest reputation [*The Athenaeum*]:–

'Unlike that of many writers, Miss Austen's fame has grown fastest since she died: there was no éclat about her first appearance: the public took time to make up its mind; and she, not having staked her hopes of happiness on success or failure, was content to wait for the decision of her claims.

Those claims have long been established beyond a question; but the merit of *first* recognizing them belongs less to reviewers than to general readers. So retired, so unmarked by literary notoriety, was the life Miss Austen led, that if any likeness was ever taken of her, none has ever been engraved [1]. With regard to her genius we must adventure a few remarks. She herself compares her productions to a little bit of ivory, two inches wide, worked upon with a brush so fine, that little effect is produced after much labour. It is so: her portraits are perfect likenesses, admirably finished, many of them gems, but it is all miniature painting; and, satisfied with being inimitable in one line, she never essayed canvass [*sic*] and oils; never tried her hands at a majestic daub. Her 'two inches of ivory' just describes her preparations for a tale of three volumes. A village – two families connected together – three or four interlopers, out of whom are to spring a little tracasserie; – and by means of village or country town visiting and gossiping a real plot shall thicken, and its 'rear of darkness' never be scattered till six pages off *finis*. The plots are simple in construction, and yet intricate in development; – the main characters, those that the reader feels sure are to love, marry, and make mischief, are introduced in the first or second chapter; the work is all done by half a dozen people; no person, scene, or sentence, is ever introduced needless to the matter in hand: – no catastrophes, or discoveries, or surprises of a grand nature are allowed – neither children nor fortunes are lost or found by accident – the mind is never taken off the level surface of life – the reader breakfasts, dines, walks, and gossips, with the various worthies, till a process of transmutation takes place in him, and he absolutely fancies himself one of the company. Yet the winding up of the plot involves a surprise: a few incidents are entangled at the beginning in the most simple and natural manner, and till the close one never feels quite sure how they are to be disentangled. Disentangled, however, they are, and that in a most satisfactory manner. The secret is, Miss Austen was a thorough mistress in the knowledge of human character; how it is acted upon by education and circumstance; and how, when once formed, it shows itself through every hour of every day, and in every speech to every person. Her conversations would be tiresome but for this ; and her personages, the fellows to whom may be met in the streets, or drank tea with at half an hour's notice, would excite no interest; but in Miss Austen's hands we see into their hearts and hopes, their motives, their struggles within themselves; and a sympathy is induced, which, if extended to daily life, and the world at large, would make the reader a more amiable person; and we must think it that reader's own fault who does not close her pages with more charity in his heart towards unpretending, if prosing, worth; with a higher estimation of simple kindness, and sincere good-will; with a quickened sense of the duty of bearing and forbearing, in domestic intercourse, and of the pleasure of adding to the little comforts even of persons who are neither wits not beauties, – who, in a word, does not feel more disposed to be benevolent. In the last posthumous tale ("Persuasion") there is a strain of a higher mood; there is still the exquisite delineation of common life, such life as we hear, and see, and make part of, with the addition of a finer, more poetic, yet equally real tone of thought and actions in the principals. If Miss Austen was sparing in her introduction of nobler characters, it was because they are scattered sparingly in life. Her death has made a chasm in our light literature – the domestic novel, with its home-born incidents, its "familiar matter of to-day," its slight array of names, and great cognisance of people and things, its confinement to country life, and total oblivion of costume, manners, the great world, and "the mirror of fashion." Every species of composition is, when good, to be admired in its way;but the revival of the domestic novel would make a pleasant interlude to the showy, sketchy novels of high life.

'Miss Austen has the merit (in our judgment most essential) of being evidently a Christian writer: a merit which is much enhanced, both on the score of good taste and of practical utility, by her religion being not at all obtrusive. She might defy the most fastidious critic to call any of her novels (as Coelebs [character in a moral novel by Hannah More] was designated) a dramatic sermon. The subject is rather alluded to, and that incidentally, than studiously brought forward and dwelt upon. In fact, she is more sparing of it than would be thought desirable by some persons; perhaps even by herself, had she consulted merely her own sentiments; but she probably introduced it as far as she thought would be generally profitable; for when the purpose of inculcating a religious principle is made too palpably prominent, many readers, if they do not throw aside the book with disgust, are apt to fortify themselves with that respectful kind of apathy with which they undergo a regular sermon, and prepare themselves as they do to swallow a dose of medication, endeavouring to get it down in large gulps, without tasting it more than is necessary.'

Perhaps these volumes may be perused by some readers who will feel a solicitude respecting the authoress, extending beyond the perishable qualities of temper, manners, taste, and talents. – We can assure all such (and the being able to do so gratifies us more than the loudest voice of human praise) that Jane Austen's hopes of immortality were built upon the Rock of ages. That she deeply felt, and devoutly acknowledged, the insignificance of all worldly attainments, and the worthlessness of all human services, in the eyes of her heavenly Father. That she had no other hope of mercy, pardon, and peace, but through the merits and sufferings of her Redeemer.

October 5 1832

1. No [professional] likeness ever was taken of Miss Austen; which the editor much laments, as he is thereby precluded from the gratification of prefixing her portrait to this edition.

3

A Niece's Recollections

Jane Anna Elizabeth Austen (known as Anna) was the daughter of Jane Austen's eldest brother James and his first wife Anne. Anna was close to her aunt from the age two, when her mother died and her father sent her to be comforted and cared for by her grandparents and aunts at Steventon Rectory. Jane spent a lot of time with Anna and helped her in her attempt to write a novel. She became a trusted confidante and advisor to her motherless niece. Anna was twenty-four when her aunt died in 1817.

In the 1860s Edward Austen-Leigh decided to write a biography of Jane Austen and asked his half-sister Anna to record her memories for him to include. The following letter, written when Anna was seventy-one years old, contains her contribution to the biography.

Although Anna protested that her memories were few and vague, she produced some interesting recollections of Jane Austen from both the early and late periods of her life, which were spent in Hampshire. She recalled that her aunt was a great favourite with children and that, unsurprisingly, she was a good storyteller. She remembered both the fun and laughter which she shared with her aunt and the more serious side of her character.

RECOLLECTIONS OF AUNT JANE
ANNA LEFROY
(1864)

Southern Hill,
Reading
Decr 1864

My dear Edward

You have asked me to put on paper my recollections of Aunt Jane, & to do so would be, both on your account & her's a labour of love if I had but a sufficiency of material.

I am sorry to say that my reminiscences are few; surprisingly so, considering how much I saw of her in childhood, & how much intercourse we had in later years. I look back to the first period but find little that I can grasp of any substance, or certainty: it seems now all so shadowy! I recollect the frequent visits of my two Aunts, & how they walked in wintry weather through the sloppy lane between Steventon and Dean in pattens [a protective clog], usually worn at that time even by Gentlewomen. I remember too their bonnets: because though precisely alike in colour, shape and material, I made it a pleasure to guess, & I believe always guessed right, which bonnet & which Aunt belonged to each other – Children do not think of Aunts, or perhaps of any grown-up people as young; yet at the time to which I now refer my Aunts must have been very young women – even a little later, when I might be 9 or 10 yrs old I thought it so very odd, to hear Grandpapa speak of them as 'the Girls'. 'Where are the Girls?' 'Are the Girls gone out?'

At the time of my birth Aunt Jane was not much over 17 – She was thus entered in the family Bible in her Father's hand writing. A very good clear hand he wrote, by the by. 'Jane Austen born 16 Decr. 1775. Privately baptised 17 Decr. 1775. Rec^{d}. Into the Church 5 Ap^{l}. 1776 Sponsors Revd. Mr. Cooke, Rector of Bookham Surry, Mrs. Jane Austen of Sevenoaks Kent, Father's Uncle's Wife, M^{rs}. Musgrave of Chinnor, Oxon.'

Aunt Jane was the general favorite [sic] *with children; her ways with them being so playful, & and her long circumstantial stories so delightful! These were continued from time to time, & begged for of course at all possible or impossible occasions; woven, as she proceeded out of nothing, but her own happy talents for invention. Ah! If but one of them could be now recovered!*

Other things have been even more completely obliterated – I have been told that one of her earliest Novels (Pride & Prejudice) was read aloud (in M.S. of course) in the Parsonage at Dean, whilst I was in the room, & not expected to listen – Listen however I did, with so much interest, & with so much talk afterwards about 'Jane & Elizabeth' that it was resolved, for prudence sake, to read no more of the story in my hearing. This was related to me years afterwards, when the Novel had been published; & it was supposed that the names might recall to my recollection that early impression. Such however did not prove to be the case. Something you may expect me to say of our Aunt's personal appearance, though in the latter years of her life it must be as well remembered by you as by me. The Figure tall & slight, but not drooping; well balanced, as was proved by her quick firm step. Her complexion of that rather rare sort which seems the peculiar property of light brunettes. A mottled skin, not fair, but perfectly clear & healthy in hue; the fine naturally curling hair, neither light nor dark; the bright hazel eyes to match, & the rather small but well shaped nose. One hardly understands how with all these advantages she could yet fail of being a decidedly handsome woman.

I have intimated that of the two Sisters Aunt Jane was generally the favorite with children, but with the young people of Godmersham it was not so. They liked her indeed as a playfellow, & as a teller of stories, but they were not really fond of her. I believe that their Mother was not, at least that she very much preferred the elder Sister. A little talent went a long way with Goodneston Bridgeses of that period; & much must have gone a long way too far. This preference lasted for a good while, nor do I think that there was ever any abatement in the love of that family for Aunt Cassandra. Time however brought, as it always does bring, new impressions or modifications of the old ones. Owing to particular circumstances there grew up during the latter years of Aunt Jane's life a great & affectionate intimacy between herself & the eldest of her nieces; & I suppose there a [sic] *few now living who can more fully appreciate the talent or revere the memory of Aunt Jane than Lady Knatchbull [Fanny Knight]. This has brought me to the period of my own greatest share of intimacy; the two years before my marriage, & the two or three years after, when we lived, as you know almost close to Chawton when the original 17 years between us seemed to shrink to 7 – or to nothing. It comes back to me now how strangely I missed her; it had become so much a habit with me to put by things in my mind with a reference to her and to say to myself, 'I shall keep this for Aunt Jane.' It was my great amusement during one summer visit at Chawton to procure Novels from a circulating Library at Alton, & after running them over to relate the stories to Aunt Jane. I may say it was her amusement also, as she sat busily stitching away at a work of charity, in which I fear I took myself no more useful part. Greatly we both enjoyed it, one piece of absurdity leading to another, till Aunt Cassan[dr]a fatigued with her own share of laughter wd. exclaim 'How* can *you both be so foolish?' & beg us to leave off – One of these Novels, written by a Mrs. Hunter of Norwich, was an exceedingly lengthy affair; there was no harm in the book, except in a most unaccountable manner the same story about the same people, most of whom I think had died before the real story began was repeated 3 or 4 times over. A copy of the note written a few weeks afterwards, in reply to one from 'Mrs. Hunter' will give you some idea of the state of the case.*

'Miss Jane Austen begs her best thanks may be conveyed to Mrs. Hunter of Norwich for the Threadpapers which she has been so kind as to send her by Mr. Austen, & which will be always very valuable on account of the spirited sketches (made it is supposed by Nicholson or Glover [landscape painters]) of the most interesting spots, Tarefield Hall, the Mill, & above all the Tomb of Howard's wife, of the faithful representation of which Miss Jane Austen is undoubtedly a good judge having spent so many summers at Tarefield Abbey the delighted guest of the worthy Mrs. Wilson. Miss Jane Austen's tears have flowed over each sweet sketch in such a way as would do Mrs. Hunter's heart

good to see; if Mrs. Hunter could understand all Miss Austen's interest in the subject she would certainly have the kindness to publish at least 4 vols more about the Flint family, & especially would give many fresh particulars on that part of it which Mrs H. has hitherto handled too briefly; viz, the history of Mary Flint's marriage with Howard.

Miss Austen cannot close this small epitome of the miniature abridgement of her thanks & admiration without expressing her sincere hope that Mrs. Hunter is provided at Norwich with a more safe conveyance to London than Alton can now boast, as the Car of Falkenstein which was the pride of that Town was overturned within the last 10 days.'

The Car of Falkenstein, Collier's, but at that time called Falkner's Coach, relates to some earlier nonsense.

Her unusually quick sense of the ridiculous inclined her to play with the trifling commonplaces of everyday life, whether as regarded people or things; but she never played with it's serious duties or responsibilities – when grave she was very *grave; I am not sure but that Aunt Cassandra's disposition was the most equally cheerful of the two. Their affection for each other was extreme; it passed the common love of sisters; and it had been so from childhood. My Grandmother talking to me once [of] by gone times, & of that particular time when my Aunts were placed at the Reading Abbey School, said that Jane was too young to make her going to school at all necessary, but it was her own doing; she* would *go with Cassandra; 'if Cassandra's head had been going to be cut off Jane would have her's cut off too' –*

They must however have been separated sometimes as Cassandra in her childhood was a good deal with Dr. and Mrs. Cooper [her aunt] at Bath – She once described to me her return to Steventon one fine summer evening. The Coopers had sent or conveyed her a good part of the journey, but my grandfather had to go, I think as far as Andover to meet her – He might have conveyed himself by Coach, but he brought his Daughter home in a Hack chaise; & almost home they were when they met Jane & Charles, the two little ones of the family, who had got as far as New down to meet the chaise, & have the pleasure of riding home in it; but who first spied the chaise tradition does not say, whether such happiness were the lawful property of Jane or Charles will never exactly be understood.

I have come to the end of my traditional lore, as well as of my personal recollections, & I am sorry that both should be so meagre & unsatisfactory; but if this attempt should incline others to do the same, even if no more, the contributions when put together may furnish a memorial of some value. You must have it in your own power to write something; & Caroline, though her recollections cannot go back as far even as your's, is, I know acquainted with some particulars of interest in the life of our Aunt; they relate to circumstances of which I never had any knowledge, but were communicated to her by the best of then living authorities, Aunt Cassandra – There may be other sources of information, if we could get at them – Letters may have been preserved, & this is the more probable as Aunt Jane's talent for letter writing was so much valued & thought so delightful amongst her own family circle.

Such gleanings however are not likely to fall to our share, & we must content ourselves, I fear, with our own reminiscences.

Believe me d[r]. Edw[d]
y[r]. affect: Sister
J. A. E. Lefroy

4

A Niece's Memoir

Caroline Mary Craven Austen was the daughter of James Austen and his second wife Mary. She enjoyed an affectionate relationship with her aunt and was a frequent visitor to Chawton Cottage, where Jane Austen spent the last years of her life.

In the 1860s when Edward Austen-Leigh asked Caroline to contribute her memories to his proposed biography she readily agreed to help. She appreciated the importance of preserving memories of their 'illustrious' aunt for future generations of the family and for the benefit of the increasing numbers of her readers.

Although Caroline was only twelve years old when Jane Austen died her powers of recall were excellent and she was able to provide her brother with a considerable amount of material. As well as her own recollections Caroline also remembered much that her mother had told her about Jane and she possessed her mother's pocket-books which contained some written memories.

Caroline added much to the memories already provided by Anna. She supplied further information about Jane's appearance, character and qualities as an aunt. She drew a picture of domestic happiness and unusual harmony within the Austen family, but also hinted at family troubles.

Caroline's detailed descriptions of Chawton Cottage and how her aunt passed her time there must have been particularly useful to Edward. She also revealed how secretive Jane was about her writing and told the story of how Emma *came to be dedicated to the Prince Regent. Caroline provided information on Jane's illness, her final days in Winchester and her death, all of which was used in the biography.*

These memories were published in 1952 by the Jane Austen Society as My Aunt Jane Austen: A Memoir *with a preface by the scholar R. W. Chapman.*

MY AUNT JANE AUSTEN: A MEMOIR CAROLINE AUSTEN (1867)

A memoir of Miss Jane Austen has often been asked for, and strangers have declared themselves willing and desirous to undertake the task of writing it – and have wondered that the family have refused to supply the necessary materials. But tho' none of her nearest relatives desired that the details of a very private and rather uneventful life should be laid before the world yet I think they would not willingly have let her memory die – and it *will* die and be lost, if no effort is made to preserve it –The grass grave in the village churchyard sinks down in a few years to the common level, and its place is no more to be found and so, to keep the remembrance of the departed a little longer in the world which they have left, we lay a stone over their graves, and inscribe upon it their name and age, and perhaps some few words of their virtues and of our own sorrow – and tho' the stone moulders and tho' the letters fade away, yet do they outlast the interest of *what* they record –We remember our dead always – but when *we* shall have joined them their memory may be said to have perished out of the earth, for no distinct idea of them remains behind, and the next generation soon forget that they ever existed –

For most of us therefore the memorial on the perishing tombstone is enough – and *more* than enough – it will tell its tale longer than anyone will care to read it – But not so for all – Every country has had its great men, whose lives have been and are still read – with unceasing interest; and so, in *some* families there has been *one* distinguished by talent or goodness, and known far beyond the home circle, whose memory ought to be preserved through more than a single generation – Such a one was my Aunt – Jane Austen –

Since her death, the public voice has placed her in the first rank of the Novellists [*sic*] of her day – given her, I may say, the first place amongst them – and it seems but right that *some* record should remain with *us* of her life and character; and that *she* herself should not be forgotten by her nearest descendants, whilst her writings still *live*, and are still spreading her fame wherever the English books are read – Her last long surviving Brother has recently died at the age of 91 – The generation who knew her is passing away – but those who are succeeding us must feel an interest in the personal character of their Great Aunt, who has made the family name in some small degree, illustrious – For *them* therefore, and for my own gratification I will try to call back my recollections of what she *was*, and what manner of life she led – It is not much that I have to tell – for I mean to relate only what I *saw* and what I *thought* myself, – I was just twelve years old when she died – therefore, I knew her only with a child's knowledge –

My first very distinct remembrance of her is in her own home at Chawton – The house belonged to her second Brother, Mr. Knight (of Godmersham and Chawton) and was by him made a comfortable residence for his Mother and sisters –The family party *there* were, my Grandmother, Mrs. Austen – my two Aunts, her daughters – and a third Aunt of *mine* – Miss Lloyd [Martha], who had made her home with *them* before I can remember, and who remained their inmate as long as Mrs. Austen lived –

The dwelling place of a favourite Author always possesses a certain interest for those who love the books that issued from it –Tho' some of my Aunt's Novels were imagined and written, in her very early days – *some* certainly at Steventon yet that it was from Chawton that after being rearranged and prepared for publication they were sent out into the world – and it is with Chawton therefore, that her name as an Author, must be identified – The house which she inhabited was in itself, not much more deserving of notice than Cowper's [William Cowper, the poet] dwelling place at Olney – and yet more than 30 years after his death, *that* was pointed out to us, as a *something* that strangers passing through the little town, *must* wish to see – Now, as the remembrance of Chawton Cottage, for so in later years it came to be called, is still pleasant to *me* – I will assume that those who never knew it, may like to have laid before them, a description of their Aunt's home – the *last* that she dwelt in – where, in the maturity of her mind, she completed the works that have given her an *English* name – where after a few years, whilst still in the prime of life, she began to droop and wither away – the home from whence she removed only in the last stage of her illness, by the persuasion of her friends, hoping against hope – and to which her sister before long had to return alone –

My Grand Father, Mr. Austen, held for many years, the adjoining Livings of Deane and Steventon – but gave up his duties to his eldest son, and settled at Bath, a very few years before his own death – For a while, his Widow and daughters remained at Bath – then they removed to Southampton – and finally settled in the village of Chawton –

Mr. Knight had been able to offer his Mother the choice of two houses – one in Kent near to Godmersham – and the other at Chawton – and she and her daughters eventually decided on the Hampshire residence.

I have been told I know not how truly, that it *had* been originally a roadside Inn – and it was well placed for such a purpose – just where the road from Winchester comes into the London and Gosport line – The fork between the two being partly occupied by a large shallow pond – which pond I believe has long since become dry ground –

The front door opened on the road, a very narrow enclosure of each side, protected the house from the possible shock of any runaway vehicle – A good sized entrance, and two parlours called drawing and dining room, made the *length* of the house; all intended originally to look on the road – but the large drawing room window was blocked-up and turned into a bookcase when Mrs. Austen took possession and another was opened at the side, which gave to view only turf and trees – A high wooden fence shut out the road (the Winchester road it was) all the length of the little domain, and trees were planted inside to form a shrubbery walk – which carried round the enclosure, gave a very sufficient space for exercise – you did not feel cramped for room; and there was a pleasant irregular mixture of hedgerow, and grass, and gravel walk and long grass for mowing, and orchard – which I imagine arose from two or three little enclosures having been thrown together, and arranged as best might be, for ladies' occupation – There was besides a good kitchen garden, large court and many out-buildings, not much occupied – and all this affluence of space was very delightful to children, and I have no doubt added considerably to the pleasure of a visit –

Everything *in*doors and *out* was well kept – the house was well furnished, and it was altogether a comfortable and ladylike establishment, tho' I beleive [*sic*] the means which supported it were but small –

The house was quite as good as the generality of Parsonage houses were *then* – and much in the same old style – the ceilings low and roughly finished – *some* bedrooms very small – *none* very large but in number sufficient to accomodate [*sic*] the inmates, and several guests –

The dining room could not be made to look anywhere *but* on the road – and *there* my Grandmother often sat for an hour or two in the morning, with her work or her writing – cheered by its sunny aspect, and by the stirring scene it afforded her.

I beleive the close vicinity of the road was really no more an evil to *her* than it was to her grandchildren. Collyer's daily coach with six horses was a sight to see! and most delightful was it to a child to have the awful stillness of night so frequently broken by the noise of passing carriages, which seemed sometimes, even to shake the bed –

The village of Chawton has, of course, long since been tranquilised – it is no more a great thoroughfare, and *other* and *many* changes have past [*sic*] over it – and if any of its visitants should fail to recognise from my description, the house by the pond – I must beg them not hastily to accuse me of having exaggerated its former pleasantness.

Twenty years ago, on being then left vacant by Aunt Cassandra's death, it was divided into habitations for the poor, and made to accomodate several families – so I was *told* – for I have never seen it since and I beleive trees have been cut down, and all that could be termed pleasure ground has reverted again to more ordinary purposes –

My visits to Chawton were frequent – I cannot tell *when* they began – they were very pleasant to me – and Aunt Jane was the great charm – As a very little girl, I was always creeping up to her, and following her whenever I *could*, in the house and out of it – I might not have remembered *this*, but for the recollection of my mother's telling me privately, I must not be troublesome to my Aunt –

Her charm to children was great sweetness of manner – she seemed to love you, and you loved her naturally in return – *This* as well as I can now recollect and analyse, was what I felt in my earliest days, before I was old enough to be amused by her cleverness – But soon came the delight of her playful talk – *Everyth*ing she could make amusing to a child – Then,as I got older, and when cousins came to share the entertainment, she would tell us the most delightful stories chiefly of Fairyland, and her Fairies had all characters of their own – The tale was invented I am sure, at the moment, and was sometimes continued for 2 or 3 days, if occasion served –

As to my Aunt's personal appearance, her's was the first face that I can remember thinking pretty, not that I *used* that word to myself, but I know I looked at her with admiration – Her face was rather *round* than long – she had a *bright* but, not a *pink* colour – a clear brown complexion and very good hazle [*sic*] eyes – She was not, I believe, an absolute beauty, but before she left Steventon she was established as a very pretty girl, in the opinion of most of her neighbours – as I learnt afterwards from some of those who still remained – Her hair, a darkish brown, curled naturally – it was in short curls round her face (for *then* ringlets were *not*.) She always wore a cap – Such was the custom with ladies who were not quite young – at least of a morning but I never saw her without one, to the best of my remembrance, either morning or evening.

I beleive my two Aunts were not accounted very good dressers, and were thought to have taken to the garb of middle age unnecessarily soon – but they were particularly neat, and they held all untidy ways in great disesteem. Of the *two*, Aunt Jane was by far my favourite – I did not *dislike* Aunt Cassandra – but if my visit had at any time chanced to fall out during *her* absence, I don't think I should have missed her – whereas, *not* to have found Aunt Jane at Chawton, *would* have been a blank indeed.

As I grew older I met with young companions at my Grandmother's – Of Capt. Charles Austen's motherless girls, *one* the eldest, Cassy – lived there chiefly, for a time – under the especial tutorage of Aunt Cassandra; and then Chawton House was for a while inhabited by Capt. Frank Austen; and *he* had many children – I beleive we were all of us, according to our different ages and natures, very fond of our Aunt Jane – and that we ever retained a strong impression of the pleasantness of Chawton life – One of my cousins, now long since dead, after he was grown up, used occasionally to go and see Aunt Cass[a] – *then* left sole inmate of the old house – and he told me once, that his visits were always a disappointment to him – for that he could not help expecting to feel particularly happy at Chawton and never till he got there, could he fully realise to himself how all its peculiar pleasures were gone –

In the time of my childhood, it was a cheerful house – my Uncles, one or another, frequently coming for a few days; and they were all pleasant in their own family – I have thought since, after having seen more of other households, *wonderfully,* as the *family* talk had much of spirit and vivacity, and it was never troubled by disagreements as it was not their habit to argue with each other – There always was perfect harmony amongst the brothers and sisters, and over my Grandmother's door might have been inscribed the text, 'Behold how good – and joyful a thing it is, brethren, to dwell together in unity.' There was firm family union, never broken but by death – tho' the time came when that union could not have been preserved if natural affection had not been by a spirit of forbearance and generosity –

Aunt Jane began her day with music – for which I conclude she had a natural taste; as she thus kept it up – tho' she had no one to teach; was never induced (as I have heard) to play in company; and none of her family cared much for it. I suppose, that she might not trouble *them*, she chose her practising time before breakfast – when she could have the room to herself – She practised regularly every morning – She played very pretty tunes, *I* thought – and I liked to stand by her and listen to them; but the music, (for I knew the books well in after years) would now be thought disgracefully easy – Much that she played from was manuscript, copied out by herself – and so neatly and correctly, that it was as easy to read as print –

At 9 o'clock she made breakfast – *that* was *her* part of the household work – The tea and sugar stores were under *her* charge – *and* the wine – Aunt Cassandra did all the rest – for my Grandmother had suffered herself to be superseded by her daughters *before* I can remember; and soon *after,* she ceased even to sit at the head of the table –

I don't beleive [*sic*] Aunt Jane observed any particular method in parcelling out her day but I think she generally sat in the drawing room till luncheon: when visitors were there, chiefly at work – She was fond of work – and she was a great adept at overcast and satin stitch – the peculiar delight of that day – General handiness and neatness were amongst her characteristics – *She* could throw the spilikens for us, better than anyone else, and she was wonderfully successful at cup and ball – She found a resource sometimes in that simple game, when she suffered from weak eyes and could not work or read for long together –

Her handwriting remains to bear testimony to its own excellence; and every note and letter of hers, was finished off *handsomely* –There was an art *then* in folding and sealing – no adhesive envelopes made all easy – some people's letters looked always loose and untidy – but *her* paper was sure to take the right folds, and *her* sealing wax to drop in the proper place –

After luncheon, my Aunts generally walked out – sometimes they went to Alton for shopping – Often, one or the other of them, to the Great House – as it was then called – when a brother was inhabiting it, to make a visit – or if the house were standing empty they liked to stroll about the grounds – sometimes to Chawton Park – a noble beech wood, just within a walk – but sometimes, but that was rarely, to call on a neighbour – They had no carriage, and their visitings did not extend far – there were a few families living in the village – but no great intimacy was kept up with any of them –they were upon *friendly* but rather *distant* terms, with all – Yet I am sure my Aunt Jane had a regard for her neighbours and felt a kindly interest in their proceedings. She liked immensely to hear all about them. They sometimes served for her amusement, but it was her own nonsense that gave zest to the gossip – She never turned *them* into ridicule – She was as far as possible from being either censorious or satirical – she never abused them or *quizzed* them –*That* was the word of the day – an ugly word, now obsolete – and the ugly practice which it bespoke, is far less prevalent *now*, under *any* name, than it was *then.* The laugh she occasionally raised was by imagining for her neighbours impossible contingencies – by relating in prose or verse some trifling incident coloured to her own fancy, or in writing a history of what they had said or done, that *could* deceive nobody – As an instance I would give her description of the pursuits of Miss Mills and Miss Yates – two young ladies of whom she knew next to nothing – they were only on a visit to a near neighbour but their names tempted her into rhyme – and so *on* she went –This was before *my* time. Mrs Lefroy knows the lines better than *I* do – I beleive she has a copy and I shall not attempt to quote them imperfectly here. To about the same date perhaps may be referred (at least it was equally before *my* time) a few chapters which I overheard – of a mock heroic story, written between herself and one of her nieces, and I doubt *not,* at *her* instigation – If I remember rightly, it had no other foundation than their having seen a neighbour passing on the coach, without having previously known that he was going to leave home – (*This* I have since been told was written entirely by the Niece only under her encouragement).

I did not often see my Aunt with a book in her hand, but I beleive [*sic*] she was fond of reading and that she *had* read and *did* read a good deal. I doubt whether she cared very much for poetry in *general;* but she was a great admirer of [George] Crabbe, and consequently she took a keen interest in finding out *who* he was – Other contemporary writers were well-known, but *his* origen [*sic*] having been obscure, his name did not announce *itself* – however by diligent enquiry she was ere long able to inform the rest of the family that he held the Living of Trowbridge, and had recently married a second time –

A very warm admirer of my Aunt's writing but a stranger in England, lately made the observation that it would be most interesting to know what had been Miss Austen's opinions on the great public events of her time – a period as she rightly observed, of the greatest interest – for my Aunt must have been a young woman, able to *think,* at the time of the French Revolution & the long disastrous chapter then begun, was closed by the Battle of Waterloo, two years before her death – anyone *might* naturally desire to know what part a mind such as her's had taken in the great strifes of war and policy which so disquieted Europe for more than 20 years – and yet, it was a question that had never before presented itself to me – and tho' I have *now* retraced my steps on *this* track, I have found absolutely nothing!

The general politics of the family were Tory – rather taken for granted I suppose, than discussed, as even my Uncles seldom talked about it – and in vain do I try to recall any word or expression of Aunt Jane's that had reference to public events – *Some* bias of course she *must* have had – but I can only *guess* to which quarter it inclined – Of her historical opinions I *am* able to record *thus* much –that she was a most loyal adherent of Charles the 1st, and that she always encouraged my youthful beleif [*sic*] in Mary Stuart's perfect innocence of all the crimes with which History has charged her memory –

My Aunt must have spent much time in writing – her desk lived in the drawing room. I often saw her writing letters on it, and I beleive she wrote much of her Novels in the same way-sitting with her family, when they were quite alone; but *I* never saw any manuscript of *that* sort, in progress – She wrote very fully to her Brothers when they were at sea, and she corresponded with many others of her family –

There is nothing in those letters which *I* have seen that would be acceptable to the public – They were very well expressed, and they must have been very interesting to those who received them – but they detailed chiefly home and family events: and she seldom committed herself *even* to an *opinion* – so that to strangers they could be *no* transcript of her mind – they would not feel that they knew her any the better for having read them –

They were rather *over*-cautious, for excellence – Her letters to Aunt

Cassandra (for they were *sometimes* separated) were, I dare say, open and confidential – My Aunt looked them over and burnt the greater part, (as she told me), 2 or 3 years before her own death – She left, or *gave* some as legacies to the Nieces – but of those that *I* have seen, several had portions cut out – Aunt Jane was so good as frequently to write to *me*; and in addressing a child, she was perfect –

When staying at Chawton, if my two cousins, Mary Jane and Cassy were there, we often had amusements in which my Aunt was very helpful – *She* was the one to whom we always looked for help – She would furnish us with what we wanted from her wardrobe, and *she* would often be the entertaining visitor in our make beleive house – She amused us in various ways – *once* I remember in giving a conversation as between myself and my two cousins, supposed to be grown up, the day after a Ball.

As I grew older, she would talk to me more seriously of my reading, and of my amusements – I had taken early to writing verse and stories, and I am sorry to think *how* I troubled her with reading them. She was very kind about it, and always had some praise to bestow but at last she warned me against spending too much time upon them – She said – how well I recollect it! that she *knew* writing stories was a great amusement, and *she* thought a harmless one – tho' many people, she was aware, thought otherwise – but that at *my* age it would be bad for me to be much taken up with my own compositions – Later still – it was after she got to Winchester, she sent me a message to this effect – That if I would take her advice, I should cease writing till I was 16, and that she had herself often wished she had *read* more, and written *less,* in the corresponding years of her own life.

She was considered to read aloud remarkably well. I did not often hear her but *once* I knew her take up a volume of Evelina [by Fanny Burney] and read a few pages of Mr. Smith and the Brangtons and I thought it was like a play. She had a very good *speaking* voice – This was the opinion of her contemporaries – and though I did not *then* think of it as a perfection, or ever hear it observed upon, yet its tones have never been forgotten – I can recall them even now – and I *know* they *were* very pleasant.

I have spoken of the family union that prevailed amongst my Grandmother's children – Aunt Jane was a very affectionate sister to all her Brothers – One of them in particular was her especial pride and delight: but of all her family, the nearest and dearest throughout her whole life was, undoubtedly her sister – her *only* sister. Aunt Cassandra was the older by 3 or 4 years, and the habit of looking up to her begun in childhood, seemed always to continue – When I was a little girl she would frequently say to me, if opportunity offered, that Aunt Cassandra could teach everything much better than *she* could – Aunt Cass^{a}. *knew* more – Aunt Cass[a]. could tell me better whatever I wanted to know – all which, I ever received in respectful silence – Perhaps she thought *my* mind wanted a turn in *that* direction, but I truly beleive she did always *really* think of her sister, as the superior to herself. The most perfect affection and confidence ever subsisted between them – and great and lasting was the sorrow of the survivor when the final separation was made –

My Aunt's life at Chawton, as far as *I* ever knew, was an easy and pleasant one – it had little variety in it, and I am not aware of any particular trials, till her own health began to fail – She stayed from home occasionally – almost entirely with the families of her different Brothers – In the Autumn of 1815 she was in London, with my Uncle, Mr. Henry Austen, then living in Hans Place – and a widower –

During her visit, he was seized with low fever and became so ill that his life was despaired of, and Aunt Cassandra and my Father were summoned to the house – *there,* for a day or two, they hourly expected his death – but a favourable turn came, and he began to recover – My Father then went home. Aunt Cass[a]. stayed on nearly a month, and Aunt Jane remained some weeks longer, to nurse the Convalescent –

It was during this stay in London, that a little gleam of Court favor [*sic*] shone upon her. She had at first published her Novels with a great desire of remaining *herself* unknown – but it was found impossible to preserve a secret that so many of the family knew and by this time, she had given up the attempt – and her name had been made public enough – tho' it was never inserted in the title page –

Two of the great Physicians of the day had attended my Uncle during his illness – I am not, at this distance of time, sufficiently sure *which* they were, as to give their names, but *one* of them had very intimate access to the Prince Regent, and continuing his visits during my Uncle's recovery, he told my Aunt one day, that the Prince was a great admirer of her Novels: that he often read them, and had a set in each of his residences – That *he,* the physician had told his Royal Highness that Miss Austen was now in London, and that by the Prince's desire, Mr. Clarke, the Librarian of Carlton House, would speedily wait upon her –

Mr. Clarke came, and endorsed all previous compliments, and invited my Aunt to see Carlton House, saying the Prince had charged him to show her the Library there, adding many civilities as to the pleasure his R.H. had received from her novels – Three had *then* been published – The invitation could not be declined – and my Aunt went, at an appointed time, to Carlton House –

She saw the Library, and I beleive, some other apartments, but the particulars of her visit, if I ever heard them, I have now forgotten – only *this*, I *do* well recollect – that in the course of it, Mr. Clarke, speaking again of the Regent's admiration of her writing, declared himself charged to say, that if Miss Austen had any other Novel forthcoming, she was quite at liberty to dedicate it to the Prince.

My Aunt made all proper acknowledgements at the moment, but had no intention of accepting the honor [*sic*] offered – until she was avised [*sic*] by some of her friends that she must consider the permission as a command –

Emma was then in the Publisher's hands – so a few lines of dedication were affixed to the 1st volume, and following still the instructions of the well informed, she sent a Copy, handsomely bound, to Carlton House – and I *suppose* it was duly acknowledged by Mr. Clarke –

My Aunt, soon after her visit to *him,* returned home, where the little adventure was talked of for a while with some interest, and afforded some amusement – In the following Spring, Mr. Henry Austen ceased to reside in London, and my Aunt was never brought so near the precincts of the Court again – nor did she ever try to recall herself to the recollection of the Physician, Librarian or Prince, and so ended this little burst of Royal Patronage.

I beleive Aunt Jane's health began to fail some time before we knew she was really ill – but she became avowedly less equal to exercise. In a letter to me she says:

'I have taken one ride on the donkey, and I like it very much, and you must try to get me quiet mild days that I may be able to go out pretty constantly – a great deal of wind does not suit me, as I still have a tendency to rhumatism [*sic*]. In short, I am but a poor Honey at present – I will be better when you can come and see us.'

A donkey carriage had been set up for my Grandmother's accomodation – but I think *she* seldom used it, and Aunt Jane found it a help to herself in getting to Alton – where, for a time, Capt. Austen had a house, after removing from his Brother's place at Chawton –

In my later visits to Chawton Cottage, I remember Aunt Jane used often to lie down after dinner – My Grandmother herself was frequently on the sofa – sometimes in the afternoon, sometimes in the evening, at no fixed period of the day, – She had not bad health for her age, and she worked often for hours in the garden, and naturally wanted rest afterwards – There was only one sofa in the room – and Aunt Jane laid upon 3 chairs which she arranged for herself – I think she had a pillow, but it never looked comfortable – She called it *her* sofa, end even when the *other* was unoccupied, *she* never took it – It seemed understood that she preferred the chairs –

I wondered and wondered – for the *real* sofa was frequently vacant, and *still* she laid in this comfortless manner – I often asked her how she *could* like the chairs best – and I suppose I worried her into telling me the reason of her choice – which was, that if *she* ever used the sofa, Grandmama would be leaving it for *her*, and would not lie down, as she did now, whenever she felt inclined –

In May,1816 my two Aunts went for a few weeks to Cheltenham – I am able to ascertain the date of *this*, and some similar occurrences, by a reference to old pocket books in my possession – It was a journey in those days, to go from Hampshire into Gloucestershire and their first stage was to Steventon – They stayed one whole day, and left my cousin Cassy to remain with us during their absence –

They made also a short stay at Mr. Fowle's at Kintbury – I beleive *that* was, as they returned – Mrs. Dexter, then Mary Jane Fowle, told me afterwards, that Aunt Jane went over the old places, and recalled old recollections associated with them, in a very particular manner – looked at them, as my cousin thought, as if she never expected to see them again – The Kintbury family, during that visit, received an impression that her health was failing – altho' they did *not* know of any particular malady.

The year 1817, the last of my Aunt's life, began it seems under good auspices.

I copy from a letter of her's to myself dated Jany. 23rd 1817 – the only letter I have which *does* bear the date of the year –

'I feel myself getting stronger than I was – and can so perfectly well walk *to* Alton, *or* back again, without the slightest fatigue that I hope to be able to do *both*, when summer comes' –

I do not know *when* the alarming symptoms of her malady came on – It was in the following March that *I* had the first idea of her being seriously ill – It had been settled that about the end of that month, or the beginning of April, I should spend a few days at Chawton, in the absence of my Father and Mother, who were just then engaged with Mrs. Leigh Perrot in arranging her late husband's affairs – it was shortly after Mr. Leigh Perrot's death – but Aunt Jane became too ill to have me in the house, and so I went instead to my sister, Mrs. Lefroy, at Wyards – The next day we walked over to Chawton to make enquiries after our Aunt – She was keeping her room but said she would see us, and we went up to her – She was in her dressing gown and was sitting quite like an invalide [*sic*] in an arm chair – but she got up, and kindly greeted us – and then pointing to seats which had been arranged for us by the fire, she said, 'There's a chair for the married lady, and a little stool for *you*, Caroline.' – It is strange, but those trifling words are the last of her's that I can remember – for I retain *no* recollection *at* all of what was said by any one in the conversation that of course ensued –

I was struck by the alteration in herself – She was very pale – her voice was weak and low and there was about her, a general appearance of debility and suffering; but I have been told that she never *had* much actual pain –

She was not equal to the exertion of talking to us, and our visit to the sick room was a very short one – Aunt Cassandra soon taking us away – I do not suppose we stayed a quarter of an hour; and *I* never saw Aunt Jane again –

I think she must have been particularly ill *that* day, and that in some degree she afterwards rallied – *I* soon went home again – but I beleive Mrs. Lefroy saw her more than once afterwards before she went to Winchester –

It was sometime in the following May, that she removed thither – Better medical advice was needed than Alton could supply – Not I beleive with much hope that any skill could effect a cure but from the natural desire of her family to place her in the best hands – Mr. Lyford was thought to be very clever so much so, as to be generally summoned far beyond his own practise – to give his opinion in cases of serious illness –

In the earlier stages of her malady, my Aunt had had the advice, in London, of one of the eminent physicians of the day –

Aunt Cassandra, of course, accompanied her sister, and they had lodgings in College Street – Their great friends Mrs. Heathcote and Miss Bigg, then living in The Close, had made all the arrangements for them, and did all they could to promote their comfort during that melancholy sojourn in Winchester.

Mr. Lyford could give no hope of recovery – He told my Mother that the duration of the illness must be very uncertain – it *might* be lingering or it might, with equal probability come to a sudden close – and that he feared the *last* period, whenever it arrived, would be one of severe suffering – but *this* was mercifully ordered otherwise – My Mother, after a little time, had joined her sisters-in-law – to make it more cheerful for them, and also to take a share of the necessary attendance – From *her,* therefore, I learned, that my Aunt's resignation and composure of spirit were such, as those who knew her well, would have hoped for and expected – She was a humble and beleiving Christian; her life had passed in the cheerful performance of all home duties, and with *no* aiming at applause, she had sought, as if by instinct to promote the happiness of all those who came within her influence – doubtless she had her reward, in the peace of mind which was granted to her in her last days –

She was quite aware of her own danger – it was no delusive hope that kept up her spirits – and there was everything to attach her to life – Tho' she had passed by the hopes and enjoyments of youth, yet its sorrows also were left behind – and Autumn is sometimes so calm and fair that it consoles us for the departure of Spring and Summer – and *thus* it might have been with *her* – She was happy in her family and in her home; and no doubt the exercise of her great talent, was a happiness also in itself – and she was just learning to feel confidence in her own success – In no human mind was there less of vanity than in her's – yet she could not *but* be pleased and gratified as her works, by slow degrees made their way in the world, with constantly increasing favour –

She had *no* cause to be weary of life, and there was much to make it very pleasant to her – We may be sure she would fain have lived on – yet she was enabled, without complaint, and without dismay, to prepare for death – She had for some time known that it *might* be approaching her; and *now* she saw it with certainty, to be very near at hand.

The religious services most suitable to her state were ministered to her, during this, the last stage of her illness – sometimes by a Brother – Two of them were Clergymen and at Winchester she was within easy distance of both –

Her sweetness of temper never failed her; she was considerate and grateful to those who attended on her, and at times, when feeling rather better, her playfulness of spirit prevailed, and she amused them even in their sadness – A Brother frequently went over for a few hours, or a day or two –

Suddenly she became much worse – Mr. Lyford thought the end was near at hand, and she beleived *herself* to be dying – and under this conviction she said all that she wished to say to those around her –

In taking then, as she thought, a last leave of my Mother, she thanked her for being there, and said, 'You have always been a kind sister to me, Mary.' – Contrary to every expectation the immediate danger passed away; she became comfortable again, and seemed really better –

My Mother then came home – but not for long as she was shortly summoned back – This was from no increase of my Aunt's illness, but because the Nurse could not be trusted for *her* share of the night attendance, having been more than once found asleep – so to relieve her from that part of her charge, Aunt Cassandra and my Mother and my Aunt's maid took the nights between them.

Aunt Jane continued very cheerful and comfortable, and there began to be a *hope* of, at least, a *respite* from death –

But soon, and suddenly, as it were, a great change came on – *not* apparently, attended with much suffering – she sank rapidly – Mr. Lyford – when he saw her, could give no further hope, and she must have felt her own state – for when he asked her if there was anything she wanted, she replied, 'Nothing but death.' Those were her last words –

They watched by her through the night, and in quietness and peace she breathed her last on the morning of 18th July, 1817 –

I need scarcely say she was dearly loved by her family – Her Brothers were very proud of her – Her literary fame, at the close of her life, was

only just spreading – but they were proud of her talents, which *they* even then estimated highly – proud of her home virtues, of her cheerful spirit – of her pleasant looks – and *each* loved afterwards to *fancy* a resemblance in some daughter of his own, to the dear 'Aunt Jane', whose perfect equal they *yet* never expected to see –
March 1867 – Written out,
At Frog Firle – Sussex

5

The First Biography

James Edward Austen-Leigh (known as Edward) was the son of Jane Austen's brother James and his second wife Mary. His relationship with his aunt was as close as that of Anna and Caroline. They all shared Jane Austen's roots in Hampshire. Edward visited his aunt often and wrote to her when he was away at school in Winchester. He was the youngest mourner at her funeral.

Edward obtained a degree from Oxford University and was ordained in 1820. He then began a long career in the church. He was vicar of Bray in Berkshire in the 1860s when he started to gather material for a biography of Jane Austen.

In addition to his own memories of his aunt and the letters she had sent him, Edward also had Anna and Caroline's recollections. His cousin Cassy Esten, Charles Austen's eldest daughter, also offered him the use of some letters of Jane's which she had inherited from her Aunt Cassandra in 1845 and two water-colour sketches of Jane painted by her sister.

Edward was not so fortunate, however, when he approached his cousin Fanny Knight for help. She was not prepared to contribute her memories and could not remember where she had put a box of Jane's letters which she had inherited. Edward was further impeded by the absence of autobiographical material, such as diaries, and the lack of public information about Jane Austen resulting from her wish to keep her authorship a secret.

Despite these obstacles Edward completed the Memoir *in less than six months and it was published in December 1869. As well as a straightforward biography it traced Jane Austen's development as a novelist, a history of the publication of her works and observations, opinions and reviews. He also outlined the growth of her fame and reputation.*

The Memoir *included four illustrations, a facsimile of Jane's handwriting and a portrait of her. The portrait was an improved version of one of the watercolour pictures painted by Cassandra Austen. As this was not thought to be a good likeness of Jane, the author of the* Memoir *had it prettified by an artist.*

There were a number of shortcomings to the Memoir *which should be noted. The most significant of these was that the author did not reveal the whole truth about some aspects of Jane's life. He did not, for example, make any mention of her brother George, the second child of George and Cassandra Austen. George, who suffered from epilepsy and other disabilities, lived away from home in the care of a local family. In the* Memoir *George's younger brothers were moved up a place in the seniority of the Austen sons, as if he did not exist. This was, no doubt, as much a reflection of the fact that George was never really a part of the Austen family as the desire of a Victorian biographer to hide an uncomfortable fact.*

Another shortcoming was the tendency of the author to digress, often at great length, possibly due to the lack of material available to him. This lack may also explain the scanty information about some important aspects of Jane's life, such as her long stays with her family in Kent during which she acquired much inspiration and material for her novels.

Despite these limitations the Memoir *was well received by the reading public and the Austen family. Caroline Austen commented, 'Perhaps never before has so small a volume attracted so much attention'. It resulted in new editions of the novels, a spate of new articles and reviews, and a demand for more information about Jane Austen and her works. To satisfy this demand a second extended edition of the* Memoir *was published in 1871. This edition contained a few more letters, a specimen of the Juvenilia, an interesting postscript to the first edition, the cancelled chapter of* Persuasion *and a précis of the first chapters of a novel which Jane Austen was working on until a few months before her death. The unpublished short story* Lady Susan *and the unfinished novel* The Watsons *were added as appendices.*

The following is the text of the second edition without the appendices.

A MEMOIR OF JANE AUSTEN JAMES EDWARD AUSTEN-LEIGH 1871

Preface

The Memoir of my Aunt, Jane Austen, has been received with more favour than I had ventured to expect. The notices taken of it in the periodical press, as well as letters addressed to me by many with whom I am not personally acquainted, show that an unabated interest is still taken in every particular that can be told about her. I am thus encouraged not only to offer a Second Edition of the Memoir, but also to enlarge it with some additional matter which I might have scrupled to intrude on the public if they had not thus seemed to call for it. In the present Edition, the narrative is somewhat enlarged, and a few more letters are added; with a short specimen of her childish stories. The cancelled chapter of 'Persuasion' is given, in compliance with wishes both publicly and privately expressed. A fragment of a story entitled 'The Watsons' is printed [1]; and extracts are given from a novel which she had begun a few months before her death; but the chief addition is a short tale never before published, called 'Lady Susan'.[1] I regret that the little which I have been able to add could not appear in my First Edition; as much of it was either unknown to me, or not at my command, when I first published; and I hope that I may claim some indulgent allowance for the difficulty of recovering little facts and feelings which had been merged half a century deep in oblivion.
NOVEMBER 17, 1870

Notes
1. *The Watsons* and *Lady Susan* are not included here.

> 'He knew of no one but himself who was inclined to the work. This is no uncommon motive. A man sees something to be done, knows of no one who will do it but himself, and so is driven to the enterprise.'
>
> HELPS' *Life of Columbus*, ch. i.

Introductory Remarks—Birth of Jane Austen—Her Family Connections—Their Influence on her Writings

More than half a century has passed away since I, the youngest of the mourners [1] attended the funeral of my dear aunt Jane in Winchester

Cathedral; and now, in my old age, I am asked whether my memory will serve to rescue from oblivion any events of her life or any traits of her character to satisfy the enquiries of a generation of readers who have been born since she died. Of events her life was singularly barren: few changes and no great crisis ever broke the smooth current of its course. Even her fame may be said to have been posthumous: it did not attain to any vigorous life till she had ceased to exist. Her talents did not introduce her to the notice of other writers, or connect her with the literary world, or in any degree pierce through the obscurity of her domestic retirement. I have therefore scarcely any materials for a detailed life of my aunt; but I have a distinct recollection of her person and character; and perhaps many may take an interest in a delineation, if any such can be drawn, of that prolific mind whence sprung the Dashwoods and Bennets, the Bertrams and Woodhouses, the Thorpes and Musgroves, who have been admitted as familiar guests to the firesides of so many families, and are known there as individually and intimately as if they were living neighbours. Many may care to know whether the moral rectitude, the correct taste, and the warm affections with which she invested her ideal characters, were really existing in the native source whence those ideas flowed, and were actually exhibited by her in the various relations of life. I can indeed bear witness that there was scarcely a charm in her most delightful characters that was not a true reflection of her own sweet temper and loving heart. I was young when we lost her; but the impressions made on the young are deep, and though in the course of fifty years I have forgotten much, I have not forgotten that 'Aunt Jane' was the delight of all her nephews and nieces. We did not think of her as being clever, still less as being famous; but we valued her as one always kind, sympathising, and amusing. To all this I am a living witness, but whether I can sketch out such a faint outline of this excellence as shall be perceptible to others may be reasonably doubted. Aided, however, by a few survivors [2] who knew her, I will not refuse to make the attempt. I am the more inclined to undertake the task from a conviction that, however little I may have to tell, no one else is left who could tell so much of her.

Jane Austen was born on December 16, 1775, at the Parsonage House of Steventon in Hampshire. Her father, the Rev. George Austen, was of a family long established in the neighbourhood of Tenterden and Sevenoaks in Kent. I believe that early in the seventeenth century they were clothiers. Hasted, in his history of Kent, says:'The clothing business was exercised by persons who possessed most of the landed property in the Weald, insomuch that almost all the ancient families of these parts, now of large estates and genteel rank in life, and some of them ennobled by titles, are sprung from ancestors who have used this great staple manufacture, now almost unknown here.' In his list of these families Hasted places the Austens, and he adds that these clothiers 'were usually called the Gray Coats of Kent; and were a body so numerous and united that at county elections whoever had their vote and interest was almost certain of being elected.' The family still retains a badge of this origin; for their livery is of that peculiar mixture of light blue and white called Kentish gray, which forms the facings of the Kentish militia.

Mr. George Austen had lost both his parents before he was nine years old. He inherited no property from them; but was happy in having a kind uncle, Mr. Francis Austen, a successful lawyer at Tunbridge, the ancestor of the Austens of Kippington, who, though he had children of his own, yet made liberal provision for his orphan nephew. The boy received a good education at Tunbridge School, whence he obtained a scholarship, and subsequently a fellowship, at St. John's College, Oxford. In 1764 he came into possession of the two adjoining Rectories of Deane and Steventon in Hampshire; the former purchased for him by his generous uncle Francis, the latter given by his cousin Mr. Knight. This was no very gross case of plurality, according to the ideas of that time, for the two villages were little more than a mile apart, and their united populations scarcely amounted to three hundred. In the same year he married Cassandra, youngest daughter of the Rev. Thomas Leigh, of the family of Leighs of Warwickshire, who, having been a fellow of All Souls, held the College living of Harpsden, near Henley-upon-Thames. Mr. Thomas Leigh was a younger brother of Dr. Theophilus Leigh, a personage well known at Oxford in his day, and his day was not a short one, for he lived to be ninety, and held the Mastership of Balliol College for above half a century. He was a man more famous for his sayings than his doings, overflowing with puns and witticisms and sharp retorts; but his most serious joke was his practical one of living much longer than had been expected or intended. He was a fellow of Corpus, and the story is that the Balliol men, unable to agree in electing one of their own number to the Mastership, chose him, partly under the idea that he was in weak health and likely soon to cause another vacancy. It was afterwards said that his long incumbency had been a judgment on the Society for having elected an *Out-College Man*.[3] I imagine that the front of Balliol towards Broad Street which has recently been pulled down must have been built, or at least restored, while he was Master, for the Leigh arms were placed under the cornice at the corner nearest to Trinity gates. The beautiful building lately erected has destroyed this record, and thus 'monuments themselves memorials need.'

His fame for witty and agreeable conversation extended beyond the bounds of the University. Mrs. Thrale [Hester Thrale diarist, author and patron of the arts], in a letter to Dr. Johnson, writes thus: 'Are you acquainted with Dr. Leigh,[4] the Master of Balliol College, and are you not delighted with his gaiety of manners and youthful vivacity, now that he is eighty-six years of age? I never heard a more perfect or excellent pun than his, when some one told him how, in a late dispute among the Privy Councillors, the Lord Chancellor struck the table with such violence that he split it. "No, no, no," replied the Master; "I can hardly persuade myself that he *split* the *table*, though I believe he *divided* the *Board.*"'

Some of his sayings of course survive in family tradition. He was once calling on a gentleman notorious for never opening a book, who took him into a room overlooking the Bath Road, which was then a great thoroughfare for travellers of every class, saying rather pompously, 'This, Doctor, I call my study.' The Doctor, glancing his eye round the room, in which no books were to be seen, replied, 'And very well named too, sir, for you know [Alexander] Pope tells us, "The proper *study* of mankind is *Man*". When my father went to Oxford he was honoured with an invitation to dine with this dignified cousin. Being a raw undergraduate, unaccustomed to the habits of the University, he was about to take off his gown, as if it were a great coat, when the old man, then considerably turned eighty, said, with a grim smile, 'Young man, you need not strip: we are not going to fight.' This humour remained in him so strongly to the last that he might almost have supplied Pope with another instance of 'the ruling passion strong in death,' for only three days before he expired, being told that an old acquaintance was lately married, having recovered from a long illness by eating eggs, and that the wits said that he had been egged on to matrimony, he immediately trumped the joke, saying, 'Then may the yoke sit easy on him.' I do not know from what common ancestor the Master of Balliol and his great-niece Jane Austen, with some others of the family, may have derived the keen sense of humour which they certainly possessed.

Mr. and Mrs. George Austen resided first at Deane, but removed in 1771 to Steventon, which was their residence for about thirty years. They commenced their married life with the charge of a little child, a son of the celebrated Warren Hastings [Governor General of Bengal 1773-1785], who had been committed to the care of Mr. Austen before his marriage, probably through the influence of his sister, Mrs. Hancock, whose husband at that time held some office under Hastings in India. Mr. Gleig, in his 'Life of Hastings,' says that his son George, the offspring of his first marriage, was sent to England in 1761 for his education, but that he had never been able to ascertain to whom this precious charge was entrusted, nor what became of him. I am able to state, from family tradition, that he died young, of what was then called putrid sore throat; and that Mrs. Austen had become so much attached to him that she always declared that his death had been as great a grief to her as if he had been a child of her own.

About this time, the grandfather of Mary Russell Mitford, Dr. Russell, was Rector of the adjoining parish of Ashe; so that the parents of two popular female writers must have been intimately acquainted with each other.

As my subject carries me back about a hundred years, it will afford occasions for observing many changes gradually effected in the manners and habits of society, which I may think it worth while to mention. They may be little things, but time gives a certain importance even to trifles, as it imparts a peculiar flavour to wine. The most ordinary articles of domestic life are looked on with some interest, if they are brought to light after being long buried; and we feel a natural curiosity to know what was done and said by our forefathers, even though it may be nothing wiser or better than what we are daily doing or saying ourselves. Some of this generation may be little aware how many conveniences, now considered to be necessaries and matters of course, were unknown to their grandfathers and grandmothers. The lane between Deane and Steventon has long been as smooth as the best turnpike road; but when the family removed from the one residence to the other in 1771, it was a mere cart track, so cut up by deep ruts as to be impassable for a light carriage. Mrs. Austen, who was not then in strong health, performed the short journey on a feather-bed, placed upon some soft articles of furniture in the waggon which held their household goods. In those days it was not unusual to set men to work with shovel and pickaxe to fill up ruts and holes in roads seldom used by carriages, on such special occasions as a funeral or a wedding. Ignorance and coarseness of language also were still lingering even upon higher levels of society than might have been expected to retain such mists. About this time, a neighbouring squire, a man of many acres, referred the following difficulty to Mr. Austen's decision: 'You know all about these sort of things. Do tell us. Is Paris in France, or France in Paris? for my wife has been disputing with me about it.' The same gentleman, narrating some conversation which he had heard between the rector and his wife, represented the latter as beginning her reply to her husband with a round oath; and when his daughter called him to task, reminding him that Mrs. Austen never swore, he replied, 'Now, Betty, why do you pull me up for nothing? that's neither here nor there; you know very well that's only *my way of telling the story.*' Attention has lately been called by a celebrated writer to the inferiority of the clergy to the laity of England two centuries ago. The charge no doubt is true, if the rural clergy are to be compared with that higher section of country gentlemen who went into parliament, and mixed in London society, and took the lead in their several counties; but it might be found less true if they were to be compared, as in all fairness they ought to be, with that lower section with whom they usually associated. The smaller landed proprietors, who seldom went farther from home than their county town, from the squire with his thousand acres to the yeoman who cultivated his hereditary property of one or two hundred, then formed a numerous class – each the aristocrat of his own parish; and there was probably a greater difference in manners and refinement between this class and that immediately above them than could now be found between any two persons who rank as gentlemen. For in the progress of civilisation, though all orders may make some progress, yet it is most perceptible in the lower. It is a process of 'levelling up;' the rear rank 'dressing up,' as it were, close to the front rank. When Hamlet mentions, as something which he had 'for *three years taken* note of,' that 'the toe of the peasant comes so near the heel of the courtier,' it was probably intended by Shakspeare [*sic*] as a satire on his own times; but it expressed a principle which is working at all times in which society makes any progress. I believe that a century ago the improvement in most country parishes began with the clergy; and that in those days a rector who chanced to be a gentleman and a scholar found himself superior to his chief parishioners in information and manners, and became a sort of centre of refinement and politeness.

Mr. Austen was a remarkably good-looking man, both in his youth and his old age. During his year of office at Oxford he had been called the 'handsome Proctor;' and at Bath, when more than seventy years old, he attracted observation by his fine features and abundance of snow-white hair. Being a good scholar he was able to prepare two of his sons for the University, and to direct the studies of his other children, whether sons or daughters, as well as to increase his income by taking pupils.

In Mrs. Austen also was to be found the germ of much of the ability which was concentrated in Jane, but of which others of her children had a share. She united strong common sense with a lively imagination, and often expressed herself, both in writing and in conversation, with epigrammatic force and point. She lived, like many of her family, to an advanced age. During the last years of her life she endured continual pain, not only patiently but with characteristic cheerfulness. She once said to me, 'Ah, my dear, you find me just where you left me – on the sofa. I sometimes think that God Almighty must have forgotten me; but I dare say He will come for me in His own good time.' She died and was buried at Chawton, January 1827, aged eighty-eight.

Her own family were so much, and the rest of the world so little, to Jane Austen, that some brief mention of her brothers and sister is necessary in order to give any idea of the objects which principally occupied her thoughts and filled her heart, especially as some of them, from their characters or professions in life, may be supposed to have had more or less influence on her writings: though I feel some reluctance in bringing before public notice persons and circumstances essentially private.

Her eldest brother James, my own father, had, when a very young man, at St. John's College, Oxford, been the originator and chief supporter of a periodical paper called 'The Loiterer,' written somewhat on the plan of the 'Spectator' [popular paper started in 1711] and its successors, but nearly confined to subjects connected with the University. In after life he used to speak very slightingly of this early work, which he had the better right to do, as, whatever may have been the degree of their merits, the best papers had certainly been written by himself. He was well read in English literature, had a correct taste, and wrote readily and happily, both in prose and verse. He was more than ten years older than Jane, and had, I believe, a large share in directing her reading and forming her taste.

Her second brother, Edward, had been a good deal separated from the rest of the family, as he was early adopted by his cousin, Mr. Knight, of Godmersham Park in Kent and Chawton House in Hampshire; and finally came into possession both of the property and the name. But though a good deal separated in childhood, they were much together in after life, and Jane gave a large share of her affections to him and his children. Mr. Knight was not only a very amiable man, kind and indulgent to all connected with him, but possessed also a spirit of fun and liveliness, which made him especially delightful to all young people.

Her third brother, Henry, had great conversational powers, and inherited from his father an eager and sanguine disposition. He was a very entertaining companion, but had perhaps less steadiness of purpose, certainly less success in life, than his brothers. He became a clergyman when middle-aged; and an allusion to his sermons will be found in one of Jane's letters. At one time he resided in London, and was useful in transacting his sister's business with her publishers.

Her two youngest brothers, Francis and Charles, were sailors during that glorious period of the British navy which comprises the close of the last and the beginning of the present century, when it was impossible for an officer to be almost always afloat, as these brothers were, without seeing service which, in these days, would be considered distinguished. Accordingly, they were continually engaged in actions of more or less importance, and sometimes gained promotion by their success. Both rose to the rank of Admiral, and carried out their flags to distant stations.

Francis lived to attain the very summit of his profession, having died, in his ninety-third year, G.C.B. and Senior Admiral of the Fleet, in 1865.

He possessed great firmness of character, with a strong sense of duty, whether due from himself to others, or from others to himself. He was consequently a strict disciplinarian; but, as he was a very religious man, it was remarked of him (for in those days, at least, it was remarkable) that he maintained this discipline without ever uttering an oath or permitting one in his presence. On one occasion, when ashore in a seaside town, he was spoken of as '*the* officer who kneeled at church;' a custom which now happily would not be thought peculiar.

Charles was generally serving in frigates or sloops; blockading harbours, driving the ships of the enemy ashore, boarding gun-boats, and frequently making small prizes. At one time he was absent from England on such services for seven years together. In later life he commanded the Bellerophon, at the bombardment of St. Jean d'Acre in 1840. In 1850 he went out in the Hastings, in command of the East India and China station, but on the breaking out of the Burmese war he transferred his flag to a steam sloop, for the purpose of getting up the shallow waters of the Irrawaddy, on board of which he died of cholera in 1852, in the seventy-fourth year of his age. His sweet temper and affectionate disposition, in which he resembled his sister Jane, had secured to him an unusual portion of attachment, not only from his own family, but from all the officers and common sailors who served under him. One who was with him at his death has left this record of him: 'Our good Admiral won the hearts of all by his gentleness and kindness while he was struggling with disease, and endeavouring to do his duty as Commander-in-chief of the British naval forces in these waters. His death was a great grief to the whole fleet. I know that I cried bitterly when I found he was dead.' The Order in Council of the Governor-General of India, Lord Dalhousie, expresses 'admiration of the staunch high spirit which, notwithstanding his age and previous sufferings, had led the Admiral to take his part in the trying service which has closed his career.'

These two brothers have been dwelt on longer than the others because their honourable career accounts for Jane Austen's partiality for the Navy, as well as for the readiness and accuracy with which she wrote about it. She was always very careful not to meddle with matters which she did not thoroughly understand. She never touched upon politics, law, or medicine, subjects which some novel writers have ventured on rather too boldly, and have treated, perhaps, with more brilliancy than accuracy. But with ships and sailors she felt herself at home, or at least could always trust to a brotherly critic to keep her right. I believe that no flaw has ever been found in her seamanship either in 'Mansfield Park' or in 'Persuasion.'

But dearest of all to the heart of Jane was her sister Cassandra, about three years her senior. Their sisterly affection for each other could scarcely be exceeded. Perhaps it began on Jane's side with the feeling of deference natural to a loving child towards a kind elder sister. Something of this feeling always remained; and even in the maturity of her powers, and in the enjoyment of increasing success, she would still speak of Cassandra as of one wiser and better than herself. In childhood, when the elder was sent to the school of a Mrs. Latournelle, in the Forbury at Reading, the younger went with her, not because she was thought old enough to profit much by the instruction there imparted, but because she would have been miserable without her sister; her mother observing that 'if Cassandra were going to have her head cut off, Jane would insist on sharing her fate.' This attachment was never interrupted or weakened. They lived in the same home, and shared the same bed-room, till separated by death. They were not exactly alike. Cassandra's was the colder and calmer disposition; she was always prudent and well judging, but with less outward demonstration of feeling and less sunniness of temper than Jane possessed. It was remarked in her family that 'Cassandra had the *merit* of having her temper always under command, but that Jane had the *happiness* of a temper that never required to be commanded.' When 'Sense and Sensibility' came out, some persons, who knew the family slightly, surmised that the two elder Miss Dashwoods were intended by the author for her sister and herself; but this could not be the case. Cassandra's character might indeed represent the '*sense*' of Elinor, but Jane's had little in common with the '*sensibility*' of Marianne. The young woman who, before the age of twenty, could so clearly discern the failings of Marianne Dashwood, could hardly have been subject to them herself.

This was the small circle, continually enlarged, however, by the increasing families of four of her brothers, within which Jane Austen found her wholesome pleasures, duties, and interests, and beyond which she went very little into society during the last ten years of her life. There was so much that was agreeable and attractive in this family party that its members may be excused if they were inclined to live somewhat too exclusively within it. They might see in each other much to love and esteem, and something to admire. The family talk had abundance of spirit and vivacity, and was never troubled by disagreements even in little matters, for it was not their habit to dispute or argue with each other: above all, there was strong family affection and firm union, never to be broken but by death. It cannot be doubted that all this had its influence on the author in the construction of her stories, in which a family party usually supplies the narrow stage, while the interest is made to revolve round a few actors.

It will be seen also that though her circle of society was small, yet she found in her neighbourhood persons of good taste and cultivated minds.

Her acquaintance, in fact, constituted the very class from which she took her imaginary characters, ranging from the member of parliament, or large landed proprietor, to the young curate or younger midshipman of equally good family; and I think that the influence of these early associations may be traced in her writings, especially in two particulars. First, that she is entirely free from the vulgarity, which is so offensive in some novels, of dwelling on the outward appendages of wealth or rank, as if they were things to which the writer was unaccustomed; and, secondly, that she deals as little with very low as with very high stations in life. She does not go lower than the Miss Steeles, Mrs. Elton, and John Thorpe, people of bad taste and underbred manners, such as are actually found sometimes mingling with better society. She has nothing resembling the Brangtons, or Mr. Dubster and his friend Tom Hicks, with whom Madame D'Arblay [Fanny Burney] loved to season her stories, and to produce striking contrasts to her well bred characters.

Notes

1. I went to represent my father, who was too unwell to attend himself, and thus I was the only one of my generation present.

2. My chief assistants have been my sisters, Mrs B. Lefroy and Miss Austen, whose recollections of our aunt are, on some points, more vivid than my own. I have not only been indebted to their memory for facts, but have sometimes used their words. Indeed some passages towards the end of the work were entirely written by the latter.

I have also to thank some of my cousins, and especially the daughters of Admiral Charles Austen, for the use of letters and papers which had passed into their hands, without which this Memoir, scanty as it is, could not have been written.

3. There seems to have been doubt as to the validity of this election; for Hearne says that it was referred to the Visitor, who confirmed it. (Hearne's *Diaries,* v.2)

4. Mrs Thrale writes Dr Lee, but there can be no doubt of the identity of the person.

Description of Steventon—Life at Steventon—Changes of Habits and Customs in the last Century

As the first twenty-five years, more than half of the brief life of Jane Austen, were spent in the parsonage of Steventon, some description of that place ought to be given. Steventon is a small rural village upon the chalk hills of north Hants, situated in a winding valley about seven miles from Basingstoke. The South-Western railway crosses it by a short embankment, and, as it curves round, presents a good view of it on the left hand to those who are travelling down the line, about three miles before entering the tunnel under Popham Beacon. It may be known to some sportsmen, as lying in one of the best portions of the Vine Hunt. It is certainly not a picturesque country; it presents no grand or extensive views; but the features are small rather than plain. The surface continually swells and sinks, but the hills are not bold, nor the valleys deep; and though it is sufficiently well clothed with woods and hedgerows, yet the poverty of the soil in most places prevents the timber from attaining a large size. Still it has its beauties. The lanes wind along in a natural curve, continually fringed with irregular borders of native turf, and lead to pleasant nooks and corners. One who knew and loved it well very happily expressed its quiet charms, when he wrote

True taste is not fastidious, nor rejects,
Because they may not come within the rule
Of composition pure and picturesque,
Unnumbered simple scenes which fill the leaves
Of Nature's sketch book.

[Extract from the poem *Lines written in the Autumn of 1817 after a recovery from sickness* by James Austen]

Of this somewhat tame country, Steventon, from the fall of the ground, and the abundance of its timber, is certainly one of the prettiest spots; yet one cannot be surprised that, when Jane's mother, a little before her marriage, was shown the scenery of her future home, she should have thought it unattractive, compared with the broad river, the rich valley, and the noble hills which she had been accustomed to behold at her native home near Henley-upon-Thames.

The house itself stood in a shallow valley, surrounded by sloping meadows, well sprinkled with elm trees, at the end of a small village of cottages, each well provided with a garden, scattered about prettily on either side of the road. It was sufficiently commodious to hold pupils in addition to a growing family, and was in those times considered to be above the average of parsonages; but the rooms were finished with less elegance than would now be found in the most ordinary dwellings. No cornice marked the junction of wall and ceiling; while the beams which supported the upper floors projected into the rooms below in all their naked simplicity, covered only by a coat of paint or whitewash: accordingly it has since been considered unworthy of being the Rectory house of a family living, and about forty-five years ago it was pulled down for the purpose of erecting a new house in a far better situation on the opposite side of the valley.

North of the house, the road from Deane to Popham Lane ran at a sufficient distance from the front to allow a carriage drive, through turf and trees. On the south side the ground rose gently, and was occupied by one of those old-fashioned gardens in which vegetables and flowers are combined, flanked and protected on the east by one of the thatched mud walls common in that country, and overshadowed by fine elms. Along the upper or southern side of this garden, ran a terrace of the finest turf, which must have been in the writer's thoughts when she described Catherine Morland's childish delight in 'rolling down the green slope at the back of the house.'

But the chief beauty of Steventon consisted in its hedgerows. A hedgerow, in that country, does not mean a thin formal line of quickset, but an irregular border of copse-wood and timber, often wide enough to contain within it a winding footpath, or a rough cart track. Under its shelter the earliest primroses, anemones, and wild hyacinths were to be found; sometimes, the first bird's-nest; and, now and then, the unwelcome adder. Two such hedgerows radiated, as it were, from the parsonage garden. One, a continuation of the turf terrace, proceeded westward, forming the southern boundary of the home meadows; and was formed into a rustic shrubbery, with occasional seats, entitled 'The Wood Walk.' The other ran straight up the hill, under the name of 'The Church Walk,' because it led to the parish church, as well as to a fine old manor-house, of Henry VIII.'s time, occupied by a family named Digweed, who have for more than a century rented it, together with the chief farm in the parish. The church itself – I speak of it as it then was, before the improvements made by the present rector –

A little spireless fane,
Just seen above the woody lane,

[From the poem *To Edward on planting a lime tree on the terrace in the meadow before the house. 1813,* by James Austen]

might have appeared mean and uninteresting to an ordinary observer; but the adept in church architecture would have known that it must have stood there some seven centuries, and would have found beauty in the very narrow early English windows, as well as in the general proportions of its little chancel; while its solitary position, far from the hum of the village, and within sight of no habitation, except a glimpse of the gray [*sic*] manor-house through its circling screen of sycamores, has in it something solemn and appropriate to the last resting-place of the silent dead. Sweet violets, both purple and white, grow in abundance beneath its south wall. One may imagine for how many centuries the ancestors of those little flowers have occupied that undisturbed, sunny nook, and may think how few living families can boast of as ancient a tenure of their land. Large elms protrude their rough branches; old hawthorns shed their annual blossoms over the graves; and the hollow yew-tree must be at least coeval with the church.

But whatever may be the beauties or defects of the surrounding scenery, this was the residence of Jane Austen for twenty-five years. This was the cradle of her genius. These were the first objects which inspired her young heart with a sense of the beauties of nature. In strolls along those wood-walks, thick-coming fancies rose in her mind, and gradually assumed the forms in which they came forth to the world. In that simple church she brought them all into subjection to the piety which ruled her in life, and supported her in death.

The home at Steventon must have been, for many years, a pleasant and prosperous one. The family was unbroken by death, and seldom visited by sorrow. Their situation had some peculiar advantages beyond those of ordinary rectories. Steventon was a family living. Mr. Knight, the patron, was also proprietor of nearly the whole parish. He never resided there, and consequently the rector and his children came to be regarded in the neighbourhood as a kind of representatives of the family. They shared with the principal tenant the command of an excellent manor, and enjoyed, in this reflected way, some of the consideration usually awarded to landed proprietors. They were not rich, but, aided by Mr. Austen's powers of teaching, they had enough to afford a good education to their sons and daughters, to mix in the best society of the neighbourhood, and to exercise a liberal hospitality to their own relations and friends. A carriage and a pair of horses were kept. This might imply a higher style of living in our days than it did in theirs. There were then no assessed taxes. The carriage, once bought, entailed little further expense; and the horses probably, like Mr. Bennet's, were often employed on farm work. Moreover, it should be remembered that a pair of horses in those days were almost necessary, if ladies were to move about at all; for neither the condition of the roads nor the style of carriage-building admitted of any comfortable vehicle being drawn by a single horse. When one looks at the few specimens still remaining of coach-building in the last century, it strikes one that the chief object of the builders must have been to combine the greatest possible weight with the least possible amount of accommodation.

The family lived in close intimacy with two cousins, Edward and Jane Cooper, the children of Mrs. Austen's eldest sister, and Dr. Cooper, the vicar of Sonning, near Reading. The Coopers lived for some years at Bath, which seems to have been much frequented in those days by clergymen retiring from work. I believe that Cassandra and Jane sometimes visited them there, and that Jane thus acquired the intimate knowledge of the topography and customs of Bath, which enabled her to write 'Northanger Abbey' long before she resided there herself. After the death of their own parents, the two young Coopers paid long visits at Steventon. Edward Cooper did not live undistinguished. When an undergraduate at Oxford, he gained the prize for Latin hexameters on 'Hortus Anglicus' in 1791; and in later life he was known by a work on prophecy, called 'The Crisis,' and other religious publications, especially for several volumes of Sermons, much preached in many pulpits in my youth. Jane Cooper was married from her uncle's house at Steventon, to Captain, afterwards Sir Thomas Williams, under whom Charles Austen served in several ships. She was a dear friend of her namesake, but was fated to become a cause of great sorrow to her, for a few years after the marriage she was suddenly killed by an accident to her carriage.

There was another cousin closely associated with them at Steventon, who must have introduced greater variety into the family circle. This was the daughter of Mr. Austen's only sister, Mrs. Hancock. This cousin had been educated in Paris, and married to a Count de Feuillade, of whom I know little more than that he perished by the guillotine during the French Revolution. Perhaps his chief offence was his rank; but it was said that the charge of 'incivism,' under which he suffered, rested on the fact of his having laid down some arable land into pasture – a sure sign of his intention to embarrass the Republican Government by producing a famine! His wife escaped through dangers and difficulties to England, was received for some time into her uncle's family, and finally married her cousin Henry Austen. During the short peace of Amiens, she and her second husband went to France, in the hope of recovering some of the Count's property, and there narrowly escaped being included amongst the *détenus*. Orders had been given by Buonaparte's government to detain all English travellers, but at the post-houses Mrs. Henry Austen gave the necessary orders herself, and her French was so perfect that she passed everywhere for a native, and her husband escaped under this protection.

She was a clever woman, and highly accomplished, after the French rather than the English mode; and in those days, when intercourse with the Continent was long interrupted by war, such an element in the society of a country parsonage must have been a rare acquisition. The sisters may have been more indebted to this cousin than to Mrs. La Tournelle's teaching for the considerable knowledge of French which they possessed. She also took the principal parts in the private theatricals in which the family several times indulged, having their summer theatre in the barn, and their winter one within the narrow limits of the dining-room, where the number of the audience must have been very limited. On these occasions, the prologues and epilogues were written by Jane's eldest brother, and some of them are very vigorous and amusing. Jane was only twelve years old at the time of the earliest of these representations, and not more than fifteen when the last took place. She was, however, an early observer, and it may be reasonably supposed that some of the incidents and feelings which are so vividly painted in the Mansfield Park theatricals are due to her recollections of these entertainments.

Some time before they left Steventon, one great affliction came upon the family. Cassandra was engaged to be married to a young clergyman [Thomas Fowle, a former pupil of her father]. He had not sufficient private fortune to permit an immediate union; but the engagement was not likely to be a hopeless or a protracted one, for he had a prospect of early preferment from a nobleman with whom he was connected both by birth and by personal friendship. He accompanied this friend to the West Indies, as chaplain to his regiment, and there died of yellow fever, to the great concern of his friend and patron, who afterwards declared that, if he had known of the engagement, he would not have permitted him to go out to such a climate. This little domestic tragedy caused great and lasting grief to the principal sufferer, and could not but cast a gloom over the whole party. The sympathy of Jane was probably, from her age, and her peculiar attachment to her sister, the deepest of all.

Of Jane herself I know of no such definite tale of love to relate. Her reviewer in the 'Quarterly' of January 1821 observes, concerning the attachment of Fanny Price to Edmund Bertram,

> The silence in which this passion is cherished, the slender hopes and enjoyments by which it is fed, the restlessness and jealousy with which it fills a mind naturally active, contented, and unsuspicious, the manner in which it tinges every event, and every reflection, are painted with a vividness and a detail of which we can scarcely conceive any one but a female, and we should almost add, a female writing from recollection, capable.

This conjecture, however probable, was wide of the mark. The picture was drawn from the intuitive perceptions of genius, not from personal experience. In no circumstance of her life was there any similarity between herself and her heroine in 'Mansfield Park.' She did not indeed pass through life without being the object of warm affection. In her youth she had declined the addresses of a gentleman [Harris Bigg-Wither] who had the recommendations of good character, and connections, and position in life, of everything, in fact, except the subtle power of touching her heart. There is, however, one passage of romance in her history with which I am imperfectly acquainted, and to which I am unable to assign name, or date, or place, though I have it on sufficient authority. Many years after her death, some circumstances induced her sister Cassandra to break through her habitual reticence, and to speak of it. She said that, while staying at some seaside place, they became acquainted with a gentleman, whose charm of person, mind, and manners was such that Cassandra thought him worthy to possess and likely to win her sister's love. When they parted, he expressed his intention of soon seeing them again; and Cassandra felt no doubt as to his motives. But they never again met. Within a short time they heard of his sudden death. I believe that, if Jane ever loved, it was this unnamed gentleman; but the acquaintance had been short, and I am unable to say whether her feelings were of such a nature as to affect her happiness.

Any description that I might attempt of the family life at Steventon, which closed soon after I was born, could be little better than a fancy-piece. There is no doubt that if we could look into the households of the clergy and the small gentry of that period, we should see some things which would seem strange to us, and should miss many more to which we are accustomed. Every hundred years, and especially a century like the last, marked by an extraordinary advance in wealth, luxury, and refinement of taste, as well as in the mechanical arts which embellish our houses, must produce a great change in their aspect. These changes are always at work; they are going on now, but so silently that we take no note of them. Men soon forget the small objects which they leave behind them as they drift down the stream of life. As [Alexander] Pope says:–

> Nor does life's stream for observation stay;
> It hurries all too fast to mark their way.

Important inventions, such as the applications of steam, gas, and electricity, may find their places in history; but not so the alterations, great as they may be, which have taken place in the appearance of our dining and drawing-rooms. Who can now record the degrees by which the custom prevalent in my youth of asking each other to take wine together at dinner became obsolete? Who will be able to fix, twenty years hence, the date when our dinners began to be carved and handed round by servants, instead of smoking before our eyes and noses on the table? To record such little matters would indeed be 'to chronicle small beer.' But, in a slight memoir like this, I may be allowed to note some of those changes in social habits which give a colour to history, but which the historian has the greatest difficulty in recovering.

At that time the dinner-table presented a far less splendid appearance than it does now. It was appropriated to solid food, rather than to flowers, fruits, and decorations. Nor was there much glitter of plate upon it; for the early dinner hour rendered candlesticks unnecessary, and silver forks had not come into general use: while the broad rounded end of the knives indicated the substitute generally used instead of them.[1]

The dinners too were more homely, though not less plentiful and savoury; and the bill of fare in one house would not be so like that in another as it is now, for family receipts were held in high estimation. A grandmother of culinary talent could bequeath to her descendant fame for some particular dish, and might influence the family dinner for many generations.

> Dos est magna parentium
> Virtus.
> ['excellence is the great legacy of parents']

One house would pride itself on its ham, another on its game-pie, and a third on its superior furmity, or tansey-pudding. Beer and home-made wines, especially mead, were more largely consumed. Vegetables were less plentiful and less various. Potatoes were used, but not so abundantly as now; and there was an idea that they were to be eaten only with roast meat. They were novelties to a tenant's wife who was entertained at Steventon Parsonage, certainly less than a hundred years ago; and when Mrs. Austen advised her to plant them in her own garden, she replied, 'No, no; they are very well for you gentry, but they must be terribly *costly to rear.*'

But a still greater difference would be found in the furniture of the rooms, which would appear to us lamentably scanty. There was a general deficiency of carpeting in sitting-rooms, bed-rooms, and passages. A pianoforte, or rather a spinnet or harpsichord, was by no means a necessary appendage. It was to be found only where there was a decided taste for music, not so common then as now, or in such great houses as would probably contain a billiard-table. There would often be but one sofa in the house, and that a stiff, angular, uncomfortable article. There were no deep easy-chairs, nor other appliances for lounging; for to lie down, or even to lean back, was a luxury permitted only to old persons or invalids. It was said of a nobleman, a personal friend of George III and a model gentleman of his day, that he would have made the tour of Europe without ever touching the back of his travelling carriage. But perhaps we should be most struck with the total absence of those elegant little articles which now embellish and encumber our drawing-room tables. We should miss the sliding bookcases and picture-stands, the letter-weighing machines and envelope cases, the periodicals and illustrated newspapers – above all, the countless swarm of photograph books which now threaten to swallow up all space. A small writing-desk, with a smaller work-box, or netting-case, was all that each young lady contributed to occupy the table; for the large family work-basket, though often produced in the parlour, lived in the closet.

There must have been more dancing throughout the country in those days than there is now: and it seems to have sprung up more spontaneously, as if it were a natural production, with less fastidiousness as to the quality of music, lights, and floor. Many country towns had a monthly ball throughout the winter, in some of which the same apartment served for dancing and tea-room. Dinner parties more frequently ended with an extempore dance on the carpet, to the music of a harpsichord in the house, or a fiddle from the village. This was always supposed to be for the entertainment of the young people, but many, who had little pretension to youth, were very ready to join in it. There can be no doubt that Jane herself enjoyed dancing, for she attributes this taste to her favourite heroines; in most of her works, a ball or a private dance is mentioned, and made of importance.

Many things connected with the ball-rooms of those days have now passed into oblivion. The barbarous law which confined the lady to one partner throughout the evening must indeed have been abolished before Jane went to balls. It must be observed, however, that this custom was in one respect advantageous to the gentleman, inasmuch as it rendered his duties more practicable. He was bound to call upon his partner the next morning, and it must have been convenient to have only one lady for whom he was obliged

> To gallop all the country over,
> The last night's partner to behold,
> And humbly hope she caught no cold.

But the stately minuet still reigned supreme; and every regular ball commenced with it. It was a slow and solemn movement, expressive of grace and dignity, rather than of merriment. It abounded in formal bows and courtesies, with measured paces, forwards, backwards and sideways, and many complicated gyrations. It was executed by one lady and gentleman, amidst the admiration, or the criticism, of surrounding spectators. In its earlier and most palmy days, as when Sir Charles and Lady Grandison [characters in Samuel Richardson's novel *The History of Sir Charles Grandison*] delighted the company by dancing it at their own wedding, the gentleman wore a dress sword, and the lady was armed with a fan of nearly equal dimensions. Addison [Joseph Addison, founder of *The Spectator*] observes that 'women are armed with fans, as men with swords, and sometimes do more execution with them.' The graceful carriage of each weapon was considered a test of high breeding. The clownish man was in danger of being tripped up by his sword getting between his legs: the fan held clumsily looked more of a burden than an ornament; while in the hands of an adept it could be made to speak a language of its own.[2] It was not everyone who felt qualified to make this public exhibition, and I have been told that those ladies who intended to dance minuets, used to distinguish themselves from others by wearing a particular kind of lappet [a flap] on their head-dress. I have heard also of another curious proof of the respect in which this dance was held. Gloves immaculately clean were considered requisite for its due performance, while gloves a little soiled were thought good enough for a country dance; and accordingly some prudent ladies provided themselves with two pairs for their several purposes. The minuet expired with the last century: but long after it had ceased to be danced publicly it was taught to boys and girls, in order to give them a graceful carriage.

Hornpipes, cotillons, and reels, were occasionally danced; but the chief occupation of the evening was the interminable country dance, in which all could join. This dance presented a great show of enjoyment, but it was not without its peculiar troubles. The ladies and gentlemen were ranged apart from each other in opposite rows, so that the facilities for flirtation, or interesting intercourse, were not so great as might have been desired by both parties. Much heart-burning and discontent sometimes arose as to *who* should stand above *whom*, and especially as to who was entitled to the high privilege of calling and leading off the first dance: and no little indignation was felt at the lower end of the room when any of the leading couples retired prematurely from their duties, and did not condescend to dance up and down the whole set. We may rejoice that these causes of irritation no longer exist; and that if such feelings as jealousy, rivalry, and discontent ever touch celestial bosoms in the modern ball-room they must arise from different and more recondite sources.

I am tempted to add a little about the difference of personal habits. It may be asserted as a general truth, that less was left to the charge and discretion of servants, and more was done, or superintended, by the masters and mistresses. With regard to the mistresses, it is, I believe, generally understood, that at the time to which I refer, a hundred years ago, they took a personal part in the higher branches of cookery, as well as in the concoction of home-made wines, and distilling of herbs for domestic medicines, which are nearly allied to the same art. Ladies did not disdain to spin the thread of which the household linen was woven. Some ladies liked to wash with their own hands their choice china after breakfast or tea. In one of my earliest child's books, a little girl, the daughter of a gentleman, is taught by her mother to make her own bed before leaving her chamber. It was not so much that they had not servants to do all these things for them, as that they took an interest in such occupations. And it must be borne in mind how many sources of interest enjoyed by this generation were then closed, or very scantily opened to ladies. A very small minority of them cared much for literature or science. Music was not a very common, and drawing was a still rarer, accomplishment; needlework, in some form or other, was their chief sedentary employment.

But I doubt whether the rising generation are equally aware how much gentlemen also did for themselves in those times, and whether some things that I can mention will not be a surprise to them. Two homely proverbs were held in higher estimation in my early days than they are now – 'The master's eye makes the horse fat;' and, 'If you would be well served, serve yourself.' Some gentlemen took pleasure in being their own gardeners, performing all the scientific, and some of the manual, work themselves. Well-dressed young men of my acquaintance, who had their coat from a London tailor, would always brush their evening suit themselves, rather than entrust it to the carelessness of a rough servant, and to the risks of dirt and grease in the kitchen; for in those days servants' halls were not common in the houses of the clergy and the smaller country gentry. It was quite natural that Catherine Morland should have contrasted the magnificence of the offices at Northanger Abbey with the few shapeless pantries in her father's parsonage. A young man who expected to have his things packed or unpacked for him by a servant, when he travelled, would have been thought exceptionally fine, or exceptionally lazy. When my uncle undertook to teach me to shoot, his first lesson was how to clean my own gun. It was thought meritorious on the evening of a hunting day, to turn out after dinner, lanthorn in hand, and visit the stable, to ascertain that the horse had been well cared for. This was of the more importance, because, previous to the introduction of clipping, about the year 1820, it was a difficult and tedious work to make a long-coated hunter dry and comfortable, and was often very imperfectly done. Of course, such things were not practised by those who had gamekeepers, and stud-grooms, and plenty of well-trained servants; but they were practised by many who were unequivocally gentlemen, and whose grandsons, occupying the same position in life, may perhaps be astonished at being told that '*such things were*.'

I have drawn pictures for which my own experience, or what I heard from others in my youth, have supplied the materials. Of course, they cannot be universally applicable. Such details varied in various circles, and were changed very gradually; nor can I pretend to tell how much of what I have said is descriptive of the family life at Steventon in Jane Austen's youth. I am sure that the ladies there had nothing to do with the mysteries of the stew-pot or the preserving-pan; but it is probable that their way of life differed a little from ours, and would have appeared to us more homely. It may be that useful articles, which would not now be produced in drawing-rooms, were hemmed, and marked, and darned in the old-fashioned parlour. But all this concerned only the outer life; there was as much cultivation and refinement of mind as now, with probably more studied courtesy and ceremony of manner to visitors; whilst certainly in that family literary pursuits were not neglected.

I remember to have heard of only two little things different from modern customs. One was, that on hunting mornings the young men usually took their hasty breakfast in the kitchen. The early hour at which hounds then met may account for this; and probably the custom began, if it did not end, when they were boys; for they hunted at an early age, in a scrambling sort of way, upon any pony or donkey that they could procure, or, in default of such luxuries, on foot. I have been told that Sir Francis Austen, when seven years old, bought on his own account, it must be supposed with his father's permission, a pony for a guinea and a half; and after riding him with great success for two seasons, sold him for a guinea more. One may wonder how the child could have so much money, and how the animal could have been obtained for so little. The same authority informs me that his first cloth suit was made from a scarlet habit, which, according to the fashion of the times, had been his mother's usual morning dress. If all this is true, the future admiral of the British Fleet must have cut a conspicuous figure in the hunting-field. The other peculiarity was that, when the roads were dirty, the sisters took long walks in pattens. This defence against wet and dirt is now seldom seen. The few that remain are banished from good society, and employed only in menial work; but a hundred and fifty years ago they were celebrated in poetry, and considered so clever a contrivance that [John] Gay in his 'Trivia,' ascribes the invention to a god stimulated by his passion for a mortal damsel, and derives the name 'Patten' from 'Patty.'

> The patten now supports each frugal dame,
> Which from the blue-eyed Patty takes the name.

But mortal damsels have long ago discarded the clumsy implement. First it dropped its iron ring and became a clog; afterwards it was fined down into the pliant galoshe – lighter to wear and more effectual to protect – a no less manifest instance of gradual improvement than [William] Cowper indicates when he traces through eighty lines of poetry his 'accomplished sofa' back to the original three-legged stool.

As an illustration of the purposes which a patten was intended to serve, I add the following epigram, written by Jane Austen's uncle, Mr. Leigh Perrot, on reading in a newspaper the marriage of Captain Foote to Miss Patten:–

Through the rough paths of life, with a patten your guard,
May you safely and pleasantly jog;
May the knot never slip, nor the ring press too hard,
Nor the *Foot* find the *Patten* a clog.

At the time when Jane Austen lived at Steventon, a work was carried on in the neighbouring cottages which ought to be recorded, because it has long ceased to exist.

Up to the beginning of the present century, poor women found profitable employment in spinning flax or wool. This was a better occupation for them than straw plaiting, inasmuch as it was carried on at the family hearth, and did not admit of gadding and gossiping about the village. The implement used was a long narrow machine of wood, raised on legs, furnished at one end with a large wheel, and at the other with a spindle on which the flax or wool was loosely wrapped, connected together by a loop of string. One hand turned the wheel, while the other formed the thread. The outstretched arms, the advanced foot, the sway of the whole figure backwards and forwards, produced picturesque attitudes, and displayed whatever of grace or beauty the work-woman might possess.[3] Some ladies were fond of spinning, but they worked in a quieter manner, sitting at a neat little machine of varnished wood, like Tunbridge ware, generally turned by the foot, with a basin of water at hand to supply the moisture required for forming the thread, which the cottager took by a more direct and natural process from her own mouth. I remember two such elegant little wheels in our own family.

It may be observed that this hand-spinning is the most primitive of female accomplishments, and can be traced back to the earliest times. Ballad poetry and fairy tales are full of allusions to it. The term 'spinster' still testifies to its having been the ordinary employment of the English young woman. It was the labour assigned to the ejected nuns by the rough earl who said, 'Go spin, ye jades, go spin.' It was the employment at which Roman matrons and Grecian princesses presided amongst their handmaids. Heathen mythology celebrated it in the three Fates spinning and measuring out the thread of human life. Holy Scripture honours it in those 'wise-hearted women' who 'did spin with their hands, and brought that which they had spun' for the construction of the Tabernacle in the wilderness: and an old English proverb carries it still farther back to the time 'when Adam delved and Eve span.' But, at last, this time-honoured domestic manufacture is quite extinct amongst us – crushed by the power of steam, overborne by a countless host of spinning jennies, and I can only just remember some of its last struggles for existence in the Steventon cottages.

Notes

1. The celebrated Beau Brummell [iconic Regency figure and arbiter of fashion], who was so intimate with George IV as to be able to quarrel with him, was born in 1771. It is reported that when he was questioned about his parents, he replied that it was long since he had heard of them, but that he imagined the worthy couple must have cut their own throats by that time, because when he last saw them they were eating peas with their knives. Yet Brummel's father had probably lived in good society; and was certainly able to put his son into a fashionable regiment, and to leave him 30,000*l.* Raikes [Thomas Raikes, 1777–1848, diarist and dandy] believes that he had been Secretary to Lord North. Thackeray's [Victorian novelist] idea that he had been a footman cannot stand against the authority of Raikes, who was intimate with the son. (Raikes's *Memoirs,* vol.ii.p.207)
2. See 'Spectator,' No. 102, on the Fan Exercise. Old gentlemen who had survived the fashion of wearing swords were known to regret the disuse of that custom, because it put an end to one way of distinguishing those who had, from those who had not, been used to good society. To wear the sword easily was an art which, like swimming and skating, required to be learned in youth. Children could practise it early with their toy swords adapted to their size.
3. Mrs. Gaskell, in her tale of 'Sylvia's Lovers,' declares that this hand-spinning rivalled harp-playing in its gracefulness.

Early Compositions—Friends at Ashe—A very old Letter—Lines on the Death of Mrs. Lefroy—Observations on Jane Austen's Letter-writing—Letters

I know little of Jane Austen's childhood. Her mother followed a custom, not unusual in those days, though it seems strange to us, of putting out her babies to be nursed in a cottage in the village. The infant was daily visited by one or both of its parents, and frequently brought to them at the parsonage, but the cottage was its home, and must have remained so till it was old enough to run about and talk; for I know that one of them, in after life, used to speak of his foster mother as 'Movie,' the name by which he had called her in his infancy. It may be that the contrast between the parsonage house and the best class of cottages was not quite so extreme then as it would be now, that the one was somewhat less luxurious, and the other less squalid. It would certainly seem from the results that it was a wholesome and invigorating system, for the children were all strong and healthy. Jane was probably treated like the rest in this respect. In childhood every available opportunity of instruction was made use of. According to the ideas of the time, she was well educated, though not highly accomplished, and she certainly enjoyed that important element of mental training, associating at home with persons of cultivated intellect. It cannot be doubted that her early years were bright and happy, living, as she did, with indulgent parents, in a cheerful home, not without agreeable variety of society. To these sources of enjoyment must be added the first stirrings of talent within her, and the absorbing interest of original composition. It is impossible to say at how early an age she began to write. There are copy books extant containing tales some of which must have been composed while she was a young girl, as they had amounted to a considerable number by the time she was sixteen. Her earliest stories are of a slight and flimsy texture, and are generally intended to be nonsensical, but the nonsense has much spirit in it. They are usually preceded by a dedication of mock solemnity to some one of her family. It would seem that the grandiloquent dedications prevalent in those days had not escaped her youthful penetration. Perhaps the most characteristic feature in these early productions is that, however puerile the matter, they are always composed in pure simple English, quite free from the over-ornamented style which might be expected from so young a writer. One of her juvenile effusions is given, as a specimen of the kind of transitory amusement which Jane was continually supplying to the family party.

THE MYSTERY.
AN UNFINISHED COMEDY.
DEDICATION.
TO THE REV. GEORGE AUSTEN

SIR,—I humbly solicit your patronage to the following Comedy, which, though an unfinished one, is, I flatter myself, as complete a *Mystery* as any of its kind.
I am, Sir, your most humble Servant,
THE AUTHOR.

THE MYSTERY, A COMEDY.
DRAMATIS PERSONAE

Men.	*Women.*
Col. ELLIOT.	FANNY ELLIOT.
OLD HUMBUG	Mrs. HUMBUG
YOUNG HUMBUG.	*and*
SIR EDWARD SPANGLE	DAPHNE.
and	
CORYDON.	

ACT I.

SCENE I.– A garden

Enter Corydon.

Corydon. But hush: I am interrupted. [Exit CORYDON.

Enter Old Humbug and his Son, talking.

Old Hum. It is for that reason that I wish you to follow my advice. Are you convinced of its propriety?

Young Hum. I am, sir, and will certainly act in the manner you have pointed out to me.

Old Hum. Then let us return to the house. [Exeunt.

SCENE II.—A parlour in Humbug's house. Mrs. Humbug and Fanny discovered at work.

Mrs. Hum. You understand me, my love?

Fanny. Perfectly, ma'am: pray continue your narration.

Mrs. Hum. Alas! it is nearly concluded; for I have nothing more to say on the subject.

Fanny. Ah! here is Daphne.

Enter Daphne.

Daphne. My dear Mrs. Humbug, how d'ye do? Oh! Fanny, it is all over.

Fanny. Is it indeed!

Mrs. Hum. I'm very sorry to hear it.

Fanny. Then 'twas to no purpose that I—

Daphne. None upon earth.

Mrs. Hum. And what is to become of—?

Daphne. Oh! 'tis all settled. (*Whispers* MRS. HUMBUG.)

Fanny. And how is it determined?

Daphne. I'll tell you. (*Whispers* FANNY.)

Mrs. Hum. And is he to—?

Daphne. I'll tell you all I know of the matter. (*Whispers* MRS. HUMBUG *and* FANNY.)

Fanny. Well, now I know everything about it, I'll go away.

Mrs. Hum. and *Daphne*. And so will I.

[*Exeunt.*

SCENE III.—*The curtain rises, and discovers* SIR EDWARD SPANGLE *reclined in an elegant attitude on a sofa fast asleep.*

Enter COL. ELLIOTT.

Col. E. My daughter is not here, I see. There lies Sir Edward. Shall I tell him the secret? No, he'll certainly blab it. But he's asleep, and won't hear me;—so I'll e'en venture. (*Goes up to* SIR EDWARD, *whispers him, and exit.*)

END OF THE FIRST ACT.

FINIS.

Her own mature opinion of the desirableness of such an early habit of composition is given in the following words of a niece [Caroline]:-

> As I grew older, my aunt would talk to me more seriously of my reading and my amusements. I had taken early to writing verses and stories, and I am sorry to think how I troubled her with reading them. She was very kind about it, and always had some praise to bestow, but at last she warned me against spending too much time upon them. She said – how well I recollect it! – that she knew writing stories was a great amusement, and *she* thought a harmless one, though many people, she was aware, thought otherwise; but that at my age it would be bad for me to be much taken up with my own compositions. Later still – it was after she had gone to Winchester – she sent me a message to this effect, that if I would take her advice I should cease writing till I was sixteen; that she had herself often wished she had read more, and written less in the corresponding years of her own life.' As this niece was only twelve years old at the time of her aunt's death, these words seem to imply that the juvenile tales to which I have referred had, some of them at least, been written in her childhood.

But between these childish effusions, and the composition of her living works, there intervened another stage of her progress, during which she produced some stories, not without merit, but which she never considered worthy of publication. During this preparatory period her mind seems to have been working in a very different direction from that into which it ultimately settled. Instead of presenting faithful copies of nature, these tales were generally burlesques, ridiculing the improbable events and exaggerated sentiments which she had met with in sundry silly romances. Something of this fancy is to be found in 'Northanger Abbey,' but she soon left it far behind in her subsequent course. It would seem as if she were first taking note of all the faults to be avoided, and curiously considering how she ought *not* to write before she attempted to put forth her strength in the right direction. The family have, rightly, I think, declined to let these early works be published. Mr. Shortreed [friend of Walter Scott] observed very pithily of Walter Scott's early rambles on the borders, 'He was makin' himsell a' the time; but he didna ken, may be, what he was about till years had passed. At first he thought of little, I dare say, but the queerness and the fun.' And so, in a humbler way, Jane Austen was 'makin' hersell,' little thinking of future fame, but caring only for 'the queerness and the fun;' and it would be as unfair to expose this preliminary process to the world, as it would be to display all that goes on behind the curtain of the theatre before it is drawn up.

It was, however, at Steventon that the real foundations of her fame were laid. There some of her most successful writing was composed at such an early age as to make it surprising that so young a woman could have acquired the insight into character, and the nice observation of manners which they display. 'Pride and Prejudice,' which some consider the most brilliant of her novels, was the first finished, if not the first begun. She began it in October 1796, before she was twenty-one years old, and completed it in about ten months, in August 1797. The title then intended for it was 'First Impressions.' 'Sense and Sensibility' was begun, in its present form, immediately after the completion of the former, in November 1797 but something similar in story and character had been written earlier under the title of 'Elinor and Marianne;' and if, as is probable, a good deal of this earlier production was retained, it must form the earliest specimen of her writing that has been given to the world. 'Northanger Abbey,' though not prepared for the press till 1803, was certainly first composed in 1798.

Amongst the most valuable neighbours of the Austens were Mr. and Mrs. Lefroy and their family. He was rector of the adjoining parish of Ashe; she was sister to Sir Egerton Brydges, to whom we are indebted for the earliest notice of Jane Austen that exists. In his autobiography, speaking of his visits at Ashe, he writes thus:–

> The nearest neighbours of the Lefroys were the Austens of Steventon. I remember Jane Austen, the novelist, as a little child. She was very intimate with Mrs. Lefroy, and much encouraged by her. Her mother was a Miss Leigh, whose paternal grandmother was sister to the first Duke of Chandos. Mr. Austen was of a Kentish family, of which several branches have been settled in the Weald of Kent, and some are still remaining there. When I knew Jane Austen, I never suspected that she was an authoress; but my eyes told me that she was fair and handsome, slight and elegant, but with cheeks a little too full.

One may wish that Sir Egerton had dwelt rather longer on the subject of these memoirs, instead of being drawn away by his extreme love for genealogies to her great-grandmother and ancestors. That great-grandmother however lives in the family records as Mary Brydges, a daughter of Lord Chandos, married in Westminster Abbey to Theophilus Leigh of Addlestrop in 1698. When a girl she had received a curious letter of advice and reproof, written by her mother from Constantinople. Mary, or 'Poll,' was remaining in England with her grandmother, Lady Bernard, who seems to have been wealthy and inclined to be too indulgent to her granddaughter. This letter is given. Any such authentic document, two hundred years old, dealing with domestic details, must possess some interest. This is remarkable, not only as a specimen of the homely language in which ladies of rank then expressed themselves, but from the sound sense which it contains. Forms of expression vary, but good sense and right principles are the same in the nineteenth that they were in the seventeenth century.

MY DEARES POLL,

Y^{r} letters by Cousin Robbert Serle arrived here not before the 27th of Aprill, yett were they hartily wellcome to us, bringing ye joyful news which a great while we had longed for of my most dear Mother & all other relations & friends good health which I beseech God continue to you all, & as I observe in y^{rs} to y^{r} Sister Betty ye extraordinary kindness of (as I may truly say) the best Moth^{r}.& Gnd Moth^{r} in the world in pinching herself to make you fine, so I cannot but admire her great good Housewifry in affording you so very plentifull an allowance, & yett to increase her Stock at the rate I find she hath done; & think I can never sufficiently mind you how very much it is y$_{r}$ duty on all occasions to pay her y^{r}. gratitude in all humble submission & obedience to all her commands soe long as you live. I must tell you 'tis to her bounty & care in y^{e} greatest measure you are like to owe y^{r} well living in this world, & as you cannot but be very sensible you are an extraordinary charge to her so it behoves you to take particular heed that in ye whole course of y^{r} life, you render her a proportionable comfort, especially since 'tis ye best way you can ever hope to make her such amends as God requires of y^{r} hands. but Poll! it grieves me a little & y^{t} I am forced to take notice of & reprove you for some vaine expressions in y^{r} lettrs to y^{r} Sister – you say concerning y^{r} allowance "you aime to bring y^{r} bread & cheese even" in this I do not discommend you, for a foule shame indeed it would be should you out run the Constable having soe liberall a provision made you for y^{r} maintenance – but ye reason you give for y^{r} resolution I cannot at all approve for you say "to spend more you can't" thats because you have it not to spend, otherwise it seems you would. So y^{t} tis y^{r} Grandmoth^{rs} discretion & not yours th^{t} keeps you from extravagancy, which plainly appears in ye close of y^{r} sentence, saying y^{t} you think it simple covetousness to save out of y^{rs} but 'tis my opinion if you lay all on y^{r} back 'tis ten tymes a greater sin & shame th^{n} to save some what out of soe large an allowance in y^{r} purse to help you at a dead lift. Child, we all know our beginning, but who knows his end? Y^{e} best use th^{t} can be made of fair weath^{r} is to provide against foule & 'tis great discretion & of noe small commendations for a young woman betymes to shew herself housewifly & frugal. Y^{r} Mother neither Maide nor wife ever yett bestowed forty pounds a yeare on herself & yett if you never fall und^{r} a worse reputation in ye world th^{n} she (I thank God for it) hath hitherto done, you need not repine at it, & you cannot be ignorant of ye difference th^{t} was between my fortune & what you are to expect. You ought *likewise to consider th^{t} you have seven brothers & sisters & you are all one man's children & therefore it is very unreasonable that one should expect to be preferred in finery soe much above all ye rest for 'tis impossible you should soe much mistake y^{r} ffather's condition as to fancy he is able to allow every one of you forty pounds a yeare a piece, for such an allowance with the charge of their diett over and above will amount to at least five hundred pounds a yeare, a sum y^{r} poor ffather can ill spare, besides doe but bethink y^{r} self what a ridiculous sight it will be when y^{r} grandmothr & you come to us to have noe less th^{n} seven waiting gentlewomen in one house, for what reason can you give why every one of y^{r} sisters should not have every one of y^{m} a Maide as well as you, & though you may spare to pay y^{r} maide's wages out of y^{r} allowance yett you take no care of ye unnecessary charge you put y^{r} ffath^{r} to in y^{r} increase of his family, whereas if it were not a piece of pride to have ye name of keeping y^{r} maide she y^{t} waits on y^{r} good Grandmother might easily doe as formerly you know she hath done, all ye business you have for a maide unless as you grow old^{r} you grow a veryer Foole which God forbid!*

Poll, you live in a place where you see great plenty & splendour but let not ye allurements of earthly pleasures tempt you to forget or neglect ye duty of a good Christian in dressing y^{r} bettr part which is y^{r} soule, as will best please God. I am not against y^{r} going decent & neate as becomes y^{r} ffathers daughter but to clothe y^{r}self rich & be running into every gaudy fashion can never become y^{r} circumstances & instead of doing you creditt & getting you a good prefer^{nt} it is ye readiest way you can take to fright all sober men from ever thinking of matching th^{m}selves with women that live above thy^{r} fortune, & if this be a wise way of spending money judge you! & besides, doe but reflect what an od sight it will be to a stranger that comes to our house to see y^{r} Grandmoth^{r} y^{r} Mothr & all y^{r} Sisters in a plane dress & you only trick^{d} up like a bartlemew-babby – you know what sort of people those are th^{t} can't faire well but they must cry rost meate now what effect could you imagine y^{r} writing in such a high straine to y^{r} Sisters could have but eithe^{r} to provoke th^{m} to envy you or murmur against us. I must tell you neith^{r} of y^{r} Sisters have ever had twenty pounds a yeare allowance from us yett, & yett they^{r} dress hath not disparaged neith^{r} th^{m} nor us & without incurring ye censure of simple covetousness they will have some what to shew out of their saving that will doe th^{m} creditt & I expect y^{t} you th^{t} are they^{r} elder Sister sh^{d} rather sett th^{m} examples of ye like nature th^{n} tempt th^{m} from treading in ye steps of their good Grandmoth^{r} & poor Moth^{r}. This is not half what might be saide on this occasion but believing thee to be a very good natured dutyfull child I sh^{d} have thought it a great deal too much but yt having in my coming hither past through many most desperate dangers I cannot forbear thinking & preparing myself for all events, & therefore not knowing how it may please God to dispose of us I conclude it my duty to God & thee my d^{r} child to lay

this matter as home to thee as I could, assuring you my daily prayers are not nor shall not be wanting that God may give you grace always to remember to make a right use of this truly affectionate counsell of y[r] poor Moth[r]. & though I speak very plaine down-right english to you yett I would not have you doubt but that I love you as hartily as any child I have & if you serve God and take good courses I promise you my kindness to you shall be according to y[r] own hart's desire, for you may be certain I can aime at nothing in what I have now writ but y[r] real good which to promote shall be y[e] study & care day & night
Of my dear Poll
thy truly affectionate Mothr.
ELIZA CHANDOS.
Pera of Galata, May y[e] 6th 1686.
P.S. – Thy ffath[r] & I send thee our blessing, & all thy broth[rs] & sist[rs] theyr service. Our harty & affectionate service to my broth[r] & sist[r] Childe & all. my dear cozens. When you see my Lady Worster & cozen Howlands pray present th[m] my most humble service.

This letter shows that the wealth acquired by trade was already manifesting itself in contrast with the straitened circumstances of some of the nobility. Mary Brydges's 'poor ffather,' in whose household economy was necessary, was the King of England's ambassador at Constantinople; the grandmother, who lived in 'great plenty and splendour,' was the widow of a Turkey merchant. But then, as now, it would seem, rank had the power of attracting and absorbing wealth.

At Ashe also Jane became acquainted with a member of the Lefroy family, who was still living when I began these memoirs, a few months ago; the Right Hon. Thomas Lefroy, late Chief Justice of Ireland. One must look back more than seventy years to reach the time when these two bright young persons were, for a short time, intimately acquainted with each other, and then separated on their several courses, never to meet again; both destined to attain some distinction in their different ways, one to survive the other for more than half a century, yet in his extreme old age to remember and speak, as he sometimes did, of his former companion, as one to be much admired, and not easily forgotten by those who had ever known her.

Mrs. Lefroy herself was a remarkable person. Her rare endowments of goodness, talents, graceful person, and engaging manners, were sufficient to secure her a prominent place in any society into which she was thrown; while her enthusiastic eagerness of disposition rendered her especially attractive to a clever and lively girl. She was killed by a fall from her horse on Jane's birthday, Dec. 16, 1804. The following lines to her memory were written by Jane four years afterwards, when she was thirty-three years old. They are given, not for their merits as poetry, but to show how deep and lasting was the impression made by the elder friend on the mind of the younger:–

TO THE MEMORY OF MRS. LEFROY.
The day returns again, my natal day;
What mix'd emotions in my mind arise!
Beloved Friend; four years have passed away
Since thou wert snatched for ever from our eyes.
The day commemorative of my birth,
Bestowing life, and light, and hope to me,
Brings back the hour which was thy last on earth.
O! bitter pang of torturing memory!
Angelic woman! past my power to praise
In language meet thy talents, temper, mind,
Thy solid worth, thy captivating grace,
Thou friend and ornament of human kind.
But come, fond Fancy, thou indulgent power;
Hope is desponding, chill, severe, to thee:
Bless thou this little portion of an hour;
Let me behold her as she used to be.
I see her here with all her smiles benign,
Her looks of eager love, her accents sweet,
That voice and countenance almost divine,
Expression, harmony, alike complete.
Listen! It is not sound alone,'tis sense,
T's genius, taste, and tenderness of soul:
T'is genuine warmth of heart, without pretence,
And purity of mind that crowns the whole.
She speaks! Tis eloquence, that grace of tongue,
So rare, so lovely, never misapplied
By her, to palliate vice, or deck a wrong:
She speaks and argues but on virtue's side.
Hers is the energy of soul sincere;
Her Christian spirit, ignorant to feign,
Seeks but to comfort, heal, enlighten, cheer,
Confer a pleasure or prevent a pain.
Can aught enhance such goodness? yes, to me
Her partial favour from my earliest years
Consummates all: ah! give me but to see
Her smile of love! The vision disappears.
'Tis past and gone. We meet no more below,
Short is the cheat of Fancy o'er the tomb.
Oh! might I hope to equal bliss to go,

To meet thee, angel, in thy future home.
Fain would I feel an union with thy fate:
Fain would I seek to draw an omen fair
From this connection in our earthly date.
Indulge the harmless weakness. Reason, spare.

The loss of their first home is generally a great grief to young persons of strong feeling and lively imagination; and Jane was exceedingly unhappy when she was told that her father, now seventy years of age, had determined to resign his duties to his eldest son, who was to be his successor in the Rectory of Steventon, and to remove with his wife and daughters to Bath. Jane had been absent from home when this resolution was taken; and, as her father was always rapid both in forming his resolutions and in acting on them, she had little time to reconcile herself to the change.

A wish has sometimes been expressed that some of Jane Austen's letters should be published. Some entire letters, and many extracts, will be given in this memoir; but the reader must be warned not to expect too much from them. With regard to accuracy of language indeed every word of them might be printed without correction. The style is always clear, and generally animated, while a vein of humour continually gleams through the whole; but the materials may be thought inferior to the execution, for they treat only of the details of domestic life. There is in them no notice of politics or public events; scarcely any discussions on literature, or other subjects of general interest. They may be said to resemble the nest which some little bird builds of the materials nearest at hand, of the twigs and mosses supplied by the tree in which it is placed; curiously constructed out of the simplest matters.

Her letters have very seldom the date of the year, or the signature of her Christian name at full length; but it has been easy to ascertain their dates, either from the post-mark, or from their contents.

The two following letters are the earliest that I have seen. They were both written in November 1800; before the family removed from Steventon. Some of the same circumstances are referred to in both.

The first is to her sister Cassandra, who was then staying with their brother Edward at Godmersham Park, Kent:–

Steventon, Saturday evening, Nov. 8th.
MY DEAR CASSANDRA,
I thank you for so speedy a return to my two last, and particularly thank you for your anecdote of Charlotte Graham and her cousin, Harriet Bailey, which has very much amused both my mother and myself. If you can learn anything farther of that interesting affair, I hope you will mention it. I have

two messages; let me get rid of them, and then my paper will be my own. Mary [wife of James Austen] fully intended writing to you by Mr. Chute's [William Chute, M.P. for Hampshire] frank, and only happened entirely to forget it, but will write soon; and my father wishes Edward to send him a memorandum of the price of the hops. The tables are come, and give general contentment. I had not expected that they would so perfectly suit the fancy of us all three, or that we should so well agree in the disposition of them; but nothing except their own surface can have been smoother. The two ends put together form one constant table for everything, and the centre piece stands exceedingly well under the glass, and holds a great deal most commodiously, without looking awkwardly. They are both covered with green baize, and send their best love. The Pembroke has got its destination by the sideboard, and my mother has great delight in keeping her money and papers locked up. The little table which used to stand there has most conveniently taken itself off into the best bedroom; and we are now in want only of the chiffonniere, which is neither finished nor come. So much for that subject; I now come to another, of a very different nature, as other subjects are very apt to be. Earle Harwood [the Harwoods lived at Deane] has been again giving uneasiness to his family and talk to the neighbourhood; in the present instance, however, he is only unfortunate, and not in fault.

About ten days ago, in cocking a pistol in the guard-room at Marcau, he accidentally shot himself through the thigh. Two young Scotch surgeons in the island were polite enough to propose taking off the thigh at once, but to that he would not consent; and accordingly in his wounded state was put on board a cutter and conveyed to Haslar Hospital, at Gosport, where the bullet was extracted, and where he now is, I hope, in a fair way of doing well. The surgeon of the hospital wrote to the family on the occasion, and John Harwood went down to him immediately, attended by James [1], whose object in going was to be the means of bringing back the earliest intelligence to Mr. and Mrs. Harwood, whose anxious sufferings, particularly those of the latter, have of course been dreadful. They went down on Tuesday, and James came back the next day, bringing such favourable accounts as greatly to lessen the distress of the family at Deane, though it will probably be a long while before Mrs. Harwood can be quite at ease. One *most material comfort, however, they have; the assurance of its being really an accidental wound, which is not only positively declared by Earle himself, but is likewise testified by the particular direction of the bullet. Such a wound could not have been received in a duel. At present he is going on very well, but the surgeon will not declare him to be in no danger.[2] Mr. Heathcote [of Hursley Park, Hants.] met with a genteel little accident the other day in hunting. He got off to lead his horse over a hedge, or a house, or something, and his horse in his haste trod upon his leg, or rather ancle [*sic*], I believe, and it is not certain whether the small bone is not broke. Martha [Lloyd] has accepted*

Mary's invitation for Lord Portsmouth's ball. He has not yet sent out his own invitations, but that *does not signify; Martha comes, and a ball there is to be. I think it will be too early in her mother's absence for me to return with her.*

Sunday Evening. – *We have had a dreadful storm of wind in the fore part of this day, which has done a great deal of mischief among our trees. I was sitting alone in the dining-room when an odd kind of crash startled me – in a moment afterwards it was repeated. I then went to the window, which I reached just in time to see the last of our two highly valued elms descend into the Sweep!!!! The other, which had fallen, I suppose, in the first crash, and which was the nearest to the pond, taking a more easterly direction, sunk among our screen of chestnuts and firs, knocking down one spruce-fir, beating off the head of another, and stripping the two corner chestnuts of several branches in its fall. This is not all. One large elm out of the two on the left-hand side as you enter what I call the elm walk, was likewise blown down; the maple bearing the weathercock was broke in two, and what I regret more than all the rest is, that all the three elms which grew in Hall's meadow, and gave such ornament to it, are gone; two were blown down, and the other so much injured that it cannot stand. I am happy to add, however, that no greater evil than the loss of trees has been the consequence of the storm in this place, or in our immediate neighbourhood. We grieve, therefore, in some comfort.*

'I am yours ever,

'J. A.'

The next letter, written four days later than the former, was addressed to Miss Lloyd, an intimate friend, whose sister (my mother) was married to Jane's eldest brother:–

Steventon, Wednesday evening, Nov. 12th.

MY DEAR MARTHA,

*I did not receive your note yesterday till after Charlotte [maidservant] had left Deane, or I would have sent my answer by her, instead of being the means, as I now must be, of lessening the elegance of your new dress for the Hurstbourne ball by the value of 3*d *[postage was paid by the recipient]. You are very good in wishing to see me at Ibthorp [home of Mrs Lloyd and Martha] so soon, and I am equally good in wishing to come to you. I believe our merit in that respect is much upon a par, our self-denial mutually strong. Having paid this tribute of praise to the virtue of both, I shall here have done with panegyric, and proceed to plain matter of fact. In about a fortnight's time I hope to be with you. I have two reasons for not being able to come before. I wish so to arrange my visit as to spend some days with you after your mother's return. In the 1st place, that I may have the pleasure of seeing her, and in the 2nd, that I may have a better* *chance of bringing you back with me. Your promise in my favour was not quite absolute, but if your will is not perverse, you and I will do all in our power to overcome your scruples of conscience. I hope we shall meet next week to talk all this over, till we have tired ourselves with the very idea of my visit before my visit begins. Our invitations for the 19th are arrived, and very curiously are they worded.[3] Mary mentioned to you yesterday poor Earle's unfortunate accident, I dare say. He does not seem to be going on very well. The two or three last posts have brought less and less favourable accounts of him. John Harwood has gone to Gosport again to-day. We have two families of friends now who are in a most anxious state; for though by a note from Catherine [Bigg] this morning there seems now to be a revival of hope at Manydown its continuance may be too reasonably doubted. Mr. Heathcote [4] however, who has broken the small bone of his leg, is so good as to be going on very well. It would be really too much to have three people to care for.*

'You distress me cruelly by your request about books. I cannot think of any to bring with me, nor have I any idea of our wanting them. I come to you to be talked to, not to read or hear reading; I can do that at home; and indeed I am now laying in a stock of intelligence to pour out on you as my share of the conversation. I am reading Henry's History of England [Robert Henry's History of Great Britain*], which I will repeat to you in any manner you may prefer, either in a loose, desultory, unconnected stream, or dividing my recital, as the historian divides it himself, into seven parts:–The Civil and Military: Religion: Constitution: Learning and Learned Men: Arts and Sciences: Commerce, Coins, and Shipping: and Manners. So that for every evening in the week there will be a different subject. The Friday's lot – Commerce, Coins, and Shipping – you will find the least entertaining; but the next evening's portion will make amends. With such a provision on my part, if you will do yours by repeating the French Grammar, and Mrs. Stent [5] will now and then ejaculate some wonder about the cocks and hens, what can we want? Farewell for a short time. We all unite in best love, and I am your very affectionate*

J. A.

The two next letters must have been written early in 1801, after the removal from Steventon had been decided on, but before it had taken place. They refer to the two brothers who were at sea, and give some idea of a kind of anxieties and uncertainties to which sisters are seldom subject in these days of peace, steamers, and electric telegraphs. At that time ships were often windbound or becalmed, or driven wide of their destination; and sometimes they had orders to alter their course for some secret service; not to mention the chance of conflict with a vessel of superior power – no improbable occurrence before the battle of Trafalgar.

Information about relatives on board men-of-war was scarce and scanty, and often picked up by hearsay or chance means; and every scrap of intelligence was proportionably valuable:–

MY DEAR CASSANDRA,

I should not have thought it necessary to write to you so soon, but for the arrival of a letter from Charles to myself. It was written last Saturday from off the Start, and conveyed to Popham Lane by Captain Boyle, on his way to Midgham. He came from Lisbon in the "Endymion." I will copy Charles's account of his conjectures about Frank: "He has not seen my brother lately, nor does he expect to find him arrived, as he met Captain Inglis at Rhodes, going up to take command of the 'Petrel,' as he was coming down; but supposes he will arrive in less than a fortnight from this time, in some ship which is expected to reach England about that time with dispatches from Sir Ralph Abercrombie."[Commander of British troops in the Mediterranean]. The event must show what sort of a conjuror Captain Boyle is. The "Endymion" has not been plagued with any more prizes. Charles spent three pleasant days in Lisbon.

They were very well satisfied with their royal passenger [6], whom they found jolly and affable, who talks of Lady Augusta as his wife, and seems much attached to her.

When this letter was written, the "Endymion" was becalmed, but Charles hoped to reach Portsmouth by Monday or Tuesday. He received my letter, communicating our plans, before he left England; was much surprised, of course, but is quite reconciled to them, and means to come to Steventon once more while Steventon is ours.

From a letter written later in the same year:–

Charles has received 30l. for his share of the privateer, and expects 10l. more; but of what avail is it to take prizes if he lays out the produce in presents to his sisters? He has been buying gold chains and topaze crosses for us. He must be well scolded. The "Endymion" has already received orders for taking troops to Egypt, which I should not like at all if I did not trust to Charles being removed from her somehow or other before she sails. He knows nothing of his own destination, he says, but desires me to write directly, as the "Endymion" will probably sail in three or four days. He will receive my yesterday's letter, and I shall write again by this post to thank and reproach him. We shall be unbearably fine.

Notes

1. James, the writer's eldest brother.
2. The limb was saved.

3. The invitation, the ball dress, and some other things in this and the preceding letter refer to a ball annually given at Hurstbourne Park, on the anniversary of the Earl of Portsmouth's marriage with his first wife. He was the Lord Portsmouth whose eccentricities afterwards became notorious, and the invitations, as well as other arrangements about these balls, were of a peculiar character.
4. The father of Sir William Heathcote, of Hursley, who was married to a daughter of Mr Bigg Wither, of Manydown, and lived in the neighbourhood.
5. A very dull old lady, then residing with Mrs Lloyd.
6. The Duke of Sussex, son of George III, married, without royal consent, to the Lady Augusta Murray.

Removal from Steventon—Residences at Bath and at Southampton—Settling at Chawton

The family removed to Bath in the spring of 1801, where they resided first at No. 4 Sydney Terrace, and afterwards in Green Park Buildings. I do not know whether they were at all attracted to Bath by the circumstance that Mrs. Austen's only brother, Mr. Leigh Perrot, spent part of every year there. The name of Perrot, together with a small estate at Northleigh in Oxfordshire, had been bequeathed to him by a great uncle. I must devote a few sentences to this very old and now extinct branch of the Perrot family; for one of the last survivors, Jane Perrot, married to a Walker, was Jane Austen's great grandmother, from whom she derived her Christian name. The Perrots were settled in Pembrokeshire at least as early as the thirteenth century. They were probably some of the settlers whom the policy of our Plantagenet kings placed in that county, which thence acquired the name of 'England beyond Wales,' for the double purpose of keeping open a communication with Ireland from Milford Haven, and of overawing the Welsh. One of the family seems to have carried out this latter purpose very vigorously; for it is recorded of him that he slew *twenty-six men* of Kemaes, a district of Wales, and *one wolf*. The manner in which the two kinds of game are classed together, and the disproportion of numbers, are remarkable; but probably at that time the wolves had been so closely killed down, that *lupicide* was become a more rare and distinguished exploit than *homicide*. The last of this family died about 1778, and their property was divided between Leighs and Musgraves, the larger portion going to the latter. Mr. Leigh Perrot pulled down the mansion, and sold the estate to the Duke of Marlborough, and the name of these Perrots is now to be found only on some monuments in the church of Northleigh.

Mr. Leigh Perrot was also one of several cousins to whom a life interest in the Stoneleigh property in Warwickshire was left, after the extinction of the earlier Leigh peerage, but he compromised his claim to the succession in his lifetime. He married a niece of Sir Montague Cholmeley of Lincolnshire. He was a man of considerable natural power, with much of the wit of his uncle, the Master of Balliol, and wrote clever epigrams and riddles, some of which, though without his name, found their way into print; but he lived a very retired life, dividing his time between Bath and his place in Berkshire called Scarlets. Jane's letters from Bath make frequent mention of this uncle and aunt.

The unfinished story, now published under the title of 'The Watsons,' must have been written during the author's residence in Bath. In the autumn of 1804 she spent some weeks at Lyme, and became acquainted with the Cobb, which she afterwards made memorable for the fall of Louisa Musgrove. In February 1805, her father died at Bath, [in fact he died on 21st January] and was buried at Walcot Church. The widow and daughters went into lodgings for a few months, and then removed to Southampton. The only records that I can find about her during those four years are the three following letters to her sister; one from Lyme, the others from Bath. They shew that she went a good deal into society, in a quiet way, chiefly with ladies; and that her eyes were always open to minute traits of character in those with whom she associated:–

Extract from a letter from Jane Austen to her Sister.

Lyme, Friday, Sept. 14 (1804).

MY DEAR CASSANDRA, – I take the first sheet of fine striped paper to thank you for your letter from Weymouth, and express my hopes of your being at Ibthorp before this time. I expect to hear that you reached it yesterday evening, being able to get as far as Blandford on Wednesday. Your account of Weymouth contains nothing which strikes me so forcibly as there being no ice in the town. For every other vexation I was in some measure prepared, and particularly for your disappointment in not seeing the Royal Family go on board on Tuesday, having already heard from Mr. Crawford [visitor or resident of Lyme] that he had seen you in the very act of being too late. But for there being no ice, what could prepare me! You found my letter at Andover, I hope, yesterday, and have now for many hours been satisfied that your kind anxiety on my behalf was as much thrown away as kind anxiety usually is. I continue quite well; in proof of which I have bathed again this morning. It was absolutely necessary that I should have the little fever and indisposition which I had: it has been all the fashion this week in Lyme. We are quite settled in our lodgings by this time, as you may suppose, and everything goes on in the usual order. The servants behave very well, and make no difficulties, though nothing

certainly can exceed the inconvenience of the offices, except the general dirtiness of the house and furniture, and all its inhabitants. I endeavour, as far as I can, to supply your place, and be useful, and keep things in order. I detect dirt in the water decanters, as fast as I can, and keep everything as it was under your administration...The ball last night was pleasant, but not full for Thursday. My father staid contentedly till half-past nine (we went a little after eight), and then walked home with James [manservant] and a lanthorn, though I believe the lanthorn was not lit, as the moon was up; but sometimes this lanthorn may be a great convenience to him. My mother and I staid about an hour later. Nobody asked me the two first dances; the two next I danced with Mr. Crawford, and had I chosen to stay longer might have danced with Mr. Granville, Mrs. Granville's son, whom my dear friend Miss A. [Armstrong] introduced to me, or with a new odd-looking man who had been eyeing me for some time, and at last, without any introduction, asked me if I meant to dance again. I think he must be Irish by his ease, and because I imagine him to belong to the honbl B.'s, who are son, and son's wife of an Irish viscount, bold queer-looking people, just fit to be quality at Lyme. I called yesterday morning (ought it not in strict propriety to be termed yester-morning?) on Miss A. and was introduced to her father and mother. Like other young ladies she is considerably genteeler than her parents. Mrs. A. sat darning a pair of stockings the whole of my visit. But do not mention this at home, lest a warning should act as an example. We afterwards walked together for an hour on the Cobb; she is very converseable in a common way; I do not perceive wit or genius, but she has sense and some degree of taste, and her manners are very engaging. She seems to like people rather too easily.
Yours affect[ly],
J. A.

Letter from Jane Austen to her sister Cassandra at Ibthorp, alluding to the sudden death of Mrs. Lloyd at that place:–

25 Gay Street (Bath), Monday,
April 8, 1805.
MY DEAR CASSANDRA, – Here is a day for you. Did Bath or Ibthorp ever see such an 8th of April? It is March and April together; the glare of the one and the warmth of the other. We do nothing but walk about. As far as your means will admit, I hope you profit by such weather too. I dare say you are already the better for change of place. We were out again last night. Miss Irvine invited us, when I met her in the Crescent, to drink tea with them, but I rather declined it, having no idea that my mother would be disposed for another evening visit there so soon; but when I gave her the message, I found her very well inclined to go; and accordingly, on leaving Chapel, we walked

to Lansdown. This morning we have been to see Miss Chamberlaine look hot on horseback. Seven years and four months ago we went to the same riding-house to see Miss [Lucy] Lefroy's performance! [1] What a different set are we now moving in! But seven years, I suppose, are enough to change every pore of one's skin and every feeling of one's mind. We did not walk long in the Crescent yesterday. It was hot and not crowded enough; so we went into the field, and passed close by S. T. and Miss S._again.[2] I have not yet seen her face, but neither her dress nor air have anything of the dash or stylishness which the Browns talked of; quite the contrary; indeed, her dress is not even smart, and her appearance very quiet. Miss Irvine says she is never speaking a word. Poor wretch; I am afraid she is en pénitence. *Here has been that excellent Mrs. Coulthart calling, while my mother was out, and I was believed to be so. I always respected her, as a good-hearted friendly woman. And the Browns have been here; I find their affidavits [a joking reference to their visiting cards] on the table. The "Ambuscade" reached Gibraltar on the 9th of March, and found all well; so say the papers. We have had no letters from anybody, but we expect to hear from Edward to-morrow, and from you soon afterwards. How happy they are at Godmersham now! I shall be very glad of a letter from Ibthorp, that I may know how you all are, but particularly yourself. This is nice weather for Mrs. J. Austen's going to Speen, and I hope she will have a pleasant visit there. I expect a prodigious account of the christening dinner; perhaps it brought you at last into the company of Miss Dundas again.*

Tuesday. – *I received your letter last night, and wish it may be soon followed by another to say that all is over; but I cannot help thinking that nature will struggle again, and produce a revival. Poor woman! May her end be peaceful and easy as the exit we have witnessed! [Probably a reference to the death of Jane's father] And I dare say it will. If there is no revival, suffering must be all over; even the consciousness of existence, I suppose, was gone when you wrote. The nonsense I have been writing in this and in my last letter seems out of place at such a time, but I will not mind it; it will do you no harm, and nobody else will be attacked by it. I am heartily glad that you can speak so comfortably of your own health and looks, though I can scarcely comprehend the latter being really approved. Could travelling fifty miles produce such an immediate change? You were looking very poorly here, and everybody seemed sensible of it. Is there a charm in a hack postchaise? But if there were, Mrs. Craven's [a relative of the Lloyds] carriage might have undone it all. I am much obliged to you for the time and trouble you have bestowed on Mary's cap, and am glad it pleases her; but it will prove a useless gift at present, I suppose. Will not she leave Ibthorp on her mother's death? As a companion you are all that Martha can be supposed to want, and in that light, under these circumstances, your visit will indeed have been well timed.*

Thursday. – *I was not able to go on yesterday; all my wit and leisure were bestowed on letters to Charles and Henry. To the former I wrote in consequence of my mother's having seen in the papers that the "Urania" was waiting at Portsmouth for the convoy for Halifax. This is nice, as it is only three weeks ago that you wrote by the "Camilla." I wrote to Henry because I had a letter from him in which he desired to hear from me very soon. His to me was most affectionate and kind, as well as entertaining; there is no merit to him in* that; *he cannot help being amusing. He offers to meet us on the sea coast, if the plan of which Edward gave him some hint takes place. Will not this be making the execution of such a plan more desirable and delightful than ever? He talks of the rambles we took together last summer with pleasing affection.*
Yours ever,
J. A.

From the same to the same.

Gay St. Sunday Evening,
April 21 (1805).
MY DEAR CASSANDRA, – I am much obliged to you for writing to me again so soon; your letter yesterday was quite an unexpected pleasure. Poor Mrs. Stent! it has been her lot to be always in the way; but we must be merciful, for perhaps in time we may come to be Mrs. Stents ourselves, unequal to anything, and unwelcome to everybody...My morning engagement was with the Cookes, and our party consisted of George and Mary, a Mr. L., Miss B. [Bendish], who had been with us at the concert, and the youngest Miss W. [Whitby] Not Julia; we have done with her; she is very ill; but Mary. Mary W.'s turn is actually come to be grown up, and have a fine complexion, and wear great square muslin shawls. I have not expressly enumerated myself among the party, but there I was, and my cousin George was very kind, and talked sense to me every now and then, in the intervals of his more animated fooleries with Miss B., who is very young, and rather handsome, and whose gracious manners, ready wit, and solid remarks, put me somewhat in mind of my old acquaintance L. L. [Lucy Lefroy]. There was a monstrous deal of stupid quizzing and common-place nonsense talked, but scarcely any wit; all that bordered on it or on sense came from my cousin George, whom altogether I like very well. Mr. B. [Bendish] seems nothing more than a tall young man. My evening engagement and walk was with Miss A.[probably Miss Armstrong], who had called on me the day before, and gently upbraided me in her turn with a change of manners to her since she had been in Bath, or at least of late. Unlucky me! that my notice should be of such consequence, and my manners so bad! She was so well disposed, and so

reasonable, that I soon forgave her, and made this engagement with her in proof of it. She is really an agreeable girl, so I think I may like her; and her great want of a companion at home, which may well make any tolerable acquaintance important to her, gives her another claim on my attention. I shall endeavour as much as possible to keep my intimacies in their proper place, and prevent their clashing. Among so many friends, it will be well if I do not get into a scrape; and now here is Miss Blashford come. I should have gone distracted if the Bullers had staid...When I tell you I have been visiting a countess this morning, you will immediately, with great justice, but no truth, guess it to be Lady Roden. No: it is Lady Leven, the mother of Lord Balgonie. On receiving a message from Lord and Lady Leven through the Mackays, declaring their intention of waiting on us, we thought it right to go to them. I hope we have not done too much, but the friends and admirers of Charles must be attended to. They seem very reasonable, good sort of people, very civil, and full of his praise.[3] We were shewn at first into an empty drawing-room, and presently in came his lordship, not knowing who we were, to apologise for the servant's mistake, and to say himself what was untrue, that Lady Leven was not within. He is a tall gentlemanlike looking man, with spectacles, and rather deaf. After sitting with him ten minutes we walked away; but Lady Leven coming out of the dining parlour as we passed the door, we were obliged to attend her back to it, and pay our visit over again. She is a stout woman, with a very handsome face. By this means we had the pleasure of hearing Charles's praises twice over. They think themselves excessively obliged to him, and estimate him so highly as to wish Lord Balgonie, when he is quite recovered, to go out to him. There is a pretty little Lady Marianne of the party, to be shaken hands with, and asked if she remembered Mr. Austen...

I shall write to Charles by the next packet, unless you tell me in the meantime of your intending to do it.

Believe me, if you chuse,
Y^r^ affᵗᵉ Sister.

Jane did not estimate too highly the 'Cousin George' mentioned in the foregoing letter; who might easily have been superior in sense and wit to the rest of the party. He was the Rev. George Leigh Cooke, long known and respected at Oxford, where he held important offices, and had the privilege of helping to form the minds of men more eminent than himself. As Tutor in Corpus Christi College, he became instructor to some of the most distinguished undergraduates of that time: amongst others to Dr. Arnold, the Rev. John Keble, and Sir John Coleridge. The latter has mentioned him in terms of affectionate regard, both in his Memoir of Keble, and in a letter which appears in Dean Stanley's 'Life of Arnold.' Mr. Cooke was also an impressive preacher of earnest awakening sermons. I remember to have heard it observed by some of my undergraduate friends that, after all, there was more good to be got from George Cooke's plain sermons than from much of the more laboured oratory of the University pulpit. He was frequently Examiner in the schools, and occupied the chair of the Sedleian Professor of Natural Philosophy, from 1810 to 1853.

Before the end of 1805, the little family party removed to Southampton. They resided in a commodious old-fashioned house in a corner of Castle Square.

I have no letters of my aunt, nor any other record of her, during her four years' residence at Southampton; and though I now began to know, and, what was the same thing, to love her myself, yet my observations were only those of a young boy, and were not capable of penetrating her character, or estimating her powers. I have, however, a lively recollection of some local circumstances at Southampton, and as they refer chiefly to things which have been long ago swept away, I will record them. My grandmother's house had a pleasant garden, bounded on one side by the old city walls; the top of this wall was sufficiently wide to afford a pleasant walk, with an extensive view, easily accessible to ladies by steps. This must have been a part of the identical walls which witnessed the embarkation of Henry V. before the battle of Agincourt, and the detection of the conspiracy of Cambridge, Scroop, and Grey, which Shakspeare has made so picturesque; when, according to the chorus in Henry V, the citizens saw

> The well-appointed King at Hampton Pier
> Embark his royalty.

Among the records of the town of Southampton, they have a minute and authentic account, drawn up at that time, of the encampment of Henry V. near the town, before his embarkment for France. It is remarkable that the place where the army was encamped, then a low level plain, is now entirely covered by the sea, and is called Westport.[4] At that time Castle Square was occupied by a fantastic edifice, too large for the space in which it stood, though too small to accord well with its castellated style, erected by the second Marquis of Lansdowne, half-brother to the well-known statesman, who succeeded him in the title. The Marchioness had a light phaeton, drawn by six, and sometimes by eight little ponies, each pair decreasing in size, and becoming lighter in colour, through all the grades of dark brown, light brown, bay, and chestnut, as it was placed farther away from the carriage. The two leading pairs were managed by two boyish postilions, the two pairs nearest to the carriage were driven in hand. It was a delight to me to look down from the window and see this fairy equipage put together; for the premises of this castle were so contracted that the whole process went on in the little space that remained of the open square. Like other fairy works, however, it all proved evanescent. Not only carriage and ponies, but castle itself, soon vanished away, 'like the baseless fabric of a vision.' On the death of the Marquis in 1809, the castle was pulled down. Few probably remember its existence; and any one who might visit the place now would wonder how it ever could have stood there.

In 1809 Mr. Knight was able to offer his mother the choice of two houses on his property; one near his usual residence at Godmersham Park in Kent; the other near Chawton House, his occasional residence in Hampshire. The latter was chosen; and in that year the mother and daughters, together with Miss Lloyd [Martha], a near connection who lived with them, settled themselves at Chawton Cottage.

Chawton may be called the *second*, as well as the *last* home of Jane Austen; for during the temporary residences of the party at Bath and Southampton she was only a sojourner in a strange land; but here she found a real home amongst her own people. It so happened that during her residence at Chawton circumstances brought several of her brothers and their families within easy distance of the house. Chawton must also be considered the place most closely connected with her career as a writer; for there it was that, in the maturity of her mind, she either wrote or rearranged, and prepared for publication the books by which she has become known to the world. This was the home where, after a few years, while still in the prime of life, she began to droop and wither away, and which she left only in the last stage of her illness, yielding to the persuasion of friends hoping against hope.

This house stood in the village of Chawton, about a mile from Alton, on the right hand side, just where the road to Winchester branches off from that to Gosport. It was so close to the road that the front door opened upon it; while a very narrow enclosure, paled in on each side, protected the building from danger of collision with any runaway vehicle. I believe it had been originally built for an inn, for which purpose it was certainly well situated. Afterwards it had been occupied by Mr. Knight's steward; but by some additions to the house, and some judicious planting and skreening [*sic*], it was made a pleasant and commodious abode. Mr. Knight was experienced and adroit at such arrangements, and this was a labour of love to him. A good-sized entrance and two sitting-rooms made the length of the house, all intended originally to look upon the road, but the large drawing-room window was blocked up and turned into a book-case, and another opened at the side which gave to view only turf and trees, as a high wooden fence and hornbeam hedge shut out the Winchester road, which skirted the whole length of the little domain. Trees were planted each side to form a shrubbery walk, carried round the enclosure, which gave a sufficient space for ladies' exercise. There was a pleasant irregular mixture of hedgerow, and gravel walk, and orchard, and long grass for mowing, arising from two or three little enclosures having been thrown together. The house itself was quite as good as the generality of parsonage-houses then were, and much in the same style; and was capable of receiving other members of the family as frequent visitors. It was sufficiently well furnished; everything inside and out was kept in good repair, and it was altogether a comfortable and ladylike establishment, though the means which supported it were not large.

I give this description because some interest is generally taken in the residence of a popular writer. Cowper's unattractive house in the street of Olney has been pointed out to visitors, and has even attained the honour of an engraving in Southey's edition of his works: but I cannot recommend any admirer of Jane Austen to undertake a pilgrimage to this spot. The building indeed still stands, but it has lost all that gave it its character. After the death of Mrs. Cassandra Austen, in 1845, it was divided into tenements for labourers, and the grounds reverted to ordinary uses.

Notes

1. Here is evidence that Jane Austen was acquainted with Bath before it became her residence in 1801.
2. A gentleman and lady lately engaged to be married.
3. It seems that Charles Austen, then first lieutenant of the *Endymion,* had had an opportunity of shewing attention and kindness to some of Lord Leven's family.
4. See Wharton's note to Johnson's and Steevens' Shakespeare.

Description of Jane Austen's person, character, and tastes

As my memoir has now reached the period when I saw a great deal of my aunt, and was old enough to understand something of her value, I will here attempt a description of her person, mind, and habits. In person she was very attractive; her figure was rather tall and slender, her step light and firm, and her whole appearance expressive of health and animation. In complexion she was a clear brunette with a rich colour; she had full round cheeks, with mouth and nose small and well formed, bright hazel eyes, and brown hair forming natural curls close round her face. If not so regularly handsome as her sister, yet her countenance had a peculiar charm of its own to the eyes of most beholders. At the time of which I am now writing, she never was seen, either morning or evening, without a cap; I believe that she and her sister were generally thought to have taken to the garb of middle age earlier than their years or their looks required; and that, though remarkably neat in their dress as in all their ways, they were scarcely sufficiently regardful of the fashionable, or the becoming.

She was not highly accomplished according to the present standard. Her sister drew well, and it is from a drawing of hers that the likeness prefixed to this volume has been taken. Jane herself was fond of music, and had a sweet voice, both in singing and in conversation; in her youth she had received some instruction on the pianoforte; and at Chawton she practised daily, chiefly before breakfast. I believe she did so partly that she might not disturb the rest of the party who were less fond of music. In the evening she would sometimes sing, to her own accompaniment, some simple old songs, the words and airs of which, now never heard, still linger in my memory.

She read French with facility, and knew something of Italian. In those days German was no more thought of than Hindostanee, as part of a lady's education. In history she followed the old guides – [Oliver] Goldsmith, [David] Hume, and [William] Robertson. Critical enquiry into the usually received statements of the old historians was scarcely begun. The history of the early kings of Rome had not yet been dissolved into legend. Historic characters lay before the reader's eyes in broad light or shade, not much broken up by details. The virtues of King Henry VIII were yet undiscovered, nor had much light been thrown on the inconsistencies of Queen Elizabeth; the one was held to be an unmitigated tyrant, and an embodied Blue Beard; the other a perfect model of wisdom and policy. Jane, when a girl, had strong political opinions, especially about the affairs of the sixteenth and seventeenth centuries. She was a vehement defender of Charles I. and his grandmother Mary; but I think it was rather from an impulse of feeling than from any enquiry into the evidences by which they must be condemned or acquitted. As she grew up, the politics of the day occupied very little of her attention, but she probably shared the feeling of moderate Toryism which prevailed in her family. She was well acquainted with the old periodicals from the 'Spectator' downwards. Her knowledge of [Samuel] Richardson's works was such as no one is likely again to acquire, now that the multitude and the merits of our light literature have called off the attention of readers from that great master. Every circumstance narrated in 'Sir Charles Grandison', all that was ever said or done in the cedar parlour, was familiar to her; and the wedding days of Lady L. and Lady G. were as well remembered as if they had been living friends. Amongst her favourite writers, [Samuel] Johnson in prose, [George] Crabbe in verse, and [William] Cowper in both, stood high. It is well that the native good taste of herself and of those with whom she lived, saved her from the snare into which a sister novelist had fallen, of imitating the grandiloquent style of Johnson. She thoroughly enjoyed Crabbe; perhaps on account of a certain resemblance to herself in minute and highly finished detail; and would sometimes say, in jest, that, if she ever married at all, she could fancy being Mrs. Crabbe; looking on the author quite as an abstract idea, and ignorant and regardless what manner of man he might be. [Walter] Scott's poetry gave her great pleasure; she did not live to make much acquaintance with his novels. Only three of them were published before her death; but it will be seen by the following extract from one of her letters, that she was quite prepared to admit the merits of 'Waverley'; and it is remarkable that, living, as she did, far apart from the gossip of the literary world, she should even then have spoken so confidently of his being the author of it: –

> Walter Scott has no business to write novels; especially good ones. It is not fair. He has fame and profit enough as a poet, and ought not to be taking the bread out of other people's mouths. I do not mean to like 'Waverley,' if I can help it, but I fear I must. I am quite determined, however, not to be pleased with Mrs. —'s,[a reference to Jane West's novel *Alicia de Lacy*] should I ever meet with it, which I hope I may not. I think I can be stout against anything written by her. I have made up my mind to like no novels really, but Miss Edgeworth's, E.'s[Edward, author of this memoir], and my own.

It was not, however, what she *knew*, but what she *was*, that distinguished her from others. I cannot better describe the fascination which she exercised over children than by quoting the words of two of her nieces. One [Caroline] says:–

> As a very little girl I was always creeping up to aunt Jane, and following her whenever I could, in the house and out of it. I might not have remembered this but for the recollection of my mother's telling me privately, that I must not be troublesome to my aunt. Her first charm to children was great sweetness of manner. She seemed to love you, and you loved her in return. This, as well as I can now recollect, was what I felt in my early days, before I was old enough to be amused by her cleverness. But soon came the delight of her playful talk. She could make everything amusing to a child. Then, as I got older, when cousins came to share the entertainment, she would tell us the most delightful stories, chiefly of Fairyland, and her fairies had all characters of their own. The tale was invented, I am sure, at the moment, and was continued for two or three days, if occasion served.

Again:–

> When staying at Chawton, with two of her other nieces, we often had amusements in which my aunt was very helpful. She was the one to whom we always looked for help. She would furnish us with what we wanted from her wardrobe; and she would be the entertaining visitor in our make-believe house. She amused us in various ways. Once, I remember, in giving a conversation as between myself and my two cousins, supposing we were all grown up, the day after a ball.

Very similar is the testimony of another niece [Anna]:–

> Aunt Jane was the general favourite with children; her ways with them being so playful, and her long circumstantial stories so delightful. These were continued from time to time, and were begged for on all possible and impossible occasions; woven, as she proceeded, out of nothing but her own happy talent for invention. Ah! if but one of them could be recovered! And again, as I grew older, when the original seventeen years between our ages seemed to shrink to seven, or to nothing, it comes back to me now how strangely I missed her. It had become so much a habit with me to put by things in my mind with a reference to her, and to say to myself, I shall keep this for aunt Jane.

A nephew of hers used to observe that his visits to Chawton, after the death of his aunt Jane, were always a disappointment to him. From old associations he could not help expecting to be particularly happy in that house; and never till he got there could he realise to himself how all its peculiar charm was gone. It was not only that the chief light in the house was quenched, but that the loss of it had cast a shade over the spirits of the survivors. Enough has been said to show her love for children, and her wonderful power of entertaining them; but her friends of all ages felt her enlivening influence. Her unusually quick sense of the ridiculous led her to play with all the common-places of everyday life, whether as regarded persons or things; but she never played with its serious duties or responsibilities, nor did she ever turn individuals into ridicule. With all her neighbours in the village she was on friendly, though not on intimate, terms. She took a kindly interest in all their proceedings, and liked to hear about them. They often served for her amusement; but it was her own nonsense that gave zest to the gossip. She was as far as possible from being censorious or satirical. She never abused them or *quizzed* them – *that* was the word of the day; an ugly word, now obsolete; and the ugly practice which it expressed is much less prevalent now than it was then. The laugh which she occasionally raised was by imagining for her neighbours, as she was equally ready to imagine for her friends or herself, impossible contingencies, or by relating in prose or verse some trifling anecdote coloured to her own fancy, or in writing a fictitious history of what they were supposed to have said or done, which could deceive nobody.

The following specimens may be given of the liveliness of mind which imparted an agreeable flavour both to her correspondence and her conversation:–

ON READING IN THE NEWSPAPERS THE MARRIAGE OF MR. GELL TO MISS GILL, OF EASTBOURNE.
At Eastbourne Mr. Gell, From being perfectly well,
Became dreadfully ill, For love of Miss Gill.
So he said, with some sighs, I'm the slave of your iis*;*
Oh, restore, if you please, By accepting my ees.

ON THE MARRIAGE OF A MIDDLE-AGED FLIRT WITH A MR. WAKE, WHOM, IT WAS SUPPOSED, SHE WOULD SCARCELY HAVE ACCEPTED IN HER YOUTH.
Maria, good-humoured, and handsome, and tall,
For a husband was at her last stake;
And having in vain danced at many a ball,
Is now happy to jump at a Wake.

We were all at the play last night to see Miss O'Neil in Isabella. I do not think she was quite equal to my expectation. I fancy I want something more than can be. Acting seldom satisfies me. I took two pocket handkerchiefs, but had very little occasion for either. She is an elegant creature, however, and hugs Mr. Young delightfully.

So, Miss B. is actually married, but I have never seen it in the papers; and one may as well be single if the wedding is not to be in print.

Once, too, she took it into her head to write the following mock panegyric on a young friend [her niece], who really was clever and handsome:–

In measured verse I'll now rehearse
The charms of lovely Anna:
And, first, her mind is unconfined
Like any vast savannah.
Ontario's lake may fitly speak
Her fancy's ample bound:
Its circuit may, on strict survey

Five hundred miles be found.
Her wit descends on foes and friends
Like famed Niagara's Fall;
And travellers gaze in wild amaze,
And listen, one and all.
Her judgment sound, thick, black, profound,
Like transatlantic groves,
Dispenses aid, and friendly shade
To all that in it roves.
If thus her mind to be defined
America exhausts,
And all that's grand in that great land
In similes it costs –
Oh how can I her person try
To image and portray?
How paint the face, the form how trace
In which those virtues lay?
Another world must be unfurled,
Another language known,
Ere tongue or sound can publish round
Her charms of flesh and bone.

I believe that all this nonsense was nearly extempore, and that the fancy of drawing the images from America arose at the moment from the obvious rhyme which presented itself in the first stanza.

The following extracts are from letters addressed to a niece [Anna] who was at that time amusing herself by attempting a novel, probably never finished, certainly never published, and of which I know nothing but what these extracts tell. They show the good-natured sympathy and encouragement which the aunt, then herself occupied in writing 'Emma,' could give to the less matured powers of the niece. They bring out incidentally some of her opinions concerning compositions of that kind:–

Extracts

Chawton, Aug. 10, 1814.

Your aunt C. does not like desultory novels, and is rather fearful that yours will be too much so; that there will be too frequent a change from one set of people to another, and that circumstances will be sometimes introduced, of apparent consequence, which will lead to nothing. It will not be so great an objection to me. I allow much more latitude than she does, and think nature and spirit cover many sins of a wandering story. And people in general do not care much about it, for your comfort...

Sept. 9.
You are now collecting your people delightfully, getting them exactly into such a spot as is the delight of my life. Three or four families in a country village is the very thing to work on; and I hope you will write a great deal more, and make full use of them while they are so very favourably arranged.

Sept. 28.
Devereux Forrester being ruined by his vanity is very good: but I wish you would not let him plunge into a 'vortex of dissipation.' I do not object to the thing, but I cannot bear the expression; it is such thorough novel slang; and so old that I dare say Adam met with it in the first novel that he opened.'

Hans Place (Nov. 1814).
I have been very far from finding your book an evil, I assure you. I read it immediately, and with great pleasure. Indeed, I do think you get on very fast. I wish other people of my acquaintance could compose as rapidly. Julian's history was quite a surprise to me. You had not very long known it yourself, I suspect; but I have no objection to make to the circumstance; it is very well told, and his having been in love with the aunt gives Cecilia an additional interest with him. I like the idea; a very proper compliment to an aunt! I rather imagine, indeed, that nieces are seldom chosen but in compliment to some aunt or other. I dare say your husband was in love with me once, and would never have thought of you if he had not supposed me dead of a scarlet fever.

Jane Austen was successful in everything that she attempted with her fingers. None of us could throw spilikins in so perfect a circle, or take them off with so steady a hand. Her performances with cup and ball were marvellous. The one used at Chawton was an easy one, and she has been known to catch it on the point above an hundred times in succession, till her hand was weary. She sometimes found a resource in that simple game, when unable, from weakness in her eyes, to read or write long together. A specimen of her clear strong handwriting is here given. Happy would the compositors for the press be if they had always so legible a manuscript to work from. But the writing was not the only part of her letters which showed superior handiwork. In those days there was an art in folding and sealing. No adhesive envelopes made all easy. Some people's letters always looked loose and untidy; but her paper was sure to take the right folds, and her sealing-wax to drop into the right place. Her needlework both plain and ornamental was excellent, and might almost have put a sewing machine to shame. She was considered especially great in satin stitch. She spent much time in these occupations, and some of her merriest talk was over clothes which she and her companions were making, sometimes for themselves, and sometimes for the poor. There still remains a curious specimen of her needlework made for a sister-in-law, my mother. In a very small bag is deposited a little rolled up housewife, furnished with minikin needles and fine thread. In the housewife is a tiny pocket, and in the pocket is enclosed a slip of paper, on which, written as with a crow quill, are these lines:–

This little bag, I hope, will prove
To be not vainly made;
For should you thread and needles want,
It will afford you aid.
And, as we are about to part,
It will serve another end:
For, when you look upon this bag,
You'll recollect your friend.

It is the kind of article that some benevolent fairy might be supposed to give as a reward to a diligent little girl. The whole is of flowered silk, and having been never used and carefully preserved, it is as fresh and bright as when it was first made seventy years ago; and shows that the same hand which painted so exquisitely with the pen could work as delicately with the needle.

I have collected some of the bright qualities which shone, as it were, on the surface of Jane Austen's character, and attracted most notice; but underneath them there lay the strong foundations of sound sense and judgment, rectitude of principle, and delicacy of feeling, qualifying her equally to advise, assist, or amuse. She was, in fact, as ready to comfort the unhappy, or to nurse the sick, as she was to laugh and jest with the lighthearted. Two of her nieces were grown up, and one of them was married, before she was taken away from them. As their minds became more matured, they were admitted into closer intimacy with her, and learned more of her graver thoughts; they know what a sympathising friend and judicious adviser they found her to be in many little difficulties and doubts of early womanhood.

I do not venture to speak of her religious principles: that is a subject on which she herself was more inclined to *think* and *act* than to *talk*, and I shall imitate her reserve; satisfied to have shown how much of Christian love and humility abounded in her heart, without presuming to lay bare the roots whence those graces grew. Some little insight, however, into these deeper recesses of the heart must be given, when we come to speak of her death.

Habits of Composition resumed after a long interval—First publication—The interest taken by the Author in the success of her Works

It may seem extraordinary that Jane Austen should have written so little during the years that elapsed between leaving Steventon and settling at Chawton; especially when this cessation from work is contrasted with her literary activity both before and after that period. It might rather have been expected that fresh scenes and new acquaintance would have called forth her powers; while the quiet life which the family led both at Bath and Southampton must have afforded abundant leisure for composition; but so it was that nothing which I know of, certainly nothing which the public have seen, was completed in either of those places. I can only state the fact, without assigning any cause for it; but as soon as she was fixed in her second home, she resumed the habits of composition which had been formed in her first, and continued them to the end of her life. The first year of her residence at Chawton seems to have been devoted to revising and preparing for the press 'Sense and Sensibility,' and 'Pride and Prejudice'; but between February 1811 and August 1816, she began and completed 'Mansfield Park,' 'Emma,' and 'Persuasion,' so that the last five years of her life produced the same number of novels with those which had been written in her early youth. How she was able to effect all this is surprising, for she had no separate study to retire to, and most of the work must have been done in the general sitting-room, subject to all kinds of casual interruptions. She was careful that her occupation should not be suspected by servants, or visitors, or any persons beyond her own family party. She wrote upon small sheets of paper which could easily be put away, or covered with a piece of blotting paper. There was, between the front door and the offices, a swing door which creaked when it was opened; but she objected to having this little inconvenience remedied, because it gave her notice when anyone was coming. She was not, however, troubled with companions like her own Mrs. Allen in 'Northanger Abbey,' whose 'vacancy of mind and incapacity for thinking were such that, as she never talked a great deal, so she could never be entirely silent; and therefore, while she sat at work, if she lost her needle, or broke her thread, or saw a speck of dirt on her gown, she must observe it, whether there were any one at leisure to answer her or not.' In that well occupied female party there must have been many precious hours of silence during which the pen was busy at the little mahogany writing-desk, [1] while Fanny Price, or Emma Woodhouse, or Anne Elliott was growing into beauty and interest. I have no doubt that I, and my sisters and cousins, in our visits to Chawton, frequently disturbed this mystic process, without having any idea of the mischief that we were doing; certainly we never should have guessed it by any signs of impatience or irritability in the writer.

As so much had been previously prepared, when once she began to publish, her works came out in quick succession. 'Sense and Sensibility' was published in 1811, 'Pride and Prejudice' at the beginning of 1813, 'Mansfield Park' in 1814, 'Emma' early in 1816; 'Northanger Abbey' and 'Persuasion' did not appear till after her death, in 1818. It will be shown farther on why 'Northanger Abbey,' though amongst the first written, was one of the last published. Her first three novels were published by Egerton, her last three by Murray. The profits of the four which had been printed before her death had not at that time amounted to seven hundred pounds.

I have no record of the publication of 'Sense and Sensibility,' nor of the author's feelings at this her first appearance before the public; but the following extracts from three letters to her sister give a lively picture of the interest with which she watched the reception of 'Pride and Prejudice,' and show the carefulness with which she corrected her compositions, and rejected much that had been written:–

Chawton, Friday, January 29 (1813).

I hope you received my little parcel by J. Bond [farm bailiff] on Wednesday evening, my dear Cassandra, and that you will be ready to hear from me again on Sunday, for I feel that I must write to you to-day. I want to tell you that I have got my own darling child from London. On Wednesday I received one copy sent down by Falkener [coachman] with three lines from Henry to say that he had given another to Charles and sent a third by the coach to Godmersham ...The advertisement is in our paper to-day for the first time: 18s. He shall ask 1l. 1s. for my two next, and 1l. 8s. for my stupidest of all. Miss B.[possibly Miss Benn] dined with us on the very day of the book's coming, and in the evening we fairly set at it, and read half the first vol. to her, prefacing that, having intelligence from Henry that such a work would soon appear, we had desired him to send it whenever it came out, and I believe it passed with her unsuspected. She was amused, poor soul! That *she could not help, you know, with two such people to lead the way, but she really does seem to admire Elizabeth. I must confess that I think her as delightful a creature as ever appeared in print, and how I shall be able to tolerate those who do not like* her *at least I do not know. There are a few typical errors; and a "said he," or a "said she," would sometimes make the dialogue more immediately clear; but "I do not write for such dull elves" as have not a great deal of ingenuity themselves. The second volume is shorter than I could wish, but the difference is not so much in reality as in look, there being a larger proportion of narrative in that part. I have lop't and crop't so successfully, however, that I imagine it must be rather shorter than*

"Sense and Sensibility" altogether. Now I will try and write of something else.

Chawton, Thursday, February 4 (1813).
MY DEAR CASSANDRA, – Your letter was truly welcome, and I am much obliged to you for all your praise; it came at a right time, for I had had some fits of disgust. Our second evening's reading to Miss B. had not pleased me so well, but I believe something must be attributed to my mother's too rapid way of getting on: though she perfectly understands the characters herself, she cannot speak as they ought. Upon the whole, however, I am quite vain enough and well satisfied enough. The work is rather too light, and bright, and sparkling; it wants shade; it wants to be stretched out here and there with a long chapter of sense, if it could be had; if not, of solemn specious nonsense, about something unconnected with the story; an essay on writing, a critique on Walter Scott, or the history of Buonaparté, or something that would form a contrast, and bring the reader with increased delight to the playfulness and epigrammatism of the general style...The greatest blunder in the printing that I have met with is in page 220, v. 3, where two speeches are made into one. There might as well be no suppers at Longbourn; but I suppose it was the remains of Mrs. Bennett's old Meryton habits.

The following letter seems to have been written soon after the last two: in February 1813:–

This will be a quick return for yours, my dear Cassandra; I doubt its having much else to recommend it; but there is no saying; it may turn out to be a very long and delightful letter. I am exceedingly pleased that you can say what you do, after having gone through the whole work, and Fanny [Knight]'s praise is very gratifying. My hopes were tolerably strong of her, *but nothing like a certainty. Her liking Darcy and Elizabeth is enough. She might hate all the others, if she would. I have her opinion under her own hand this morning, but your transcript of it, which I read first, was not, and is not, the less acceptable. To* me *it is of course all praise, but the more exact truth which she sends you is good enough...Our party on Wednesday was not unagreeable, though we wanted a master of the house less anxious and fidgety, and more conversable. Upon Mrs. —'s mentioning that she had sent the rejected addresses [*Rejected Addresses or, The New Theatrum Poetarum *(1812) by James and Horatio Smith] to Mrs. H., I began talking to her a little about them, and expressed my hope of their having amused her. Her answer was, "Oh dear yes, very much, very droll indeed, the opening of the house, and the striking up of the fiddles!" What she meant, poor woman, who shall say? I sought no farther. As soon as a whist party was formed, and a round table* *threatened, I made my mother an excuse and came away, leaving just as many for* their *round table as there were at Mrs. Grant's.[2] I wish they might be as agreeable a set. My mother is very well, and finds great amusement in glove-knitting, and at present wants no other work. We quite run over with books. She has got Sir John Carr's 'Travels in Spain,' and I am reading a Society [Chawton Book Society] octavo, an 'Essay on the Military Police and Institutions of the British Empire,' by Capt. Pasley of the Engineers, a book which I protested against at first, but which upon trial I find delightfully written and highly entertaining. I am as much in love with the author as I ever was with Clarkson or Buchanan, or even the two Mr. Smiths of the city. The first soldier I ever sighed for; but he does write with extraordinary force and spirit. Yesterday, moreover, brought us 'Mrs. Grant's Letters,' with Mr. White's compliments; but I have disposed of them, compliments and all, to Miss P., and amongst so many readers or retainers of books as we have in Chawton, I dare say there will be no difficulty in getting rid of them for another fortnight, if necessary. I have disposed of Mrs. Grant for the second fortnight to Mrs. —. It can make no difference to* her *which of the twenty-six fortnights in the year the 3 vols. lie on her table. I have been applied to for information as to the oath taken in former times of Bell, Book, and Candle, but have none to give. Perhaps you may be able to learn something of its origin where you now are. Ladies who read those enormous great stupid thick quarto volumes which one always sees in the breakfast parlour there must be acquainted with everything in the world. I detest a quarto. Capt. Pasley's book is too good for their society. They will not understand a man who condenses his thoughts into an octavo. I have learned from Sir J. Carr that there is no Government House at Gibraltar. I must alter it to the Commissioner's. [This is a reference to* Mansfield Park *in which Jane wrote about a Government House in Gibraltar.]'*

The following letter belongs to the same year, but treats of a different subject. It describes a journey from Chawton to London, in her brother's curricle, and shows how much could be seen and enjoyed in course of a long summer's day by leisurely travelling amongst scenery which the traveller in an express train now rushes through in little more than an hour, but scarcely sees at all:–

Sloane Street, Thursday, May 20 (1813).
MY DEAR CASSANDRA,

Before I say anything else, I claim a paper full of halfpence on the drawing-room mantel-piece; I put them there myself, and forgot to bring them with me. I cannot say that I have yet been in any distress for money, but I chuse to have my due, as well as the Devil. How lucky we were in our weather yesterday! This wet morning makes one more sensible of it. We had no rain of any consequence. The head of the curricle was put half up three or four times, but our share of the showers was very trifling, though they seemed to be heavy all round us, when we were on the Hog's-back [the road along the chalk ridge between Farnham and Guildford], and I fancied it might then be raining so hard at Chawton as to make you feel for us much more than we deserved. Three hours and a quarter took us to Guildford, where we staid barely two hours, and had only just time enough for all we had to do there; that is, eating a long and comfortable breakfast, watching the carriages, paying Mr. Harrington [a Guildford shopkeeper], and taking a little stroll afterwards. From some views which that stroll gave us, I think most highly of the situation of Guildford. We wanted all our brothers and sisters to be standing with us in the bowling-green, and looking towards Horsham. I was very lucky in my gloves – got them at the first shop I went to, though I went into it rather because it was near than because it looked at all like a glove shop, and gave only four shillings for them; after which everybody at Chawton will be hoping and predicting that they cannot be good for anything, and their worth certainly remains to be proved; but I think they look very well. We left Guildford at twenty minutes before twelve (I hope somebody cares for these minutiae), and were at Esher in about two hours more. I was very much pleased with the country in general. Between Guildford and Ripley I thought it particularly pretty, also about Painshill; and from a Mr. Spicer's grounds at Esher, which we walked into before dinner, the views were beautiful. I cannot say what we did not see, but I should think there could not be a wood, or a meadow, or palace, or remarkable spot in England that was not spread out before us on one side or other. Claremont [a Palladian mansion in Esher, Surrey] is going to be sold: a Mr. Ellis has it now. It is a house that seems never to have prospered. After dinner we walked forward to be overtaken at the coachman's time, and before he did overtake us we were very near Kingston. I fancy it was about half-past six when we reached this house – a twelve hours' business, and the horses did not appear more than reasonably tired. I was very tired too, and glad to get to bed early, but am quite well to-day. I am very snug in the front drawing-room all to myself, and would not say "thank you" for any company but you. The quietness of it does me good. I have contrived to pay my two visits, though the weather made me a great while about it, and left me only a few minutes to sit with Charlotte Craven [3]. She looks very well, and her hair is done up with an elegance to do credit to any education. Her manners are as unaffected and pleasing as ever. She had heard from her mother to-day. Mrs. Craven spends another fortnight at Chilton. I saw nobody but Charlotte, which pleased me best. I was shewn upstairs into a drawing-room, where she came to me, and the appearance of the room, so totally unschool-like, amused me very much; it was full of modern elegancies.

'Yours very affec[tly]*.,*
J.A.

The next letter, written in the following year, contains an account of another journey to London, with her brother Henry, and reading with him the manuscript of 'Mansfield Park':-

Henrietta Street, Wednesday, March 2 (1814).
MY DEAR CASSANDRA,

You were wrong in thinking of us at Guildford last night: we were at Cobham. On reaching G. we found that John [coachman] and the horses were gone on. We therefore did no more than we had done at Farnham – sit in the carriage while fresh horses were put in, and proceeded directly to Cobham, which we reached by seven, and about eight were sitting down to a very nice roast fowl, &c. We had altogether a very good journey, and everything at Cobham was comfortable. I could not pay Mr. Harrington! That was the only alas! of the business. I shall therefore return his bill, and my mother's 2l., *that you may try your luck. We did not begin reading till Bentley Green. Henry's approbation is hitherto even equal to my wishes. He says it is different from the other two, but does not appear to think it at all inferior. He has only married Mrs. R. I am afraid he has gone through the most entertaining part. He took to Lady B. and Mrs. N. most kindly, and gives great praise to the drawing of the characters. He understands them all, likes Fanny, and, I think, foresees how it will all be. I finished the "Heroine" last night, and was very much amused by it. I wonder James did not like it better. It diverted me exceedingly. We went to bed at ten. I was very tired, but slept to a miracle, and am lovely to-day, and at present Henry seems to have no complaint. We left Cobham at half-past eight, stopped to bait and breakfast at Kingston, and were in this house considerably before two. Nice smiling Mr. Barlowe [a member of staff in Henry Austen's bank] met us at the door and, in reply to enquiries after news, said that peace was generally expected [the Treaty of Paris was signed a few weeks later]. I have taken possession of my bedroom, unpacked my bandbox, sent Miss P.'s two letters to the twopenny post, been visited by Md. B.[Madame Bigeon, Henry Austen's housekeeper], and am now writing by myself at the new table in the front room. It is snowing. We had some snowstorms yesterday, and a smart frost at night, which gave us a hard road from Cobham to Kingston; but as it was then getting dirty and heavy, Henry had a pair of leaders put on to the bottom of Sloane St. His own horses, therefore, cannot have had hard work. I watched for* veils *as we drove through the streets, and had the pleasure of seeing several upon vulgar heads. And now, how do you all do? – you in particular, after the worry of yesterday and the day before. I hope Martha had a pleasant visit again,*

and that you and my mother could eat your beef-pudding. Depend upon my thinking of the chimney-sweeper as soon as I wake to-morrow. Places are secured at Drury Lane for Saturday, but so great is the rage for seeing [Edmund] Kean that only a third and fourth row could be got; as it is in a front box, however, I hope we shall do pretty well – Shylock, a good play for Fanny [Jane's niece] – she cannot be much affected, I think. Mrs. Perigord [Henry Austen's servant] has just been here. She tells me that we owe her master for the silk-dyeing. My poor old muslin has never been dyed yet. It has been promised to be done several times. What wicked people dyers are. They begin with dipping their own souls in scarlet sin. It is evening. We have drank tea, and I have torn through the third vol. of the "Heroine." I do not think it falls off. It is a delightful burlesque, particularly on the Radcliffe [Ann Radcliffe, author of Gothic novels] style. Henry is going on with "Mansfield Park." He admires H. Crawford: I mean properly, as a clever, pleasant man. I tell you all the good I can, as I know how much you will enjoy it. We hear that Mr. Kean is more admired than ever. There are no good places to be got in Drury Lane for the next fortnight, but Henry means to secure some for Saturday fortnight, when you are reckoned upon. Give my love to little Cass. I hope she found my bed comfortable last night. I have seen nobody in London yet with such a long chin as Dr. Syntax [character in a comic poem], nor anybody quite so large as Gogmagolicus [a legendary giant].
'Yours affly.,
J. Austen.

Notes
1. This mahogany desk, which has done good service to the public, is now in the possession of my sister Miss Austen.
2. At this time, February 1813, 'Mansfield Park' was nearly finished.
3. The present Lady Pollen, of Redenham, near Andover, then at a school in London.

Seclusion from the literary world—Notice from the Prince Regent—Correspondence with Mr. Clarke—Suggestions to alter her style of writing

Jane Austen lived in entire seclusion from the literary world: neither by correspondence, nor by personal intercourse was she known to any contemporary authors. It is probable that she never was in company with any person whose talents or whose celebrity equalled her own; so that her powers never could have been sharpened by collision with superior intellects, nor her imagination aided by their casual suggestions. Whatever she produced was a genuine home-made article. Even during the last two or three years of her life, when her works were rising in the estimation of the public, they did not enlarge the circle of her acquaintance. Few of her readers knew even her name, and none knew more of her than her name. I doubt whether it would be possible to mention any other author of note, whose personal obscurity was so complete. I can think of none like her, but of many to contrast with her in that respect. Fanny Burney, afterwards Madame D'Arblay, was at an early age petted by Dr. Johnson, and introduced to the wits and scholars of the day at the tables of Mrs. Thrale [Hester Thrale, writer and hostess to the literati] and Sir Joshua Reynolds [portrait painter]. Anna Seward [poet], in her self-constituted shrine at Lichfield, would have been miserable, had she not trusted that the eyes of all lovers of poetry were devoutly fixed on her. Joanna Baillie [poet and dramatist] and Maria Edgeworth [novelist] were indeed far from courting publicity; they loved the privacy of their own families, one with her brother and sister in their Hampstead villa, the other in her more distant retreat in Ireland; but fame pursued them, and they were the favourite correspondents of Sir Walter Scott. Crabbe, who was usually buried in a country parish, yet sometimes visited London, and dined at Holland House [a social centre for politicians and the literati], and was received as a fellow-poet by [Thomas] Campbell, [Thomas] Moore, and [Samuel] Rogers; and on one memorable occasion he was Scott's guest at Edinburgh, and gazed with wondering eyes on the incongruous pageantry with which George IV. was entertained in that city. Even those great writers [Wordsworth, Coleridge and their circle] who hid themselves amongst lakes and mountains associated with each other; and though little seen by the world were so much in its thoughts that a new term, 'Lakers,' was coined to designate them. The chief part of Charlotte Brontë's life was spent in a wild solitude compared with which Steventon and Chawton might be considered to be in the gay world; and yet she attained to personal distinction which never fell to Jane's lot. When she visited her kind publisher in London, literary men and women were invited purposely to meet her: [William] Thackeray bestowed upon her the honour of his notice; and once in Willis's [1] Rooms she had to walk shy and trembling through an avenue of lords and ladies, drawn up for the purpose of gazing at the author of 'Jane Eyre.' Miss Mitford [Mary Russell Mitford], too, lived quietly in 'Our Village,' devoting her time and talents to the benefit of a father scarcely worthy of her; but she did not live there unknown. Her tragedies gave her a name in London. She numbered Milman and Talfourd [nineteenth century men of letters] amongst her correspondents; and her works were a passport to the society of many who would not otherwise have sought her. Hundreds admired Miss Mitford on account of her writings for one who ever connected the idea of Miss Austen with the press. A few years ago, a gentleman visiting Winchester Cathedral desired to be shown Miss Austen's grave. The verger, as he pointed it out, asked, 'Pray, sir, can you tell me whether there was anything particular about that lady; so many people want to know where she was buried?' During her life the ignorance of the verger was shared by most people; few knew that 'there was anything particular about that lady.'

It was not till towards the close of her life, when the last of the works that she saw published was in the press, that she received the only mark of distinction ever bestowed upon her; and that was remarkable for the high quarter whence it emanated rather than for any actual increase of fame that it conferred. It happened thus. In the autumn of 1815 she nursed her brother Henry through a dangerous fever and slow convalescence at his house in Hans Place. He was attended by one of the Prince Regent's physicians. All attempts to keep her name secret had at this time ceased, and though it had never appeared on a title-page, all who cared to know might easily learn it: and the friendly physician was aware that his patient's nurse was the author of 'Pride and Prejudice.' Accordingly he informed her one day that the Prince was a great admirer of her novels; that he read them often, and kept a set in every one of his residences; that he himself therefore had thought it right to inform his Royal Highness that Miss Austen was staying in London, and that the Prince had desired Mr. Clarke, the librarian of Carlton House, to wait upon her. The next day Mr. Clarke made his appearance, and invited her to Carlton House, saying that he had the Prince's instructions to show her the library and other apartments, and to pay her every possible attention. The invitation was of course accepted, and during the visit to Carlton House Mr. Clarke declared himself commissioned to say that if Miss Austen had any other novel forthcoming she was at liberty to dedicate it to the Prince. Accordingly such a dedication was immediately prefixed to 'Emma,' which was at that time in the press.

Mr. Clarke was the brother of Dr. Clarke, the traveller and mineralogist, whose life has been written by Bishop Otter. Jane found in him not only a very courteous gentleman, but also a warm admirer of her talents; though it will be seen by his letters that he did not clearly apprehend the limits of her powers, or the proper field for their exercise. The following correspondence took place between them.

Feeling some apprehension lest she should make a mistake in acting on the verbal permission which she had received from the Prince, Jane addressed the following letter to Mr. Clarke:–

Nov. 15, 1815.

SIR, – I must take the liberty of asking you a question. Among the many flattering attentions which I received from you at Carlton House on Monday last was the information of my being at liberty to dedicate any future work to His Royal Highness the Prince Regent, without the necessity of any solicitation on my part. Such, at least, I believed to be your words; but as I am very anxious to be quite certain of what was intended, I entreat you to have the goodness to inform me how such a permission is to be understood, and whether it is incumbent on me to show my sense of the honour, by inscribing the work now in the press to His Royal Highness; I should be equally concerned to appear either presumptuous or ungrateful.'

The following gracious answer was returned by Mr. Clarke, together with a suggestion which must have been received with some surprise:–

Carlton House, Nov. 16, 1815.

DEAR MADAM, – It is certainly not incumbent *on you to dedicate your work now in the press to His Royal Highness; but if you wish to do the Regent that honour either now or at any future period I am happy to send you that permission, which need not require any more trouble or solicitation on your part.*

Your late works, Madam, and in particular "Mansfield Park," reflect the highest honour on your genius and your principles. In every new work your mind seems to increase its energy and power of discrimination. The Regent has read and admired all your publications.

Accept my best thanks for the pleasure your volumes have given me. In the perusal of them I felt a great inclination to write and say so. And I also, dear Madam, wished to be allowed to ask you to delineate in some future work the habits of life, and character, and enthusiasm of a clergyman, who should pass his time between the metropolis and the country, who should be something like [James] Beattie's Minstrel –

Silent when glad, affectionate tho' shy,
And in his looks was most demurely sad;
And now he laughed aloud, yet none knew why.

Neither Goldsmith, nor La Fontaine in his "Tableau de Famille," have in my mind quite delineated an English clergyman, at least of the present day, fond of and entirely engaged in literature, no man's enemy but his own. Pray, dear Madam, think of these things.

Believe me at all times with sincerity and respect, your faithful and obliged servant,

J. S. CLARKE, Librarian.

The following letter, written in reply, will show how unequal the author of

'Pride and Prejudice' felt herself to delineating an enthusiastic clergyman of the present day, who should resemble Beattie's Minstrel:–

Dec. 11.

DEAR SIR, – My 'Emma' is now so near publication that I feel it right to assure you of my not having forgotten your kind recommendation of an early copy for Carlton House, and that I have Mr. Murray's promise of its being sent to His Royal Highness, under cover to you, three days previous to the work being really out. I must make use of this opportunity to thank you, dear Sir, for the very high praise you bestow on my other novels. I am too vain to wish to convince you that you have praised them beyond their merits. My greatest anxiety at present is that this fourth work should not disgrace what was good in the others. But on this point I will do myself the justice to declare that, whatever may be my wishes for its success, I am strongly haunted with the idea that to those readers who have preferred "Pride and Prejudice" it will appear inferior in wit, and to those who have preferred "Mansfield Park" inferior in good sense. Such as it is, however, I hope you will do me the favour of accepting a copy. Mr. Murray will have directions for sending one. I am quite honoured by your thinking me capable of drawing such a clergyman as you gave the sketch of in your note of Nov. 16th. But I assure you I am not. *The comic part of the character I might be equal to, but not the good, the enthusiastic, the literary. Such a man's conversation must at times be on subjects of science and philosophy, of which I know nothing; or at least be occasionally abundant in quotations and allusions which a woman who, like me, knows only her own mother tongue, and has read little in that, would be totally without the power of giving. A classical education, or at any rate a very extensive acquaintance with English literature, ancient and modern, appears to me quite indispensable for the person who would do any justice to your clergyman; and I think I may boast myself to be, with all possible vanity, the most unlearned and uninformed female who ever dared to be an authoress.*
Believe me, dear Sir,
Your obliged and faithful hum^bl Ser^t.
JANE AUSTEN.[2]

Mr. Clarke, however, was not to be discouraged from proposing another subject. He had recently been appointed chaplain and private English secretary to Prince Leopold, who was then about to be united to the Princess Charlotte; and when he again wrote to express the gracious thanks of the Prince Regent for the copy of 'Emma' which had been presented, he suggests that "an historical romance illustrative of the august House of Cobourg would just now be very interesting," and might very properly be dedicated to Prince Leopold. This was much as if Sir William Ross [portrait painter] had been set to paint a great battle-piece; and it is amusing to see with what grave civility she declined a proposal which must have struck her as ludicrous, in the following letter:–

MY DEAR SIR, – I am honoured by the Prince's thanks and very much obliged to yourself for the kind manner in which you mention the work. I have also to acknowledge a former letter forwarded to me from Hans Place. I assure you I felt very grateful for the friendly tenor of it, and hope my silence will have been considered, as it was truly meant, to proceed only from an unwillingness to tax your time with idle thanks. Under every interesting circumstance which your own talents and literary labours have placed you in, or the favour of the Regent bestowed, you have my best wishes. Your recent appointments I hope are a step to something still better. In my opinion, the service of a court can hardly be too well paid, for immense must be the sacrifice of time and feeling required by it.

'You are very kind in your hints as to the sort of composition which might recommend me at present, and I am fully sensible that an historical romance, founded on the House of Saxe Cobourg, might be much more to the purpose of profit or popularity than such pictures of domestic life in country villages as I deal in. But I could no more write a romance than an epic poem. I could not sit seriously down to write a serious romance under any other motive than to save my life; and if it were indispensable for me to keep it up and never relax into laughing at myself or at other people, I am sure I should be hung before I had finished the first chapter. No, I must keep to my own style and go on in my own way; and though I may never succeed again in that, I am convinced that I should totally fail in any other.

I remain, my dear Sir,
Your very much obliged, and sincere friend,
J. AUSTEN.
Chawton, near Alton, April 1, 1816.

Mr. Clarke should have recollected the warning of the wise man,

Force not the course of the river.' If you divert it from the channel in which nature taught it to flow, and force it into one arbitrarily cut by yourself, you will lose its grace and beauty.

But when his free course is not hindered,
He makes sweet music with the enamelled stones,
Giving a gentle kiss to every sedge
He overtaketh in his pilgrimage:
And so by many winding nooks he strays
With willing sport.

[Slight misquote from Shakespeare's *Two Gentlemen of Verona*]

All writers of fiction, who have genius strong enough to work out a course of their own, resist every attempt to interfere with its direction. No two writers could be more unlike each other than Jane Austen and Charlotte Brontë; so much so that the latter was unable to understand why the former was admired, and confessed that she herself 'should hardly like to live with her ladies and gentlemen, in their elegant but confined houses;' but each writer equally resisted interference with her own natural style of composition. Miss Brontë, in reply to a friendly critic, who had warned her against being too melodramatic, and had ventured to propose Miss Austen's works to her as a study, writes thus:–

> Whenever I *do* write another book, I think I will have nothing of what you call "melodrama." I *think* so, but I am not sure. I *think*, too, I will endeavour to follow the counsel which shines out of Miss Austen's "mild eyes," to finish more, and be more subdued; but neither am I sure of that. When authors write best, or, at least, when they write most fluently, an influence seems to waken in them which becomes their master – which will have its way – putting out of view all behests but its own, dictating certain words, and insisting on their being used, whether vehement or measured in their nature, new moulding characters, giving unthought of turns to incidents, rejecting carefully elaborated old ideas, and suddenly creating and adopting new ones. Is it not so? And should we try to counteract this influence? Can we indeed counteract it?[3]

The playful raillery with which the one parries an attack on her liberty, and the vehement eloquence of the other in pleading the same cause and maintaining the independence of genius, are very characteristic of the minds of the respective writers.

The suggestions which Jane received as to the sort of story that she ought to write were, however, an amusement to her, though they were not likely to prove useful; and she has left amongst her papers one entitled, 'Plan of a novel according to hints from various quarters.' The names of some of those advisers are written on the margin of the manuscript opposite to their respective suggestions.

Heroine to be the daughter of a clergyman, who after having lived much in the world had retired from it, and settled on a curacy with a very small fortune of his own. The most excellent man that can be imagined, perfect in character, temper, and manner, without the smallest drawback or peculiarity to prevent his being the most delightful companion to his daughter from one year's end to the other. Heroine faultless in character, beautiful in person, and possessing every possible accomplishment. Book to open with father and daughter conversing in long speeches, elegant language, and a tone of high serious sentiment. The father induced, at his daughter's earnest request, to relate to her the past events of his life. Narrative to reach through the greater part of the first volume; as besides all the circumstances of his attachment to her mother, and their marriage, it will comprehend his going to sea as chaplain to a distinguished naval character about the court; and his going afterwards to court himself, which involved him in many interesting situations, concluding with his opinion of the benefits of tithes being done away with...From this outset the story will proceed, and contain a striking variety of adventures. Father an exemplary parish priest, and devoted to literature; but heroine and father never above a fortnight in one place: he being driven from his curacy by the vile arts of some totally unprincipled and heartless young man, desperately in love with the heroine, and pursuing her with unrelenting passion. No sooner settled in one country of Europe, than they are compelled to quit it, and retire to another, always making new acquaintance, and always obliged to leave them. This will of course exhibit a wide variety of character. The scene will be for ever shifting from one set of people to another, but there will be no mixture, all the good will be unexceptionable in every respect. There will be no foibles or weaknesses but with the wicked, who will be completely depraved and infamous, hardly a resemblance of humanity left in them. Early in her career, the heroine must meet with the hero: all perfection, of course, and only prevented from paying his addresses to her by some excess of refinement. Wherever she goes, somebody falls in love with her, and she receives repeated offers of marriage, which she refers wholly to her father, exceedingly angry that he should not be the first applied to. Often carried away by the anti-hero, but rescued either by her father or the hero. Often reduced to support herself and her father by her talents, and work for her bread; continually cheated, and defrauded of her hire; worn down to a skeleton, and now and then starved to death. At last, hunted out of civilised society, denied the poor shelter of the humblest cottage, they are compelled to retreat into Kamtschatka, where the poor father quite worn down, finding his end approaching, throws himself on the ground, and after four or five hours of tender advice and parental admonition to his miserable child, expires in a fine burst of literary enthusiasm, intermingled with invectives against the holders of tithes. Heroine inconsolable for some time, but afterwards crawls back towards her former country, having at least twenty narrow escapes of falling into the hands of anti-hero; and at last, in the very nick of time, turning a corner to avoid him, runs into the arms of the hero himself, who, having just shaken off the scruples which fettered him before, was at the very moment setting off in pursuit of her. The tenderest and completest *éclaircissement* takes place, and they are happily united. Throughout the whole work heroine to be in the most elegant society, and living in high style.'

Since the first publication of this memoir, Mr. Murray of Albemarle Street has very kindly sent to me copies of the following letters, which his father received from Jane Austen, when engaged in the publication of 'Emma.' The increasing cordiality of the letters shows that the author felt that her interests were duly cared for, and was glad to find herself in the hands of a publisher whom she could consider as a friend.

Her brother had addressed to Mr. Murray a strong complaint of the tardiness of a printer:–

23 Hans Place, Thursday, November 23 (1815).

SIR, – My brother's note last Monday has been so fruitless, that I am afraid there can be but little chance of my writing to any good effect; but yet I am so very much disappointed and vexed by the delays of the printers, that I cannot help begging to know whether there is no hope of their being quickened. Instead of the work being ready by the end of the present month, it will hardly, at the rate we now proceed, be finished by the end of the next; and as I expect to leave London early in December, it is of consequence that no more time should be lost. Is it likely that the printers will be influenced to greater dispatch and punctuality by knowing that the work is to be dedicated, by permission, to the Prince Regent? If you can make that circumstance operate, I shall be very glad. My brother returns 'Waterloo' with many thanks for the loan of it. We have heard much of Scott's account of Paris [4]. If it be not incompatible with other arrangements, would you favour us with it, supposing you have any set already opened? You may depend upon its being in careful hands.

I remain, Sir, your ob^{t}. humble Se^{t}.

J. AUSTEN.

Hans Place, December 11 (1815).

DEAR SIR, – As I find that "Emma" is advertised for publication as early as Saturday next, I think it best to lose no time in settling all that remains to be settled on the subject, and adopt this method as involving the smallest tax on your time.

In the first place, I beg you to understand that I leave the terms on which the trade should be supplied with the work entirely to your judgment, entreating you to be guided in every such arrangement by your own experience of what is most likely to clear off the edition rapidly. I shall be satisfied with whatever you feel to be best. The title-page must be "Emma, dedicated by permission to H.R.H. the Prince Regent." And it is my particular wish that one set should be completed and sent to H.R.H. two or three days before the work is generally public. It should be sent under cover to the Rev. J. S. Clarke, Librarian, Carlton

House. I shall subjoin a list of those persons to whom I must trouble you to forward also a set each, when the work is out; all unbound, with "From the Authoress" in the first page.

I return you, with very many thanks, the books you have so obligingly supplied me with. I am very sensible, I assure you, of the attention you have paid to my convenience and amusement. I return also "Mansfield Park," as ready for a second edition, I believe, as I can make it. I am in Hans Place till the 16th. From that day inclusive, my direction will be Chawton, Alton, Hants.

I remain, dear Sir,

Yr faithful humb. Servt

J. AUSTEN.

I wish you would have the goodness to send a line by the bearer, stating the day *on which the set will be ready for the Prince Regent.*

Hans Place, December 11 (1815).

DEAR SIR, – I am much obliged by yours, and very happy to feel everything arranged to our mutual satisfaction. As to my direction about the title-page, it was arising from my ignorance only, and from my having never noticed the proper place for a dedication. I thank you for putting me right. Any deviation from what is usually done in such cases is the last thing I should wish for. I feel happy in having a friend to save me from the ill effect of my own blunder.

Yours, dear Sir, &c.

J. AUSTEN.

Chawton, April 1, 1816.

DEAR SIR, – I return you the "Quarterly Review" with many thanks. The Authoress of "Emma" has no reason, I think, to complain of her treatment in it, except in the total omission of "Mansfield Park." I cannot but be sorry that so clever a man as the Reviewer of "Emma" should consider it as unworthy of being noticed. You will be pleased to hear that I have received the Prince's thanks for the handsome *copy I sent him of "Emma." Whatever he may think of* my *share of the work, yours seems to have been quite right.*

In consequence of the late event in Henrietta Street, [Henry Austen's recent bankruptcy] I must request that if you should at any time have anything to communicate by letter, you will be so good as to write by the post, directing to me (Miss J. Austen), Chawton, near Alton; and that for anything of a larger bulk, you will add to the same direction, by Collier's Southampton coach.

I remain, dear Sir,

Yours very faithfully,

J. AUSTEN.

About the same time the following letters passed between the Countess of Morley and the writer of 'Emma.' I do not know whether they were personally acquainted with each other, nor in what this interchange of civilities originated:–

The Countess of Morley to Miss J. Austen.
Saltram, December 27 (1815).

MADAM, – I have been most anxiously waiting for an introduction to "Emma," and am infinitely obliged to you for your kind recollection of me, which will procure me the pleasure of her acquaintance some days sooner than I should otherwise have had it. I am already become intimate with the Woodhouse family, and feel that they will not amuse and interest me less than the Bennetts, Bertrams, Norrises, and all their admirable predecessors. I can give them no higher praise.
I am, Madam, your much obliged
F. MORLEY.

Miss J. Austen to the Countess of Morley.

MADAM, – Accept my thanks for the honour of your note, and for your kind disposition in favour of "Emma." In my present state of doubt as to her reception in the world, it is particularly gratifying to me to receive so early an assurance of your Ladyship's approbation. It encourages me to depend on the same share of general good opinion which "Emma's" predecessors have experienced, and to believe that I have not yet, as almost every writer of fancy does sooner or later, overwritten myself.
I am, Madam,
Your obliged and faithful Servt.
J. AUSTEN.
December 31, 1815.

Notes

1. See Mrs Gaskell's 'Life of Miss Bronte' vol.ii.p.215.
2. It was her pleasure to boast of greater ignorance than she had any just claim to. She knew more than her mother tongue, for she knew a good deal of French and a little Italian.
3. Mrs Gaskell's 'Life of Miss Bronte,' vol.ii.p.53.
4. This must have been 'Paul's Letters to his Kinsfolk.'

Slow growth of her fame—Ill success of first attempts at publication—Two Reviews of her works contrasted

Seldom has any literary reputation been of such slow growth as that of

Jane Austen. Readers of the present day know the rank that is generally assigned to her. They have been told by Archbishop Whately, in his review of her works, and by Lord Macaulay [Thomas Babington Macaulay, historian], in his review of Madame D'Arblay's, the reason why the highest place is to be awarded to Jane Austen, as a truthful drawer of character, and why she is to be classed with those who have approached nearest, in that respect, to the great master Shakspeare [*sic*]. They see her safely placed, by such authorities, in her niche, not indeed amongst the highest orders of genius, but in one confessedly her own, in our British temple of literary fame; and it may be difficult to make them believe how coldly her works were at first received, and how few readers had any appreciation of their peculiar merits. Sometimes a friend or neighbour, who chanced to know of our connection with the author, would condescend to speak with moderate approbation of 'Sense and Sensibility,' or 'Pride and Prejudice'; but if they had known that we, in our secret thoughts, classed her with Madame D'Arblay or Miss Edgeworth, or even with some other novel writers of the day whose names are now scarcely remembered, they would have considered it an amusing instance of family conceit. To the multitude her works appeared tame and commonplace [1], poor in colouring, and sadly deficient in incident and interest. It is true that we were sometimes cheered by hearing that a different verdict had been pronounced by more competent judges: we were told how some great statesman or distinguished poet held these works in high estimation; we had the satisfaction of believing that they were most admired by the best judges, and comforted ourselves with Horace's 'satis est Equitem mihi plaudere' [It is enough if the knights applaud me]. So much was this the case, that one of the ablest men of my acquaintance [2] said, in that kind of jest which has much earnest in it, that he had established it in his own mind, as a new test of ability, whether people *could* or *could not* appreciate Miss Austen's merits.

But though such golden opinions were now and then gathered in, yet the wide field of public taste yielded no adequate return either in praise or profit. Her reward was not to be the quick return of the cornfield, but the slow growth of the tree which is to endure to another generation. Her first attempts at publication were very discouraging. In November, 1797, her father wrote the following letter to Mr. Cadell:–

Sir, – I have in my possession a manuscript novel, comprising 3 vols., about the length of Miss Burney's "Evelina." As I am well aware of what consequence it is that a work of this sort sh^d^ make its first appearance under a respectable name, I apply to you. I shall be much obliged therefore if you will inform me whether you choose to be concerned in it, what will be the expense of publishing it at the author's risk, and what you will venture to

advance for the property of it, if on perusal it is approved of. Should you give any encouragement, I will send you the work.
I am, Sir, your humble Servant,
GEORGE AUSTEN
Steventon, near Overton, Hants,
1st Nov. 1797.

This proposal was declined by return of post! The work thus summarily rejected must have been 'Pride and Prejudice.'

The fate of 'Northanger Abbey' was still more humiliating. It was sold, in 1803, to a publisher in Bath [this is incorrect, it was sold to the London publisher Richard Crosby], for ten pounds, but it found so little favour in his eyes, that he chose to abide by his first loss rather than risk farther expense by publishing such a work. It seems to have lain for many years unnoticed in his drawers; somewhat as the first chapters of 'Waverley' lurked forgotten amongst the old fishing-tackle in Scott's cabinet. Tilneys, Thorpes, and Morlands consigned apparently to eternal oblivion! But when four novels of steadily increasing success had given the writer some confidence in herself, she wished to recover the copyright of this early work. One of her brothers undertook the negotiation. He found the purchaser very willing to receive back his money, and to resign all claim to the copyright. When the bargain was concluded and the money paid, but not till then, the negotiator had the satisfaction of informing him that the work which had been so lightly esteemed was by the author of 'Pride and Prejudice.' I do not think that she was herself much mortified by the want of early success. She wrote for her own amusement. Money, though acceptable, was not necessary for the moderate expenses of her quiet home. Above all, she was blessed with a cheerful contented disposition, and an humble mind; and so lowly did she esteem her own claims, that when she received 150*l*. from the sale of 'Sense and Sensibility,' she considered it a prodigious recompense for that which had cost her nothing. It cannot be supposed, however, that she was altogether insensible to the superiority of her own workmanship over that of some contemporaries who were then enjoying a brief popularity. Indeed a few touches in the following extracts from two of her letters show that she was as quicksighted to absurdities in composition as to those in living persons.

Mr. C.'s opinion is gone down in my list; but as my paper relates only to "Mansfield Park," I may fortunately excuse myself from entering Mr. D's. I will redeem my credit with him by writing a close imitation of "Self-Control" [by Mary Brunton], as soon as I can. I will improve upon it. My heroine shall not only be wafted down an American river in a boat by herself. She shall cross the Atlantic in the same way; and never stop till she reaches Gravesend.

*We have got "Rosanne" [*Rosanne: or A Father's Labour Lost *by Laetitia Matilda Hawkins] in our Society, and find it much as you describe it; very good and clever, but tedious. Mrs. Hawkins' great excellence is on serious subjects. There are some very delightful conversations and reflections on religion: but on lighter topics I think she falls into many absurdities; and, as to love, her heroine has very comical feelings. There are a thousand improbabilities in the story. Do you remember the two Miss Ormsdens introduced just at last? Very flat and unnatural. Mad*[elle]*. Cossart is rather my passion.*

Two notices of her works appeared in the 'Quarterly Review.' One in October 1815, and another, more than three years after her death, in January 1821. The latter article is known to have been from the pen of Whately, afterwards Archbishop of Dublin.[3] They differ much from each other in the degree of praise which they award, and I think also it may be said, in the ability with which they are written. The first bestows some approval, but the other expresses the warmest admiration. One can scarcely be satisfied with the critical acumen of the former writer, who, in treating of 'Sense and Sensibility,' takes no notice whatever of the vigour with which many of the characters are drawn, but declares that 'the interest and *merit* of the piece depends *altogether* upon the behaviour of the elder sister!' Nor is he fair when, in 'Pride and Prejudice,' he represents Elizabeth's change of sentiments towards Darcy as caused by the sight of his house and grounds. But the chief discrepancy between the two reviewers is to be found in their appreciation of the commonplace and silly characters to be found in these novels. On this point the difference almost amounts to a contradiction, such as one sometimes sees drawn up in parallel columns, when it is desired to convict some writer or some statesman of inconsistency. The Reviewer, in 1815, says: 'The faults of these works arise from the minute detail which the author's plan comprehends. Characters of folly or simplicity, such as those of old Woodhouse and Miss Bates, are ridiculous when first presented, but if too often brought forward, or too long dwelt on, their prosing is apt to become as tiresome in fiction as in real society.' The Reviewer, in 1821, on the contrary, singles out the fools as especial instances of the writer's abilities, and declares that in this respect she shows a regard to character hardly exceeded by Shakspeare himself. These are his words: 'Like him (Shakspeare) she shows as admirable a discrimination in the character of fools as of people of sense; a merit which is far from common. To invent indeed a conversation full of wisdom or of wit requires that the writer should himself possess ability; but the converse does not hold good, it is no fool that can describe fools well; and many who have succeeded pretty well in painting superior characters have failed in giving individuality to those weaker ones which it is necessary to introduce in order to give a faithful representation of real life: they exhibit to us mere folly in the abstract, forgetting that to the eye of the skilful naturalist the insects on a leaf present as wide differences as exist between the lion and the elephant. Slender, and Shallow, and Aguecheek, as Shakspeare has painted them, though equally fools, resemble one another no more than Richard, and Macbeth, and Julius Caesar; and Miss Austen's [4] Mrs. Bennet, Mr. Rushworth, and Miss Bates are no more alike than her Darcy, Knightley, and Edmund Bertram. Some have complained indeed of finding her fools too much like nature, and consequently tiresome. There is no disputing about tastes; all we can say is, that such critics must (whatever deference they may outwardly pay to received opinions) find the "Merry Wives of Windsor" and "Twelfth Night" very tiresome; and that those who look with pleasure at Wilkie's pictures, or those of the Dutch school, must admit that excellence of imitation may confer attraction on that which would be insipid or disagreeable in the reality. Her minuteness of detail has also been found fault with; but even where it produces, at the time, a degree of tediousness, we know not whether that can justly be reckoned a blemish, which is absolutely essential to a very high excellence. Now it is absolutely impossible, without this, to produce that thorough acquaintance with the characters which is necessary to make the reader heartily interested in them. Let any one cut out from the "Iliad" or from Shakspeare's plays everything (we are far from saying that either might not lose some parts with advantage, but let him reject everything) which is absolutely devoid of importance and interest *in itself*; and he will find that what is left will have lost more than half its charms. We are convinced that some writers have diminished the effect of their works by being scrupulous to admit nothing into them which had not some absolute and independent merit. They have acted like those who strip off the leaves of a fruit tree, as being of themselves good for nothing, with the view of securing more nourishment to the fruit, which in fact cannot attain its full maturity and flavour without them.

The world, I think, has endorsed the opinion of the later writer; but it would not be fair to set down the discrepancy between the two entirely to the discredit of the former. The fact is that, in the course of the intervening five years, these works had been read and reread by many leaders in the literary world. The public taste was forming itself all this time, and 'grew by what it fed on.' These novels belong to a class which gain rather than lose by frequent perusals, and it is probable that each Reviewer represented fairly enough the prevailing opinions of readers in the year when each wrote.

Since that time, the testimonies in favour of Jane Austen's works have been continual and almost unanimous. They are frequently referred to as models; nor have they lost their first distinction of being especially acceptable to minds of the highest order. I shall indulge myself by collecting into the next chapter instances of the homage paid to her by such persons.

Notes

1. A greater genius than my aunt shared with her the imputation of being *commonplace.* Lockhart, speaking of the low estimation in which Scott's conversational powers were held in the literary and scientific society of Edinburgh, says : 'I think the epithet most in vogue concerning it was "commonplace."' He adds, however, that one of the most eminent of that society was of a different opinion, 'who, when some glib youth chanced to echo in his hearing the consolatory tenet of local mediocrity, answered quietly, "I have the misfortune to think differently from you – in my humble opinion Walter Scott's *sense* is a still more wonderful thing than his genius."' – Lockhart's *Life of Scott,*vol.iv.chap.v.
2. The late Mr R. H. Cheney.
3. Lockhart had supposed that this article had been written by Scott, because it exactly accorded with the opinions which Scott had often been heard to express, but he learned afterwards that it had been written by Whately; and Lockhart, who became the Editor of the Quarterly, must have had the means of knowing the truth. (See Lockhart's *Life of Sir Walter Scott,* vol.v.p.158) I remember that, at the time when the review came out, it was reported in Oxford that Whately had written the article at the request of the lady whom he afterwards married.
4. In transcribing this passage I have taken the liberty so far to correct it as to spell her name properly with an 'e.'

Opinions expressed by eminent persons—Opinions of others of less eminence—Opinion of American readers

Into this list of the admirers of my Aunt's works, I admit those only whose eminence will be universally acknowledged. No doubt the number might have been increased.

[Robert] Southey, in a letter to Sir Egerton Brydges, says:

> You mention Miss Austen. Her novels are more true to nature, and have, for my sympathies, passages of finer feeling than any others of

> this age. She was a person of whom I have heard so well and think so highly, that I regret not having had an opportunity of testifying to her the respect which I felt for her.

It may be observed that Southey had probably heard from his own family connections of the charm of her private character. A friend of hers, the daughter of Mr. Bigge Wither, of Manydown Park near Basingstoke, was married to Southey's uncle, the Rev. Herbert Hill, who had been useful to his nephew in many ways, and especially in supplying him with the means of attaining his extensive knowledge of Spanish and Portuguese literature. Mr. Hill had been Chaplain to the British Factory at Lisbon, where Southey visited him and had the use of a library in those languages which his uncle had collected. Southey himself continually mentions his uncle Hill in terms of respect and gratitude.

> S. T. Coleridge,would sometimes burst out into high encomiums of Miss Austen's novels as being, 'in their way, perfectly genuine and individual productions'.

> I remember Miss Mitford's saying to me: 'I would almost cut off one of my hands, if it would enable me to write like your aunt with the other.'

The biographer of Sir J. Mackintosh says

> Something recalled to his mind the traits of character which are so delicately touched in Miss Austen's novels...He said that there was genius in sketching out that new kind of novel He was vexed for the credit of the "Edinburgh Review" that it had left her unnoticed [1]... The "Quarterly" had done her more justice...It was impossible for a foreigner to understand fully the merit of her works. Madame de Staël [French woman of letters], to whom he had recommended one of her novels, found no interest in it; and in her note to him in reply said it was "vulgaire": and yet, he said, nothing could be more true than what he wrote in answer: "There is no book which that word would so little suit."... Every village could furnish matter for a novel to Miss Austen. She did not need the common materials for a novel, strong emotions, or strong incidents. [2]

It was not, however, quite impossible for a foreigner to appreciate these works; for Mons. Guizot [Francois Guizot, philosopher and historian] writes thus:

> I am a great novel reader, but I seldom read German or French novels.

> The characters are too artificial. My delight is to read English novels, particularly those written by women. "C'est toute une école de morale." Miss Austen, Miss Ferrier, &c., form a school which in the excellence and profusion of its productions resembles the cloud of dramatic poets of the great Athenian age.

In the 'Keepsake' [an annual miscellany] of 1825 the following lines appeared, written by Lord Morpeth, afterwards seventh Earl of Carlisle, and Lord-Lieutenant of Ireland, accompanying an illustration of a lady reading a novel.

> Beats thy quick pulse o'er Inchbald's thrilling leaf,
> Brunton's high moral, Opie's deep wrought grief?
> Has the mild chaperon claimed thy yielding heart?
> Carroll's dark page, Trevelyan's gentle art?
> Or is it thou, all perfect Austen? Here
> Let one poor wreath adorn thy early bier
> That scarce allowed thy modest youth to claim
> Its living portion of thy certain fame!
> Oh! Mrs. Bennett! Mrs. Norris too!
> While memory survives we'll dream of you.
> And Mr. Woodhouse, whose abstemious lip
> Must thin, but not too thin, his gruel sip.
> Miss Bates, our idol, though the village bore,
> And Mrs. Elton, ardent to explore,
> While the clear style flows on without pretence,
> With unstained purity, and unmatched sense,
> Or, if a sister e'er approached the throne,
> She called the rich 'inheritance' her own.

The admiration felt by Lord Macaulay would probably have taken a very practical form, if his life had been prolonged. I have the authority of his sister, Lady Trevelyan, for stating that he had intended to undertake the task upon which I have ventured. He purposed to write a memoir of Miss Austen, with criticisms on her works, to prefix it to a new edition of her novels, and from the proceeds of the sale to erect a monument to her memory in Winchester Cathedral. Oh! that such an idea had been realised! That portion of the plan in which Lord Macaulay's success would have been most certain might have been almost sufficient for his object. A memoir written by him would have been a monument.

I am kindly permitted by Sir Henry Holland [doctor to Queen Victoria] to give the following quotation from his printed but unpublished recollections of his past life:–

> I have the picture still before me of Lord Holland lying on his bed, when attacked with gout, his admirable sister, Miss Fox, beside him reading aloud, as she always did on these occasions, some one of Miss Austen's novels, of which he was never wearied. I well recollect the time when these charming novels, almost unique in their style of humour, burst suddenly on the world. It was sad that their writer did not live to witness the growth of her fame.

My brother-in-law, Sir Denis Le Marchant, has supplied me with the following anecdotes from his own recollections:–

> When I was a student at Trinity College, Cambridge, Mr. Whewell, then a Fellow and afterwards Master of the College, often spoke to me with admiration of Miss Austen's novels. On one occasion I said that I had found "Persuasion" rather dull. He quite fired up in defence of it, insisting that it was the most beautiful of her works. This accomplished philosopher was deeply versed in works of fiction. I recollect his writing to me from Caernarvon, where he had the charge of some pupils, that he was weary of *his* stay, for he had read the circulating library twice through.
>
> During a visit I paid to Lord Lansdowne, at Bowood, in 1846, one of Miss Austen's novels became the subject of conversation and of praise, especially from Lord Lansdowne, who observed that one of the circumstances of his life which he looked back upon with vexation was that Miss Austen should once have been living some weeks in his neighbourhood without his knowing it.
>
> I have heard Sydney Smith [editor of *The Edinburgh Review*], more than once, dwell with eloquence on the merits of Miss Austen's novels. He told me he should have enjoyed giving her the pleasure of reading her praises in the "Edinburgh Review." "Fanny Price" was one of his prime favourites.

I close this list of testimonies, this long 'Catena Patrum' [list of authorities], with the remarkable words of Sir Walter Scott, taken from his diary for March 14, 1826 [3]

> Read again, for the third time at least, Miss Austen's finely written novel of "Pride and Prejudice." That young lady had a talent for describing the involvements and feelings and characters of ordinary life, which is to me the most wonderful I ever met with. The big Bow-Wow strain I can do myself like any now going; but the exquisite touch which renders

> ordinary common-place things and characters interesting from the truth of the description and the sentiment is denied to me. What a pity such a gifted creature died so early!

The well-worn condition of Scott's own copy of these works attests that they were much read in his family. When I visited Abbotsford, a few years after Scott's death, I was permitted, as an unusual favour, to take one of these volumes in my hands. One cannot suppress the wish that she had lived to know what such men thought of her powers, and how gladly they would have cultivated a personal acquaintance with her. I do not think that it would at all have impaired the modest simplicity of her character; or that we should have lost our own dear 'Aunt Jane' in the blaze of literary fame.

It may be amusing to contrast with these testimonies from the great, the opinions expressed by other readers of more ordinary intellect. The author herself has left a list of criticisms which it had been her amusement to collect, through means of her friends. This list contains much of warm-hearted sympathising praise, interspersed with some opinions which may be considered surprising.

> One lady could say nothing better of 'Mansfield Park,' than that it was 'a mere novel.'
>
> Another owned that she thought 'Sense and Sensibility' and 'Pride and Prejudice' downright nonsense; but expected to like 'Mansfield Park' better, and having finished the first volume, hoped that she had got through the worst.
>
> Another did not like 'Mansfield Park.' Nothing interesting in the characters. Language poor.
>
> One gentleman read the first and last chapters of 'Emma,' but did not look at the rest because he had been told that it was not interesting.
>
> The opinions of another gentleman about 'Emma' were so bad that they could not be reported to the author.

'Quot homines, tot sententiae' [as many opinions as there are men].

Thirty-five years after her death there came also a voice of praise from across the Atlantic. In 1852 the following letter was received by her brother Sir Francis Austen:–

Boston, Massachusetts, U.S.A.
6th Jan. 1852.

Since high critical authority has pronounced the delineations of character in the works of Jane Austen second only to those of Shakspeare [*sic*], transatlantic admiration appears superfluous; yet it may not be uninteresting to her family to receive an assurance that the influence of her genius is extensively recognised in the American Republic, even by the highest judicial authorities. The late Mr. Chief Justice Marshall, of the supreme Court of the United States, and his associate Mr. Justice Story, highly estimated and admired Miss Austen, and to them we owe our introduction to her society. For many years her talents have brightened our daily path, and her name and those of her characters are familiar to us as "household words." We have long wished to express to some of her family the sentiments of gratitude and affection she has inspired, and request more information relative to her life than is given in the brief memoir prefixed to her works.

Having accidentally heard that a brother of Jane Austen held a high rank in the British Navy, we have obtained his address from our friend Admiral Wormley, now resident in Boston, and we trust this expression of our feeling will be received by her relations with the kindness and urbanity characteristic of Admirals of *her creation*. Sir Francis Austen, or one of his family, would confer a great favour by complying with our request The autograph of his sister, or a few lines in her handwriting, would be placed among our chief treasures.

The family who delight in the companionship of Jane Austen, and who present this petition, are of English origin. Their ancestor held a high rank among the first emigrants to New England, and his name and character have been ably represented by his descendants in various public stations of trust and responsibility to the present time in the colony and state of Massachusetts. A letter addressed to Miss Quincey, care of the Honble Josiah Quincey, Boston, Massachusetts, would reach its destination.

Sir Francis Austen returned a suitable reply to this application; and sent a long letter of his sister's, which, no doubt, still occupies the place of honour promised by the Quincey family.

Notes

1. Incidentally she had received high praise in Lord Macaulay's Review of Madame D'Arblay's Works in the 'Edinburgh'.
2. *Life of Sir J. Mackintosh,*vol.ii.p.472.
3. Lockhart's *Life of Scott,*vol.vi.chap.vii.

Observations on the Novels

It is not the object of these memoirs to attempt a criticism on Jane Austen's novels. Those particulars only have been noticed which could be illustrated by the circumstances of her own life; but I now desire to offer a few observations on them, and especially on one point, on which my age renders me a competent witness – the fidelity with which they represent the opinions and manners of the class of society in which the author lived early in this century. They do this the more faithfully on account of the very deficiency with which they have been sometimes charged – namely, that they make no attempt to raise the standard of human life, but merely represent it as it was. They certainly were not written to support any theory or inculcate any particular moral, except indeed the great moral which is to be equally gathered from an observation of the course of actual life – namely, the superiority of high over low principles, and of greatness over littleness of mind. These writings are like photographs, in which no feature is softened; no ideal expression is introduced, all is the unadorned reflection of the natural object; and the value of such a faithful likeness must increase as time gradually works more and more changes in the face of society itself. A remarkable instance of this is to be found in her portraiture of the clergy. She was the daughter and the sister of clergymen, who certainly were not low specimens of their order: and she has chosen three of her heroes from that profession; but no one in these days can think that either Edmund Bertram or Henry Tilney had adequate ideas of the duties of a parish minister. Such, however, were the opinions and practice then prevalent among respectable and conscientious clergymen before their minds had been stirred, first by the Evangelical, and afterwards by the High Church movement which this century has witnessed. The country may be congratulated which, on looking back to such a fixed landmark, can find that it has been advancing instead of receding from it.

The long interval that elapsed between the completion of 'Northanger Abbey' in 1798, and the commencement of 'Mansfield Park' in 1811, may sufficiently account for any difference of style which may be perceived between her three earlier and her three later productions. If the former showed quite as much originality and genius, they may perhaps be thought to have less of the faultless finish and high polish which distinguish the latter. The characters of the John Dashwoods, Mr. Collins, and the Thorpes stand out from the canvas with a vigour and originality which cannot be surpassed; but I think that in her last three works are to be found a greater refinement of taste, a more nice sense of propriety, and a deeper insight into the delicate anatomy of the human heart, marking the difference between the brilliant girl and the mature woman. Far from being one of those who have over-written themselves, it may be affirmed that her fame would have stood on a narrower and less firm basis, if she had not lived to resume her pen at Chawton.

Some persons have surmised that she took her characters from individuals with whom she had been acquainted. They were so life-like that it was assumed that they must once have lived, and have been transferred bodily, as it were, into her pages. But surely such a supposition betrays an ignorance of the high prerogative of genius to create out of its own resources imaginary characters, who shall be true to nature and consistent in themselves. Perhaps, however, the distinction between keeping true to nature and servilely copying any one specimen of it is not always clearly apprehended. It is indeed true, both of the writer and of the painter, that he can use only such lineaments as exist, and as he has observed to exist, in living objects; otherwise he would produce monsters instead of human beings; but in both it is the office of high art to mould these features into new combinations, and to place them in the attitudes, and impart to them the expressions which may suit the purposes of the artist; so that they are nature, but not exactly the same nature which had come before his eyes; just as honey can be obtained only from the natural flowers which the bee has sucked; yet it is not a reproduction of the odour or flavour of any particular flower, but becomes something different when it has gone through the process of transformation which that little insect is able to effect. Hence, in the case of painters, arises the superiority of original compositions over portrait painting. Reynolds was exercising a higher faculty when he designed Comedy and Tragedy contending for Garrick, than when he merely took a likeness of that actor. The same difference exists in writings between the original conceptions of Shakspeare and some other creative geniuses, and such full-length likenesses of individual persons, 'The Talking Gentleman' for instance, as are admirably drawn by Miss Mitford. Jane Austen's powers, whatever may be the degree in which she possessed them, were certainly of that higher order. She did not copy individuals, but she invested her own creations with individuality of character. A reviewer in the 'Quarterly' speaks of an acquaintance who, ever since the publication of 'Pride and Prejudice,' had been called by his friends Mr. Bennet, but the author did not know him. Her own relations never recognised any individual in her characters; and I can call to mind several of her acquaintance whose peculiarities were very tempting and easy to be caricatured of whom there are no traces in her pages. She herself, when questioned on the subject by a friend, expressed a dread of what she called such an 'invasion of social proprieties.' She said that she thought it quite fair to note peculiarities and weaknesses, but that it was her desire to create, not to reproduce; 'besides,' she added, 'I am too proud of my gentlemen to admit that they were only Mr. A. or Colonel B.' She did not, however, suppose that her imaginary characters were of a higher order than are to be found in nature; for she said, when speaking of two of her great favourites, Edmund Bertram and Mr. Knightley: 'They are very far from being what I know English gentlemen often are.'

She certainly took a kind of parental interest in the beings whom she had created, and did not dismiss them from her thoughts when she had finished her last chapter. We have seen, in one of her letters, her personal affection for Darcy and Elizabeth; and when sending a copy of 'Emma' to a friend [her niece Anna] whose daughter had been lately born, she wrote thus: 'I trust you will be as glad to see my "Emma," as I shall be to see your Jemima.' She was very fond of Emma, but did not reckon on her being a general favourite; for, when commencing that work, she said, 'I am going to take a heroine whom no one but myself will much like.' She would, if asked, tell us many little particulars about the subsequent career of some of her people. In this traditionary way we learned that Miss Steele never succeeded in catching the Doctor; that Kitty Bennet was satisfactorily married to a clergyman near Pemberley, while Mary obtained nothing higher than one of her uncle Philip's clerks, and was content to be considered a star in the society of Meriton; that the 'considerable sum' given by Mrs. Norris to William Price was one pound; that Mr. Woodhouse survived his daughter's marriage, and kept her and Mr. Knightley from settling at Donwell, about two years; and that the letters placed by Frank Churchill before Jane Fairfax, which she swept away unread, contained the word 'pardon.' Of the good people in 'Northanger Abbey' and 'Persuasion' we know nothing more than what is written: for before those works were published their author had been taken away from us, and all such amusing communications had ceased for ever.

Declining health of Jane Austen—Elasticity of her spirits—Her resignation and humility—Her death

Early in the year 1816 some family troubles [Henry Austen's bankruptcy and disappointment over the will of James Leigh Perrot] disturbed the usually tranquil course of Jane Austen's life; and it is probable that the inward malady, which was to prove ultimately fatal, was already felt by her; for some distant friends [1] whom she visited in the spring of that year, thought that her health was somewhat impaired, and observed that she went about her old haunts, and recalled old recollections connected with them in a particular manner, as if she did not expect ever to see them again. It is not surprising that, under these circumstances, some of her letters were of a graver tone than had been customary with her, and expressed resignation rather than cheerfulness. In reference to these troubles in a letter to her brother Charles, after mentioning that she had been laid up with an attack of bilious fever, she says: 'I live up stairs for the present and am coddled. I am the only one of the party who has been so silly, but a weak body must excuse weak nerves.' And again, to another correspondent: 'But I am getting too near complaint; it has been the appointment of God, however secondary causes may have operated.' But the elasticity of her spirits soon recovered their tone. It was in the latter half of that year that she addressed the two following lively letters to a nephew [the author of this memoir], one while he was at Winchester School, the other soon after he had left it:–

Chawton, July 9, 1816.

MY DEAR EDWARD. – Many thanks. A thank for every line, and as many to Mr. W. Digweed for coming. We have been wanting very much to hear of your mother, and are happy to find she continues to mend, but her illness must have been a very serious one indeed. When she is really recovered, she ought to try change of air, and come over to us. Tell your father that I am very much obliged to him for his share of your letter, and most sincerely join in the hope of her being eventually much the better for her present discipline. She has the comfort moreover of being confined in such weather as gives one little temptation to be out. It is really too bad, and has been too bad for a long time, much worse than any one can bear, and I begin to think it will never be fine again. This is a finesse *of mine, for I have often observed that if one writes about the weather, it is generally completely changed before the letter is read. I wish it may prove so now, and that when Mr. W. Digweed reaches Steventon to-morrow, he may find you have had a long series of hot dry weather. We are a small party at present, only grandmamma, Mary Jane [Frank's daughter], and myself. Yalden's coach cleared off the rest yesterday. I am glad you recollected to mention your being come home. [2] My heart began to sink within me when I had got so far through your letter without its being mentioned. I was dreadfully afraid that you might be detained at Winchester by severe illness, confined to your bed perhaps, and quite unable to hold a pen, and only dating from Steventon in order, with a mistaken sort of tenderness, to deceive me. But now I have no doubt of your being at home. I am sure you would not say it so seriously unless it actually were so. We saw a countless number of post-chaises full of boys pass by yesterday morning [3] – full of future heroes, legislators, fools, and villains. You have never thanked me for my last letter, which went by the cheese [with the delivery of cheese]. I cannot bear not to be thanked. You will not pay us a visit yet of course; we must not think of it. Your mother must get well first, and you must go to*

Oxford and not *be elected; after that a little change of scene may be good for you, and your physicians I hope will order you to the sea, or to a house by the side of a very considerable pond. [4]_Oh! it rains again. It beats against the window. Mary Jane and I have been wet through once already to-day; we set off in the donkey-carriage for Farringdon, as I wanted to see the improvement Mr. Woolls is making, but we were obliged to turn back before we got there, but not soon enough to avoid a pelter all the way home. We met Mr. Woolls. I talked of its being bad weather for the hay, and he returned me the comfort of its being much worse for the wheat. We hear that Mrs. S. [Mrs Sclater of Tangier Park, Hampshire] does not quit Tangier: why and wherefore? Do you know that our Browning [manservant] is gone? You must prepare for a William when you come, a good-looking lad, civil and quiet, and seeming likely to do. Good bye. I am sure Mr. W. D. [5] will be astonished at my writing so much, for the paper is so thin that he will be able to count the lines if not to read them.*
Yours affec[ly],
JANE AUSTEN

In the next letter will be found her description of her own style of composition, which has already appeared in the notice prefixed to 'Northanger Abbey' and 'Persuasion':–

Chawton, Monday, Dec. 16th (1816).

MY DEAR E., – One reason for my writing to you now is, that I may have the pleasure of directing to you Esq[re]. I give you joy of having left Winchester. Now you may own how miserable you were there; now it will gradually all come out, your crimes and your miseries—how often you went up by the Mail to London and threw away fifty guineas at a tavern, and how often you were on the point of hanging yourself, restrained only, as some ill-natured aspersion upon poor old Winton has it, by the want of a tree within some miles of the city. Charles Knight [Jane's nephew] and his companions passed through Chawton about 9 this morning; later than it used to be. Uncle Henry and I had a glimpse of his handsome face, looking all health and good humour. I wonder when you will come and see us. I know what I rather speculate upon, but shall say nothing. We think uncle Henry in excellent looks. Look at him this moment, and think so too, if you have not done it before; and we have the great comfort of seeing decided improvement in uncle Charles, both as to health, spirits, and appearance. And they are each of them so agreeable in their different way, and harmonise so well, that their visit is thorough enjoyment. Uncle Henry writes very superior sermons. You and I must try to get hold of one or two, and put them into our novels: it would be a fine help to a volume; and we could make our heroine read it aloud on a Sunday evening, just as well as Isabella Wardour, in the "Antiquary" [by Walter Scott] is made to read the "History of the Hartz Demon" in the ruins of St. Ruth, though I believe, on recollection, Lovell is the reader. By the bye, my dear E., I am quite concerned for the loss your mother mentions in her letter. Two chapters and a half to be missing is monstrous! It is well that I *have not been at Steventon lately, and therefore cannot be suspected of purloining them: two strong twigs and a half towards a nest of my own would have been something. I do not think, however, that any theft of that sort would be really very useful to me. What should I do with your strong, manly, vigorous sketches, full of variety and glow? How could I possibly join them on to the little bit (two inches wide) of ivory on which I work with so fine a brush, as produces little effect after much labour?*

You will hear from uncle Henry how well Anna is. She seems perfectly recovered. Ben was here on Saturday, to ask uncle Charles and me to dine with them, as to-morrow, but I was forced to decline it, the walk is beyond my strength (though I am otherwise very well), and this is not a season for donkey-carriages; and as we do not like to spare uncle Charles, he has declined it too. Tuesday. *Ah, ah! Mr. E. I doubt your seeing uncle Henry at Steventon to-day. The weather will prevent your expecting him, I think. Tell your father, with aunt Cass's love and mine, that the pickled cucumbers are extremely good, and tell him also – "tell him what you will." No, don't tell him what you will, but tell him that grandmamma begs him to make Joseph Hall [tenant of Mrs Austen] pay his rent, if he can.*

You must not be tired of reading the word uncle, *for I have not done with it. Uncle Charles thanks your mother for her letter; it was a great pleasure to him to know that the parcel was received and gave so much satisfaction, and he begs her to be so good as to give three shillings for him to Dame Staples, which shall be allowed for in the payment of her debt here.*

Adieu, Amiable! I hope Caroline behaves well to you.
Yours affec^{ly},
J. AUSTEN.

I cannot tell how soon she was aware of the serious nature of her malady. By God's mercy it was not attended with much suffering; so that she was able to tell her friends as in the foregoing letter, and perhaps sometimes to persuade herself that, excepting want of strength, she was 'otherwise very well;' but the progress of the disease became more and more manifest as the year advanced. The usual walk was at first shortened, and then discontinued; and air was sought in a donkey-carriage. Gradually, too, her habits of activity within the house ceased, and she was obliged to lie down much. The sitting-room contained only one sofa, which was frequently occupied by her mother, who was more than seventy years old. Jane would never use it, even in her mother's absence; but she contrived a sort of couch for herself with two or three chairs, and was pleased to say that this arrangement was more comfortable to her than a real sofa. Her reasons for this might have been left to be guessed, but for the importunities of a little niece, which obliged her to explain that if she herself had shown any inclination to use the sofa, her mother might have scrupled being on it so much as was good for her.

It is certain, however, that the mind did not share in this decay of the bodily strength. 'Persuasion' was not finished before the middle of August in that year; and the manner in which it was then completed affords proof that neither the critical nor the creative powers of the author were at all impaired. The book had been brought to an end in July; and the re-engagement of the hero and heroine effected in a totally different manner in a scene laid at Admiral Croft's lodgings. But her performance did not satisfy her. She thought it tame and flat, and was desirous of producing something better. This weighed upon her mind, the more so probably on account of the weak state of her health; so that one night she retired to rest in very low spirits. But such depression was little in accordance with her nature, and was soon shaken off. The next morning she awoke to more cheerful views and brighter inspirations: the sense of power revived; and imagination resumed its course. She cancelled the condemned chapter, and wrote two others, entirely different, in its stead. The result is that we possess the visit of the Musgrove party to Bath; the crowded and animated scenes at the White Hart Hotel; and the charming conversation between Capt. Harville and Anne Elliot, overheard by Capt. Wentworth, by which the two faithful lovers were at last led to understand each other's feelings. The tenth and eleventh chapters of 'Persuasion' then, rather than the actual winding-up of the story, contain the latest of her printed compositions, her last contribution to the entertainment of the public. Perhaps it may be thought that she has seldom written anything more brilliant; and that, independent of the original manner in which the *dénouement* is brought about, the pictures of Charles Musgrove's good-natured boyishness and of his wife's jealous selfishness would have been incomplete without these finishing strokes. The cancelled chapter exists in manuscript. It is certainly inferior to the two which were substituted for it: but it was such as some writers and some readers might have been contented with; and it contained touches which scarcely any other hand could have given, the suppression of which may be almost a matter of regret. [6]

The following letter was addressed to her friend Miss Bigg, then staying at Streatham with her sister, the wife of the Reverend Herbert Hill, uncle of Robert Southey. It appears to have been written three days before she began her last work, which will be noticed in another chapter; and shows that she was not at that time aware of the serious nature of her malady:–

Chawton, January 24, 1817.

MY DEAR ALETHEA, – I think it time there should be a little writing between us, though I believe the epistolary debt is on your side, and I hope this will find all the Streatham party well, neither carried away by the flood, nor rheumatic through the damps. Such mild weather is, you know, delightful to us, and though we have a great many ponds, and a fine running stream through the meadows on the other side of the road, it is nothing but what beautifies us and does to talk of. I *have certainly gained strength through the winter and am not far from being well; and I think I understand my own case now so much better than I did, as to be able by care to keep off any serious return of illness. I am convinced that* bile *is at the bottom of all I have suffered, which makes it easy to know how to treat myself. You will be glad to hear thus much of me, I am sure. We have just had a few days' visit from Edward, who brought us a good account of his father, and the very circumstance of his coming at all, of his father's being able to spare him, is itself a good account. He grows still, and still improves in appearance, at least in the estimation of his aunts, who love him better and better, as they see the sweet temper and warm affections of the boy confirmed in the young man: I tried hard to persuade him that he must have some message for William, [7] but in vain... This is not a time of year for donkey-carriages, and our donkeys are necessarily having so long a run of luxurious idleness that I suppose we shall find they have forgotten much of their education when we use them again. We do not use two at once however; don't imagine such excesses... Our own new clergyman [8] is expected here very soon, perhaps in time to assist Mr. Papillon on Sunday. I shall be very glad when the first hearing is over. It will be a nervous hour for our pew, though we hear that he acquits himself with as much ease and collectedness, as if he had been used to it all his life. We have no chance we know of seeing you between Streatham and Winchester: you go the other road and are engaged to two or three houses; if there should be any change, however, you know how welcome you would be... We have been reading the "Poet's Pilgrimage to Waterloo", [by Robert Southey] and generally with much approbation. Nothing will please all the world, you know; but parts of it suit me better than much that he has written before. The opening*—the proem *I believe he calls it—is very beautiful. Poor man! one cannot but grieve for the loss of the son so fondly described. Has he at all recovered it? What do Mr. and Mrs. Hill know about his present state?*

Yours affly

J. AUSTEN.

The real object of this letter is to ask you for a receipt, but I thought it genteel not to let it appear early. We remember some excellent orange wine at Manydown, made from Seville oranges, entirely or chiefly. I should be very much obliged to you for the receipt, if you can command it within a few weeks.

On the day before, January 23rd, she had written to her niece in the same hopeful tone:

I feel myself getting stronger than I was, and can so perfectly walk to *Alton,* or *back again without fatigue, that I hope to be able to do* both *when summer comes.*

Alas! summer came to her only on her deathbed. March 17th is the last date to be found in the manuscript on which she was engaged; and as the watch of the drowned man indicates the time of his death, so does this final date seem to fix the period when her mind could no longer pursue its accustomed course.

And here I cannot do better than quote the words of the niece to whose private records of her aunt's life and character I have been so often indebted:–

I do not know how early the alarming symptoms of her malady came on. It was in the following March that I had the first idea of her being seriously ill. It had been settled that about the end of that month, or the beginning of April, I should spend a few days at Chawton, in the absence of my father and mother, who were just then engaged with Mrs. Leigh Perrot in arranging her late husband's affairs; but Aunt Jane became too ill to have me in the house, and so I went instead to my sister Mrs. Lefroy at Wyards'. The next day we walked over to Chawton to make enquiries after our aunt. She was then keeping her room, but said she would see us, and we went up to her. She was in her dressing gown, and was sitting quite like an invalid in an arm-chair, but she got up and kindly greeted us, and then, pointing to seats which had been arranged for us by the fire, she said, "There is a chair for the married lady, and a little stool for you, Caroline."[9] It is strange, but those trifling words were the last of hers that I can remember, for I retain no recollection of what was said by anyone in the conversation that ensued. I was struck by the alteration in herself. She was very pale, her voice was weak and low, and there was about her a general appearance of debility and suffering; but I have been told that she never had much acute pain. She was not equal to the exertion of talking to us, and our visit to the sick room was a very short one, Aunt Cassandra soon taking us away. I do not suppose we stayed a quarter of an hour; and I never saw Aunt Jane again.

In May 1817 she was persuaded to remove to Winchester, for the sake of medical advice from Mr. Lyford. The Lyfords have, for some generations, maintained a high character in Winchester for medical skill, and the Mr. Lyford of that day was a man of more than provincial reputation, in whom great London practitioners expressed confidence. Mr. Lyford spoke encouragingly. It was not, of course, his business to extinguish hope in his patient, but I believe that he had, from the first, very little expectation of a permanent cure. All that was gained by the removal from home was the satisfaction of having done the best that could be done, together with such alleviations of suffering as superior medical skill could afford.

Jane and her sister Cassandra took lodgings in College Street. They had two kind friends living in the Close, Mrs. Heathcote and Miss Bigg, the mother and aunt of the present Sir Wm. Heathcote of Hursley, between whose family and ours a close friendship has existed for several generations. These friends did all that they could to promote the comfort of the sisters, during that sad sojourn in Winchester, both by their society, and by supplying those little conveniences in which a lodging-house was likely to be deficient. It was shortly after settling in these lodgings that she wrote to a nephew [the author of this memoir] the following characteristic letter, no longer, alas in her former strong, clear hand.

Mrs. David's, College St., Winton,
Tuesday, May 27th.

There is no better way, my dearest E., of thanking you for your affectionate concern for me during my illness than by telling you myself, as soon as possible, that I continue to get better. I will not boast of my handwriting; neither that nor my face have yet recovered their proper beauty, but in other respects I gain strength very fast. I am now out of bed from 9 in the morning to 10 at night: upon the sofa, it is true, but I eat my meals with aunt Cassandra in a rational way, and can employ myself, and walk from one room to another. Mr. Lyford says he will cure me, and if he fails, I shall draw up a memorial and lay it before the Dean and Chapter, and have no doubt of redress from that pious, learned, and disinterested body. Our lodgings are very comfortable. We have a neat little drawing-room with a bow window overlooking Dr. Gabell's [headmaster of Winchester College] [10] garden. Thanks to the kindness of your father and mother in sending me their carriage, my journey hither on Saturday was performed with very little fatigue, and had it been a fine day, I think I should have felt none; but it distressed me to see uncle Henry and Wm. Knight, who kindly attended us on horseback, riding in the rain almost the whole way. We expect a visit from them to-morrow, and hope they will stay the night; and on Thursday, which is a confirmation and a holiday, we are to get Charles [Jane's nephew] out to breakfast. We have had but one visit from him, *poor fellow, as he is in sick-room, but he hopes to be out to-night. We see Mrs. Heathcote every day, and William is to call upon us soon. God bless you, my dear E. If ever you are ill, may you be as tenderly nursed as*

I have been. May the same blessed alleviations of anxious, sympathising friends be yours: and may you possess, as I dare say you will, the greatest blessing of all in the consciousness of not being unworthy of their love. I *could not feel this.*
Your very affec[te] *Aunt*
J. A.

The following extract from a letter which has been before printed, written soon after the former, breathes the same spirit of humility and thankfulness:–

I will only say further that my dearest sister, my tender, watchful, indefatigable nurse, has not been made ill by her exertions. As to what I owe her, and the anxious affection of all my beloved family on this occasion, I can only cry over it, and pray God to bless them more and more.

Throughout her illness she was nursed by her sister, often assisted by her sister-in-law, my mother. Both were with her when she died. Two of her brothers, who were clergymen, lived near enough to Winchester to be in frequent attendance, and to administer the services suitable for a Christian's death-bed. While she used the language of hope to her correspondents, she was fully aware of her danger, though not appalled by it. It is true that there was much to attach her to life. She was happy in her family; she was just beginning to feel confidence in her own success; and, no doubt, the exercise of her great talents was an enjoyment in itself. We may well believe that she would gladly have lived longer; but she was enabled without dismay or complaint to prepare for death. She was a humble, believing Christian. Her life had been passed in the performance of home duties, and the cultivation of domestic affections, without any self-seeking or craving after applause. She had always sought, as it were by instinct, to promote the happiness of all who came within her influence, and doubtless she had her reward in the peace of mind which was granted her in her last days. Her sweetness of temper never failed. She was ever considerate and grateful to those who attended on her. At times, when she felt rather better, her playfulness of spirit revived, and she amused them even in their sadness. Once, when she thought herself near her end, she said what she imagined might be her last words to those around her, and particularly thanked her sister-in-law for being with her, saying: 'You have always been a kind sister to me, Mary.' When the end at last came, she sank rapidly, and on being asked by her attendants whether there was anything that she wanted, her reply was, '*Nothing but death*.' These were her last words. In quietness and peace she breathed her last on the morning of July 18, 1817.

On the 24th of that month she was buried in Winchester Cathedral, near the centre of the north aisle, almost opposite to the beautiful chantry tomb of William of Wykeham. A large slab of black marble in the pavement marks the place. Her own family only attended the funeral. Her sister returned to her desolated home, there to devote herself, for ten years, to the care of her aged mother; and to live much on the memory of her lost sister, till called many years later to rejoin her. Her brothers went back sorrowing to their several homes. They were very fond and very proud of her. They were attached to her by her talents, her virtues, and her engaging manners; and each loved afterwards to fancy a resemblance in some niece or daughter of his own to the dear sister Jane, whose perfect equal they yet never expected to see.

Notes

1. The Fowles, of Kintbury in Berkshire.
2. It seems that her young correspondent, after dating from his home, had been so superfluous as to state in his letter that he was returned home, and thus to have drawn on himself this banter.
3. The road by which many Winchester boys returned home ran close to Chawton Cottage.
4. There was, though it no longer exists, a pond close to Chawton Cottage, at the junction of the Winchester and Gosport roads.
5. Mr Digweed, who conveyed the letters to and from Chawton, was the gentleman named [in Chapter 2], as renting the old manor-house and the large farm at Steventon.
6. This cancelled chapter is now printed, in compliance with the requests addressed to me from several quarters.
7. Miss Bigg's nephew, the present Sir William Heathcote, of Hursley.
8. Her brother Henry, who had been ordained late in life.
9. The writer was at that time under twelve years old.
10. It was the corner house in College Street, at the entrance to Commoners.

The Cancelled Chapter (Chap. X.) of 'Persuasion'

With all this knowledge of Mr. Elliot and this authority to impart it, Anne left Westgate Buildings, her mind deeply busy in revolving what she had heard, feeling, thinking, recalling, and foreseeing everything, shocked at Mr. Elliot, sighing over future Kellynch, and pained for Lady Russell, whose confidence in him had been entire. The embarrassment which must be felt from this hour in his presence! How to behave to him? How to get rid of him? What to do by any of the party at home? Where to be blind?

Where to be active? It was altogether a confusion of images and doubts – a perplexity, an agitation which she could not see the end of. And she was in Gay Street, and still so much engrossed that she started on being addressed by Admiral Croft, as if he were a person unlikely to be met there. It was within a few steps of his own door.

'You are going to call upon my wife,' said he. 'She will be very glad to see you.'

Anne denied it.

'No! she really had not time, she was in her way home;' but while she spoke the Admiral had stepped back and knocked at the door, calling out,

'Yes, yes; do go in; she is all alone; go in and rest yourself.'

Anne felt so little disposed at this time to be in company of any sort, that it vexed her to be thus constrained, but she was obliged to stop.

'Since you are so very kind,' said she, 'I will just ask Mrs. Croft how she does, but I really cannot stay five minutes. You are sure she is quite alone?'

The possibility of Captain Wentworth had occurred; and most fearfully anxious was she to be assured – either that he was within, or that he was not – *which* might have been a question.

'Oh yes! quite alone, nobody but her mantua-maker with her, and they have been shut up together this half-hour, so it must be over soon.'

'Her mantua-maker! Then I am sure my calling now would be most inconvenient. Indeed you must allow me to leave my card and be so good as to explain it afterwards to Mrs. Croft.'

'No, no, not at all – not at all – she will be very happy to see you. Mind, I will not swear that she has not something particular to say to you, but *that* will all come out in the right place. I give no hints. Why, Miss Elliot, we begin to hear strange things of you (smiling in her face). But you have not much the look of it, as grave as a little judge!'

Anne blushed.

'Aye, aye, that will do now, it is all right. I thought we were not mistaken.'

She was left to guess at the direction of his suspicions; the first wild idea had been of some disclosure from his brother-in-law, but she was ashamed the next moment, and felt how far more probable it was that he should be meaning Mr. Elliot. The door was opened, and the man evidently beginning to *deny* his mistress, when the sight of his master stopped him. The Admiral enjoyed the joke exceedingly. Anne thought his triumph over Stephen rather too long. At last, however, he was able to invite her up stairs, and stepping before her said, 'I will just go up with you myself and show you in. I cannot stay, because I must go to the Post-Office, but if you will only sit down for five minutes I am sure Sophy will come, and you will find nobody to disturb you – there is nobody but Frederick here,' opening the door as he spoke. Such a person to be passed over as nobody to *her*! After being allowed to feel quite secure, indifferent, at her ease, to have it burst on her that she was to be the next moment in the same room with him! No time for recollection! for planning behaviour or regulating manners! There was time only to turn pale before she had passed through the door, and met the astonished eyes of Captain Wentworth, who was sitting by the fire, pretending to read, and prepared for no greater surprise than the Admiral's hasty return.

Equally unexpected was the meeting on each side. There was nothing to be done, however, but to stifle feelings, and to be quietly polite, and the Admiral was too much on the alert to leave any troublesome pause. He repeated again what he had said before about his wife and everybody, insisted on Anne's sitting down and being perfectly comfortable – was sorry he must leave her himself, but was sure Mrs. Croft would be down very soon, and would go upstairs and give her notice directly. Anne *was* sitting down, but now she arose, again to entreat him not to interrupt Mrs. Croft and re-urge the wish of going away and calling another time. But the Admiral would not hear of it; and if she did not return to the charge with unconquerable perseverance, or did not with a more passive determination walk quietly out of the room (as certainly she might have done), may she not be pardoned? If she *had* no horror of a few minutes' tête-à-tête with Captain Wentworth, may she not be pardoned for not wishing to give him the idea that she had? She reseated herself, and the Admiral took leave, but on reaching the door, said –

'Frederick, a word with *you* if you please.'

Captain Wentworth went to him, and instantly, before they were well out of the room, the Admiral continued –

'As I am going to leave you together, it is but fair I should give you something to talk of; and so, if you please – '

Here the door was very firmly closed, she could guess by which of the two – and she lost entirely what immediately followed, but it was impossible for her not to distinguish parts of the rest, for the Admiral, on the strength of the door's being shut, was speaking without any management of voice, though she could hear his companion trying to check him. She could not doubt their being speaking of her. She heard her own name and Kellynch repeatedly. She was very much disturbed. She knew not what to do, or what to expect, and among other agonies felt the possibility of Captain Wentworth's not returning into the room at all, which, after her consenting to stay, would have been – too bad for language. They seemed to be talking of the Admiral's lease of Kellynch. She heard him say something of the lease being signed – or not signed – *that* was not likely to be a very agitating subject, but then followed –

'I hate to be at an uncertainty. I must know at once. Sophy thinks the same.'

Then in a lower tone Captain Wentworth seemed remonstrating, wanting to be excused, wanting to put something off.

'Phoo, phoo,' answered the Admiral, 'now is the time; if you will not speak, I will stop and speak myself.'

'Very well, sir, very well, sir,' followed with some impatience from his companion, opening the door as he spoke –

'You will then, you promise you will?' replied the Admiral in all the power of his natural voice, unbroken even by one thin door.

'Yes, sir, yes.' And the Admiral was hastily left, the door was closed, and the moment arrived in which Anne was alone with Captain Wentworth.

She could not attempt to see how he looked, but he walked immediately to a window as if irresolute and embarrassed, and for about the space of five seconds she repented what she had done – censured it as unwise, blushed over it as indelicate. She longed to be able to speak of the weather or the concert, but could only compass the relief of taking a newspaper in her hand. The distressing pause was over, however; he turned round in half a minute, and coming towards the table where she sat, said in a voice of effort and constraint –

'You must have heard too much already, Madam, to be in any doubt of my having promised Admiral Croft to speak to you on a particular subject, and this conviction determines me to do so, however repugnant to my – to all my sense of propriety to be taking so great a liberty! You will acquit me of impertinence I trust, by considering me as speaking only for another, and speaking by necessity; and the Admiral is a man who can never be thought impertinent by one who knows him as you do. His intentions are always the kindest and the best, and you will perceive he is actuated by none other in the application which I am now, with – with very peculiar feelings – obliged to make.' He stopped, but merely to recover breath, not seeming to expect any answer. Anne listened as if her life depended on the issue of his speech. He proceeded with a forced alacrity:–

'The Admiral, Madam, was this morning confidently informed that you were – upon my soul, I am quite at a loss, ashamed (breathing and speaking quickly) – the awkwardness of *giving* information of this kind to one of the parties – you can be at no loss to understand me. It was very confidently said that Mr. Elliot – that everything was settled in the family for a union between Mr. Elliot and yourself. It was added that you were to live at Kellynch – that Kellynch was to be given up. This the Admiral knew could not be correct. But it occurred to him that it might be the *wish* of the parties. And my commission from him, Madam, is to say, that if the family wish is such, his lease of Kellynch shall be cancelled, and he and my sister will provide themselves with another home, without imagining themselves to be doing anything which under similar circumstances would not be done for *them*. This is all, Madam. A very few words in reply from you will be sufficient. That *I* should be the person commissioned on this subject is extraordinary! and believe me, Madam, it is no less painful. A very few words, however, will put an end to the awkwardness and distress we may *both* be feeling.'

Anne spoke a word or two, but they were unintelligible; and before she could command herself, he added, 'If you will only tell me that the Admiral may address a line to Sir Walter, it will be enough. Pronounce only the words, *he may*, and I shall immediately follow him with your message.'

'No, Sir,' said Anne; 'there is no message. You are misin – the Admiral is misinformed. I do justice to the kindness of his intentions, but he is quite mistaken. There is no truth in any such report.'

He was a moment silent. She turned her eyes towards him for the first time since his re-entering the room. His colour was varying, and he was looking at her with all the power and keenness which she believed no other eyes than his possessed.

'No truth in any such report?' he repeated. 'No truth in any *part* of it?'

'None.'

He had been standing by a chair, enjoying the relief of leaning on it, or of playing with it. He now sat down, drew it a little nearer to her, and looked with an expression which had something more than penetration in it – something softer. Her countenance did not discourage. It was a silent but a very powerful dialogue; on his supplication, on hers acceptance. Still a little nearer, and a hand taken and pressed; and 'Anne, my own dear Anne!' bursting forth in all the fulness of exquisite feeling, – and all suspense and indecision were over. They were re-united. They were restored to all that had been lost. They were carried back to the past with only an increase of attachment and confidence, and only such a flutter of present delight as made them little fit for the interruption of Mrs. Croft when she joined them not long afterwards. *She*, probably, in the observations of the next ten minutes saw something to suspect; and though it was hardly possible for a woman of her description to wish the mantua-maker had imprisoned her longer, she might be very likely wishing for some excuse to run about the house, some storm to break the windows above, or a summons to the Admiral's shoemaker below. Fortune favoured them all, however, in another way, in a gentle, steady rain, just happily set in as the Admiral returned and Anne rose to go. She was earnestly invited to stay dinner. A note was despatched to Camden Place, and she staid – staid till ten at night; and during that time the husband and wife, either by the wife's contrivance, or by simply going on in their usual way, were frequently out of the room together – gone upstairs to hear a noise, or downstairs to settle their accounts, or upon the landing to trim the lamp. And these precious moments were turned to so good an account that all the most anxious feelings of the past were gone through. Before they parted at night, Anne had the felicity of being assured that in the first place (so far from being altered for the worse), she had gained inexpressibly in personal loveliness; and that as to character, hers was now fixed on his mind as *perfection* itself, maintaining the just medium of fortitude and gentleness – that he had never ceased to love and prefer her, though it had been only at Uppercross that he had learnt to do her justice, and only at Lyme that he had begun to understand his own feelings; that at Lyme he had received lessons of more than one kind – the passing admiration of Mr. Elliot had at least *roused* him, and the scene on the Cobb, and at Captain Harville's, had fixed her superiority. In his preceding attempts to attach himself to Louisa Musgrove (the attempts of anger and pique), he protested that he had continually felt the impossibility of really caring for Louisa, though till *that day*, till the leisure for reflection which followed it, he had not understood the perfect excellence of the mind with which Louisa's could so ill bear comparison; or the perfect, the unrivalled hold it possessed over his own. There he had learnt to distinguish between the steadiness of principle and the obstinacy of self-will, between the darings of heedlessness and the resolution of a collected mind; there he had seen everything to exalt in his estimation the woman he had lost, and there had begun to deplore the pride, the folly, the madness of resentment, which had kept him from trying to regain her when thrown in his way. From that period to the present had his penance been the most severe. He had no sooner been free from the horror and remorse attending the first few days of Louisa's accident, no sooner had begun to feel himself alive again, than he had begun to feel himself, though alive, not at liberty.

He found that he was considered by his friend Harville an engaged man. The Harvilles entertained not a doubt of a mutual attachment between him and Louisa; and though this to a degree was contradicted instantly, it yet made him feel that perhaps by *her* family, by everybody, by *herself* even, the same idea might be held, and that he was not *free* in honour, though if such were to be the conclusion, too free alas! in heart. He had never thought justly on this subject before, and he had not sufficiently considered that his excessive intimacy at Uppercross must have its danger of ill consequence in many ways; and that while trying whether he could attach himself to either of the girls, he might be exciting unpleasant reports if not raising unrequited regard.

He found too late that he had entangled himself, and that precisely as he became thoroughly satisfied of his not *caring* for Louisa at all, he must regard himself as bound to her if her feelings for him were what the Harvilles supposed. It determined him to leave Lyme, and await her perfect recovery elsewhere. He would gladly weaken by any *fair* means whatever sentiment or speculations concerning them might exist; and he went therefore into Shropshire, meaning after a while to return to the Crofts at Kellynch, and act as he found requisite.

He had remained in Shropshire, lamenting the blindness of his own pride and the blunders of his own calculations, till at once released from Louisa by the astonishing felicity of her engagement with Benwick.

Bath – Bath had instantly followed in *thought*, and not long after in *fact*. To Bath – to arrive with hope, to be torn by jealousy at the first sight of Mr. Elliot; to experience all the changes of each at the concert; to be miserable by the morning's circumstantial report, to be now more happy than language could express, or any heart but his own be capable of.

He was very eager and very delightful in the description of what he had felt at the concert; the evening seemed to have been made up of exquisite moments. The moment of her stepping forward in the octagon room to speak to him, the moment of Mr. Elliot's appearing and tearing her away, and one or two subsequent moments, marked by returning hope or increasing despondency, were dwelt on with energy.

'To see you,' cried he, 'in the midst of those who could not be my well-wishers; to see your cousin close by you, conversing and smiling, and feel all the horrible eligibilities and proprieties of the match! To consider it as the certain wish of every being who could hope to influence you! Even if your own feelings were reluctant or indifferent, to consider what powerful support would be his! Was it not enough to make the fool of me which I appeared? How could I look on without agony? Was not the very sight of the friend who sat behind you; was not the recollection of what had been, the knowledge of her influence, the indelible, immovable impression of what persuasion had once done – was it not all against me?'

'You should have distinguished,' replied Anne. 'You should not have suspected me now; the case so different, and my age so different. If I was wrong in yielding to persuasion once, remember it was to persuasion exerted on the side of safety, not of risk. When I yielded, I thought it was to duty; but no duty could be called in aid here. In marrying a man indifferent to me, all risk would have been incurred, and all duty violated.'

'Perhaps I ought to have reasoned thus,' he replied; 'but I could not. I could not derive benefit from the late knowledge I had acquired of your character. I could not bring it into play; it was overwhelmed, buried, lost in those earlier feelings which I had been smarting under year after year. I could think of you only as one who had yielded, who had given me up, who had been influenced by anyone rather than by me. I saw you with the very person who had guided you in that year of misery. I had no reason to believe her of less authority now. The force of habit was to be added.'

'I should have thought,' said Anne, 'that my manner to yourself might have spared you much or all of this.'

'No, no! Your manner might be only the ease which your engagement to another man would give. I left you in this belief; and yet – I was determined to see you again. My spirits rallied with the morning, and I felt that I had still a motive for remaining here. The Admiral's news, indeed, was a revulsion; since that moment I have been divided what to do, and had it been confirmed, this would have been my last day in Bath.'

There was time for all this to pass, with such interruptions only as enhanced the charm of the communication, and Bath could hardly contain any other two beings at once so rationally and so rapturously happy as during that evening occupied the sofa of Mrs. Croft's drawing-room in Gay Street.

Captain Wentworth had taken care to meet the Admiral as he returned into the house, to satisfy him as to Mr. Elliot and Kellynch; and the delicacy of the Admiral's good-nature kept him from saying another word on the subject to Anne. He was quite concerned lest he might have been giving her pain by touching on a tender part – who could say? She might be liking her cousin better than he liked her; and, upon recollection, if they had been to marry at all, why should they have waited so long? When the evening closed, it is probable that the Admiral received some new ideas from his wife, whose particularly friendly manner in parting with her gave Anne the gratifying persuasion of her seeing and approving. It had been such a day to Anne; the hours which had passed since her leaving Camden Place had done so much! She was almost bewildered – almost too happy in looking back. It was necessary to sit up half the night, and lie awake the remainder, to comprehend with composure her present state, and pay for the overplus of bliss by headache and fatigue.

Then follows Chapter XI., i.e. *XII. in the published book and at the end is written –*
Finis, July 18, 1816.

The Last Work

Jane Austen was taken from us: how much unexhausted talent perished with her, how largely she might yet have contributed to the entertainment of her readers, if her life had been prolonged, cannot be known; but it is certain that the mine at which she had so long laboured was not worked out, and that she was still diligently employed in collecting fresh materials from it. 'Persuasion' had been finished in August 1816; some time was probably given to correcting it for the press; but on the 27th of the following January, according to the date on her own manuscript, she began a new novel, and worked at it up to the 17th of March. The chief part of this manuscript is written in her usual firm and neat hand, but some of the latter pages seem to have been first traced in pencil, probably when she was too weak to sit long at her desk, and written over in ink afterwards. The quantity produced does not indicate any decline of power or industry, for in those seven weeks twelve chapters had been completed. It is more difficult to judge of the quality of a work so little advanced. It had received no name; there was scarcely any indication what the course of the story was to be, nor was any heroine yet perceptible, who, like Fanny Price, or Anne Elliot, might draw round her the sympathies of the reader. Such an unfinished fragment cannot be presented to the public; but I am persuaded that some of Jane Austen's admirers will be glad to learn something about the latest creations which were forming themselves in her mind; and therefore, as some of the principal characters were already sketched in with a vigorous hand, I will try to give an idea of them, illustrated by extracts from the work.

The scene is laid at Sanditon, a village on the Sussex coast, just struggling into notoriety as a bathing-place, under the patronage of the two principal proprietors of the parish, Mr. Parker and Lady Denham.

Mr. Parker was an amiable man, with more enthusiasm than judgment, whose somewhat shallow mind overflowed with the one idea of the prosperity of Sanditon, together with a jealous contempt of the rival village of Brinshore, where a similar attempt was going on. To the regret of his much-enduring wife, he had left his family mansion, with all its ancestral comforts of gardens, shrubberies, and shelter, situated in a valley some miles inland, and had built a new residence – a Trafalgar House – on the bare brow of the hill overlooking Sanditon and the sea, exposed to every wind that blows; but he will confess to no discomforts, nor suffer his family to feel any from the change. The following extract brings him before the reader, mounted on his hobby:–

> He wanted to secure the promise of a visit, and to get as many of the family as his own house would hold to follow him to Sanditon as soon as possible; and, healthy as all the Heywoods undeniably were, he foresaw that every one of them would be benefitted by the sea. He held it indeed as certain that no person, however upheld for the present by fortuitous aids of exercise and spirit in a semblance of health, could be really in a state of secure and permanent health without spending at least six weeks by the sea every year. The sea air and sea-bathing together were nearly infallible; one or other of them being a match for every disorder

> of the stomach, the lungs, or the blood. They were anti-spasmodic, anti-pulmonary, anti-bilious, and anti-rheumatic. Nobody could catch cold by the sea; nobody wanted appetite by the sea; nobody wanted spirits; nobody wanted strength. They were healing, softening, relaxing, fortifying, and bracing, seemingly just as was wanted; sometimes one, sometimes the other. If the sea breeze failed, the sea-bath was the certain corrective; and when bathing disagreed, the sea breeze was evidently designed by nature for the cure. His eloquence, however, could not prevail. Mr. and Mrs. Heywood never left home...The maintenance, education, and fitting out of fourteen children demanded a very quiet, settled, careful course of life; and obliged them to be stationary and healthy at Willingden. What prudence had at first enjoined was now rendered pleasant by habit. They never left home, and they had a gratification in saying so.

Lady Denham's was a very different character. She was a rich vulgar widow, with a sharp but narrow mind, who cared for the prosperity of Sanditon only so far as it might increase the value of her own property. She is thus described:-

> Lady Denham had been a rich Miss Brereton, born to wealth, but not to education. Her first husband had been a Mr. Hollis, a man of considerable property in the country, of which a large share of the parish of Sanditon, with manor and mansion-house, formed a part. He had been an elderly man when she married him; her own age about thirty. Her motives for such a match could be little understood at the distance of forty years, but she had so well nursed and pleased Mr. Hollis that at his death he left her everything – all his estates, and all at her disposal. After a widowhood of some years she had been induced to marry again. The late Sir Harry Denham, of Denham Park, in the neighbourhood of Sanditon, succeeded in removing her and her large income to his own domains; but he could not succeed in the views of permanently enriching his family which were attributed to him. She had been too wary to put anything out of her own power, and when, on Sir Harry's death, she returned again to her own house at Sanditon, she was said to have made this boast, "that though she had got nothing but her title from the family, yet she had given nothing for it." For the title it was to be supposed that she married.
>
> Lady Denham was indeed a great lady, beyond the common wants of society; for she had many thousands a year to bequeath, and three distinct sets of people to be courted by:– her own relations, who might very reasonably wish for her original thirty thousand pounds among them; the legal heirs of Mr. Hollis, who might hope to be more indebted

to her sense of justice than he had allowed them to be to his; and those members of the Denham family for whom her second husband had hoped to make a good bargain. By all these, or by branches of them, she had, no doubt, been long and still continued to be well attacked; and of these three divisions Mr. Parker did not hesitate to say that Mr. Hollis's kindred were the least in favour, and Sir Harry Denham's the most. The former, he believed, had done themselves irremediable harm by expressions of very unwise resentment at the time of Mr. Hollis's death: the latter, to the advantage of being the remnant of a connection which she certainly valued, joined those of having been known to her from their childhood, and of being always at hand to pursue their interests by seasonable attentions. But another claimant was now to be taken into account: a young female relation whom Lady Denham had been induced to receive into her family. After having always protested against any such addition, and often enjoyed the repeated defeat she had given to every attempt of her own relations to introduce 'this young lady, or that young lady,' as a companion at Sanditon House, she had brought back with her from London last Michaelmas a Miss Clara Brereton, who bid fair to vie in favour with Sir Edward Denham, and to secure for herself and her family that share of the accumulated property which they had certainly the best right to inherit.

Lady Denham's character comes out in a conversation which takes place at Mr. Parker's tea-table.

The conversation turned entirely upon Sanditon, its present number of visitants, and the chances of a good season. It was evident that Lady Denham had more anxiety, more fears of loss than her coadjutor. She wanted to have the place fill faster, and seemed to have many harassing apprehensions of the lodgings being in some instances underlet. To a report that a large boarding-school was expected she replies, 'Ah, well, no harm in that. They will stay their six weeks, and out of such a number who knows but some may be consumptive, and want asses' milk; and I have two milch asses at this very time. But perhaps the little Misses may hurt the furniture. I hope they will have a good sharp governess to look after them.' But she wholly disapproved of Mr. Parker's wish to secure the residence of a medical man amongst them. 'Why, what should we do with a doctor here? It would only be encouraging our servants and the poor to fancy themselves ill, if there was a doctor at hand. Oh, pray let us have none of that tribe at Sanditon: we go on very well as we are. There is the sea, and the downs, and my milch asses: and I have told Mrs. Whitby that if anybody enquires for a chamber horse, they may be supplied at a fair rate (poor Mr. Hollis's chamber horse, as good as

> new); and what can people want more? I have lived seventy good years in the world, and never took physic, except twice: and never saw the face of a doctor in all my life on my own account; and I really believe if my poor dear Sir Harry had never seen one neither, he would have been alive now. Ten fees, one after another, did the men take who sent him out of the world. I beseech you, Mr. Parker, no doctors here.'

This lady's character comes out more strongly in a conversation with Mr. Parker's guest, Miss Charlotte Heywood. Sir Edward Denham with his sister Esther and Clara Brereton have just left them.

> Charlotte accepted an invitation from Lady Denham to remain with her on the terrace, when the others adjourned to the library. Lady Denham, like a true great lady, talked, and talked only of her own concerns, and Charlotte listened. Taking hold of Charlotte's arm with the ease of one who felt that any notice from her was a favour, and communicative from the same sense of importance, or from a natural love of talking, she immediately said in a tone of great satisfaction, and with a look of arch sagacity:-
>
> 'Miss Esther wants me to invite her and her brother to spend a week with me at Sanditon House, as I did last summer, but I shan't. She has been trying to get round me every way with her praise of this and her praise of that; but I saw what she was about. I saw through it all. I am not very easily taken in, my dear.'
>
> Charlotte could think of nothing more harmless to be said than the simple enquiry of, 'Sir Edward and Miss Denham?'
>
> 'Yes, my dear; my young folks, as I call them, sometimes: for I take them very much by the hand, and had them with me last summer, about this time, for a week – from Monday to Monday – and very delighted and thankful they were. For they are very good young people, my dear. I would not have you think that I only notice them for poor dear Sir Harry's sake. No, no; they are very deserving themselves, or, trust me, they would not be so much in my company. I am not the woman to help anybody blindfold. I always take care to know what I am about, and who I have to deal with before I stir a finger. I do not think I was ever overreached in my life; and that is a good deal for a woman to say that has been twice married. Poor dear Sir Harry (between ourselves) thought at first to have got more, but (with a bit of a sigh) he is gone, and we must not find fault with the dead. Nobody could live happier together than us: and he was a very honourable man, quite the gentleman, of ancient family; and when he died I gave Sir Edward his gold watch.'
>
> This was said with a look at her companion which implied its right to produce a great impression; and seeing no rapturous astonishment in Charlotte's countenance, she added quickly,

'He did not bequeath it to his nephew, my dear; it was no bequest; it was not in the will. He only told me, and that but once, that he should wish his nephew to have his watch; but it need not have been binding, if I had not chose it.'

'Very kind indeed, very handsome!' said Charlotte, absolutely forced to affect admiration.'

'Yes, my dear; and it is not the only kind thing I have done by him. I have been a very liberal friend to Sir Edward; and, poor young man, he needs it bad enough. For, though I am only the dowager, my dear, and he is the heir, things do not stand between us in the way they usually do between those two parties. Not a shilling do I receive from the Denham estate. Sir Edward has no payments to make me. He don't stand uppermost, believe me; it is I that help him.'

'Indeed! he is a very fine young man, and particularly elegant in his address.'

This was said chiefly for the sake of saying something; but Charlotte directly saw that it was laying her open to suspicion, by Lady Denham's giving a shrewd glance at her, and replying,

'Yes, yes; he's very well to look at; and it is to be hoped that somebody of large fortune will think so; for Sir Edward must marry for money. He and I often talk that matter over. A handsome young man like him will go smirking and smiling about, and paying girls compliments, but he knows he must marry for money. And Sir Edward is a very steady young man, in the main, and has got very good notions.'

'Sir Edward Denham,' said Charlotte, 'with such personal advantages, may be almost sure of getting a woman of fortune, if he chooses it.'

This glorious sentiment seemed quite to remove suspicion.

'Aye, my dear, that is very sensibly said; and if we could but get a young heiress to Sanditon. But heiresses are monstrous scarce! I do not think we have had an heiress here, nor even a Co., since Sanditon has been a public place. Families come after families, but, as far as I can learn, it is not one in a hundred of them that have any real property, landed or funded. An income, perhaps, but no property. Clergymen, may be, or lawyers from town, or half-pay officers, or widows with only a jointure; and what good can such people do to anybody? Except just as they take our empty houses, and (between ourselves) I think they are great fools for not staying at home. Now, if we could get a young heiress to be sent here for her health, and, as soon as she got well, have her fall in love with Sir Edward! And Miss Esther must marry somebody of fortune, too. She must get a rich husband. Ah! young ladies that have no money are very much to be pitied.' After a short pause: 'If Miss Esther thinks to talk me into inviting them to come and stay at Sanditon House, she will find herself mistaken. Matters are altered with me since last summer, you know: I have Miss Clara with me now, which makes a great difference. I should not choose to have my two housemaid's time taken up all the morning in dusting out bedrooms. They have Miss Clara's room to put to rights, as well as mine, every day. If they had hard work, they would want higher wages.'

Charlotte's feelings were divided between amusement and indignation. She kept her countenance, and kept a civil silence; but without attempting to listen any longer, and only conscious that Lady Denham was still talking in the same way, allowed her own thoughts to form themselves into such meditation as this:– 'She is thoroughly mean; I had no expectation of anything so bad. Mr. Parker spoke too mildly of her. He is too kind-hearted to see clearly, and their very connection misleads him. He has persuaded her to engage in the same speculation, and because they have so far the same object in view, he fancies that she feels like him in other things; but she is very, very mean. I can see no good in her. Poor Miss Brereton! And it makes everybody mean about her. This poor Sir Edward and his sister! how far nature meant them to be respectable I cannot tell; but they are obliged to be mean in their servility to her; and I am mean, too, in giving her my attention with the appearance of coinciding with her. Thus it is when rich people are sordid.'

Mr. Parker has two unmarried sisters of singular character. They live together; Diana, the younger, always takes the lead, and the elder follows in the same track. It is their pleasure to fancy themselves invalids to a degree and in a manner never experienced by others; but, from a state of exquisite pain and utter prostration, Diana Parker can always rise to be officious in the concerns of all her acquaintance, and to make incredible exertions where they are not wanted.

It would seem that they must be always either very busy for the good of others, or else extremely ill themselves. Some natural delicacy of constitution, in fact, with an unfortunate turn for medicine, especially quack medicine, had given them an early tendency at various times to various disorders. The rest of their suffering was from their own fancy, the love of distinction, and the love of the wonderful. They had charitable hearts and many amiable feelings; but a spirit of restless activity, and the glory of doing more than anybody else, had a share in every exertion of benevolence, and there was vanity in all they did, as well as in all they endured.

These peculiarities come out in the following letter of Diana Parker to her brother:-

MY DEAR TOM, – We were much grieved at your accident, and if you had not described yourself as having fallen into such very good hands,

I should have been with you at all hazards the day after receipt of your letter, though it found me suffering under a more severe attack than usual of my old grievance, spasmodic bile, and hardly able to crawl from my bed to the sofa. But how were you treated? Send me more particulars in your next. If indeed a simple sprain, as you denominate it, nothing would have been so judicious as friction – friction by the hand alone, supposing it could be applied immediately. Two years ago I happened to be calling on Mrs. Sheldon, when her coachman sprained his foot, as he was cleaning the carriage, and could hardly limp into the house; but by the immediate use of friction alone, steadily persevered in (I rubbed his ancle with my own hands for four hours without intermission), he was well in three days...Pray never run into peril again in looking for an apothecary on our account; for had you the most experienced man in his line settled at Sanditon, it would be no recommendation to us. We have entirely done with the whole medical tribe. We have consulted physician after physician in vain, till we are quite convinced that they can do nothing for us, and that we must trust to our knowledge of our own wretched constitutions for any relief; but if you think it advisable for the interests of the place to get a medical man there, I will undertake the commission with pleasure, and have no doubt of succeeding. I could soon put the necessary irons in the fire. As for getting to Sanditon myself, it is an impossibility. I grieve to say that I cannot attempt it, but my feelings tell me too plainly that in my present state the sea-air would probably be the death of me; and in truth I doubt whether Susan's nerves would be equal to the effort. She has been suffering much from headache, and six leeches a day, for ten days together, relieved her so little that we thought it right to change our measures; and being convinced on examination that much of the evil lay in her gums, I persuaded her to attack the disorder there. She has accordingly had three teeth drawn, and is decidedly better; but her nerves are a good deal deranged, she can only speak in a whisper, and fainted away this morning on poor Arthur's trying to suppress a cough.'

Within a week of the date of this letter, in spite of the impossibility of moving, and of the fatal effects to be apprehended from the sea-air, Diana Parker was at Sanditon with her sister. She had flattered herself that by her own indefatigable exertions, and by setting at work the agency of many friends, she had induced two large families to take houses at Sanditon. It was to expedite these politic views that she came; and though she met with some disappointment of her expectation, yet she did not suffer in health.

Such were some of the *dramatis personae*, ready dressed and prepared for their parts. They are at least original and unlike any that the author had produced before. The success of the piece must have depended on the skill with which these parts might be played; but few will be inclined to distrust the skill of one who had so often succeeded. If the author had lived to complete her work, it is probable that these personages might have grown into as mature an individuality of character, and have taken as permanent a place amongst our familiar acquaintance, as Mr. Bennet, or John Thorp, Mary Musgrove, or Aunt Norris herself.

Postscript

When first I was asked to put together a memoir of my aunt, I saw reasons for declining the attempt. It was not only that, having passed the three score years and ten usually allotted to man's strength, and being unaccustomed to write for publication, I might well distrust my ability to complete the work, but that I also knew the extreme scantiness of the materials out of which it must be constructed. The grave closed over my aunt fifty-two years ago; and during that long period no idea of writing her life had been entertained by any of her family. Her nearest relatives, far from making provision for such a purpose, had actually destroyed many of the letters and papers by which it might have been facilitated. They were influenced, I believe, partly by an extreme dislike to publishing private details, and partly by never having assumed that the world would take so strong and abiding an interest in her works as to claim her name as public property. It was therefore necessary for me to draw upon recollections rather than on written documents for my materials; while the subject itself supplied me with nothing striking or prominent with which to arrest the attention of the reader. It has been said that the happiest individuals, like nations during their happiest periods, have no history. In the case of my aunt, it was not only that her course of life was unvaried, but that her own disposition was remarkably calm and even. There was in her nothing eccentric or angular; no ruggedness of temper; no singularity of manner; none of the morbid sensibility or exaggeration of feeling, which not unfrequently accompanies great talents, to be worked up into a picture. Hers was a mind well balanced on a basis of good sense, sweetened by an affectionate heart, and regulated by fixed principles; so that she was to be distinguished from many other amiable and sensible women only by that peculiar genius which shines out clearly enough in her works, but of which a biographer can make little use. The motive which at last induced me to make the attempt is exactly expressed in the passage prefixed to these pages. I thought that I saw something to be done: knew of no one who could do it but myself, and so was driven to the enterprise. I am glad that I have been able to finish my work. As a family record it can scarcely fail to be interesting to those relatives who must ever set a high value on their connection with Jane Austen, and to them I especially dedicate it; but as I have been asked to do so, I also submit it to the censure of the public, with all its faults both of deficiency and redundancy. I know that its value in their eyes must depend, not on any merits of its own, but on the degree of estimation in which my aunt's works may still be held; and indeed I shall esteem it one of the strongest testimonies ever borne to her talents, if for her sake an interest can be taken in so poor a sketch as I have been able to draw.

BRAY VICARAGE :
Sept. 7, 1869.

The following is a postscript which was printed at the end of the first edition of this memoir but omitted from the second.

Since these pages were in type, I have read with astonishment the strange misrepresentation of my aunt's manners given by Miss Mitford in a letter which appears in her lately-published Life, vol. i. p. 305. Miss Mitford does not profess to have known Jane Austen herself, but to report what had been told her by her mother. Having stated that her mother '*before her marriage*' was well acquainted with Jane Austen and her family, she writes thus:– 'Mamma says that she was *then* the prettiest, silliest, most affected, husband-hunting butterfly she ever remembers.' The editor of Miss Mitford's Life very properly observes in a note how different this description is from 'every other account of Jane Austen from whatever quarter.' Certainly it is so totally at variance with the modest simplicity of character which I have attributed to my aunt, that if it could be supposed to have a semblance of truth, it must be equally injurious to her memory and to my trustworthiness as her biographer. Fortunately I am not driven to put my authority in competition with that of Miss Mitford, nor to ask which ought to be considered the better witness in this case; because I am able to prove by a reference to dates that Miss Mitford must have been under a mistake, and that her mother could not possibly have known what she was supposed to have reported; inasmuch as Jane Austen, at the time referred to, was a little girl.

Mrs. Mitford was the daughter of Dr. Russell, Rector of Ashe, a parish adjoining Steventon, so that the families of Austen and Russell must at that time have been known to each other. But the date assigned by Miss Mitford for the termination of the acquaintance is the time of her mother's marriage. This took place in October 1785, when Jane, who had been born in December 1775, was not quite ten years old. In point of fact, however, Miss Russell's opportunities of observing Jane Austen must have come to an end still earlier: for upon Dr. Russell's death, in January

1783, his widow and daughter removed from the neighbourhood, so that all intercourse between the families ceased when Jane was little more than seven years old.

All persons who undertake to narrate from hearsay things which are supposed to have taken place before they were born are liable to error, and are apt to call in imagination to the aid of memory: and hence it arises that many a fancy piece has been substituted for genuine history.

I do not care to correct the inaccurate account of Jane Austen's manners in after life: because Miss Mitford candidly expresses a doubt whether she had not been misinformed on that point.

Nov. 17, 1869

6

The Letters of Jane Austen

Edward Hugessen Knatchbull Hugessen, the first Lord Brabourne, was the eldest son of Jane Austen's "favourite niece" Fanny Knatchbull (née Knight). Fanny was the daughter of Jane's brother Edward and his wife Elizabeth.

In 1882, on the death of his mother, Lord Brabourne found a box containing ninety-six letters written by Jane Austen and the original manuscript of the short story Lady Susan. *The box and its contents had been left to Fanny by her aunt Cassandra Austen, Jane's sister, to whom most of the letters had been written.*

The interest in Jane Austen had continued unabated since the publication of the Memoir *in 1869. As the letters had not been available to the author of that work, Lord Brabourne decided to publish them to throw additional light on Jane Austen's life. He was satisfied that 'no-one living can, I think, have any possible just cause of annoyance at their publication.'*

Lord Brabourne edited the letters and they were published, in two volumes, by Richard Bentley in 1884. They were dedicated, rather grandly, to Queen Victoria, who, according to Lord Brabourne, "so highly appreciated the works of Jane Austen". A copy of a portrait by Johann Zoffany, believed to be of Jane Austen as a child, was published opposite the title of Volume One.

The first volume contained three biographical chapters, two chapters on the novels and letters from January 1796 to June 1808. The second volume contained letters from October 1808 to July 1817 and some verses written by members of the Austen family which were enclosed in one of the letters. Lord Brabourne also appended other material of interest, some of which came from James Edward Austen-Leigh's Memoir. *The letters were divided into sections which were each introduced with information to add to the interest of the reader.*

The letters published by Lord Brabourne were only a portion of the vast number of letters which Jane Austen, who was a prolific letter writer, must have written. Jane's letters were private and she would not have envisaged that they would be read by anyone other than the recipient. With this in mind Cassandra Austen destroyed a number of her sister's letters which she did not want future generations of the family to read and parts were cut out of some of the letters which she left to family members. Nevertheless, a few of the surviving letters contain remarks which could be regarded as unkind, but it should be remembered that these were not intended to be read by anyone else. Cassandra destroyed all of her own letters to Jane.

The letters added considerably to the existing knowledge of Jane Austen's life in Hampshire, her illness and her death. They provided new information about her visits to Kent and London, and the years spent in Bath and Southampton. Not only did Austen's witty correspondence provide an insight into her character, her interests and her family but it also opened a window onto the lives of the gentry and aristocracy in the England of her time.

Lord Brabourne's biographical chapters contained useful new material and brought the story of her family members up to date. In his chapters on Austen's novels Lord Brabourne set them into the context of eighteenth century literature and the wider canon of English literature. He also explained why he agreed with the 'popular approbation' of the novels 'which has already stamped these books as among the greatest of English novels'.

The following is the full text of Lord Brabourne's edition of the letters with the exception of copies of pages from an account book and some inventories belonging to a relation of Jane Austen by marriage, which were included as appendices.

LETTERS OF JANE AUSTEN
EDITED
WITH AN INTRODUCTION AND CRITICAL REMARKS
BY EDWARD, LORD BRABOURNE
IN TWO VOLUMES

TO
THE QUEEN'S MOST EXCELLENCY MAJESTY
MADAM,

It was the knowledge that your Majesty so highly appreciated the works of Jane Austen which emboldened me to ask permission to dedicate to your Majesty these volumes, containing as they do numerous letters of that authoress, of which, as her great-nephew, I have recently become possessed. These letters are printed, with the exception of a very few omissions which appeared obviously desirable, just as they were written, and if there should be found in them, or in the chapters which accompany them, anything which may interest or amuse your Majesty, I shall esteem myself doubly fortunate in having been the means of bringing them under your Majesty's notice.

I am, Madam,
Your Majesty's very humble and obedient subject,
BRABOURNE.

Introduction

It is right that some explanation should be given of the manner in which the letters now published came into my possession.

The Rev. J. E. Austen Leigh, nephew to Jane Austen, and first cousin to my mother Lady Knatchbull, published in 1869 'a Memoir' of his aunt, and supplemented it by a second and enlarged edition in the following year, to which he added the hitherto unpublished tale, 'Lady Susan,' for the publication of which he states in his preface that he had 'lately received permission from the author's niece, Lady Knatchbull, of Provender, in Kent, to whom the autograph copy was given.' It seems that the autograph copy of another unpublished tale, 'The Watsons,' had been given to Mr. Austen Leigh's half-sister, Mrs. Lefroy, and that each recipient took a copy of what was given to the other, by which means Mr. Austen Leigh became acquainted with the existence and contents of 'Lady Susan,' and knowing that it was the property of my mother, wrote to ask her permission to attach it to, and publish it with, the second edition of his 'Memoir.' My mother was at that time unable to attend to business, and my youngest sister, who lived with her, replied to the request, giving the desired permission on her behalf, but stating at the same time that the autograph copy had been lost for the last six years, that any letters which existed could not be found, and that my mother was not in a fit state to allow of any search being made. It so happened that no reference was made to me, and I only knew of the request having been made and granted when I saw the tale in print. But on my mother's death, in December 1882, all her papers came into my possession, and I not only found the original copy of 'Lady Susan' – in Jane Austen's own handwriting – among the other books in the Provender library, but a square box full of letters, fastened up carefully in separate packets, each of which was endorsed 'For Lady Knatchbull,' in the handwriting of my great-aunt, Cassandra Austen, and with which was a paper endorsed, in my mother's handwriting, 'Letters from my dear Aunt Jane Austen, and two from Aunt Cassandra after her decease,' which paper contained the letters written to my mother herself. The box itself had been endorsed by my mother as follows: – 'Letters from Aunt Jane to Aunt Cassandra at different periods of her life – a few to me – and some from Aunt Cass. to me after At. Jane's death.'

This endorsement bears the date August, 1856, and was probably made the last time my mother looked at the letters. At all events, a comparison of these letters with some quoted by Mr. Austen Leigh makes it abundantly clear that they have never been in his hands, and that they are now presented to the public for the first time. Indeed, it is much to be regretted that the 'Memoir' should have been published without the additional light which many of these letters throw upon the Life, though of course no blame attaches to Mr. Austen Leigh in the matter.

The opportunity, however, having been lost, and 'Lady Susan' already published, it remained for me to consider whether the letters which had come into my possession were of sufficient public interest to justify me in giving them to the world. They had evidently, for the most part, been left to my mother by her Aunt Cassandra Austen; they contain the confidential outpourings of Jane Austen's soul to her beloved sister, interspersed with many family and personal details which, doubtless, she would have told to no other human being. But to-day, more than seventy long years have rolled away since the greater part of them were written; no one now living can, I think, have any possible just cause of annoyance at their publication, whilst, if I judge rightly, the public never took a deeper or more lively interest in all that concerns Jane Austen than at the present moment. Her works, slow in their progress towards popularity, have achieved it with the greater certainty, and have made an impression the more permanent from its gradual advance. The popularity continues, although the customs and manners which Jane Austen describes have changed and varied so much as to belong in a great measure to another age. But the reason of its continuance is not far to seek. Human nature is the same in all ages of the world, and 'the inimitable Jane' (as an old friend of mine used always to call her) is true to Nature from first to last. She does not attract our imagination by sensational descriptions or marvellous plots; but, with so little 'plot' at all as to offend those who read only for excitement, she describes men and women exactly as men and women really are, and tells her tale of ordinary, everyday life with such truthful delineation, such bewitching simplicity, and, moreover, with such purity of style and language, as have rarely been equalled, and perhaps never surpassed.

This being the case, it has seemed to me that the letters which show what her own 'ordinary, everyday life' was, and which afford a picture of her such as no history written by another person could give so well, are likely to interest a public which, both in Great Britain and America, has learned to appreciate Jane Austen. It will be seen that they are ninety-four in number, ranging in date from 1796 to 1816 – that is to say, over the last twenty years of her life. Some other letters, written to her sister Cassandra, appear in Mr. Austen Leigh's book, and it would seem that at Cassandra's death, in 1845, the correspondence must have been divided, and whilst the bulk of it came to my mother, a number of letters passed into the possession of Mr. Austen Leigh's sisters, from whom he obtained them. These he made use of without being aware of the existence of the rest.

However this may be, it is certain that I am now able to present to the public entirely new matter, from which may be gathered a fuller and more complete knowledge of Jane Austen and her 'belongings' than could otherwise have been obtained. Miss Tytler [Sarah Tytler, author of *Jane Austen and Her Works* 1880], indeed, has made a praiseworthy effort to impart to the world information respecting the life and works of her favourite authoress, but her 'Life' is little more than a copy of Mr. Austen Leigh's Memoir. I attempt no 'Memoir' that can properly be so called, but I give the letters as they were written, with such comments and explanations as I think may add to their interest. I am aware that in some of the latter I have wandered somewhat far away from Jane Austen, having been led aside by allusions which awaken old memories and recall old stories. But whilst my 'addenda' may be read or skipped as the reader pleases, they do not detract from the actual value of the genuine letters which I place before him. These, I think, can hardly fail to be of interest to all who desire to know more of the writer; and, although they form no continuous narrative and record no stirring events, it will be remarked that, amid the most ordinary details and most commonplace topics, every

now and then sparkle out the same wit and humour which illuminate the pages of 'Pride and Prejudice,' 'Mansfield Park,' 'Emma,' &c., and which have endeared the name of Jane Austen to many thousands of readers in English speaking homes.
BRABOURNE.
May 1884

Letters of Jane Austen

Godmersham and Goodnestone
My great-aunt, Jane Austen, died on July 18,1817. As circumstances over which I had no control prevented my appearance in the world until twelve years later, I was unfortunately debarred from that personal acquaintance with her and her surroundings which would have enabled me to describe both with greater accuracy of detail than I can at present hope to attain. I feel, however, that I have some claim to undertake the task which I am about to commence, from the fact that my mother, the eldest daughter of the Edward Austen so often alluded to in the accompanying letters, was the favourite niece of Aunt Jane, and that the latter's name has been a household word in my family from the earliest period of my recollection. It is of my mother that Jane Austen writes to her sister Cassandra (October 7, 1808), 'I am greatly pleased with your account of Fanny; I found her in the summer just what you describe, almost another sister, and could not have supposed that a neice [1] would ever have been so much to me. She is quite after one's own heart.' And it is *to* my mother that her Aunt Cassandra writes in 1817, after her sister's death: 'I believe she was better known to you than to any human being besides myself.' The memory of 'Aunt Jane' was so constantly and so tenderly cherished by my mother, and I have always heard her spoken of in such terms of affection, that I feel very much as if I must have known her myself, and I am not content to let these letters go forth to the world without such additional information as I am able to impart with respect to the people and things of whom and of which they treat.

In order to be properly interested in a biography or in biographical letters, it is necessary that the reader should know something of the 'dramatis personae,' so as to feel as nearly as possible as if they were personal acquaintances; and if this desirable point is once reached, the amusement to be found in the narrative is sensibly increased. Of course it is very possible to fall into the error of going too much into detail, and provoking the exclamation, 'What has this got to do with Jane Austen?' I think that this is an exclamation very likely to be made by some of those who may peruse these volumes; but, on the other hand, I am inclined to believe that, upon the whole, it is better to give too much than too little information. For my own part, I confess that, if I read letters of this kind at all, I like to know as much as is to be known about the people and places mentioned. To leave me at the end of my perusal uncertain as to the fate of some of the people, or as to the present condition of the places, is to my mind a distinct fraud upon the good nature which has induced me to take sufficient interest in them to read the book. I like to know whom John married, what became of Mary, who lives at A___, and whether B____is still in the possession of the same family; and, such being my view of the case, I have endeavoured to give as much information as I could about everybody and everything. At the distance of time from which these letters were written, it is next to impossible not to miss, and perhaps occasionally misunderstand, some of the allusions; but, for the most part, I hope and think this has been avoided.

To a considerable extent, the letters tell their own story, the first being written in 1796, when the writer was not yet twenty-one – the last in 1816, the year before she died. The 'Memoir' published by Mr. Austen Leigh gives an outline of Jane Austen's history which these letters will do much to fill up and complete; but there are some points which he has left untouched, and others upon which he was not in possession of the information which I am now able to impart. For instance, Mr. Austen Leigh speaks of letters written in November, 1800, as 'the earliest letters' he has seen, whereas the present collection comprises more than twenty which were written before that time. Again, he quotes a sentence written in April, 1805, as 'evidence that Jane Austen was acquainted with Bath before it became her residence in 1801,' the fact of which acquaintance, the reason for it and the manner in which it came about, will all be found in these letters.

It is not my desire or intention to attempt a regular biography of Jane Austen, by which I mean an account of the events of her life set down in chronological order and verified with historical precision. In truth, the real beauty of Jane Austen's life really consisted in its being uneventful: *it* was emphatically a home life, and *she* the light and blessing of a home circle. When it has been said that she was born at Steventon Rectory on December 16, 1775, that the family moved to Bath in 1801, that her father died there in January, 1805, that she subsequently went with her mother to Southampton, in 1809 settled at Chawton, and went in 1817 to die at Winchester, the whole record of the life has been nearly completed; its beauty is to be found in the illustrations which these letters afford, revealing to us as they do more of the character and inner life of the writer than could be discovered by the mere dry recital of events.

To judge the letters fairly, however, and to understand them as they ought to be understood to make them interesting, I think it is very desirable to arrive at a more complete knowledge than has hitherto been possible for the general public, of the circumstances under which they were written, and the places to and from which they were addressed.

Of Steventon, where the first half of Jane Austen's life was passed, there is little to be said beyond what has already been told by Mr. Austen Leigh. But it is interesting to enquire how it was that Steventon became Jane Austen's home, and the more so since it was through the same channel that her family became interested in Godmersham Park and Chawton House, from or to the former of which many of her letters were addressed, and near to the latter of which was the home where she passed the later period of her life. In fact, before one can thoroughly understand and feel at home with the people of whom Jane Austen writes, and who were the friends and companions of her life, one should know something of the history of Godmersham and Goodnestone, in Kent, as well as of Steventon and Chawton, in Hampshire; and I am bound to say, speaking from personal experience, that the more we know about them, the better we shall like them.

I will take Godmersham first, partly because I know it best, and partly because it obliges me to enter upon a genealogical sketch which is required in order to trace the way in which this place became connected with Jane Austen and Jane Austen with the place. Godmersham Park is situated in one of the most beautiful parts of Kent, namely, in the Valley of the Stour, which lies between Ashford and Canterbury. Soon after you pass the Wye Station of the railway from the former to the latter place, you see Godmersham Church on your left hand, and just beyond it comes into view the wall which shuts off the shrubberies and pleasure grounds of the great house from the road; close to the church nestles the home farm, and beyond it the rectory, with lawn sloping down to the River Stour, which, for a distance of nearly a mile, runs through the east end of the park. A little beyond the church you see the mansion, between which and the railroad lies the village, divided by the old high road from Ashford to Canterbury, nearly opposite Godmersham. The Valley of the Stour makes a break in that ridge of chalk hills (the proper name of which is the Backbone of Kent) which runs from Dover to Folkestone, and from Folkestone by Lyminge, Norton, Stowting, Brabourne, and Brook to Wye, where the break occurs, and on the other side of the valley the hills appear again, running down from Chilham, past Godmersham to Challock and Eastwell, and away behind Charing and Lenham. So that Godmersham Park, beyond the house, is upon the chalk downs, and on its further side is bounded by King's Wood, a large tract of woodland containing many hundred acres and possessed by several different owners. It is a healthy as well as a lovely situation, with Chilham Park to the north and Eastwell Park to the south, six and a half miles from

Ashford and eight miles from Canterbury, and within an easy drive from the quaint little town of Wye.

Godmersham formerly belonged to the ancient family of Brodnax, one of whom lived in the reign of Henry V., and married Alicie Scappe, from whom descended various generations of the name, who seem to have lived either at Hythe, Burmarsh, or Cheriton – all places in Kent adjoining each other – until we come to Thomas Brodnax, of Godmersham,who, having married, first a Gilbert, and then a Brockman, of Beachborough, died in 1602. His great-grandson William, having married the daughter of Thomas Digges, of Chilham, was knighted, either for that reason or a better, in 1664, and left a son William, who married, first a Coppin and then a May, and died in 1726.

It is through Thomas Brodnax, the son of this last-named William, that the Austen family became connected with Godmersham. He changed his name, doubtless for very good cause, first in 1727 to May (his mother's name), and then, in 1738, to Knight. As Thomas May Knight he ended his life, in 1781, aged eighty years, and of him Hasted, the Kentish historian, says that 'he was a gentleman whose eminent worth ought not here to pass unnoticed; whose high character for upright conduct and integrity stamped a universal confidence and authority on all he said and did, which rendered his life as honourable as it was good, and caused his death to be lamented by everyone as a public loss.'

It was this Thomas May Knight's marriage with which we have now to deal, and to do so in a satisfactory manner we must turn to the genealogical tree of the Austens, who are, according to Hasted, 'a family of ancient standing in Kent,' and one of whom, John Austen, of Broadford, not only died there, in 1620, but was comfortably buried in the parish church, where are – or were – hung his coat of arms in commemoration of the event. From him descended John Austen, of Gravehurst and Broadford, who died in 1705, aged seventy-six, having had a son John and a daughter Jane by his wife Jane Atkins. The son married Elizabeth Weller, had a son William, and then died the year before his father. The daughter married Stephen Stringer, and had a daughter named Hannah. William Austen and Hannah Stringer being thus first cousins, the former married Rebecca Hampson, and had a son George, who was Jane Austen's father; the latter married William Monk, and had a daughter Jane, who married Thomas May Knight, of Godmersham Park and Chawton House. This latter couple had one son, Thomas Knight, who married Catherine, daughter of Wadham Knatchbull, Canon and Prebendary of Durham,and, having no children, Mr. Knight adopted Edward Austen, George Austen's second son [he was, in fact, the third son], and, dying in 1794, left him all his property, subject to his widow's life interest.

It will be seen by the foregoing account how it was that the Austens became concerned with Godmersham, and it will also be seen that the various county histories which Mr. Austen Leigh follows, in saying that Mr. Thomas Knight left his property to 'his cousin Edward Austen,' certainly make the most of the relationship. All that the two could fairly say was that their great-grandfather and great-grandmother were brother and sister, and their grandfather and grandmother first cousins; but, according to the present ideas of the world, it is somewhat straining a point to claim the relationship of 'cousin' for the second generation after the indisputable first-cousinship. I believe, however, that, as a matter of fact, Mr. Knight had no nearer relations than this branch of the family, and personally I have no objection to the relationship having been established and accepted in this case, since thereby Edward Austen, who was my much repected grandfather, became possessed of large property, which enabled him, by an early marriage, to bring about that satisfactory relationship with my unworthy self, When Mr. Knight (who was member for Kent for a short time [1774] during his father's lifetime) died in 1794, being then under sixty years of age, his widow, as will appear from the letters, gave up her property to Edward Austen, to whom it would otherwise have come only at her decease. She reserved a certain income for herself, retired to Canterbury, and settled down in a house known as 'White Friars,' so called from the Augustine or 'White Friars' (though the appellation more properly belonged to the Carmelites), who formerly possessed it, and from whom it passed through various hands till it came by marriage into the possession of the Papillons of Acrise, from whom Mr. W. O. Hammond, of St. Albans Court, bought it, lived there for a time, and then sold it to Mrs. Knight, who inhabited it until her death in October 1812. In November 1812 Edward Austen and his family took the name of Knight.

Mrs. Knight (*nee* Catherine Knatchbull) lived on the best of terms with those who succeeded her at Godmersham. She was a very superior woman, with a good understanding and highly cultivated mind; she was my mother's godmother, and I shall add to the present collection of letters two of hers, one to my mother and the other to my father, Sir Edward Knatchbull, which I think are of some interest. Mrs. Knight was not only a very superior, but a very beautiful woman, if we may judge from her picture, by Romney, which now hangs in the dining-room at Chawton House, and is enough to make anyone proud of being related to her. It was, as I have said, the adoption of my maternal grandfather Edward Austen, by Mr. Knight, which enabled the former to marry; and this brings me to the connection of Jane Austen and her family with Goodnestone, which shall duly be set forth in a manner which will throw light upon many of the characters in our play. For the 'Elizabeth' to whom frequent reference is made throughout these letters, being the wife chosen by my revered grandfather, and consequently occupying the undoubted position of my maternal grandmother, was a daughter of the family of Sir Brook Bridges, of Goodnestone, which family requires immediate and careful attention.

Now there are two Goodnestones in Kent (pronounced 'Gunstone'), between which let the unwary reader fall into no error. Goodnestone 'next Faversham' is a different place altogether from *our* Goodnestone, which is 'next Wingham,'and is in old records written Godwinceston, 'which name,' says Hasted, 'it took from Earl Godwin, once owner of it.' Goodnestone was not the original seat of the Bridges race. Collins tells us that 'this family has been of good antiquity in Ireland, where several of the branches thereof have now considerable estates; but the first that settled in England was John Bridges of South Littleton, in Worcestershire, who, on November 14, 1578, purchased an house and lands at Alcester, in Warwickshire. His grandson, John Bridges, settled at Hackney, and was the father of Col. John Bridges, whose second son, Brooke, was the first Bridges who possessed Goodnestone. For we find from Hasted that in the reign of Queen Anne one Sir Thos. Engham sold it to Brook Bridges, of Grove, auditor of the imprest, who new built the mansion, and died possessed of it in 1717. 'He built,' says Collins, 'a very handsome house, and very much improv'd the gardens, and along the side of the *terras* walks, stand the busts of the twelve Caesars, in marble, larger than the life; they were brought from Rome, and cost about 600*l*.' His son, who was created a baronet in 1718, married, first, Margaret Marsham, daughter of Sir Robt. Marsham and sister of the first Lord Romney; secondly, Mary, daughter of Sir Thomas Hales, of Bekesbourne.

It is necessary to go back as far as this, in order to show the connection and kinship of various persons to whom allusion is made in some of the Godmersham and Goodnestone letters. Sir Brook left two children by his first wife: Margaret, who married John Plumptre, Esq., of Fredville near Wingham, M.P. for Nottingham in 1750, and died without children (with which a second wife amply supplied him), and Brook, who succeeded him as second baronet in March, 1728. This Sir Brook married Anne, daughter of Sir Thomas Palmer, of Wingham (of whom more anon), but died during his shrievalty (May 23, 1733), after which a posthumous child was born to him, who is a person of great consequence to my history, as will be presently seen when I come to speak of his children. He, being the third Sir Brook, married Fanny Fowler, daughter of Christopher Fowler, Esq., of Graces, Essex, who, to judge by her picture, of which there are several copies in the family, did credit to his taste. It may be properly here remarked that through this lady's mother, Frances Mildmay, came the claim to the Fitzwalter peerage, which the fifth Sir Brook so nearly sustained before the Committee of Privileges of the House of Lords in later years, that no one ever quite knew how he failed to get it, any more than they understood the species of wild justice by which a peerage of the same name, but *not* the same peerage, was eventually given to, and died with him. The third Sir Brook and Fanny Fowler (who died March 15, 1825) had ten children, all of whom are mentioned, some of them frequently, in these letters. There were four sons, of whom William, the eldest, became the fourth baronet upon the death of his father in 1791, took the name of Brook by Act of Parliament, married Eleanor Foote, the daughter of John Foote, Esq., banker, of London, and by her (who died in 1806) had two sons, Sir Brook (who succeeded him, married his first cousin Fanny Cage, was created Lord Fitzwalter, of Woodham Walter, Sussex, in 1868, and died without issue in 1875) and George, who married Louisa, daughter of Chas. Chaplin, Esq., M.P. of Blankney, Lincolnshire, and succeeded his brother as sixth baronet. The fourth Sir Brook also left a daughter Eleanor, who married in 1828 the Rev. Henry Western Plumptre, third son of Mr. Plumptre, of Fredville, and had a large family.

But I am descending into modern times far too rapidly, having yet to deal with the seven younger children of the third Sir Brook and Fanny Fowler. The second son was Henry, who also took the name of Brook, married in 1795 Jane, daughter of Sir Thos. Pym Hales, and had sundry children who need not here be specified. The other two sons were Brook Edward and Brook John, who also married, but who do not signify to us at present. It is with the daughters that we are more concerned, for four of the six married – three of them in the same year – and to them or their children we have constant references in the letters before us. Fanny married Lewis Cage, of Milgate, the family place, two and a half miles from Maidstone, and was the mother of Fanny Cage, who, as has been already mentioned, married her cousin Sir Brook, and as Lady Fitzwalter died without issue in 1874. Sophia married William Deedes, Esq., of Sandling, near Hythe, became the mother of no less than twenty children, and died in 1844. Elizabeth married Edward Austen, and had eleven children, of whom my mother was the eldest, and fifteen years later, in 1806, Harriet Mary married the Rev. Geo. Moore, Rector of Canterbury, and eldest son of the then Archbishop of Canterbury, by whom she also had a numerous family.

I cannot forbear interrupting my geneaological narrative here, in the hope that my lady readers will be interested in the matter which causes the interruption, inasmuch as it relates to the manners and customs of just a hundred years ago with regard to matrimonial engagements. I have the letters in which Fanny Fowler, Lady Bridges, announces the coming marriages of her three elder daughters; they were written to her husband's half-brother's (Chas. Fielding) wife, and being interesting, although very remotely connected with 'Jane Austen,' if I may not properly insert them, as I shall venture to do, in the appendix to these volumes, what is the use of having an appendix at all? I shall certainly do so, for the benefit of all those mothers who have daughters, married or to be married, in order that they may see and appreciate the manner in which my beloved great-grandmother bore the loss (by marriage) of three daughters in one year. Besides these three and Mrs. Moore, however, she had two daughters to console her, neither of whom was married. Marianne (mentioned in the thirty-fifth letter, who was a confirmed invalid all her life, and died in 1811) and Louisa. The latter, who is mentioned in letter sixty-six as having gone with her mother to Bath in 1813, lived many years, much loved and respected by my generation, who knew her as 'Great-Aunt Louisa,' and often saw her at Godmersham and Goodnestone, at the latter of which she died in June 1856. When Sir Brook, the third baronet, died in 1791, his widow retired to Goodnestone Farm, and lived there with these two unmarried daughters and the two Miss Cages, Fanny and Sophia, who came to her after the death of their parents, the latter having died within a few months of each other.

I have now shown, as I hope with sufficient clearness, how the two Kentish places, Godmersham and Goodnestone, became connected with the life of Jane Austen; Godmersham, as the home of her brother Edward; Goodnestone, as the home of his wife Elizabeth; and, in the genealogical sketches which I have given, I have shown something of those interweaving and interwoven relationships of the eastern part of Kent which have given rise to the saying that 'in Kent they are all first cousins.' But I cannot forbear saying a few more words in this place upon Kentish relationships, which will assist in explaining some other allusions in our letters, and without which I should really feel as if I had been guilty of an inexcusable omission.

My mother, who took a deep interest in all family matters, and was an infallible authority upon questions connected with county genealogoy, always began her elucidation of any point relating to her mother's family with the following words: 'Once upon a time there were three Miss Palmers.' As nobody is at all likely to dispute this fact at the present day, I pause to remark that the Palmers were an old Kentish family, of Wingham, and the first baronet, Sir Thomas, was raised to that dignity in 1621. Of him says Hasted, 'He so constantly resided at Wingham that he is said to have kept sixty Christmases without intermission in this mansion with great hospitality.' Sir Thomas had three sons, each of whom was knighted, and from him descended the father of the three ladies whose doings I am about to commemorate. Their names were Mary, Elizabeth and Anne. Mary became the second wife of Daniel, seventh Earl of Winchilsea, by whom she had four daughters, of whom only one, Heneage, married, her husband being Sir George Osborn, of Chicksands Priory, Bedfordshire.

Elizabeth Palmer married Edward Finch, fifth brother of the said Daniel, seventh Earl of Winchilsea, who took the name of Hatton under the will of his aunt, the widow of Viscount Hatton, and died in 1771, leaving a son George. Meanwhile, the second, third, and fourth brothers lived and died, and only the second brother, William, left a son. He accomplished this by marrying twice: first, Lady Anne Douglas, who had no children; secondly, Lady Charlotte Fermor, whose son George succeeded his uncle Daniel as eighth Earl of Winchilsea, but died unmarried in 1826.

Meanwhile, George Finch-Hatton, the son of Edward, and therefore first cousin to George, the eighth earl, had died, after having married Lady Elizabeth Mary Murray, daughter of the Earl of Mansfield, and left three children, of whom the eldest, George William, succeeded as ninth Earl of Winchilsea, in 1826. This is the 'George Hatton' several times mentioned in the letters from Godmersham.

But, in following up the Finches and Hattons, I have left Anne, the third Miss Palmer, too long alone, and must hasten back to her, with many apologies. She was the lady who, as has been already mentioned, married the second Sir Brook Bridges; but, whether the honour of the alliance, or the responsibilities of the office of High Sheriff of the county, or some other cause, brought about the catastrophe, certain it is that Sir Brook left her a widow, as has already been stated, in 1733; and, in 1737, she took to herself a second husband, in the person of Charles Fielding, second son of Basil, fourth Earl of Denbigh, by whom she had two sons and two daughters before her death in 1743. This lady's second son Charles was a commodore in the navy; he married Sophia Finch, sister of George Finch, eighth Earl of Winchilsea, and daughter of William and Lady Charlotte Finch (nee Fermor). Lady Charlotte was governess to the children of King George III, and her daughter, Mrs. Charles Fielding, lived with her at Windsor and St. James', so her children were brought up with the Royal Family. This will explain the various references to members of the Fielding family which will be found in Jane Austen's letters; and, though I feel rather ashamed of having inflicted upon my readers such a dull chapter of genealogy, those who care to do so will be able to identify by its aid many of the people who were her contemporaries, friends, and relations.

Austens and Knights

In the preceding chapter I have dealt pretty fully with the relationships which accrued to Jane Austen through the marriage of her brother Edward to Elizabeth Bridges, and her consequent connection with Godmersham and Goodnestone.

Before, however, I come to speak of her non-Kentish relations, it may be as well to specify the children of that marriage, the elder of whom are constantly mentioned in the letters. The 'Fanny' whose name occurs so often, and to whom some of the later letters are addressed, is Fanny Catherine, the eldest child of the marriage, who was born on January 23, 1793. A son may be pardoned for saying (especially when it is simply and literally true) that never was a more exemplary life passed than that of his mother. Upon October 10, 1808, just before she had completed her sixteenth year, her mother (the 'Elizabeth' of the letters) died very suddenly, leaving ten children besides herself, the youngest quite a baby. From that moment my mother took charge of the family, watched over her brothers and sisters, was her father's right hand and mainstay, and proved herself as admirable in that position as afterwards in her married life. She married my father, Sir Edward Knatchbull, as his second wife, on October 24, 1820, when she had nearly completed her twenty-eighth year,and died on Christmas morning, 1882, being within four weeks of completing her ninetieth year. Besides her, the children of my grandfather and grandmother consisted of six boys and four girls.

Edward, the eldest son, married twice, and left several children by both marriages. He lived at Chawton House during his father's lifetime, and after the latter's death, in November 1852, he spent a large sum in repairing and remodelling Godmersham, intending to live there, but never did so, sold a large portion of the property to Lord Sondes (whose Kentish estate of Lees Court was and is adjoining), and finally disposed of the rest, with the house, to Mr. Lister Kaye; and, at his death in 1878, left Chawton House and property to his eldest son by his second wife, Adela, daughter of John Portal, Esq., of Freefolk, in the county of Hants. The second son, George Thomas, is the 'ittle Dordy' of the letters, and seems to have been a particular pet of Jane's. He was one of those men who were clever enough to do almost anything, but live to their lives'end very comfortably doing nothing. The most remarkable achievement of his which I am able to record was his winning a *50l* prize in the lottery in 1804, when quite a child, an event duly chronicled in her pocket-book of that year by my mother, who kept a regular journal of family events from very early childhood. Subsequently, my respected uncle was mighty at cricket, and one of the first, if not *the* first, who introduced the practice of 'round' bowling instead of the old-fashioned 'underhand.' He was very well informed, agreeable, a pleasant companion, and always popular with his nephews and nieces; but I know of nothing else which he did worthy of mention, except marry in 1837 as kind-hearted a woman as ever lived in the person of Hilare, daughter of Admiral Sir Robt. Barlow, and widow of the second Lord Nelson. They had no children, and passed a great deal of their time on the Continent. She died in 1857, and he survived her ten years, dying in August 1867.

The next brother, Henry, married his first cousin, Sophia Cage, sister of Lady Bridges, and afterwards the daughter of the Rev. E. Northey, and died in 1843. He left two children, one by each wife, and the fourth brother, William, left several also, having married three times, and held the rectory of Steventon until his death in 1873.

But as he, together with the two younger sons, Charles Bridges and Brook John (the former of whom died unmarried in October 1867, and the latter left no children, and died in 1878), were too young to be more than casually mentioned in 'At. Jane's correspondence, it is needless to give further particulars about them. All the sons of the marriage of Edward Austen and Elizabeth Bridges have passed away at the present time of writing, but two of the four younger daughters are still with us. I had written 'three,' but alas! even while these pages are passing through my hands, another has been taken – namely, Elizabeth, the 'Lizzie' of the letters, who married, in 1818, Edward Royd Rice, Esq., of Dane Court, near Sandwich, Kent, had a numerous family, and died in April of the present year. Those who are left are Marianne, still unmarried, and Louisa, who married Lord George Hill, as his second wife, the first having been her sister Cassandra, who died in 1842.

This record will serve to explain many allusions in the letters, but I have still to deal with the 'inimitable Jane's' kith and kin in Hampshire and further abroad. Her own immediate family consisted of five [in fact six] brothers and the one sister, Cassandra, some three years older than herself, to whom most of 'the letters' are addressed.

I remember 'Great-Aunt Cassandra' very well, which is not extraordinary, considering that she only died in the spring of 1845, when I was nearly sixteen years old. All through her life she was a constant visitor at her brother's house at Godmersham, and it was to this circumstance, and to the consequent separation of the sisters, that we owe most of our letters. As the penny post had not been invented in those good old times, people wrote less frequently and took more pains with their letters than is now the general habit, and we shall find several allusions to the 'franks' which could at that time (and indeed up to 1840) be given by members of Parliament, who were thus enabled to oblige their friends by saving them the heavy postage of their letters.

However, franks or no franks, it is very certain that the two sisters wrote to each other letters which may fairly be called voluminous, and my great regret is that, in presenting to the public so many of Jane's letters to Cassandra, I cannot add to their value by producing any of Cassandra's to Jane, of which the latter gave us sufficient hints to make us feel that they must have been of an amusing and interesting character. In all probability, however, when Jane Austen died in 1817, and all her papers and letters came into her sister's possession, the latter did not think her own letters worth preserving, and they were accordingly destroyed.

From my recollection of 'Great-Aunt Cassandra' in her latter days she must have been a very sensible, charming, and agreeable person. Of her earlier life I cannot tell more than is told in Mr. Austen Leigh's Memoir and may be gathered from her sister's letters. If the engagement to a young clergyman, who died in the West Indies before it could be fulfilled, was to her a lasting sorrow, it was not one which interfered with her cheerful disposition and temperament, so far at least as we younger people could tell, and all my recollections of her are pleasant. The warmest affection doubtless existed between the two sisters, but indeed, so far as my experience goes of Austens and Knights, I should say that there has seldom been a family in which family affection and unity has existed in a stronger degree.

Jane Austen's eldest brother was James, the husband of the 'Mary' to whom such frequent allusions are made, who was Mary Lloyd before she married, the mother of Mr. Austen Leigh, the writer of the Memoir, and the sister of Elizabeth, who was Mrs. Fowle of Kintbury, and of Martha, who is so often mentioned, and who eventually married Sir Francis Austen, one of Jane's younger brothers, and died in 1843. Neither she, however, nor her sister Mary was the first wife of their respective husbands. James Austen first married Anne, daughter of General Mathew, who presented him with one only daughter before she shuffled off this mortal coil. This daughter, however, is of some importance to our present purpose, partly because, her name being Jane Anna Elizabeth, she is the 'Anna' frequently referred to in our letters, and partly because, in November 1814, she thought fit to marry the Rev. Benjamin Lefroy, afterwards Rector of Ashe (the 'Ben' of the letters, who died in 1829), and thus gives me a peg upon which to hang a few other Lefroys, and show how they come to be so often mentioned by 'At. Jane.' Mrs. B. Lefroy had one son and six daughtes, and died in 1872.

Once upon a time there was a Thomas Lefroy, of Canterbury, who married a Phoebe Thomson of Kenfield (an estate not far from that cathedral city), and had a son Anthony, who lived some time at Leghorn, married Elizabeth Langlois, and begat two sons, the one of whom was named Anthony, while the other rejoiced in the appellation of Isaac Peter George. Now, Anthony attained to the position of Lieutenant-Colonel of the 9th Dragoons, which fully justified him in marrying Anne Gardiner in 1769, and subsequently dying in 1819. Before achieving the latter feat, however, he became the father of the 'Tom Lefroy' of our letters, who was eventually known to the world as the Right Hon. Thos. Lefroy, Lord Chief Justice of Ireland, and one of the ablest lawyers of his day.

Meanwhile Isaac Peter George Lefroy became Fellow of All Souls, Rector of Ashe, near Steventon, and Compton, in Surrey, husband of Anne Brydges, of Wotton, Kent (sister of Sir Egerton Brydges), and father of two sons, the younger of whom was the Benjamin who married our 'Anna,' whilst the elder was John Henry George, of Ewshott House, Farnham, who also became Rector of Ashe and Compton, married a Cottrell, and died in 1823, when his brother Benjamin succeeded him in the living of Ashe, the three presentations to which had been purchased by Mr Langlois. He must have been immediately preceded in the rectory by Dr. Russell, the grandfather of Mary Russell Mitford, to whose family we shall also find allusions in the earlier letters. There was a great intimacy between the rectories of Ashe and Steventon, and Mrs. Lefroy was a valued friend of Jane's up to the time of her death, in 1804, which was occasioned by a fall from her horse.

After this little Lefroy interlude I must return to James Austen, who is keeping all the rest of his family waiting in the most unconscionable manner.

I have already said that his second wife was Mary Lloyd, who bare him two children, 'James Edward' and 'Caroline Mary Craven,' and died in 1843, having survived her husband twenty-four years. He only survived his sister Jane two years, and died at Steventon in December 1819. James Edward, the writer of the Memoir, married Emma, daughter of Charles Smith, Esq., of Suttons, and died in 1874, leaving a numerous family. He took the name of Leigh in addition to that of Austen, having inherited Scarlets, in Berkshire, under the will of the widow of his maternal uncle James Leigh Perrot, 'of whom more anon,' as the old chroniclers say. His widow died in 1876, and his sister Caroline, who never married, died in 1880.

Of Edward Austen I have told in the account of Godmersham, so I come next to Henry, of whom his nephew, Mr. Austen Leigh, tells us that he 'had great conversational powers, and inherited from his father an eager and sanguine disposition. He was a very entertaining companion, but had perhaps less steadiness of purpose, certainly less success in life, than his brothers.' This picture is doubtless drawn with fidelity, and the facts seem to be, as far as I can discover them, that my worthy great-uncle's want of 'steadiness and purpose' was evinced by his trying various professions, one after the other, without achieving any particular success in any. I gather from the letters before us that his sister gauged his character pretty well, and did not anticipate much success for his career. He seems to have had a hankering after a soldier's life for some time; then he went into a bank in Alton. He afterwards became Receiver General for Oxfordshire, and also a banker in London; and, whilst he lived there, helped his sister Jane with her publishing business. In 1816 his bank broke, upon which he became a clergyman, and went out as chaplain to Berlin in 1818. He married twice, which seems to have been the general habit of the family, his first wife being his first cousin Madame de Feuillade, nee Eliza

Hancock. Mr. Austen Leigh is mistaken in saying his grandfather, George Austen had only one sister. He had two, who rejoiced in the euphonious names of 'Philadelphia' and 'Leonora.' The latter died single, the former married Mr. Hancock, and her daughter married the Comte de Feuillade, and when he had been unlucky enough to be guillotined in the French Revolution, took her cousin Henry *en secondes noces,* died in 1813, and left him inconsolable until 1820, when he consoled himself with Eleanor, daughter of Henry Jackson, of London, by his wife, who was one of the Papillons of Acrise. He had no children, and died in 1850 at Tunbridge Wells, having, I believe, had no preferment except the living of Steventon, which, on the death of his brother James in 1819, he held for a short time, until his nephew, William Knight, was old enough to take it –a comfortable family arrangement.

I cannot leave Henry Austen without giving to my readers the only example of his 'conversational powers' with which I am acquainted, and which illustrates the dry, quaint humour which was a characteristic of some of the family. He is said to have been driving on one occasion with a relation in one of the rough country lanes near Steventon, when the pace at which the postchaise was advancing did not satisfy his eager temperament. Putting his head out of the window, he cried out to the postillion, 'Get on, boy! Get on, will you?' The 'boy' turned round in his saddle, and replied: 'I *do* get on, sir, where I can!' 'You stupid fellow!' was the rejoinder. 'Any fool can do that. I want you to get on *where you can't !'*

Of the two sailor brothers of Jane Austen – Francis and Charles – Mr. Austen Leigh gives a fuller history than of the others, because he thinks that 'their honourable career accounts for Jane Austen's partiality for the navy, as well as for the readiness and accuracy with which she wrote about it.' However this may be, there can be no doubt that their career was most honourable, and that they were both of them as good examples of British sailors as could well be furnished. I believe that both of them were much loved in their profession, as they certainly were by their relations, old and young. The 'Memoir' tells us that Francis Austen was upon one occasion spoken of as '*the* officer who kneeled at church,' which reminds me of an anecdote which my mother used to tell of one admiral having whispered to the other at the commencement of Divine Service, 'Brother, what do you think it is that people mostly say into their hats when they come into church? For my part, I always say, "For what I am going to receive the Lord make me truly thankful."' And I am not prepared to say that he could have improved on the petition.

As I am upon anecdotes, let me tell one also of Sir Francis Austen, since it shall never be said that I omitted that which I have heard of him all my life as one of the things *most like himself* that he ever did.

He was exceedingly precise, and spoke always with due deliberation, let the occasion be what it might, never having been known to hurry himself in his speech for any conceivable reason. It so fell out, then, that whilst in some foreign seas where sharks and similar unpleasant creatures abound, a friend, or sub-officer of his (I know not which), was bathing from the ship. Presently Sir Francis called out to him in his usual tone and manner, 'Mr. Pakenham, you are in danger of a shark – a shark of the blue species! You had better return to the ship.' 'Oh! Sir Francis; you are joking are you not?' 'Mr. Pakenham, I am not given to joking. If you do not immediately return, soon will the shark eat you.' Whereupon Pakenham, becoming alive to his danger, acted upon the advice thus deliberately given, saved himself 'by the skin of his teeth' from the shark.

Another anecdote of 'Uncle Frank' occurs to me, bearing upon the exact precision which was one of his characteristics. On one occasion he is said to have visited a well-known watchmaker, one of whose chronometers he had taken with him during an absence of five years, and which was still in excellent order. After looking carefully at it, the watchmaker remarked, with conscious pride, 'Well, Sir Francis, it seems to have varied none at all.' Very slowly, and very gravely, came the answer: 'Yes, it *has* varied – *eight seconds!*'

Sir Francis lived to be nearly ninety-three, and died at his house, Portsdown Lodge, in 1865, just twenty years after his sister Cassandra had died at the same place. He also was twice married, first to Mary Gibson of Ramsgate, who died in 1823, and then to the Martha Lloyd of our letters. At the time of his death he was a G.C.B., and Senior Admiral of the Fleet, just before his attainment to which dignity he thus wrote to one of his nieces, in 1862:–

'And now with reference to my nomination as Rear Admiral of the United Kingdom. It is an appointment held by patent under the Great Seal; and, though honourable, is certainly in my case not a lucrative office, as I am compelled, to qualify for holding it, to resign my good-service pension of 300 *l.* a year. The salary is, I believe, about the same, but there are very heavy fees of office to be paid, which will absorb at least one quarter of the salary. This ought not to be so. It is a national reproach that an officer should have to pay for honours conferred on him by his sovereign, and which we may presume were fairly earned. It is true I had the opportunity of retaining the pension, and refusing the other; but who, after reaching nearly the top of the list (I have only two above me), would like to refuse so distinguished an honour?'

This private little expression of discontent, from a man of a contented and happy disposition, seems so just that I could not refrain from inserting it here, but will say no more of 'Uncle Frank,' save that he had twelve children by his first wife, and that his eldest son married his first cousin, the daughter of his brother Charles, Fanny by name.

The said Charles also served with distinction, and died of cholera in 1852, in a steam sloop on the Irrawaddy, literally at the post of duty. He, too followed the family custom of marrying twice, his first wife being Miss Fanny Palmer, of Bermuda, who had three daughters, and died young; and his second, her sister Harriet, by whom he had two boys. He was a man of a singularly sweet temper and disposition, and I cannot help quoting from Mr. Austen Leigh the record left of him by 'one who was with him at his death.' 'Our good admiral won the hearts of all by his gentleness and kindness while he was struggling with disease and endeavouring to do his duty as Commander-in-Chief of the British naval forces in these waters. His death was a great grief to the whole fleet. I know that I cried bitterly when I found he was dead.'

A great many allusions to her sailor brothers will be found in Jane's letters, and in her delight at their promotion and interest in their profession one is forcibly reminded of 'Fanny Price' and her beloved brother William, although in the latter case the intervention of an ardent lover procured for young Price that which a proper family pride induces me to believe was obtained by my great-uncles by their own merits.

These, then, were the members of the family of Steventon Rectory; and between them all, as indeed may be gathered from the letters before us, the warmest affection always existed. If proof of this were needed, it is afforded by the numerous and affectionate references to her brothers to which I have alluded, and by the sympathy for each other which crops up whenever we have the opportunity of observing it. How anxiously 'Frank's' promotion is expected; how welcome is the presence of 'our own particular little brother' Charles; how assiduous is Jane in her attendance upon Henry in his illness, and how promptly his brother Edward hurries to London when he is informed of it! All these are signs and tokens of the warmth of family feeling, the brotherly and sisterly affection, which, in the case of the Austens, certainly went to show that 'blood is thicker than water,' in some races at least, and which bound together the members of this family by bonds which time could never sever, distance never lessen, prosperity never diminish, and sorrow only tend to strengthen and cement.

Besides the brothers and sisters of whom we hear so much in her letters, Jane Austen had uncles and aunts whose individuality one must get well into one's head in order to understand her allusions.

I have already mentioned her father's two sisters, and her mother's brother, Mr. Leigh Perrot, who inherited from a great uncle his additional name and a small property to justify the addition. He married a Lincolnshire Cholmeley (Jane by name – she died in 1836), and lived sometimes at

Bath and sometimes at Scarlets. Bath was also patronised by Dr. Cooper, the Incumbent of Sonning, near Reading, which was very unkind of him, because, as he married Jane Austen's aunt – her mother's eldest sister, Jane Leigh – he could have taken no surer means to confuse a biographer who seeks to identify the 'Uncle' and 'Aunt' to whom Jane constantly alludes in her Bath letters. Had he foreseen the difficulty no doubt he would have lived somewhere else; but, as matters stand at present, it is just possible that (although I have made every enquiry in order to prevent it) I may occasionally have mistaken the avuncular allusions in some of the letters, in which case I beg to apologise to the wronged uncle, and am thankful to reflect that it makes no great difference to anybody.

Steventon and Chawton, Winchester

Since it may very likely happen that these volumes may fall into the hands of persons who have not read Mr. Austen Leigh's 'Memoir,' it is but right that, with the assistance which it affords me, I should, without attempting a regular biography, give some brief account of an existence to which, in my humble judgment, the world is so much indebted. I have already described the relations by whom Jane was surrounded, and given such an account of her family as it seemed necessary to attach to her letters. I have not as yet, however, spoken of the home in which she was born or of the county in which the greater part of her life was passed.

Steventon – which is also written 'Stephington' in Warner's 'History of Hampshire,' and 'Stivetune' in Domesday Book – had the honour of being her birthplace; for in the rectory of that quiet village she came into the world on December 16, 1775. Steventon, as Mr. Austen Leigh tells us, is situated 'upon the chalk hills of North Hants, in a winding valley about seven miles from Basingstoke.' The house, standing in the valley, was somewhat better than the ordinary parsonage-houses of the day; the old-fashioned hedgerows were beautiful, and the country around sufficiently picturesque for those who have the good taste to admire country scenery. As, however, the house has been pulled down for some sixty years, a new one built on the other side of the valley, and the church 'restored' (a word of somewhat equivocal meaning), it is useless to attempt a description of things which exist no longer. The living was in the gift of Mr. Knight, of Chawton (and Godmersham), to whom also nearly the whole parish belonged, and hence it was that Jane's father, the Rev. Geo. Austen, obtained the preferment, whilst the living of the adjacent parish of Deane came to him as the gift of his uncle, Francis Austen, his father's brother, who married a Motley, went to Sevenoaks, had a son Francis, who took his mother's name, bought Kippington, and established a branch of the Austens there. Mr. George Austen held these two livings in 1764, and moved from Deane to Steventon in 1771, four years before the birth of his daughter Jane. In speaking of his marriage with Cassandra Leigh, Mr. Austen Leigh mentions her uncle, Dr. Theophilus Leigh, who lived to be ninety, and was master of Balliol College for above half a century. The story is told of him that he was elected – being a 'Corpus' man – 'under the idea that he was in weak health and likely soon to cause another vacancy.' This was the story always told of the venerable President of Magdalen, Dr. Routh, who died in his hundredth year, having, according to tradition, outlived several generations of men who, during their lifetimes, were considered to be certain to succeed him. But whilst, as an old Magdalen man, I cannot allow Dr. Theophilus Leigh to monopolise the position with which he is credited by this story, I am quite ready to believe that it has been told of him as well as Dr. Routh, and probably also of every other head of a college who has attained to patriarchal age.

All the early part of Jane Austen's life was passed at Steventon, save and except the time occupied in those visits of some of which our letters speak. *How* it was passed, what were her habits and what her occupations, will be better gathered from the letters themselves than from any description which I could collect from the imperfect data before me or invent for myself. It is very clear, however, that Jane Austen was by no means averse to amusement, appreciated a ball as much as anybody, and got all the enjoyment she could out of life, as a sensible young woman might have been expected to do. I have been told that I might very well have left out all those parts of her letters which refer to the details of dress and the descriptions of her gowns and other raiment which she gives her sister. I am, however, of a contrary opinion; that which does not interest one person may be precisely that which pleases another, and to alter or omit the apparently insignificant parts of a large picture may have a prejudicial effect upon the whole. Besides, it is something in the nature of a comfort to ordinary persons to find that so superior a being as Jane Austen concerned herself about such trifles as the 'fit' of a gown or the colour of a stocking, and I am glad to be in a position to afford the slightest comfort to anybody. Of the sweetness of her temper, and the bright, 'sunshiny' character of her disposition, no one can doubt who has heard her spoken of by those who personally knew her, and I do not think these letters will alter the general opinion. Here and there, it is true, there may be sentences which hardly seem to be written in a kindly vein towards those to whom they refer; but it must never be forgotten that these sentences were written only for the eyes of a sister who thoroughly knew and appreciated the spirit of fun in which they flowed from Jane's pen, and in which they were meant to be taken, and that they never would have been written or spoken so as to give pain to the people mentioned. Indeed, it should always be borne in mind during the perusal of these letters that, although, as I have before pointed out, a vein of good-natured satire might generally be found, alike in the letters and conversations of many of the Austen family, it always *was* good-natured, and no malice ever lurked beneath. No-one, I imagine, was in reality ever more kind-hearted and considerate of the feelings of others than Jane Austen, and certainly no one was ever better loved or more sorrowfully lamented by the relations whom she left behind her.

Apart from the visits which I have mentioned, Jane's existence seems to have glided on in uninterrupted tranquillity in that old parsonage-house at Steventon, until the year 1800, when her father made up his mind to give up the active duties of his parish and retire to Bath, for which, as he was then some seventy years of age, he can scarcely be blamed. He accomplished his purpose in the following year, when he did not, as has been stated, resign his living to his son, but placed him in the house and parish as his *locum tenens,* in which capacity he continued to act during the rest of his father's lifetime.

There is little more to say about Stevenotn, save that one anecdote occurs to me which may be as well recorded. At one time the Rev. George Austen took pupils. It seems that a word which is pronounced 'rice' (though I will not vouch for the spelling) was formerly used in Hampshire to signify 'faggots' or 'underwood,' and upon one occasion a pupil was heard to observe to another with a deep sigh, that he was afraid they would have nothing but rice puddings for some time to come, for he had heard Mrs. Austen say that 'a wagon-load of *rice*' had come in that morning.

When the death of Mr. Austen occurred early in 1805, the widow and daughters moved into lodgings in Gay Street, and remained in Bath for some months, and Mr. Austen Leigh gives us a letter of Jane's from Gay Street, written in April, in which occurs the following characteristic remark about an individual into whose identity I have not thought it necessary to enquire: 'Poor Mrs. Stent! [a friend of Mrs Lloyd, who lived in reduced circumstances] it has been her lot to be always in the way; but we must be merciful, for perhaps in time we may come to be Mrs Stents ourselves, unequal to anything, and unwelcome to everybody.'

I do not know why the family chose Southampton as their next residence, but so it was, and there they lived for the next four years, in a house with a pleasant garden attached, close to the old city walls, and in a locality which took its name, 'Castle Square,' from, or, at all events, was 'occupied by, a fantastic edifice,' says Mr. Austen Leigh, which was of a 'castellated style,' and had been built by the second Marquis of Lansdowne. Of Jane's life at Southampton there is little more to be learned than can be gathered from the letters written from Castle Square, and most of these are so occupied with family affairs, and the death of her brother's wife at Godmersham, that they tell us less of her own doings than might otherwise have been the case. So far as we can judge, she seems to have had a certain amount of society at Southampton, and to have liked her life there as well as could have been expected. The change to Chawton in 1809, however, could not have been unwelcome. Mr. Knight was then able to offer to his mother and sisters the choice between a house on his Hampshire property and one upon his estate in Kent. The latter must have been either Eggarton or Bilting, both within easy distance of Godmersham; but I suppose that the associations connected with Hampshire caused the selection of Chawton Cottage, and there was passed the remainder of Jane's life; there were composed or completed most of her novels. 'Chawton Cottage' had formerly been the steward's house, enlarged and improved by Mr. Knight; there was nothing particular about it; the vicinity to the high road was somewhat inconvenient, but balanced by its proximity to the 'great house,' and it seems to have answered very well the purpose for which Mr. Knight had converted it into a habitable residence.

Mr. Austen Leigh gives a kindly warning to admirers of Jane Austen who might take it into their heads to make a pilgrimage to the place. There is nothing in it either beautiful or romantic, nothing to associate it with the memory of the immortal Jane. When Cassandra Austen died in 1845, it was turned into dwellings for labourers, and so altered that it cannot now be seen as it was in Jane's days. Very recently I paid a visit to it, whilst staying at Chawton House, in order that I might satisfy myself with my own eyes as to its present condition. As you come through the village of Chawton, along the road from Alton, the cottage is the last building upon your right hand, at the turning where the Winchester road branches off to the right, just before you reach the park in which stands Chawton House. It is built in rather a straggling, irregular style, and as you stand opposite it in the road, the first thing that strikes you is, that a large window between the door and the end of the cottage furthest from Alton has at some time or other been bricked up. This was, I believe, the window of the drawing-room of the house when Jane's family lived there, and this part of the place has now been converted into a labourer's club – an excellent institution, of which it would be well if there were more in England. I entered this club, the windows of which look away from the road, and there, perhaps upon the very spot where Jane had often sat in old days was a young labourer diligently perusing the 'Standard,' whilst opposite to him another was engaged on the 'Graphic,' and a third was contemplating with evident satisfaction the arrival of a foaming glass of beer, having, to judge from his appearance, just come from a hard day's work. There are three dwellings in the building besides the club; a low range of out-buildings, probably little touched since Jane's days, flanks the cottage on the Alton side, and behind it is a large garden, now divided among the cottagers, extending beyond the building, also on the further side, and altogether of sufficient size to have afforded plenty of space for the former occupants to indulge their taste for flowers and shrubs, and to have quiet walks therein when they wished for privacy. I pictured to myself the figure of Jane Austen walking up and down, intent upon deciding the fate of one of her heroes or heroines, or maturing the plot of her next book. This, however, required a somewhat strong effort of imagination, inasmuch as no signs of shrubs or walks remain, the ground is all under cultivation, and the only living creatures which met my view were two worthy rustics engaged in ordinary agricultural work. After you pass the cottage, a few hundred yards further along the road, you arrive at a gate on your left, on entering which you face Chawton House, an old Elizabethan-mansion built on rising ground, which is about two hundred yards from the gate, the beautiful little church standing upon your right hand when you have advanced about half-way from the gate to the house. This place has long been the seat of the Knight family, one of whom (William) had a lease of it in 1525 from Sir Thomas West, Lord Delawarr, who had acquired it through his wife, Elizabeth, one of the three daughters and co-heiresses of Sir John Bonvile. This William Knight's son John bought the house, and left a son Nicholas, who purchased the manor, advowson, and other lands, since which time it has remained in the family. The present house was mostly built by John Knight, in 1588, but it seems to have been originally a much larger building, although now quite large enough, and certainly comfortable enough, for any reasonable mortals. This John Knight appears as a subscriber of fifty pounds on the 27th May, 1588, among the 'names of persons in Hampshire who contributed to the funds raised by Queen Elizabeth to defray the expenses in resisting the Spanish Armada.' His descendants were devoted Royalists in the Civil Wars, and there is now at Chawton, among other interesting relics, a small ornament in the shape of a head of King Charles the First, said to have been given to his friends on the scaffold, which has come down from Sir Richard Knight, who was knighted for his services rendered to the Royal cause. This gentleman's name also appears among the list of those chosen by King Charles the Second at the restoration to be invested with the Order of the Royal Oak, which order was, after all, never established, the project being abandoned under the apprehension that it might perpetuate dissensions which were better consigned to oblivion. There is a handsome monument of white and black marble in a recess on the south side of the chancel in Chawton Church, whereon this Sir Richard Knight is represented by a full-length cumbent figure of white marble, in armour, holding a staff of office in his right hand.

The near neighbourhood of Chawton House must have been a great advantage and pleasure to Jane during her life at the cottage from 1809 until 1817. About half a mile from her old home there is a very large beech wood, 'Chawton Park' by name, in which the trees are magnificent, and there is no underwood to prevent those who are privileged to do so from walking beneath their shade. The wood belongs to the owner of Chawton House, and one can imagine it to have been a favourite haunt of Jane's. Whether she indulged herself in roaming there or not, however, I imagine her life to have been altogether very happy, because she was all the time with her own people, occupied in the home pursuits in which she delighted, having always her literary resources to fall back upon, and being cheered from time to time by visits to and from the relations she loved. There are no strange or exciting events to relate, no adventures to chronicle; the even tenor of her life affords no materials from which a romantic story could be woven, and I can only once again refer to the letters to tell their own tale. Alas! it is not a long one. Her health was evidently failing in the latter part of the year 1816, and in May of the following year the two sisters went together to Winchester, from which Jane was never to return. They took lodgings in the corner house of College Street, of which Jane writes that 'they are very comfortable. We have a neat little drawing room, with a bow-window overlooking Dr. Gabell's [headmaster of Winchester College] garden.' During the next two months Cassandra nursed her beloved sister with unfailing tenderness and assiduity. She was assisted from time to time by her sister-in-law, Mrs. James Austen (the 'Mary' of the letters), and her brothers James and Henry were able to be frequently with her. Cassandra's letters, herewith published, tell all that is to be told of Jane Austen's last days on earth, and tell it in language at once simple and pathetic. On July 18th she died, and on the 24th she was buried in Winchester Cathedral, 'near the centre of the north aisle, almost opposite to the beautiful chantry tomb of William of Wykeham,' the place of burial being marked by a large slab of black marble in the pavement, bearing the following inscription:–

> In memory of JANE AUSTEN, youngest daughter of the late Revd. George Austen, formerly Rector of Steventon, in this County. She departed this life on July 18, 1817, aged 41, after a long illness, supported with the patience and hope of a Christian. The benevolence of her heart, the sweetness of her temper, and the extraordinary endowments of her mind, obtained the regard of all who knew her, and the warmest love of her immediate connexions. Their grief is in proportion to their affection; they know their loss to be irreparable, but in their deepest affliction they are consoled by a firm, though humble,

hope that her charity, devotion, faith, and purity have rendered her soul acceptable in the sight of her Redeemer.

Mr. Austen Leigh, the writer of the memoir, subsequently inserted a brass in the north wall, near the grave, with an inscription denoting that it was to 'JANE AUSTEN, known to many by her writings, endeared to her family by the varied charms of her character, and ennobled by Christian faith and piety.' This appropriate text is added – 'She openeth her mouth with wisdom, and in her tongue is the law of kindness.' – Prov. xxxi.26.

Such are the memorials which the pious affection of relatives has erected over the last resting-place of Jane Austen, but a memorial more enduring has been created by her own hand. It is something to be able to say of any author or authoress that their works may be read without fear of harm; it is something more to be able to say, as we can truly say in this case, that, whilst in Jane Austen's books instruction and amusement are happily blended, the innate purity of her soul shines throughout each story and upon every page, and the mind of the reader is insensibly led to a love of all that is moral and virtuous and a distaste for anything that is the reverse. Jane did not live to enjoy the full knowledge of the popularity which was destined to be hers, but of it and of her it may be permitted to her relatives to be proud; and proud they are to believe that wherever the English language is read and spoken her works stand and will remain an everlasting memorial of genius turned to good account and talents exercised for the benefit and improvement of mankind.

The Novels

I was going to devote my next chapter entirely to Jane Austen's novels, when I recollected that such a chapter could by no means be made complete without referring to other novels and novelists at the same time. Such a chapter may be at once discarded by those who do not care for the subject, or who are satisfied to read and enjoy their novels without being troubled with my criticisms. But the theme is one too enticing for me to leave untouched, especially as I belong to the family which Jane Austen tells us were in her day 'great novel-readers,' and am not ashamed to confess that I have read as many as most people, and shall probably read a great many more. Novels are the sugar-plums of literature, and a library without novels would be as deficient as a childhood without sugar-plums, although neither the one nor the other would be satisfactory if unsupplied with something of a more substantial character.

I think it is immensely interesting to read side by side and compare the different styles of the novels which have charmed successive generations, and, in discussing Jane Austen's works, to contrast those of other writers who wrote practically for the same generation.

Several passages in our letters show us that Jane Austen was well acquainted with some at least of Richardson's novels. Of the general popularity of these works at the time of their publication I imagine there can be no doubt; and, indeed, this need cause one no surprise, if one supposes the British public to have accepted as an accurate estimate of them all, that which their talented author gives of 'Pamela' in his preface to the edition of 1742, which is so deliciously modest that I cannot forbear to transcribe it:–

> If to Divert and Entertain, and at the same time to Instuct and Improve, the Minds of the Youth of both sexes:
> If to inculcate Religion and Morality in so easy and agreeable a manner, as shall render them equally delightful and profitable:
> If to set forth, in the most exemplary lights, the Parental, the Filial, and the Social Duties:
> If to paint Vice in its proper Colours, to make it deservedly Odious; and to set Virtue in its own amiable Light, and to make it look Lovely:
> If to draw characters with Justness, and to support them distinctly.

And, after a few more 'ifs' of the same sort:–

> If to effect all these good Ends, in so probable, so natural, so lively a manner, as shall engage the Passions of every sensible Reader, and attach their regard to the story:
> If these be laudable or worthy recommendations, the Editor of the following Letters *ventures to assert that all these ends are obtained here, together.*

No doubt if all these desirable ends were thus secured, the popularity which the works of Samuel Richardson enjoyed, both at home and abroad, is accounted for without further trouble; and, even if the panegyric be deemed somewhat too highly drawn for acceptance in its entirety, the fact that the novels have been translated and published in most other countries must be accepted as evidence of their intrinsic merit.

Nevertheless, whatever attractions English society once found in 'Pamela,' 'Clarissa,' and 'Sir Charles Grandison,' I fancy that in the present day there are few people who would not find them insufferably dull, and still fewer who would not raise more serious objections both to the matters of which they treat and to the manner of their treatment. Certainly there is in these books a great deal of plain-speaking; a spade is called a spade, and there is much from which that which we now call good taste and delicacy would recoil.

One must make allowance, I suppose, for the advance of time and improvement of manners; and as 'Sir Charles Grandison' (the last of the three) was published some fifty years before Jane Austen wrote, these works must be considered as belonging altogether to another generation. Moreover, if we allow that their general tendency, at least, was to decry vice and exalt virtue, I am afraid that this is more than we can say of many of the 'sensational' novels which are so largely read in the present day. Take any one of these and you will find that, if crime is not actually made attractive, it is generally excused or extenuated; sympathy for the criminal is created or suggested, the story teems with startling incidents, and the best praise which can probably be accorded to the book is the somewhat negative recommendation that it has no particular tendency at all.

It certainly was not books of such a character and complexion which Jane Austen had in view in that spirited defence of novels and novel-readers which we find at the end of the fifth chapter of 'Northanger Abbey,' where, after describing it as the habit of Catherine Morland and Isabella Thorpe upon a rainy morning 'to shut themselves up, and read novels together,' she goes on 'Yes, novels; for I will not adopt that ungenerous and impolitic custom so common with novel-writers, of degrading by their contemptuous censure the very performances to the number of which they are themselves adding,' ... 'there seems almost a general wish of decrying the capacity and undervaluing the labour of the novelist, and of slighting the performances which have only genius, wit, and taste to recommend them. "I am no novel-reader," such is the common cant. "And what are you reading, Miss?" "Oh, it is only a novel," replies the young lady; while she lays down her book with affected indifference or momentary shame. "It is *only* 'Cecilia,' or 'Camilla,' or 'Belinda,'" or, in short, *only* some work in which the greatest powers of the mind are displayed, in which the most thorough knowledge of human nature, the happiest delineation of its varieties, the liveliest effusions of wit and humour, are conveyed to the world in the best chosen language.'

The mention of Miss Burney's novels in this passage reminds me of the frequent comparisons which have been instituted between her works and those of Jane Austen, and as I like to be in the fashion, I will add one more to the number of those who have compared the two.

My own taste for novel-reading commenced at a very early age; strange to say, such works of fiction had a greater attraction for me than the Latin grammar or even the Greek Testament, and having access to my father's library, which contained, amid a multitude of other literature, most of the best novels which had been published for many years past, I was enabled to indulge my taste to the full, and probably read a great deal more than was good for me. I well remember how in those days days I delighted in 'Evelina,' 'Cecilia,' and 'Camilla,' and I have little doubt that my verdict would have then been given in favour of Miss Burney, if I had been obliged to give a preference to one authoress over the other. But, on looking back to-day, I can fairly say that, if I have read these three novels three times over since those days (which I rather doubt), I have certainly perused Jane Austen's books five or six times as often, and much more frequently my special favourites, which I give here in their order of merit: 'Pride and Prejudice,' 'Mansfield Park,' and 'Emma.' These rank, to my mind, among the few books which one can take up again and again, and recur to particular passages and scenes which never seem to tire one in the reading. Miss Bronte's 'Jane Eyre' and 'Villette' are of the same class; Charles Reade's 'It is Never too Late to Mend,' Blackmore's 'Lorna Doone,' and Henry Kingsley's 'Ravenshoe' also may be admitted, but I do not remember any more, excepting always those masterpieces with which Dickens and Thackeray have adorned English literature, and some of those works which have made the names of Walter Scott and Bulwer household words among their countryman.

I own that I cannot place in the same rank any one of Miss Burney's novels. As far as plot and incident are concerned, there is perhaps something more of both to be discovered than in Jane Austen's works; but one of the principal merits of the latter is, that they excite a continuous interest in the mind of the reader, in spite of that absence of plot and incident which is really conspicuous on looking back at the conclusion of the book. Take, for instance, 'Sense and Sensibility': the whole story may be compressed into half-a-dozen sentences, and there is nothing exciting or sensational about it. But the characters of the two sisters, Elinor and Marianne, are sustained with wonderful fidelity throughout, and the reader is captivated by delineations of everyday life so simple and so true to nature as amply to supply the want of 'plot.' To this standard Miss Burney never seems to me to approach, or to come within a mile of Jane Austen, whilst in some instances she approximates both to the vulgar and the horrible, neither of which is to be found in the pages of the immortal Jane. The scenes in 'Evelina' in which the unfortunate Madame Duval is victimised by the French-hating Captain Mirvan (a character to read of which makes an Englishman blush for his nationality), the courtship of Mr. Dubster, and the whole character of Mrs. Mittin in 'Camilla,' as well as the eccentricities of Mr. Briggs in 'Cecilia,' certainly savour of vulgarity, whilst the 'horrible' is exemplified by the suicide of Mr. Harrell in 'Cecilia,' the death of Bellamy in 'Camilla,' and sundry other harrowing passages which season Miss Burney's performances. It may be said, perhaps, that she wrote for an earlier generation than Jane Austen, but the novels of both were published within the same forty years – i.e. between 1778 and 1818 – a proximity of publication which seems to render legitimate the comparison between the two. 'Evelina' was published in 1778, 'Cecilia' in 1782, 'Camilla' in 1796, and the 'Wanderer' in 1813; whilst Jane Austen's 'Sense and Sensibility' and 'Pride and Prejudice' were written, as we know, in 1796, although not published until 1811 and 1813; 'Northanger Abbey' was written in 1798, though not published until after the death of the authoress, in 1817; and 'Mansfield Park' and 'Emma' were published in 1814 and 1815.

I mention the 'Wanderer' with some hesitation, because I think it must be admitted to be so sadly inferior to Miss Burney's earlier novels, that her reputation must stand upon those first three, without the 'prestige' of which I cannot think that the 'Wanderer' would ever have met with any public fame. But, even with regard to these three, there is another remark which occurs to me as being one justified by the facts of the case, and which appears to establish the superiority of the one writer over the other. There must be admitted to be originality in some of Miss Burney's characters, as well as skill in the manner of their introduction and the description of their conduct. But what one character can we fix upon to remember, as we cannot help remembering the creations of Jane Austen; who, throughout all Miss Burney's novels, can be held to rival the provokingly silly Mrs. Bennet, so delightful in her folly, the insufferable Mr. Collins, the detestable Mrs. Norris, the inimitable Miss Bates, and a score more of the figures which Miss Austen places upon the canvas, in such a manner as to make us all feel that they are not only real living people, but personal acquaintances of our own?

It must certainly be conceded that there is much more of excitement to be found in the novels of Miss Burney than in those of Jane Austen; her heroines are placed in much more extraordinary situations; like loadstones, wherever they appear, they attract lovers; and the conduct of some of the latter is so violently extravagant as to have an appearance of unreality, which detracts from the interest of the story. Still it must be confessed that 'Evelina,' 'Cecilia,' and 'Camilla are all pleasant reading, and in each novel the heroine always satisfactorily escapes from her troubles and trials, and marries the right person in the most desirable and orthodox manner. This is only right and proper. I have no patience with authors who excite in our hearts an interest, more or less kind, for their heroes and heroines, and then harrow our feelings by either killing them or leaving them in a state of misfortune and misery. That is the sole fault I find with Charlotte Bronte's 'Villette,' wherein her 'Professor' is left in such a condition that we may suppose him either drowned in the Atlantic during a particularly stormy autumn, or happily rescued from that terrible fate, the probabilities all pointing to the catastrophe, and the possibility of the reverse being only insinuated in a gentle manner, which leads us to suppose that such good fortune can scarcely have occurred. It is said that Miss Bronte had meant to have killed her hero without doubt, but, deterred by the remonstrances of her father, conceded so much as to leave his fate in uncertainty; but, for my own part, I would rather have known the worst, and have read that last page again and again, with a feeling of disappointment and regret that there should have been any doubt left about the matter.

I have lately been reading the 'Diary and Letters' of Madame D'Arblay (Miss Burney), and cannot help saying that I find as great a contrast between the letters of the two authoresses as between their novels. It may be said that it is hardly fair to compare the private letters of one sister to another, such as those which I now give to the world, with those which were probably written, if not with a view to publication, at least with an idea that they might some day be published. I cannot, however, admit the unfairness and, if I did, I feel that I should be bringing a graver charge against Miss Burney than I intend to do – namely, the charge of having habitually 'made up' her letters for the public eye. Such letters are not really letters, in the sense in which we use the word as ordinarily applied to the written communications between relations and friends, wherein they express to each other their thought and describe their actions, with no intention that these should be known beyond the immediate circle in which the person moves to whom the letters are written. I assume Miss Burney's letters to be genuine, according to this view, and I say that neither they nor her Diary could ever have been written by Jane Austen. They are the records of a life which was lived much more before the world than the life of Jane and, without wishing in any degree to disparage the writer, I must say that they chronicle the praise and approval which she received both in public and in private, after a fashion, and to an extent from which the more sensitive and delicate nature of Jane Austen would have instinctively shrunk. It would have been impossible for her to have written – even for her own private perusal – the flattering words which it delighted Miss Burney to inscribe in her Diary as having been spoken of or to herself, and these letters are remarkable rather for the paucity than the frequency of allusions to her own writings. In fact, whilst Madame D'Arblay's 'Diary and Letters' tell us all about herself, who and what she was, how she lived, and with whom she passed her time – all, in short, that we could possibly desire to know about her and her proceedings – Jane Austen's letters, on the contrary, leave us to find out all these things for ourselves, and to regret that no further or more minute record is in existence. Of course I may be accused of partiality for my own relative in arriving at this result of a comparison between two authoresses both of whom have deserved well of the public, and each of whom may be appreciated and admired without decrying the other. Still, considering that, as far as concerns education outside her own home, general intercourse with the world and opportunities of observation, the advantage was certainly rather on the side of Miss Burney, I think it is but due to Jane Austen to maintain, as I confidently do, the great superiority of her writings in point of correctness of tone and taste, purity of style and language, and fidelity of description.

It is a less easy matter to compare her, as she has been compared, with Charlotte Bronte, or with our still more modern novelists, George Eliot and Charlotte Yonge. All these three have achieved for themselves the honour of elevating and purifying the aspirations of mankind, at the same time that in their several styles of fiction they have afforded to the world an infinite variety of intellectual amusement.

Of George Eliot and Charlotte Yonge I do not desire to write to-day. The one has been too recently taken from us to allow of the impartial discussion of her works, which, however meritorious, cannot be accurately gauged until further time has elapsed; for a book is, in this respect, like a beautiful landscape, and requires distance to develop it in its greater or smaller perfection. The other still lives to delight a large number of admiring readers, and, therefore, I prefer to say no more of her writings, except that I am quite sure that no one has ever been the worse, while very many have been greatly the better, for reading them.

With regard to Charlotte Bronte, who, like Jane Austen, was a clergyman's daughter, I would observe that her writings resemble Jane's in this one respect – that they take their complexion and character from the scenery and surroundings of her home – different altogether as were the two homes and the two writers. I have already confessed my partiality for 'Jane Eyre' and 'Villette,' and for these books, as well as for their authoress, I again avow an immense admiration. But they are books which Jane Austen never could or would have written, and some of the most interesting characters are such as it would never have entered into her mind to conceive. It never would have occurred to her, for instance, to take for a hero such a man as Mr. Rochester, who, having been so unfortunate as to marry a mad wife, thinks it perfectly legitimate to take a second during the lifetime of the first, without a hint to the intended victim of the true state of the case. Nor, in all probability, would she ever have thought of representing the sad victim as continuing to cherish such a devoted love for the man who had so proposed to wrong her, as to induce her to return, after a becoming interval, for a last look at the mansion in which the wrong had been so nearly perpetrated, and, finding that the mansion and mad wife had been conveniently burnt together, and the would-be bigamist crippled and blinded by the same happy event, to come lovingly back to him, and marry him as contentedly as if nothing particular had happened. These characters, however, *did* occur to Charlotte Bronte, and her delineation of them is such as to make them attractive by their very defects, and to carry her readers along with them, in spite of all the moral considerations which ought, I suppose, to deter us from reading about, and still more from liking, such naughty people. The truth is, that the style of the two writers is so dissimilar, the scenes and characters of which they treat are so entirely different, that it is hardly possible to compare them without doing injustice to one or the other. Fortunately, it is both possible and permissible to delight at one and the same time in the novels of both, and to appreciate the one without in the smallest degree underrating the other. I can honestly say that this is so in my own case, and that, loving them both, I do not care to compare them.

Jane Austen did not rush hastily before the public, nor was she encouraged by any rapid or extraordinary success. Mr. Austen Leigh gives us a letter which her father wrote to Mr. Cadell, the publisher, in November 1797, evidently referring to 'Pride and Prejudice,' which, under the name of 'False Impressions,' [this is a mistake, the name was *First Impressions*] had been her earliest production.

Sir. – I have in my possession a manuscript novel, comprising 3 vols., about the length of Miss Burney's 'Evelina.' As I am well aware of what consequence it is that a work of this sort should make its first appearance under a respectable name, I apply to you. I shall be much obliged, therefore, if you will inform me if you choose to be concerned in it, what will be the expense of publishing it at the author's risk, and what you will venture to advance for the property of it, if on perusal it is approved of? Should you give any encouragement, I will send you the work.
I am, Sir, your humble servant,
George Austen
Steventon, Overton, Hants,
November1, 1797.

This proposal, we are told, was declined by return of post, which the publisher must have regretted in subsequent years, though not with a deeper sorrow than the publisher at Bath [he was, in fact, a London publisher], who went so far as to buy 'Northanger Abbey' for 10 *l.*,and having laid it aside as worthless, was subsequently induced to return it, which he gladly did, for the same money, and was afterwards informed that it was by the author of 'Pride and Prejudice,' and other works which had then established the reputation of the authoress. It was Henry Austen who thus gained the manuscript, and disappointed the original purchaser by the subsequent disclosure of the state of the case.

Of the keen interest which Jane took in her books we have evidence in some of the letters in these volumes, and also in those which Mr. Austen Leigh has already given to the world. In one of the latter (January 29, 1813) she writes to her sister of 'Pride and Prejudice':–

I want to tell you that I have got my own darling child from London. On Wednesday I received one copy sent down by Falkener [manager or driver of the London to Southampton coach], with three lines from Henry to say that he had given another to Charles, and sent a third by the coach to Godmersham.

She is particularly enamoured of that creation of her own brain who has doubtless inspired the same sentiment in many other people – 'Elizabeth Darcy' (nee Bennet) – and of my mother's views upon the same subject she writes that:–

Fanny's praise is very gratifying. My hopes were tolerably strong of her, *but nothing like a certainty. Her liking Darcy and Elizabeth is enough. She might hate all the others, if she would.*

Although I have said that Jane Austen would never have chronicled all the laudatory remarks which might have been made, of and to her, by the admirers of her books, it must not be thought that I intend to represent her by any means as insensible to their praise or careless of the approbation which she received. This would have been unnatural, and therefore inconsistent with Jane's character. She undoubtedly appreciated the approval of her friends and the world, although she probably never anticipated the extent to which that approval would ultimately reach. Indeed, during her lifetime it was by no means general, and some of the criticisms which she herself collected are of a very contrary character. 'Mansfield Park' is called 'a mere novel,' 'Sense and Sensibility' and 'Pride and Prejudice' are stigmatized as 'downright nonsense.' Jane's language is called 'poor,' 'Emma' is declared to be 'not interesting,' and sundry opinions of an unfavourable tendency are recorded, which at the present day would be scouted as heretical by the literary world, but which only show the entirely different views which people are able to take upon the same subject.

It is refreshing to turn to such a genuine instance of admiration as that which I find narrated in a letter from Lady George Hill to my mother (her sister) in 1856. Speaking of the widow of Sir Guy Campbell, she says:–

Lady Campbell is "Pamela's" daughter and Lord Edwd. Fitzgerald's, and a most ardent admirer and enthusiastic lover of Aunt Jane's works. Aunt

Cassandra herself would be satisfied at her appreciation of them – nothing ever like them before or since. When she heard I was her niece she was in exstasies. "My dear, is it possible, are you Jane Austen's niece? that I should never have known that before! – come and tell me about her – do you remember her? was she pretty? wasn't she pretty? Oh, if I could but have seen her – Macaulay [Thomas Babington Macaulay, historian] says she is second to Shakespeare. I was at Bowood when Lord Lansdowne heard of her death – you cannot think how grieved and affected he was." I told her you *were her great friend and used to correspond with her. "Oh! write and ask her if she can only send me* one *of her own real letters, and tell me any and every particular she may know about her life, self, everything, I should be so delighted! Pray do write and ask her. The Archbishop of Dublin is another of her staunch admirers, and we have such long conversations about her." Then off she went, talking over and repeating parts of every one of the books, &c.*

This is by no means a solitary instance of the enthusiasm with which Jane's works are admired, and which has induced me to believe that anything connected with her which has not hitherto seen the light may not be unacceptable to those who, in a greater or less degree, share the opinions of Lady Campbell.

I have spoken elsewhere of Miss Tytler's Life of Jane Austen as being little more than a reproduction of Mr. Austen Leigh's 'Memoir.' I have, I confess, a much greater objection to her manner of treating the novels; for, although she speaks of touching them 'with a reverent hand,' she appears to me to have done just the reverse, and to have given an account of each book, sometimes in Jane Austen's words, with a running commentary, but generally in her own words, paraphrasing the original in such a manner as to spoil the symmetry of the work and destroy much of the beauty of the literary structure. Jane Austen's works did not, and do not, require this kind of handling. They should be read just as they were written, and it may be truly said of them that no books are more suitable for reading aloud. If *well* read, by a person who can understand the characters, and is in sympathy with the spirit of the book, they are admirably adapted for this purpose; but as a great number of people dislike anything of the kind, it is a comfort to be able to add that they are equally delightful to read to oneself. The reviews of these books which have already appeared, and the general knowledge of them which is possessed by the public, deter me from entering into any lengthy criticism of their peculiar excellences or occasional defects, nor do I think it either necessary or desirable to introduce quotations from novels which are so well known and appreciated by the great body of the readers of fiction.

There are, however, some few remarks which occur to me which may not be out of place, when we are considering the life and character of the gifted authoress of these works, and the circumstances under which they were written.

My first observation, then, is to the effect, that in all her books the heroes are decidedly inferior to the heroines; their characters less vigorously drawn, and themselves less interesting to the reader. There they are; because every heroine requires a hero; but in every case it is *she* and not *he* who is the prominent figure in the play.

Let us take the six novels into view. 'Pride and Prejudice' gives us Darcy; 'Sense and Sensibility,' Edward Ferrars; 'Northanger Abbey,' Henry Tilney; 'Mansfield Park,' Edmund Bertram; 'Emma,' Mr. Knightley; and 'Persuasion,' Captain Wentworth. Then look at the six heroines to match – Elizabeth Bennet (she is sometimes spoken of in the novel as 'Eliza Bennet,' and it is noticeable in our letters that Jane constantly calls her Elizabeths 'Eliza'), Elinor Dashwood, Catherine Morland, Fanny Price, Emma Woodhouse, and Anne Elliot – how much more we seem to know and to sympathise with the women than with the men throughout!

Darcy is really the only one for whom I feel much regard. He was certainly proud – a fault with which his education and surroundings had much to do; and, after all, it is perhaps not a wholly inexcusable pride which causes a man to hesitate before seeking to ally himself to a family of which the mother is insufferably vulgar and silly, several of the daughters objectionable, and the connections of a rank in life inferior to his own. Before his own heart was touched, it was neither wrong nor unnatural that he should strive to deter his friend Bingley from such a connection; and when he found himself vanquished by the charms of Elizabeth, he got rid of his pride with a rapidity as commendable as that with which the lady dismissed her 'prejudice.' I think that we are told more of Darcy than of most of Jane's other heroes, and the gradual alteration of Elizabeth's opinion of him as his character becomes better understood, and consequently better appreciated by her, is told and worked out in the most admirable manner. The gentleman's disposition was not one which made him likely to be the victim of a hasty attachment, and we watch with interest the stuggle which goes on in his mind before he allows his growing love for Elizabeth to conquer his objections to her family. When this result has been accomplished, the lady is still perfectly unaware of the conquest which she has achieved, and his declaration to her at the parsonage, where she is on a visit to her friend, Charlotte Collins, takes her entirely by surprise. This is a very good scene in itself, and marks an epoch in the hero's life; for her contumelious rejection of his advances has a marvellous effect upon him, to the very great improvement of his character. He accepts her decision in a manner which would have made it difficult for an ordinary writer to bring the two together again except by some strange and unusual method. Jane, however, manages it all in a most natural manner. Some words of Elizabeth regarding his two greatest offences – the abstracting of her sister's lover and the supposed wrongs of Wickham – induce him to write a long letter of explananation, which commences the change in the lady's heart, and from that moment Darcy only appears during the rest of the story in the most amiable light. I reject altogether the idea that the beauties of Pemberley had any effect in inducing Elizabeth to reconsider her refusal, and the sole doubt which remains upon my mind is the extent to which gratitude for his generous behaviour to her sister Lydia and her worthless husband really supplied the place of a warmer feeling in Elizabeth's heart. Gratitude, however, is a soil in which love readily grows and thrives, and in this instance the two may very well have existed and flourished side by side.

But, after Darcy, what hero have we in whom it is possible to feel any deep interest such as that which attaches us to several of the heroines? Edward Ferrers scarcely inspires much respect. Whatever excuse there may be for his conduct, he certainly behaves in such a manner as to induce Elinor to believe him attached to herself, whilst all the time he was engaged to another woman; for, if this had not been the case, the discovery of the engagement would not have filled the sensible heroine with such astonishment and dismay. His engagement was a boyish entanglement from which a man of any strength of character would have freed himself as soon as he found how much he had mistaken his own feelings, and how unsuited he and the lady were to each other, whilst there is something ludicrous in the rapidity with which, the very moment that his fool of brother has conveniently taken her off his hands, he hurries off to Elinor, to make her happy by the assurance that he had really been all the while false to the lady whom he had still proposed to marry, and had loved her and her alone, although perfectly prepared to sacrifice her to his absurd 'engagement,' His readiness, moreover, to become a clergyman because clerical preferment was found for him does not add to the attractiveness of his character; but Jane's picture of a clergyman is generally that of a second son who enters the profession in order to hold a family living, an idea not unnatural in the daughter of one who was himself the possessor of one of those benefices.

Our two next heroes, Henry Tilney and Edmund Bertram, are to be classed in this category. Of the former, indeed, we know very little. A ball-room acquaintance at Bath, whose father, being deceived as to Catherine Morland's position and fortune, invites her to Northanger, and courts her on his son's behalf until he finds out the mistake, we really know nothing more of this hero than that he displays a certain amount of amiable good sense in his conversations with Catherine, and a creditable degree of firmness in refusing to give her up at his father's command, or to root out of his heart that love which had been fostered, if not absolutely planted therein, by the paternal hand. The best we can say of this hero is that, if we knew him more, we should probably like him better.

Of Edmund Bertram we know a good deal more, and he should perhaps rank next to Darcy in order of merit. His uniform kindness to his little cousin (which won her heart from the first), his superiority to the other members of his family, and general good conduct throughout the story, entitle him to our respect, if not to something more. We cannot help feeling sorry that he did not show a little more firmness in the matter of the theatricals, but are pleased at his readiness to give Fanny Price (at a time when he was not the least in love with her) the full credit which she deserved for her conduct upon that trying occasion. He may be blamed for having been attracted by the fascinations of Miss Crawford, when Fanny was there to be compared with her, but this was one of the most natural things in the world. Miss Crawford undoubtedly *was* fascinating, and moreover had, and showed precisely that kind of predilection for Edmund which is so delightful to a young man when evinced by a pretty, clever, and agreeable person of the other sex. Besides, Fanny's perfections being before his eyes every day, naturally struck him less than those of her rival, and he went on comfortably considering his affection for his cousin to be of the most quiet and brotherly description, until the exigencies of the story compelled him to find out that it was something of a different nature. Take him all in all, I must own Edmund Bertram to be, after all, a hero above the average of such people, and one less inferior to the heroine than any other of his class in the six novels, excepting always Darcy, to whom I remain faithful; inasmuch as I think there is more power in his character and more masterly touches in its delineation.

I frankly confess that I never could endure Mr. Knightley. He interfered too much, he judged other people rather too quickly and too harshly, he was too old for Emma, and being the elder brother of her elder sister's husband, there was something incongruous in the match which I could never bring myself to approve. To tell the truth, I always wanted Emma to marry Frank Churchill, and so did Mr. and Mrs. Weston. Mr. Knightley, however, is an eminently respectable hero – too respectable, in fact, to be a hero at all; he does not seem to rise above the standard of respectability into that of heroism; and I should have disputed his claim to the position had he not satisfactorily established it beyond all possible doubt by marrying the heroine. But I have never felt satisfied with the marriage, and feel very sure that Emma was not nearly so happy as she pretended. I am certain that he frequently lectured her, was jealous of every agreeable man that ventured to say a civil word to her, and evinced his intellectual superiority by such a plethora of eminently sensible conversations, as either speedily hurried her to an untimely grave, or induced her to run away with somebody possessed of an inferior intellect, but more endearing qualities.

As to Captain Wentworth we are really told so little that there is nothing to say, except that he was a most faithful lover, but would have been wiser if he had not waited so long before letting the object of his affections know that such was the case. There is something pleasant about all Jane's sailors. Her sailor brothers were good examples of their class, and from them she probably drew her ideas. Not a word can be said against Captain Wentworth, and I sincerely hope that he and his Anne lived very happily all the rest of their lives.

But now let us turn from heroes to heroines, and I shall hardly know how to praise enough. Let Elizabeth Bennet stand forth; she is, to my mind, the most delightful character that ever condescended to display her perfections in a novel. She is not so intensely sweet and amiable as Anne Elliot, so sternly sensible as Elinor Dashwood, so simple and grateful as Fanny Price, so 'superior' as Emma; but not one of them all can equal her as a heroine of romance, and that principally because there is nothing romantic about her. She is drawn with such an exquisite touch that she is far more like a personal acquaintance than one 'in a book;' one enters into her feelings, understands her thoughts, her hopes and her fears, and cannot help taking the same sort of interest in her proceedings as if she was one's own relation. How cleverly is the line drawn which separates her and Jane from the rest of the Bennet family, to whom they were as much superior as if they had been the children of other parents! How keenly we share her discomfort at the vulgarity of her mother and the folly of her younger sisters; how warmly we appreciate her solicitude for Jane, and her anger against those who had separated that beloved sister from the man for whom she cared; how well we understand the warmth of honest sympathetic indignation with which she received Wickham's account of his ill-treatment by Mr. Darcy, and the equally honest contrition she experienced when she discovered how much that indignation had been misplaced; with what interest do we watch the gradual change of her opinion of Darcy, as the mists which have enveloped his character are gradually cleared away; and how heartily do we rejoice at her ultimate decision to accept the man who so well deserved her, and at the opportunity, created by the most bitter opponent of the marriage, which happily brought him a second time to her feet!

I do not know any character in any novel that ever was written whose career from first to last, throughout the whole book, one follows with such intense and continuous interest as that of this charming Elizabeth. There are several scenes to which I might call special attention, as illustrative of her character; but I will be content with one, to my mind the most delicious and inimitable scene in the whole book – I mean the interview between Elizabeth and Lady Catherine de Burgh, when the latter, furious at the report that her nephew Mr. Darcy is about to marry Elizabeth, drives over, in all the dignity and grandeur which can be imparted by a chaise and four, to insist upon its being immediately contradicted. If it were possible that our admiration of Elizabeth could be increased, her conduct and language during this trying interview would certainly accomplish such a result. The calmness and self-possession with which she encounters the arrogant insolence of her visitor, the courageous and undaunted spirit with which she refuses to be bullied and brow-beaten, and the acute but perfectly civil manner in which she holds her own, and puts her adversary entirely in the wrong throughout the whole of the conversation, are described with a rare talent, and the whole scene is one which, both in its conception and execution, is undoubtedly one of the most excellent that ever was written.

I could dwell with delight upon Elizabeth for a much longer time, but in my comparison of heroes and heroines I can only afford a short space to each, and therefore hurry on to 'Sense and Sensibility,' where Elinor and Marianne Dashwood are the two prominent figures, and I suppose that the former, being 'Sense,' has the best claim to the heroine's niche. She is certainly an excellent young woman, though, to my mind, less interesting than some of her sister heroines. It undoubtedly was a position the reverse of pleasant to be made the unwilling confidant of a girl so inferior to herself in good-breeding and refinement as Lucy Steele, and to receive as the first great secret the news that her own lover was engaged to this obnoxious young woman. It was disagreeable, too, to have a sister whose 'sensibility' took the form of love-sick extravagances which must have constantly grated against Elinor's 'sense,' and who, by carrying her hysterical sentimentality so far as nearly to die of it, caused a disagreeable interruption to the tranquillity of their domestic life. But, under all these circumstances, Elinor evinced a fortitude and self-control which must command our respect if it does not attract our admiration; she takes a common-sense view of everything which occurs, submits with proper resignation to things which appear inevitable, condoles with and comforts her sister in her love disappointment without disclosing her own much greater reason to be heart-broken, and contentedly accepts and settles down with her lover when time and the vagaries of Miss Lucy Steele have enabled him to declare himself in his true colours. Altogether she is an admirably-drawn character, and the contrast between her 'sense' and the 'sensibility' of Marianne, so well depicted and sustained, elevates her, at her sister's expense, to a very creditable place among the list of heroines.

Upon the whole, I think Catherine Morland the least interesting of the aforesaid list, and yet she is the heroine of such an interesting story, that I feel sorry as soon as I have written the words. I am consoled, however, by the reflection that the authoress begins her book by the remark that in her early youth nobody would ever have supposed Catherine to have been born a heroine. She was the daughter of a clergyman, one of a large family, rather uninformed, very romantic, and, for the rest of it, a good-tempered, well-disposed, and good-looking girl, with no very marked characteristic or striking ability, or anything else to distinguish her from the common herd of girls. She is made interesting by the story, and as she generally takes a right view of things, is grateful for any kindness shown to her, shrinks from vulgarity, takes naturally to good things and people, and behaves with great propriety in the different positions in which she is placed, one can forgive her too great fondness for romances replete with horrors, and the readiness with which she harbours the suspicion that General Tilney had made away with his wife. We are able, upon the whole, to take her to our affections as a commendable specimen of the heroine tribe, although certainly eclipsed by other creations of the same fertile brain.

Fanny Price is altogether of a different calibre, and, according to my opinion, contests with Emma Woodhouse the second place after Elizabeth Bennet. They are, of course, very different people in many respects, but as a matter of taste I am inclined to give the preference to Fanny. She is so gentle, so grateful, so ready to do a kindness to any and everybody, so submissive to Aunt Norris, so thoughtful for Lady Bertram, so good a daughter, so loving a sister, such an affectionate cousin, such a true and faithful friend, that one is inclined to wonder how a character can have been drawn with so few faults as to be near perfection, and yet so natural that it is impossible not to recognize it as a true picture. From her first entry into Mansfield Park down to the very end of the story, our hearts go out to Fanny Price, and we love her with a steady and unvarying love. She wins our sympathy from the moment we make her acquaintance, and keeps it throughout her whole career. She had something to bear, too, during her sojourn in her uncle's house. There are few things more difficult to endure than injustice, and of this Aunt Norris inflicted a perpetual and unlimited amount upon the devoted head of her long-suffering niece. But there are worse things to endure in life than even the injustice of an ill-conditioned old aunt. It must have been a sore trial to Fanny to see Mary Crawford stealing from her that which she prized beyond everything else – her cousin Edmund's affection – and a sorer trial still to see him bestowing that affection upon a woman who, with all her beauty and other attractions, did not come up to Fanny's standard, and whom she could not deem worthy of her cousin. Very trying, too, must have been those conversations with Edmund, wherein, doubtful of himself and of Miss Crawford, he spoke of the latter to Fanny, evidently seeking to be strengthened and encouraged by her in his affection for her rival; and trying, too, and in no ordinary degree, must have been the friendship of that rival for herself, especially when it took the form of endeavouring to secure her acceptance of Henry Crawford for her husband. But Fanny came well and nobly out of every ordeal. The same simple, quiet, honest determination to do what her conscience told her to be right, which sustained her in that severe trial in the matter of the theatricals in the absence of Sir Thomas, stood her equally in good stead throughout all her other troubles and trials. If we admire Elizabeth Bennet most, I really think that, upon the whole, we love Fanny Price best. It is impossible not to love such a thoroughly unselfish character, and I think she must be admitted to be one of the best of heroines and most charming of people.

The partisans of 'Emma' must forgive me for placing her only third on the list. She is a very charming creature, and all the more so for not having been drawn faultless, but with just enough imperfection to set her off, without taking her out of the category of ordinary mortals, to whom absolute perfection is an impossibility. Her propensity for match-making was decidedly objectionable, but as she failed so signally in this respect, it was probably its own punishment. Left the mistress of her father's house at an early age by the marriage of her sister, Emma ran a good chance of being spoiled, and such would probably have been her fate but for the excellent governess provided for her in the person of Miss Taylor, who became an equally excellent wife for Mr. Weston just before the commencement of the story. Still, Miss Emma seems to have been tolerably self-willed, and to have been possessed of an independent spirit of her own, and a confidence in her own judgment which the adulation of her neighbours must have considerably increased. One does not exactly see *why* Emma Woodhouse should have been regarded as a little goddess in her own neighbourhood, but such appears to have been the case, and she is depicted throughout the story as the intellectual superior of everybody else, except Mr Knightley, who treats her more like an elder brother than a lover, administers to her a well-deserved rebuke upon the occasion of her making an unkindly satirical remark to poor Miss Bates, and graciously marries her when he finds that he has been mistaken in supposing her attached to Frank Churchill. 'Emma' is undoubtedly a well-drawn character, and one that enjoys a deserved popularity; but I confess that she is not my favourite heroine, as she is the favourite of many admirers of 'Jane Austen's' novels, and had I been the hero of the piece, I am by no means sure that I should not have preferred to marry Jane Fairfax, who, despite her mistake in entering into a secret engagement with Frank Churchill, is a sweet and womanly character, and would have required less looking after and management than the 'superior' Emma.

I have but little to say of 'Anne Elliot,' the heroine of 'Persuasion,' but that little is good. With a worldly father and unsympathetic elder sister, her early life, after the loss of her mother, was not of the happiest description, nor had its happiness been increased by the breaking off of her engagement with Lieutenant Wentworth, their mutual attachment having been thwarted by that want of pecuniary resources which so often operates as a barrier in similar cases. Anne Elliot, taking after her mother rather than her father, was of a sweet disposition, amiable in every relation of life, and so faithful to her first love as to have been quite ready to 'take up' with him again when he came home eight years later with the rank of Captain, and his sister's husband, Admiral Crofts, had taken Kellynch, Sir Walter Elliot's family place. The gentleman, however, from timidity, doubt of her affection, and afterwards from the report that she was to marry her rich but profligate cousin, Mr. Elliot, held aloof, and did not renew his former suit. Sweet, modest, tender-hearted, womanly Anne Elliot behaved just as she should have done under such a condition of affairs. Of course she never obtruded herself upon her lover in the slightest degree, or took any steps to let him know the unchanged state of her affections. She remained true to him throughout all temptations to the contrary, refused her cousin, kept her secret with proper reserve until the right moment and opportunity arrived, and then without hesitation forgave Captain Wentworth his doubts and delay, owned her continued affection without any pretence of concealment, and obtained the husband for whom she had so long waited, and whom she so well deserved. We do not hear so much of Anne Elliot as of some of Jane's other heroines, but we hear enough to sympathise with her from first to last, to appreciate the sweetness of her character, and to wish her every possible happiness in her married life.

At the conclusion of my list of heroines I retain my opinion of their superiority to the heroes of these novels, with the additional remark that perhaps this may result from the fact that they are created by the hand of a woman, who might be better able to understand and describe the feelings and actions of her own than those of the other sex. Still, it must be allowed that she shows a marvellous knowledge of both, and that few, if any, men who have attempted novel-writing have equalled either the male or female creations of the 'inimitable Jane.'

It would occupy more time and space than I can afford if I were to criticize in detail one half or one quarter of the prominent characters in these novels. I have spoken elsewhere of a certain want of 'plot' and 'incident,' but this I say in praise rather than blame, the wonder being at the manner in which the books are made so intensely interesting with so little of either. Perhaps the truth lies in the fact that, whilst a weak or imperfectly drawn character requires some exciting events to make it interesting, Jane's characters are so well drawn as to be interesting under the most trivial and ordinary circumstances.

Take one instance from 'Pride and Prejudice.' There is nothing very remarkable in a man having married a silly wife, although one is inclined to wonder that a person with such a keen sense of humour and lively appreciation of the folly of other people as Mr. Bennet should have been caught by a pretty face when handicapped by such intense and silly vulgarity as that which his wife displayed. Such things *did* happen in Jane Austen's days, and probably happen still; but for all that one may wonder on, consoling oneself with the reflection that the man must always be punished for the rest of his life. But the remarkable thing is, that out of this somewhat ordinary couple Jane manages to create two very amusing characters, whose daily conversations required no stirring events of any kind to make them so interesting as to cause the reader always to wish they were longer. Mr. Bennet bore his fate with more equanimity than many men would have done, and his quaint, dry remarks are irrestibly comic, and almost as amusing as the absurdities of his better-half.

Mr. Collins, again, is really only a not uncommon character slightly exaggerated. But the exaggeration is carried out after a fashion so delightfully clever that Mr. Collins becomes one of the very best characters in the book, and his letters are not to be equalled. The announcement of his intention to visit Longbourn House, with the scarcely concealed view of marrying one of his cousins by way of atonement for being next in the entail, and, therefore, the future possessor of their home on their father's death, is our first introduction to this worthy individual, and we are at once led to expect amusement from such a character. The reality, however, even surpasses our anticipations. His conversations are charming; the self-assurance with which he proposes to Elizabeth, the readiness with which he consoles himself with her friend, Charlotte Lucas; above all, the grateful servility with which he accepts the crumbs which fall from Lady Catherine de Burgh's table, and magnifies her with continuous adoration – all combine to enhance our admiration of the skill which could draw such a character with a touch which makes it amusingly ridiculous without being unnaturally absurd. But perhaps the letter in which he condoles with Mr. Bennet on the occasion of Lydia's elopement, and that in which he warns Elizabeth against marrying Lady Catherine's nephew without the consent of that august potentate, are two of the finest pieces of composition in the book. The first is simply inimitable, and the second falls little short of it.

The Collins episode in this book suggests a comparison with that of Mr.

Elton in 'Emma.' In each case the gentleman is refused by the heroine, and in each marries somebody else with very little delay. Mr. Collins, however, has the advantage both in the wife he selects and the behaviour which he adopts. He cheerfully accepts the situation, receives Elizabeth at the parsonage, and only revenges himself by parading before her eyes as much as possible the inestimable advantages conferred upon him by the vicinity of Rosings.

Mr. Elton, a man equally conceited but of greater ability, shows himself to be more little-minded in a similar situation, for he evidently resents his refusal to the end of the chapter, and both he and his disagreeable wife lose no opportunity of sneering at and decrying Emma, who had not only been guilty of the unpardonable offence of rejecting his advances, but had bitterly wounded his vanity by believing them to have been intended for Harriet Smith. Perhaps Mr. Collins's innate and intense satisfaction with himself and all that belonged to him may have had some share in inducing him to forgive Elizabeth when he had secured Charlotte; but at all events he shines in comparison with Mr Elton, and should have all the credit he deserves.

The character of Lady Catherine de Burgh has sometimes been deemed exaggerated; but in Jane Austen's days the deference paid to rank and position was far greater than at present, and an arrogant woman, accustomed to have her own way and impatient of contradiction, is, I suppose, pretty much the same kind of being in all ages of the world. If there is any criticism which may fairly be made, it is the total want of good-breeding which Lady Catherine, supposed to be a well-bred woman, exhibits in her conversations with those whom she deems her inferiors, whose feelings she apparently seeks to outrage every minute in the most unnecessary manner, and to whom she speaks after a fashion utterly at variance with the present usages of society. Some allowance must of course be made for the change in times and manners which has taken place, but in this one particular it is difficult not to incline to the opinion that the character is a little exaggerated. She is splendid, however, in the interview with Elizabeth, to which I have already alluded, and as a set-off to the heroine, as well as to Mr. Collins, is perfection. Indeed, one of the most delicious things in the whole book is the way in which her arrogant interference is made to punish itself, and causes her to impart to Darcy that which he might not otherwise have discovered – namely, that change in Elizabeth's feelings which encourages him to approach her once more. The way in which he does this is very natural, and exceedingly well told, and, in fact, there is hardly a page in this book which does not excite our wonder that it should have been written by a girl of twenty-one, ignorant of the world outside her own family circle.

There is more 'finish' about 'Emma,' and, perhaps, also about 'Mansfield

Park,' but, take it all in all, 'Pride and Prejudice' is the most wonderful production of the authoress.

One comfort in Jane's novels lies in the fact that, as I have already observed of Miss Burney's works, they all end in the happy marriage of her heroines, so that we are left in no sad uncertainty as to their respective fates. An elopement or two on the part of their relatives (Lydia Bennet and Julia Bertram to wit) only adds to their own respectability by the contrast, and they themselves are always people of the greatest propriety and most unblemished character. This is just as it should be, for we are bound to take a more or less tender interest in the heroine of the book, and it is decidedly preferable to experience this feeling for a well-conducted and respectable young woman than for the doubtful and sometimes really disreputable heroines whom we encounter too often in more modern novels. Jane's heroines never transgress the bounds of conventional good-behaviour. They enjoy their dancing, their novel-reading, their innocent flirtations, and other similar amusements which enlivened the society of their day; but they indulge in no extravagances, do nothing out of the common way, and are a model set of heroines whom nobody but Jane could have made so entertaining and interesting as she has certainly done. They all deserve to marry comfortably – which seems to have been Jane's idea of the true object of a girl's life – and it is impossible to grudge their deserts to such meritorious people.

This leads me to another observation upon the drift and tendency of these novels. I think they really do all that the author of 'Pamela' declares that he does in the self-laudatory preface which I have quoted. They make virtue lovely, and vice the reverse; they show how the one brings its own reward, the other its own punishment, and without ever preaching to us, they continually impress upon our minds lessons of a purifying and elevating tendency. The different motives which influence men and women in various circumstances of life – the special faults which beset certain natures – the effects which those faults produce upon others, the opposite results of a religious training and of a mere worldly education; all these are drawn by the master-hand of a great artist, and are brought before us with a fidelity of description which can hardly fail to impress the reader.

There is very little direct mention of religion, as a mainspring of action, in any of Jane Austen's books. In the 'religious novels' of which the literary world has had a copious supply during the last fifty years, religion is often introduced in such a manner as doubtless to satisfy the godly reader, but effectually to deter the worldling from the perusal of the work. People are represented as so habitually pious, so fond of church-going and church-restoring, and so very much better than the common run of men, that the book does not attract those whose lives are less exemplary, and who feel that the narrative is of worlds outside and apart from their own. There is nothing of this in Jane's books. So far from any parade of religion, there is so little allusion to anything if the kind that it would be a misnomer to apply the term 'religious novel' to any of her works. But yet, throughout them all, the moral and virtuous thoughts and actions, which can spring only from a mind imbued with the principles of religion, are constantly brought before us, in such a manner as to command our respect, and to afford us, at the same time, an example of the way in which such thoughts can be cherished, and such actions performed, without any separation from the world, or the necessity of conducting ourselves differently from other people. There is a purity of thought as well as of style, an undercurrent of refinement, and an imperceptible suggestion of good which have not improbably had more salutary effects than any 'religious' novels that have ever been written. But I will indulge myself in no further criticism. Popular approbation has already stamped these books as among the greatest of English novels. I am glad of the opportunity of throwing such further light upon the life of the writer as can be afforded by those of her letters which remain to us, and I only regret that I have not more materials from which to furnish the lovers of her works still further details of the life of Jane Austen.

Letters

1796

The first two letters which I am able to present to my readers were written from Steventon to Jane Austen's sister Cassandra in January, 1796. The most interesting allusion, perhaps, is to her 'young Irish friend,' who would seem by the context to have been the late Lord Chief Justice of Ireland, though at the time of writing only 'Mr. Tom Lefroy.' I have no means of knowing how serious the 'flirtation' between the two may have been, or whether it was to this that Mr. Austen Leigh refers when he tells us that 'in her youth she had declined the addresses of a gentleman who had the recommendations of good character and connections, and position in life, of everything, in fact, except the subtle power of touching her heart.' I am inclined, however, upon the whole, to think, from the tone of the letters, as well as from some passages in later letters, that this little affair had nothing to do with the 'addresses' referred to, any more than with that 'passage of romance in her history' with which Mr. Austen Leigh was himself so 'imperfectly acquainted' that he can only tell us that there *was* a gentleman whom the sisters met 'whilst staying at some seaside place,' whom Cassandra Austen thought worthy of her sister Jane, and likely to gain her affection, but who very provokingly died suddenly after having expressed his 'intention of soon seeing them again.' Mr. Austen Leigh thinks that, 'if Jane ever loved, it was this unnamed gentleman'; but I have never met with any evidence upon the subject, and from all I have heard of 'Aunt Jane,' I strongly incline to the opinion that, whatever passing inclination she may have felt for anyone during her younger days (and that there was once such an inclination is, I believe, certain), she was too fond of home, and too happy among her own relations, to have sought other ties, unless her heart had been really won, and that this was a thing which never actually happened. Her allusion (letter two) to the day on which 'I am to flirt my last with Tom Lefroy' rather negatives the idea that there was anything serious between the two, whilst a later reference (letter ten) to Mrs. Lefroy's 'friend' seems to intimate that, whoever the latter may have been, any attachment which existed was rather on the side of the gentleman than of the lady, and was not recognized by her as being of a permanent nature.

The first letter is written on her sister Cassandra's birthday, and is directed to her at Kintbury, where she seems to have been staying with her friend Elizabeth Fowle (often referred to in these letters as "Eliza"), *née* Lloyd, whose sister was the 'Mary' who 'would never have guessed' the 'tall clergyman's' name, and who afterwards married the 'James' (Jane's brother) who was taken into the carriage as an encouragement to his improved dancing. Elizabeth Lloyd married the Rev. Fulwar Craven Fowle, who was the Vicar of Kintbury, near Newbury. Mr. Fowle was, I have always heard, a good sportsman, a good preacher, and a man of some humour. He had a hunter at one time which he named 'Biscay,' because it was 'a great roaring bay.' He commanded a troop of Volunteers in the war-time, and King George the Third is reported to have said of him that he was 'the best preacher, rider to hounds, and cavalry officer in Berks.'

The Harwoods of Deane were country neighbours of whom we shall find frequent mention. They were a very old Hampshire family, living upon their own property, which was formerly much larger than at the date of our letters, and which, I believe, has now passed away altogether from its former possessors. Close to Deane is Ashe, of which Mr. Lefroy was rector, and Ashe Park, now occupied by Col. R. Portal, and in 1796 belonging to Mr. Portal, of Laverstoke, was at that time occupied by the family of St. John. The Rivers family lived, I believe, at Worthy Park, Kingsworthy, and I imagine the Miss Deanes to have been of the family of that name living in Winchester. One member of this family has since held the neighbouring living of Bighton. The Lyfords were medical men, father and son, living at Basingstoke. It will be noted that one of them attended Mrs. George Austen in the illness mentioned in the earlier letters, and it was one of the same family who was Jane Austen's doctor in her last illness at Winchester. In a little volume concerning the 'Vine hunt' which he printed privately in 1865, Mr. Austen Leigh tells a good story of the grandfather of the 'John Lyford' here mentioned, 'a fine tall man, with such a flaxen wig as is not to be seen or conceived by this generation.' He knew nothing about fox-hunting, but had a due and proper regard for those who indulged in it, and it is recorded of him that upon one occasion, having accidentally fallen in with Mr. Chute's hounds when checked, he caused great confusion by galloping up in a very excited state, waving his hat, and exclaiming 'Tally-ho! Mr. Chute. Tally-ho! Mr. Chute.' Not that he had seen the fox, but because he imagined that 'Tally-ho!' was the word with which fox-hunters ordinarily greeted each other in the field.

Among the people mentioned as having been at 'the Harwoods' ball' were several who deserve notice. 'Mr. Heathcote' was William, the brother of Sir Thomas, the fourth Baronet of Hursley. Two years after the date of this letter, viz., in 1798, he married Elizabeth, daughter of Lovelace Bigg Wither, Esq., of Manydown; he was Prebendary of Winchester, and pre-deceasing his brother, his son William succeeded the latter as fifth baronet in 1825, sat for Hants in five Parliaments, and afterwards for Oxford University for fourteen years. He was made a Privy Councillor in 1870, and lived till 1881, very greatly respected and beloved by a large circle of friends. In 1796 the Heathcotes lived at Worting, a house in a village of the same name, situate about five or six miles from Steventon. Mr. J. Portal was Mr. Portal, of Freefolk House, near Overton. He married twice, and, living till 1848, was succeeded by the eldest son of his second wife, Melville Portal, who was afterwards for a short time member for North Hants. Mr. John Portal's eldest daughter by his first marriage was Caroline, who married Edward Austen's fourth son William. Adela, one of his daughters by his second wife, became the second wife of the 'little Edward' mentioned in the letters, who was the eldest son of the same Edward Austen, Jane's brother, the owner of Godmersham and Chawton. She died in 1870. Mr. Portal's brother William lived at Laverstoke, which, as well as Ashe Park, belonged to him. Mr. Bigg Wither, of Manydown, had two other daughters besides Mrs. Heathcote, namely, Alithea, with whom 'James danced,' and Catherine, who afterwards married the Rev. Herbert Hill, who enjoyed the double distinction of being Southey's uncle and (at one time) chaplain to the British factory at Lisbon. 'Ibthorp' was a house near Lord Portsmouth's place, Hurstbourne, where lived as a widow Mrs. Lloyd, the mother of Eliza, Martha, and Mary. Her husband, the Rev. Nowys Lloyd, had held the two livings of Enbourne near Newbury and Bishopston, Wilts, and at the latter place fell in love with 'Martha Craven,'who was living there with an 'Aunt Willoughby,' having run away from a mother whom family tradition alleges to have treated her badly. Mrs. Lloyd died in April, 1805, when the Austens were at Bath. The Coopers, whose arrival is expected in the first, and announced in the second letter, were Dr. Cooper, already mentioned as having married Jane Austen's aunt, Jane Leigh, with his wife and their two children, Edward and Jane, of whom we shall frequently hear. I have no means of knowing who is referred to as 'Warren,' but there was, and is, a Hampshire family of that name, of Worting House, Basingstoke, and it may very likely be one of them, since they were of course near neighbours, and likely to be intimate at Steventon. Neither can I bring proof positive as to the identity of Mr. Benjamin Portal, which is the more to be regretted because a person with such 'handsome' eyes deserves to be identified. There was, however, a certain clergyman, the Rev. William Portal, a member of the Freefolk and Laverstoke family, who had a wife, seven sons, and the Rectory of Stoke Charity in Hants. None of these sons married, but, judging by dates, some of them must have been living about 1796, and probably Benjamin was one of them.

The third letter of 1796 is dated from London, where the writer had evidently stopped for a night on her way from Steventon to Rowling, a journey which in those days was a much more serious affair than at present, when a few hours of railroad take us comfortably from one place to the other. Rowling was and is a small place belonging to the Bridges family, being about a mile distant from Goodnestone. Edward Austen, Jane's brother, lived there at this time, though whether his brother-in-law, Sir Brook, let it or lent it to him I cannot say. Probably the former; at any rate, here he lived, and here were his three eldest children born. The subsequent letters (four to seven inclusive) were written whilst Jane was visiting her brother, and are full of touches of her own quaint humour. Mrs. Knight had not left Godmersham at this time, but was about to do so, and my grandfather and grandmother were going to take possession. The 'Mr. and Mrs. Cage' were Lewis Cage and his wife, Fanny Bridges. Harriet and Louisa were the two unmarried sisters of the latter; Edward, their brother, and the 'Mr. and Mrs. Bridges' must have been Henry Bridges, next brother to Sir Brook (fourth baronet), who was Rector of Danbury and Woodham Ferrers, in Essex, who had married Jane Hales the year before this letter was written. Sir Thomas Hales, his father-in-law, was M. P. for Dover, and had four daughters besides Jane, of whom the two youngest, Harriet and Caroline, are here mentioned. Harriet died unmarried, Caroline married Mr. Gore in 1798. Sir Thomas had died in 1773, and was succeeded by his son of the same name, who dying in 1824, and having only one daughter, the baronetcy became extinct. The allusion to 'Camilla in Mr. Dubster's summer-house' (to whom Jane likens herself when her brother's absence obliged her to stay at Rowling till he should return to escort her home) will be understood by those who have perused Miss Burney's novel of that name, and to those who have not will, I hope, be an inducement to do so, as it will certainly repay the perusal. Lady Waltham was the wife of Lord Waltham, and a great friend of Lady Bridges.

There are other allusions to things and people scattered throughout these letters, to understand which it is necessary to bear in mind that they are often made in the purest spirit of playful nonsense, and are by no means to be taken as grave and serious expressions of opinion or statement of facts. When, for instance, speaking of Mrs. Knight, the widow of Godmersham, she says 'it is imagined that she will shortly be married again,' and in the next letter speaks of her brother Edward as intending to get some of a vacant farm into his occupation, 'if he can cheat Sir Brook enough in the agreement,' she is writing in the same spirit of fun as when she presently tells us that her brother had thoughts of 'taking the name of Claringbould,' that 'Mr. Richard Harvey's match is put off till he has got a better Christian name,' and that two gentlemen about to marry 'are to have one wife between them.' Mrs. Knight was advanced in years at the time, and her marrying a second time a very unlikely thing to occur; and I suppose no man ever lived who was less likely to 'cheat' or take advantage of another than my grandfather, Edward Austen. It is in the same vein of fun, or of originality, if the phrase be better, that she speaks (letter seven) of 'the Captain John Gore, commanded by the Triton,' instead of 'the Triton,' commanded by Captain John Gore,' and, in the postscript to the same letter, of her brother Frank being 'much pleased with the prospect of having Captain Gore under his command,' when of course the relative position of the two was precisely the reverse. Many people will think this explanation superfluous, but I have so often met with matter-of-fact individuals who persist in taking everything in its plain and literal sense, that I think it well to make it. It is to this day a peculiarity of some of the Austens (and doubtless not confined to them) to talk and write nonsense to each other which, easily understood between themselves at the time, might have a curious appearance if published a hundred years hence. Such expressions as a 'chutton mop' for 'a mutton chop,'to clerge (i. e. to perform the duties of a clergyman), and to 'ronge' – i. e. 'to affect with a pleasing melancholy' – are well enough when used and appreciated in family letters and conversations, but might give rise to curious dissertations upon the different use of particular English words at different times, if given without comment or explanation to the public, whilst the literal interpretation of things said in jest to those who understood the jest at the time would cause the most serious mistakes as to the real meaning of the writer and the spirit in which she wrote.

The sixth and seventh letters are full of local and personal allusions of more or less interest. The dinner-party at Nackington is pleasantly described, and the wealth of Mr. Milles referred to in the pretended expectation expressed that he would have advanced money to a person with whom he had no relationship which might have induced such generosity. It was natural that Lady Sondes' picture should be found in her father's house, for in that relationship stood Mr. Milles to her. She was at this time living at Lees Court with her husband, who did not die until ten years later. Bifrons was at this time in the possession of the Taylor family, from whom it afterwards passed to the Conynghams; but I do not know to whom Jane refers as the individual upon whom she once fondly doated, although the 'once' could not have been very long before, as at this time she had not yet completed her twenty-first year. Mrs. Joan Knatchbull lived in Canterbury. She was the only sister of Sir Wyndham Knatchbull, who died in 1763, when the title and estates went to his uncle. The other people referred to in these letters are either dealt with in the preliminary chapters, or do not appear to require further notice, having little to do with Jane or her family. [Jane's siblings James, Edward, Henry, Frank, Cassandra and Charles, and their families are mentioned frequently throughout the letters].

I

Steventon: Saturday (January 9).

In the first place I hope you will live twenty-three years longer. Mr. Tom Lefroy's birthday was yesterday, so that you are very near of an age.

After this necessary preamble I shall proceed to inform you that we had an exceeding good ball last night, and that I was very much disappointed at not seeing Charles Fowle of the party, as I had previously heard of his being invited. In addition to our set at the Harwoods' ball, we had the Grants, St. Johns, Lady Rivers, her three daughters and a son, Mr. and Miss Heathcote, Mrs. Lefevre, two Mr. Watkins, Mr. J. Portal, Miss Deanes, two Miss Ledgers, and a tall clergyman who came with them, whose name Mary would never have guessed.

We were so terrible good as to take James in our carriage, though there were three of us before, but indeed he deserves encouragement for the very great improvement which has lately taken place in his dancing. Miss Heathcote is pretty, but not near so handsome as I expected. Mr. H. began with Elizabeth, and afterwards danced with her again; but they do not know *how* to be particular. *I flatter myself, however, that they will profit by the three successive lessons which I have given them.*

You scold me so much in the nice long letter which I have this moment received from you, that I am almost afraid to tell you how my Irish friend [Tom Lefroy] and I behaved. Imagine to yourself everything most profligate and shocking in the way of dancing and sitting down together. I can expose *myself however, only* once more, *because he leaves the country soon after next Friday, on which day we* are to *have a dance at Ashe after all. He is a very gentlemanlike, good-looking, pleasant young man, I assure you. But as to our having ever met, except at the three last balls, I cannot say much; for he is so excessively laughed at about me at Ashe, that he is ashamed of coming to Steventon, and ran away when we called on Mrs. Lefroy a few days ago.*

We left Warren at Dean Gate, in our way home last night, and he is now on his road to town. He left his love, &c., to you, and I will deliver it when we meet. Henry goes to Harden to-day in his way to his Master's degree. We shall feel the loss of these two most agreeable young men exceedingly, and shall have nothing to console us till the arrival of the Coopers on Tuesday. As they will stay here till the Monday following, perhaps Caroline will go to the Ashe ball with me, though I dare say she will not.

I danced twice with Warren last night, and once with Mr. Charles Watkins, and, to my inexpressible astonishment, I entirely escaped John Lyford. I was forced to fight hard for it, however. We had a very good supper, and the greenhouse was illuminated in a very elegant manner.

We had a visit yesterday morning from Mr. Benjamin Portal, whose eyes are as handsome as ever. Everybody is extremely anxious for your return, but as you cannot come home by the Ashe ball, I am glad that I have not fed them with false hopes. James danced with Alithea, and cut up the turkey last night with great perseverance. You say nothing of the silk stockings; I flatter myself, therefore, that Charles has not purchased any, as I cannot very well afford to pay for them; all my money is spent in buying white gloves and pink persian. I wish Charles had been at Manydown, because he would have given you some description of my friend, and I think you must be impatient to hear something about him.

Henry is still hankering after the Regulars, and as his project of purchasing the adjutancy of the Oxfordshire is now over, he has got a scheme in his head about getting a lieutenancy and adjutancy in the 86th, a new-raised regiment, which he fancies will be ordered to the Cape of Good Hope. I heartily hope that he will, as usual, be disappointed in this scheme. We have trimmed up and given away all the old paper hats of Mamma's manufacture; I hope you will not regret the loss of yours.

After I had written the above, we received a visit from Mr. Tom Lefroy and his cousin George. The latter is really very well-behaved now; and as for the other, he has but one fault, which time will, I trust, entirely remove – it is that his morning coat is a great deal too light. He is a very great admirer of Tom Jones [hero of the eponymous novel by Henry Fielding], and therefore wears the same coloured clothes, I imagine, which he *did when he was wounded.*

Sunday. – *By not returning till the 19th, you will exactly contrive to miss seeing the Coopers, which I suppose it is your wish to do. We have heard nothing from Charles for some time. One would suppose they must have sailed by this time, as the wind is so favourable. What a funny name Tom [Cassandra's fiancé Tom Fowle] has got for his vessel! But he has no taste in names, as we well know, and I dare say he christened it himself. I am sorry for the Beaches' loss of their little girl, especially as it is the one so much like me.*

I condole with Miss M. [Miss Murdon who lived at Kintbury Rectory] on her losses and with Eliza [Mrs Fowle] on her gains, and am ever yours,

J. A.

To Miss Austen,

Rev. Mr. Fowle's, Kintbury, Newbury.

II

Steventon: Thursday (January 16)

I have just received yours and Mary's [Mary Lloyd] letter, and I thank you both, though their contents might have been more agreeable. I do not at all expect to see you on Tuesday, since matters have fallen out so unpleasantly; and if you are not able to return till after that day, it will hardly be possible for us to send for you before Saturday, though for my own part I care so little about the ball that it would be no sacrifice to me to give it up for the sake of seeing you two days earlier. We are extremely sorry for poor Eliza's illness. I trust, however, that she has continued to recover since you wrote, and that you will none of you be the worse for your attendance on her. What a good-for-nothing fellow Charles is to bespeak the stockings! I hope he will be too hot all the rest of his life for it!

I sent you a letter yesterday to Ibthorp, which I suppose you will not receive at Kintbury. It was not very long or very witty, and therefore if you never receive it, it does not much signify. I wrote principally to tell you that the Coopers were arrived and in good health. The little boy is very like Dr. Cooper, and the little girl is to resemble Jane, they say.

Our party to Ashe to-morrow night will consist of Edward Cooper, James (for a ball is nothing without him*), Buller, who is now staying with us, and I. I look forward with great impatience to it, as I rather expect to receive an offer from my friend in the course of the evening. I shall refuse him, however, unless he promises to give away his white coat.*

I am very much flattered by your commendation of my last letter, for I write only for fame, and without any view to pecuniary emolument.

Edward [Cooper] is gone to spend the day with his friend, John Lyford, and does not return till to-morrow. Anna [daughter of James Austen] is now here; she came up in her chaise to spend the day with her young cousins, but she does not much take to them or to anything about them, except Caroline's spinning-wheel. I am very glad to find from Mary that Mr. and Mrs. Fowle [Tom Fowle's parents] are pleased with you. I hope you will continue to give satisfaction.

How impertinent you are to write to me about Tom [Tom Fowle, Cassandra's fiancé], as if I had not opportunities of hearing from him myself! The last *letter that I received from him was dated on Friday, 8th, and he told me that if the wind should be favourable on Sunday, which it proved to be, they were to sail from Falmouth on that day. By this time, therefore, they are at Barbadoes, I suppose. The Rivers are still at Manydown, and are to be at Ashe to-morrow. I intended to call on the Miss Biggs yesterday had the weather been tolerable. Caroline, Anna, and I have just been devouring some cold souse, and it would be difficult to say which enjoyed it most.*

Tell Mary that I make over Mr. Heartley and all his estate to her for her sole use and benefit in future, and not only him, but all my other admirers into the bargain wherever she can find them, even the kiss which C. Powlett wanted to give me, as I mean to confine myself in future to Mr. Tom Lefroy, for whom I don't care sixpence. Assure her also, as a last and indubitable proof of Warren's indifference to me, that he actually drew that gentleman's picture for me, and delivered it to me without a sigh.

Friday. – *At length the day is come on which I am to flirt my last with Tom Lefroy, and when you receive this it will be over. My tears flow as I write at the melancholy idea. Wm. Chute called here yesterday. I wonder what he means by being so civil. There is a report that Tom [Chute] is going to be married to a Lichfield lass. John Lyford and his sister bring Edward home today, dine with us, and we shall all go together to Ashe. I understand that we are to draw for partners. I shall be extremely impatient to hear from you again, that I may know how Eliza is, and when you are to return.*

With best love, &c., I am affectionately yours,

J. AUSTEN.

Miss Austen,

The Rev. Mr. Fowle's, Kintbury, Newbury.

III

Cork Street: Tuesday morn (August, 1796).

MY DEAR CASSANDRA,

Here I am once more in this scene of dissipation and vice, and I begin already to find my morals corrupted. We reached Staines yesterday, I do not (know) when, without suffering so much from the heat as I had hoped to do. We set off again this morning at seven o'clock, and had a very pleasant drive, as the morning was cloudy and perfectly cool. I came all the way in the chaise from Hertford Bridge.

Edward and Frank are both gone out to seek their fortunes; the latter is to return soon and help us seek ours. The former we shall never see again. We are to be at Astley's [an equestrian circus] to-night, which I am glad of. Edward has heard from Henry this morning. He has not been at the races at all, unless his driving Miss Pearson [his fiancée] over to Rowling one day can be so called. We shall find him there on Thursday.

I hope you are all alive after our melancholy parting yesterday, and that you pursued your intended avocation with success. God bless you! I must leave off, for we are going out.

Yours very affectionately,

J. AUSTEN.

Everybody's love.

IV

Rowling: Thursday (September 1).

MY DEAREST CASSANDRA,

The letter which I have this moment received from you has diverted me beyond moderation. I could die of laughter at it, as they used to say at school. You are indeed the finest comic writer of the present age.

Since I wrote last, we have been very near returning to Steventon so early as next week. Such, for a day or two, was our dear brother Henry's scheme, but at present matters are restored, not to what they were, for my absence seems likely to be lengthened still farther. I am sorry for it, but what can I do?

Henry leaves us to-morrow for Yarmouth, as he wishes very much to consult his physician there, on whom he has great reliance. He is better than he was when he first came, though still by no means well. According to his present plan, he will not return here till about the 23rd, and bring with him, if he can, leave of absence for three weeks, as he wants very much to have some shooting at Godmersham, whither Edward and Elizabeth are to remove very early in October. If this scheme holds, I shall hardly be at Steventon before the middle of that month; but if you cannot do without me, I could return, I suppose, with Frank if he ever goes back. He enjoys himself here very much, for he has just learnt to turn, and is so delighted with the employment, that he is at it all day long.

I am sorry that you found such a conciseness in the strains of my first letter. I must endeavour to make you amends for it, when we meet, by some elaborate details, which I shall shortly begin composing.

I have had my new gown made up, and it really makes a very superb surplice. I am sorry to say that my new coloured gown is very much washed out, though I charged everybody to take great care of it. I hope yours is so too. Our men had but indifferent weather for their visit to Godmersham, for it rained great part of the way there and all the way back. They found Mrs. Knight [Edward Austen's adoptive mother] remarkably well and in very good spirits. It is imagined that she will shortly be married again. I have taken little George once in my arms since I have been here, which I thought very kind. I have told Fanny about the bead of her necklace, and she wants very much to know where you found it.

To-morrow I shall be just like Camilla in Mr. Dubster's summer-house, for my Lionel will have taken away the ladder by which I came here, or at least by which I intended to get away, and here I must stay till his return. My situation, however, is somewhat preferable to hers, for I am very happy here, though I should be glad to get home by the end of the month. I have no idea that Miss Pearson will return with me.

What a fine fellow Charles is, to deceive us into writing two letters to him at Cork! I admire his ingenuity extremely, especially as he is so great a gainer by it.

Mr. and Mrs. Cage and Mr. and Mrs. Bridges dined with us yesterday. Fanny seemed as glad to see me as anybody, and inquired very much after you, whom she supposed to be making your wedding-clothes. She is as handsome as ever, and somewhat fatter. We had a very pleasant day, and some liqueurs *in the evening. Louisa's [Bridges] figure is very much improved; she is as stout [healthy] again as she was. Her face, from what I could see of it one evening, appeared not at all altered. She and the gentlemen walked up here on Monday night – she came in the morning with the Cages from Hythe.*

Lady Hales, with her two youngest daughters, have been to see us. Caroline is not grown at all coarser than she was, nor Harriet at all more delicate. I am glad to hear so good an account of Mr. Charde [Jane's music tutor], and only fear that my long absence may occasion his relapse. I practise every day as much as I can – I wish it were more for his sake. I have heard nothing of Mary Robinson [possibly a maid] since I have been (here). I expect to be well scolded for daring to doubt, whenever the subject is mentioned.

Frank has turned a very nice little butterchurn for Fanny. I do not believe that any of the party were aware of the valuables they had left behind; nor can I hear anything of Anna's gloves. Indeed I have not inquired at all about them hitherto.

We are very busy making Edward's shirts, and I am proud to say that I am the neatest worker of the party. They say that there are a prodigious number of birds hereabouts this year, so that perhaps I *may kill a few. I am glad to hear so good an account of Mr. Limprey and J. Lovett. I know nothing of my mother's handkerchief, but I dare say I shall find it soon.*
I am very affectionately yours,
JANE.
Miss Austen, Steventon, Overton, Hants.

V

Rowling: Monday (September 5).
MY DEAR CASSANDRA,

I shall be extremely anxious to hear the event of your ball, and shall hope to receive so long and minute an account of every particular that I shall be tired of reading it. Let me know how many, besides their fourteen selves and Mr. and Mrs. Wright, Michael will contrive to place about their coach, and how many of the gentlemen, musicians, and waiters, he will have persuaded to come in their shooting-jackets. I hope John Lovett's accident will not prevent his attending the ball, as you will otherwise be obliged to dance with Mr. Tincton the whole evening. Let me know how J. Harwood deports himself without the Miss Biggs, and which of the Marys will carry the day with my brother James.

We were at a ball on Saturday, I assure you. We dined at Goodnestone, and in the evening danced two country-dances and the Boulangeries. I opened the ball with Edward Bridges; the other couples were Lewis Cage and Harriet, Frank and Louisa, Fanny and George. Elizabeth played one country-dance, Lady Bridges the other, which she made Henry dance with her, and Miss Finch played the Boulangeries.

In reading over the last three or four lines, I am aware of my having expressed myself in so doubtful a manner that, if I did not tell you to the contrary, you might imagine it was Lady Bridges who made Henry dance with her at the same time that she was playing, which, if not impossible, must appear a very improbable event to you. But it was Elizabeth who danced. We supped there, and walked home at night under the shade of two umbrellas.

To-day the Goodnestone party begins to disperse and spread itself abroad. Mr. and Mrs. Cage and George repair to Hythe. Lady Waltham, Miss Bridges, and Miss Mary Finch to Dover, for the health of the two former. I have never seen Marianne at all. On Thursday Mr. and Mrs. Bridges return to Danbury; Miss Harriet Hales accompanies them to London on her way to Dorsetshire.

Farmer Claringbould died this morning, and I fancy Edward means to get some of his farm, if he can cheat Sir Brook enough in the agreement.

We have just got some venison from Godmersham, which the two Mr. Harveys are to dine on to-morrow, and on Friday or Saturday the Goodnestone people are to finish their scraps. Henry went away on Friday, as he purposed, without fayl. You will hear from him soon, I imagine, as he talked of writing to Steventon shortly. Mr. Richard Harvey is going to be married; but as it is a great secret, and only known to half the neighbourhood, you must not mention it. The lady's name is Musgrave.

I am in great distress. I cannot determine whether I shall give Richis [maidservant] half a guinea or only five shillings when I go away. Counsel me, amiable Miss Austen, and tell me which will be the most.

We walked Frank last night to Crixhall Ruff, and he appeared much edified. Little Edward was breeched yesterday for good and all, and was whipped into the bargain.

Pray remember me to everybody who does not inquire after me; those who do, remember me without bidding. Give my love to Mary Harrison, and tell her I wish, whenever she is attached to a young man, some respectable *Dr. Marchmont [character in the novel* Camilla*] may keep them apart for five volumes...*

VI

Rowling: Thursday (September 15).
MY DEAR CASSANDRA,

We have been very gay since I wrote last; dining at Nackington [home of the Milles family], returning by moonlight, and everything quite in style, not to mention Mr. Claringbould's funeral which we saw go by on Sunday.

I believe I told you in a former letter that Edward had some idea of taking the name of Claringbould; but that scheme is over, though it would be a very eligible as well as a very pleasant plan, would anyone advance him money enough to begin on. We rather expected Mr. Milles to have done so on Tuesday; but to our great surprise nothing was said on the subject, and unless it is in your power to assist your brother with five or six hundred pounds, he must entirely give up the idea.

At Nackington we met Lady Sondes' picture over the mantel-piece in the dining-room, and the pictures of her three children in an ante room, besides Mr. Scott, Miss Fletcher, Mr. Toke, Mr. J. Toke, and the Archdeacon Lynch. Miss Fletcher and I were very thick, but I am the thinnest of the two. She wore her purple muslin, which is pretty enough, though it does not become her complexion. There are two traits in her character which are pleasing – namely, she admires Camilla [the novel], and drinks no cream in her tea. If you should ever see Lucy [Lefroy], you may tell her that I scolded Miss Fletcher for her negligence in writing, as she desired me to do, but without being able to bring her to any proper sense of shame – that Miss Fletcher says in her defence, that as everybody whom Lucy knew when she was in Canterbury has now left it, she has nothing at all to write to her about. By everybody, *I suppose Miss Fletcher means that a new set of officers have arrived there. But this is a note of my own.*

Mrs. Milles, Mr. John Toke, and in short everybody of any sensibility enquired in tender strains after you, and I took an opportunity of assuring Mr. J. T. that neither he nor his father need longer keep themselves single for you.

We went in our two carriages to Nackington; but how we divided I shall leave you to surmise, merely observing that, as Elizabeth and I were without either hat or bonnet, it would not have been very convenient for us to go in the chaise. We went by Bifrons [home of the Taylor family], and I contemplated with a melancholy pleasure the abode of him on whom I once fondly doated. We dine to-day at Goodnestone, to meet my Aunt Fielding from Margate and a Mr. Clayton, her professed admirer – at least so I imagine. Lady Bridges has received very good accounts of Marianne, who is already certainly the better for her bathing.

So His Royal Highness Sir Thomas Williams [husband of Jane's cousin Jane] has at length sailed; the papers say 'on a cruise.' But I hope they are gone to Cork, or I shall have written in vain. Give my love to Jane, as she arrived at Steventon yesterday, I dare say.

I sent a message to Mr. Digweed from Edward in a letter to Mary Lloyd which she ought to receive to-day; but as I know that the Harwoods are not very exact as to their letters, I may as well repeat it to you. Mr. Digweed is to be informed that illness has prevented Seward's [farm bailiff] coming over to look at the repairs intended at the farm, but that he will come as soon as he can. Mr. Digweed may also be informed, if you think proper, that Mr. and Mrs. Milles are to dine here to-morrow, and that Mrs. Joan Knatchbull is to be asked to meet them. Mr. Richard Harvey's match is put off till he has got a better Christian name, of which he has great hopes.

Mr. Children's two sons are both going to be married, John and George. They are to have one wife between them, a Miss Holwell, who belongs to the Black Hole at Calcutta. I depend on hearing from James very soon; he promised me an account of the ball, and by this time he must have collected his ideas enough after the fatigue of dancing to give me one.

Edward and Fly [nickname of Frank Austen] went out yesterday very early in a couple of shooting jackets, and came home like a couple of bad shots, for they killed nothing at all. They are out again to-day, and are not yet returned. Delightful sport! They are just come home, Edward with his two brace, Frank with his two and a half. What amiable young men!

Friday. – *Your letter and one from Henry are just come, and the contents of both accord with my scheme more than I had dared expect. In one particular I could wish it otherwise, for Henry is very indifferent indeed. You must not expect us quite so early, however, as Wednesday, the 20th – on that day se'nnight, according to our present plan, we may be with you. Frank had never any idea of going away before Monday, the 26th. I shall write to Miss Mason immediately and press her returning with us, which Henry thinks very likely and particularly eligible.*

Buy Mary Harrison's gown by all means. You shall have mine for ever so much money, though, if I am tolerably rich when I get home, I shall like it very much myself.

As to the mode of our travelling to town, I *want to go in a stage-coach, but Frank will not let me. As you are likely to have the Williams and Lloyds with you next week, you would hardly find room for us then. If anyone wants anything in town, they must send their commissions to Frank, as* I *shall merely pass through it. The tallow-chandler is Penlington, at the Crown and Beehive, Charles Street, Covent Garden.*

Miss Austen, Steventon, Overton, Hants.

VII

Rowling: Sunday (September 18.)

MY DEAR CASSANDRA,

This morning has been spent in doubt and deliberation, in forming plans and removing difficulties, for it ushered in the day with an event which I had not intended should take place so soon by a week. Frank has received his appointment on board the 'Captain John Gore,' commanded by the 'Triton,' and will therefore be obliged to be in town on Wednesday; and though I have every disposition in the world to accompany him on that day, I cannot go on the uncertainty of the Pearsons being at home, as I should not have a place to go to in case they were from home.

I wrote to Miss P. on Friday, and hoped to receive an answer from her this morning, which would have rendered everything smooth and easy, and would have enabled us to leave this place to-morrow, as Frank, on first receiving his appointment, intended to do. He remains till Wednesday merely to accommodate me. I have written to her again to-day, and desired her to answer it by return of post. On Tuesday, therefore, I shall positively know whether they can receive me on Wednesday. If they cannot, Edward has been so good as to promise to take me to Greenwich on the Monday following, which was the day before fixed on, if that suits them better. If I have no answer at all on Tuesday, I must suppose Mary is not at home, and must wait till I do *hear, as, after having invited her to go to Steventon with me, it will not quite do to go home and say no more about it.*

My father will be so good as to fetch home his prodigal daughter from town, I hope, unless he wishes me to walk the hospitals, enter at the Temple, or mount guard at St. James'. It will hardly be in Frank's power to take me home – nay, it certainly will not. I shall write again as soon as I get to Greenwich.

What dreadful hot weather we have! It keeps one in a continual state of inelegance.

If Miss Pearson should return with me, pray be careful not to expect too much beauty. I will not pretend to say that on a first view *she quite answered the opinion I had formed of her. My mother, I am sure, will be disappointed if she does not take great care. From what I remember of her picture, it is no great resemblance.*

I am very glad that the idea of returning with Frank occurred to me; for as to Henry's coming into Kent again, the time of its taking place is so very uncertain that I should be waiting for dead men's shoes. *I had once determined to go with Frank to-morrow and take my chance, &c., but they dissuaded me from so rash a step, as I really think on consideration it would have been; for if the Pearsons were not at home, I should inevitably fall a sacrifice to the arts of some fat woman who would make me drunk with small beer.*

Mary is brought to bed of a boy – both doing very well. I shall leave you to guess what Mary I mean. Adieu, with best love to your agreeable inmates. Don't let the Lloyds go on any account before I return, unless Miss P. is of the party. How ill I have written! I begin to hate myself.

Yours ever,

J. AUSTEN.

The 'Triton' is a new 32 frigate just launched at Deptford. Frank is much pleased with the prospect of having Captain Gore under his command.

Miss Austen, Steventon, Overton, Hants.

1798, 1799

The next division of letters comprises those written in 1798 and in January 1799. The first is written from Dartford, evidently the first stage of a journey home to Steventon from Godmersham, where Mr. and Mrs. George Austen had been visiting their son Edward in his new abode, probably for the first time, since he could not have been settled there for more than a year; and there is a graphic account of the loss and recovery of Jane's writing and dressing boxes, which appear to have had a narrow escape from a voyage to the West Indies. From this and the following letters, it would seem that Mrs. Austen was in delicate health, and apparently thought herself worse than was really the case. At any rate, she rallied from the attack of which she complained at this time, and lived happily on until 1827, when she died at the ripe age of eighty-eight, having survived her husband twenty-two and her daughter Jane ten years. The other nine letters are all written from Steventon, and record the details of the everyday life in Jane Austen's home. She manages the household for her mother, visits the poor, enjoys such society as the neighbourhood affords, and fills her letters with such gossip about things and people as would be likely to interest her sister. Most of the people to whom she alludes will be identified by reference to the introductory chapters of this book, and of others there is nothing more to be said than that they were country neighbours of various stations in life, to whom attaches no particular interest as far as Jane Austen is concerned. The Digweeds were brothers who occupied a fine old Elizabethan manor-house and a large farm in Steventon, which belonged to the Knight family until Mr. E. Knight (son of E. Austen) sold it to the Duke of Wellington, and the late Duke sold it in 1874 to Mr. Harris. An attempt to restore it failed, and eventually a new house was built some fifty yards from the old one; but, although the latter was turned into stables, its appearance in front at least was not injured, and there is a charming view of it across the lawn from the drawing-room of the new house. Previous to its sale to the present owner, the Digweed family had occupied the manor house for more than 150 years, but not being Irish tenants, I suppose they got no compensation for 'disturbance.'

'John Bond' was Mr. Austen's 'factotum' in his farming operations. There is an anecdote extant relating to this worthy which may as well be told here: Mr. Austen used to join Mr. Digweed in buying twenty or thirty sheep, and that all might be fair, it was their custom to open the pen, and the first half of the sheep which ran out were counted as belonging to the rector. Going down to the fold on one occasion after this process had been gone through, Mr. Austen remarked one sheep among his lot larger and finer than the rest. 'Well, John,'he observed to Bond, who was with him, 'I think we have had the best of the luck with Mr. Digweed today, in getting that sheep.' 'Maybe not so much in the luck as you think, sir,' responded the faithful John. 'I see'd her the moment I come in, and set eyes on the sheep, so when we opened the pen I just giv'd her a `huck' with my stick, and out a run.'

There is an allusion in the sixteenth to 'First Impressions' – her original name for the work afterwards published as 'Pride and Prejudice' – which shows that, as regards this book at least, her having written it was no secret from her family. It is singular that it should have remained so long unpublished, but at all events this proves that it was no hasty production, but one which had been well considered, and submitted to the judgment of others long before it was given to the public. Jane changed the name of another novel also between composition and publication, 'Sense and Sensibility' having been at first entitled 'Elinor and Marianne.'

In the same letter there is an observation about 'Mrs. Knight's giving up the Godmersham estate to Edward being no such prodigious act of generosity after all,' which was certainly not intended seriously, or if so, was written under a very imperfect knowledge of the facts. I have seen the letters which passed upon the occasion. The first is from Mrs. Knight, offering to give up the property in the kindest and most generous terms, and this when she was not much above forty years of age, and much attached to the place. Then comes my grandfather's answer, deprecating the idea of her making such a sacrifice, and saying that he and his wife were already well enough off through Mrs. Knight's kindness, and could not endure that she should leave for their sakes a home which she loved so much. Mrs. Knight replies that it was through her great affection for my grandfather that her late husband had adopted him, that she loved him as if he was her own son, that his letter had strengthened her in her resolution to give up the property to him, and that she considered there were duties attaching to the possession of landed property which could not be discharged by a woman so well as by a man. She reminds him how that the poor had always been liberally treated by the Godmersham family, and expresses her happiness at feeling that he will do his duty in this and other respects, and that she shall spend the rest of her days near enough to see much of him and his wife. I am quite sure that my grandfather was most gratefully fond of Mrs. Knight, and considered her conduct, as indeed it was, an act of affectionate generosity.

VIII

'Bull and George,' Dartford:
Wednesday (October 24)
MY DEAR CASSANDRA,

You have already heard from Daniel [Godmersham coachman], I conclude, in what excellent time we reached and quitted Sittingbourne, and how very well my mother bore her journey thither. I am now able to send you a continuation of the same good account of her. She was very little fatigued on her arrival at this place, has been refreshed by a comfortable dinner, and now seems quite stout. It wanted five minutes of twelve when we left Sittingbourne, from whence we had a famous pair of horses, which took us to Rochester in an hour and a quarter; the postboy seemed determined to show my mother that Kentish drivers were not always tedious, and really drove as fast as Cax.

Our next stage was not quite so expeditiously performed; the road was heavy and our horses very indifferent. However, we were in such good time, and my mother bore her journey so well, that expedition was of little importance to us; and as it was, we were very little more than two hours and a half coming hither, and it was scarcely past four when we stopped at the inn. My mother took some of her bitters at Ospringe, and some more at Rochester, and she ate some bread several times.

We have got apartments up two pair of stairs, as we could not be otherwise accommodated with a sitting-room and bed-chambers on the same floor, which we wished to be. We have one double-bedded and one single-bedded room; in the former my mother and I are to sleep. I shall leave you to guess who is to occupy the other. We sate down to dinner a little after five, and had some beefsteaks and a boiled fowl, but no oyster sauce.

I should have begun my letter soon after our arrival but for a little adventure which prevented me. After we had been here a quarter of an hour it was discovered that my writing and dressing boxes had been by accident put into a chaise which was just packing off as we came in, and were driven away towards Gravesend in their way to the West Indies. No part of my property could have been such a prize before, for in my writing-box was all my worldly wealth, 7l., and my dear Harry's deputation [authority from Edward Austen to his tenant Harry Digweed to shoot on his land]. Mr. Nottley [landlord of the Bull and George inn] immediately despatched a man and horse after the chaise, and in half an hour's time I had the pleasure of being as rich as ever; they were got about two or three miles off.

My day's journey has been pleasanter in every respect than I expected. I have been very little crowded and by no means unhappy. Your watchfulness with regard to the weather on our accounts was very kind and very effectual. We had one heavy shower on leaving Sittingbourne, but afterwards the clouds cleared away, and we had a very bright chrystal *afternoon.*

My father is now reading the 'Midnight Bell,' which he has got from the library, and mother sitting by the fire. Our route to-morrow is not determined. We have none of us much inclination for London, and if Mr. Nottley will give us leave, I think we shall go to Staines through Croydon and Kingston, which will be much pleasanter than any other way; but he is decidedly for Clapham and Battersea. God bless you all!

Yours affectionately,

J. A.

I flatter myself that itty Dordy *[her nephew George] will not forget me at least under a week. Kiss him for me.*

Miss Austen, Godmersham Park,

Faversham, Kent

IX

Steventon: Saturday (October 27)

MY DEAR CASSANDRA,

Your letter was a most agreeable surprise to me to-day, and I have taken a long sheet of paper to show my gratitude.

We arrived here yesterday between four and five, but I cannot send you quite so triumphant an account of our last day's journey as of the first and second. Soon after I had finished my letter from Staines, my mother began to suffer from the exercise or fatigue of travelling, and she was a good deal indisposed. She had not a very good night at Staines, but bore her journey better than I had expected, and at Basingstoke, where we stopped more than half an hour, received much comfort from a mess of broth and the sight of Mr. Lyford, who recommended her to take twelve drops of laudanum when she went to bed as a composer, which she accordingly did.

James called on us just as we were going to tea, and my mother was well enough to talk very cheerfully to him before she went to bed. James seems to have taken to his old trick of coming to Steventon in spite of Mary's reproaches, for he was here before breakfast and is now paying us a second visit. They were to have dined here to-day, but the weather is too bad. I have had the pleasure of hearing that Martha is with them. James fetched her from Ibthorp on Thursday, and she will stay with them till she removes to Kintbury.

We met with no adventures at all in our journey yesterday, except that our trunk had once nearly slipped off, and we were obliged to stop at Hartley to have our wheels greased.

Whilst my mother and Mr. Lyford were together I went to Mrs. Ryder's and bought what I intended to buy, but not in much perfection. There were no narrow braces for children and scarcely any notting silk; but Miss Wood [Mrs Ryder's assistant], as usual, is going to town very soon, and will lay in a fresh stock. I gave 2s. 3d. *a yard for my flannel, and I fancy it is not very good, but it is so disgraceful and contemptible an article in itself that its being comparatively good or bad is of little importance. I bought some Japan ink likewise, and next week shall begin my operations on my hat, on which you know my principal hopes of happiness depend.*

I am very grand indeed; I had the dignity of dropping out my mother's laudanum last night. I carry about the keys of the wine and closet, and twice since I began this letter have had orders to give in the kitchen. Our dinner was very good yesterday, and the chicken boiled perfectly tender; therefore I shall not be obliged to dismiss Nanny [servant] on that account.

Almost everything was unpacked and put away last night. Nanny chose to do it, and I was not sorry to be busy. I have unpacked the gloves and placed yours in your drawer. Their colour is light and pretty, and I believe exactly what we fixed on.

Your letter was chaperoned here by one from Mrs. Cooke [cousin of Jane's mother], in which she says that 'Battleridge' [a tale written by Mrs Cooke] is not to come out before January, and she is so little satisfied with Cawthorn's dilatoriness that she never means to employ him again.

Mrs. Hall, of Sherborne, was brought to bed yesterday of a dead child, some weeks before she expected, owing to a fright. I suppose she happened unawares to look at her husband.

There has been a great deal of rain here for this last fortnight, much more than in Kent, and indeed we found the roads all the way from Staines most disgracefully dirty. Steventon lane has its full share of it, and I don't know when I shall be able to get to Deane.

I hear that Martha is in better looks and spirits than she has enjoyed for a long time, and I flatter myself she will now be able to jest openly about Mr. W.[a man whom Martha Lloyd had hoped to marry]

The spectacles which Molly [maidservant] found are my mother's, the scissors my father's. We are very glad to hear such a good account of your patients [Elizabeth Austen and her new baby], little and great. My dear itty Dordy's remembrance of me is very pleasing to me – foolishly pleasing, because I know it will be over so soon. My attachment to him will be more durable. I shall think with tenderness and delight on his beautiful and smiling countenance and interesting manner until a few years have turned him into an ungovernable, ungracious fellow.

The books from Winton [Winchester] are all unpacked and put away; the binding has compressed them most conveniently, and there is now very good room in the bookcase for all that we wish to have there. I believe the servants were very glad to see us. Nanny was, I am sure. She confesses that it was very dull, and yet she had her child with her till last Sunday. I understand that there are some grapes left, but I believe not many; they must be gathered as soon as possible, or this rain will entirely rot them.

I am quite angry with myself for not writing closer; why is my alphabet so much more sprawly than yours? Dame Tilbury's daughter has lain in. Shall I give her any of your baby clothes? The laceman was here only a few days ago. How unfortunate for both of us that he came so soon! Dame Bushell washes for us only one week more, as Sukey has got a place. John Steevens' wife undertakes our purification. She does not look as if anything she touched would ever be clean, but who knows? We do not seem likely to have any other maidservant at present, but Dame Staples will supply the place of one. Mary has hired a young girl from Ashe who has never been out to service to be her scrub, but James fears her not being strong enough for the place.

Earle Harwood has been to Deane lately, as I think Mary wrote us word, and his family then told him that they would receive his wife, if she continued to behave well for another year. He was very grateful, as well he might, their behaviour throughout the whole affair has been particularly kind. Earle and his wife live in the most private manner imaginable at Portsmouth, without keeping a servant of any kind. What a prodigious innate love of virtue she must have, to marry under such circumstances!

It is now Saturday evening, but I wrote the chief of this in the morning. My mother has not been down at all to-day; the laudanum made her sleep a good deal, and upon the whole I think she is better. My father and I dined by ourselves. How strange! He and John Bond are now very happy together, for I have just heard the heavy step of the latter along the passage.

James Digweed called to-day, and I gave him his brother's deputation. Charles Harwood, too, has just called to ask how we are, in his way from Dummer, whither he has been conveying Miss Garrett [relation of the Harwoods], who is going to return to her former residence in Kent. I will *leave off, or I shall not have room to add a word to-morrow.*

Sunday. – *My mother has had a very good night, and feels much better to-day.*

I have received my Aunt's [Jane Leigh Perrot] letter, and thank you for your scrap. I will write to Charles soon. Pray give Fanny and Edward a kiss from me, and ask George if he has got a new song for me. 'Tis really very kind of my Aunt to ask us to Bath again; a kindness that deserves a better return than to profit by it.

Yours ever,

J. A.

Miss Austen, Godmersham Park,
Faversham, Kent

X

Saturday, November 17, 1798.
MY DEAR CASSANDRA,

If you paid any attention to the conclusion of my last letter, you will be satisfied, before you receive this, that my mother has had no relapse, and that Miss Debary comes. The former continues to recover, and though she does not gain strength very rapidly, my expectations are humble enough not to outstride her improvements. She was able to sit up nearly eight hours yesterday, and to-day I hope we shall do as much...So much for my patient – now for myself.

Mrs. Lefroy did come last Wednesday, and the Harwoods came likewise, but very considerately paid their visit before Mrs. Lefroy's arrival, with whom, in spite of interruptions both from my father and James, I was enough alone to hear all that was interesting, which you will easily credit when I tell you that of her nephew [Tom] she said nothing at all, and of her friend [Revd Samuel Blackall, whom Mrs Lefroy had introduced to Jane as a possible husband] very little. She did not once mention the name of the former to me, and I was too proud to make any enquiries; but on my father's afterwards asking where he was, I learnt that he was gone back to London in his way to Ireland, where he is called to the Bar and means to practise.

She showed me a letter which she had received from her friend a few weeks ago (in answer to one written by her to recommend a nephew of Mrs. Russell to his notice at Cambridge), towards the end of which was a sentence to this effect: 'I am very sorry to hear of Mrs. Austen's illness. It would give me particular pleasure to have an opportunity of improving my acquaintance with that family – with a hope of creating to myself a nearer interest. But at present I cannot indulge any expectation of it.' This is rational enough; there is less love and more sense in it than sometimes appeared before, and I am very well satisfied. It will all go on exceedingly well, and decline away in a very reasonable manner. There seems no likelihood of his coming into Hampshire this Christmas, and it is therefore most probable that our indifference will soon be mutual, unless his regard, which appeared to spring from knowing nothing of me at first, is best supported by never seeing me.

Mrs. Lefroy made no remarks in the letter, nor did she indeed say anything about him as relative to me. Perhaps she thinks she has said too much already. She saw a great deal of the Mapletons while she was in Bath. Christian is still in a very bad state of health, consumptive, and not likely to recover.

Mrs. Portman is not much admired in Dorsetshire; the good-natured world, as usual, extolled her beauty so highly, that all the neighbourhood have had the pleasure of being disappointed.

My mother desires me to tell you that I am a very good housekeeper, which I have no reluctance in doing, because I really think it my peculiar excellence, and for this reason – I always take care to provide such things as please my own appetite, which I consider as the chief merit in housekeeping. I have had some ragout veal, and I mean to have some haricot mutton to-morrow. We are to kill a pig soon.

There is to be a ball at Basingstoke next Thursday. Our assemblies have very kindly declined ever since we laid down the carriage, so that dis-convenience and dis-inclination to go have kept pace together.

My father's affection for Miss Cuthbert [who lived near Godmersham] is as lively as ever, and he begs that you will not neglect to send him intelligence of her or her brother, whenever you have any to send. I am likewise to tell you that one of his Leicestershire sheep, sold to the butcher last week, weighed 27 lb. and 1/4 per quarter.

I went to Deane with my father two days ago to see Mary, who is still plagued with the rheumatism, which she would be very glad to get rid of, and still more glad to get rid of her child, of whom she is heartily tired. Her nurse is come and has no particular charm either of person or manner; but as all the Hurstbourne world pronounce her to be the best nurse that ever was, Mary expects her attachment to increase.

What fine weather this is! Not very becoming perhaps early in the morning, but very pleasant out of doors at noon, and very wholesome – at least everybody fancies so, and imagination is everything. To Edward, however, I really think dry weather of importance. I have not taken to fires yet.

I believe I never told you that Mrs. Coulthard and Anne, late of Manydown, are both dead, and both died in childbed. We have not regaled Mary with this news. Harry St. John is in Orders, has done duty at Ashe, and performs very well.

I am very fond of experimental housekeeping, such as having an ox-cheek now and then, I shall have one next week, and I mean to have some little dumplings put into it, that I may fancy myself at Godmersham.

I hope George was pleased with my designs. Perhaps they would have suited him as well had they been less elaborately finished; but an artist cannot do anything slovenly. I suppose baby grows and improves.

Sunday. – *I have just received a note from James to say that Mary was brought to bed last night, at eleven o'clock, of a fine little boy [James Edward Austen], and that everything is going on very well. My mother had desired to know nothing of it before it should be all over, and we were clever enough to prevent her having any suspicion of it, though Jenny, who had been left here by her mistress, was sent for home...*

I called yesterday on Betty Londe, who enquired particularly after you, and said she seemed to miss you very much, because you used to call in upon her very often. This was an oblique reproach at me, which I am sorry to have merited, and from which I will profit. I shall send George another picture when I write next, which I suppose will be soon, on Mary's account. My mother continues well.

Yours,

J. A.

Miss Austen, Godmersham.

XI

Steventon: Sunday (November 25).

MY DEAR SISTER,

I expected to have heard from you this morning, but no letter is come. I shall not take the trouble of announcing to you any more of Mary's children, if, instead of thanking me for the intelligence, you always sit down and write to James. I am sure nobody can desire your letters so much as I do, and I don't think anybody deserves them so well.

Having now relieved my heart of a great deal of malevolence, I will proceed to tell you that Mary continues quite well, and my mother tolerably so. I saw the former on Friday, and though I had seen her comparatively hearty the Tuesday before, I was really amazed at the improvement which three days had made in her. She looked well, her spirits were perfectly good, and she spoke much more vigorously than Elizabeth did when we left Godmersham. I had only a glimpse at the child, who was asleep; but Miss Debary told me that his eyes were large, dark, and handsome. She *looks much as she used to do, is netting herself a gown in worsteds, and wears what Mrs. Birch [friend of Jane's mother] would call a* pot hat. *A short and compendious history of Miss Debary!*

I suppose you have heard from Henry himself that his affairs are happily settled. We do not know who furnishes the qualification [creditworthiness to become Paymaster in the Oxfordshire Militia]. Mr. Mowell would have readily given it, had not all his Oxfordshire property been engaged for a similar purpose to the Colonel. Amusing enough!

Our family affairs are rather deranged at present, for Nanny has kept her bed these three or four days, with a pain in her side and fever, and we are forced to have two charwomen, which is not very comfortable. She is considerably better now, but it must still be some time, I suppose, before she is able to do anything. You and Edward will be amused, I think, when you know that Nanny Littlewart [maidservant] dresses my hair.

The ball on Thursday was a very small one indeed, hardly so large as an Oxford smack. There were but seven couples, and only twenty-seven people in the room.

The Overton Scotchman [pedlar] has been kind enough to rid me of some of my money, in exchange for six shifts and four pair of stockings. The Irish is not so fine as I should like it; but as I gave as much money for it as I intended, I have no reason to complain. It cost me 3s. 6d. *per yard. It is rather finer, however, than our last, and not so harsh a cloth.*

We have got 'Fitz-Albini' [novel by Samuel Egerton Brydges, brother of Mrs Lefroy]; my father has bought it against my private wishes, for it does not quite satisfy my feelings that we should purchase the only one of Egerton's works of which his family are ashamed. That these scruples, however, do not at all interfere with my reading it, you will easily believe. We have neither of us yet finished the first volume. My father is disappointed – I *am not, for I expected nothing better. Never did any book carry more internal evidence of its author. Every sentiment is completely Egerton's. There is very little story, and what there is is told in a strange, unconnected way. There are many characters introduced, apparently merely to be delineated. We have not been able to recognise any of them hitherto, except Dr. and Mrs. Hey and Mr. Oxenden, who is not very tenderly treated.*

You must tell Edward that my father gives 25s. *apiece to Seward for his last lot of sheep, and, in return for this news, my father wishes to receive some of Edward's pigs.*

We have got Boswell's 'Tour to the Hebrides,' and are to have his 'Life of Johnson'; and, as some money will yet remain in Burdon's [bookseller] hands, it is to be laid out in the purchase of Cowper's works. This would please Mr. Clarke, could he know it.

By the bye, I have written to Mrs. Birch among my other writings, and so I hope to have some account of all the people in that part of the world before long. I have written to Mrs. E. Leigh [relative of Jane's mother], too, and Mrs. Heathcote has been ill-natured enough to send me a letter of enquiry; so that altogether I am tolerably tired of letter-writing, and, unless I have anything new to tell you of my mother or Mary, I shall not write again for many days; perhaps a little repose may restore my regard for a pen. Ask little Edward whether Bob Brown [probably a manservant at Godmersham] wears a great coat this cold weather.

Miss Austen, Godmersham Park.

XII

Steventon: December 1.

MY DEAR CASSANDRA,

I am so good as to write to you again thus speedily, to let you know that I have just heard from Frank. He was at Cadiz, alive and well, on October 19, and had then very lately received a letter from you, written as long ago as when the 'London' was at St. Helen's. But his raly *latest intelligence of us was in one from me of September 1, which I sent soon after we got to Godmersham. He had written a packet full for his dearest friends in England, early in October, to go by the 'Excellent'; but the 'Excellent' was not sailed, nor likely to sail, when he despatched this to me. It comprehended letters for both of us, for Lord Spencer [First Lord of the Admiralty], Mr. Daysh [clerk in the Navy Ticket Office], and the East India Directors. Lord St. Vincent had left the fleet when he wrote, and was gone to Gibraltar, it was said to superintend the fitting out of a private expedition from thence against some of the enemies' ports; Minorca or Malta were conjectured to be the objects.*

Frank writes in good spirits, but says that our correspondence cannot be so easily carried on in future as it has been, as the communication between Cadiz and Lisbon is less frequent than formerly. You and my mother, therefore, must not alarm yourselves at the long intervals that may divide his letters. I address this advice to you two as being the most tender-hearted of the family.

My mother made her entrée *into the dressing-room through crowds of admiring spectators yesterday afternoon, and we all drank tea together for the. first time these five weeks. She has had a tolerable night, and bids fair for a continuance in the same brilliant course of action to-day...*

Mr. Lyford was here yesterday; he came while we were at dinner, and partook of our elegant entertainment. I was not ashamed at asking him to sit down to table, for we had some pease-soup, a sparerib, and a pudding. He wants my mother to look yellow and to throw out a rash, but she will do neither.

I was at Deane yesterday morning. Mary was very well, but does not gain bodily strength very fast. When I saw her so stout on the third and sixth days, I expected to have seen her as well as ever by the end of a fortnight.

James went to Ibthorp yesterday to see his mother and child. Letty [maidservant] is with Mary at present, of course exceedingly happy, and in raptures with the child. Mary does not manage matters in such a way as to make me want to lay in myself. She is not tidy enough in her appearance; she has no dressing-gown to sit up in; her curtains are all too thin, and things are not in that comfort and style about her which are necessary to make such a situation an enviable one. Elizabeth was really a pretty object with her nice clean cap put on so tidily and her dress so uniformly white and orderly. We live entirely in the dressing-room now, which I like very much; I always feel so much more elegant in it than in the parlour.

No news from Kintbury yet. Eliza sports with our impatience. [She, too, was expecting a baby.] She was very well last Thursday. Who is Miss Maria Montresor going to marry, and what is to become of Miss Mulcaster?

I find great comfort in my stuff gown, but I hope you do not wear yours too often. I have made myself two or three caps to wear of evenings since I came home, and they save me a world of torment as to hair-dressing, which at present gives me no trouble beyond washing and brushing, for my long hair is always plaited up out of sight, and my short hair curls well enough to want no papering. I have had it cut lately by Mr. Butler.

There is no reason to suppose that Miss Morgan is dead after all. Mr. Lyford gratified us very much yesterday by his praises of my father's mutton, which they all think the finest that was ever ate. John Bond begins to find himself grow old, which John Bonds ought not to do, and unequal to much hard work; a man is therefore hired to supply his place as to labour, and John himself is to have the care of the sheep. There are not more people engaged than before, I believe; only men instead of boys. I fancy so at least, but you know my stupidity as to such matters. Lizzie Bond [daughter of John] is just apprenticed to Miss Small, so we may hope to see her able to spoil gowns in a few years.

My father has applied to Mr. May [brewer] for an alehouse for Robert [possibly husband of Nanny Hilliard], at his request, and to Mr. Deane [brewer], of Winchester, likewise. This was my mother's idea, who thought he would be proud to oblige a relation of Edward in return for Edward's accepting his money. He sent a very civil answer indeed, but has no house vacant at present. May expects to have an empty one soon at Farnham, so perhaps Nanny may have the honour of drawing ale for the Bishop [Farnham Castle was a residence of the Bishop of Winchester]. I shall write to Frank to-morrow.

Charles Powlett gave a dance on Thursday, to the great disturbance of all his neighbours, of course, who, you know, take a most lively interest in the state of his finances, and live in hopes of his being soon ruined.

We are very much disposed to like our new maid; she knows nothing of a dairy, to be sure, which, in our family, is rather against her, but she is to be taught it all. In short, we have felt the inconvenience of being without a maid so long, that we are determined to like her, and she will find it a hard matter to displease us. As yet, she seems to cook very well, is uncommonly stout, and says she can work well at her needle.

Sunday. – *My father is glad to hear so good an account of Edward's pigs, and desires he may be told, as encouragement to his taste for them, that Lord Bolton is particularly curious in* his *pigs, has had pigstyes of a most elegant construction built for them, and visits them every morning as soon as he rises.*

Affectionately yours,

J. A.

Miss Austen, Godmersham Park,

Faversham.

XIII

Steventon: Tuesday (December 18).

MY DEAR CASSANDRA,

Your letter came quite as soon as I expected, and so your letters will always do, because I have made it a rule not to expect them till they come, in which I think I consult the ease of us both.

It is a great satisfaction to us to hear that your business is in a way to be settled, and so settled as to give you as little inconvenience as possible. You are very welcome to my father's name and to his services if they are ever required in it. I shall keep my ten pounds too, to wrap myself up in next winter.

I took the liberty a few days ago of asking your black velvet bonnet to lend me its cawl, which it very readily did, and by which I have been enabled to give a considerable improvement of dignity to cap, which was before too nidgetty to please me. I shall wear it on Thursday, but I hope you will not be offended with me for following your advice as to its ornaments only in part. I still venture to retain the narrow silver round it, put twice round without any bow, and instead of the black military feather shall put in the coquelicot one as being smarter, and besides coquelicot is to be all the fashion this winter. After the ball I shall probably make it entirely black.

I am sorry that our dear Charles begins to feel the dignity of ill-usage. My father will write to Admiral Gambier. He must have already received so much satisfaction from his acquaintance and patronage of Frank, that he will be delighted, I dare say, to have another of the family introduced to him. I think it would be very right in Charles to address Sir Thomas [Williams] on the occasion, though I cannot approve of your scheme of writing to him (which you communicated to me a few nights ago) to request him to come home and convey you to Steventon. To do you justice, however, you had some doubts of the propriety of such a measure yourself.

I am very much obliged to my dear little George for his message – for his love at least; his duty, I suppose, was only in consequence of some hint of my favourable intentions towards him from his father or mother. I am sincerely rejoiced, however, that I ever was born, since it has been the means of procuring him a dish of tea. Give my best love to him.

This morning has been made very gay to us by visits from our two lively neighbours, Mr. Holder and Mr. John Harwood.

I have received a very civil note from Mrs. Martin, requesting my name as a subscriber to her library which opens January 14, and my name, or rather yours, is accordingly given. My mother finds the money. Mary subscribes too, which I am glad of, but hardly expected. As an inducement to subscribe, Mrs. Martin tells me that her collection is not to consist only of novels, but of every kind of literature, &c. She might have spared this pretension to our family, who are great novel-readers and not ashamed of being so; but it was necessary, I suppose, to the self-consequence of half her subscribers.

I hope and imagine that Edward Taylor is to inherit all Sir Edward Dering's *fortune as well as all his own father's. I took care to tell Mrs. Lefroy of your calling on her mother, and she seemed pleased with it.*

I enjoyed the hard black frosts of last week very much, and one day while they lasted walked to Deane by myself. I do not know that I ever did such a thing in my life before.

Charles Powlett has been very ill, but is getting well again. His wife is discovered to be everything that the neighbourhood could wish her, silly and cross as well as extravagant. Earle Harwood and his friend Mr. Bailey came to Deane yesterday, but are not to stay above a day or two. Earle has got the appointment to a prison-ship at Portsmouth, which he has been for some time desirous of having, and he and his wife are to live on board for the future.

We dine now at half-past three, and have done dinner, I suppose, before you begin. We drink tea at half-past six. I am afraid you will despise us. My father reads Cowper to us in the morning, to which I listen when I can. How do you spend your evenings? I guess that Elizabeth works [does needlework], that you read to her, and that Edward goes to sleep. My mother continues hearty; her appetite and nights are very good, but she sometimes complains of an asthma, a dropsy, water in her chest, and a liver disorder.

*The third Miss Irish Lefroy is going to be married to a Mr. Courteney, but whether James or Charles I do not know. Miss Lyford is gone into Suffolk with her brother and Miss Lodge [fiancee of John Lyford]. Everybody is now very busy in making up an income for the two latter. Miss Lodge has only 800*l*. of her own, and it is not supposed that her father can give her much; therefore the good offices of the neighbourhood will be highly acceptable. John Lyford means to take pupils.*

James Digweed has had a very ugly cut – how could it happen? It happened by a young horse which he had lately purchased, and which he was trying to back into its stable; the animal kicked him down with his forefeet, and kicked a great hole in his head; he scrambled away as soon as he could, but was stunned for a time, and suffered a good deal of pain afterwards. Yesterday he got upon the horse again, and, for fear of something worse, was forced to throw himself off.

Wednesday. – *I have changed my mind, and changed the trimmings of my cap this morning; they are now such as you suggested. I felt as if I should not prosper if I strayed from your directions, and I think it makes me look more like Lady Conyngham now than it did before, which is all that one lives for now. I believe I* shall *make my new gown like my robe, but the back of the latter is all in a piece with the tail, and will seven yards enable me to copy it in that respect?*

Mary went to church on Sunday, and had the weather been smiling, we should have seen her here before this time. Perhaps I may stay at Manydown as long as Monday, but not longer. Martha sends me word that she is too busy to write to me now, and but for your letter I should have supposed her deep in the study of medicine preparatory to their removal from Ibthorp. The letter to Gambier goes to-day.

I expect a very stupid ball; there will be nobody worth dancing with, and nobody worth talking to but Catherine[Bigg], for I believe Mrs. Lefroy will not be there. Lucy [Lefroy] is to go with Mrs. Russell.

People get so horridly poor and economical in this part of the world that I have no patience with them. Kent is the only place for happiness; everybody is rich there. I must do similar justice, however, to the Windsor neighbourhood. I have been forced to let James and Miss Debary have two sheets of your drawing-paper, but they shan't have any more; there are not above three or four left, besides one of a smaller and richer sort. Perhaps you may want some more if you come through town in your return, or rather buy some more, for your wanting it will not depend on your coming through town, I imagine.

I have just heard from Martha and Frank: his letter was written on November 12. All well and nothing particular.

J. A.

Miss Austen, Godmersham Park, Faversham.

XIV

Steventon: Monday night (December 24).

MY DEAR CASSANDRA,

I have got some pleasant news for you which I am eager to communicate, and therefore begin my letter sooner, though I shall not send *it sooner than usual.*

Admiral Gambier, in reply to my father's application, writes as follows: – 'As it is usual to keep young officers in small vessels, it being most proper on account of their inexperience, and it being also a situation where they are more in the way of learning their duty, your son has been continued in the 'Scorpion'; but I have mentioned to the Board of Admiralty his wish to be in a frigate, and when a proper opportunity offers and it is judged that he has taken his turn in a small ship, I hope he will be removed. With regard to your son now in the 'London' I am glad I can give you the assurance that his promotion is likely to take place very soon, as Lord Spencer has been so good as to say he would include him in an arrangement that he proposes making in a short time relative to some promotions in that quarter.'

There! I may now finish my letter and go and hang myself, for I am sure I can neither write nor do anything which will not appear insipid to you after this. Now *I really think he will soon be made, and only wish we could communicate our foreknowledge of the event to him whom it principally concerns. My father has written to Daysh [at the Navy Office] to desire that he will inform us, if he can, when the commission is sent. Your chief wish is now ready to be accomplished; and could Lord Spencer [First Lord of the Admiralty] give happiness to Martha [possibly the sisters hoped that she would fall in love with Frank] at the same time, what a joyful heart he would make of yours!*

I have sent the same extract of the sweets of Gambier to Charles, who, poor fellow, though he sinks into nothing but an humble attendant on the hero of the piece, will, I hope, be contented with the prospect held out to him. By what the Admiral says, it appears as if he had been designedly kept in the 'Scorpion.' But I will not torment myself with conjectures and suppositions; facts shall satisfy me.

Frank had not heard from any of us for ten weeks when he wrote to me on November 12 in consequence of Lord St. Vincent being removed to Gibraltar. When his commission is sent, however, it will not be so long on its road as our letters, because all the Government despatches are forwarded by land to his lordship from Lisbon with great regularity.

I returned from Manydown this morning, and found my mother certainly in no respect worse than when I left her. She does not like the cold weather, but that we cannot help. I spent my time very quietly and very pleasantly with Catherine. Miss Blackford is agreeable enough. I do not want people to be very agreeable, as it saves me the trouble of liking them a great deal. I found only Catherine and her when I got to Manydown on Thursday. We dined together and went together to Worting to seek the protection of Mrs. Clarke, with whom were Lady Mildmay, her eldest son, and a Mr. and Mrs. Hoare.

Our ball was very thin, but by no means unpleasant. There were thirty-one people, and only eleven ladies out of the number, and but five single women in the room. Of the gentlemen present you may have some idea from the list of my partners – Mr. Wood, G. Lefroy, Rice, a Mr. Butcher (belonging to the Temples, a sailor and not of the 11th Light Dragoons), Mr. Temple (not the horrid one of all), Mr. Wm. Orde (cousin to the Kingsclere man), Mr. John Harwood, and Mr. Calland, who appeared as usual with his hat in his hand, and stood every now and then behind Catherine and me to be talked to and abused for not dancing. We teased him, however, into it at last. I was very glad to see him again after so long a separation, and he was altogether rather the genius and flirt of the evening. He enquired after you.

There were twenty dances, and I danced them all, and without any fatigue. I was glad to find myself capable of dancing so much, and with so much satisfaction as I did; from my slender enjoyment of the Ashford balls (as assemblies for dancing) I had not thought myself equal to it, but in cold weather and with few couples I fancy I could just as well dance for a week together as for half an hour. My black cap was openly admired by Mrs. Lefroy, and secretly I imagine by everybody else in the room.

Tuesday. – *I thank you for your long letter, which I will endeavour to deserve by writing the rest of this as closely as possible. I am full of joy at much of your information; that you should have been to a ball, and have danced at it, and supped with the Prince [Prince William Frederick, in Kent on military duty], and that you should meditate the purchase of a new muslin gown, are delightful circumstances.* I *am determined to buy a handsome one whenever I can, and I am so tired and ashamed of half my present stock, that I even blush at the sight of the wardrobe which contains them. But I will not be much longer libelled by the possession of my coarse spot; I shall turn it into a petticoat very soon. I wish you a merry Christmas, but* no *compliments of the season.*

Poor Edward! It is very hard that he, who has everything else in the world that he can wish for, should not have good health too. But I hope with the assistance of stomach complaints, faintnesses, and sicknesses, he will soon be restored to that blessing likewise. If his nervous complaint proceeded from a suppression of something that ought to be thrown out, which does not seem unlikely, the first of these disorders may really be a remedy, and I sincerely wish it may, for I know no one more deserving of happiness without alloy than Edward is.

I cannot determine what to do about my new gown; I wish such things were to be bought ready-made. I have some hopes of meeting Martha at the christening [of James Edward Austen] at Deane next Tuesday, and shall see what she can do for me. I want to have something suggested which will give me no trouble of thought or direction.

Again I return to my joy that you danced at Ashford, and that you supped with the Prince. I can perfectly comprehend Mrs. Cage's distress and perplexity. She has all those kind of foolish and incomprehensible feelings which would make her fancy herself uncomfortable in such a party. I love her, however, in spite of all her nonsense. Pray give 't'other Miss Austen's' compliments to Edward Bridges when you see him again.

I insist upon your persevering in your intention of buying a new gown; I am sure you must want one, and as you will have 5l. *due in a week's, time, I am certain you may afford it very well, and if you think you cannot, I will give you the body-lining.*

Of my charities to the poor since I came home you shall have a faithful account. I have given a pair of worsted stockings to Mary Hutchins, Dame Kew, Mary Steevens, and Dame Staples; a shift to Hannah Staples, and a shawl to Betty Dawkins; amounting in all to about half a guinea. But I have no reason to suppose that the Battys *would accept of anything, because I have not made them the offer.*

I am glad to hear such a good account of Harriet Bridges [sister of Elizabeth Austen]; she goes on now as young ladies of seventeen ought to do, admired and admiring, in a much more rational way than her three elder sisters, who had so little of that kind of youth. I dare say she fancies Major

Elkington [this should read Elrington] as agreeable as Warren, and if she can think so, it is very well.

I was to have dined at Deane to-day, but the weather is so cold that I am not sorry to be kept at home by the appearance of snow. We are to have company to dinner on Friday: the three Digweeds and James. We shall be a nice silent party, I suppose. Seize upon the scissors as soon as you possibly can on the receipt of this. I only fear your being too late to secure the prize.

The Lords of the Admiralty will have enough of our applications at present, for I hear from Charles that he has written to Lord Spencer himself to be removed. I am afraid his Serene Highness will be in a passion, and order some of our heads to be cut off.

My mother wants to know whether Edward has ever made the hen-house which they planned together. I am rejoiced to hear from Martha that they certainly continue at Ibthorp, and I have just heard that I am sure of meeting Martha at the christening.

You deserve a longer letter than this; but it is my unhappy fate seldom to treat people so well as they deserve...God bless you!

Yours affectionately,
JANE AUSTEN.

Wednesday. – *The snow came to nothing yesterday, so I* did *go to Deane, and returned home at nine o'clock at night in the little carriage, and without being very cold.*

Miss Austen, Godmersham Park,
Faversham, Kent.

XV

Steventon: Friday (December 28).
MY DEAR CASSANDRA,

Frank is made. He was yesterday raised to the rank of Commander, and appointed to the 'Petterel' sloop, now at Gibraltar. A letter from Daysh has just announced this, and as it is confirmed by a very friendly one from Mr. Mathew [father of James Austen's first wife whose niece was married to Admiral Gambier] to the same effect, transcribing one from Admiral Gambier to the General, we have no reason to suspect the truth of it.

As soon as you have cried a little for joy, you may go on, and learn farther that the India House have taken Captain Austen's *petition into consideration – this comes from Daysh – and likewise that Lieutenant Charles John Austen is removed to the 'Tamar' frigate – this comes from the Admiral. We cannot find out where the 'Tamar' is, but I hope we shall now see Charles here at all events.*

This letter is to be dedicated entirely to good news. If you will send my father an account of your washing and letter expenses, &c., he will send you a draft for the amount of it, as well as for your next quarter, and for Edward's rent. If you don't buy a muslin gown now on the strength of this money and Frank's promotion, I shall never forgive you.

Mrs. Lefroy has just sent me word that Lady Dorchester meant to invite me to her ball on January 8, which, though an humble blessing compared with what the last page records, I do not consider as any calamity.

I cannot write any more now, but I have written enough to make you very happy, and therefore may safely conclude.

Yours affectionately,

JANE.

Miss Austen, Godmersham Park.

XVI

Steventon: Tuesday (January 8).

MY DEAR CASSANDRA,

You must read your letters over five *times in future before you send them, and then, perhaps, you may find them as entertaining as I do. I laughed at several parts of the one which I am now answering.*

Charles is not come yet, but he must come this morning, or he shall never know what I will do to him. The ball at Kempshott is this evening, and I have got him an invitation, though I have not been so considerate as to get him a partner. But the cases are different between him and Eliza Bailey, for he is not in a dying way, and may therefore be equal to getting a partner for himself. I believe I told you that Monday was to be the ball night, for which, and for all other errors into which I may ever have led you, I humbly ask your pardon.

Elizabeth is very cruel about my writing music, and, as a punishment for her, I should insist upon always writing out all hers for her in future, if I were not punishing myself at the same time.

I am tolerably glad to hear that Edward's income is so good a one – as glad as I can be at anybody's being rich except you and me – and I am thoroughly rejoiced to hear of his present to you.

I am not to wear my white satin cap to-night, after all; I am to wear a mamalone [marmaluke, Egyptian style] cap instead, which Charles Fowle sent to Mary, and which she lends me. It is all the fashion now; worn at the opera, and by Lady Mildmays at Hackwood balls. I hate describing such things, and I dare say you will be able to guess what it is like. I have got over the dreadful epocha of mantua-making much better than I expected. My gown is made very much like my blue one, which you always told me sat very well, with only these variations: the sleeves are short, the wrap fuller, the apron comes over it, and a band of the same completes the whole.

I assure you that I dread the idea of going to Brighton as much as you do, but I am not without hopes that something may happen to prevent it.

F— has lost his election at B—, [these letters may have been deleted by Cassandra because they would have identified family members] and perhaps they may not be able to see company for some time. They talk of going to Bath, too, in the spring, and perhaps they may be overturned in their way down, and all laid up for the summer.

Wednesday. – *I have had a cold and weakness in one of my eyes for some days, which makes writing neither very pleasant nor very profitable, and which will probably prevent my finishing this letter myself. My mother has undertaken to do it for me, and I shall leave the Kempshott ball for her.*

You express so little anxiety about my being murdered under Ash Park Copse by Mrs. Hulbert's servant, that I have a great mind not to tell you whether I was or not, and shall only say that I did not return home that night or the next, as Martha kindly made room for me in her bed, which was the shut-up one in the new nursery. Nurse and the child slept upon the floor, and there we all were in some confusion and great comfort. The bed did exceedingly well for us, both to lie awake in and talk till two o'clock, and to sleep in the rest of the night. I love Martha better than ever, and I mean to go and see her, if I can, when she gets home. We all dined at the Harwoods' on Thursday, and the party broke up the next morning.

This complaint in my eye has been a sad bore to me, for I have not been able to read or work in any comfort since Friday, but one advantage will be derived from it, for I shall be such a proficient in music by the time I have got rid of my cold, that I shall be perfectly qualified in that *science at least to take Mr. Roope's [music master to the Finch-Hatton family] office at Eastwell next summer; and I am sure of Elizabeth's recommendation, be it only on Harriet's account. Of my talent in drawing I have given specimens in my letters to you, and I have nothing to do but to invent a few hard names for the stars.*

Mary grows rather more reasonable about her child's beauty, and says that she does not think him really handsome; but I suspect her moderation to be something like that of W— W—'s mamma. Perhaps Mary has told you that they are going to enter more into dinner parties; the Biggs and Mr. Holder dine there to-morrow, and I am to meet them. I shall sleep there. Catherine has the honour of giving her name to a set, which will be composed of two Withers, two Heathcotes, a Blackford, and no Bigg except herself. She congratulated me last night on Frank's promotion, as if she really felt the joy she talked of.

My sweet little George! I am delighted to hear that he has such an inventive genius as to face-making. I admired his yellow wafer very much, and hope he will choose the wafer for your next letter. I wore my green shoes last night, and took my white *fan with me; I am very glad he never threw it into the river.*

Mrs. Knight giving up the Godmersham estate to Edward was no such prodigious act of generosity after all, it seems, for she has reserved herself an income out of it still; this ought to be known, that her conduct may not be overrated. I rather think Edward shows the most magnanimity of the two, in accepting her resignation with such incumbrances.

The more I write, the better my eye gets, so I shall at least keep on till it is quite well, before I give up my pen to my mother.

Mrs. Bramston's little movable apartment was tolerably filled last night by herself, Mrs. H. Blackstone, her two daughters, and me. I do not like the Miss Blackstones; indeed, I was always determined not to like them, so there is the less merit in it. Mrs. Bramston was very civil, kind, and noisy. I spent a very pleasant evening, chiefly among the Manydown party. There was the same kind of supper as last year, and the same want of chairs. There were more dancers than the room could conveniently hold, which is enough to constitute a good ball at any time.

I do not think I was very much in request. People were rather apt not to ask me till they could not help it; one's consequence, you know, varies so much at times without any particular reason. There was one gentleman, an officer of the Cheshire, a very good-looking young man, who, I was told, wanted very much to be introduced to me, but as he did not want it quite enough to take much trouble in effecting it, we never could bring it about.

I danced with Mr. John Wood again, twice with a Mr. South, a lad from Winchester, who, I suppose, is as far from being related to the bishop of that diocese [whose name was North] as it is possible to be, with G. Lefroy, and J. Harwood, who, I think, takes to me rather more than he used to do. One of my gayest actions was sitting down two dances in preference to having Lord Bolton's eldest son for my partner, who danced too ill to be endured. The Miss Charterises were there, and played the parts of the Miss Edens with great spirit. Charles never came. Naughty Charles! I suppose he could not get superseded in time.

Miss Debary has replaced your two sheets of drawing-paper with two of superior size and quality; so I do not grudge her having taken them at all now. Mr. Ludlow and Miss Pugh of Andover are lately married, and so is Mrs. Skeete of Basingstoke, and Mr. French, chemist, of Reading.

I do not wonder at your wanting to read 'First Impressions' again, so seldom as you have gone through it, and that so long ago. I am much obliged to you for meaning to leave my old petticoat behind you. I have long secretly wished it might be done, but had not courage to make the request.

Pray mention the name of Maria Montresor's lover when you write next. My mother wants to know it, and I have not courage to look back into your letters to find it out.

I shall not be able to send this till to-morrow, and you will be disappointed on Friday; I am very sorry for it, but I cannot help it.

The partnership between Jeffereys, Toomer, and Legge [partners in a

Basingstoke bank] dissolved; the two latter are melted away into nothing, and it is to be hoped that Jeffereys will soon break, for the sake of a few heroines whose money he may have. I wish you joy of your birthday twenty times over.

I shall be able to send this to the post to-day which exalts me to the utmost pinnacle of human felicity, and makes me bask in the sunshine of prosperity, or gives me any other sensation of pleasure in studied language which you may prefer. Do not be angry with me for not filling my sheet, and believe me yours affectionately,

J. A.

Miss Austen, Godmersham Park,
Faversham.

XVII

Steventon: Monday (January 21)
MY DEAR CASSANDRA,

I will endeavour to make this letter more worthy your acceptance than my last, which was so shabby a one that I think Mr. Marshall [postmaster] could never charge you with the postage. My eyes have been very indifferent since it was written, but are now getting better once more; keeping them so many hours open on Thursday night, as well as the dust of the ball-room, injured them a good deal. I use them as little as I can, but you know, and Elizabeth knows, and everybody who ever had weak eyes knows, how delightful it is to hurt them by employment, against the advice and entreaty of all one's friends.

Charles leaves us to-night. The 'Tamar' is in the Downs [anchorage off Ramsgate and Deal, Kent], and Mr. Daysh advises him to join her there directly, as there is no chance of her going to the westward. Charles does not approve of this at all, and will not be much grieved if he should be too late for her before she sails, as he may then hope to get into a better station. He attempted to go to town last night, and got as far on his road thither as Dean Gate; but both the coaches were full, and we had the pleasure of seeing him back again. He will call on Daysh to-morrow to know whether the 'Tamar' has sailed or not, and if she is still at the Downs he will proceed in one of the night coaches to Deal. I want to go with him, that I may explain the country to him properly between Canterbury and Rowling, but the unpleasantness of returning by myself deters me. I should like to go as far as Ospringe with him very much indeed, that I might surprise you at Godmersham.

Martha writes me word that Charles was very much admired at Kintbury, and Mrs. Lefroy never saw anyone so much improved in her life, and thinks him handsomer than Henry. He appears to far more advantage here than he did at Godmersham, not surrounded by strangers and neither oppressed by a pain in his face or powder in his hair.

James christened Elizabeth Caroline [daughter of Fulwar Craven and Eliza Fowle] on Saturday morning, and then came home. Mary, Anna, and Edward have left us of course; before the second went I took down her answer to her cousin Fanny.

*Yesterday came a letter to my mother from Edward Cooper to announce, not the birth of a child, but of a living; for Mrs. Leigh has begged his acceptance of the Rectory of Hamstall-Ridware in Staffordshire, vacant by Mr. Johnson's death. We collect from his letter that he means to reside there, in which he shows his wisdom. Staffordshire is a good way off; so we shall see nothing more of them till, some fifteen years hence, the Miss Coopers are presented to us, fine, jolly, handsome, ignorant girls. The living is valued at 140*l. *a year, but perhaps it may be improvable. How will they be able to convey the furniture of the dressing-room so far in safety?*

Our first cousins seem all dropping off very fast. One is incorporated into the family, another dies, and a third goes into Staffordshire. We can learn nothing of the disposal of the other living. I have not the smallest notion of Fulwar's having it. Lord Craven has probably other connections and more intimate ones, in that line, than he now has with the Kintbury family.

Our ball on Thursday was a very poor one, only eight couple and but twenty-three people in the room; but it was not the ball's fault, for we were deprived of two or three families by the sudden illness of Mr. Wither, who was seized that morning at Winchester with a return of his former alarming complaint. An express was sent off from thence to the family; Catherine and Miss Blackford were dining with Mrs. Russell. Poor Catherine's distress must have been very great. She was prevailed on to wait till the Heathcotes could come from Wintney, and then with those two and Harris [Bigg Wither] proceeded directly to Winchester. In such a disorder his danger, I suppose, must always be great; but from this attack he is now rapidly recovering, and will be well enough to return to Manydown, I fancy, in a few days.

It was a fine thing for conversation at the ball. But it deprived us not only of the Biggs, but of Mrs. Russell too, and of the Boltons and John Harwood, who were dining there likewise, and of Mr. Lane, who kept away as related to the family. Poor man! – I mean Mr. Wither – his life is so useful, his character so respectable and worthy, that I really believe there was a good deal of sincerity in the general concern expressed on his account.

Our ball was chiefly made up of Jervoises and Terrys, the former of whom were apt to be vulgar, the latter to be noisy. I had an odd set of partners: Mr. Jenkins, Mr. Street, Col. Jervoise, James Digweed, J. Lyford, and Mr. Biggs, a friend of the latter. I had a very pleasant evening, however, though you will probably find out that there was no particular reason for it; but I do not think it worth while to wait for enjoyment until there is some real opportunity for it. Mary behaved very well, and was not at all fidgetty. For the history of her adventures at the ball I refer you to Anna's letter.

When you come home you will have some shirts to make up for Charles. Mrs. Davies [draper] frightened him into buying a piece of Irish when we were in Basingstoke. Mr. Daysh supposes that Captain Austen's commission has reached him by this time.

Tuesday. – *Your letter has pleased and amused me very much. Your essay on happy fortnights is highly ingenious, and the talobert skin made me laugh a good deal. Whenever I fall into misfortune, how many jokes it ought to furnish to my acquaintance in general, or I shall die dreadfully in their debt for entertainment.*

It began to occur to me before you mentioned it that I had been somewhat silent as to my mother's health for some time, but I thought you could have no difficulty in divining its exact state – you, who have guessed so much stranger things. She is tolerably well – better upon the whole than she was some weeks ago. She would tell you herself that she has a very dreadful cold in her head at present; but I have not much compassion for colds in the head without fever or sore throat.

Our own particular little brother [Charles] got a place in the coach last night, and is now, I suppose, in town. I have no objection at all to your buying our gowns there, as your imagination has pictured to you exactly such a one as is necessary to make me happy. You quite abash me by your progress in notting, for I am still without silk. You must get me some in town or in Canterbury; it should be finer than yours.

I thought Edward would not approve of Charles being a crop [having his hair cut], and rather wished you to conceal it from him at present, lest it might fall on his spirits and retard his recovery. My father furnishes him with a pig from Cheesedown [farm]; it is already killed and cut up, but it is not to weigh more than nine stone; the season is too far advanced to get him a larger one. My mother means to pay herself for the salt and the trouble of ordering it to be cured by the sparibs, the souse, and the lard. We have had one dead lamb.

I congratulate you on Mr. E. Hatton's good fortune. I suppose the marriage will now follow out of hand. Give my compliments to Miss Finch.

What time in March may we expect your return in? I begin to be very tired of answering people's questions on that subject, and, independent of that, *I shall be very glad to see you at home again, and then if we can get Martha and shirk...who will be so happy as we?*

I think of going to Ibthorp in about a fortnight. My eyes are pretty well, I thank you, if you please.

Wednesday, 23rd. – *I wish my dear Fanny many returns of this day, and that she may on every return enjoy as much pleasure as she is now receiving from her doll's-beds.*

I have just heard from Charles, who is by this time at Deal. He is to be Second Lieutenant, which pleases him very well. The 'Endymion' is come into the Downs, which pleases him likewise. He expects to be ordered to Sheerness shortly, as the 'Tamar' has never been refitted.

My father and mother made the same match for you last night, and are very much pleased with it. He *is a beauty of my mother's.*

Yours affectionately,

JANE.

Miss Austen, Godmersham Park,

Faversham,

1799

The third division consists of four letters written from Bath in May and June, 1799, when Mr. and Mrs. Austen of Godmersham had taken a house for a month, in order that the former might 'try the waters' for the benefit of his health, which was supposed to be delicate; the experiment seems to have been successful, for he lived fifty-three years longer, dying at Godmersham in December, 1852, at the good old age of eighty-two. Cassandra had stayed at home with her father at Steventon, and Mrs. Austen and Jane had accompanied the Godmersham party. These letters contain little more than ordinary chit-chat, and for the most part explain themselves. There is another allusion to 'Pride and Prejudice' under the name of 'First Impressions,' which Martha Lloyd seems to have been allowed to read; another proof that this work at least was read and talked over in the family long before it was published.

XVIII

13, Queen's Square, Friday (May 17)

MY DEAREST CASSANDRA,

Our journey yesterday went off exceedingly well; nothing occurred to alarm or delay us. We found the roads in excellent order, had very good horses all the way, and reached Devizes with ease by four o'clock. I suppose John [coachman] has told you in what manner we were divided when we left Andover, and no alteration was afterwards made. At Devizes we had comfortable rooms and a good dinner, to which we sat down about five; amongst other things we had asparagus and a lobster, which made me wish for you, and some cheesecakes, on which the children made so delightful a supper as to endear the town of Devizes to them for a long time.

Well, here we are at Bath; we got here about one o'clock, and have been arrived just long enough to go over the house, fix on our rooms, and be very well pleased with the whole of it. Poor Elizabeth has had a dismal ride of it from Devizes, for it has rained almost all the way, and our first view of Bath has been just as gloomy as it was last November twelvemonth.

I have got so many things to say, so many things equally important, that I know not on which to decide at present, and shall therefore go and eat with the children.

We stopped in Paragon as we came along, but as it was too wet and dirty for us to get out, we could only see Frank, who told us that his master was very indifferent, but had had a better night last night than usual. In Paragon we met Mrs. Foley and Mrs. Dowdeswell with her yellow shawl airing out, and at the bottom of Kingsdown Hill we met a gentleman in a buggy, who, on minute examination, turned out to be Dr. Hall – and Dr. Hall in such very deep mourning that either his mother, his wife, or himself must be dead. These are all of our acquaintances who have yet met our eyes.

I have some hopes of being plagued about my trunk; I had *more a few hours ago, for it was too heavy to go by the coach which brought Thomas and Rebecca [servants] from Devizes; there was reason to suppose that it might be too heavy likewise for any other coach, and for a long time we could hear of no waggon to convey it. At last, however, we unluckily discovered that one was just on the point of setting out for this place, but at any rate the trunk cannot be here till to-morrow; so far we are safe, and who knows what may not happen to procure a farther delay?*

I put Mary's letter into the post-office at Andover with my own hand.

We are exceedingly pleased with the house; the rooms are quite as large as we expected. Mrs. Bromley [landlady] is a fat woman in mourning, and a little black kitten runs about the staircase. Elizabeth has the apartment within the drawing-room; she wanted my mother to have it, but as there was no bed in the inner one, and the stairs are so much easier of ascent, or my mother so much stronger than in Paragon as not to regard the double flight, it is settled for us to be above, where we have two very nice-sized rooms, with dirty [this may be a misreading of dimity] quilts and everything comfortable. I have the outward and larger apartment, as I ought to have; which is quite as large as our bedroom at home, and my mother's is not materially less. The beds are both as large as any at Steventon, and I have a very nice chest of drawers and a closet full of shelves – so full indeed that there is nothing else in it, and it should therefore be called a cupboard rather than a closet, I suppose.

Tell Mary that there were some carpenters at work in the inn at Devizes this morning, but as I could not be sure of their being Mrs. W. Fowle's relations, I did not make myself known to them.

I hope it will be a tolerable afternoon. When first we came, all the umbrellas were up, but now the pavements are getting very white again.

My mother does not seem at all the worse for her journey, nor are any of us, I hope, though Edward seemed rather fagged last night, and not very brisk this morning; but I trust the bustle of sending for tea, coffee, and sugar, &c., and going out to taste a cheese himself, will do him good.

There was a very long list of arrivals here in the newspaper yesterday, so that we need not immediately dread absolute solitude; and there is a public breakfast in Sydney Gardens every morning, so that we shall not be wholly starved.

Elizabeth has just had a very good account of the three little boys [the younger children had remained behind at Godmersham] I hope you are very busy and very comfortable. I find no difficulty in closing my eyes. I like our situation very much; it is far more cheerful than Paragon, and the prospect from the drawing-room window, at which I now write, is rather picturesque, as it commands a prospective view of the left side of Brock Street, broken by three Lombardy poplars in the garden of the last house in Queen's Parade.

I am rather impatient to know the fate of my best gown, but I suppose it will be some days before Frances [maidservant] can get through the trunk. In the meantime I am, with many thanks for your trouble in making it, as well as marking my silk stockings,

Yours very affectionately,

JANE.

A great deal of love from everybody.

Miss Austen, Steventon, Overton, Hants.

XIX

13, Queen's Square, Sunday (June 2).

MY DEAR CASSANDRA,

I am obliged to you for two letters, one from yourself and the other from Mary, for of the latter I knew nothing till on the receipt of yours yesterday, when the pigeon-basket was examined, and I received my due. As I have written to her since the time which ought to have brought me hers, I suppose she will consider herself, as I choose to consider, still in my debt.

I will lay out all the little judgment I have in endeavouring to get such stockings for Anna as she will approve; but I do not know that I shall execute Martha's commission at all, for I am not fond of ordering shoes; and, at any rate, they shall all have flat heels.

What must I tell you of Edward? Truth or falsehood. I will try the former, and you may choose for yourself another time. He was better yesterday than he had been for two or three days before – about as well as while he was at Steventon. He drinks at the Hetling Pump, is to bathe to-morrow, and try electricity on Tuesday. He proposed the latter himself to Dr. Fellowes, who made no objection to it, but I fancy we are all unanimous in expecting no advantage from it. At present I have no great notion of our staying here beyond the month.

I heard from Charles last week; they were to sail on Wednesday.

My mother seems remarkably well. My uncle overwalked himself at first, and can now only travel in a chair, but is otherwise very well.

My cloak is come home. I like it very much, and can now exclaim with delight, like J. Bond at hay-harvest, 'This is what I have been looking for these three years.' I saw some gauzes in a shop in Bath Street yesterday at only 4d. *a yard, but they were not so good or so pretty as mine. Flowers are very much worn, and fruit is still more the thing. Elizabeth has a bunch of strawberries, and I have seen grapes, cherries, plums, and apricots. There are likewise almonds and raisins, French plums, and tamarinds at the grocers', but I have never seen any of them in hats. A plum or greengage would cost three shillings; cherries and grapes about five, I believe, but this is at some of the dearest shops. My aunt has told me of a very cheap one, near Walcot Church, to which I shall go in quest of something for you. I have never seen an old woman at the pump-room.*

Elizabeth has given me a hat, and it is not only a pretty hat, but a pretty style *of hat too. It is something like Eliza's, only, instead of being all straw, half of it is narrow purple ribbon. I flatter myself, however, that you can understand very little of it from this description. Heaven forbid that I should ever offer such encouragement to explanations as to give a clear one on any occasion myself! But I must write no more of this...*

I spent Friday evening with the Mapletons, and was obliged to submit to being pleased in spite of my inclination. We took a very charming walk from six to eight up Beacon Hill, and across some fields, to the village of Charlecombe, which is sweetly situated in a little green valley, as a village with such a name ought to be. Marianne is sensible and intelligent, and even Jane, considering how fair she is, is not unpleasant. We had a Miss North and a Mr. Gould of our party; the latter walked home with me after tea. He is a very young man, just entered Oxford, wears spectacles, and has heard that 'Evelina' was written by Dr. Johnson.

I am afraid I cannot undertake to carry Martha's shoes home, for, though we had plenty of room in our trunks when we came, we shall have many more things to take back, and I must allow besides for my *packing.*

There is to be a grand gala on Tuesday evening in Sydney Gardens, a concert, with illuminations and fireworks. To the latter Elizabeth and I look forward with pleasure, and even the concert will have more than its usual charm for me, as the gardens are large enough for me to get pretty well beyond the reach of its sound. In the morning Lady Willoughby is to present the colours to some corps, or Yeomanry, or other, in the Crescent, and that such festivities may have a proper commencement, we think of going to...

I am quite pleased with Martha and Mrs. Lefroy for wanting the pattern of our caps, but I am not so well pleased with your giving it to them. Some wish, some prevailing wish, is necessary to the animation of everybody's mind, and in gratifying this you leave them to form some other which will not probably be half so innocent. I shall not forget to write to Frank. Duty and love, &c

Yours affectionately,
JANE.

My uncle is quite surprised at my hearing from you so often; but as long as we can keep the frequency of our correspondence from Martha's uncle we will not fear our own.
Miss Austen, Steventon.

XX

13, Queen Square, Tuesday (June 11).
MY DEAR CASSANDRA,

Your letter yesterday made me very happy. I am heartily glad that you have escaped any share in the impurities of Deane, and not sorry, as it turns out, that our stay here has been lengthened. I feel tolerably secure of our getting away next week, though it is certainly possible that we may remain till Thursday the 27th. I wonder what we shall do with all our intended visits this summer! I should like to make a compromise with Adlestrop, Harden, and Bookham, that Martha's spending the summer at Steventon should be considered as our respective visits to them all.

Edward has been pretty well for this last week, and as the waters have never disagreed *with him in any respect, we are inclined to hope that he will derive advantage from them in the end. Everybody encourages us in this expectation, for they all say that the effect of the waters cannot be negative, and many are the instances in which their benefit is felt afterwards more than on the spot. He is more comfortable here than I thought he would be, and so is Elizabeth, though they will both, I believe, be very glad to get away – the latter especially, which one can't wonder at* somehow. *So much for Mrs. Piozzi. [Hester Thrale, woman of letters] I had some thoughts of writing the whole of my letter in her style, but I believe I shall not.*

Though you have given me unlimited powers concerning your sprig, I cannot determine what to do about it, and shall therefore in this and in every other future letter continue to ask your farther directions. We have been to the cheap shop, and very cheap we found it, but there are only flowers made there, no fruit; and as I could get four or five very pretty sprigs of the former for the same money which would procure only one Orleans plum – in short, could get more for three or four shillings than I could have means of bringing home – I cannot decide on the fruit till I hear from you again. Besides, I cannot help thinking that it is more natural to have flowers grow out of the head than fruit. What do you think on that subject?

I would not let Martha read 'First Impressions' again upon any account, and am very glad that I did not leave it in your power. She is very cunning, but I saw through her design; she means to publish it from memory, and one more perusal must enable her to do it. As for 'Fitzalbini,' when I get home she shall have it as soon as ever she will own that Mr. Elliott is handsomer than Mr. Lance, that fair men are preferable to black; for I mean to take every opportunity of rooting out her prejudices.

Benjamin Portal is here. How charming that is! I do not exactly know why, but the phrase followed so naturally that I could not help putting it down. My mother saw him the other day, but without making herself known to him.

I am very glad you liked my lace, and so are you, and so is Martha, and we are all glad together. I have got your cloak home, which is quite delightful – as delightful at least as half the circumstances which are called so.

I do not know what is the matter with me to-day, but I cannot write quietly; I am always wandering away into some exclamation or other. Fortunately I have nothing very particular to say.

We walked to Weston one evening last week, and liked it very much. Liked what *very much? Weston? No,* walking *to Weston. I have not expressed myself properly, but I hope you will understand me.*

We have not been to any public place lately, nor performed anything out of the common daily routine of No. 13, Queen Square, Bath. But to-day we were to have dashed away at a very extraordinary rate, by dining out, had it not so happened that we did not go.

Edward renewed his acquaintance lately with Mr. Evelyn, who lives in the Queen's Parade, and was invited to a family dinner, which I believe at first Elizabeth was rather sorry at his accepting; but yesterday Mrs. Evelyn called on us, and her manners were so pleasing that we liked the idea of going very much. The Biggs would call her a nice woman. But Mr. Evelyn, who was indisposed yesterday, is worse to-day, and we are put off.

It is rather impertinent to suggest any household care to a housekeeper, but I just venture to say that the coffee-mill will be wanted every day while Edward is at Steventon, as he always drinks coffee for breakfast.

Fanny desires her love to you, her love to grandpapa, her love to Anna, and her love to Hannah; the latter is particularly to be remembered. Edward desires his love to you, to grandpapa, to Anna, to little Edward, to Aunt James and Uncle James, and he hopes all your turkeys and ducks, and chicken and guinea fowls are very well; and he wishes you very much to send him a printed letter, and so does Fanny – and they both rather think they shall answer it.

'On more accounts than one you wished our stay here to be lengthened beyond last Thursday.' There is some mystery in this. What have you going on in Hampshire besides the itch *from which you want to keep us?*

Dr. Gardiner was married yesterday to Mrs. Percy and her three daughters.

Now I will give you the history of Mary's veil, in the purchase of which I have so considerably involved you that it is my duty to economise for you in the flowers. I had no difficulty in getting a muslin veil for half a guinea, and not much more in discovering afterwards that the muslin was thick, dirty, and ragged, and therefore would by no means do for a united gift. I changed it consequently as soon as I could, and, considering what a state my imprudence had reduced me to, I thought myself lucky in getting a black lace one for sixteen shillings. I hope the half of that sum will not greatly exceed what you had intended to offer upon the altar of sister-in-law affection. Yours affectionately, JANE.

They [the Bigg sisters] do not seem to trouble you much from Manydown. I have long wanted to quarrel with them, and I believe I shall take this opportunity. There is no denying that they are very capricious – for they like to enjoy their elder sister's company when they can.

Miss Austen, Steventon, Overton, Hants.

XXI

13, Queen Square, Wednesday (June 19).

MY DEAR CASSANDRA,

The children were delighted with your letters, as I fancy they will tell you themselves before this is concluded. Fanny expressed some surprise at the wetness of the wafers, but it did not lead to any suspicion of the truth.

Martha and you were just in time with your commissions, for two o'clock on Monday was the last hour of my receiving them. The office is now closed.

John Lyford's history is a melancholy one. I feel for his family, and when I know that his wife was really fond of him, I will feel for her too, but at present I cannot help thinking their loss the greatest.

Edward has not been well these last two days; his appetite has failed him, and he has complained of sick and uncomfortable feelings, which, with other symptoms, make us think of the gout; perhaps a fit of it might cure him, but I cannot wish it to begin at Bath. He made an important purchase yesterday: no less so than a pair of coach-horses. His friend Mr. Evelyn found them out and recommended them, and if the judgment of a Yahoo [a reference to Gulliver's Travels *by Jonathan Swift] can ever be depended on, I suppose it may now, for I believe Mr. Evelyn has all his life thought more of horses than of anything else. Their colour is black and their size not large; their price sixty guineas, of which the chair mare was taken as fifteen – but this is of course to be a secret.*

Mrs. Williams need not pride herself upon her knowledge of Dr. Mapleton's success here; she knows no more than everybody else knows in Bath. There is not a physician in the place who writes so many prescriptions as he does. I cannot help wishing that Edward had not been tied down to Dr. Fellowes, for, had he come disengaged, we should all have recommended Dr. Mapleton; my uncle and aunt as earnestly as ourselves. I do not see the Miss Mapletons very often, but just as often as I like; we are always very glad to meet, and I do not wish to wear out our satisfaction.

Last Sunday we all drank tea in Paragon; my uncle is still in his flannels, but is getting better again.

On Monday Mr. Evelyn was well enough for us to fulfil our engagement with him; the visit was very quiet and uneventful – pleasant enough. We met only another Mr. Evelyn, his cousin, whose wife came to tea.

Last night we were in Sydney Gardens again, as there was a repetition of the gala which went off so ill on the 4th. We did not go till nine, and then were in very good time for the fireworks, which were really beautiful, and surpassing my expectation; the illuminations too were very, pretty. The weather was as favourable as it was otherwise a fortnight ago. The play on Saturday is, I hope, *to conclude our gaieties here, for nothing but a lengthened stay will make it otherwise. We go with Mrs. Fellowes.*

Edward will not remain at Steventon longer than from Thursday to the following Monday, I believe, as the rent-day is to be fixed for the consecutive *Friday.*

I can recollect nothing more to say at present; perhaps breakfast may assist my ideas. I was deceived – my breakfast supplied only two ideas – that the rolls were good and the butter bad. But the post has been more friendly to me – it has brought me a letter from Miss Pearson.

You may remember that I wrote to her above two months ago about the parcel under my care; and as I had heard nothing from her since, I thought myself obliged to write again, two or three days ago, for after all that has passed [the broken engagement between Henry Austen and Miss Pearson] I was determined that the correspondence should never cease through my means. This second letter has produced an apology for her silence, founded on the illness of several of the family. The exchange of packets is to take place through the medium of Mr. Nutt, probably one of the sons belonging to Woolwich Academy, who comes to Overton in the beginning of July. I am tempted to suspect from some parts of her letter that she has a matrimonial project in view. I shall question her about it when I answer her letter, but all this you know is en mystère *between ourselves.*

Edward has seen the apothecary to whom Dr. Millman recommended him, a sensible, intelligent man, since I began this, and he attributes his present little feverish indisposition to his having ate something unsuited to his stomach. I do not understand that Mr. Anderton suspects the gout at all; the occasional particular glow in the hands and feet, which we considered as a symptom of that disorder, he only calls the effect of the water in promoting a better circulation of the blood.

I cannot help thinking from your account of Mrs. E. H. [Harwood] that Earle's vanity has tempted him to invent the account of her former way of life, that his triumph in securing her might be greater; I dare say she was nothing but an innocent country girl in fact. Adieu! I shall not write again before Sunday, unless anything particular happens.

Yours ever,

JANE.

We shall be with you on Thursday to a very late dinner – later, I suppose, than my father will like for himself – but I give him leave to eat one before. You must give us something very nice, for we are used to live well.

Miss Austen, Steventon, Overton,

1800, 1801

These are all addressed to Godmersham, where Cassandra was staying with her brother Edward. 'Heathcote and Chute forever,' in the first letter (No. 22), refers to the two Conservative members, who again stood and were returned without a contest in 1802. Mr. William Chute, of the Vine, in the parish of Sherborn St. John, Basingstoke, was a mighty fox-hunter, and the founder of the celebrated pack which has since been called by the name of his house. He was elected M. P. for Hants in 1795. Camden mentions this seat in the following laudatory words, after the description of Basing House:–

> Neere unto this house, the Vine sheweth itselfe, a very faire place, and mansion house of the Baron Sands, so named of the vines there, which wee have had in Britaine, since Probus the emperour's time, rather for shade than fruit. For, hee permitted the Britaines to have vines. The first of these Barons was Sir William Sands, whom King Henry the Eighth advanced to that dignitie, being Lord Chamberlaine unto him, and having much amended his estate by marrying Margerie Bray, daughter and heire of John Bray, and cousin to Sir Reinold Bray, a most worthy Knight of the Order of the Garter, and a right noble Banneret: whose son Thomas Lord Sands was grandfather to William L. Sands that now liveth.

Warner has, in his 'History of Hampshire,' an interesting account of this place and of the Sands family, concluding thus: 'About 1654, the ancient family mansion of the Vine, together with the estate, was sold, in those unhappy times, to Chaloner Chute, Esq., a lawyer, who, in 1656, was returned member for Middlesex; and again for the same place in the Parliament of Richard Cromwell; and also Speaker of the House, but from the anxiety of his mind respecting the tumults, he was so ill, that the Parliament chose another Speaker, until his health should be re-established; but that never happened: he dying April 15, 1659.' Anthony Chute, says Warner, 'stood the famous contested election for the county' in 1734, and afterwards sat for Yarmouth and subsequently for Newport in the Isle of Wight. A collateral branch of Chutes, from Norfolk, came into this property in 1776.

An allusion in letter No. 24 (written November 20, 1800) to James Digweed's compliment to Cassandra respecting the fall of two elms, suggests the quotation from a letter published by Mr. Austen Leigh, of the date of November 8, in that same year:–

> Sunday evening. We have had a dreadful storm of wind in the fore-part of this day which has done a great deal of mischief among our trees. I was sitting alone in the dining-room when an odd kind of crash startled me; in a moment afterwards it was repeated. I then went to the window, which I reached just in time to see the last of our two highly valued elms descend into the sweep; the other, which had fallen, I suppose, in the first crash, and which was the nearest to the pond, taking a more easterly direction, sank among our screen of chestnuts and firs, knocking down one spruce fir, breaking off the head of another, and stripping the two corner chestnuts of several branches in its fall. This is not all. One large elm out of the two on the left-hand side as you enter what I call the elm walk was likewise blown down; the maple bearing the weather-cock was broke in two, and what I regret more than all the rest is, that all the three elms which grew in Hall's meadow and gave such ornament to it are gone; two were blown down, and the other so much injured that it cannot stand. I am happy to add, however, that no greater evil than the loss of the trees has been the consequence of the storm in this place, or in our immediate neighbourhood; we grieve, therefore, in some comfort.

In this same twenty-fourth letter occurs the sentence, 'You and George walking to Eggerton!' Eggerton, or more properly Eggarton, was an old manor-house near Godmersham, on the other side of the river. It formerly belonged – that is to say, so long ago as the reign of Queen Elizabeth – to the Scots of Scot's Hall, from whose possession it passed through several hands until it came into those of the Gott family, one of whom left it to the co-heiresses of William Western Hugessen of Provender; and when these two ladies married respectively Sir Edward Knatchbull (my grandfather) and Sir Joseph Banks, this property was sold to Jane, a sister of Mr. Thomas Knight. Another of his sisters, Mrs. Elizabeth Knight, was of weak intellect, and after the two sisters had resided first at Bilting, she was moved to Eggarton, a larger and more convenient house, and two lady attendants, Miss Cuthbert and her sister Maria, were engaged to look after her, which they did for many years. It was to these ladies that the visits from Godmersham were paid. Eggarton House stood on the east side of Godmersham, in the parish of Crundale, near a wood, which went by the name of Purr Wood, and was eventually pulled down by my grandfather, Mr. Knight, who did not care to let it, being so near Godmersham.

The twenty-fifth letter is almost entirely taken up with remarks upon the preparations for leaving Steventon and settling at Bath, which event occurred in 1801, and does not seem to have been regretted by Jane as much as one would have expected. But the fact is that she was very little dependent upon the world outside her own family, and carried with her wherever she went occupations and resources of her own which did not require to be supplemented by extraneous assistance. Her home was wherever her own people were, and whether at Steventon, Bath, or elsewhere, her cheerful temperament was even and unvaried, and assured her own happiness as well as that of those with whom she lived.

The other letters in this division do not seem to require further explanation.

XXII

Steventon: Saturday evening (October 25).

MY DEAR CASSANDRA,

I am not yet able to acknowledge the receipt of any parcel from London, which I suppose will not occasion you much surprise. I was a little disappointed to-day, but not more so than is perfectly agreeable, and I hope to be disappointed again to-morrow, as only one coach comes down on Sundays.

You have had a very pleasant journey of course and have found Elizabeth and all the children very well on your arrival at Godmersham, and I congratulate you on it. Edward is rejoicing this evening, I dare say, to find himself once more at home, from which he fancies he has been absent a great while. His son left behind him the very fine chestnuts which had been selected for planting at Godmersham, and the drawing of his own which he had intended to carry to George; the former will therefore be deposited in the soil of Hampshire instead of Kent, the latter I have already consigned to another element.

We have been exceedingly busy ever since you went away. In the first place we have had to rejoice two or three times every day at your having such very delightful weather for the whole of your journey, and in the second place we have been obliged to take advantage of the very delightful weather ourselves by going to see almost all our neighbours.

On Thursday we walked to Deane, yesterday to Oakley Hall and Oakley, and to-day to Deane again. At Oakley Hall we did a great deal – eat some sandwiches all over mustard, admired Mr. Bramston's porter, and Mrs. Bramston's transparencies, and gained a promise from the latter of two roots of heartsease, one all yellow and the other all purple, for you. At Oakley we bought ten pair of worsted stockings and a shift; the shift is for Betty Dawkins, as we find she wants it more than a rug; she is one of the most grateful of all whom Edward's charity has reached, or at least she expresses herself more warmly than the rest, for she sends him a "sight of thanks."

This morning we called at the Harwoods', and in their dining-room found 'Heathcote and Chute forever.' Mrs. William Heathcote and Mrs. Chute – the first of whom took a long ride yesterday morning with Mrs. Harwood into Lord Carnarvon's park, and fainted away in the evening, and the second walked down from Oakley Hall attended by Mrs. Augusta Bramston; they had meant to come on to Steventon afterwards, but we knew a trick worth two of that. If I had thought of it in time, I would have said something civil to her about Edward's never having had any serious idea of calling on Mr. Chute while he was in Hampshire; but unluckily it did not occur to me. Mrs. Heathcote is gone home to-day; Catherine had paid her an early visit at Deane in the morning, and brought a good account of Harris [Bigg-Wither].

James went to Winchester Fair yesterday, and bought a new horse, and Mary has got a new maid – two great acquisitions; one comes from Folly farm, is about five years old, used to draw, and thought very pretty, and the other is niece to Dinah at Kintbury.

James called by my father's desire on Mr. Bayle [cabinet maker] to inquire into the cause of his being so horrid. Mr. Bayle did not attempt to deny his being horrid, and made many apologies for it; he did not plead his having a drunken self, he talked only of a drunken foreman, &c., and gave hopes of the tables being at Steventon on Monday se'nnight next. We have had no letter since you left us, except one from Mr. Serle of Bishopstoke to inquire the character of James Elton.

Our whole neighbourhood is at present very busy grieving over poor Mrs. Martin, who has totally failed in her business, and had very lately an execution in her house. Her own brother and Mr. Rider are the principal creditors, and they have seized her effects in order to prevent other people's doing it. There has been the same affair going on, we are told, at Wilson's, and my hearing nothing of you makes me apprehensive that you, your fellow travellers, and all your effects, might be seized by the bailiffs when you stopt at the house, and sold altogether for the benefit of the creditors.

In talking of Mr. Deedes' new house, Mrs. Bramston told us one circumstance, which, that we should be ignorant of it before, must make Edward's conscience fly into his face; she told us that one of the sitting rooms at Sandling, an oval room, with a bow at one end, has the very remarkable and singular feature of a fireplace with a window, the centre window of the bow, exactly over the mantel-piece.

Sunday. – *This morning's unpromising aspect makes it absolutely necessary for me to observe once more how peculiarly fortunate you have been in your weather, and then I will drop the subject forever. Our improvements have advanced very well; the bank along the elm wall is sloped down for the reception of thorns and lilacs, and it is settled that the other side of the path is to continue turfed, and to be planted with beech, ash, and larch.*

Monday. – *I am glad I had no means of sending this yesterday, as I am now able to thank you for executing my commission so well. I like the gown very much, and my mother thinks it very ugly. I like the stockings also very much, and greatly prefer having two pair only of that quality to three of an inferior sort. The combs are very pretty, and I am much obliged to you for your present, but am sorry you should make me so many. The pink shoes are not particularly beautiful, but they fit me very well; the others are faultless. I am glad that I have still my cloak to expect.*

Among my other obligations, I must not omit to remember your writing me so long a letter in a time of such hurry. I am amused by your going to Milgate at last, and glad that you have so charming a day for your journey home.

My father approves his stockings very highly, and finds no fault with any part of Mrs. Hancock's bill except the charge of 3s. 6d. *for the packing-box.*

The weather does not know how to be otherwise than fine. I am surprised that Mrs. Marriot should not be taller. Surely you have made a mistake. Did Mr. Roland [possibly a hairdresser] make you look well?

Yours affectionately,

J. A.

Miss Austen, Godmersham Park,
Faversham, Kent.

XXIII

Steventon: Saturday (November 1)

MY DEAR CASSANDRA,

You have written, I am sure, though I have received no letter from you since your leaving London; the post, and not yourself, must have been unpunctual.

*We have at last heard from Frank; a letter from him to you came yesterday, and I mean to send it on as soon as I can get a ditto (*that *means a frank), which I hope to do in a day or two.* En attendant, *you must rest satisfied with knowing that on the 8th of July the "Petterel," with the rest of the Egyptian squadron, was off the Isle of Cyprus, whither they went from Jaffa for provisions, &c., and whence they were to sail in a day or two for Alexandria, there to wait the result of the English proposals for the evacuation of Egypt. The rest of the letter, according to the present fashionable style of composition, is chiefly descriptive. Of his promotion he knows nothing; of prizes he is guiltless.*

Your letter is come; it came, indeed, twelve lines ago, but I could not stop to acknowledge it before, and I am glad it did not arrive till I had completed my first sentence, because the sentence had been made ever since yesterday, and I think forms a very good beginning.

Your abuse of our gowns amuses but does not discourage me; I shall take mine to be made up next week, and the more I look at it the better it pleases me. My cloak came on Tuesday, and, though I expected a good deal, the beauty of the lace astonished me. It is too handsome to be worn – almost too handsome to be looked at. The glass is all safely arrived also, and gives great satisfaction. The wine-glasses are much smaller than I expected, but I suppose it is the proper size. We find no fault with your manner of performing any of our commissions, but if you like to think yourself remiss in any of them, pray do.

My mother was rather vexed that you could not go to Penlington's [tallow chandler], but she has since written to him, which does just as well. Mary is disappointed, of course, about her locket, and of course delighted about the mangle, which is safe at Basingstoke. You will thank Edward for it on their behalf, &c., &c., and, as you know how much it was wished for, will not feel that you are inventing gratitude.

Did you think of our ball on Thursday evening, and did you suppose me at it? You might very safely, for there I was. On Wednesday morning it was settled that Mrs. Harwood, Mary, and I should go together, and shortly afterwards a very civil note of invitation for me came from Mrs. Bramston, who wrote I believe as soon as as she knew of the ball. I might likewise have gone with Mrs. Lefroy, and therefore, with three methods of going, I must have been more at the ball than anyone else. I dined and slept at Deane; Charlotte [maidservant] and I did my hair, which I fancy looked very indifferent, nobody abused it, however, and I retired delighted with my success.

It was a pleasant ball, and still more good than pleasant, for there were nearly sixty people, and sometimes we had seventeen couple. The Portsmouths, Dorchesters, Boltons, Portals, and Clerks were there, and all the meaner and more usual &c., &c.'s. There was a scarcity of men in general, and a still greater scarcity of any that were good for much. I danced nine dances out of ten – five with Stephen Terry, T. Chute, and James Digweed, and four with Catherine. There was commonly a couple of ladies standing up together, but not often any so amiable as ourselves.

I heard no news, except that Mr. Peters, who was not there, is supposed to be particularly attentive to Miss Lyford. You were inquired after very prettily, and I hope the whole assembly now understands that you are gone into Kent, which the families in general seemed to meet in ignorance of. Lord Portsmouth surpassed the rest in his attentive recollection of you, inquired more into the length of your absence, and concluded by desiring to be 'remembered to you when I wrote next.'

Lady Portsmouth had got a different dress on, and Lady Bolton is much improved by a wig. The three Miss Terries were there, but no Annie; which was a great disappointment to me. I hope the poor girl had not set her heart on her appearance that evening so much as I had. Mr. Terry is ill, in a very low way. I said civil things to Edward for Mr. Chute, who amply returned them by declaring that, had he known of my brother's being at Steventon, he should have made a point of calling upon him to thank him for his civility about the Hunt.

I have heard from Charles, and am to send his shirts by half-dozens as they are finished; one set will go next week. The 'Endymion' is now waiting only for orders, but may wait for them perhaps a month. Mr. Coulthard [1] was unlucky in very narrowly missing another unexpected guest at Chawton, for Charles had actually set out and got half way thither in order to spend one day with Edward, but turned back on discovering the distance to be considerably more than he had fancied, and finding himself and his horse to be very much tired. I should regret it the more if his friend Shipley had been of the party, for Mr. Coulthard might not have been so well pleased to see only one come at a time.

Miss Harwood is still at Bath, and writes word that she never was in better health, and never more happy. Joshua Wakeford died last Saturday, and my father buried him on Thursday. A deaf Miss Fonnereau is at Ashe, which has prevented Mrs. Lefroy's going to Worting or Basingstoke during the absence of Mr. Lefroy.

*My mother is very happy in the prospect of dressing a new doll which Molly [maidservant] has given Anna. My father's feelings are not so enviable, as it appears that the farm cleared 300*l*. last year. James and Mary went to Ibthorp for one night last Monday, and found Mrs. Lloyd not in very good looks. Martha has been lately at Kintbury, but is probably at home by this time. Mary's promised maid has jilted her, and hired herself elsewhere. The Debaries persist in being afflicted at the death of their uncle, of whom they now say they saw a great deal in London. Love to all. I am glad George remembers me.*

Yours very affectionately,

J. A.

I am very unhappy. In re-reading your letter I find I might have spared myself any intelligence of Charles. To have written only what you knew before! You may guess how much I feel. I wore at the ball your favourite gown, a bit of muslin of the same round my head, bordered with Mrs. Cooper's [Jane's aunt] band, and one little comb.

Miss Austen, Godmersham Park.

1. Coulthard rented Chawton House at this time.

XXIV

Steventon: Thursday (November 20).
MY DEAR CASSANDRA,

Your letter took me quite by surprise this morning; you are very welcome, however, and I am very much obliged to you. I believe I drank too much wine last night at Hurstbourne; I know not how else to account for the shaking of my hand to-day. You will kindly make allowance therefore for any indistinctness of writing, by attributing it to this venial error.

Naughty Charles did not come on Tuesday, but good Charles came yesterday morning. About two o'clock he walked in on a Gosport hack. His feeling equal to such a fatigue is a good sign, and his feeling no fatigue in it a still better. He walked down to Deane to dinner; he danced the whole evening, and to-day is no more tired than a gentleman ought to be.

Your desiring to hear from me on Sunday will, perhaps, bring you a more particular account of the ball than you may care for, because one is prone to think much more of such things the morning after they happen, than when time has entirely driven them out of one's recollection.

It was a pleasant evening; Charles found it remarkably so, but I cannot tell why, unless the absence of Miss Terry, towards whom his conscience reproaches him with being now perfectly indifferent, was a relief to him. There were only twelve dances, of which I danced nine, and was merely prevented from dancing the rest by the want of a partner. We began at ten, supped at one, and were at Deane before five. There were but fifty people in the room; very few families indeed from our side of the county, and not many more from the other. My partners were the two St. Johns, Hooper, Holder, and very prodigious Mr. Mathew, with whom I called the last, and whom I liked the best of my little stock.

There were very few beauties, and such as there were were not very handsome. Miss Iremonger did not look well, and Mrs. Blount was the only one much admired. She appeared exactly as she did in September, with the same broad face, diamond bandeau, white shoes, pink husband, and fat neck. The two Miss Coxes were there: I traced in one the remains of the vulgar, broad-featured girl who danced at Enham eight years ago; the other is refined into a nice, composed-looking girl, like Catherine Bigg. I looked at Sir Thomas Champneys and thought of poor Rosalie [their cousin Eliza's maid who had been the object of Sir Thomas' attention]; I looked at his daughter, and thought her a queer animal with a white neck. Mrs. Warren, I was constrained to think, a very fine young woman, which I much regret. She danced away with great activity. Her husband is ugly enough, uglier even than his cousin John; but he does not look so very old. The Miss Maitlands are both prettyish, very like Anne [their aunt and James Austen's first wife], with brown skins, large dark eyes, and a good deal of nose. The General [General Mathew, father of Anne and Mrs Maitland] has got the gout, and

Mrs. Maitland the jaundice. Miss Debary, Susan, and Sally, all in black, but without any statues, made their appearance, and I was as civil to them as circumstances would allow me.

They told me nothing new of Martha. I mean to go to her on Thursday, unless Charles should determine on coming over again with his friend Shipley for the Basingstoke ball, in which case I shall not go till Friday. I shall write to you again, however, before I set off, and I shall hope to hear from you in the meantime. If I do not stay for the ball, I would not on any account do so uncivil a thing by the neighbourhood as to set off at that very time for another place, and shall therefore make a point of not being later than Thursday morning.

Mary said that I looked very well last night. I wore my aunt's gown and handkerchief, and my hair was at least tidy, which was all my ambition. I will now have done with the ball, and I will moreover go and dress for dinner.

Thursday evening. – *Charles leaves us on Saturday, unless Henry should take us in his way to the island, of which we have some hopes, and then they will probably go together on Sunday.*

The young lady whom it is expected that Sir Thomas is to marry is Miss Emma Wabshaw; she lives somewhere between Southampton and Winchester, is handsome, accomplished, amiable, and everything but rich. He is certainly finishing his house in a great hurry. Perhaps the report of his being to marry a Miss Fanshawe might originate in his attentions to this very lady – the names are not unlike.

Summers has made my gown very well indeed, and I get more and more pleased with it. Charles does not like it, but my father and Mary do. My mother is very much resigned to it; and as for James, he gives it the preference over everything of the kind he ever saw, in proof of which I am desired to say that if you like to sell yours Mary will buy it.

We had a very pleasant day on Monday at Ashe, we sat down fourteen to dinner in the study, the dining-room being not habitable from the storms having blown down its chimney. Mrs. Bramston talked a good deal of nonsense, which Mr. Bramston and Mr. Clerk seemed almost equally to enjoy. There was a whist and a casino table, and six outsiders. [Henry] Rice and Lucy [Lefroy] made love, Mat. Robinson fell asleep, James and Mrs. Augusta alternately read Dr. Finnis' pamphlet on the cow-pox, and I bestowed my company by turns on all.

On inquiring of Mrs. Clerk, I find that Mrs. Heathcote made a great blunder in her news of the Crookes and Morleys. It is young Mr. Crook who is to marry the second Miss Morley, and it is the Miss Morleys instead of the second Miss Crooke who were the beauties at the music meeting. This seems a more likely tale, a better devised imposture.

The three Digweeds all came on Tuesday, and we played a pool at commerce. James Digweed left Hampshire to-day. I think he must be in love with you, from his anxiety to have you go to the Faversham balls, and likewise from his supposing that the two elms fell from their grief at your absence. Was not it a gallant idea? It never occurred to me before, but I dare say it was so.

Hacker has been here to-day putting in the fruit trees. A new plan has been suggested concerning the plantation of the new inclosure of the right-hand side of the elm walk: the doubt is whether it would be better to make a little orchard of it by planting apples, pears, and cherries, or whether it should be larch, mountain ash, and acacia. What is your opinion? I say nothing, and am ready to agree with anybody.

You and George walking to Eggerton! What a droll party! Do the Ashford people still come to Godmersham church every Sunday in a cart? It is you *that always disliked Mr. N. Toke so much, not I. I do not like his wife, and I do not like Mr. Brett, but as for Mr. Toke, there are few people whom I like better.*

Miss Harwood and her friend have taken a house fifteen miles from Bath; she writes very kind letters, but sends no other particulars of the situation. Perhaps it is one of the first houses in Bristol.

Farewell; Charles sends you *his best love and Edward his worst. If you think the distinction improper, you may take the worst yourself. He will write to you when he gets back to his ship, and in the meantime desires that you will consider me as*

Your affectionate sister,

J. A.

Friday. – *I have determined to go on Thursday, but of course not before the post comes in. Charles is in very good looks indeed. I had the comfort of finding out the other evening who all the fat girls with long noses were that disturbed me at the 1st H. ball. They all prove to be Miss Atkinsons of En— [illegible].*

I rejoice to say that we have just had another letter from our dear Frank. It is to you, very short, written from Larnica in Cyprus, and so lately as October 2. He came from Alexandria, and was to return there in three or four days, knew nothing of his promotion, and does not write above twenty lines, from a doubt of the letter's ever reaching you, and an idea of all letters being opened at Vienna. He wrote a few days before to you from Alexandria by the 'Mercury,' sent with despatches to Lord Keith. Another letter must be owing to us besides this, one *if not* two*; because none of these are to me. Henry comes to-morrow, for one night only.*

My mother has heard from Mrs. E. Leigh. Lady Saye and Seale and her daughter are going to remove to Bath. Mrs. Estwick [niece of Lady Saye and Sele] is married again to a Mr. Sloane, a young man under age, without the knowledge of either family. He bears a good character, however.

Miss Austen, Godmersham Park,

Faversham, Kent.

XXV

Steveton: Saturday (January 3).

MY DEAR CASSANDRA,

As you have by this time received my last letter, it is fit that I should begin another, and I begin with the hope, which is at present uppermost in my mind, that you often wore a white gown in the morning at the time of all the gay parties being with you.

Our visit at Ash Park, last Wednesday, went off in a come-çá *way. We met Mr. Lefroy and Tom Chute, played at cards, and came home again. James and Mary dined here on the following day, and at night Henry set off in the mail for London. He was as agreeable as ever during his visit, and has not lost anything in Miss Lloyd's estimation.*

Yesterday we were quite alone – only our four selves; but to-day the scene is agreeably varied by Mary's driving Martha to Basingstoke, and Martha's afterwards dining at Deane.

My mother looks forward with as much certainty as you can do to our keeping two maids; my father is the only one not in the secret. We plan having a steady cook and a young, giddy housemaid, with a sedate, middle-aged man, who is to undertake the double office of husband to the former and sweetheart to the latter. No children, of course, to be allowed on either side.

You feel more for John Bond than John Bond deserves. I am sorry to lower his character, but he is not ashamed to own himself that he has no doubt at all of getting a good place, and that he had even an offer many years ago from a Farmer Paine of taking him into his service whenever he might quit my father's.

There are three parts of Bath which we have thought of as likely to have houses in them – Westgate Buildings, Charles Street, and some of the short streets leading from Laura Place or Pulteney Street.

Westgate Buildings, though quite in the lower part of the town, are not badly situated themselves. The street is broad, and has rather a good appearance. Charles Street, however, I think, is preferable. The buildings are new, and its nearness to Kingsmead Fields would be a pleasant circumstance. Perhaps you may remember, or perhaps you may forget, that Charles Street leads from the Queen Square Chapel to the two Green Park Streets.

The houses in the streets near Laura Place I should expect to be above our price. Gay Street would be too high, except only the lower house on the left-hand side as you ascend. Towards that *my mother has no disinclination; it used to be lower rented than any other house in the row, from some inferiority in the apartments. But above all others her wishes are at present fixed on the corner house in Chapel Row, which opens into Prince's Street. Her knowledge of it, however, is confined only to the outside, and therefore she is equally uncertain of its being really desirable as of its being to be had.*

In the meantime she assures you that she will do everything in her power to avoid Trim Street, although you have not expressed the fearful presentiment of it which was rather expected.

We know that Mrs. Perrot will want to get us into Oxford Buildings, but we all unite in particular dislike of that part of the town, and therefore hope to escape. Upon all these different situations you and Edward may confer together, and your opinion of each will be expected with eagerness.

As to our pictures, the battle-piece, Mr. Nibbs, Sir William East, and all the old heterogeneous miscellany, manuscript, Scriptural pieces dispersed over the house, are to be given to James. Your own drawings will not cease to be your own, and the two paintings on tin will be at your disposal. My mother says that the French agricultural prints in the best bedroom were given by Edward to his two sisters. Do you or he know anything about it?

She has written to my aunt, and we are all impatient for the answer. I do not know how to give up the idea of our both going to Paragon in May. Your *going I consider as indispensably necessary, and I shall not like being left behind; there is no place here or hereabouts that I shall want to be staying at, and though, to be sure, the keep of two will be more than of one, I will endeavour to make the difference less by disordering my stomach with Bath buns; and as to the* trouble *of accommodating us, whether there are one or two, it is much the same.*

According to the first plan, my mother and our two selves are to travel down together, and my father follow us afterwards in about a fortnight or three weeks. We have promised to spend a couple of days at Ibthorp in our way. We must all meet at Bath, you know, before we set out for the sea, and, everything considered, I think the first plan as good as any.

My father and mother, wisely aware of the difficulty of finding in all Bath such a bed as their own, have resolved on taking it with them; all the beds, indeed, that we shall want are to be removed – viz., besides theirs, our own two, the best for a spare one, and two for servants; and these necessary articles will probably be the only material ones that it would answer to send down. I do not think it will be worth while to remove any of our chests of drawers; we shall be able to get some of a much more commodious sort, made of deal, and painted to look very neat; and I flatter myself that for little comforts of all kinds our apartment will be one of the most complete things of the sort all over Bath, Bristol included.

We have thought at times of removing the sideboard, or a Pembroke table, or some other piece of furniture, but, upon the whole, it has ended in thinking that the trouble and risk of the removal would be more than the advantage of having them at a place where everything may be purchased. Pray send your opinion.

Martha has as good as promised to come to us again in March. Her spirits are better than they were.

I have now attained the true art of letter-writing, which we are always told is to express on paper exactly what one would say to the same person by word of mouth. I have been talking to you almost as fast as I could the whole of this letter.

Your Christmas gaieties are really quite surprising; I think they would satisfy even Miss Walter [their cousin Phylly Walter] herself. I hope the ten shillings won by Miss Foote may make everything easy between her and her cousin Frederick. So Lady Bridges, in the delicate language of Coulson Wallop, is in for it *[pregnant]! I am very glad to hear of the Pearsons' good fortune. It is a piece of promotion which I know they looked forward to as very desirable some years ago, on Captain Lockyer's illness. It brings them a considerable increase of income and a better house.*

My mother bargains for having no trouble at all in furnishing our house in Bath, and I have engaged for your willingly undertaking to do it all. I get more and more reconciled to the idea of our removal. We have lived long enough in this neighbourhood: the Basingstoke balls are certainly on the decline, there is something interesting in the bustle of going away, and the prospect of spending future summers by the sea or in Wales is very delightful. For a time we shall now possess many of the advantages which I have often thought of with envy in the wives of sailors or soldiers. It must not be generally known, however, that I am not sacrificing a great deal in quitting the country, or I can expect to inspire no tenderness, no interest, in those we leave behind.

The threatened Act of Parliament [probably to relieve social distress during the harsh winter] does not seem to give any alarm.

My father is doing all in his power to increase his income, by raising his tithes, &c., and I do not despair of getting very nearly six hundred a year.

In what part of Bath do you mean to place your bees? We are afraid of the South Parade's being too hot.

Monday. – *Martha desires her best love, and says a great many kind things about spending some time with you in March, and depending on a large return from us both in the autumn. Perhaps I may not write again before Sunday.*

Yours affectionately,

J. A.

Miss Austen, Godmersham Park,
Faversham, Kent.

XXVI

Steventon: Thursday (January 8).

MY DEAR CASSANDRA,

The 'perhaps' which concluded my last letter being only a 'perhaps,' will not occasion your being overpowered with surprise, I dare say, if you should *receive this before Tuesday, which, unless circumstances are very perverse, will be the case. I received yours with much general philanthropy, and still more peculiar good will, two days ago; and I suppose I need not tell you that it was very long, being written on a foolscap sheet, and very entertaining, being written by you.*

Mr. Payne [cousin of the Austens] has been dead long enough for Henry to be out of mourning for him before his last visit, though we knew nothing of it till about that time. Why he died, or of what complaint, or to what noblemen he bequeathed his four daughters in marriage, we have not heard.

I am glad that the Wildmans are going to give a ball, and hope you will not fail to benefit both yourself and me by laying out a few kisses in the purchase of a frank. I believe you are right in proposing to delay the cambric muslin, and I submit with a kind of voluntary reluctance.

Mr. Peter Debary has declined Deane curacy; he wishes to be settled near London. A foolish reason! as if Deane were not near London in comparison of Exeter or York. Take the whole world through, and he will find many more places at a greater distance from London than Deane than he will at a less. What does he think of Glencoe or Lake Katherine?

I feel rather indignant that any possible objection should be raised against so valuable a piece of preferment, so delightful a situation! – that Deane should not be universally allowed to be as near the metropolis as any other country villages. As this is the case, however, as Mr. Peter Debary has shown himself a Peter in the blackest sense of the word, we are obliged to look elsewhere for an heir; and my father has thought it a necessary compliment to James Digweed to offer the curacy to him, though without considering it as either a desirable or an eligible situation for him. Unless he is in love with Miss Lyford, I think he had better not be settled exactly in this neighbourhood; and unless he is very much in love with her indeed, he is not likely to think a salary of 50l. *equal in value or efficiency to one of* 75l.

Were you *indeed to be considered as one of the fixtures of the house! – but you were never actually erected in it either by Mr. Egerton Brydges or Mrs. Lloyd [previous tenants].*

Martha and I dined yesterday at Deane to meet the Powletts and Tom Chute, which we did not fail to do. Mrs. Powlett was at once expensively and nakedly dressed; we have had the satisfaction of estimating her lace and her muslins; and she said too little to afford us much other amusement.

Mrs. John Lyford is so much pleased with the state of widowhood as to be going to put in for being a widow again; she is to marry a Mr. Fendall, a banker in Gloucester, a man of very good fortune, but considerably older than herself, and with three little children. Miss Lyford has never been here yet; she can come only for a day, and is not able to fix the day.

I fancy Mr. Holder will have the farm, and without being obliged to depend on the accommodating spirit of Mr. William Portal; he will probably have it for the remainder of my father's lease. This pleases us all much better than its falling into the hands of Mr. Harwood or Farmer Twitchen. Mr. Holder is to come in a day or two to talk to my father on the subject, and then John Bond's interest will not be forgotten.

I have had a letter to-day from Mrs. Cooke. Mrs. Laurel [neighbour of the Cookes] is going to be married to a Mr. Hinchman, a rich East Indian. I hope Mary will be satisfied with this proof of her cousin's existence and welfare, and cease to torment herself with the idea of his bones being bleaching in the sun on Wantage Downs [Jane jokingly confuses Mr Hinchman with a cousin of Mary's with a similar name].

Martha's visit is drawing towards its close, which we all four sincerely regret. The wedding day [wedding anniversary of James and Mary Austen] is to be celebrated on the 16th, because the 17th falls on Saturday; and a day or two before the 16th Mary will drive her sister to Ibthorp to find all the festivity she can in contriving for everybody's comfort, and being thwarted or teased by almost everybody's temper. Fulwar, Eliza, and Tom Chute are to be of the party. I know of nobody else. I was asked, but declined it.

Eliza has seen Lord Craven at Barton, and probably by this time at Kintbury, where he was expected for one day this week. She found his manners very pleasing indeed. The little flaw of having a mistress now living with him at Ashdown Park seems to be the only unpleasing circumstance about him. From Ibthorp, Fulwar and Eliza are to return with James and Mary to Deane.

The Prices are not *to have an house on Weyhill; for the present he has lodgings in Andover, and they are in view of a dwelling hereafter in Appleshaw, that village of wonderful elasticity, which stretches itself out for the reception of everybody who does not wish for a house on Speen Hill.*

Pray give my love to George [her nephew]; tell him that I am very glad to hear he can skip so well already, and that I hope he will continue to send me word of his improvement in the art.

I think you judge very wisely in putting off your London visit, and I am mistaken if it be not put off for some time. You speak with such noble resignation of Mrs. Jordan [actress] and the Opera House, that it would be an insult to suppose consolation required; but to prevent you thinking with regret of this rupture of your engagement with Mr. Smithson [friend of Henry Austen], I must assure you that Henry suspects him to be a great miser.

Friday. – *No answer from my aunt [Leigh Perrot]. She has no time for writing, I suppose, in the hurry of selling furniture, packing clothes, and preparing for their removal to Scarletts.*

You are very kind in planning presents for me to make, and my mother has shown me exactly the same attention; but as I do not choose to have generosity dictated to me, I shall not resolve on giving my cabinet to Anna till the first thought of it has been my own.

Sidmouth is now talked of as our summer abode. Get all the information, therefore, about it that you can from Mrs. C. Cage.

My father's old ministers are already deserting him to pay their court to his son. The brown mare, which, as well as the black, was to devolve on James at our removal, has not had patience to wait for that, and has settled herself even now at Deane. The death of Hugh Capet [possibly a horse], which, like that of Mr. Skipsey [possibly another horse], though undesired, was not wholly unexpected, being purposely effected, has made the immediate possession of the mare very convenient, and everything else I suppose will be seized by degrees in the same manner. Martha and I work at the books every day.

Yours affectionately,

J. A.

Miss Austen, Godmersham Park,

Faversham, Kent.

XXVII

Steventon: Wednesday (January 14).

Poor Miss Austen! It appears to me that I have rather oppressed you of late by the frequency of my letters. You had hoped not to hear from me again before Tuesday, but Sunday showed you with what a merciless sister you had to deal. I cannot recall the past, but you shall not hear from me quite so often in future.

Your letter to Mary was duly received before she left Dean with Martha yesterday morning, and it gives us great pleasure to know that the Chilham ball was so agreeable, and that you danced four dances with Mr. Kemble. Desirable, however, as the latter circumstance was, I cannot help wondering at its taking place. Why did you dance four dances with so stupid a man? Why not rather dance two of them with some elegant brother officer who was struck with your appearance as soon as you entered the room?

Martha left you her best love. She will write to you herself in a short time; but, trusting to my memory rather than her own, she has nevertheless desired me to ask you to purchase for her two bottles of Steele's lavender water when you are in town, provided you should go to the shop on your own account, otherwise you may be sure that she would not have you recollect the request.

James dined with us yesterday, wrote to Edward in the evening, filled three sides of paper, every line inclining too much towards the northeast, and the very first line of all scratched out, and this morning he joins his lady in the fields of Elysium and Ibthorp.

Last Friday was a very busy day with us. We were visited by Miss Lyford and Mr. Bayle. The latter began his operations in the house, but had only time to finish the four sitting-rooms; the rest is deferred till the spring is more advanced and the days longer. He took his paper of appraisement away with him, and therefore we only know the estimate he has made of one or two articles of furniture which my father particularly inquired into. I understand, however, that he was of opinion that the whole would amount to more than two hundred pounds, and it is not imagined that this will comprehend the brewhouse and many other, &c., &c.

Miss Lyford was very pleasant, and gave my mother such an account of the houses in Westgate Buildings, where Mrs. Lyford lodged four years ago, as made her think of a situation there with great pleasures but your opposition will be without difficulty decisive, and my father, in particular, who was very well inclined towards the Row before, has now ceased to think of it entirely. At present the environs of Laura Place seem to be his choice. His views on the subject are much advanced since I came home; he grows quite ambitious, and actually requires now a comfortable and a creditable-looking house.

On Saturday Miss Lyford went to her long home that is to say, it was a long way off – and soon afterwards a party of fine ladies issuing from a well-known commodious green vehicle, their heads full of Bantam cocks and Galinies [hens], entered the house – Mrs. Heathcote, Mrs. Harwood, Mrs. James Austen, Miss Bigg, Miss Jane Blachford. [They were considering buying Mrs Austen's poultry.]

Hardly a day passes in which we do not have some visitor or other: yesterday came Mrs. Bramstone, who is very sorry that she is to lose us, and afterwards Mr. Holder, who was shut up for an hour with my father and James in a most awful manner. John Bond est a lui.

Mr. Holder was perfectly willing to take him on exactly the same terms with my father, and John seems exceedingly well satisfied. The comfort of not changing his home is a very material one to him, and since such are his unnatural feelings, his belonging to Mr. Holder is the every thing needful; but otherwise there would have been a situation offering to him, which I had thought of with particular satisfaction, viz., under Harry Digweed, who, if John had quitted Cheesedown, would have been eager to engage him as superintendent at Steventon, would have kept a horse for him to ride about on, would probably have supplied him with a more permanent home, and I think would certainly have been a more desirable master altogether.

John and Corbett are not to have any concern with each other – there are to be two farms and two bailiffs. We are of opinion that it would be better in only one.

This morning brought my aunt's reply, and most thoroughly affectionate is its tenor. She thinks with the greatest pleasure of our being settled in Bath – it is an event which will attach her to the place more than anything else could do, &c., &c. She is, moreover, very urgent with my mother not to delay her visit in Paragon, if she should continue unwell, and even recommends her spending the whole winter with them. At present and for many days past my mother has been quite stout, and she wishes not to be obliged by any relapse to alter her arrangements.

Mr. and Mrs. Chamberlayne are in Bath, lodging at the Charitable Repository; I wish the scene may suggest to Mrs. C. the notion of selling her black beaver bonnet for the relief of the poor. Mrs. Welby [niece of Mrs Leigh Perrot] has been singing duets with the Prince of Wales.

*My father has got above 500 volumes to dispose of; I want James to take them at a venture at half a guinea a volume. The whole repairs of the parsonage at Deane, inside and out, coachbox, basket and dickey will not much exceed 100*l.

Have you seen that Major Byng, a nephew of Lord Torrington, is dead? That must be Edmund.

Friday. – *I thank you for yours, though I should have been more grateful for it if it had not been charged 8*d. *instead of 6*d.*, which has given me the torment of writing to Mr. Lambould [postmaster] on the occasion. I am rather surprised at the revival of the London visit; but Mr. Doricourt [character in the play* Belle Stratagem *by Hannah Cowley] has travelled – he knows best.*

That James Digweed has refused Deane curacy I suppose he has told you himself, though probably the subject has never been mentioned between you. Mrs. Milles flatters herself falsely, it has never been Mrs. Rice's wish to have her son settled near herself; and there is now a hope entertained of her relenting in favour of Deane.

Mrs. Lefroy and her son-in-law were here yesterday; she tries not to be sanguine, but he was in excellent spirits. I rather wish they may have the curacy. It would be an amusement to Mary to superintend their household management, and abuse them for expense, especially as Mrs. L. means to advise them to put their washing out.

Yours affectionately,

J. A.

Miss Austen, Godmersham Park,
Faversham, Kent.

XXVIII

Steventon: Wednesday (January 21).

Expect a most agreeable letter, for not being overburdened with subject (having nothing at all to say), I shall have no check to my genius from beginning to end.

Well, and so Frank's letter has made you very happy, but you are afraid he would not have patience to stay for the 'Haarlem,' which you wish him to have done as being safer than the merchantman. Poor fellow! to wait from the middle of November to the end of December, and perhaps even longer, it must be sad work; especially in a place where the ink is so abominably pale. What a surprise to him it must have been on October 20, to be visited, collared, and thrust out of the 'Petterell' by Captain Inglis. He kindly passes over the poignancy of his feelings in quitting his ship, his officers, and his men.

What a pity it is that he should not be in England at the time of this promotion, because he certainly would have had an appointment, so everybody says, and therefore it must be right for me to say it too. Had he been really here, the certainty of the appointment, I dare say, would not have been half so great, but as it could not be brought to the proof his absence will be always a lucky source of regret.

Eliza [Fowle] talks of having read in a newspaper that all the 1st lieutenants of the frigates whose captains were to be sent into line-of-battle ships were to be promoted to the rank of commanders. If it be true, Mr. Valentine may afford himself a fine Valentine's knot, and Charles may perhaps become 1st of the 'Endymion,' though I suppose Captain Durham is too likely to bring a villain with him under that denomination.

I dined at Deane yesterday, as I told you I should, and met the two Mr. Holders. We played at vingt-un, which, as Fulwar was unsuccessful, gave him an opportunity of exposing himself as usual [he was supposedly a bad loser].

Eliza says she is quite well, but she is thinner than when we saw her last, and not in very good looks. I suppose she has not recovered from the effects of her illness in December. She cuts her hair too short over her forehead, and does not wear her cap far enough upon her head; in spite of these many disadvantages, however, I can still admire her beauty. They all dine here to-day; much good may it do us all.

William [Fowle] and Tom [Fowle] are much as usual; Caroline [Cooper] is improved in her person; I think her now really a pretty child. She is still very shy, and does not talk much.

Fulwar goes next month into Gloucestershire, Leicestershire, and Warwickshire, and Eliza spends the time of his absence at Ibthorp and Deane; she hopes, therefore, to see you before it is long.

Lord Craven was prevented by company at home from paying his visit at Kintbury, but, as I told you before, Eliza is greatly pleased with him, and they seem likely to be on the most friendly terms.

Martha returns into this country next Tuesday, and then begins her two visits at Deane.

I expect to see Miss Bigg every day to fix the time for my going to Manydown; I think it will be next week, and I shall give you notice of it, if I can, that you may direct to me there.

The neighbourhood have quite recovered the death of Mrs. Rider [haberdasher]; so much so, that I think they are rather rejoiced at it now; her things were so very dear! and Mrs. Rogers is to be all that is desirable. Not even death itself can fix the friendship of the world.

You are not to give yourself the trouble of going to Penlingtons when you are in town; my father is to settle the matter when he goes there himself; you are only to take special care of the bills of his in your hands, and I dare say will not be sorry to be excused the rest of the business.

Thursday. – *Our party yesterday was very quietly pleasant. Today we all attack Ashe Park, and to-morrow I dine again at Deane. What an eventful week!*

Eliza left me a message for you, which I have great pleasure in delivering: she will write to you and send you your money next Sunday. Mary has likewise a message: she will be much obliged to you if you can bring her the pattern of the jacket and trousers, or whatever it is that Elizabeth's boys wear when they are first put into breeches; so if you could bring her an old suit itself, she would be very glad, but that I suppose is hardly done.

I am happy to hear of Mrs. Knight's amendment, whatever might be her complaint.

The Wylmots being robbed must be an amusing thing to their acquaintance, and I hope it is as much their pleasure as it seems their avocation to be subjects of general entertainment.

I have a great mind not to acknowledge the receipt of your letter, which I have just had the pleasure of reading, because I am so ashamed to compare the sprawling lines of this with it. But if I say all that I have to say, I hope I have no reason to hang myself.

Caroline [Cooper] was only brought to bed on the 7th of this month, so that her recovery does seem pretty rapid. I have heard twice from Edward [Caroline's brother] on the occasion, and his letters have each been exactly what they ought to be – cheerful and amusing. He dares not write otherwise to me, *but perhaps he might be obliged to purge himself from the guilt of writing nonsense by filling his shoes with whole peas for a week afterwards. Mrs. G. [Girle, Edward's grandmother] has left him 100l., his wife and son 500l. each.*

I join with you in wishing for the environs of Laura Place, but do not venture to expect it. My mother hankers after the Square [Queens Square] dreadfully, and it is but natural to suppose that my uncle will take her *part. It would be very pleasant to be near Sydney Gardens; we might go into the labyrinth every day.*

You need not endeavour to match my mother's morning calico; she does not mean to make it up any more.

Why did not J. D. [James Digweed] make his proposals to you? I suppose he went to see the cathedral, that he might know how he should like to be married in it.

Fanny shall have the boarding-school [one of Jane's childhood books], as soon as her papa gives me an opportunity of sending it; and I do not know whether I may not by that time have worked myself into so generous a fit as to give it to her forever.

We have a ball on Thursday too; I expect to go to it from Manydown. Do not be surprised, or imagine that Frank is come, if I write again soon; it will only be to say that I am going to M., and to answer your question about my gown.

Miss Austen, Godmersham Park,
Faversham, Kent.

XXIX

Steventon: Sunday (January 25).

I have nothing to say about Manydown, but I write because you will expect to hear from me, and because if I waited another day or two, I hope your visit to Goodnestone would make my letter too late in its arrival. I dare say I shall be at M. in the course of this week, but as it is not certain you will direct to me at home.

I shall want two new coloured gowns for the summer, for my pink one will not do more than clear me from Steventon. I shall not trouble you, however, to get more than one of them, and that is to be a plain brown cambric muslin, for morning wear; the other, which is to be a very pretty yellow and white cloud, I mean to buy in Bath. Buy two brown ones, if you please, and both of a length, but one longer than the other – it is for a tall woman. Seven yards for my mother, seven yards and a half for me; a dark brown, but the kind of brown is left to your own choice, and I had rather they were different, as it will be always something to say, to dispute about which is the prettiest. They must be cambric muslin.

How do you like this cold weather? I hope you have all been earnestly praying for it as a salutary relief from the dreadful mild and unhealthy season preceding it, fancying yourself half putrified from the want of it, and that now you all draw into the fire, complain that you never felt such bitterness of cold before, that you are half starved, quite frozen, and wish the mild weather back again with all your hearts.

Your unfortunate sister was betrayed last Thursday into a situation of the utmost cruelty. I arrived at Ashe Park before the party from Deane, and was shut up in the drawing-room with Mr. Holder alone for ten minutes. I had some thoughts of insisting on the housekeeper or Mary Corbett [maidservant] being sent for, and nothing could prevail on me to move two steps from the door, on the lock of which I kept one hand constantly fixed. We met nobody but ourselves, played at vingt-un again, and were very cross.

On Friday I wound up my four days of dissipation by meeting William Digweed at Deane, and am pretty well, I thank you, after it. While I was there a sudden fall of snow rendered the roads impassable, and made my journey home in the little carriage much more easy and agreeable than my journey down.

Fulwar and Eliza left Deane yesterday. You will be glad to hear that Mary is going to keep another maid. I fancy Sally is too much of a servant to find time for everything, and Mary thinks Edward is not so much out of doors as he ought to be; there is therefore to be a girl in the nursery.

I would not give much for Mr. Price's chance of living at Deane; he builds his hope, I find, not upon anything that his mother has written, but upon the effect of what he has written himself. He must write a great deal better than those eyes indicate if he can persuade a perverse and narrow-minded woman to oblige those whom she does not love.

Your brother Edward makes very honourable mention of you, I assure you, in his letter to James, and seems quite sorry to part with you. It is a great comfort to me to think that my cares have not been thrown away, and that you are respected in the world. Perhaps you may be prevailed on to return with him and Elizabeth into Kent, when they leave us in April, and I rather suspect that your great wish of keeping yourself disengaged has been with that view. Do as you like; I have overcome my desire of your going to Bath with my mother and me. There is nothing which energy will not bring one to.

Edward Cooper is so kind as to want us all to come to Hamstall this summer, instead of going to the sea, but we are not so kind as to mean to do it. The summer after, if you please, Mr. Cooper, but for the present we greatly prefer the sea to all our relations.

I dare say you will spend a very pleasant three weeks in town. I hope you will see everything worthy of notice, from the Opera House to Henry's office in Cleveland Court; and I shall expect you to lay in a stock of intelligence that may procure me amusement for a twelvemonth to come. You will have a turkey from Steventon while you are there, and pray note down how many full courses of exquisite dishes M. Halavant [Henry Austen's chef] converts it into.

I cannot write any closer. Neither my affection for you nor for letter-writing can stand out against a Kentish visit. For a three-months' absence I can be a very loving relation and a very excellent correspondent, but beyond that I degenerate into negligence and indifference.

I wish you a very pleasant ball on Thursday, and myself another, and Mary and Martha a third, but they will not have theirs till Friday, as they have a scheme for the Newbury Assembly.

Nanny's husband is decidedly against her quitting service in such times as these, and I believe would be very glad to have her continue with us. In some respects she would be a great comfort, and in some we should wish for a different sort of servant. The washing would be the greatest evil. Nothing is settled, however, at present with her, but I should think it would be as well for all parties if she could suit herself in the meanwhile somewhere nearer her husband and child than Bath. Mrs. H. Rice's place would be very likely to do for her. It is not many, as she is herself aware, that she is qualified for.

My mother has not been so well for many months as she is now.

Adieu.

Yours sincerely,

J. A.

Miss Austen, Godmersham Park,
Faversham, Kent.

1801

Mr. and Mrs. Leigh Perrot were the uncle and aunt who lived at Paragon, Bath, and it would seem that the Steventon family, having made up their mind to settle in Bath upon Mr. George Austen's giving over his clerical duties to his son, made the Perrot's house their head-quarters whilst they looked about for a fitting abode. Cassandra Austen seems to have been visiting, first at Mrs. Lloyd's and then at Kintbury, for to these places the letters are addressed. They have not many allusions which require explanation, being chiefly occupied by observations regarding the search for a house, the people whom Jane encountered at Bath, and the news they heard about the sale of their effects at Steventon Rectory. I suppose 'the Chamberlaynes' to have been the family of the Rev. Thomas Chamberlayne, rector and patron of Charlton, who married in 1799 Maria Francesca, daughter of Captain Robert Walker, R,N., and whose eldest son is described in 'Burke's Landed Gentry' as Thomas Chamberlayne, of Cranbury Park and Weston Grove, Hants – which, by the way, the unwary reader must not confound with the Weston to which Jane and Mrs. Chamberlayne walked, which was, of course, the Weston by Bath, celebrated for the battle of 1643, in which the Royalist Sir Bevil Grenville lost his life, and which was fought on Lansdown, mostly in this parish, from which the present Marquis of that name takes his title.

It will be seen that there is an 'hiatus' in the letters after 1801, for I have discovered none between May in that year and August 1805. During this period the family lived in Bath, first at No.4 Sydney Terrace, and afterwards in Green Park Buildings, until Mr. Austen's death. Before the move to Southampton, which occurred later in the same year, Jane went to pay a visit to her relations in Kent, from which county the next letters were written.

XXX

Paragon: Tuesday (May 5).

MY DEAR CASSANDRA,

I have the pleasure of writing from my own *room up two pair of stairs, with everything very comfortable about me.*

Our journey here was perfectly free from accident or event; we changed horses at the end of every stage, and paid at almost every turn-pike. We had charming weather, hardly any dust, and were exceedingly agreeable, as we did not speak above once in three miles.

Between Luggershall and Everley we made our grand meal, and then with admiring astonishment perceived in what a magnificent manner our support had been provided for. We could not with the utmost exertion consume above the twentieth part of the beef. The cucumber will, I believe, be a very acceptable present, as my uncle talks of having inquired the price of one lately, when he was told a shilling.

We had a very neat chaise from Devizes; it looked almost as well as a gentleman's, at least as a very shabby gentleman's; in spite of this advantage, however, we were above three hours coming from thence to Paragon, and it was half after seven by your clocks before we entered the house.

Frank, whose black head was in waiting in the Hall window, received us very kindly; and his master and mistress did not show less cordiality. They both look very well, though my aunt has a violent cough. We drank tea as soon as we arrived, and so ends the account of our journey, which my mother bore without any fatigue.

How do you do to-day? I hope you improve in sleeping – I think you must, because I *fall off; I have been awake ever since five and sooner; I fancy I had too much clothes over me; I thought I* should *by the feel of them before I went to bed, but I had not courage to alter them. I am warmer here without any fire than I have been lately with an excellent one.*

Well, and so the good news is confirmed, and Martha triumphs. My uncle and aunt seemed quite surprised that you and my father were not coming sooner.

I have given the soap and the basket, and each have been kindly received. One *thing only among all our concerns has not arrived in safety: when I got into the chaise at Devizes I discovered that your drawing ruler was broke in two; it is just at the top where the cross-piece is fastened on. I beg pardon.*

There is to be only one more ball – next Monday is the day. The Chamberlaynes are still here. I begin to think better of Mrs. C—, and upon recollection believe she has rather a long chin than otherwise, as she remembers us in Gloucestershire when we were very charming young women.

The first view of Bath in fine weather does not answer my expectations; I think I see more distinctly through rain. The sun was got behind everything, and the appearance of the place from the top of Kingsdown was all vapour, shadow, smoke, and confusion.

I fancy we are to have a house in Seymour Street, or thereabouts. My uncle and aunt both like the situation. I was glad to hear the former talk of all the houses in New King Street as too small; it was my own idea of them. I had not been two minutes in the dining-room before he questioned me with all his accustomary eager interest about Frank and Charles, their views and intentions. I did my best to give information.

*I am not without hopes of tempting Mrs. Lloyd to settle in Bath; meat is only 8*d. *per pound, butter 12*d.*, and cheese 9 1/2*d. *You must carefully conceal from her, however, the exorbitant price of fish: a salmon has been sold at 2*s. *9*d. *per pound the whole fish. The Duchess of York's removal is expected to make that article more reasonable – and till it really appears so, say nothing about salmon.*

Tuesday night. – *When my uncle went to take his second glass of water I walked with him, and in our morning's circuit we looked at two houses in Green Park Buildings, one of which pleased me very well. We walked all over it except into the garret; the dining-room is of a comfortable size, just as large as you like to fancy it; the second room about 14 ft. square. The apartment over the drawing-room pleased me particularly, because it is divided into two, the smaller one a very nice-sized dressing-room, which upon occasion might admit a bed. The aspect is south-east. The only doubt is about the dampness of the offices, of which there were symptoms.*

Wednesday. – *Mrs. Mussell has got my gown, and I will endeavour to explain what her intentions are. It is to be a round gown, with a jacket and a frock front, like Cath. Bigg's, to open at the side. The jacket is all in one with the body, and comes as far as the pocket-holes – about half a quarter of a yard deep, I suppose, all the way round, cut off straight at the corners with a broad hem. No fulness appears either in the body or the flap; the back is quite plain in this form* [figure]*, and the sides equally so. The front is sloped round to the bosom and drawn in, and there is to be a frill of the same to put on occasionally when all one's handkerchiefs are dirty – which frill* must *fall back. She is to put two breadths and a-half in the tail, and no gores – gores not being so much worn as they were. There is nothing new in the sleeves: they are to be plain, with a fulness of the same falling down and gathered up underneath, just like some of Martha's, or perhaps a little longer. Low in the back behind, and a belt of the same. I can think of nothing more, though I am afraid of not being particular enough.*

My mother has ordered a new bonnet, and so have I; both white strip, trimmed with white ribbon. I find my straw bonnet looking very much like other people's, and quite as smart. Bonnets of cambric muslin on the plan of Lady Bridges' are a good deal worn, and some of them are very pretty; but I shall defer one of that sort till your arrival. Bath is getting so very empty that I am not afraid of doing too little. Black gauze cloaks are worn as much as anything. I shall write again in a day or two. Best love.

Yours ever,

J. A.

We have had Mrs. Lillingstone and the Chamberlaynes to call on us. My mother was very much struck with the odd looks of the two latter; I *have only seen* her. *Mrs. Busby drinks tea and plays at cribbage here to-morrow; and on Friday, I believe, we go to the Chamberlaynes'. Last night we walked by the Canal.*

Miss Austen, Mrs. Lloyd's, Up Hurstbourne,
Andover.

XXXI

Paragon: Tuesday (May 12).
MY DEAR CASSANDRA,

My mother has heard from Mary, and I have heard from Frank; we therefore know something now of our concerns in distant quarters; and you, I hope, by some means or other are equally instructed, for I do not feel inclined to transcribe the letter of either.

You know from Elizabeth, I dare say, that my father and Frank, deferring their visit to Kippington on account of Mr. M. Austen's [1] absence, are to be at Godmersham to-day; and James, I dare say, has been over to Ibthorp by this time to inquire particularly after Mrs. Lloyd's health, and forestall whatever intelligence of the sale I might attempt to give; sixty-one guineas and a-half for the three cows gives one some support under the blow of only eleven guineas for the tables. Eight for my pianoforte is about what I really expected to get; I am more anxious to know the amount of my books, especially as they are said to have sold well.

My adventures since I wrote last have not been numerous; but such as they are, they are much at your service.

We met not a creature at Mrs. Lillingstone's, and yet were not so very stupid, as I expected, which I attribute to my wearing my new bonnet and being in good looks. On Sunday we went to church twice, and after evening service walked a little in the Crescent fields, but found it too cold to stay long.

Yesterday morning we looked into a house in Seymour Street, which there is reason to suppose will soon be empty; and as we are assured from many quarters that no inconvenience from the river is felt in those buildings, we are at liberty to fix in them if we can. But this house was not inviting; the largest room downstairs was not much more than fourteen feet square, with a western aspect.

In the evening, I hope you honoured my toilette and ball with a thought; I dressed myself as well as I could, and had all my finery much admired at home. By nine o'clock my uncle, aunt, and I entered the rooms, and linked Miss Winstone on to us. Before tea it was rather a dull affair; but then the before tea did not last long, for there was only one dance, danced by four couple. Think of four couple, surrounded by about an hundred people, dancing in the Upper Rooms at Bath.

After tea we cheered up; the breaking up of private parties sent some scores more to the ball, and though it was shockingly and inhumanly thin for this place, there were people enough, I suppose, to have made five or six very pretty Basingstoke assemblies.

I then got Mr. Evelyn to talk to, and Miss T. to look at; and I am proud to say that though repeatedly assured that another in the same party was the She, I fixed upon the right one from the first. A resemblance to Mrs. L. was my guide. She is not so pretty as I expected; her face has the same defect of baldness as her sisters, and her features not so handsome; she was highly rouged, and looked rather quietly and contentedly silly than anything else.

Mrs. B. and two young women were of the same party, except when Mrs. B. thought herself obliged to leave them to run round the room after her drunken husband. His avoidance, and her pursuit, with the probable intoxication of both, was an amusing scene.

The Evelyns returned our visit on Saturday; we were very happy to meet, and all that; they are going to-morrow into Gloucestershire to the Dolphins for ten days. Our acquaintance, Mr. Woodward, is just married to a Miss Rowe, a young lady rich in money and music.

I thank you for your Sunday's letter, it is very long and very agreeable. I fancy you know many more particulars of our sale than we do; we have heard the price of nothing but the cows, bacon, hay, hops, tables, and my father's chest of drawers and study table. Mary is more minute in her account of their own gains than in ours; probably being better informed in them. I will attend to Mrs. Lloyd's commission and to her abhorrence of musk when I write again.

I have bestowed three calls of inquiry on the Mapletons, and I fancy very beneficial ones to Marianne, as I am always told that she is better. I have not seen any of them. Her complaint is a bilious fever.

I like my dark gown very much indeed, colour, make, and everything; I mean to have my new white one made up now, in case we should go to the rooms again next Monday, which is to be really the last time.

Wednesday. – Another stupid party last night; perhaps if larger they might be less intolerable, but here there were only just enough to make one card-table, with six people to look on and talk nonsense to each other. Lady Fust, Mrs. Busby, and a Mrs. Owen sat down with my uncle to whist, within five minutes after the three old Toughs came in, and there they sat, with only the exchange of Adm. Stanhope for my uncle, till their chairs were announced.

I cannot anyhow continue to find people agreeable; I respect Mrs. Chamberlayne for doing her hair well, but cannot feel a more tender sentiment. Miss Langley is like any other short girl, with a broad nose and wide mouth, fashionable dress and exposed bosom. Adm. Stanhope is a gentleman-like man, but then his legs are too short and his tail too long. Mrs.

Stanhope could not come; I fancy she had a private appointment with Mr. Chamberlayne, whom I wished to see more than all the rest.

My uncle has quite got the better of his lameness, or at least his walking with a stick is the only remains of it. He and I are soon to take the long-planned walk to the Cassoon [the canal basin], and on Friday we are all to accompany Mrs. Chamberlayne and Miss Langley to Weston.

My mother had a letter yesterday from my father; it seems as if the W. Kent Scheme was entirely given up. He talks of spending a fortnight at Godmersham, and then returning to town.

Yours ever,

J. A.

Excepting a slight cold, my mother is very well; she has been quite free from feverish or bilious complaints since her arrival here.

Miss Austen, Mrs. Lloyd's,
Hurstbourn Tarrant, Andover.

1. Francis Motley-Austen, who bought Kippington from Sir Chas. Farnaby.

XXXII

Paragon: Thursday (May 21)

MY DEAR CASSANDRA,

To make long sentences upon unpleasant subjects is very odious, and I shall therefore get rid of the one now uppermost in my thoughts as soon as possible.

Our views on G. P. Buildings seem all at an end; the observation of the damps still remaining in the offices of an house which has been only vacated a week, with reports of discontented families and putrid fevers, has given the coup de grace. *We have now nothing in view. When you arrive, we will at least have the pleasure of examining some of these putrefying houses again; they are so very desirable in size and situation, that there is some satisfaction in spending ten minutes within them.*

I will now answer the inquiries in your last letter. I cannot learn any other explanation of the coolness between my aunt and Miss Bond than that the latter felt herself slighted by the former's leaving Bath last summer without calling to see her before she went. It seems the oddest kind of quarrel in the world. They never visit, but I believe they speak very civilly if they meet. My uncle and Miss Bond certainly do.

*The four boxes of lozenges, at 1s. 1 1/2*d. *per box, amount, as I was told, to 4*s. 6d.*, and as the sum was so trifling, I thought it better to pay at once than contest the matter.*

I have just heard from Frank. My father's plans are now fixed; you will see him at Kintbury on Friday, and, unless inconvenient to you, we are to see you both here on Monday, the 1st of June. Frank has an invitation to Milgate, which I believe he means to accept.

Our party at Ly. Fust's was made up of the same set of people that you have already heard of – the Winstones, Mrs. Chamberlayne, Mrs. Busby, Mrs. Franklyn, and Mrs. Maria Somerville; yet I think it was not quite so stupid as the two preceding parties here.

The friendship between Mrs. Chamberlayne and me which you predicted has already taken place, for we shake hands whenever we meet. Our grand walk to Weston was again fixed for yesterday, and was accomplished in a very striking manner. Every one of the party declined it under some pretence or other except our two selves, and we had therefore a tête-à-tête, *but* that *we should equally have had after the first two yards had half the inhabitants of Bath set off with us.*

It would have amused you to see our progress. We went up by Sion Hill, and returned across the fields. In climbing a hill Mrs. Chamberlayne is very capital; I could with difficulty keep pace with her, yet would not flinch for the world. On plain ground I was quite her equal. And so we posted away under a fine hot sun, she *without any parasol or any shade to her hat, stopping for nothing, and crossing the churchyard at Weston with as much expedition as if we were afraid of being buried alive. After seeing what she is equal to, I cannot help feeling a regard for her. As to agreeableness, she is much like other people.*

Yesterday evening we had a short call from two of the Miss Arnolds [cousins of Mrs Austen], who came from Chippenham on business. They are very civil, and not too genteel, and upon hearing that we wanted a house, recommended one at Chippenham.

This morning we have been visited again by Mrs. and Miss Holder; they wanted us to fix an evening for drinking tea with them, but my mother's still remaining cold allows her to decline everything of the kind. As I *had a separate invitation, however, I believe I shall go some afternoon. It is the fashion to think them both very detestable, but they are so civil, and their gowns look so white and so nice (which, by the bye, my aunt thinks an absurd pretension in this place), that I cannot utterly abhor them, especially as Miss Holder owns that she has no taste for music.*

After they left us I went with my mother to help look at some houses in New King Street, towards which she felt some kind of inclination, but their size has now satisfied her. They were smaller than I expected to find them; one in particular out of the two was quite monstrously little; the best of the sitting-rooms not so large as the little parlour at Steventon, and the second room in every floor about capacious enough to admit a very small single bed.

We are to have a tiny party here to-night. I hate tiny parties, they force one into constant exertion. Miss Edwards and her father, Mrs. Busby and her nephew, Mr. Maitland, and Mrs. Lillingstone are to be the whole; and I am prevented from setting my black cap at Mr. Maitland by his having a wife and ten children.

My aunt has a very bad cough – do not forget to have heard about that *when you come – and I think she is deafer than ever. My mother's cold disordered her for some days, but she seems now very well. Her resolution as to remaining here begins to give way a little; she will not like being left behind, and will be glad to compound matters with her enraged family.*

You will be sorry to hear that Marianne Mapleton's disorder has ended fatally. She was believed out of danger on Sunday, but a sudden relapse carried her off the next day. So affectionate a family must suffer severely; and many a girl on early death has been praised into an angel, I believe, on slighter pretensions to beauty, sense, and merit than Marianne.

Mr. Bent seems bent *upon being very detestable, for he values the books at only 70*l*. The whole world is in a conspiracy to enrich one part of our family at the expense of another. Ten shillings for Dodsley's Poems, however, please me to the quick, and I do not care how often I sell them for as much. When Mrs. Bramston has read them through I will sell them again. I suppose you can hear nothing of your magnesia?*

Friday. – *You have a nice day for your journey, in whatever way it is to be performed, whether in the Debary's coach or on your own twenty toes.*

When you have made Martha's bonnet you must make her a cloak of the same sort of materials; they are very much worn here, in different forms – many of them just like her black silk spencer, with a trimming round the armholes instead of sleeves, some are long before, and some long all round, like C. Bigg's. Our party last night supplied me with no new idea for my letter.

Yours ever,

J. A.

The Pickfords are in Bath, and have called here. She is the most elegant-looking woman I have seen since I left Martha; he *is as raffish in his appearance as I would wish every disciple of Godwin [William Godwin, political philosopher and novelist] to be. We drink tea to-night with Mrs. Busby. I scandalised her nephew cruelly; he has but three children instead of ten.*

Best love to everybody.

Miss Austen, the Rev. F. C. Fowle's,

Kintbury, Newbury.

1805

The thirty-third letter begins with an account of a visit to Eastwell Park, where lived George Hatton and his wife, Lady Elizabeth (*née* Murray). The two boys, George and Daniel, to whom reference is made, were the late Earl of Winchilsea (ninth earl, who succeeded his cousin in

1826), and his brother, who subsequently married Lady Louisa Greville (daughter of the Earl of Warwick), and was Rector of Great Weldon, Northamptonshire, and Chaplain to the Queen. Lady Gordon and Miss Anne Finch were the sisters of the owner of Eastwell Park, the former of whom married Sir Jenison William Gordon, K. C. B., and the latter died unmarried. Goodnestone Farm, to which the first letter was written, and from which Jane afterwards writes, is a comfortable house very near the great house, which has generally been inhabited as a dower house or by some younger member of the Bridges family, to whom it belongs. "Harriot" means Harriet Bridges, as this was the year before she married Mr. Moore. It will be noticed that Jane always has a good word for her when she speaks of her, which, considering the freedom of her general remarks upon her acquaintance, is a high testimony to character, which was doubtless deserved. It must be admitted that my beloved great-aunt was a careless speller. She invariably spells 'niece' 'neice' in these letters, and in that now before me she spells Lady Bridges' name 'Brydges' twice, which I note to remark that the Goodnestone family spell their name with an 'i,' the Wootton family with a 'y,' which makes a difference, though I cannot describe it in the same terms as Mr. Justice Haliburton (Sam Slick) once used to me in the House of Commons, when, having occasion to write his name, I asked him if I should spell it with one 'l' or two. 'Sir,' he replied, 'on no account with more than one; *there is an `l' of a difference*.' The Knatchbulls who are mentioned as having stayed at Godmersham at this time were Captain Charles Knatchbull, R. N., son of Wadham Knatchbull, Chancellor and Prebendary of Durham, who had married his cousin Frances, only daughter and heiress of Major Norton Knatchbull (youngest son of the fourth Hatch baronet), of Babington, Somersetshire, which place Captain Charles now possessed in right of his wife.

The Duke of Gloucester, whose death put off the Deal ball, was the brother of King George the Third, who died in his 62d year. At the time of his death he commanded a regiment of Guards, and was Warden and Keeper of the New Forest, Ranger of Windsor Forest and of Hampton Court Park, and Chancellor of Dublin University.

The Marianne mentioned in the thirty-fifth letter as being strikingly like 'Catherine Bigg' was a younger daughter of Sir Brook and Lady Bridges (Fanny Fowler), who was an invalid and died unmarried in 1811.

XXXIII

Godmersham Park: Saturday (August 24).
MY DEAR CASSANDRA,

How do you do; and how is Harriot's cold? I hope you are at this time sitting down to answer these questions.

Our visit to Eastwell was very agreeable; I found Ly. Gordon's manners as pleasing as they had been described, and saw nothing to dislike in Sir Janison, excepting once or twice a sort of sneer at Mrs. Anne Finch. He was just getting into talk with Elizabeth as the carriage was ordered, but during the first part of the visit he said very little.

Your going with Harriot was highly approved of by everyone, and only too much applauded as an act of virtue on your part. I said all I could to lessen your merit. The Mrs. Finches were afraid you would find Goodnestone very dull; I wished when I heard them say so that they could have heard Mr. E. Bridges' solicitude on the subject, and have known all the amusements that were planned to prevent it.

They were very civil to me, as they always are; fortune was also very civil to me in placing Mr. E. Hatton by me at dinner. I have discovered that Lady Elizabeth, for a woman of her age and situation, has astonishingly little to say for herself, and that Miss Hatton has not much more. Her eloquence lies in her fingers; they were most fluently harmonious.

George is a fine boy, and well behaved, but Daniel chiefly delighted me; the good humour of his countenance is quite bewitching. After tea we had a cribbage-table, and he and I won two rubbers of his brother and Mrs. Mary. Mr. Brett was the only person there, besides our two families.

It was considerably past eleven before we were at home, and I was so tired as to feel no envy of those who were at Ly. Yates' ball. My good wishes for its being a pleasant one were, I hope, successful.

Yesterday was a very quiet day with us; my noisiest efforts were writing to Frank, and playing at battledore and shuttlecock with William; he and I have practised together two mornings, and improve a little; we have frequently kept it up three *times, and once or twice* six.

The two Edwards went to Canterbury in the chaise, and found Mrs. Knight, as you found her, I suppose, the day before, cheerful but weak. Fanny was met walking with Miss Sharp and Miss Milles, the happiest being in the world; she sent a private message to her mamma implying as much. 'Tell mamma that I am quite Palmerstone!'[a reference to the book Letters from Mrs Palmerstone to her Daughters, inculcating Morality by Entertaining Narratives *by Rachel Hunter] If little Lizzy used the same language she would, I dare say, send the same message from Goodnestone.*

In the evening we took a quiet walk round the farm, with George and Henry to animate us by their races and merriment. Little Edward is by no means better, and his papa and mamma have determined to consult Dr. Wilmot. Unless he recovers his strength beyond what is now probable, his brothers will return to school without him, and he will be of the party to Worthing. If sea-bathing should be recommended he will be left there with us, but this is not thought likely to happen.

I have been used very ill this morning: I have received a letter from Frank which I ought to have had when Elizabeth and Henry had theirs, and which in its way from Albany to Godmersham has been to Dover and Steventon. It was finished on ye 16th, and tells what theirs told before as to his present situation; he is in a great hurry to be married, and I have encouraged him in it, in the letter which ought to have been an answer to his. He must think it very strange that I do not acknowledge the receipt of his, when I speak of those of the same date to Eliz. and Henry; and to add to my injuries, I forgot to number mine on the outside.

I have found your white mittens; they were folded up within my clean nightcap, and send their duty to you.

Elizabeth has this moment proposed a scheme which will be very much for my pleasure if equally convenient to the other party; it is that when you return on Monday, I should take your place at Goodnestone for a few days. Harriot cannot be insincere, let her try for it ever so much, and therefore I defy her to accept this self-invitation of mine, unless it be really what perfectly suits her. As there is no time for an answer, I shall go in the carriage on Monday, and can return with you, if my going on to Goodnestone is at all inconvenient.

The Knatchbulls come on Wednesday to dinner, and stay only till Friday morning at the latest. Frank's letter to me is the only one that you or I have received since Thursday.

Mr. Hall walked off this morning to Ospringe, with no inconsiderable booty. He charged Elizabeth 5s. for every time of dressing her hair, and 5s. for every lesson to Sace, allowing nothing for the pleasures of his visit here, for meat, drink, and lodging, the benefit of country air, and the charms of Mrs. Salkeld's and Mrs. Sace's society.[1] Towards me he was as considerate as I had hoped for from my relationship to you, charging me only 2s. 6d. for cutting my hair, though it was as thoroughly dressed after being cut for Eastwell as it had been for the Ashford assembly. He certainly respects either our youth or our poverty.

My writing to you to-day prevents Elizabeth writing to Harriot, for which evil I implore the latter's pardon. Give my best love to her, and kind remembrance to her brothers.

Yours very affectionately,

J. A.

You are desired to bring back with you Henry's picture of Rowling for the Misses Finches.

As I find, on looking into my affairs, that instead of being very rich I am likely to be very poor, I cannot afford more than ten shillings for Sackree [nursemaid]; but as we are to meet in Canterbury I need not have mentioned this. It is as well, however, to prepare you for the sight of a sister sunk in poverty, that it may not overcome your spirits.

Elizabeth hopes you will not be later here on Monday than five o'clock, on Lizzy's account.

We have heard nothing from Henry since he went. Daniel told us that he went from Ospringe in one of the coaches.
Miss Austen, Goodnestone Farm, Wingham.

1. The Godmersham housekeeper and lady's-maid.

XXXIV

Goodnestone Farm: Tuesday (August 27).
MY DEAR CASSANDRA,

We had a very pleasant drive from Canterbury, and reached this place about half-past four, which seemed to bid fair for a punctual dinner at five; but scenes of great agitation awaited us, and there was much to be endured and done before we could sit down to table.

Harriot found a letter from Louisa Hatton, desiring to know if she and her brothers were to be at the ball at Deal on Friday, and saying that the Eastwell family had some idea of going to it, and were to make use of Rowling if they did; and while I was dressing she came to me with another letter in her hand, in great perplexity. It was from Captain Woodford, containing a message from Lady Forbes, which he had intended to deliver in person, but had been prevented from doing.

The offer of a ticket for this grand ball, with an invitation to come to her house at Dover before and after it, was Lady Forbes' message. Harriot was at first very little inclined, or rather totally disinclined, to profit by her ladyship's attention; but at length, after many debates, she was persuaded by me and herself together to accept the ticket. The offer of dressing and sleeping at Dover she determined on Marianne's account to decline, and her plan is to be conveyed by Lady Elizabeth Hatton.

I hope their going is by this time certain, and will be soon known to be so. I think Miss H. would not have written such a letter if she had not been all but sure of it, and a little more. I am anxious on the subject, from the fear of being in the way if they do not come to give Harriot a conveyance. I proposed and pressed being sent home on Thursday, to prevent the possibility of being in the wrong place, but Harriot would not hear of it.

There is no chance of tickets for the Mr. Bridgeses, as no gentlemen but of the garrison are invited.

With a civil note to be fabricated to Lady F., and an answer written to Miss H., you will easily believe that we could not begin dinner till six. We were agreeably surprised by Edward Bridges' company to it. He had been, strange to tell, too late for the cricket match, too late at least to play himself, and, not being asked to dine with the players, came home. It is impossible to do justice to the hospitality of his attentions towards me; he made a point of ordering toasted cheese for supper entirely on my account.

We had a very agreeable evening, and here I am before breakfast writing to you, having got up between six and seven; Lady Brydges' room must be good for early rising.

Mr. Sankey was here last night, and found his patient [Marianne Bridges] better, but I have heard from a maid-servant that she has had but an indifferent night.

Tell Elizabeth that I did not give her letter to Harriot till we were in the carriage, when she received it with great delight, and could read it in comfort.

As you have been here so lately, I need not particularly describe the house or style of living, in which all seems for use and comfort; nor need I be diffuse on the state of Lady Brydges' bookcase and corner-shelves upstairs. What a treat to my mother to arrange them!

Harriot is constrained to give up all hope of seeing Edward here to fetch me, as I soon recollected that Mr. and Mrs. Charles Knatchbull's being at Godmersham on Thursday must put it out of the question.

Had I waited till after breakfast, the chief of all this might have been spared. The Duke of Gloucester's death sets my heart at ease [because it led to cancellation of the ball at Deal], though it will cause some dozens to ache. Harriot's is not among the number of the last; she is very well pleased to be spared the trouble of preparation. She joins me in best love to you all, and will write to Elizabeth soon. I shall be very glad to hear from you, that we may know how you all are, especially the two Edwards.

I have asked Sophie [Cage] if she has anything to say to Lizzy in acknowledgment of the little bird, and her message is that, with her love, she is very glad Lizzy sent it. She volunteers, moreover, her love to little Marianne, with the promise of bringing her a doll the next time she goes to Godmersham.

John [Bridges] is just come from Ramsgate, and brings a good account of the people there. He and his brother, you know, dine at Nackington; we are to dine at four, that we may walk afterwards. As it is now two, and Harriot has letters to write, we shall probably not get out before.

Yours affectionately,

J. A.

Three o'clock. – *Harriot is just come from Marianne, and thinks her upon the whole better. The sickness has not returned, and a headache is at present her chief complaint, which Henry [Bridges] attributes to the sickness.*

Miss Austen, Edward Austen's, Esq.

Godmersham Park, Faversham.

XXXV

Goodnestone Farm: Friday (August 30).

MY DEAR CASSANDRA,

I have determined on staying here till Monday. Not that there is any occasion for it on Marianne's account, as she is now almost as well as usual, but Harriot is so kind in her wishes for my company that I could not resolve on leaving her to-morrow, especially as I have no reason to give for its necessity. It would be inconvenient to me to stay with her longer than the beginning of next week, on account of my clothes, and therefore I trust it will suit Edward to fetch or send for me on Monday, or Tuesday if Monday should be wet. Harriot has this moment desired me to propose his coming hither on Monday, and taking me back the next day.

The purport of Elizabeth's letter makes me anxious to hear more of what we are to do and not to do, and I hope you will be able to write me your own plans and opinions to-morrow. The journey to London is a point of the first expediency, and I am glad it is resolved on, though it seems likely to injure our Worthing scheme. I expect that we *are to be at Sandling, while* they *are in town.*

It gives us great pleasure to hear of little Edward's being better, and we imagine, from his mamma's expressions, that he is expected to be well enough to return to school with his brothers.

Marianne was equal to seeing me two days ago; we sat with her for a couple of hours before dinner, and the same yesterday, when she was evidently better, more equal to conversation, and more cheerful than during our first visit. She received me very kindly, and expressed her regret in not having been able to see you.

She is, of course, altered since we saw her in October, 1794. Eleven years could not pass away even in health without making some change, but in her case it is wonderful that the change should be so little. I have not seen her to advantage, as I understand she has frequently a nice colour, and her complexion has not yet recovered from the effects of her late illness. Her face is grown longer and thinner, and her features more marked, and the likeness which I remember to have always seen between her and Catherine Bigg is stronger than ever, and so striking is the voice and manner of speaking that I seem to be really hearing Catherine, and once or twice have been on the point of calling Harriot 'Alethea.' She is very pleasant, cheerful, and interested in everything about her, and at the same time shows a thoughtful, considerate, and decided turn of mind.

Edward Bridges dined at home yesterday; the day before he was at St. Albans; to-day he goes to Broome, and to-morrow to Mr. Hallett's, which latter engagement has had some weight in my resolution of not leaving Harriot till Monday.

We have walked to Rowling on each of the two last days after dinner, and very great was my pleasure in going over the house and grounds. We have also found time to visit all the principal walks of this place, except the walk round the top of the park, which we shall accomplish probably to-day.

Next week seems likely to be an unpleasant one to this family on the matter of game. The evil intentions of the Guards [it was feared that the movement of the Grenadier and Coldstream Guards between Deal and

Chatham would disturb the game birds and the men may be tempted to poach them] are certain, and the gentlemen of the neighbourhood seem unwilling to come forward in any decided or early support of their rights. Edward Bridges has been trying to arouse their spirits, but without success. Mr. Hammond, under the influence of daughters and an expected ball, declares he will do nothing.

Harriot hopes my brother will not mortify her by resisting all her plans and refusing all her invitations; she has never yet been successful with him in any, but she trusts he will now make her all the amends in his power by coming on Monday. She thanks Elizabeth for her letter, and you may be sure is not less solicitous than myself for her going to town.

Pray say everything kind for us to Miss Sharpe, who could not regret the shortness of our meeting in Canterbury more than we did. I hope she returned to Godmersham as much pleased with Mrs. Knight's beauty and Miss Milles' judicious remarks as those ladies respectively were with hers. You must send me word that you have heard from Miss Irvine.

I had almost forgot to thank you for your letter. I am glad you recommended 'Gisborne,' for having begun, I am pleased with it, and I had quite determined not to read it.

I suppose everybody will be black for the D. of G. Must we buy lace, or will ribbon do?

We shall not be at Worthing so soon as we have been used to talk of, shall we? This will be no evil to us, and we are sure of my mother and Martha being happy together. Do not forget to write to Charles. As I am to return so soon, we shall not send the pincushions.

Yours affectionately,

J. A.

You continue, I suppose, taking hartshorn, and I hope with good effect.

Miss Austen, Edward Austen's, Esq.

Godmersham Park, Faversham.

1807

There are no letters of 1806, so that this batch were written after the Austens had been established at Southampton for more than a year. 'Our guests' in the thirty-sixth letter were James and Mary, who had been staying with their relations in Castle Square. There is little to observe in the rest of the letter, although one is glad to find that Captain Foote was not put out of temper by having to eat underdone mutton, and that Mrs. Austen's finances were in a satisfactory condition at the commencement of the new year.

'Clarentine' is, of course, Miss S. S. Burney's work, which other people besides Jane have thought 'foolish.' It is a novel of the most ordinary description, and not one which she would have been likely to approve.

There is a playful allusion in these letters to the chance of Martha Lloyd's marriage; Jane could not foresee that this event would be delayed until her own brother Frank sought the lady's affection many years later.

XXXVI

Southampton: Wednesday (January 7).

MY DEAR CASSANDRA,

You were mistaken in supposing I should expect your letter on Sunday; I had no idea of hearing from you before Tuesday, and my pleasure yesterday was therefore unhurt by any previous disappointment. I thank you for writing so much; you must really have sent me the value of two letters in one. We are extremely glad to hear that Elizabeth is so much better, and hope you will be sensible of still further amendment in her when you return from Canterbury.

Of your visit there I must now speak 'incessantly'; it surprises, but pleases me more, and I consider it as a very just and honourable distinction of you, and not less to the credit of Mrs. Knight. I have no doubt of your spending your time with her most pleasantly in quiet and rational conversation, and am so far from thinking her expectations of you will be deceived, that my only fear is of your being so agreeable, so much to her taste, as to make her wish to keep you with her for ever. If that should be the case, we must remove to Canterbury, which I should not like so well as Southampton.

When you receive this, our guests will be all gone or going; and I shall be left to the comfortable disposal of my time, to ease of mind from the torments of rice puddings and apple dumplings, and probably to regret that I did not take more pains to please them all.

Mrs. J. Austen has asked me to return with her to Steventon; I need not give my answer; and she has invited my mother to spend there the time of Mrs. F[rank]. A[usten]'s confinement, which she seems half inclined to do.

A few days ago I had a letter from Miss Irvine, and as I was in her debt, you will guess it to be a remonstrance, not a very severe one, however; the first page is in her usual retrospective, jealous, inconsistent style, but the remainder is chatty and harmless. She supposes my silence may have proceeded from resentment of her not having written to inquire particularly after my hooping cough, &c. She is a funny one.

I have answered her letter, and have endeavoured to give something like the truth with as little incivility as I could, by placing my silence to the want of subject in the very quiet way in which we live. Phebe [maidservant] has repented, and stays. I have also written to Charles, and I answered Miss Buller's letter by return of post, as I intended to tell you in my last.

Two or three things I recollected when it was too late, that I might have told you; one is, that the Welbys have lost their eldest son by a putrid fever at Eton, and another that Tom Chute is going to settle in Norfolk.

23. Pulteney Bridge, Bath. Jane's homes in Sydney Place and Gay Street were close to this elegant bridge.

24. Royal Crescent, Bath, 1788. This famous crescent was close to all Jane's homes in Bath.

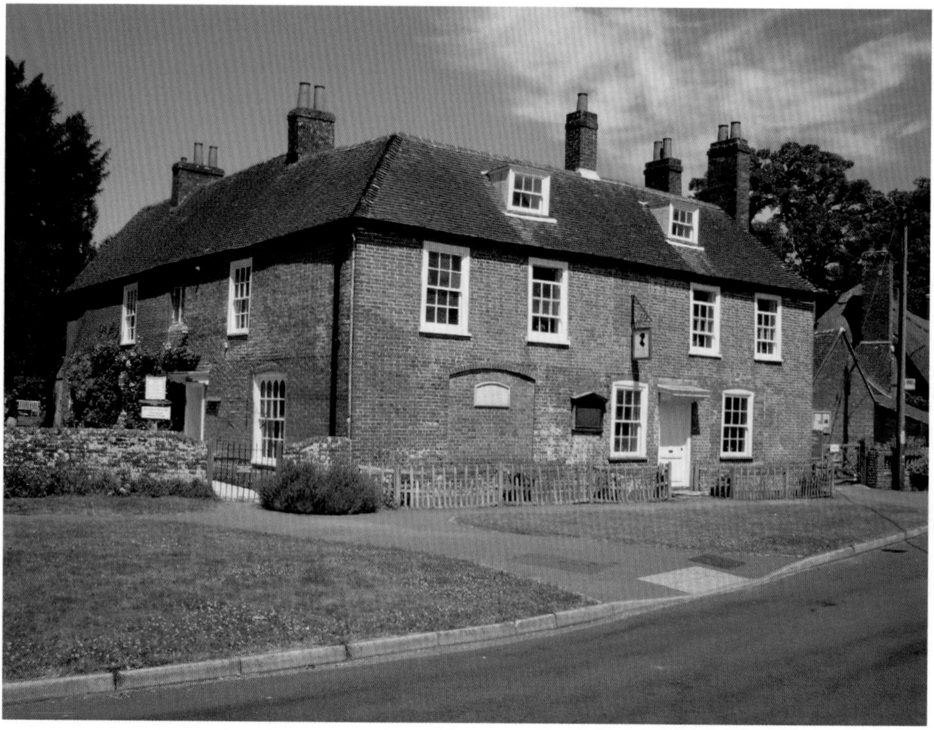

25. Chawton House Museum, formerly Chawton Cottage, Jane's last home.

26. The church of St Nicholas, Chawton, where Jane worshipped when she lived nearby.

27. Courtyard and outbuildings, Chawton House Museum.

At that moment she first perceived him
He stopt to look in.

Left: 28. Victorian illustration of a scene from *Sense and Sensibility.*

Right: 29. Victorian illustration of a scene from *Emma.*

Put round her shoulders by Mr. Crawford's quicker hands.—P. 226.

30. Victorian illustration of a scene from *Mansfield Park*.

'"Now be sincere; did you admire me for my impertinence?"'

31. Victorian illustration of a scene from *Pride and Prejudice*.

Placed it before Anne.

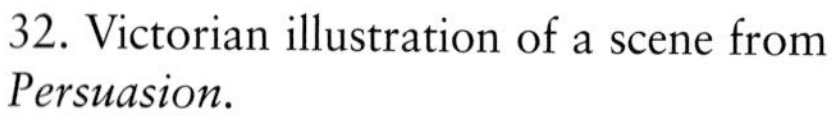

32. Victorian illustration of a scene from *Persuasion*.

The same kind of delicate flattery.

33. Victorian illustration of a scene from *Northanger Abbey*.

On reading in the Newspaper, the Marriage of "Mr. Gell of Eastbourne to Miss Gill."

Of Eastbourne Mr Gell
From being perfectly well
Became dreadfully ill
For the love of Miss Gill

So he said with some sighs
"I'm the slave of your <u>eyes</u>.
Oh! restore if you please
By accepting my <u>ease</u>."

J. A.

34. Jane's handwriting.

35. Silhouettes of Jane's father, mother and sister.

36. Carlton House, Pall Mall, the home of the Prince Regent. Jane visited Carlton House in 1816 at his invitation.

37. Winchester Cathedral where Jane is buried.

Right: 38. 8 College Street, Winchester, where Jane spent the last two months of her life and where she died on 18 July 1817.

Below left: 39. Jane Austen, a portrait by Cassandra Austen.

Below right: 40. The title page of the second edition of *A Memoir of Jane Austen* by James Edward Austen-Leigh.

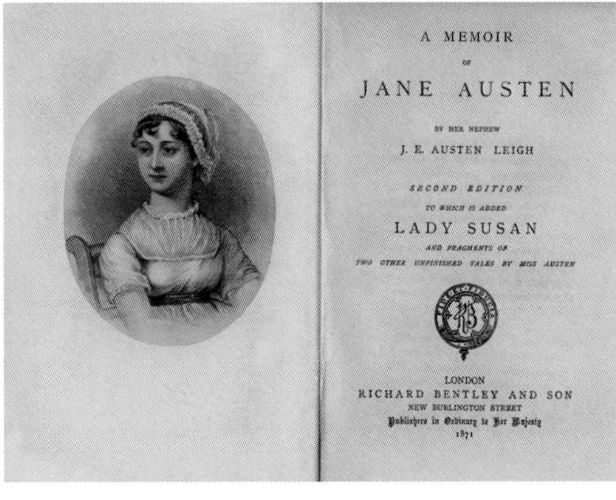

A MEMOIR

OF

JANE AUSTEN

BY HER NEPHEW

J. E. AUSTEN LEIGH

SECOND EDITION

TO WHICH IS ADDED

LADY SUSAN

AND FRAGMENTS OF

TWO OTHER UNFINISHED TALES BY MISS AUSTEN

LONDON

RICHARD BENTLEY AND SON

NEW BURLINGTON STREET

Publishers in Ordinary to Her Majesty

1871

JANE AUSTEN
Born December 16th 1775
Died July 18th 1817
WORSHIPPED HERE

This tablet was erected to her memory by
her great grandniece Emma Austen-Leigh 1936

Above:
41. James Edward Austen-Leigh, Jane's nephew and the author of the first biography of her.

Left: 42. Tablet in Steventon church.

You have scarcely ever mentioned Lizzy since your being at Godmersham. I hope it is not because she is altered for the worse.

I cannot yet satisfy Fanny as to Mrs. Foote's baby's name, and I must not encourage her to expect a good one, as Captain Foote is a professed adversary to all but the plainest; he likes only Mary, Elizabeth, Anne, &c. Our best chance is of 'Caroline,' which in compliment to a sister seems the only exception.

He dined with us on Friday, and I fear will not soon venture again, for the strength of our dinner was a boiled leg of mutton, underdone even for James; and Captain Foote has a particular dislike to underdone mutton, but he was so good-humoured and pleasant that I did not much mind his being starved. He gives us all the most cordial invitation to his house in the country, saying just what the Williams [Sir Thomas and his second wife] ought to say to make us welcome. Of them we have seen nothing since you left us, and we hear that they are just gone to Bath again, to be out of the way of further alterations at Brooklands.

Mrs. F. A. has had a very agreeable letter from Mrs. Dickson, who was delighted with the purse, and desires her not to provide herself with a christening dress, which is exactly what her young correspondent wanted; and she means to defer making any of the caps as long as she can, in hope of having Mrs. D.'s present in time to be serviceable as a pattern. She desires me to tell you that the gowns were cut out before your letter arrived, but that they are long enough for Caroline. The Beds, *as I believe they are called, have fallen to Frank's share to continue, and of course are cut out to admiration.*

'Alphonsine' did not do. We were disgusted in twenty pages, as, independent of a bad translation, it has indelicacies which disgrace a pen hitherto so pure; and we changed it for the 'Female Quixotte,' which now makes our evening amusement; to me a very high one, as I find the work quite equal to what I remembered it. Mrs. F. A., to whom it is new, enjoys it as one could wish; the other Mary, I believe, has little pleasure from that or any other book.

My mother does not seem at all more disappointed than ourselves at the termination of the family treaty [regarding a Leigh family inheritance]; she thinks less of that *just now than of the comfortable state of her own finances, which she finds on closing her year's accounts beyond her expectation, as she begins the new year with a balance of 30*l*. in her favour; and when she has written her answer to my aunt, which you know always hangs a little upon her mind, will be above the world entirely. You will have a great deal of unreserved discourse with Mrs. K., I dare say, upon this subject, as well as upon many other of our family matters. Abuse everybody but me.*

Thursday. – *We expected James yesterday, but he did not come; if he comes at all now, his visit will be a very short one, as he must return to-morrow, that Ajax [possibly a servant] and the chair may be sent to Winchester on*

Saturday. Caroline's new pelisse depended upon her mother's being able or not to come so far in the chair; how the guinea that will be saved by the same means of return is to be spent I know not. Mrs. J. A. does not talk much of poverty now, though she has no hope of my brother's being able to buy another horse next *summer.*

Their scheme against Warwickshire continues, but I doubt the family's being at Stoneleigh so early as James says he must go, which is May.

*My mother is afraid I have not been explicit enough on the subject of her wealth; she began 1806 with 68*l.*, she begins 1807 with 99*l.*, and this after 32*l. *purchase of stock. Frank, too, has been settling his accounts and making calculations, and each party feels quite equal to our present expenses; but much increase of house rent would not do for either. Frank limits himself, I believe, to four hundred a year.*

You will be surprised to hear that Jenny [maidservant] is not yet come back; we have heard nothing of her since her reaching Itchingswell, and can only suppose that she must be detained by illness in somebody or other, and that she has been each day expecting to be able to come on the morrow. I am glad I did not know beforehand that she was to be absent during the whole or almost the whole of our friends being with us, for though the inconvenience has not been nothing, I should have feared still more. Our dinners have certainly suffered not a little by having only Molly's head and Molly's hands to conduct them; she fries better than she did, but not like Jenny.

We did not *take our walk on Friday, it was too dirty, nor have we yet done it; we may perhaps do something like it to-day, as after seeing Frank skate, which he hopes to do in the meadows by the beech [this should read 'beach'], we are to treat ourselves with a passage over the ferry. It is one of the pleasantest frosts I ever knew, so very quiet. I hope it will last some time longer for Frank's sake, who is quite anxious to get some skating; he tried yesterday, but it would not do.*

Our acquaintance increase too fast. He was recognized lately by Admiral Bertie, and a few days since arrived the Admiral and his daughter Catherine to wait upon us. There was nothing to like or dislike in either. To the Berties are to be added the Lances, with whose cards we have been endowed, and whose visit Frank and I returned yesterday. They live about a mile and three-quarters from S. to the right of the new road to Portsmouth, and I believe their house is one of those which are to be seen almost anywhere among the woods on the other side of the Itchen. It is a handsome building, stands high, and in a very beautiful situation.

We found only Mrs. Lance at home, and whether she boasts any offspring besides a grand pianoforte did not appear. She was civil and chatty enough, and offered to introduce us to some acquaintance in Southampton, which we gratefully declined.

I suppose they must be acting by the orders of Mr. Lance of Netherton in this civility, as there seems no other reason for their coming near us. They will not come often, I dare say. They live in a handsome style and are rich, and she seemed to like to be rich, and we gave her to understand that we were far from being so; she will soon feel therefore that we are not worth her acquaintance.

You must have heard from Martha by this time. We have had no accounts of Kintbury since her letter to me.

Mrs. F. A. has had one fainting fit lately; it came on as usual after eating a hearty dinner, but did not last long.

I can recollect nothing more to say. When my letter is gone, I suppose I shall.

Yours affectionately,

J. A.

I have just asked Caroline if I should send her love to her godmama, to which she answered 'Yes.'

Miss Austen, Godmersham Park,
Faversham, Kent.

XXXVII

Southampton: February 8.

MY DEAREST CASSANDRA,

My expectation of having nothing to say to you after the conclusion of my last seems nearer truth than I thought it would be, for I feel to have but little. I need not, therefore, be above acknowledging the receipt of yours this morning, or of replying to every part of it which is capable of an answer, and you may accordingly prepare for my ringing the changes of the glads and sorrys for the rest of the page.

Unluckily, however, I see nothing to be glad of, unless I make it a matter of joy that Mrs. Wylmot has another son, and that Lord Lucan has taken a mistress, both of which events are, of course, joyful to the actors; but to be sorry I find many occasions. The first is, that your return is to be delayed, and whether I ever get beyond the first is doubtful. It is no use to lament. I never heard that even Queen Mary's lamentation did her any good, and I could not, therefore, expect benefit from mine. We are all sorry, and now that subject is exhausted.

I heard from Martha yesterday. She spends this week with the Harwoods, goes afterwards with James and Mary for a few days to see Peter Debary and two of his sisters at Eversley, the living of which he has gained on the death of Sir R. Cope, and means to be here on the 24th, which will be Tuesday fortnight. I shall be truly glad if she can keep to her day, but dare not depend on it, and am so apprehensive of farther detention, that, if nothing else occurs to create it, I cannot help thinking she will marry Peter Debary.

It vexed me that I could not get any fish for Kintbury while their family was large, but so it was; and till last Tuesday I could procure none. I then sent them four pair of small soles, and should be glad to be certain of their arriving in good time, but I have heard nothing about them since, and had rather hear nothing than evil. They cost six shillings, and as they travelled in a basket which came from Kintbury a few days before with poultry, &c., I insist upon treating you with the booking, whatever it may be. *You are only eighteen pence in my debt.*

Mrs. E. Leigh did not make the slightest allusion to my uncle's business, as I remember telling you at the time, but you shall have it as often as you like. My mother wrote to her a week ago.

Martha's rug is just finished, and looks well, though not quite so well as I had hoped. I see no fault in the border, but the middle is dingy. My mother desires me to say that she will knit one for you as soon as you return to choose the colours and pattern.

I am sorry I have affronted you on the subject of Mr. Moore, but I do not mean ever to like him; and as to pitying a young woman merely because she cannot live in two places at the same time, and at once enjoy the comforts of being married and single, I shall not attempt it, even for Harriet. You see I have a spirit as well as yourself.

Frank and Mary cannot at all approve of your not being at home in time to help them in their finishing purchases, and desire me to say that, if you are not, they will be as spiteful as possible, and choose everything in the style most likely to vex you – knives that will not cut, glasses that will not hold, a sofa without a seat, and a book-case without shelves.

Our garden is putting in order by a man who bears a remarkably good character, has a very fine complexion, and asks something less than the first. The shrubs which border the gravel walk, he says, are only sweetbriar and roses, and the latter of an indifferent sort; we mean to get a few of a better kind, therefore, and at my own particular desire he procures us some syringas. I could not do without a syringa, for the sake of Cowper's line. We talk also of a laburnum. The border under the terrace wall is clearing away to receive currants and gooseberry bushes, and a spot is found very proper for raspberries.

The alterations and improvements within doors, too, advance very properly, and the offices will be made very convenient indeed. Our dressing table is constructing on the spot, out of a large kitchen table belonging to the house, for doing which we have the permission of Mr. Husket, Lord Lansdown's [the Austen's landlord] painter – domestic painter, I should call him, for he lives in the castle. Domestic chaplains have given way to this more necessary office, and I suppose whenever the walls want no touching up he is employed about my lady's face.

The morning was so wet that I was afraid we should not be able to see our little visitor, but Frank, who alone could go to church, called for her after service, and she is now talking away at my side and examining the treasures of my writing-desk drawers – very happy, I believe. Not at all shy, of course. Her name is Catherine [Foote], and her sister's Caroline. She is something like her brother, and as short for her age, but not so well-looking.

What is become of all the shyness in the world? Moral as well as natural diseases disappear in the progress of time, and new ones take their place. Shyness and the sweating sickness have given way to confidence and paralytic complaints.

I am sorry to hear of Mrs. Whitfield's increasing illness, and of poor Marianne Bridges having suffered so much; these are some of my sorrows; and that Mrs. Deedes is to have another child I suppose I may lament.

The death of Mrs. W. K. [Wyndham Knatchbull] we had seen. I had no idea that anybody liked her, and therefore felt nothing for any survivor, but I am now feeling away on her husband's account, and think he had better marry Miss Sharpe.

I have this instant made my present, and have the pleasure of seeing it smiled over with genuine satisfaction. I am sure I may, on this occasion, call Kitty Foote, as Hastings did H. Egerton, my 'very valuable friend.'

Evening. – *Our little visitor has just left us, and left us highly pleased with her; she is a nice, natural, open-hearted, affectionate girl, with all the ready civility which one sees in the best children in the present day; so unlike anything that I was myself at her age, that I am often all astonishment and shame. Half her time was spent at spillikins, which I consider as a very valuable part of our household furniture, and as not the least important benefaction from the family of Knight to that of Austen.*

But I must tell you a story. Mary [Frank's wife] has for some time had notice from Mrs. Dickson of the intended arrival of a certain Miss Fowler in this place. Miss F. is an intimate friend of Mrs. D., and a good deal known as such to Mary. On Thursday last she called here while we were out. Mary found, on our return, her card with only her name on it, and she had left word that she would call again. The particularity of this made us talk, and, among other conjectures, Frank said in joke, 'I dare say she is staying with the Pearsons.' The connection of the names struck Mary, and she immediately recollected Miss Fowler's having been very intimate with persons so called, and, upon putting everything together, we have scarcely a doubt of her being actually staying with the only family in the place whom we cannot visit.

What a contretemps*! in the language of France. What an unluckiness! in that of Madame Duval [character in the novel* Evelina*]. The black gentleman has certainly employed one of his menial imps to bring about this complete, though trifling, mischief. Miss F. has never called again, but we are in daily expectation of it. Miss P. has, of course, given her a proper understanding of* *the business. It is evident that Miss F. did not expect or wish to have the visit returned, and Frank is quite as much on his guard for his wife as we could desire for her sake or our own.*

We shall rejoice in being so near Winchester when Edward [her nephew] belongs to it, and can never have our spare bed filled more to our satisfaction than by him. Does he leave Eltham at Easter?

We are reading 'Clarentine,' and are surprised to find how foolish it is. I remember liking it much less on a second reading than at the first, and it does not bear a third at all. It is full of unnatural conduct and forced difficulties, without striking merit of any kind.

Miss Harrison is going into Devonshire, to attend Mrs. Dusantoy, as usual. Miss J. is married to young Mr. G., and is to be very unhappy. He swears, drinks, is cross, jealous, selfish, and brutal. The match makes her family miserable, and has occasioned his *being disinherited.*

The Browns are added to our list of acquaintance. He commands the Sea Fencibles here, under Sir Thomas [Williams], and was introduced at his own desire by the latter when we saw him last week. As yet the gentlemen only have visited, as Mrs. B. is ill, but she is a nice-looking woman, and wears one of the prettiest straw bonnets in the place.

Monday. – *The garret beds are made, and ours will be finished to-day. I had hoped it would be finished on Saturday, but neither Mrs. Hall nor Jenny was able to give help enough for that, and I have as yet done very little, and Mary nothing at all. This week we shall do more, and I should like to have all the five beds completed by the end of it. There will then be the window curtains, sofa-cover, and a carpet to be altered.*

I should not be surprised if we were to be visited by James again this week; he gave us reason to expect him soon, and if they go to Eversley he cannot come next week.

There, I flatter myself I have constructed you a smartish letter, considering my want of materials, but, like my dear Dr. Johnson, I believe I have dealt more in notions than facts.

I hope your cough is gone and that you are otherwise well, and remain, with love,
Yours affectionately,
J.A.
Miss Austen, Godmersham Park,
Faversham, Kent.

XXXVIII

Southampton: Friday (February 20).
MY DEAR CASSANDRA,

We have at last heard something of Mr. Austen's [John Austen of Broadford, Kent] will. It is believed at Tunbridge that he has left everything after the death of his widow to Mr. M. [Motley] Austen's third son John; and, as the said John was the only one of the family who attended the funeral, it seems likely to be true. Such ill-gotten wealth can never prosper.

I really have very little to say this week, and do not feel as if I should spread that little into the show of much. I am inclined for short sentences.

Mary will be obliged to you to take notice how often Elizabeth nurses her baby in the course of twenty-four hours, how often it is fed, and with what; you need not trouble yourself to write the result of your observations, your return will be early enough for the communication of them. You are recommended to bring away some flower seeds from Godmersham, particularly mignonette seed.

My mother has heard this morning from Paragon. My aunt talks much of the violent colds prevailing in Bath, from which my uncle has suffered ever since their return, and she has herself a cough much worse than any she ever had before, subject as she has always been to bad ones. She writes in good humour and cheerful spirits, however. The negotiation between them and Adlestrop [the financial settlement regarding the Stoneleigh inheritance] so happily over, indeed, what can have power to vex her materially?

Elliston, she tells us, has just succeeded to a considerable fortune on the death of an uncle. I would not have it enough to take him from the stage; she [his wife] should quit her business, and live with him in London.

We could not pay our visit on Monday; the weather altered just too soon, and we have since had a touch of almost everything in the weather way; two of the severest frosts since the winter began, preceded by rain, hail, and snow. Now we are smiling again.

Saturday. – I have received your letter, but I suppose you do not expect me to be gratified by its contents. I confess myself much disappointed by this repeated delay of your return, for though I had pretty well given up all idea of your being with us before our removal, I felt sure that March would not pass quite away without bringing you. Before April comes, of course, something else will occur to detain you. But as you are happy, all this is selfishness, of which here is enough for one page.

Pray tell Lizzy that if I had imagined her teeth to be really out, I should have said before what I say now, that it was a very unlucky fall indeed, that I am afraid it must have given her a great deal of pain, and that I dare say her mouth looks very comical.

I am obliged to Fanny for the list of Mrs. Coleman's children, whose names I had not, however, quite forgot; the new one I am sure will be Caroline. I have got Mr. Bowen's [apothecary] recipe for you; it came in my aunt's letter.

You must have had more snow at Godmersham than we had here; on Wednesday morning there was a thin covering of it over the fields and roofs *of the houses, but I do not think there was any left the next day. Everybody used to Southampton says that snow never lies more than twenty-four hours near it, and, from what we have observed ourselves, it is very true.*

Frank's going into Kent depends, of course, upon his being unemployed; but as the First Lord, after promising Lord Moira that Captain A. should have the first good frigate that was vacant, has since given away two or three fine ones, he has no particular reason to expect an appointment now. He, *however, has scarcely spoken about the Kentish journey. I have my information chiefly from her, and she considers her own going thither as more certain if he should be at sea than if not.*

Frank has got a very bad cough, for an Austen; but it does not disable him from making very nice fringe for the drawing-room curtains.

Mrs. Day has now got the carpet in hand, and Monday I hope will be the last day of her employment here. A fortnight afterwards she is to be called again from the shades of her red-checked bed in an alley near the end of the High Street, to clean the new house and air the bedding.

We hear that we are envied our house by many people, and that the garden is the best in the town. There will be green baize enough for Martha's room and ours, not to cover them, but to lie over the part where it is most wanted, under the dressing table. Mary is to have a piece of carpeting for the same purpose; my mother says she *does not want any, and it may certainly be better done without in her rooms than in Martha's and ours, from the difference of their aspect.*

I recommend Mrs. Grant's letters, as a present to the latter; what they are about, and how many volumes they form, I do not know, having never heard of them but from Miss Irvine, who speaks of them as a new and much-admired work, and as one which has pleased her highly. I have inquired for the book here, but find it quite unknown.

I believe I *put five breadths of linsey also into my flounce; I know I found it wanted more than I had expected, and that I should have been distressed if I had not bought more than I believed myself to need for the sake of the even measure, on which we think so differently. A light morning gown will be a very necessary purchase for you, and I wish you a pretty one. I shall buy such things whenever I am tempted, but as yet there is nothing of the sort to be seen.*

We are reading Barretti's other book, and find him dreadfully abusive of poor Mrs. Sharpe. I can no longer take his part against you, as I did nine years ago.

Sunday. – *This post has brought our Martha's own assurance of her coming on Tuesday evening, which nothing is now to prevent except William [Jane's nephew] should send her word that there is no* remedy *[slang word used by Winchester College boys for a holiday] on that day. Her letter was put into the post at Basingstoke on their return from*

Eversley, where she says they have spent their time very pleasantly. She does not own herself in any danger of being tempted back again, however, and as she signs by her maiden name, we are at least to suppose her not married yet.

They must have had a cold visit, but as she found it agreeable I suppose there was no want of blankets, and we may trust to her sister's taking care that her love of many should be known. She sends me no particulars, having time only to write the needful.

I wish you a pleasant party to-morrow, and not more than you like of Miss Hatton's neck. Lady B. [first wife of Sir Brook Bridges] must have been a shameless woman if she named H. Hales as within her husband's reach. It is a piece of impertinence, indeed, in a woman to pretend to fix on any one, as if she supposed it could be only ask and have. A widower with three children has no right to look higher than his daughter's governess.

I am forced to be abusive for want of subject, having really nothing to say. When Martha comes she will supply me with matter; I shall have to tell you how she likes the house, and what she thinks of Mary.

You must be very cold to-day at Godmersham. We are cold here. I expect a severe March, a wet April, and a sharp May. And with this prophecy I must conclude.

My love to everybody.

Yours affectionately,

J. AUSTEN.

Miss Austen, Godmersham Park,
Faversham, Kent.

1808

These letters were written during a visit which Jane and her brother James and his wife paid to Godmersham at this time. There is a graphic description of the arrival of the two ladies and their reception by their relations, and a pleasant account of the life at Godmersham, which Edward Austen had greatly improved, inside and out, since his accession to the property in 1798. 'Bentigh' and 'the Temple plantations' deserve a word of notice. The former was once a ploughed field, but when my grandfather first came to Godmersham he planted it with underwood, and made gravel walks through it, planted an avenue of trees on each side of the principal walk, and added it to the shrubberies. The family always walked through it on their way to church, leaving the shrubberies by a little door in the wall, at the end of the private grounds, which brought them out just opposite the church. The same improving hand planted also a great deal on the other (east) side of the river, where was a pretty sort of summer-house called 'The Temple,' built by one of the preceding owners of the place. The road at that time ran nearer to the house than the present turnpike road; it formerly divided the river from the park, and the hill called 'the Canterbury Hill' was also planted by my grandfather, and is the plantation to which reference is here made.

'Edward and Caroline' are James and Mary Austen's children – the writer of the 'Memoir' who was now nearly ten years old, and his little sister.

The fortieth commences with an account of a visit to Canterbury, wherein is a kindly mention of Mrs. Knight (Catherine Knatchbull) and a criticism on Mr. Moore (Harriet Bridges' husband), who does not seem to have been a favourite of Jane's, although she never varies in her affectionate mention of his wife. Mrs. Knight seems to have been very generously disposed towards other members of the Austen family besides her husband's heir, for her 'very agreeable present' is here gratefully acknowledged, and both Cassandra and Jane stayed with her at different times at the White Friars house.

'Buckwell' is an old-fashioned farmhouse, belonging to the Godmersham property, and situate on the Ashford road, within an easy drive. The 'dragging' of the fish-pond does not seem to have tempted Jane, but it is a kind of sport which has a peculiar fascination of its own, though scarcely so great as that of 'letting the water off' from a well-stocked pond. There are few more delightful pastimes than this to school-boys who have the good fortune to have pond-owning fathers; the patience which has to be exercised whilst the water slowly drains away is amply rewarded when the depth has become sufficiently reduced to allow of the sight of the carp and tench splashing about in evident astonishment at the extraordinary change which is taking place in their usually quiet home. Then, when enough water has been drained off to allow it, how gloriously exciting is the plunge into the mud, and the capture of the fish in small landing nets, varied by the eager chase after the eels, whose twistings and windings are enough to baffle the most experienced holder of eel-tongs, and whose capture is the climax of the sport. This, however, is not strictly germane to Jane Austen, whom I do not suspect of having ever waded after eels in her life, and who upon the occasion of the present less exciting amusement stayed quietly at home. In the same letter the expression: 'I initiated her into the mysteries of Inmanism' requires explanation. Mrs. Inman was the aged widow of a former clergyman at Godmersham, who lived at the park-keeper's house ('Old Hills'), and it was one of the 'treats' of the Godmersham children to walk up to her with fruit after dessert. She was blind, and used to walk about the park with a gold-headed walking-stick, and leaning on the arm of her faithful servant Nanny Part. She died in September, 1815.

'John Bridges,' who had grown 'old and black,' was Brook John, younger brother of the reigning Sir Brook. Strange to say, he married the sister of his eldest brother's second wife, Miss Hawley – as Edward married the sister of the first wife, Miss Foote – a rare example of confidence in a fraternal selection of a family from which to choose a partner for life. John Bridges had the curacy of Moldash (which was attached to the living of Godmersham), and lived some time with his sister and brother-in-law, with whose children he was a great favourite. He hunted (which was a common qualification with clergymen in those days), had delicate health, and died in 1812, leaving no children. His widow afterwards married Mr. Bramston, of Skreens, in Essex. She was the 'Aunt Charlotte' of the Godmersham family, and died in 1848.

The forty-first letter mentions 'Mr. Knatchbull of Provender' as being at the White Friars. This was my father, afterwards the Right Hon. Sir Edward Knatchbull, who subsequently represented Kent from the death of his father in 1819 to 1830, and East Kent from 1832 to 1845. At this time he had been two years married to his first wife, Annabella-Christiana, daughter of Sir John Honywood. Provender had been the property of the two Hugessen co-heiresses, Mary (Lady Knatchbull) and Dorothy (Lady Banks), wife of the Right Hon. Sir Joseph Banks, and through this channel came into my father's and, ultimately, into my possession. 'Charles Graham,' rector of Barham, and brother to my grandfather Sir E. Knatchbull's second wife, was always intimate at Hatch, as was, in after years, his only son, a most popular young man, who was unhappily drowned at Oxford whilst an undergraduate of Trinity College in that University. The 'Lady Knatchbull' here mentioned was my grandfather's third wife, Mary Hawkins, co-heiress of Nash Court, near Faversham. Curiously enough this property, which was sold, has come back to a descendant of this lady, one of whose daughters, Eleanor Knatchbull, married the fourth Lord Sondes, and the late owner of Nash Court, Mr. Ladd, lately bequeathed it (subject to the life interest of his wife) to one of the younger sons of the fifth Lord (now the first Earl) Sondes – his neighbour at Lees Court, which adjoins it.

The Knatchbulls who 'returned into Somersetshire' were the branch of the Hatch family already mentioned in the sixth division of letters.

The Lady Bridges mentioned in the forty-second letter was not the then baronet's wife, Miss Foote, who had died two years before, but his mother, 'Fanny Fowler,' who at this time was living at Goodnestone Farm at the Dower-house.

XXXIX

Godmersham: Wednesday (June 15).

MY DEAR CASSANDRA,

Where shall I begin? Which of all my important nothings shall I tell you first? At half after seven yesterday morning Henry saw us into our own carriage, and we drove away from the Bath Hotel; which, by-the-bye, had been found most uncomfortable quarters – very dirty, very noisy, and very ill-provided. James began his journey by the coach at five. Our first eight miles were hot; Deptford Hill brought to my mind our hot journey into Kent fourteen years ago; but after Blackheath we suffered nothing, and as the day advanced it grew quite cool. At Dartford, which we reached within the two hours and three-quarters, we went to the Bull, the same inn at which we breakfasted in that said journey, and on the present occasion had about the same bad butter.

At half-past ten we were again off, and, travelling on without any adventure reached Sittingbourne by three. Daniel was watching for us at the door of the George, and I was acknowledged very kindly by Mr. and Mrs. Marshall [landlords], to the latter of whom I devoted my conversation, while Mary went out to buy some gloves. A few minutes, of course, did for Sittingbourne; and so off we drove, drove, drove, and by six o'clock were at Godmersham.

Our two brothers were walking before the house as we approached, as natural as life. Fanny and Lizzy met us in the Hall with a great deal of pleasant joy; we went for a few minutes into the breakfast parlour, and then proceeded to our rooms. Mary has the Hall chamber. I am in the Yellow room – very literally – for I am writing in it at this moment. It seems odd to me to have such a great place all to myself, and to be at Godmersham without you is also odd.

You are wished for, I assure you: Fanny, who came to me as soon as she had seen her Aunt James to her room, and stayed while I dressed, was as energetic as usual in her longings for you. She is grown both in height and size since last year, but not immoderately, looks very well, and seems as to conduct and manner just what she was and what one could wish her to continue.

Elizabeth, who was dressing when we arrived, came to me for a minute attended by Marianne, Charles, and Louisa, and, you will not doubt, gave me a very affectionate welcome. That I had received such from Edward also I need not mention; but I do, you see, because it is a pleasure. I never saw him look in better health, and Fanny says he is perfectly well. I cannot praise Elizabeth's looks, but they are probably affected by a cold. Her little namesake has gained in beauty in the last three years, though not all that Marianne has lost. Charles is not quite so lovely as he was. Louisa is much as I expected, and Cassandra I find handsomer than I expected, though at present disguised by such a violent breaking-out that she does not come down after dinner. She has charming eyes and a nice open countenance, and seems likely to be very lovable. Her size is magnificent.

I was agreeably surprised to find Louisa Bridges [Elizabeth's sister] still here. She looks remarkably well (legacies are very wholesome diet), and is just what she always was. John [Bridges] is at Sandling. You may fancy our dinner party therefore; Fanny, of course, belonging to it, and little Edward, for that day. He was almost too happy, his happiness at least made him too talkative.

It has struck ten; I must go to breakfast.

Since breakfast I have had a tête-à-tête *with Edward in his room; he wanted to know James's plans and mine, and from what his own now are I think it already nearly certain that I shall return when they do, though not with them. Edward will be going about the same time to Alton, where he has business with Mr. Trimmer [lawyer], and where he means his son should join him; and I shall probably be his companion to that place, and get on afterwards somehow or other.*

I should have preferred a rather longer stay here certainly, but there is no prospect of any later conveyance for me, as he does not mean to accompany Edward on his return to Winchester, from a very natural unwillingness to leave Elizabeth [who was expecting her eleventh baby] at that time. I shall at any rate be glad not to be obliged to be an incumbrance on those who have brought me here, for, as James has no horse, I must feel in their carriage that I am taking his place. We were rather crowded yesterday, though it does not become me to say so, as I and my boa were of the party, and it is not to be supposed but that a child of three years of age [Caroline] was fidgety.

I need scarcely beg you to keep all this to yourself, lest it should get round by Anna's means. She is very kindly inquired after by her friends here, who all regret her not coming with her father and mother.

I left Henry, I hope, free from his tiresome complaint, in other respects well, and thinking with great pleasure of Cheltenham and Stoneleigh.

The brewery scheme is quite at an end: at a meeting of the subscribers last week it was by general, and I believe very hearty, consent dissolved.

The country is very beautiful. I saw as much as ever to admire in my yesterday's journey.

Thursday. – *I am glad to find that Anna was pleased with going to Southampton, and hope with all my heart that the visit may be satisfactory to everybody. Tell her that she will hear in a few days from her mamma, who would have written to her now but for this letter.*

Yesterday passed quite à la *Godmersham: the gentlemen rode about Edward's farm, and returned in time to saunter along Bentigh with us; and after dinner we visited the Temple Plantations, which, to be sure, is a Chevalier Bayard of a plantation. James and Mary are much struck with the beauty of the place. To-day the spirit of the thing is kept up by the two brothers being gone to Canterbury in the chair.*

I cannot discover, even through Fanny, that her mother is fatigued by her attendance on the children. I have, of course, tendered my services, and when Louisa is gone, who sometimes hears the little girls read, will try to be accepted in her stead. She will not be here many days longer. The Moores are partly expected to dine here to-morrow or Saturday.

I feel rather languid and solitary – perhaps because I have a cold; but three years ago we were more animated with you and Harriot and Miss Sharpe. We shall improve, I dare say, as we go on.

I have not yet told you how the new carriage is liked – very well, very much indeed, except the lining, which does look rather shabby.

I hear a very bad account of Mrs. Whitefield [wife of the vicar of Godmersham]; a very good one of Mrs. Knight, who goes to Broadstairs next month. Miss Sharpe is going with Miss Bailey to Tenby. The Widow Kennet succeeds to the post of laundress.

Would you believe it my trunk is come already; and, what completes the wondrous happiness, nothing is damaged. I unpacked it all before I went to bed last night, and when I went down to breakfast this morning presented the rug, which was received most gratefully, and met with universal admiration. My frock is also given, and kindly accepted.

Friday. – *I have received your letter, and I think it gives me nothing to be sorry for but Mary's [Frank's wife] cold, which I hope is by this time better. Her approbation of her child's hat makes me very happy. Mrs. J. A. bought one at Gayleard's for Caroline, of the same shape, but brown and with a feather.*

I hope Huxham [physician whose Tincture of Bark Cassandra was taking] is a comfort to you; I am glad you are taking it. I shall probably have an opportunity of giving Harriot your message tomorrow; she does not come here, they have not a day to spare, but Louisa and I are to go to her in the morning. I send your thanks to Eliza by this post in a letter to Henry.

Lady Catherine is Lord Portmore's daughter. I have read Mr. Jefferson's case [Revd T. Jefferson, author of Two Sermons*] to Edward, and he desires to have his name set down for a guinea and his wife's for another; but does not wish for more than one copy of the work. Your account of Anna gives me pleasure. Tell her, with my love, that I like her for liking the quay. Mrs. J. A. seems rather surprised at the Maitlands drinking tea with you, but that does not prevent my approving it. I hope you had not a disagreeable evening with Miss Austen [of Ensbury, Dorset, may have been a relation of the Hampshire Austens] and her niece. You know how interesting the purchase of a sponge-cake is to me.*

I am now just returned from Eggerton; Louisa [Bridges] and I walked together and found Miss Maria [Cuthbert] at home. Her sister we met on our way back. She *had been to pay her compliments to Mrs. Inman, whose chaise was seen to cross the park while we were at dinner yesterday.*

I told Sackree [nursemaid] that you desired to be remembered to her, which pleased her; and she sends her duty, and wishes you to know that she has been into the great world. She went on to town after taking William to

Eltham, and, as well as myself, saw the ladies go to Court on the 4th. She had the advantage indeed of me in being in the Palace.

Louisa [Edward and Elizabeth's daughter] is not so handsome as I expected, but she is not quite well. Edward and Caroline seem very happy here; he has nice playfellows in Lizzy and Charles. They and their attendant have the boys' attic. Anna will not be surprised that the cutting off her hair is very much regretted by several of the party in this house; I am tolerably reconciled to it by considering that two or three years may restore it again.

You are very important with your Captain Bulmore and Hotel Master, and I trust, if your trouble overbalances your dignity on the occasion, it will be amply repaid by Mrs. Craven's approbation, and a pleasant scheme to see her.

Mrs. Cooke has written to my brother James to invite him and his wife to Bookham in their way back, which, as I learn through Edward's means, they are not disinclined to accept, but that my being with them would render it impracticable, the nature of the road affording no conveyance to James. I shall therefore make them easy on that head as soon as I can.

I have a great deal of love to give from everybody.

Yours most affectionately,

JANE.

My mother will be glad to be assured that the size of the rug does perfectly well. It is not to be used till winter.

Miss Austen, Castle Square, Southampton.

XL

Godmersham: Thursday (June 20).

MY DEAR CASSANDRA,

I will first talk of my visit to Canterbury, as Mrs. J. A.'s letter to Anna cannot have given you every particular of it which you are likely to wish for. I had a most affectionate welcome from Harriot, and was happy to see her looking almost as well as ever. She walked with me to call on Mrs. Brydges, when Elizabeth and Louisa went to Mrs. Milles'. Mrs. B. was dressing, and could not see us, and we proceeded to the White Friars, where Mrs. K. was alone in her drawing room, as gentle, and kind, and friendly as usual. She inquired after everybody, especially my mother and yourself. We were with her a quarter of an hour before Elizabeth and Louisa, hot from Mrs. Baskerville's shop, walked in; they were soon followed by the carriage, and another five minutes brought Mr. Moore himself, just returned from his morning ride.

Well, and what do I think of Mr. Moore? I will not pretend in one meeting to dislike *him, whatever Mary may say, but I can honestly assure her that I saw nothing in him to admire. His manners, as you have always said, are gentleman-like, but by no means winning. He made one formal inquiry after you.*

I saw their little girl, and very small and very pretty she is. Her features are as delicate as Mary Jane's, with nice dark eyes; and if she had Mary Jane's fine colour she would be quite complete. Harriot's fondness for her seems just what is amiable and natural, and not foolish. I saw Caroline [Mr Moore's daughter by his first wife] also, and thought her very plain.

Edward's plan for Hampshire does not vary; he only improves it with the kind intention of taking me on to Southampton, and spending one whole day with you; and, if it is found practicable, Edward, jun., will be added to our party for that one day also, which is to be Sunday, the 10th of July. I hope you may have beds for them. We are to begin our journey on the 8th, and reach you late on the 9th.

This morning brought me a letter from Mrs. Knight, containing the usual fee, and all the usual kindness. She asks me to spend a day or two with her this week, to meet Mrs. C. Knatchbull, who, with her husband, comes to the White Friars to-day, and I believe I shall go. I have consulted Edward, and think it will be arranged for Mrs. J. A.'s going with me one morning, my staying the night, and Edward's driving me home the next evening. Her very agreeable present will make my circumstances quite easy. I shall reserve half for my pelisse. I hope by this early return I am sure of seeing Catherine [Bigg] and Alethea [Bigg]; and I propose that, either with or without them, you and I and Martha shall have a snug fortnight while my mother is at Steventon.

We go on very well here. Mary finds the children less troublesome than she expected, and, independent of them, there is certainly not much to try the patience or hurt the spirits at Godmersham. I initiated her yesterday into the mysteries of Inman-ism. The poor old lady is as thin and cheerful as ever, and very thankful for a new acquaintance. I had called on her before with Elizabeth and Louisa.

I find John Bridges grown very old and black, but his manners are not altered; he is very pleasing, and talks of Hampshire with great admiration.

Pray let Anna have the pleasure of knowing that she is remembered with kindness, both by Mrs. Cooke and Miss Sharpe. Her manners must be very much worsted by your description of them, but I hope they will improve by this visit.

Mrs. Knight finished her letter with, 'Give my best love to Cassandra when you write to her.' I shall like spending a day at the White Friars very much.

We breakfasted in the library this morning for the first time, and most of the party have been complaining all day of the heat; but Louisa and I feel alike as to weather, and are cool and comfortable.

Wednesday. – *The Moores came yesterday in their curricle, between* one and two o'clock, and immediately after the noonshine [snack] which succeeded their arrival a party set off for Buckwell, to see the pond dragged – Mr. Moore, James, Edward, and James; Edward on horseback, John Bridges driving Mary in his gig. The rest of us remained quietly and comfortably at home.

We had a very pleasant dinner, at the lower end of the table at least; the merriment was chiefly between Edward, Louisa, Harriot, and myself. Mr. Moore did not talk so much as I expected, and I understand from Fanny that I did not see him at all as he is in general. Our being strangers made him so much more silent and quiet. Had I had no reason for observing what he said and did, I should scarcely have thought about him. His manners to her want tenderness, and he was a little violent at last about the impossibility of her going to Eastwell. I cannot see any unhappiness in her, however, and as to kind-heartedness, &c., she is quite unaltered. Mary was disappointed in *her* beauty, and thought *him* very disagreeable; James admires *her*, and finds *him* conversable and pleasant.

I sent my answer by them to Mrs. Knight, my double acceptance of her note and her invitation, which I wrote without much effort, for I was rich, and the rich are always respectable, whatever be their style of writing.

I am to meet Harriot [Moore] at dinner to-morrow. It is one of the audit days, and Mr. M. dines with the Dean, who is just come to Canterbury. On Tuesday there is to be a family meeting at Mrs. C. Milles's: Lady Bridges and Louisa from Goodnestone, the Moores, and a party from this house – Elizabeth, John Bridges, and myself. It will give me pleasure to see Lady B.; she is now quite well. Louisa goes home on Friday, and John with her, but he returns the next day. These are our engagements; make the most of them.

Mr. Waller is dead, I see. I cannot grieve about it, nor, perhaps, can his widow very much. Edward began cutting sanfoin on Saturday, and, I hope, is likely to have favourable weather. The crop is good.

There has been a cold and sore-throat prevailing very much in this house lately; the children have almost all been ill with it, and we were afraid Lizzy was going to be very ill one day. She had specks and a great deal of fever. It went off, however, and they are all pretty well now.

I want to hear of your gathering strawberries; we have had them three times here. I suppose you have been obliged to have in some white wine, and must visit the store closet a little oftener than when you were quite by yourselves.

One begins really to expect the St. Albans [Frank's ship] now, and I wish she may come before Henry goes to Cheltenham, it will be so much more convenient to him. He will be very glad if Frank can come to him in London, as his own time is likely to be very precious, but does not depend on it. I shall not forget Charles next week.

So much did I write before breakfast, and now, to my agreeable surprise, I have to acknowledge another letter from you. I had not the least notion of hearing before to-morrow, and heard of Russell's [manservant] being about to pass the windows without any anxiety. You are very amiable and very clever to write such long letters; every page of yours has more lines than this, and every line more words than the average of mine. I am quite ashamed; but you have certainly more little events than we have. Mr. Lyford supplies you with a great deal of interesting matter (matter intellectual, not physical), but I have nothing to say of Mr. Scudamore. [1]

And now, that is such a sad, stupid attempt at wit about matter that nobody can smile at it, and I am quite out of heart. I am sick of myself and my bad pens. I have no other complaint, however; my languor is entirely removed.

Ought I to be very much pleased with "Marmion"? As yet I am not. James reads it aloud in the evening – the short evening, beginning at about 10, and broken by supper.

Happy Mrs. Harrison and Miss Austen! You seem to be always calling on them. I am glad your various civilities have turned out so well, and most heartily wish you success and pleasure in your present engagement. I shall think of you to-night as at Netley, and to-morrow too, that I may be quite sure of being right, and therefore I guess you will not go to Netley at all.

This is a sad story about Mrs. P. [Powlett who eloped with Lord S.] I should not have suspected such a thing. She stayed the Sacrament, I remember, the last time that you and I did. A hint of it, with initials, was in yesterday's 'Courier,' and Mr. Moore guessed it to be Lord S., believing there was no other Viscount S. in the peerage, and so it proved, Lord Viscount S. not being there.

Yes, I enjoy my apartment very much, and always spend two or three hours in it after breakfast. The change from Brompton quarters [Henry's home] to these is material as to space. I catch myself going on to the hall chamber now and then.

Little Caroline looks very plain among her cousins; and though she is not so headstrong or humoursome as they are, I do not think her at all more engaging. Her brother is to go with us to Canterbury to-morrow, and Fanny completes the party. I fancy Mrs. K. [Knight] feels less interest in that branch of the family than any other. I dare say she will do her duty, *however, by the boy. His Uncle Edward talks nonsense to him delightfully; more than he can always understand. The two Morrises [probably the children of the Revd James Morrice of Betshanger] are come to dine and spend the day with him.*

Mary wishes my mother to buy whatever she thinks necessary for Anna's shifts, and hopes to see her at Steventon soon after the 9th of July, if that time is as convenient to my mother as any other. I have hardly done justice to what she means on the subject, as her intention is that my mother should come at whatever time she likes best. They will be at home on the 9th.

I always come in for a morning visit from Crundale, and Mr. and Mrs. Filmer have just given me my due. He and I talked away gaily of Southampton, the Harrisons, Wallers, &c.

Fanny sends her best love to you all, and will write to Anna very soon.

Yours very affectionately,

JANE.

I want some news from Paragon.

I am almost sorry that Rose Hill Cottage should be so near suiting us, as it does not quite.

Miss Austen, Castle Square, Southampton.

[1]The doctor who attended the Godmersham family. He lived at Wye.

XLI

Godmersham: Sunday (June 26).

MY DEAR CASSANDRA,

I am very much obliged to you for writing to me on Thursday, and very glad that I owe the pleasure of hearing from you again so soon to such an agreeable cause; but you will not be surprised, nor perhaps so angry as I should be, to find that Frank's history has reached me before in a letter from Henry. We are all very happy to hear of his health and safety; he wants nothing but a good prize to be a perfect character.

This scheme to the island is an admirable thing for his wife; she will not feel the delay of his return in such variety. How very kind of Mrs. Craven to ask her! I think I quite understand the whole island arrangements, and shall be very ready to perform my part in them. I hope my mother will go, and I trust it is certain that there will be Martha's bed for Edward when he brings me home. What can you do with Anna? for her bed will probably be wanted for young Edward. His father writes to Dr. Goddard to-day to ask leave, and we have the pupil's authority for thinking it will be granted.

I have been so kindly pressed to stay longer here, in consequence of an offer of Henry's to take me back some time in September, that, not being able to detail all my objections to such a plan, I have felt myself obliged to give Edward and Elizabeth one private reason for my wishing to be at home in July. They feel the strength of it and say no more, and one can rely on their secrecy. After this I hope we shall not be disappointed of our friend's visit; my honour as well as my affection will be concerned in it. [1]

Elizabeth has a very sweet scheme of our accompanying Edward into Kent next Christmas. A legacy might make it very feasible – a legacy is our sovereign good. In the meanwhile, let me remember that I have now some *money to spare, and that I wish to have my name put down as a subscriber to Mr. Jefferson's [*Two Sermons*] works. My last letter was closed before it occurred to me how possible, how right, and how gratifying such a measure would be.*

Your account of your visitors' good journey, voyage, and satisfaction in everything gave me the greatest pleasure. They have nice weather for their introduction to the island, and I hope, with such a disposition to be pleased, their general enjoyment is as certain as it will be just. Anna's being interested in the embarkation shows a taste that one values. Mary Jane's delight in the water is quite ridiculous. Elizabeth supposes Mrs. Hall [maid at Castle Square, Southampton] will account for it by the child's knowledge of her father's being at sea.

Mrs. J. A. hopes, as I said in my last, to see my mother soon after her return home, and will meet her at Winchester on any day she will appoint.

And now I believe I have made all the needful replies and communications, and may disport myself as I can on my Canterbury visit.

It was a very agreeable visit. There was everything to make it so – kindness, conversation, variety, without care or cost. Mr. Knatchbull, from Provender, was at the W. Friars when we arrived, and stayed dinner, which, with Harriot, who came, as you may suppose, in a great hurry, ten minutes after the time, made our number six. Mr. K. went away early; Mr. Moore succeeded him, and we sat quietly working and talking till 10, when he ordered his wife away, and we adjourned to the dressing-room to eat our tart and jelly. Mr. M. was not unagreeable, though nothing seemed to go right with him. He is a sensible man and tells a story well.

Mrs. C. Knatchbull and I breakfasted tête-à-tête *the next day, for her husband was gone to Mr. Toke's, and Mrs. Knight had a sad headache which kept her in bed. She had had too much company the day before. After my coming, which was not till past two, she had Mrs. Milles, of Nackington, a Mrs. and Miss Gregory, and Charles Graham; and she told me it had been so all the morning.*

Very soon after breakfast on Friday, Mrs. C. K., who is just what we have always seen her, went with me to Mrs. Brydges, and Mrs. Moore's, paid some other visits while I remained with the latter, and we finished with Mrs. C. Milles, who luckily was not at home, and whose new house is a very convenient short cut from the Oaks to the W. Friars.

We found Mrs. Knight up and better; but early as it was – only 12 o'clock – we had scarcely taken off our bonnets before company came – Ly. Knatchbull and her mother; and after them succeeded Mrs. White, Mrs. Hughes and her two children, Mr. Moore, Harriot and Louisa, and John Bridges, with such short intervals between any as to make it a matter of wonder to me that Mrs. K. and I should ever have been ten minutes alone or have had any leisure for comfortable talk, yet we had time to say a little of everything. Edward came to dinner, and at 8 o'clock he and I got into the chair, and the pleasures of my visit concluded with a delightful drive home.

Mrs. and Miss Brydges seemed very glad to see me. The poor old lady looks much as she did three years ago, and was very particular in her inquiries after my mother. And from her and from the Knatchbulls I have all manner of kind compliments to give you both.

As Fanny writes to Anna by this post I had intended to keep my letter for another day, but, recollecting that I must keep it two, I have resolved rather to finish and send it now. The two letters will not interfere, I dare say; on the contrary, they may throw light on each other.

Mary begins to fancy, because she has received no message on the subject, that Anna does not mean to answer her letter, but it must be for the pleasure of fancying it. I think Elizabeth better and looking better than when we came.

Yesterday I introduced James to Mrs. Inman; in the evening John Bridges returned from Goodnestone, and this morning, before we had left the breakfast table, we had a visit from Mr. Whitfield [vicar of Godmersham], whose object, I imagine, was principally to thank my eldest brother for his assistance. Poor man! he has now a little intermission of his excessive solicitude on his wife's account, as she is rather better. James does duty at Godmersham to-day.

The Knatchbulls had intended coming here next week, but the rent-day makes it impossible for them to be received, and I do not think there will be any spare time afterwards. They return into Somersetshire by way of Sussex and Hants, and are to be at Fareham and, perhaps, may be in Southampton, on which possibility I said all that I thought right, and, if they are in the place, Mrs. K. has promised to call in Castle Square; it will be about the end of July. She seems to have a prospect, however, of being in that county again in the spring for a longer period, and will spend a day with us if she is.

You and I need not tell each other how glad we shall be to receive attention from, or pay it to anyone connected with, Mrs. Knight. I cannot help regretting that now, when I feel enough her equal to relish her society, I see so little of the latter.

The Milles of Nackington dine here on Friday, and perhaps the Hattons. It is a compliment as much due to me as a call from the Filmers.

When you write to the island, Mary will be glad to have Mrs. Craven informed, with her love, that she is now sure it will not be in her power to visit Mrs. Craven during her stay there, but that if Mrs. Craven can take Steventon in her way back it will be giving my brother and herself great pleasure. She also congratulates her namesake [Frank's wife] on hearing from her husband. That said namesake is rising in the world; she was thought excessively improved in her late visit. Mrs. Knight thought her so last year. Henry sends us the welcome information of his having had no face-ache since I left them.

You are very kind in mentioning old Mrs. Williams so often. Poor creature! I cannot help hoping that each letter may tell of her sufferings being over. If she wants sugar I should like to supply her with it.

The Moores went yesterday to Goodnestone, but return to-morrow. After Tuesday we shall see them no more, though Harriot is very earnest with Edward to take Wrotham in his journey, but we shall be in too great a hurry to get nearer to it than Wrotham Gate. He wishes to reach Guildford on Friday night, that we may have a couple of hours to spare for Alton. I shall be sorry to pass the door at Seale [home of the Walter family] without calling, but it must be so; and I shall be nearer to Bookham [home of the Cooke family] than I could wish in going from Dorking to Guildford; but till I have a travelling purse of my own I must submit to such things.

The Moores leave Canterbury on Friday, and go for a day or two to Sandling. I really hope Harriot is altogether very happy, but she cannot feel quite so much at her ease with her husband as the wives she has been used to.

Good-bye. I hope you have been long recovered from your worry on Thursday morning, and that you do not much mind not going to the Newbury races. I am withstanding those of Canterbury. Let that strengthen you.

Yours very sincerely,

JANE.

Miss Austen, Castle Square, Southampton.

[1] I have no clue to this reason.

XLII

Godmersham: Thursday (June 30).

MY DEAR CASSANDRA,

I give you all joy of Frank's return, which happens in the true sailor way, just after our being told not to expect him for some weeks. The wind has been very much against him, but I suppose he must be in our neighbourhood by this time. Fanny is in hourly expectation of him here. Mary's visit in the island is probably shortened by this event. Make our kind love and congratulations to her.

What cold disagreeable weather, ever since Sunday! I dare say you have fires every day. My kerseymere spencer is quite the comfort of our evening walks.

Mary thanks Anna for her letter, and wishes her to buy enough of her new coloured frock to make a shirt handkerchief. I am glad to hear of her Aunt Maitland's [her mother's sister] kind present. We want you to send us Anna's height, that we may know whether she is as tall as Fanny; and pray can you tell me of any little thing that would be probably acceptable to Mrs. F. A.? I wish to bring her something: has she a silver knife, or would you recommend a brooch? I shall not spend more than half a guinea about it.

Our Tuesday's engagement went off very pleasantly; we called first on Mrs. Knight, and found her very well; and at dinner had only the Milles' of Nackington, in addition to Goodnestone and Godmersham, and Mrs. Moore. Lady Bridges looked very well, and would have been very agreeable, I am sure, had there been time enough for her to talk to me; but as it was, she could only be kind and amiable, give one good-humoured smiles, and make friendly inquiries. Her son Edward was also looking very well, and with manners as unaltered as hers. In the evening came Mr. Moore, Mr. Toke, Dr. and Mrs. Walsby, and others. One card-table was formed, the rest of us sat and talked, and at half after nine we came away.

Yesterday my two brothers went to Canterbury, and J. Bridges left us for London in his way to Cambridge, where he is to take his master's degree.

Edward and Caroline and their mamma have all had the Godmersham cold, the former with sore-throat and fever, which his looks are still suffering from. He *is very happy here, however, but I believe the little girl will be glad to go home; her cousins are too much for her. We are to have Edward, I find, at Southampton, while his mother is in Berkshire for the races, and are very likely to have his father too. If circumstances are favourable, that will be a good time for our scheme to Beaulieu.*

Lady E. Hatton called here a few mornings ago, her daughter Elizth. with her, who says as little as ever, but holds up her head and smiles, and is to be at the races. Annamaria was there with Mrs. Hope, but we are to see her here to-morrow.

So much was written before breakfast; it is now half-past twelve, and, having heard Lizzy read, I am moved down into the library for the sake of fire, which agreeably surprised us when we assembled at ten, and here in warm and happy solitude proceed to acknowledge this day's letter.

We give you credit for your spirited voyage, and are very glad it was accomplished so pleasantly, and that Anna enjoyed it so much. I hope you are not the worse for the fatigue; but to embark at four you must have got up at three, and most likely had no sleep at all. Mary's not choosing to be at home occasions a general small surprise. As to Martha, she has not the least chance in the world of hearing from me again, and I wonder at her impudence in proposing it. I assure you I am as tired of writing long letters as you can be. What a pity that one should still be so fond of receiving them!

Fanny Austen's [a Kentish cousin] match is quite news, and I am sorry she has behaved so ill. There is some comfort to us in her misconduct, that we have not a congratulatory letter to write.

James and Edward are gone to Sandling to-day – a nice scheme for James, as it will show him a new and fine country. Edward certainly excels in doing the honours to his visitors, and providing for their amusement. They come back this evening.

Elizabeth talks of going with her three girls to Wrotham while her husband is in Hampshire; she is improved in looks since we first came, and, excepting a cold, does not seem at all unwell. She is considered, indeed, as more than usually active for her situation and size. I have tried to give James pleasure by telling him of his daughter's taste, but if he felt he did not express it. I rejoice in it very sincerely.

Henry talks, or rather writes, of going to the Downes, if the 'St. Albans' continues there, but I hope it will be settled otherwise. I had everybody's congratulations on her arrival at Canterbury. It is pleasant to be among people who know one's connections and care about them, and it amuses me to hear John Bridges talk of 'Frank.' I have thought a little of writing to the Downs, but I shall not, it is so very certain that he would be somewhere else when my letter got there.

Mr. Tho. Leigh is again in town, or was very lately. Henry met with him last Sunday in St. James's Church. He owned being come up unexpectedly on business, which we of course think can be only one *business, and he came post from Adlestrop in one day, which if it could be doubted before, convinces Henry that he will live for ever.*

Mrs. Knight is kindly anxious for our good, and thinks Mr. L. P. [Leigh Perrot] must be desirous for his family's *sake to have everything settled. Indeed I do not know where we are to get our legacy, but we will keep a sharp look-out. Lady B. was all in prosperous black the other day.*

A letter from Jenny Smallbone to her daughter [Caroline Austen's nursemaid] brings intelligence which is to be forwarded to my mother – the calving of a cow at Steventon. I am also to give her mamma's love to Anna, and say that as her papa talks of writing her a letter of comfort she will not *write, because she knows it would certainly prevent his doing so.*

When are calculations ever right? I could have sworn that Mary must have heard of the 'St. Albans' return, and would have been wild to come home or to be doing something. Nobody ever feels or acts, suffers or enjoys, as one expects.

I do not at all regard Martha's disappointment in the island; she will like it the better in the end. I cannot help thinking and re-thinking of your going to the island so heroically. It puts me in mind of Mrs. Hastings' voyage down the Ganges [in 1782 the wife of Warren Hastings voyaged down the Ganges to tend to her sick husband, an event which was recorded in a painting], and, if we had but a room to retire into to eat our fruit, we would have a picture of it hung there.

Friday, July 1. – *The weather is mended, which I attribute to my writing about it; and I am in hopes, as you make no complaint, though on the water and at four in the morning, that it has not been so cold with you.*

It will be two years to-morrow since we left Bath for Clifton, with what happy feelings of escape!

This post has brought me a few lines from the amiable Frank, but he gives us no hope of seeing him here. We are not unlikely to have a peep at Henry, who, unless the 'St. Albans' moves quickly, will be going to the Downs, and who will not be able to be in Kent without giving a day or two to Godmersham.

James has heard this morning from Mrs. Cooke, in reply to his offer of taking Bookham in his way home, which is kindly accepted; and Edwd. has had a less agreeable answer from Dr. Goddard, who actually refuses the petition. Being once fool enough to make a rule of never letting a boy go away an hour before the breaking-up hour, he is now fool enough to keep it. We are all disappointed. His letter brings a double disappointment, for he has no room for George this summer.

My brothers returned last night at ten, having spent a very agreeable day in the usual routine. They found Mrs. D. [Deedes] at home, and Mr. D. returned from business abroad to dinner. James admires the place very much, and thinks the two eldest girls handsome, but Mary's beauty has the preference. The number of children struck him a good deal, for not only are their own eleven all at home, but the three little Bridgeses are also with them.

James means to go once more to Canty. to see his friend Dr. Marlowe, who is coming about this time. I *shall hardly have another opportunity of going there. In another week I shall be at home, and there, my having been at Godmersham will seem like a dream, as my visit at Brompton seems already.*

The orange wine will want our care soon. But in the meantime, for elegance and ease and luxury, the Hattons and Milles' dine here to-day, and I shall eat ice and drink French wine, and be above vulgar economy. Luckily the pleasures of friendship, of unreserved conversation, of similarity of taste and opinions, will make good amends for orange wine.

Little Edwd. is quite well again.

Yours affectionately, with love from all,

J. A.

Miss Austen, Castle Square, Southampton.

1808, 1809

These letters were written at a time when the first great misfortune fell upon the Godmersham family, in the loss of the wife and mother so tenderly loved by all. In the last week of September Elizabeth Austen was confined with her youngest child, and on the 8th of October, after eating a hearty dinner, she was suddenly seized with sickness, and expired before the serious nature of her attack had been fully realised. The first two letters of the series, written just before this event, are in Jane's usual and cheerful spirit, and require no particular comment. The third (No. 45) was Jane's first communication to her sister after the melancholy news from Godmersham, and this and the two subsequent letters are principally upon the same subject. The forty-eighth letter alludes to the approaching marriage of Edward Bridges [1] with Harriet Foote, the sister of his brother Sir Brook's late wife. There are also allusions in this letter to some matters connected with her own mother's (the Leigh) family, which are of no public interest; nor is there anything in the forty-ninth to which I need call attention. In the fiftieth Jane alludes (as elsewhere in subsequent letters) to Lady Sondes' second marriage. This lady was Mary Elizabeth, only daughter of Richard Milles, Esq., of Elmham, Norfolk, who married, in 1785, Lewis Thomas, the second Lord Sondes, who died in 1806, and she subsequently married General Sir Henry Tucker Montresor, K.C.B., of Denne Hill. She died in 1818, leaving several children by her first, but none by her second husband, who married twice again, first Annetta, daughter of the Rev. Edward Cage, Rector of Eastling, by whom he left a family, and lastly Miss Fairman, who survived him many years, but had no children.

I do not know what 'deed' Sir Brook Bridges was supposed to be 'making up his mind to' during the *tête-à-tête* to which allusion is made in the letter, unless it was the deed of taking for his second wife Dorothy, eldest daughter of Sir Henry Hawley, which he actually accomplished in December of the next year. Probably, however, Jane was jokingly alluding to the probability of his proposing to Cassandra herself. This is the last letter of the year, for the next bears the date of January, 1809. It alludes to the illness of Mrs. E. Leigh, who would seem by the context to have been the mother of Mrs. Cooke, and, as George Cooke was 'the Reverend George Leigh Cooke,' we may gather, without searching more closely the family pedigree, that these were Jane's relations on the mother's side, of whom she saw a good deal from time to time, after taking 'Bookham' in her way to and from Steventon. [2]

I have no record of the visit to Godmersham, to the prospect of which allusion is made in this letter, and it is to be regretted that there are no letters after January, 1809, for more than two years, though, of course, many must have been written. These January letters do not contain any other allusions which appear to require explanation, or regarding which explanation would be of any general interest.

[1] Edward Bridges had the living of Lenham, his visits from which to Godmersham are referred to in subsequent letters. He afterwards went to Wingham, where he died, in 1825, leaving a large family.
[2] I find that the Rev. Mr. Cooke, Rector of Bookham, was one of Jane's god-parents – the others were Mrs. Jane Austen of Sevenoaks and Mrs. Musgrave, born Jane Huggins, and wife of Dr James Musgrave, whose mother was Catherine Perrot.

XLIII

Castle Square: Saturday (October 1)
MY DEAR CASSANDRA,

Your letter this morning was quite unexpected, and it is well that it brings such good news to counterbalance the disappointment to me of losing my first sentence, which I had arranged full of proper hopes about your journey, intending to commit them to paper to-day, and not looking for certainty till to-morrow.

We are extremely glad to hear of the birth of the child [Brook John], and trust everything will proceed as well as it begins. His mamma has our best wishes, and he our second best for health and comfort – though I suppose, unless he has our best too, we do nothing for her. *We are glad it was all over before your arrival, and I am most happy to find who the godmother is to be. My mother was some time guessing the names.*

Henry's present to you gives me great pleasure, and I shall watch the weather for him at this time with redoubled interest.

We have had four brace of birds lately, in equal lots, from Shalden and Neatham.

Our party at Mrs. Duer's produced the novelties of two old Mrs. Pollens and Mrs. Heywood, with whom my mother made a quadrille table; and of Mrs. Maitland and Caroline, and Mr. Booth without his sisters, at commerce. I have got a husband for each of the Miss Maitlands; Colonel Powlett and his brother have taken Argyle's inner house, and the consequence is so natural that I have no ingenuity in planning it. If the brother should luckily be a little sillier than the Colonel, what a treasure for Eliza [Maitland]!

Mr. Lyford called on Tuesday to say that he was disappointed of his son and daughter's coming, and must go home himself the following morning; and as I was determined that he should not lose every pleasure, I consulted him on my complaint. He recommended cotton, moistened with oil of sweet almonds, and it has done me good. I hope, therefore, to have nothing more to do with Eliza's [Mrs Henry Austen] receipt than to feel obliged to her for giving it, as I very sincerely do.

Mrs. Tilson's remembrance gratifies me, and I will use her patterns if I can.

I have just finished a handkerchief for Mrs. James Austen, which I expect her husband to give me an opportunity of sending to her ere long. Some fine day in October will certainly bring him to us in the garden, between three and four o'clock. She *hears that Miss Bigg is to be married in a fortnight. I wish it may be so.*

About an hour and a-half after your toils on Wednesday ended, ours began. At seven o'clock Mrs. Harrison, her two daughters and two visitors, with Mr. Debary and his eldest sister, walked in.

A second pool of commerce, and all the longer by the addition of the two girls, who during the first had one corner of the table and spillikens to themselves, was the ruin of us; it completed the prosperity of Mr. Debary, however, for he won them both.

Mr. Harrison came in late, and sat by the fire, for which I envied him, as we had our usual luck of having a very cold evening. It rained when our company came, but was dry again before they left us.

The Miss Ballards are said to be remarkably well-informed; their manners are unaffected and pleasing, but they do not talk quite freely enough to be agreeable, nor can I discover any right they had by taste or feeling to go their late tour.

Miss Austen and her nephew are returned, but Mr. Choles [servant] is still absent. 'Still absent,' say you. 'I did not know that he was gone anywhere;' neither did I know that Lady Bridges was at Godmersham at all, till I was told of her being still *there, which I take, therefore, to be the most approved method of announcing arrivals and departures.*

Mr. Choles is gone to drive a cow to Brentford, and his place is supplied to us by a man who lives in the same sort of way by odd jobs, and among other capabilities has that of working in a garden, which my mother will not forget if we ever have another garden here. In general, however, she thinks much more of Alton, and really expects to move there.

Mrs. Lyell's 130 guineas rent have made a great impression. To the purchase of furniture, whether here or there, she is quite reconciled, and talks of the trouble *as the only evil. I depended upon Henry's liking the Alton plan, and expect to hear of something perfectly unexceptionable there, through him.*

Our Yarmouth division [Frank and family] seem to have got nice lodgings; and, with fish almost for nothing and plenty of engagements and plenty of each other, must be very happy.

My mother has undertaken to cure six hams for Frank; at first it was a distress, but now it is a pleasure. She desires me to say that she does not doubt your making out the star pattern very well, as you have the breakfast-room rug to look at.

We have got the second volume of 'Espriella's Letters,' and I read it aloud by candle-light. The man describes well, but is horribly anti-English. He deserves to be the foreigner he assumes.

Mr. Debary went away yesterday, and I, being gone with some partridges to St. Maries, lost his parting visit.

I have heard to-day from Miss Sharpe [Jane's friend, the former governess at Godmersham, now working as companion to a Miss Bailey], and find that she returns with Miss B. to Hinckley, and will continue there at least till about Christmas, when she thinks they may both travel southward. Miss B., however, is probably to make only a temporary absence from Mr. Chessyre [her medical attendant], and I should not wonder if Miss Sharpe were to continue with her; unless anything more eligible offer she certainly will. She describes Miss B as very anxious that she should do so.

Sunday. – *I had not expected to hear from you again so soon, and am much obliged to you for writing as you did; but now, as you must have a great deal of the business upon your hands, do not trouble yourself with me for the present; I shall consider silence as good news, and not expect another letter from you till Friday or Saturday.*

You must have had a great deal more rain than has fallen here; cold enough it has been, but not wet, except for a few hours on Wednesday evening, and I could have found nothing more plastic than dust to stick in; now, indeed, we are likely to have a wet day, and, though Sunday, my mother begins it without any ailment.

Your plants were taken in one very cold, blustering day, and placed in the dining-room, and there was a frost the very same night. If we have warm weather again they are to be put out of doors; if not, my mother will have them conveyed to their winter quarters. I gather some currants every now and then, when I want either fruit or employment.

Pray tell my little goddaughter [Louisa Austen] that I am delighted to hear of her saying her lesson so well.

You have used me ill: you have been writing to Martha without telling me of it, and a letter which I sent her on Wednesday to give her information of you must have been good for nothing. I do not know how to think that something will not happen to prevent her returning by the 10th; and if it does, I shall not much regard it on my own account, for I am now got into such a way of being alone that I do not wish even for her.

The Marquis [of Landsowne] has put off being cured for another year; after waiting some weeks in vain for the return of the vessel he had agreed for, he is gone into Cornwall to order a vessel built for himself by a famous man in that country, in which he means to go abroad a twelvemonth hence.

Everybody who comes to Southampton finds it either their duty or pleasure to call upon us; yesterday we were visited by the eldest Miss Cotterel [a Steventon neighbour], just arrived from Waltham. Adieu! With love to all,
Yours affectionately,
J. A.

We had two pheasants last night from Neatham. To-morrow evening is to be given to the Maitlands. We are just asked to meet Mrs. Heywood and Mrs. Duer.

Miss Austen, Edward Austen's, Esq.
Godmersham Park, Faversham, Kent.

XLIV

Castle Square: Friday (October 7).

MY DEAR CASSANDRA,

Your letter on Tuesday gave us great pleasure, and we congratulate you all upon Elizabeth's hitherto happy recovery; tomorrow, or Sunday, I hope to hear of its advancing in the same style. We are also very glad to know that you are so well yourself, and pray you to continue so.

I was rather surprised on Monday by the arrival of a letter for you, from your Winchester correspondent [her nephew Edward, son of James], who seemed perfectly unsuspicious of your being likely to be at Godmersham. I took complete possession of the letter by reading, paying for, and answering it; and he will have the biscuits to-day – a very proper day for the purpose, though I did not think of it at the time.

I wish my brother joy of completing his thirtieth year, and hope the day will be remembered better than it was six years ago.

The masons are now repairing the chimney, which they found in such a state as to make it wonderful that it should have stood so long, and next to impossible that another violent wind should not blow it down. We may, therefore, thank you *perhaps for saving us from being thumped with old bricks. You are also to be thanked by Eliza's [their maid] desire for your present to her of dyed satin, which is made into a bonnet, and I fancy surprises her by its good appearance.*

My mother is preparing mourning for Mrs. E. K.; she has picked her old silk pelisse to pieces, and means to have it dyed black for a gown – a very interesting scheme, though just now a little injured by finding that it must be placed in Mr. Wren's hands, for Mr. Chambers is gone. As for Mr. Floor, he is at present rather low in our estimation. How is your blue gown? Mine is all to pieces. I think there must have been something wrong in the dye, for in places it divided with a touch. There was four shillings thrown away, to be added to my subjects of never-failing regret.

We found ourselves tricked into a thorough party at Mrs. Maitland's, a quadrille and a commerce table, and music in the other room. There were two pools at commerce, but I would not play more than one, for the stake was three shillings, and I cannot afford to lose that twice in an evening. The Miss M.'s were as civil and as silly as usual.

You know of course that Martha comes to-day, yesterday brought us notice of it, and the spruce beer is brewed in consequence.

On Wednesday I had a letter from Yarmouth, to desire me to send Mary's flannels and furs, &c.; and, as there was a packing case at hand, I could do it without any trouble.

On Tuesday evening Southampton was in a good deal of alarm for about an hour: a fire broke out soon after nine at Webb's, the pastry-cook, and burnt for some time with great fury. I cannot learn exactly how it originated; at the time it was said to be their bakehouse, but now I hear it was in the back of their dwelling-house, and that one room was consumed.

The flames were considerable: they seemed about as near to us as those at Lyme [where there was a fire in November 1803], and to reach higher. One could not but feel uncomfortable, and I began to think of what I should do if it came to the worst; happily, however, the night was perfectly still, the engines were immediately in use, and before ten the fire was nearly extinguished, though it was twelve before everything was considered safe, and a guard was kept the whole night. Our friends the Duers were alarmed, but not out of their good sense or benevolence.

I am afraid the Webbes have lost a great deal, more perhaps from ignorance or plunder than the fire; they had a large stock of valuable china, and, in order to save it, it was taken from the house and thrown down anywhere.

The adjoining house, a toyshop, was almost equally injured, and Hibbs, whose house comes next, was so scared from his senses that he was giving away all his goods, valuable laces, &c., to anybody who would take them.

The crowd in the High Street, I understand, was immense; Mrs. Harrison, who was drinking tea with a lady at Millar's, could not leave at twelve o'clock. Such are the prominent features of our fire. Thank God they were not worse!

Saturday. – *Thank you for your letter, which found me at the breakfast table with my two companions.*

I am greatly pleased with your account of Fanny; I found her in the summer just what you describe, almost another sister; and could not have supposed that a niece would ever have been so much to me. She is quite after one's own heart; give her my best love, and tell her that I always think of her with pleasure.

I am much obliged to you for inquiring about my ear, and am happy to say that Mr. Lyford's prescription has entirely cured me. I feel it a great blessing to hear again.

Your gown shall be unpicked, but I do not remember its being settled so before.

Martha was here by half-past six, attended by Lyddy [maid]; they had some rain at last, but a very good journey on the whole; and if looks and words may be trusted Martha is very happy to be returned. We receive her with Castle Square weather; it has blown a gale from the N.W. ever since she came, and we feel ourselves in luck that the chimney was mended yesterday.

She brings several good things for the larder, which is now very rich; we had a pheasant and hare the other day from the Mr. Grays of Alton. Is this to entice us to Alton, or to keep us away? Henry [who was an associate of a bank in Alton] had probably some share in the two last baskets from that neighbourhood, but we have not seen so much of his hand-writing, even as a direction to either.

Martha was an hour and half in Winchester, walking about with the three boys and at the pastry cook's. She thought Edward grown, and speaks with the same admiration as before of his manners; she saw in George a little likeness to his Uncle Henry.

I am glad you are to see Harriot; give my love to her. I wish you may be able to accept Lady Bridges' invitation, though I *could not her son Edward's [this could refer to a marriage proposal]; she is a nice woman and honours me by her remembrance.*

Do you recollect whether the Manydown family sent about their wedding cake? Mrs. Dundas has set her heart upon having a piece from her friend Catherine, and Martha, who knows what importance she attaches to this sort of thing, is anxious for the sake of both that there should not be a disappointment.

Our weather, I fancy, has been just like yours; we have had some *very delightful days, our 5th and 6th were what the 5th and 6th of October should always be, but we have always wanted a fire* within *doors, at least except for just the middle of the day.*

Martha does not find the key which you left in my charge for her suit the keyhole, and wants to know whether you think you can have mistaken it. It should open the interior of her high drawers, but she is in no hurry about it.

Sunday. – *It is cold enough now for us to prefer dining upstairs to dining below without a fire, and being only three we manage it very well, and to-day with two more we shall do just as well, I dare say. Miss Foote and Miss Wethered are coming.*

My mother is much pleased with Elizabeth's admiration of the rug; and pray tell Elizabeth that the new mourning gown is to be made double only *in the body and sleeves.*

Martha thanks you for your message, and desires you may be told, with her best love, that your wishes are answered, and that she is full of peace and comfort here. I do not think, however, that here she will remain a great while; she does not herself expect that Mrs. Dundas will be able to do with her long. She wishes *to stay with us till Christmas, if possible. Lyddy goes home to-morrow: she seems well, but does not mean to go to service at present.*

The Wallops are returned. Mr. John Harrison has paid his visit of duty and is gone. We have got a new physician, a Dr. Percival, the son of a famous Dr. Percival, of Manchester, who wrote moral tales for Edward to give to me.

When you write again to Catherine [Bigg], thank her on my part for her very kind and welcome mark of friendship; I shall value such a brooch very much. Good-bye, my dearest Cassandra.

Yours very affectionately, J. A.

Have you written to Mrs. E. Leigh? Martha will be glad to find Anne in work at present, and I am as glad to have her so found. We must turn our black pelisses into new, for velvet is to be very much worn this winter.

Miss Austen, Edward Austen's, Esq.
Godmersham Park, Faversham, Kent.

XLV

Castle Square (October 13).
MY DEAREST CASSANDRA,

I have received your letter, and with most melancholy anxiety was it expected, for the sad news [of the death of Elizabeth Austen] reached us last night, but without any particulars. It came in a short letter to Martha from her sister, begun at Steventon and finished in Winchester.

We have felt – we do feel – for you all, as you will not need to be told: for you, for Fanny, for Henry, for Lady Bridges, and for dearest Edward, whose loss and whose sufferings seem to make those of every other person nothing. God be praised that you can say what you do of him: that he has a religious mind to bear him up, and a disposition that will gradually lead him to comfort.

My dear, dear Fanny, I am so thankful that she has you with her! You will be everything to her; you will give her all the consolation that human aid can give. May the Almighty sustain you all, and keep you, my dearest Cassandra, well; but for the present I dare say you are equal to everything.

You will know that the poor boys [Edward and George, the sons of Edward and Elizabeth] are at Steventon. Perhaps it is best for them, as they will have more means of exercise and amusement there than they could have with us, but I own myself disappointed by the arrangement. I should have loved to have them with me at such a time. I shall write to Edward by this post.

We shall, of course, hear from you again very soon, and as often as you can write. We will write as you desire, and I shall add Bookham. Hamstall, I suppose, you write to yourselves, as you do not mention it.

What a comfort that Mrs. Deedes is saved from present misery and alarm! But it will fall heavy upon poor Harriot; and as for Lady B. [Bridges], but that her fortitude does seem truly great, I should fear the effect of such a blow, and so unlooked for. I long to hear more of you all. Of Henry's anguish I think with grief and solicitude; but he will exert himself to be of use and comfort.

With what true sympathy our feelings are shared by Martha you need not be told; she is the friend and sister under every circumstance.

We need not enter into a panegyric on the departed, but it is sweet to think of her great worth, of her solid principles, of her true devotion, her excellence in every relation of life. It is also consolatory to reflect on the shortness of the sufferings which led her from this world to a better.

Farewell for the present, my dearest sister. Tell Edward that we feel for him and pray for him.

Yours affectionately,
J. AUSTEN.

I will write to Catherine.

Perhaps you can give me some directions about mourning.

Miss Austen, Edward Austen's, Esq.
Godmersham Park, Faversham, Kent.

XLVI

Castle Square: Saturday night (October 15).
MY DEAR CASSANDRA,

Your accounts make us as comfortable as we can expect to be at such a time. Edward's loss is terrible, and must be felt as such, and these are too early days indeed to think of moderation in grief, either in him or his afflicted daughter, but soon we may hope that our dear Fanny's sense of duty to that beloved father will rouse her to exertion. For his sake, and as the most acceptable proof of love to the spirit of her departed mother, she will try to be tranquil and resigned. Does she feel you to be a comfort to her, or is she too much overpowered for anything but solitude?

Your account of Lizzy is very interesting. Poor child! One must hope the impression will *be strong, and yet one's heart aches for a dejected mind of eight years old.*

I suppose you see the corpse? How does it appear? We are anxious to be assured that Edward will not attend the funeral, but when it comes to the point I think he must feel it impossible.

Your parcel shall set off on Monday, and I hope the shoes will fit; Martha and I both tried them on. I shall send you such of your mourning as I think most likely to be useful, reserving for myself your stockings and half the velvet, in which selfish arrangement I know I am doing what you wish.

I *am to be in bombazeen and crape, according to what we are told is universal* here, *and which agrees with Martha's previous observation. My mourning, however, will not impoverish me, for by having my velvet pelisse fresh lined and made up, I am sure I shall have no occasion* this winter *for anything new of that sort. I take my cloak for the lining, and shall send yours on the chance of its doing something of the same for you, though I believe your pelisse is in better repair than mine.* One *Miss Baker makes my gown and the other my bonnet, which is to be silk covered with crape.*

I have written to Edward Cooper, and hope he will not send one of his letters of cruel comfort to my poor brother; and yesterday I wrote to Alethea Bigg, in reply to a letter from her. She tells us in confidence that Catherine is to be married on Tuesday se'nnight. Mr. Hill is expected at Manydown in the course of the ensuing week.

We are desired by Mrs. Harrison and Miss Austen to say everything proper for them to yourself and Edward on this sad occasion, especially that nothing but a wish of not giving additional trouble where so much is inevitable prevents their writing themselves to express their concern. They seem truly to feel concern.

I am glad you can say what you do of Mrs. Knight and of Goodnestone in general; it is a great relief to me to know that the shock did not make any of them ill. But what a task was yours to announce it! Now *I hope you are not overpowered with letter-writing, as Henry [Austen] and John [Bridges] can ease you of many of your correspondents.*

Was Mr. Scudmore in the house at the time, was any application attempted, and is the seizure at all accounted for?

Sunday. – *As Edward's letter to his son is not come here, we know that you must have been informed as early as Friday of the boys being at Steventon, which I am glad of.*

Upon your letter to Dr. Goddard's [headmaster of Winchester College] being forwarded to them, Mary wrote to ask whether my mother wished to have her grandsons sent to her. We decided on their remaining where they were, which I hope my brother will approve of. I am sure he will do us the justice of believing that in such a decision we sacrificed inclination to what we thought best.

I shall write by the coach to-morrow to Mrs. J. A., and to Edward, about their mourning, though this day's post will probably bring directions to them on that subject from yourselves. I shall certainly make use of the opportunity of addressing our nephew on the most serious of all concerns, as I naturally did in my letter to him before. The poor boys are, perhaps, more comfortable at Steventon than they could be here, but you will understand my feelings *with respect to it.*

To-morrow will be a dreadful day for you all. Mr. Whitfield's will be a severe duty [1] Glad shall I be to hear that it is over.

That you are forever in our thoughts you will not doubt. I see your mournful party in my mind's eye under every varying circumstance of the day; and in the evening especially figure to myself its sad gloom: the efforts to talk, the frequent summons to melancholy orders and cares, and poor Edward, restless in misery, going from one room to another, and perhaps not seldom upstairs, to see all that remains of his Elizabeth. Dearest Fanny must now look upon herself as his prime source of comfort, his dearest friend; as the being who is gradually to supply to him, to the extent that is possible, what he has lost. This consideration will elevate and cheer her.

Adieu. You cannot write too often, as I said before. We are heartily rejoiced that the poor baby gives you no particular anxiety. Kiss dear Lizzy for us. Tell Fanny that I shall write in a day or two to Miss Sharpe.

My mother is not ill.

Yours most truly,

J. AUSTEN.

Tell Henry that a hamper of apples is gone to him from Kintbury, and that Mr. Fowle [Tom, son of Fulwar, now a midshipman under Charles Austen's command] intended writing on Friday (supposing him in London) to beg that the charts, &c. may be consigned to the care of the Palmers [Charles Austen's in-laws]. Mrs. Fowle has also written to Miss Palmer to beg she will send for them.

Miss Austen, Edward Austen's, Esq.
Godmersham Park, Faversham, Kent.

1. Mr. Whitfield was the Rector of Godmersham at this time, having come there in 1778.

XLVII

Castle Square: Monday (October 24).
MY DEAR CASSANDRA,

Edward and George came to us soon after seven on Saturday, very well, but very cold, having by choice travelled on the outside, and with no great coat but what Mr. Wise, the coachman, good-naturedly spared them of his, as they sat by his side. They were so much chilled when they arrived, that I was afraid they must have taken cold; but it does not seem at all the case; I never saw them looking better.

They behave extremely *well in every respect, showing quite as much feeling as one wishes to see, and on every occasion speaking of their father with the liveliest affection. His letter was read over by each of them yesterday, and with many tears; George sobbed aloud, Edward's tears do not flow so easily; but as far as I can judge they are both very properly impressed by what has happened. Miss Lloyd, who is a more impartial judge than I can be, is exceedingly pleased with them.*

George is almost a new acquaintance to me, and I find him in a different way as engaging as Edward.

We do not want amusement: bilbocatch, at which George is indefatigable; spillikins, paper ships, riddles, conundrums, and cards, with watching the flow and ebb of the river, and now and then a stroll out, keep us well employed; and we mean to avail ourselves of our kind papa's consideration, by not returning to Winchester till quite the evening of Wednesday.

Mrs. J. A. had not time to get them more than one suit of clothes; their others are making here, and though I do not believe Southampton is famous for tailoring, I hope it will prove itself better than Basingstoke. Edward has an old black coat, which will save his *having a second new one; but I find that black pantaloons are considered by them as necessary, and of course one would not have them made uncomfortable by the want of what is usual on such occasions.*

Fanny's letter was received with great pleasure yesterday, and her brother sends his thanks and will answer it soon. We all saw what she wrote, and were very much pleased with it.

To-morrow I hope to hear from you, and to-morrow we must think of poor Catherine [Bigg, who had recently married]. To-day Lady Bridges is the heroine of our thoughts, and glad shall we be when we can fancy the meeting over. There will then be nothing so very bad for Edward to undergo.

The 'St. Albans,' I find, sailed on the very day of my letters reaching Yarmouth, so that we must not expect an answer at present; we scarcely feel, however, to be in suspense, or only enough to keep our plans [to move from Southampton] to ourselves. We have been obliged to explain them to our young visitors, in consequence of Fanny's letter, but we have not yet mentioned them to Steventon. We are all quite familiarised to the idea ourselves; my mother only wants Mrs. Seward [occupant of Chawton Cottage] to go out at Midsummer.

What sort of a kitchen garden is there? Mrs. J. A. expresses her fear of our settling in Kent, and, till this proposal [Edward Austen's offer of Chawton Cottage] was made, we began to look forward to it here; my mother was actually talking of a house at Wye. It will be best, however, as it is.

Anne has just given her mistress warning; she is going to be married; I wish she would stay her year.

On the subject of matrimony, I must notice a wedding in the Salisbury paper, which has amused me very much, Dr. Phillot to Lady Frances St. Lawrence. She *wanted to have a husband I suppose, once in her life, and* he *a Lady Frances.*

I hope your sorrowing party were at church yesterday, and have no longer that *to dread. Martha was kept at home by a cold, but I went with my two nephews, and I saw Edward was much affected by the sermon, which, indeed, I could have supposed purposely addressed to the afflicted, if the text had not naturally come in the course of Dr. Mant's observations on the Litany: 'All that are in danger, necessity, or tribulation,' was the subject of it. The weather did not allow us afterwards to get farther than the quay, where George was very happy as long as we could stay, flying about from one side to the other, and skipping on board a collier immediately.*

In the evening we had the Psalms and Lessons, and a sermon at home, to which they were very attentive; but you will not expect to hear that they did not return to conundrums the moment it was over. *Their aunt has written pleasantly of them, which was more than I hoped.*

While I write now, George is most industriously making and naming paper ships, at which he afterwards shoots with horse-chestnuts brought from Steventon on purpose; and Edward equally intent over the 'Lake of Killarney,' twisting himself about in one of our great chairs.

Tuesday. – *Your close-written letter makes me quite ashamed of my wide lines; you have sent me a great deal of matter, most of it very welcome. As to your lengthened stay, it is no more than I expected, and what must be, but you cannot suppose I like it.*

All that you say of Edward is truly comfortable; I began to fear that when the bustle of the first week was over, his spirits might for a time be more depressed; and perhaps one must still expect something of the kind. If you *escape a bilious attack, I shall wonder almost as much as rejoice. I am glad you mentioned where Catherine goes to-day; it is a good plan, but sensible people may generally be trusted to form such.*

The day began cheerfully, but it is not likely to continue what it should, for them or for us. We had a little water party *yesterday; I and my two nephews went from the Itchen Ferry up to Northam, where we landed, looked into the 74 [a naval warship in the process of being built], and walked home, and it was so much enjoyed that I had intended to take them to Netley to-day; the tide is just right for our going immediately after moonshine [this should read 'noonshine', an archaic form of nuncheon meaning a snack], but I am afraid there will be rain; if we cannot get so far, however, we may perhaps go round from the ferry to the quay.*

I had not proposed doing more than cross the Itchen yesterday, but it proved so pleasant, and so much to the satisfaction of all, that when we reached the middle of the stream we agreed to be rowed up the river; both the boys rowed great part of the way, and their questions and remarks, as well as their enjoyment, were very amusing; George's inquiries were endless, and his eagerness in everything reminds me often of his Uncle Henry.

Our evening was equally agreeable in its way: I introduced speculation *[a card game], and it was so much approved that we hardly knew how to leave off.*

Your idea of an early dinner to-morrow is exactly what we propose, for, after writing the first part of this letter, it came into my head that at this time of year we have not summer evenings. We shall watch the light to-day, that we may not give them a dark drive to-morrow.

They send their best love to papa and everybody, with George's thanks for the letter brought by this post. Martha begs my brother may be assured of her interest in everything relating to him and his family, and of her sincerely partaking our pleasure in the receipt of every good account from Godmersham.

Of Chawton I think I can have nothing more to say, but that everything you say about it in the letter now before me will, I am sure, as soon as I am able to read it to her, make my mother consider the plan with more and more pleasure. We had formed the same views on H. Digweed's farm.

A very kind and feeling letter is arrived to-day from Kintbury. Mrs. Fowle's sympathy and solicitude on such an occasion you will be able to do justice to, and to express it as she wishes to my brother. Concerning you, *she says: 'Cassandra will, I know, excuse my writing to her; it is not to save myself but* her *that I omit so doing. Give my best, my kindest love to her, and tell her I feel for her as I know she would for me on the same occasion, and that I most sincerely hope her health will not suffer.'*

We have just had two hampers of apples from Kintbury, and the floor of our little garret is almost covered. Love to all.

Yours very affectionately,

J.A.

Miss Austen, Edward Austen's, Esq.

Godmersham Park, Faversham, Kent.

XLVIII

Castle Square: Sunday (November 21).

Your letter, my dear Cassandra, obliges me to write immediately, that you may have the earliest notice of Frank's intending, if possible, to go to Godmersham exactly at the time now fixed for your visit to Goodnestone.

He resolved, almost directly on the receipt of your former letter, to try for an extension of his leave of absence, that he might be able to go down to you for two days, but charged me not to give you any notice of it, on account of the uncertainty of success. Now, however, I must give it, and now perhaps he may be giving it himself; for I am just in the hateful predicament of being obliged to write what I know will somehow or other be of no use.

He meant to ask for five days more, and if they were granted, to go down by Thursday night's mail, and spend Friday and Saturday with you; and he considered his chance of succeeding by no means bad. I hope it will take place as he planned, and that your arrangements with Goodnestone may admit of suitable alteration.

Your news of Edward Bridges was quite *news, for I have had no letter from Wrotham. I wish him happy with all my heart, and hope his choice may turn out according to his own expectations, and beyond those of his family; and I dare say it will. Marriage is a great improver, and in a similar situation Harriet may be as amiable as Eleanor. As to money, that will come, you may be sure, because they cannot do without it. When you see him again, pray give him our congratulations and best wishes. This match will certainly set John [Bridges] and Lucy [Foote] going.*

There are six bedchambers at Chawton; Henry wrote to my mother the other day, and luckily mentioned the number, which is just what we wanted to be assured of. He speaks also of garrets for store places, one of which she immediately planned fitting up for Edward's man-servant; and now perhaps it must be for our own; for she is already quite reconciled to our keeping one. The difficulty of doing without one had been thought of before. His name shall be Robert, if you please.

Before I can tell you of it, you will have heard that Miss Sawbridge is married. It took place, I believe, on Thursday. Mrs. Fowle has for some time been in the secret, but the neighbourhood in general were quite unsuspicious. Mr. Maxwell was *tutor to the young Gregorys – consequently, they must be one of the happiest couples in the world, and either of them worthy of envy, for* she *must be excessively in love, and he mounts from nothing to a comfortable home. Martha has heard him very highly spoken of. They continue for the present at Speen Hill.*

I have a Southampton match to return for your Kentish one, Captain G. Heathcote and Miss A. Lyell. I have it from Alethea, and like it, because I had made it before.

Yes, the Stoneleigh business [the inheritance of the Stoneleigh estate] is concluded, but it was not till yesterday that my mother was regularly informed of it, though the news had reached us on Monday evening by way of Steventon. My aunt [Leigh Perrot] says as little as may be on the subject by way of information, and nothing at all by way of satisfaction. She reflects on Mr. T. Leigh's dilatoriness, and looks about with great diligence and success for inconvenience and evil, among which she ingeniously places the danger of her new housemaids catching cold on the outside of the coach, when she goes down to Bath, for a carriage makes her sick.

John Binns has been offered their place, but declines it; as she supposes, because he will not wear a livery. Whatever be the cause, I like the effect.

In spite of all my mother's long and intimate knowledge of the writer, she was not up to the expectation of such a letter as this; the discontentedness of it shocked and surprised her – but I *see nothing in it out of nature, though a sad nature.*

She does not forget to wish for Chambers [a former maid], you may be sure. No particulars are given, not a word of arrears mentioned, though in her letter to James they were in a general way *spoken of. The amount of them is a matter of conjecture, and to my mother a most interesting one; she cannot fix any time for their beginning with any satisfaction to herself but Mrs. Leigh's death, and Henry's two thousand pounds neither agrees with that period nor any other. I did not like to own our previous information of what was intended last July, and have therefore only said that if we could see Henry we might hear many particulars, as I had understood that some confidential conversation had passed between him and Mr. T. L. [Leigh] at Stoneleigh.*

We have been as quiet as usual since Frank and Mary left us; Mr. Criswick called on Martha that very morning on his way home again from Portsmouth, and we have had no visitor since.

We called on the Miss Lyells one day, and heard a good account of Mr. Heathcote's canvass, the success of which, of course, exceeds his expectations. Alethea in her letter hopes for my interest, *which I conclude means Edwards's, and I take this opportunity, therefore, of requesting that he will bring in Mr. Heathcote. Mr. Lane told us yesterday that Mr. H. had behaved very handsomely, and waited on Mr. Thistlethwaite, to say that if* he *(Mr. T.) would stand,* he *(Mr. H.) would not oppose him; but Mr. T. declined it, acknowledging himself still smarting under the payment of late electioneering costs.*

The Mrs. Hulberts, we learn from Kintbury, come to Steventon this week, and bring Mary Jane Fowle with them on her way to Mrs. Nunes; she returns at Christmas with her brother.

Our *brother we may perhaps see in the course of a few days, and we mean to take the opportunity of his help to go one night to the play. Martha ought to see the inside of the theatre once while she lives in Southampton, and I think she will hardly wish to take a second view.*

The furniture of Bellevue is to be sold to-morrow, and we shall take it in our usual walk, if the weather be favourable.

How could you have a wet day on Thursday? With us it was a prince of days, the most delightful we have had for weeks; soft, bright, with a brisk wind from the southwest; everybody was out and talking of spring, and Martha and I did not know how to turn back. On Friday evening we had some very blowing weather – from 6 to 9, I think we never heard it worse, even here. And one night we had so much rain that it forced its way again into the store closet, and though the evil was comparatively slight and the mischief nothing, I had some employment the next day in drying parcels, &c. I have now moved still more out of the way.

Martha sends her best love, and thanks you for admitting her to the knowledge of the pros and cons about Harriet Foote; she has an interest in all such matters. I am also to say that she wants to see you. Mary Jane [Frank Austen's daughter] missed her papa and mama a good deal at first, but now does very well without them. I am glad to hear of little John's being better; and hope your accounts of Mrs. Knight will also improve. Adieu! remember me affectionately to everybody, and believe me,

Ever yours,

J. A.

Miss Austen, Edward Austen's, Esq.

Godmersham Park, Faversham, Kent.

XLIX

Castle Square: Friday (December 9).

Many thanks, my dear Cassandra, to you and Mr. Deedes for your joint and agreeable composition, which took me by surprise this morning. He has certainly great merit as a writer; he does ample justice to his subject, and, without being diffuse, is clear and correct; and though I do not mean to compare his epistolary powers with yours, or to give him the same portion of my gratitude, he certainly has a very pleasing way of winding up a whole, and speeding truth into the world.

'But all this,' as my dear Mrs. Piozzi [in Letters to and from the late Samuel Johnson*] says, 'is flight and fancy, and nonsense, for my master has his great casks to mind and I have my little children.' It is* you, *however, in this instance, that have the little children, and* I *that have the great cask, for we are brewing spruce beer again; but my meaning really is, that I am extremely foolish in writing all this unnecessary stuff when I have so many matters to write about that my paper will hardly hold it all. Little matters they are, to be sure, but highly important.*

In the first place, Miss Curling [cousin of Mrs Frank Austen] is actually at Portsmouth, which I was always in hopes would not happen. I wish her no worse, however, than a long and happy abode there. Here *she would probably be dull, and I am sure she would be troublesome.*

The bracelets are in my possession, and everything I could wish them to be. They came with Martha's pelisse, which likewise gives great satisfaction.

Soon after I had closed my last letter to you we were visited by Mrs. Dickens and her sister-in-law, Mrs. Bertie, the wife of a lately-made Admiral. Mrs. F. A. [1] I believe, was their first object, but they put up with us very kindly, and Mrs. D., finding in Miss Lloyd a friend of Mrs. Dundas, had another motive for the acquaintance. She seems a really agreeable woman – that is, her manners are gentle, and she knows a great many of our connections in West Kent. Mrs. Bertie lives in the Polygon, and was out when we returned her visit, which are her *two virtues.*

A larger circle of acquaintance, and an increase of amusement, is quite in character with our approaching removal. Yes, I mean to go to as many balls as possible, that I may have a good bargain. Everybody is very much concerned at our going away, and everybody is acquainted with Chawton, and speaks of it as a remarkably pretty village, and everybody knows the house we describe, but nobody fixes on the right.

I am very much obliged to Mrs. Knight for such a proof of the interest she takes in me, and she may depend upon it that I will *marry Mr. Papillon, [rector of Chawton] whatever may be his reluctance or my own. I owe her much more than such a trifling sacrifice.*

Our ball was rather more amusing than I expected. Martha liked it very much, and I did not gape till the last quarter of an hour. It was past nine before we were sent for and not twelve when we returned. The room was tolerably full, and there were, perhaps, thirty couple of dancers. The melancholy part was, to see so many dozen young women standing by without partners, and each of them with two ugly naked shoulders.

It was the same room in which we danced fifteen years ago. I thought it all over, and in spite of the shame of being so much older, felt with thankfulness that I was quite as happy now as then. We paid an additional shilling for our tea, which we took as we chose in an adjoining and very comfortable room.

There were only four dances, and it went to my heart that the Miss Lances (one of them, too, named Emma) should have partners only for two. You will not expect to hear that I *was asked to dance, but I was – by the gentleman whom we met* that Sunday *with Captain D'Auvergne. We have always kept up a bowing acquaintance since, and, being pleased with his black eyes, I spoke to him at the ball, which brought on me this civility; but I do not know his name, and he seems so little at home in the English language, that I believe his black eyes may be the best of him. Captain D'Auvergne has got a ship.*

Martha and I made use of the very favourable state of yesterday for walking, to pay our duty at Chiswell. We found Mrs. Lance at home and alone, and sat out three other ladies who soon came in. We went by the ferry, and returned by the bridge, and were scarcely at all fatigued.

Edward must have enjoyed the last two days. You, I presume, had a cool drive to Canterbury. Kitty Foote came on Wednesday, and her evening visit began early enough for the last part, the apple pie, of our dinner, for we never dine now till five.

Yesterday I – or, rather, you – had a letter from Nanny Hilliard [maid at Steventon rectory], the object of which is, that she would be very much obliged to us if we would get Hannah a place. I am sorry that I cannot assist her; if you can, let me know, as I shall not answer the letter immediately. Mr. Sloper is married again, not much to Nanny's, or anybody's satisfaction. The lady was governess to Sir Robert's natural children, and seems to have nothing to recommend her. I do not find, however, that Nanny is likely to lose her place in consequence. She says not a word of what service she wishes for Hannah, or what Hannah can do, but a nursery, I suppose, or something of that kind, must be the thing.

*Having now cleared away my smaller articles of news, I come to a communication of some weight; no less than that my uncle and aunt [2] are going to allow James 100*l. *a year. We hear of it through Steventon. Mary sent us the other day an extract from my aunt's letter on the subject, in which the donation is made with the greatest kindness, and intended as a compensation for his loss in the conscientious refusal of Hampstead living; 100*l. *a year being all that he had at the time called its worth, as I find it was always intended at Steventon to divide the real income with Kintbury.*

Nothing can be more affectionate than my aunt's language in making the present, and like-wise in expressing her hope of their being much more together in future than, to her great regret, they have of late years been. My expectations for my mother do not rise with this event. We will allow a little more time, however, before we fly out.

If not prevented by parish business, James comes to us on Monday. The Mrs. Hulberts and Miss Murden [relation of the Fowles] are their guests at present, and likely to continue such till Christmas. Anna comes home on the 19th. The hundred a year begins next Lady-day.

I am glad you are to have Henry with you again; with him and the boys you cannot but have a cheerful, and at times even a merry, Christmas. Martha is so [MSS. torn].

We want to be settled at Chawton in time for Henry to come to us for some shooting in October, at least, or a little earlier, and Edward may visit us after taking his boys back to Winchester. Suppose we name the 4th of September. Will not that do?

I have but one thing more to tell you. Mrs. Hill [wife of Dr Hill, rector of Holy Rood, Southampton and Church Oakley in Hampshire] called on my mother yesterday while we were gone to Chiswell, and in the course of the visit asked her whether she knew anything of a clergyman's family of the name of Alford, *who had resided in our part of Hampshire. Mrs. Hill had been applied to as likely to give some information of them on account of their probable vicinity to Dr. Hill's living, by a lady, or for a lady, who had known Mrs. and the two Miss Alfords in Bath, whither they had removed, it seems, from Hampshire, and who now wishes to convey to the Miss Alfords some work or trimming which she has been doing for them; but the mother and daughters have left Bath, and the lady cannot learn where they are gone to. While my mother gave us the account, the probability of its being ourselves occurred to us, and it had previously struck herself...what makes it more likely, and even indispensably to be us, is that she mentioned Mr. Hammond as now having the living or curacy which the father had had. I cannot think who our kind lady can be, but I dare say we shall not like the work.*

Distribute the affectionate love of a heart not so tired as the right hand belonging to it.

Yours ever sincerely,

J. A.

Miss Austen, Edward Austen's, Esq.

Godmersham Park, Faversham, Kent.

1. Frank Austen.
2. Mr. and Mrs. Leigh Perrot.

L

Castle Square: Tuesday (December 27).

MY DEAR CASSANDRA,

I can now write at leisure and make the most of my subjects, which is lucky, as they are not numerous this week.

Our house was cleared by half-past eleven on Saturday, and we had the satisfaction of hearing yesterday that the party reached home in safety soon after five.

I was very glad of your letter this morning, for, my mother taking medicine, Eliza [maidservant] keeping her bed with a cold, and Choles not coming, made us rather dull and dependent on the post. You tell me much that gives me pleasure, but I think not much to answer. I wish I could *help you in your needle-work. I have two hands and a new thimble that lead a very easy life.*

Lady Sondes' match surprises, but does not offend me; had her first marriage been of affection, or had there been a grown-up single daughter, I should not have forgiven her; but I consider everybody as having a right to marry once *in their lives for love, if they can, and provided she will now leave off having bad headaches and being pathetic, I can allow her, I can* wish *her, to be happy.*

Do not imagine that your picture of your tête-à-tête *with Sir B. [Sir Brook Bridges] makes any change in our expectations here; he could not be really reading, though he held the newspaper in his hand; he was making up his mind to the deed, and the manner of it. I think you will have a letter from him soon.*

I heard from Portsmouth yesterday, and as I am to send them more clothes, they cannot be expecting a very early return to us. Mary's face is pretty well, but she must have suffered a great deal with it; an abscess was formed and opened.

Our evening party on Thursday produced nothing more remarkable than Miss Murden's coming too, though she had declined it absolutely in the morning, and sitting very ungracious and very silent with us from seven o'clock till half after eleven, for so late was it, owing to the chairmen, before we got rid of them.

The last hour, spent in yawning and shivering in a wide circle round the fire, was dull enough, but the tray had admirable success. The widgeon [duck] and the preserved ginger were as delicious as one could wish. But as to our black butter [a preserve], do not decoy anybody to Southampton by such a lure, for it is all gone. The first pot was opened when Frank and Mary were here, and proved not at all what it ought to be; it was neither solid nor entirely sweet, and on seeing it Eliza remembered that Miss Austen had said she did not think it had been boiled enough. It was made, you know, when we were absent. Such being the event of the first pot, I would not save the second, and we therefore ate it in unpretending privacy; and though not what it ought to be, part of it was very good.

James means to keep three horses on this increase of income; at present he has but one. Mary wishes the other two to be fit to carry women, and in the purchase of one Edward will probably be called upon to fulfil his promise to his godson. We have now pretty well ascertained James's income to be eleven hundred pounds, curate paid, which makes us very happy – the ascertainment as well as the income.

Mary does not talk of the garden; it may well be a disagreeable subject to her, but her husband is persuaded that nothing is wanting to make the first new one good but trenching, which is to be done by his own servants and John Bond, by degrees, not at the expense which trenching the other amounted to.

I was happy to hear, chiefly for Anna's sake, that a ball at Manydown was once more in agitation; it is called a child's ball, and given by Mrs. Heathcote to Wm. Such was its beginning at least, but it will probably swell into something more. Edward was invited during his stay at Manydown, and it is to take place between this and Twelfth-day. Mrs. Hulbert has taken Anna a pair of white shoes on the occasion.

I forgot in my last to tell you that we hear, by way of Kintbury and the Palmers, that they were all well at Bermuda in the beginning of Nov.

Wednesday. – *Yesterday must have been a day of sad remembrance at Gm. [Edward Austen's wedding anniversary] I am glad it is over. We spent Friday evening with our friends at the boarding-house, and our curiosity was gratified by the sight of their fellow-inmates, Mrs. Drew and Miss Hook, Mr. Wynne and Mr. Fitzhugh; the latter is brother to Mrs. Lance, and very much the gentleman. He has lived in that house more than twenty years, and, poor man! is so totally deaf that they say he could not hear a cannon, were it fired close to him; having no cannon at hand to make the experiment, I took it for granted, and talked to him a little with my fingers, which was funny enough. I recommended him to read 'Corinna'.*

Miss Hook is a well-behaved, genteelish woman; Mrs. Drew well behaved, without being at all genteel. Mr. Wynne seems a chatty and rather familiar young man. Miss Murden was quite a different creature this last evening from what she had been before, owing to her having with Martha's help found a situation in the morning, which bids very fair for comfort. When she leaves Steventon, she comes to board and lodge with Mrs. Hookey, the chemist – for there is no Mr. Hookey. I cannot say that I am in any hurry for the conclusion of her present visit, but I was truly glad to see her comfortable in mind and spirits; at her age, perhaps, one may be as friendless oneself, and in similar circumstances quite as captious.

My mother has been lately adding to her possessions in plate – a whole tablespoon and a whole dessert-spoon, and six whole teaspoons – which makes our sideboard border on the magnificent. They were mostly the produce of old or useless silver. I have turned the 11s. in the list into 12s., and the card looks all the better; a silver tea-ladle is also added, which will at least answer the purpose of making us sometimes think of John Warren [possibly a former pupil of Jane's father].

I have laid Lady Sondes' case before Martha, who does not make the least objection to it, and is particularly pleased with the name of Montresor. I do not agree with her there, but I like his rank very much, and always affix the ideas of strong sense and highly elegant manners to a general.

I must write to Charles next week. You may guess in what extravagant terms of praise Earle Harwood speaks of him. He is looked up to by everybody in all America.

I shall not tell you anything more of Wm. Digweed's china, as your silence on the subject makes you unworthy of it. Mrs. H. Digweed looks forward with great satisfaction to our being her neighbours. I would have her enjoy the idea to the utmost, as I suspect there will not be much in the reality. With equal pleasure we anticipate an intimacy with her husband's bailiff and his wife, who live close by us, and are said to be remarkably good sort of people.

Yes, yes, we will have a pianoforte, as good a one as can be got for thirty guineas, and I will practise country dances, that we may have some amusement for our nephews and nieces, when we have the pleasure of their company.

Martha sends her love to Henry, and tells him that he will soon have a bill of Miss Chaplin's, about 14l., to pay on her account; but the bill shall not be sent in till his return to town. I hope he comes to you in good health, and in spirits as good as a first return to Godmersham can allow. With his nephews he will force himself to be cheerful, till he really is so. Send me some intelligence of Eliza [Mrs Henry Austen]; it is a long while since I have heard of her.

We have had snow on the ground here almost a week; it is now going, but Southampton must boast no longer. We all send our love to Edward junior and his brothers, and I hope Speculation is generally liked.

Fare you well.

Yours affectionately,

J. AUSTEN.

My mother has not been out of doors this week, but she keeps pretty well. We have received through Bookham an indifferent account of your godmother [Mrs Elizabeth Leigh].

Miss Austen, Edward Austen's, Esq.

Godmersham Park, Faversham, Kent.

LI

Castle Square: Tuesday (January 10).

I am not surprised, my dear Cassandra, that you did not find my last letter very full of matter, and I wish this may not have the same deficiency; but we are doing nothing ourselves to write about, and I am therefore quite dependent upon the communications of our friends, or my own wits.

This post brought me two interesting letters, yours and one from Bookham, in answer to an inquiry of mine about your good godmother, of whom we had lately received a very alarming account from Paragon. Miss Arnold [cousin of Mrs Austen] was the informant then, and she spoke of Mrs. E. L. having been very dangerously ill, and attended by a physician from Oxford.

Your letter to Adlestrop may perhaps bring you information from the spot, but in case it should not, I must tell you that she is better; though Dr. Bourne cannot yet call her out of danger; such was the case last Wednesday, and Mrs. Cooke's having had no later account is a favourable sign. I am to hear again from the latter next week, but not this, if everything goes on well.

Her disorder is an inflammation on the lungs, arising from a severe chill, taken in church last Sunday three weeks; her mind all pious composure, as may be supposed. George Cooke was there when her illness began; his brother has now taken his place. Her age and feebleness considered, one's fears cannot but preponderate, though her amendment has already surpassed the expectation of the physician at the beginning. I am sorry to add that Becky [probably a maid of Elizabeth Leigh] is laid up with a complaint of the same kind.

I am very glad to have the time of your return at all fixed; we all rejoice in it, and it will not be later than I had expected. I dare not hope that Mary and Miss Curling may be detained at Portsmouth so long or half so long; but it would be worth twopence to have it so.

The 'St. Albans' [under the command of Frank Austen] perhaps may soon be off to help bring home what may remain by this time of our poor army, [this refers to the retreat to Corunna of Sir John Moore's army and the battle there] whose state seems dreadfully critical. The 'Regency' seems to have been heard of only here; my most political correspondents make no mention of it. Unlucky that I should have wasted so much reflection on the subject.

I can now answer your question to my mother more at large, and likewise more at small – with equal perspicuity and minuteness; for the very day of our leaving Southampton is fixed; and if the knowledge is of no use to Edward, I am sure it will give him pleasure. Easter Monday, April 3, is the day; we are to sleep that night at Alton, and be with our friends at Bookham the next, if they are then at home; there we remain till the following Monday, and on Tuesday, April 11, hope to be at Godmersham. If the Cookes are absent, we shall finish our journey on the 5th. These plans depend of course upon the weather, but I hope there will be no settled cold to delay us materially.

To make you amends for being at Bookham, it is in contemplation to spend a few days at Baiton Lodge in our way out of Kent. The hint of such a visit is most affectionately welcomed by Mrs. Birch [friend of Mrs Austen], in one of her odd, pleasant letters lately, in which she speaks of us with the usual distinguished kindness, declaring that she shall not be at all satisfied unless a very handsome present is made us immediately from one quarter.

Fanny's not coming with you is no more than we expected, and as we have not the hope of a bed for her, and shall see her so soon afterwards at Godmersham, we cannot wish it otherwise.

William will be quite recovered, I trust, by the time you receive this. What a comfort his cross-stitch must have been! Pray tell him that I should like to see his work very much. I hope our answers this morning have given satisfaction; we had great pleasure in Uncle Deedes' packet; and pray let Marianne know, in private, that I think she is quite right to work a rug for Uncle John's coffee urn, and that I am sure it must give great pleasure to herself now, and to him when he receives it.

The preference of Brag over Speculation does not greatly surprise me, I believe, because I feel the same myself; but it mortifies me deeply, because Speculation was under my patronage; and, after all, what is there so delightful in a pair royal of Braggers? It is but three nines or three knaves, or a mixture of them. When one comes to reason upon it, it cannot stand its ground against Speculation – of which I hope Edward is now convinced. Give my love to him if he is.

The letter from Paragon before mentioned was much like those which had preceded it, as to the felicity of its writer. They found their house so dirty and so damp that they were obliged to be a week at an inn. John Binns had behaved most unhandsomely and engaged himself elsewhere. They have *a man, however, on the same footing, which my aunt does not like, and she finds both him and the new maidservant very, very inferior to Robert and Martha. Whether they mean to have any other domestics does not appear, nor whether they are to have a carriage while they are in Bath.*

The Holders are as usual, though I believe it is not very usual for them to be happy, which they now are at a great rate, in Hooper's marriage. The Irvines are not mentioned. The American lady [reference to Memoirs of an American Lady *by Caroline Schuyler] improved as we went on; but still the same faults in part recurred.*

We are now in Margiana, and like it very well indeed. We are just going to set off for Northumberland to be shut up in Widdrington Tower, where there must be two or three sets of victims already immured under a very fine villain.

Wednesday. – *Your report of Eliza's [Mrs Henry Austen] health gives me great pleasure, and the progress of the bank is a constant source of satisfaction. With such increasing profits; tell Henry that I hope he will not work poor High-diddle so hard as he used to do.*

Has your newspaper given a sad story of a Mrs. Middleton, wife of a farmer in Yorkshire, her sister, and servant, being almost frozen to death in the late weather, her little child quite so? I hope the sister is not our friend Miss Woodd, and I rather think her brother-in-law had moved into Lincolnshire, but their name and station accord too well. Mrs. M. and the maid are said to be tolerably recovered, but the sister is likely to lose the use of her limbs.

Charles' rug will be finished to-day, and sent to-morrow to Frank, to be consigned by him to Mr. Turner's care; and I am going to send 'Marmion' out with it – very generous in me, I think.

As we have no letter from Adlestrop, we may suppose the good woman [Elizabeth Leigh] was alive on Monday, but I cannot help expecting bad news from thence or Bookham in a few days. Do you continue quite well?

Have you nothing to say of your little name-sake [Edward's daughter Cassandra Jane]? We join in love and many happy returns.

Yours affectionately,

J. AUSTEN.

The Manydown ball was a smaller thing than I expected, but it seems to have made Anna very happy. At her *age it would not have done for* me.

Miss Austen, Edward Austen's, Esq.

Godmersham Park, Faversham, Kent.

LII

Castle Square: Tuesday (January 17).

MY DEAR CASSANDRA,

I am happy to say that we had no second letter from Bookham last week. Yours has brought its usual measure of satisfaction and amusement, and I beg your acceptance of all the thanks due on the occasion. Your offer of cravats is very kind, and happens to be particularly adapted to my wants, but it was an odd thing to occur to you.

Yes, we have got another fall of snow, and are very dreadful; everything seems to turn to snow this winter.

I hope you have had no more illness among you, and that William will be soon as well as ever. His working a footstool for Chawton is a most agreeable surprise to me, and I am sure his grandmamma will value it very much as a proof of his affection and industry, but we shall never have the heart to put our feet upon it. I believe I must work a muslin cover in satin stitch to keep it from the dirt. I long to know what his colours are. I guess greens and purples.

Edward and Henry have started a difficulty respecting our journey, which, I must own with some confusion, had never been thought of by us; but if the former expected by it to prevent our travelling into Kent entirely he will be disappointed, for we have already determined to go the Croydon road on leaving Bookham and sleep at Dartford. Will not that do? There certainly does seem no convenient resting place on the other road.

Anna went to Clanville last Friday, and I have hopes of her new aunt's [Mrs Brownlow Mathew], being really worth her knowing. Perhaps you may never have heard that James and Mary paid a morning visit there in form some weeks ago, and Mary, though by no means disposed to like her, was very much pleased with her indeed. Her *praise, to be sure, proves nothing more than Mrs. M.'s being civil and attentive to them, but her being so is in favour of her having good sense. Mary writes of Anna as improved in person, but gives her no other commendation. I am afraid her absence now may deprive her of one pleasure, for that silly Mr. Hammond is actually to give his ball on Friday.*

We had some reason to expect a visit from Earle Harwood and James this week, but they do not come. Miss Murden arrived last night at Mrs. Hookey's, [owner of a lodging house] as a message and a basket announced to us. You will therefore return to an enlarged and, of course, improved society here, especially as the Miss Williamses are come back.

We were agreeably surprised the other day by a visit from your beauty and mine, each in a new cloth mantle and bonnet; and I daresay you will value yourself much on the modest propriety of Miss W.'s taste, hers being purple and Miss Grace's scarlet.

I can easily suppose that your six weeks here will be fully occupied, were it only in lengthening the waists of your gowns. I have pretty well arranged my spring and summer plans of that kind, and mean to wear out my spotted muslin before I go. You will exclaim at this, but mine really has signs of feebleness, which, with a little care, may come to something.

Martha and Dr. Mant are as bad as ever; he runs after her in the street to apologise for having spoken to a gentleman while she *was near him the day before. Poor Mrs. Mant can stand it no longer; she is retired to one of her married daughter's.*

When William returns to Winchester Mary Jane [Fowle] is to go to Mrs. Nune's [mistress of a boarding school] for a month, and then to Steventon for a fortnight, and it seems likely that she and her Aunt Martha may travel into Berkshire together.

We shall not have a month of Martha after your return, and that month will be a very interrupted and broken one, but we shall enjoy ourselves the more when we can *get a quiet half-hour together.*

To set against your new novel, of which nobody ever heard before, and perhaps never may again, we have got 'Ida of Athens,' by Miss Owenson, which must be very clever, because it was written, as the authoress says, in three months. We have only read the preface yet, but her 'Irish Girl' does not make me expect much. If the warmth of her language could affect the body it might be worth reading in this weather.

Adieu! I must leave off to stir the fire and call on Miss Murden.

Evening. – *I have done them both, the first very often. We found our friend as comfortable as she can ever allow herself to be in cold weather. There is a very neat parlour behind the shop for her to sit in, not very light indeed, being* à la *Southampton, the middle of three deep, but very lively from the frequent sound of the pestle and mortar. [The landlady also kept a chemist's shop].*

We afterwards called on the Miss Williamses, who lodge at Durantoy's.

Miss Mary only was at home, and she is in very indifferent health. Dr. Hackett came in while we were there, and said that he never remembered such a severe winter as this in Southampton before. It is bad, but we do not suffer as we did last year, because the wind has been more N.E. than N.W.

For a day or two last week my mother was very poorly with a return of one *of her old complaints, but it did not last long, and seems to have left nothing bad behind it. She began to talk of a serious illness, her two last having been preceded by the same symptoms, but, thank heaven! she is now quite as well as one can expect her to be in weather which deprives her of exercise.*

Miss M. conveys to us a third volume of sermons [from their cousin, Revd. Edward Cooper], from Hamstall, just published, and which we are to like better than the two others; they are professedly practical, *and for the use of country congregations. I have just received some verses in an unknown hand, and am desired to forward them to my nephew Edward at Godmersham.*

Alas! poor Brag, thou boastful game!
What now avails thine empty name?
Where now thy more distinguished fame?
My day is o'er, and thine the same,
For thou, like me, art thrown aside
At Godmersham, this Christmas tide;
And now across the table wide
Each game save brag or spec. is tried.
Such is the mild ejaculation
Of tender-hearted speculation.

Wednesday. – *I expected to have a letter from somebody to-day, but I have not. Twice every day I think of a letter from Portsmouth.*

Miss Murden has been sitting with us this morning. As yet she seems very well pleased with her situation. The worst part of her being in Southampton will be the necessity of one walking with her now and then, for she talks so loud that one is quite ashamed; but our dining hours are luckily very different, which we shall take all reasonable advantage of.

The Queen's birthday moves the Assembly to this night instead of last, and, as it is always fully attended, Martha and I expect an amusing show. We were in hopes of being independent of other companions by having the attendance of Mr. Austen and Captain Harwood; but, as they fail us, we are obliged to look out for other help, and have fixed on the Wallops as least likely to be troublesome. I have called on them this morning and found them very willing, and I am sorry that you must wait a whole week for the particulars of the evening. I propose being asked to dance by our acquaintance Mr. Smith, now Captain Smith, *who has lately re-appeared in Southampton, but I shall decline it. He saw Charles last August.*

What an alarming bride Mrs—must have been; such a parade is one of the most immodest pieces of modesty that one can imagine. To attract *notice could have been her only wish. It augurs ill for her family; it announces not* great *sense, and therefore ensures boundless influence.*

I hope Fanny's visit is now taking place. You have said scarcely anything of her lately, but I trust you are as good friends as ever.

Martha sends her love, and hopes to have the pleasure of seeing you when you return to Southampton. You are to understand this message as being merely for the sake of a message to oblige me.

Yours affectionately,

J. AUSTEN.

Henry never sent his love to me in your last, but I send him mine.

Miss Austen, Edward Austen's, Esq.

Godmersham Park, Faversham, Kent.

LIII

Castle Square: Tuesday (January 24).

MY DEAR CASSANDRA,

I will give you the indulgence of a letter on Thursday this week, instead of Friday, but I do not require you to write again before Sunday, provided I may believe you and your finger going on quite well. Take care of your precious self; do not work too hard. Remember that Aunt Cassandras are quite as scarce as Miss Beverleys. [1]

I had the happiness yesterday of a letter from Charles, but I shall say as little about it as possible, because I know that *excruciating Henry will have had a letter likewise, to make all my intelligence valueless. It was written at Bermuda on the 7th and 10th of December. All well, and Fanny still only in expectation of being otherwise. [Fanny's first baby was due]. He had taken a small prize in his late cruise – a French schooner, laden with sugar; but bad weather parted them, and she had not yet been heard of. His cruise ended December 1st. My September letter was the latest he had received.*

This day three weeks you are to be in London, and I wish you better weather; not but that you may have worse, for we have now nothing but ceaseless snow or rain and insufferable dirt to complain of; no tempestuous winds nor severity of cold. Since I wrote last we have had something of each, but it is not genteel to rip up old grievances.

You used me scandalously by not mentioning Edward Cooper's sermons. I tell you everything, and it is unknown the mysteries you conceal from me; and, to add to the rest, you persevere in giving a final e to invalid, thereby putting it out of one's power to suppose Mrs. E. Leigh, even for a moment, a veteran soldier. She, good woman, is, I hope, destined for some further placid enjoyment of her own excellence in this world, for her recovery advances exceedingly well.

I had this pleasant news in a letter from Bookham last Thursday, but, as the letter was from Mary instead of her mother, you will guess her account was not equally good from home. Mrs. Cooke had been confined to her bed some days by illness, but was then better, and Mary wrote in confidence of her continuing to mend. I have desired to hear again soon.

You rejoice me by what you say of Fanny. I hope she will not turn good-for-nothing this ever so long. We thought of and talked of her yesterday with sincere affection, and wished her a long enjoyment of all the happiness to which she seems born. While she gives happiness to those about her she is pretty sure of her own share.

I am gratified by her having pleasure in what I write, but I wish the knowledge of my being exposed to her discerning criticism may not hurt my style, by inducing too great a solicitude. I begin already to weigh my words and sentences more than I did, and am looking about for a sentiment, an illustration, or a metaphor in every corner of the room. Could my ideas flow as fast as the rain in the store-closet it would be charming.

We have been in two or three dreadful states within the last week, from the melting of the snow, &c., and the contest between us and the closet has now ended in our defeat. I have been obliged to move almost everything out of it, and leave it to splash itself as it likes.

You have by no means raised my curiosity after Caleb [a reference to Coelebs in Search of a Wife *by Hannah More]. My disinclination for it before was affected, but now it is real. I do not like the evangelicals. Of course I shall be delighted when I read it, like other people, but till I do I dislike it.*

I am sorry my verses did not bring any return from Edward. I was in hopes they might, but I suppose he does not rate them high enough. It might be partiality, but they seemed to me purely classical – just like Homer and Virgil, Ovid and Propria que Maribus.

I had a nice brotherly letter from Frank the other day, which, after an interval of nearly three weeks, was very welcome. No orders were come on Friday, and none were come yesterday, or we should have heard to-day. I had supposed Miss C. [Curling] would share her cousin's room here, but a message in this letter proves the contrary. I will make the garret as comfortable as I can, but the possibilities of that apartment are not great.

My mother has been talking to Eliza [maid] about our future home, and she, *making no difficulty at all of the sweetheart, is perfectly disposed to continue with us, but till she has written home for* mother's *approbation cannot quite decide.* Mother *does not like to have her so far off. At Chawton she will be nine or ten miles nearer, which I hope will have its due influence.*

As for Sally, she means to play John Binns [a servant who turned down employment with the Leigh Perrots] with us, in her anxiety to belong to our household again. Hitherto she appears a very good servant.

You depend upon finding all your plants dead, I hope. They look very ill, I understand.

Your silence on the subject of our ball makes me suppose your curiosity too great for words. We were very well entertained, and could have stayed longer but for the arrival of my list shoes to convey me home, and I did not like to keep them waiting in the cold. The room was tolerably full, and the ball opened by Miss Glyn. The Miss Lances had partners, Captain Dauvergne's friend appeared in regimentals, Caroline Maitland had an officer to flirt with, and Mr. John Harrison was deputed by Captain Smith, being himself absent, to ask me to dance. Everything went well, you see, especially after we had tucked Mrs. Lance's neckerchief in behind and fastened it with a pin.

We had a very full and agreeable account of Mr. Hammond's ball from Anna last night; the same fluent pen has sent similar information, I know, into Kent. She seems to have been as happy as one could wish her, and the complacency of her mamma in doing the honours of the evening [Mary Austen took on the role of hostess as Mr Hammond was unmarried] must have made her pleasure almost as great. The grandeur of the meeting was beyond my hopes. I should like to have seen Anna's looks and performance, but that sad cropped head must have injured the former.

Martha pleases herself with believing that if I had kept her counsel you would never have heard of Dr. M.'s [Mant] late behaviour, as if the very slight manner in which I mentioned it could have been all on which you found your judgment. I do not endeavour to undeceive her, because I wish her happy, at all events, and know how highly she prizes happiness of any kind. She is, moreover, so full of kindness for us both, and sends you in particular so many good wishes about your finger, that I am willing to overlook a venial fault, and as Dr. M. is a clergyman, their attachment, however immoral, has a decorous air. Adieu, sweet You. This is grievous news from Spain. It is well that Dr. Moore was spared the knowledge of such a son's [John Moore] death.

Yours affectionately,

J. AUSTEN.

Anna's hand gets better and better; it begins to be too good for any consequence.

We send best love to dear little Lizzy and Marianne in particular.

The Portsmouth paper gave a melancholy history of a poor mad woman, escaped from confinement, who said her husband and daughter, of the name of Payne, lived at Ashford, in Kent. Do you own them?

Miss Austen, Edward Austen's, Esq.
Godmersham Park, Faversham, Kent.

1. 'Cecilia' Beverley, the heroine of Miss Burney's novel.

LIV

Castle Square: Monday (January 30).
MY DEAR CASSANDRA,

I was not much surprised yesterday by the agreeable surprise of your letter, and extremely glad to receive the assurance of your finger being well again.

Here is such a wet day as never was seen. I wish the poor little girls had better weather for their journey [Lizzie and Marianne Austen's journey to boarding school] ; they must amuse themselves with watching the raindrops down the windows. Sackree [their nursemaid], I suppose, feels quite broken-hearted. I cannot have done with the weather without observing how delightfully mild it is; I am sure Fanny must enjoy it with us. Yesterday was a very blowing day; we got to church, however, which we had not been able to do for two Sundays before.

I am not at all ashamed about the name of the novel, having been guilty of no insult towards your handwriting; the diphthong I always saw, but knowing how fond you were of adding a vowel wherever you could, I attributed it to that alone, and the knowledge of the truth does the book no service; the only merit it could have was in the name of Caleb, which has an honest, unpretending sound, but in Coelebs there is pedantry and affectation. Is it written only to classical scholars?

I shall now try to say only what is necessary, I am weary of meandering; so expect a vast deal of small matter, concisely told, in the next two pages.

Mrs. Cooke has been very dangerously ill, but is now, I hope, safe. I had a letter last week from George, Mary being too busy to write, and at that time the disorder was called of the typhus kind, and their alarm considerable, but yesterday brought me a much better account from Mary, the origin of the complaint being now ascertained to be bilious, and the strong medicines requisite promising to be effectual. Mrs. E. L. [Elizabeth Leigh] is so much recovered as to get into the dressing-room every day.

A letter from Hamstall gives us the history of Sir. Tho. Williams's return. The Admiral, whoever he might be, took a fancy to the 'Neptune,' and having only a worn-out 74 [warship] to offer in lieu of it, Sir Tho. declined such a command, and is come home passenger. Lucky man! to have so fair an opportunity of escape. I hope his wife allows herself to be happy on the occasion, and does not give all her thoughts to being nervous.

A great event happens this week at Hamstall in young Edward's removal to school. He is going to Rugby, and is very happy in the idea of it; I wish his happiness may last, but it will be a great change to become a raw school-boy from being a pompous sermon-writer and a domineering brother. It will do him good, I dare say.

Caroline [Cooper] has had a great escape from being burnt to death lately. As her husband gives the account, we must believe it true. Miss Murden is gone – called away by the critical state of Mrs. Pottinger, who has had another severe stroke, and is without sense or speech. Miss Murden wishes to return to Southampton if circumstances suit, but it must be very doubtful.

We have been obliged to turn away Cholles, he grew so very drunken and negligent, and we have a man in his place called Thomas.

Martha desires me to communicate something concerning herself which she knows will give you pleasure, as affording her very particular satisfaction – it is, that she is to be in town this spring with Mrs. Dundas. I need not dilate on the subject. You understand enough of the whys and wherefores to enter into her feelings, and to be conscious that of all possible arrangements it is the one most acceptable to her. She goes to Barton on leaving us, and the family remove to town in April.

What you tell me of Miss Sharpe is quite new, and surprises me a little; I feel, however, as you do. She is born, poor thing! to struggle with evil, and her continuing with Miss B. is, I hope, a proof that matters are not always so very bad between them as her letters sometimes represent.

Jenny's [maidservant] marriage I had heard of, and supposed you would do so too from Steventon, as I knew you were corresponding with Mary at the time. I hope she will not sully the respectable name she now bears.

Your plan for Miss Curling is uncommonly considerate and friendly, and such as she must surely jump at. Edward's going round by Steventon, as I understand he promises to do, can be no reasonable objection; Mrs. J. Austen's hospitality is just of the kind to enjoy such a visitor.

We were very glad to know Aunt Fanny [this should read Aunt Fatty, a relative of the Bridges family] was in the country when we read of the fire [at St James' Palace]. Pray give my best compliments to the Mrs. Finches, if they are at Gm. I am sorry to find that Sir J. Moore has a mother living, but though a very heroic son he might not be a very necessary one to her happiness. Deacon Morrell [possibly a former pupil of Jane's father, who never married] may be more to Mrs. Morrell.

I wish Sir John had united something of the Christian with the hero in his death. Thank heaven! we have had no one to care for particularly among the troops – no one, in fact, nearer to us than Sir John himself. Col. Maitland is safe and well; his mother and sisters were of course anxious about him, but there is no entering much into the solicitudes of that family.

My mother is well, and gets out when she can with the same enjoyment, and apparently the same strength, as hitherto. She hopes you will not omit begging Mrs. Seward to get the garden cropped for us, supposing she leaves the house too early to make the garden any object to herself. We are very desirous of receiving your account of the house, for your observations will have a motive which can leave nothing to conjecture and suffer nothing from want of memory. For one's own dear self, one ascertains and remembers everything.

Lady Sondes is an impudent woman to come back into her old neighbourhood again; I suppose she pretends never to have married before, and wonders how her father and mother came to have her christened Lady Sondes.

The store closet, I hope, will never do so again, for much of the evil is proved to have proceeded from the gutter being choked up, and we have had it cleared. We had reason to rejoice in the child's [Frank's daughter Mary Jane] absence at the time of the thaw, for the nursery was not habitable. We hear of similar disasters from almost everybody.

No news from Portsmouth [from Frank and Mary]. We are very patient. Mrs. Charles Fowle desires to be kindly remembered to you. She is warmly interested in my brother and his family.
Yours very affectionately,

J. AUSTEN.
Miss Austen, Edward Austen's, Esq.
Godmersham Park, Faversham, Kent.

1811

The first three of these are from Sloane Street, where Jane was at this time visiting her brother Henry and his wife Eliza, to whom frequent reference is made. They are lively letters, and she seems to have enjoyed herself thoroughly, and to have had plenty of amusement of one sort and another. 'The D'Entraigues and Comte Julien' were doubtless friends of 'Eliza,' whose first husband had been a Frenchman; the Cookes and Tilsons I have already mentioned, and nobody else in the fifty-fifth letter seems to require special attention. The fifty-sixth contains some interesting allusions to 'S. and S.' ('Sense and Sensibility'), from which I gather that some of her home critics had thought that she put the incomes of her heroes and heroines either too low or too high. It may be remarked that, as she told us in another letter that Elizabeth was her favourite character in 'Pride and Prejudice' so, with regard to the novel now under discussion, she has most reliance on a favourable reception for its heroine Elinor. Then comes an amusing description of her sister-in-law's musical party, where the drawing-room becoming too hot (an example constantly followed with fidelity by modern drawing-rooms under similar circumstances), Jane stood in the passage surrounded by gentlemen (just as other Janes have frequently done), and no doubt contributed greatly to the pleasure of the evening. I cannot pretend to interpret the message sent to 'Fanny' respecting the 'first glee,' which is written in a 'gibberish' probably only understood by the sender and receiver of the same. We must therefore be satisfied with knowing that 'the music was extremely good,' that the professionals, who were paid for it, sang very well, and the amateurs, who were not paid for it, would not sing at all. The Play was a favourite amusement of Jane's; she seems to have gone to one or more every time she was in London. One is sorry to gather from this letter that Eliza caught cold from getting out of her carriage into the night air when the horses 'actually gibbed,' and one wonders what '*that* quarter' was from which Aunt Jane supposed that 'the alloy of Fanny's happiness' would come; but, having no clue to the mystery, one can do no more than wonder. From the fifty-seventh letter we gather that Mr. W. K. (Wyndham Knatchbull) thought Jane 'a pleasant-looking young woman,' and we have another 'gibberish' message to Fanny, and in a reference to a lady who is 'most happily married' to a gentleman who 'is very religious and has got black whiskers,' one detects a touch of that peculiar humour which so often amuses us in the novels.

The fifty-eighth letter imparts the interesting intelligence of a cousin's marriage, which I find duly authenticated by 'Burke's Landed Gentry,' which chronicles the fact that General Orde's first wife was Margaret Maria Elizabeth, eldest daughter of Wm. Beckford, Esq., of Fonthill, Wilts, and that they were married in 1811, her sister 'Susan Euphemia' having married the tenth Duke of Hamilton (then Marquis of Douglas) in 1810; but how these ladies were cousins to Jane Austen I cannot make out, and am not disposed to stop and inquire. 'Poor John Bridges!' probably refers to his state of health. He married Charlotte Hawley in 1810, and died in 1812, and having lived much at Godmersham, it was natural that 'our own dear brother' (Mr. Knight) should be affected by his illness and early death. Mrs. Harding, who came from Dummer (a little village five miles from Basingstoke) to Chawton with the Terrys, was Dionysia, daughter of Sir Bouchier Wrey, wife of Richard Harding, Esq., of Upcott, and sister to Mrs. Nicholas Toke, of Godinton, whom she had therefore a perfect right to resemble if she pleased, but it seems that she did *not*. We learn from this letter that Jane had 'uncomfortable feelings' in thunderstorms, that several clerical changes in the neighbourhood were impending, and that Mr. Prowting [1] had opened a gravel-pit, but there is nothing in these circumstances which seems to call for remark. The fifty-ninth letter opens with a project for a visit from Miss Sharpe, and the rest of it is filled with various details which may be left to speak for themselves. The sixtieth refers to difficulties relating to the proposed Sharpe visit, but tells of a 'very pleasant' one made to Chawton by Henry Austen and Mr. Tilson, and informs us, writing on Thursday, June 6, that they 'began peas on Sunday' exactly two days before the orthodox time, which from King George the Third's accession until his death was always held to be 'the good King's Birthday' – namely, June 4 – so that the loyal inmates of Chawton Cottage should have restrained their appetites until the Tuesday. There is not much more in this letter, and then we have unfortunately another gap of nearly two letterless years, there being none in my collection from June 6, 1811, until May 24, 1813.

1. The Prowtings were a family who had lived on their own property in Chawton for some 200 years, and a descendant still lives there.

LV

Sloane St.: Thursday (April 18).

MY DEAR CASSANDRA,

I have so many little matters to tell you of, that I cannot wait any longer before I begin to put them down. I spent Tuesday in Bentinck Street. The Cookes called here and took me back, and it was quite a Cooke day, for the Miss Rolles [friends of the Cookes] paid a visit while I was there, and Sam Arnold [cousin of Mrs Austen] dropped in to tea.

The badness of the weather disconcerted an excellent plan of mine – that of calling on Miss Beckford again; but from the middle of the day it rained incessantly. Mary and I, after disposing of her father and mother, went to the Liverpool Museum and the British Gallery, and I had some amusement at each, though my preference for men and women always inclines me to attend more to the company than the sight.

Mrs. Cooke regrets very much that she did not see you when you called; it was owing to a blunder among the servants, for she did not know of our visit till we were gone. She seems tolerably well, but the nervous part of her complaint, I fear, increases, and makes her more and more unwilling to part with Mary.

I have proposed to the latter that she should go to Chawton with me, on the supposition of my travelling the Guildford road, and she, I do believe, would be glad to do it, but perhaps it may be impossible; unless a brother can be at home at that time, it certainly must. George comes to them to-day.

I did not see Theo. till late on Tuesday; he was gone to Ilford, but he came back in time to show his usual nothing-meaning, harmless, heartless civility. Henry, who had been confined the whole day to the bank, took me in his way home, and, after putting life and wit into the party for a quarter of an hour, put himself and his sister into a hackney coach.

I bless my stars that I have done with Tuesday. But, alas! Wednesday was likewise a day of great doings, for Manon [Eliza Austen's maid] and I took our walk to Grafton House, and I have a good deal to say on that subject.

I am sorry to tell you that I am getting very extravagant, and spending all my money, and, what is worse for you, I have been spending yours too; for in a linendraper's shop to which I went for checked muslin, and for which I was obliged to give seven shillings a yard, I was tempted by a pretty-coloured muslin, and bought ten yards of it on the chance of your liking it; but, at the same time, if it should not suit you, you must not think yourself at all obliged to take it; it is only 3s. 6d. *per yard, and I should not in the least mind keeping the whole. In texture it is just what we prefer, but its resemblance to green crewels, I must own, is not great, for the pattern is a small red spot. And now I believe I have done all my commissions except Wedgwood.*

I liked my walk very much; it was shorter than I had expected, and the weather was delightful. We set off immediately after breakfast, and must have reached Grafton House by half-past 11; but when we entered the shop the whole counter was thronged, and we waited full *half an hour before we could be attended to. When we were served, however, I was very well satisfied with my purchases – my bugle trimming at* 2s. 4d. *and three pair silk stockings for a little less than* 12s. *a pair.*

In my way back who should I meet but Mr. Moore, just come from Beckenham. I believe he would have passed me if I had not made him stop, but we were delighted to meet. I soon found, however, that he had nothing new to tell me, and then I let him go.

Miss Burton has made me a very pretty little bonnet, and now nothing can satisfy me but I must have a straw hat, of the riding-hat shape, like Mrs. Tilson's; and a young woman in this neighbourhood is actually making me one. I am really very shocking, but it will not be dear at a Guinea. Our pelisses are 17s. *each; she charges only* 8s. *for the making, but the buttons seem expensive – are expensive, I might have said, for the fact is plain enough.*

We drank tea again yesterday with the Tilsons [Mr Tilson was Henry Austen's banking partner], and met the Smiths [friends of Henry]. I find all these little parties very pleasant. I like Mrs. S.; Miss Beaty is good-humour itself, and does not seem much besides. We spend to-morrow evening with them, and are to meet the Coln. and Mrs. Cantelo *Smith [probably a joke, Charles Cantelo was a singer] you have been used to hear of, and, if she is in good humour, are likely to have excellent singing.*

To-night I might have been at the play; Henry had kindly planned our going together to the Lyceum, but I have a cold which I should not like to make worse before Saturday, so I stay within all this day.

Eliza is walking out by herself. She has plenty of business on her hands just now, for the day of the party is settled, and drawing near. Above 80 people are invited for next Tuesday evening, and there is to be some very good music – five professionals, three of them glee singers, besides amateurs. Fanny will listen to this. One of the hirelings is a Capital on the harp, from which I expect great pleasure. The foundation of the party was a dinner to Henry Egerton and Henry Walter, but the latter leaves town the day before.

I am sorry, as I wished her *prejudice to be done away, but should have been more sorry if there had been no invitation.*

I am a wretch, to be so occupied with all these things as to seem to have no thoughts to give to people and circumstances which really supply a far more lasting interest – the society in which you are; but I do think of you all, I assure you, and want to know all about everybody, and especially about your visit to the W. Friars; 'mais le moyen' not to be occupied by one's own concerns?

Saturday. – *Frank is superseded in the 'Caledonia.' Henry brought us this news yesterday from Mr. Daysh, and he heard at the same time that Charles may be in England in the course of a month. Sir Edward Pollen succeeds Lord Gambier in his command, and some captain of his succeeds Frank; and I believe the order is already gone out. Henry means to inquire farther to-day. He wrote to Mary on the occasion. This is something to think of. Henry is convinced that he will have the offer of something else, but does not think it will be at all incumbent on him to accept it; and then follows, what will he do? and where will he live?*

I hope to hear from you to-day. How are you as to health, strength, looks, &c.? I had a very comfortable account from Chawton yesterday.

If the weather permits, Eliza and I walk into London this morning. She *is in want of chimney lights for Tuesday, and I of an ounce of darning cotton. She has resolved not to venture to the play to-night. The D'Entraigues and Comte Julien cannot come to the party, which was at first a grief, but she has since supplied herself so well with performers that it is of no consequence; their not coming has produced our going to them to-morrow evening, which I like the idea of. It will be amusing to see the ways of a French circle.*

I wrote to Mrs. Hill a few days ago, and have received a most kind and satisfactory answer. Any time the first week in May exactly suits her, and therefore I consider my going as tolerably fixed. I shall leave Sloane Street on the 1st or 2nd, and be ready for James on the 9th, and, if his plan alters, I can take care of myself. I have explained my views here, and everything is smooth and pleasant; and Eliza talks kindly of conveying me to Streatham.

We met the Tilsons yesterday evening, but the singing Smiths sent an excuse, which put our Mrs. Smith out of humour.

We are come back, after a good dose of walking and coaching, and I have the pleasure of your letter. I wish I had James's verses, but they were left at Chawton. When I return thither, if Mrs. K. will give me leave, I will send them to her.

Our first object to-day was Henrietta St., to consult with Henry in consequence of a very unlucky change of the play for this very night – 'Hamlet' instead of 'King John' – and we are to go on Monday to 'Macbeth' instead; but it is a disappointment to us both.

Love to all.
Yours affectionately,
JANE.
Miss Austen, Edward Austen's, Esq.
Godmersham Park, Faversham, Kent.

LVI

Sloane St.: Thursday (April 25).
MY DEAREST CASSANDRA,

I can return the compliment by thanking you for the unexpected pleasure of your *letter yesterday, and as I like unexpected pleasure, it made me very happy; and, indeed, you need not apologise for your letter in any respect, for it is all very fine, but not* too *fine, I hope, to be written again, or something like it.*

I think Edward will not suffer much longer from heat; by the look of things this morning I suspect the weather is rising into the balsamic north-east. It has been hot here, as you may suppose, since it was so hot with you, but I have not suffered from it at all, nor felt it in such a degree as to make me imagine it would be anything in the country. Everybody has talked of the heat, but I set it all down to London.

I give you joy of our new nephew [Frank Austen's son Henry], and hope if he ever comes to be hanged it will not be till we are too old to care about it. It is a great comfort to have it so safely and speedily over. The Miss Curlings must be hard worked in writing so many letters, but the novelty of it may recommend it to them*; mine was from Miss Eliza, and she says that my brother may arrive to-day.*

No, indeed, I am never too busy to think of S. and S. I can no more forget it than a mother can forget her sucking child; and I am much obliged to you for your inquiries. I have had two sheets to correct, but the last only brings us to Willoughby's first appearance. Mrs. K. regrets in the most flattering manner that she must wait till *May, but I have scarcely a hope of its being out in June. Henry does not neglect it; he* has *hurried the printer, and says he will see him again to-day. It will not stand still during his absence, it will be sent to Eliza.*

The Incomes *remain as they were, but I will get them altered if I can. I am very much gratified by Mrs. K's interest in it; and whatever may be the event of it as to my credit with her, sincerely wish her curiosity could be satisfied sooner than is now probable. I think she will like my Elinor, but cannot build on anything else.*

Our party went off extremely well. There were many solicitudes, alarms, and vexations, beforehand, of course, but at last everything was quite right. The rooms were dressed up with flowers, &c., and looked very pretty. A glass for the mantlepiece was lent by the man who is making their own. Mr.

Egerton and Mr. Walter came at half-past five, and the festivities began with a pair of very fine soals.

Yes, Mr. Walter – for he postponed his leaving London on purpose – which did not give much pleasure at the time, any more than the circumstance from which it rose – his calling on Sunday and being asked by Henry to take the family dinner on that day, which he did; but it is all smoothed over now, and she likes him very well.

At half-past seven arrived the musicians in two hackney coaches, and by eight the lordly company began to appear. Among the earliest were George and Mary Cooke, and I spent the greater part of the evening very pleasantly with them. The drawing-room being soon hotter than we liked, we placed ourselves in the connecting passage, which was comparatively cool, and gave us all the advantage of the music at a pleasant distance, as well as that of the first view of every new comer.

I was quite surrounded by acquaintances, especially gentlemen; and what with Mr. Hampson, Mr. Seymour, Mr. W. Knatchbull, Mr. Guillemarde, Mr. Cure, a Captain Simpson, brother to the *Captain Simpson, besides Mr. Walter and Mr. Egerton, in addition to the Cookes, and Miss Beckford, and Miss Middleton, I had quite as much upon my hands as I could do.*

Poor Miss B. has been suffering again from her old complaint, and looks thinner than ever. She certainly goes to Cheltenham the beginning of June. We were all delight and cordiality of course. Miss M. seems very happy, but has not beauty enough to figure in London.

Including everybody we were sixty-six – which was considerably more than Eliza had expected, and quite enough to fill the back drawing-room and leave a few to be scattered about in the other and in the passage.

The music was extremely good. It opened (tell Fanny) with 'Poike de Parp pirs praise pof Prapela'; and of the other glees I remember, 'In peace love tunes,' 'Rosabelle,' 'The Red Cross Knight,' and 'Poor Insect.' Between the songs were lessons on the harp, or harp and pianoforte together; and the harp-player was Wiepart, whose name seems famous, though new to me. There was one female singer, a short Miss Davis, all in blue, bringing up for the public line, whose voice was said to be very fine indeed; and all the performers gave great satisfaction by doing what they were paid for, and giving themselves no airs. No amateur could be persuaded to do anything.

The house was not clear till after twelve. If you wish to hear more of it, you must put your questions, but I seem rather to have exhausted than spared the subject.

This said Captain Simpson told us, on the authority of some other Captain just arrived from Halifax, that Charles was bringing the 'Cleopatra' home, and that she was probably by this time in the Channel; but, as Captain S. was certainly in liquor, we must not quite depend on it. It must give one a sort of expectation, however, and will prevent my writing to him any more. I would rather he should not reach England till I am at home, and the Steventon party gone.

My mother and Martha both write with great satisfaction of Anna's behaviour. She is quite an Anna with variations, but she cannot have reached her last, for that is always the most flourishing and showy; she is at about her third or fourth, which are generally simple and pretty.

Your lilacs are in leaf, ours *are in bloom. The horse-chestnuts are quite out, and the elms almost. I had a pleasant walk in Kensington Gardens on Sunday with Henry, Mr. Smith, and Mr. Tilson; everything was fresh and beautiful.*

We did *go to the play after all on Saturday. We went to the Lyceum, and saw the 'Hypocrite,' an old play taken from Molière's 'Tartuffe,' and were well entertained. Dowton and Mathews were the good actors; Mrs. Edwin was the heroine, and her performance is just what it used to be. I have no chance of seeing Mrs. Siddons; she* did *act on Monday, but, as Henry was told by the boxkeeper that he did not think she would, the plans, and all thought of it, were given up. I should particularly have liked seeing her in 'Constance,' and could swear at her with little effort for disappointing me.*

Henry has been to the Water-Colour Exhibition, which opened on Monday, and is to meet us there again some morning. If Eliza cannot go (and she has a cold at present) Miss Beaty will be invited to be my companion. Henry leaves town on Sunday afternoon, but he means to write soon himself to Edward, and will tell his own plans.

The tea is this moment setting out.

Do not have your coloured muslin unless you really want it, because I am afraid I could not send it to the coach without giving trouble here.

Eliza caught her cold on Sunday in our way to the D'Entraigues. The horses actually gibbed on this side of Hyde Park Gate: a load of fresh gravel made it a formidable hill to them, and they refused the collar; I believe there was a sore shoulder to irritate. Eliza was frightened and we got out, and were detained in the evening air several minutes. The cold is in her chest, but she takes care of herself, and I hope it may not last long.

This engagement prevented Mr. Walter's staying late – he had his coffee and went away. Eliza enjoyed her evening very much, and means to cultivate the acquaintance; and I see nothing to dislike in them but their taking quantities of snuff. Monsieur, the old Count, is a very fine-looking man, with quiet manners, good enough for an Englishman, and, I believe, is a man of great information and taste. He has some fine paintings, which delighted Henry as much as the son's music gratified Eliza; and among them a miniature of Philip V. of Spain, Louis XIV.'s grandson, which exactly suited my *capacity. Count Julien's performance is very wonderful.*

We met only Mrs. Latouche and Miss East, and we are just now engaged to spend next Sunday evening at Mrs. L.'s, and to meet the D'Entraigues, but M. le Comte must do without Henry. If he would but speak English, I *would take to him.*

Have you ever mentioned the leaving off tea to Mrs. K.? Eliza has just spoken of it again. The benefit she *has found from it in sleeping has been very great.*

I shall write soon to Catherine [Hill] to fix my day, which will be Thursday. We have no engagement but for Sunday. Eliza's cold makes quiet advisable. Her party is mentioned in this morning's paper. I am sorry to hear of poor Fanny's state. From that *quarter, I suppose, is to be the alloy of her happiness. I* will *have no more to say.*

Yours affectionately,

J.A.

Give my love particularly to my goddaughter.

Miss Austen, Edward Austen's, Esq.

Godmersham Park, Faversham.

LVII

Sloane St.: Tuesday.

MY DEAR CASSANDRA,

I had sent off my letter yesterday before yours came, which I was sorry for; but as Eliza has been so good as to get me a frank, your questions shall be answered without much further expense to you.

The best direction to Henry at Oxford will be The Blue Boar, Cornmarket.

I do not *mean to provide another trimming for my pelisse, for I am determined to spend no more money; so I shall wear it as it is, longer than I ought, and then – I do not know.*

My head-dress was a bugle-band like the border to my gown, and a flower of Mrs. Tilson's. I depended upon hearing something of the evening from Mr. W. K. [Wyndham Knatchbull], and am very well satisfied with his notice of me – 'A pleasing-looking young woman' – that must do; one cannot pretend to anything better now; thankful to have it continued a few years longer!

It gives me sincere pleasure to hear of Mrs. Knight's having had a tolerable night at last, but upon this occasion I wish she had another name, for the two nights *jingle very much.*

We have tried to get 'Self-control,' but in vain. I should *like to know what her estimate is, but am always half afraid of finding a clever novel* too clever, *and of finding my own story and my own people all forestalled.*

Eliza has just received a few lines from Henry to assure her of the good conduct of his mare. He slept at Uxbridge on Sunday, and wrote from Wheatfield.

We were not claimed by Hans Place yesterday, but are to dine there to-day.

Mr. Tilson called in the evening, but otherwise we were quite alone all day; and, after having been out a great deal, the change was very pleasant.

I like your opinion of Miss Atten [this should read Allen] much better than I expected, and have now hopes of her staying a whole twelvemonth. By this time I suppose she is hard at it, governing away. Poor creature! I pity her, though they are *my nieces.*

Oh! yes, I remember Miss Emma Plumbtree's local *consequence perfectly.*
I am in a dilemma, for want of an Emma,
Escaped from the lips of Henry Gipps.
[Emma and Gipps became engaged later that year]

But, really, I was never much more put to it than in continuing an answer to Fanny's former message. What is there to be said on the subject? Pery pell, or pare pey? or po; or at the most, Pi, pope, pey, pike, pit.

I congratulate Edward on the Weald of Kent Canal Bill being put off till another Session [Edward was a magistrate], as I have just had the pleasure of reading. There is always something to be hoped from delay.
Between Session and Session
The first Prepossession
May rouse up the Nation,
And the villainous Bill
May be forced to lie still.
Against wicked men's will

There is poetry for Edward and his daughter. I am afraid I shall not have any for you.

I forgot to tell you in my last that our cousin, Miss Payne, called in on Saturday, and was persuaded to stay dinner. She told us a great deal about her friend Lady Cath. Brecknell, who is most happily married, and Mr. Brecknell is very religious, and has got black whiskers.

I am glad to think that Edward has a tolerable day for his drive to Goodnestone, and very *glad to hear of his kind promise of bringing you to town. I hope everything will arrange itself favourably. The 16th is now to be Mrs. Dundas's day.*

I mean, if I can, to wait for your return before I have my new gown made up, from a notion of their making up to more advantage together; and, as I find the muslin is not so wide as it used to be, *some contrivance may be necessary. I expect the skirt to require one-half breadth cut in gores, besides two whole breadths.*

Eliza has not yet quite resolved on inviting Anna, but I think she will.
Yours very affectionately,
JANE.

LVIII

Chawton: Wednesday (May 29).

It was a mistake of mine, my dear Cassandra, to talk of a tenth child at Hamstall. I had forgot there were but eight already.

Your inquiry after my uncle and aunt were most happily timed, for the very same post brought an account of them. They are again at Gloucester House enjoying fresh air, which they seem to have felt the want of in Bath, and are tolerably well, but not more than tolerable. My aunt does not enter into particulars, but she does not write in spirits, and we imagine that she has never entirely got the better of her disorder in the winter. Mrs. Welby takes her out airing in her barouche, which gives her a headache – a comfortable proof, I suppose, of the uselessness of the new carriage when they have got it.

You certainly must have heard before I can tell you that Col. Orde has married our cousin, Margt. Beckford, the Marchess. of Douglas's sister. The papers say that her father disinherits her, but I think too well of an Orde to suppose that she has not a handsome independence of her own.

The chicken are all alive and fit for the table, but we save them for something grand. Some of the flower seeds are coming up very well, but your mignonette makes a wretched appearance. Miss Benn has been equally unlucky as to hers. She has seed from four different people, and none of it comes up. Our young piony at the foot of the fir-tree has just blown and looks very handsome, and the whole of the shrubbery border will soon be very gay with pinks and sweet-williams, in addition to the columbines already in bloom. The syringas, too, are coming out. We are likely to have a great crop of Orleans plumbs, but not many greengages – on the standard scarcely any, three or four dozen, perhaps, against the wall. I believe I told you differently when I first came home, but I can now judge better than I could then.

I have had a medley and satisfactory letter this morning from the husband and wife at Cowes [Frank and Mary Austen]; and, in consequence of what is related of their plans, we have been talking over the possibility of inviting them here in their way from Steventon, which is what one should wish to do, and is, I daresay, what they expect; but, supposing Martha to be at home, it does not seem a very easy thing to accommodate so large a party. My mother offers to give up her room to Frank and Mary, but there will then be only the best for two maids and three children.

They go to Steventon about the 22nd, and I guess – for it is quite a guess – will stay there from a fortnight to three weeks.

I must not venture to press Miss Sharpe's coming at present; we may hardly be at liberty before August.

Poor John Bridges! we are very sorry for his situation [his poor health] and for the distress of the family. [Marianne Bridges had recently died] Lady B. is in one way severely tried. And our own dear brother suffers a great deal, I dare say, on the occasion.

I have not much to say of ourselves. Anna is nursing a cold caught in the arbour at Faringdon, that she may be able to keep her engagement to Maria M. [Middleton] this evening, when I suppose she will make it worse.

She did not return from Faringdon till Sunday, when H. B. [Harriet Benn] walked home with her, and drank tea here. She was with the Prowtings almost all Monday. She went to learn to make feather trimmings of Miss Anna, and they kept her to dinner, which was rather lucky, as we were called upon to meet Mrs. and Miss Terry the same evening at the Digweeds; and, though Anna was of course invited too, I think it always safest to keep her away from the family lest she should be doing too little or too much. [Anna's engagement to Michael Terry, now broken off, had been difficult for both families].

Mrs. Terry, Mary, and Robert, with my aunt Harding and her daughter, came from Dummer for a day and a night – all very agreeable and very much delighted with the new house and with Chawton in general.

We sat upstairs and had thunder and lightning as usual. I never knew such a spring for thunderstorms as it has been. Thank God! we have had no bad ones here. I thought myself in luck to have my uncomfortable feelings shared by the mistress of the house, as that procured blinds and candles. It had been excessively hot the whole day. Mrs. Harding is a good-looking woman, but not much like Mrs. Toke [her sister], inasmuch as she is very brown and has scarcely any teeth; she seems to have some of Mrs. Toke's civility. Miss H. is an elegant, pleasing, pretty-looking girl, about nineteen, I suppose, or nineteen and a half, or nineteen and a quarter, with flowers in her head and music at her finger ends. She plays very well indeed. I have seldom heard anybody with more pleasure. They were at Godington four or five years ago. My cousin, Flora Long, was there last year.

My *name is Diana [Harding]. How does Fanny like it? What a change in the weather! We have a fire again now.*

Harriet Benn sleeps at the Great House to-night and spends to-morrow with us; and the plan is that we should all walk with her to drink tea at Faringdon, for her mother is now recovered, but the state of the weather is not very promising at present.

Miss Benn has been returned to her cottage since the beginning of last week, and has now just got another girl; she comes from Alton. For many days Miss B. had nobody with her but her niece Elizabeth, who was delighted to be her visitor and her maid. They both dined here on Saturday while Anna was at Faringdon; and last night an accidental meeting and a sudden impulse produced Miss Benn and Maria Middleton [the Middletons were tenants of Chawton House] at our tea-table.

If you have not heard it is very fit you should, that Mr. Harrison has had the living of Fareham given him by the Bishop, and is going to reside there; and now it is said that Mr. Peach (beautiful wiseacre) wants to have the curacy of Overton, and, if he does *leave Wootton, James Digweed wishes to go there. Fare you well,*

Yours affectionately,
JANE AUSTEN.

The chimneys at the Great House are done. Mr. Prowting has opened a gravel pit, very conveniently for my mother, just at the mouth of the approach to his house; but it looks a little as if he meant to catch all his company. Tolerable gravel.

Miss Austen, Godmersham Park,
Faversham, Kent.

LIX

Chawton: Friday (May 31).
MY DEAR CASSANDRA,

I have a magnificent project. The Cookes have put off their visit to us; they are not well enough to leave home at present, and we have no chance of seeing them till I do not know when – probably never, in this house.

This circumstance has made me think the present time would be favourable for Miss Sharpe's coming to us; it seems a more disengaged period with us than we are likely to have later in the summer. If Frank and Mary do come, it can hardly be before the middle of July, which will be allowing a reasonable length of visit for Miss Sharpe, supposing she begins it when you return; and if you and Martha do not dislike the plan, and she can avail herself of it, the opportunity of her being conveyed hither will be excellent.

I shall write to Martha by this post, and if neither you nor she make any objection to my proposal, I shall make the invitation directly, and as there is no time to lose, you must write by return of post if you have any reason for not wishing it done. It was her intention, I believe, to go first to Mrs. Lloyd, but such a means of getting here may influence her otherwise.

We have had a thunder-storm again this morning. Your letter came to comfort me for it.

I have taken your hint, slight as it was, and have written to Mrs. Knight, and most sincerely do I hope it will not be in vain. I cannot endure the idea of her giving away her own wheel, and have told her no more than the truth, in saying that I could never use it with comfort. I had a great mind to add that, if she persisted in giving it, I would spin nothing with it but a rope to hang myself, but I was afraid of making it appear a less serious matter of feeling than it really is.

I am glad you are so well yourself, and wish everybody else were equally so. I will not say that your mulberry-trees are dead, but I am afraid they are not alive. We shall have pease soon. I mean to have them with a couple of ducks from Wood Barn, and Maria Middleton, towards the end of next week.

From Monday to Wednesday Anna is to be engaged at Faringdon, in order that she may come in for the gaieties of Tuesday (the 4th), on Selbourne Common [to celebrate the King's birthday], where there are to be volunteers and felicities of all kinds. Harriet B.[Benn] is invited to spend the day with the John Whites, and her father and mother have very kindly undertaken to get Anna invited also.

Harriot and Eliza dined here yesterday, and we walked back with them to tea. Not my mother – she has a cold which affects her in the usual way, and was not equal to the walk. She is better this morning, and I hope will soon physick away the worst part of it. It has not confined her; she has got out every day that the weather has allowed her.

Poor Anna is also suffering from her *cold, which is worse to-day, but as she has no sore throat I hope it may spend itself by Tuesday. She had a delightful evening with the Miss Middletons – syllabub, tea, coffee, singing, dancing, a hot supper, eleven o'clock, everything that can be imagined agreeable. She desires her best love to Fanny, and will answer her letter before she leaves Chawton, and engages to send her a particular account of the Selbourne day.*

We cannot agree as to which is the eldest of the two Miss Plumbtrees; send us word. Have you remembered to collect pieces for the patchwork? We are now at a stand-still. I got up here to look for the old map, and can now tell you that it shall be sent to-morrow; it was among the great parcel in the dining-room. As to my debt of 3s. 6d. *to Edward, I must trouble you to pay it when you settle with him for your boots.*

We began our China tea three days ago, and I find it very good. My companions know nothing of the matter. As to Fanny and her twelve pounds in a twelvemonth, she may talk till she is as black in the face as her own tea, but I cannot believe her – more likely twelve pounds to a quarter.

I have a message to you from Mrs. Cooke. The substance of it is that she hopes you will take Bookham in your way home and stay there as long as you can, and that when you must leave them they will convey you to Guildford. You may be sure that it is very kindly worded, and that there is no want of attendant compliments to my brother and his family.

I am very sorry for Mary [Cooke], but I have some comfort in there being two curates now lodging in Bookham, besides their own Mr. Waineford from Dorking, so that I think she must fall in love with one or the other.

How horrible it is to have so many people killed! And what a blessing that one cares for none of them! [A response to the Battle of Albuera]

I return to my letter-writing from calling on Miss Harriot Webb, who is short and not quite straight, and cannot pronounce an R any better than her sisters; but she has dark hair, a complexion to suit, and, I think, has the pleasantest countenance and manner of the three – the most natural. She appears very well pleased with her new home, and they are all reading with delight Mrs. H. More's recent publication.

You cannot imagine – it is not in human nature to imagine – what a nice walk we have round the orchard. The row of beech look very well indeed, and so does the young quickset hedge in the garden. I hear to-day that an apricot has been detected on one of the trees. My mother is perfectly convinced now *that she shall not be overpowered by her cleftwood, and I believe would rather have more than less.*

Strange to tell, Mr. Prowting was not *at Miss Lee's wedding, but his daughters had some cake, and Anna had her share of it.*

I continue to like our old cook quite as well as ever, and, but that I am afraid to write in her praise, I could say that she seems just the servant for us. Her cookery is at least tolerable; her pastry is the only deficiency.

God bless you, and I hope June will find you well, and bring us together.

Yours ever,

JANE.

I hope you understand that I do not expect you to write on Sunday if you like my plan. I shall consider silence as consent.

Miss Austen, Edward Austen's, Esq.

Godmersham Park, Faversham.

LX

Chawton: Thursday (June 6).

By this time, my dearest Cassandra, you know Martha's plans. I was rather disappointed, I confess, to find that she could not leave town till after ye 24th, as I had hoped to see you here the week before. The delay, however, is not great, and everything seems generally arranging itself for your return very comfortably.

I found Henry perfectly pre-disposed to bring you to London if agreeable to yourself; he has not fixed his day for going *into Kent, but he must be back again before ye 20th. You may, therefore, think with something like certainty of the close of your Godmersham visit, and will have, I suppose, about a week for Sloane Street. He travels in his gig, and should the weather be tolerable I think you must have a delightful journey.*

I have given up all idea of Miss Sharpe's travelling with you and Martha, for though you are both all compliance with my scheme, yet as you *knock off a week from the end of her visit,* Martha *rather more from the beginning, the thing is out of the question.*

I have written to her to say that after the middle of July we shall be happy to receive her, and I have added a welcome if she could make her way hither directly, *but I do not expect that she will. I have also sent our invitation to Cowes.*

We are very sorry for the disappointment you have all had in Lady B.'s [Bridges] illness; but a division of the proposed party is with you by this time, and I hope may have brought you a better account of the rest.

Give my love and thanks to Harriot, who has written me charming things of your looks, and diverted me very much by poor Mrs. C. Milles's continued perplexity.

I had a few lines from Henry on Tuesday to prepare us for himself and his friend, and by the time that I had made the sumptuous provision of a neck of mutton on the occasion, they drove into the court; but lest you should not immediately recollect in how many hours a neck of mutton may be certainly procured, I add that they came a little after twelve, both tall and well, and in their different degrees agreeable.

It was a visit of only twenty-four hours, but very pleasant while it lasted. Mr. Tilson took a sketch of the Great House before dinner, and after dinner we all three walked to Chawton Park, [1] meaning to go into it, but it was too dirty, and we were obliged to keep on the outside. Mr. Tilson admired the trees very much, but grieved that they should not be turned into money.

My mother's cold is better, and I believe she only wants dry weather to be very well. It was a great distress to her that Anna should be absent during her uncle's visit, a distress which I could not share. She does not return from Faringdon till this evening, and I doubt not has had plenty of the miscellaneous, unsettled sort of happiness which seems to suit her best. We hear from Miss Benn, who was on the Common with the Prowtings, that she was very much admired by the gentlemen in general.

I like your new bonnets exceedingly; yours is a shape which always looks well, and I think Fanny's particularly becoming to her.

On Monday I had the pleasure of receiving, unpacking, and approving our Wedgwood ware. It all came very safely, and upon the whole is a good match, though I think they might have allowed us rather larger leaves, especially in such a year of fine foliage as this. One is apt to suppose that the woods about Birmingham must be blighted. There was no bill with the goods, but that shall not screen them from being paid. I mean to ask Martha to settle the account. It will be quite in her way, for she is just now sending my mother a breakfast set from the same place.

I hope it will come by the waggon to-morrow; it is certainly what we want, and I long to know what it is like, and as I am sure Martha has great pleasure in making the present, I will not have any regret. We have considerable dealings with the waggons at present: a hamper of port and brandy from Southampton is now in the kitchen.

Your answer about the Miss Plumbtrees proves you as fine a Daniel as ever Portia was; for I maintained Emma to be the eldest.

We began pease on Sunday, but our gatherings are very small, not at all like the gathering in the 'Lady of the Lake' [by Walter Scott]. Yesterday I had the agreeable surprise of finding several scarlet strawberries quite ripe; had you been at home, this would have been a pleasure lost. There are more gooseberries and fewer currants than I thought at first. We must buy currants for our wine.

The Digweeds are gone down to see the Stephen Terrys at Southampton, and catch the King's birthday [celebrations] at Portsmouth. Miss Papillon called on us yesterday, looking handsomer than ever. Maria Middleton and Miss Benn dine here to-morrow.

We are not to enclose any more letters to Abingdon Street [possibly the home of Mrs Dundas], as perhaps Martha has told you,

I had just left off writing and put on my things for walking to Alton, when Anna and her friend Harriot called in their way thither, so we went together. Their business was to provide mourning against the King's death [he was very ill but recovered], and my mother has had a bombasin bought for her. I am not sorry to be back again, for the young ladies had a great deal to do, and without much method in doing it.

Anna does not come home till to-morrow morning. She has written I find to Fanny, but there does not seem to be a great deal to relate of Tuesday. I had hoped there might be dancing.

Mrs. Budd died on Sunday evening. I saw her two days before her death, and thought it must happen soon. She suffered much from weakness and restlessness almost to the last. Poor little Harriot seems truly grieved. You have never mentioned Harry [Edward Austen's son Henry]; how is he?

With love to you all,
Yours affectionately,
J. A.
Miss Austen, Edward Austen's, Esq.
Godmersham Park, Faversham.

[1] A large beech wood extending for a long distance upon a hill about a mile from Chawton: the trees are magnificent.

1813

The eleventh division of the letters includes those written during that which I believe to have been Jane Austen's last visit to Godmersham. With regard to most of these later letters, I have derived much assistance from my mother's old pocket-books, in which she regularly kept her diary from the time she was eleven years old until she was unable to write. During the earlier years there are only casual entries relating to Aunt Jane. As, for instance: 'June 18, 1807. – Papa brought me a packet from Southampton containing a letter from Aunt Cassandra, and a note and long strip of beautiful work as a present from Aunt Jane.' Then in September of the same year the visit of 'grandmamma and Aunts Cassandra and Jane Austen' to Chawton House is duly chronicled, and in 1808 'Aunt Jane's' stay at Godmersham for a week, accompanied by her brother James and his wife. There is also an interesting entry of the date of September 28, 1811: 'Letter from At. Cass. to beg we would not mention that Aunt Jane wrote 'Sense and Sensibility.' But, although many passages both in our letters and the pocket-books evince the affection which from a very early period existed between the aunt and the niece, the time when that affection seems to have ripened into more intimate friendship was in 1812, during a visit which my mother, in company with her father and cousin, 'Fanny Cage' (afterwards Lady Bridges), paid to Chawton Great House in that year. They arrived there on April 14, and stayed until May 7, when they returned to Kent, paying Oxford a visit on their way. My mother had at this time just completed her nineteenth year, and she and her aunt seem to have been much together during this visit. Unfortunately I have no letters bearing the date of this particular year; probably because the sisters were more than usually together at Chawton Cottage; but during the next three years I am able, by a comparison of the letters and the pocket-books, to trace Jane's movements with greater ease, and in somewhat more of detail.

And here there comes to me a great source of grief – namely, that although I have five letters addressed by 'Aunt Jane' to my mother during the years 1814-16, the pocket-books show the receipt in those same years of upwards of *thirty* letters from the same aunt, which would be invaluable for our present purpose, but which I fear must have been destroyed, with the exception of those which I have already found, and now publish.

Miss Knight, the 'Marianne' of our letters, known to and loved by all *my* generation of the family as 'Aunt May,' who succeeded my mother in the management of the Godmersham household, and reigned there, to her own happiness and that of everybody about her, until my grandfather's death, thus writes of the intimacy between her sister and aunt:–

'Your dear mother, being so many years older than the rest of us, was a friend and companion of the two aunts, Cassandra and Jane, particularly of the latter, and they had all sorts of secrets together, whilst we were only children.' That this was the case is abundantly shown by the five letters above mentioned, from which we shall see that the aunt and niece opened their hearts to each other, and wrote in the most unreserved manner. The pocket-book of 1812 chronicled many 'walks with Aunt Jane' during that month at Chawton, but none of the 'secrets' are told, nor is there anything which illustrates the life of our heroine, if I may apply such a term to one who would have been amused beyond measure at the idea of its application to herself.

The ten letters of 1813 were written – the first from Sloane Street, in May, the next two from Henrietta Street (to which locality her brother Henry had moved from Sloane Street), in September, and the seven following from Kent, and are all addressed to her sister at Chawton. In that year Godmersham required painting, and the family moved off to Chawton in April, and stayed there for six months, during which time the friendship between the aunt and niece grew and increased, as the entries in the pocket-books prove to demonstration.

June 6th. – 'Aunt Jane and I had a very interesting conversation.'
June 22nd. – 'Aunt Jane and I had a delicious morning together.'
June 23rd. – 'Aunt Jane and I walked to Alton together.'
July —. – 'Had leeches on for headache. Aunt Jane came and sat with me.'
August 1st. – 'Spent the evening with Aunt Jane.'

But, in fact, the whole diary is a continuous record of meetings between the relations; every day it is either 'The Cottage dined here' or 'we dined at the Cottage,' 'Aunt Jane drank tea with us,' &c., &c. The first letter of this series was written whilst Jane was on a visit to her brother Henry, with whom she returned to Chawton on June 1. It contains some interesting allusions to 'Pride and Prejudice' from which we may gather that the authoress had an ideal 'Jane' (Mrs. Bingley) and 'Elizabeth' (Mrs. Darcy), and that she succeeded in finding a satisfactory likeness of the first, but not of the second, in the picture galleries which she visited. I am not much surprised at this circumstance, for with all her beauty and sweetness, Jane Bingley is a less uncommon character than her sister Elizabeth, upon whom the authoress had exerted all her power, and was proportionately attached to this most successful creation of her brain. The special message to 'Fanny' upon this point reminds me of another entry in this year's diary: 'We finished 'Pride and Prejudice'. I have often heard my mother speak of 'Aunt Jane' reading some of her own works aloud to her; perhaps this refers to one of the occasions on which she did so. How delightful it must have been to hear those life-like characters described by the lips of the very person who had called them into existence!

It will be seen from another paragraph in this letter that my mother had written her aunt a letter in the character of 'Miss Darcy' which made her 'laugh heartily.' It was their habit to talk over the characters of Aunt Jane's books together, and if I only had it in my power to add some of their conversations to these letters I have no doubt that they would prove highly interesting to my readers. Jane returned with the Godmersham family to Kent early in September, and her letters from Henrietta Street were written during the short stay which the party made with Henry Austen on their homeward journey. I am able to fix the dates by the pocket-books. On Tuesday, September 14, my mother writes: 'Papa and Aunt Jane, Lizzie, Marianne, and I left Chawton at nine, and got to Uncle Henry Austen's house in Henrietta Street in good time.' The letters of the 14th and 16th tell the story of their doings, which the diary summarises pretty accurately: 'We shopped all day; a complete bustle' on the 15th; and on the 16th: 'We called on Mrs. Tilson, and were all *Spenced*,' Spence being the individual who was apparently entrusted with the superintendence of the teeth of the Godmersham family. The allusions in the letter to the visit to Covent Garden are also corroborated by entries in the pocket-book, which prove the amusement which was derived by the younger members of the party as well as by their aunt. The Mr. Tilson mentioned in the London letters was one of Henry Austen's partners in the bank.

'Miss Clewes,' after whom Jane inquires, was governess at Godmersham, whom my mother had engaged for her younger sisters, and whom she describes in her diary as 'a treasure.' She had been preceded by Miss Sharpe, who was my mother's own governess, and is often mentioned in these letters. Miss Clewes lived nearly eight years at Godmersham. The diary continues, under date of Friday, the 17th: 'We left town at eight, and reached dear Godmersham before six.'

During the next two months Jane remained in Kent, and here again the comparison with the pocket-books enables me to make out the allusions in the letters. 'Her sister in Lucina, Mrs. H. Gipps' (Letter 64), was, before her marriage, 'Emma Plumptre,'whose sister, 'Mary P.,' was a great friend of my mother's; her other two chief friends being 'Mary Oxenden,' daughter of Sir Henry Oxenden, of Broome, afterwards Mrs. Hammond, and 'Fanny Cage,' of all three of whom we find frequent mention in the letters. The 'Mr. K.s' who 'came a little before dinner on Monday' were Messrs. Wyndham and Charles Knatchbull, the first and second sons of my grandfather, Sir Edward Knatchbull, by his second wife, Frances Graham, and 'their lovely Wadham' was their cousin, son of Wyndham Knatchbull, of London, and afterwards the owner (on his brother William's death) of Babington, in Somersetshire. Wyndham Knatchbull was twenty-seven in 1813, as he was born in 1786. He was afterwards the Rev. Dr. Knatchbull, Rector of Smeeth-cum-Aldington, and died in 1868, at the age of eighty-two.

'We hear a great deal about George Hatton's wretchedness.' I remember hearing from my mother that the gentleman here referred to had 'a great disappointment' in early life, but who the lady was or whether this was the 'wretchedness' I cannot say. Perhaps it had nothing to do with love, and was only caused by the death of his great-aunt, Lady Charlotte Finch (*née* Fermor), who died in June, 1813. But I am bound to say that I have a letter before me which says, 'all the young ladies were in love with George Hatton – he was very handsome and agreeable, danced very well, and flirted famously.' At any rate, Aunt Jane rightly surmised that his 'quick feelings' would not kill him, for he lived to be Earl of Winchilsea, and to marry three times, his last wife being Fanny Margaretta, eldest daughter of Mr. Rice, of Dane Court, and the 'Lizzie' of our letters. He died in 1858, and those who in later life knew the warm-hearted generosity of his nature, the sterling worth of his character and excellence of his disposition, will not be surprised to hear of that general popularity in youth which he undoubtedly enjoyed. I may mention with regard to the letter now before us, that he got over his 'wretchedness' in due time, for early in the following June my mother's diary records: 'The intended marriage of George Hatton and Lady Charlotte Graham announced,' which duly took place on July 26, and on the 30th the entry occurs 'saw the bride and bridegroom pass to Eastwell in proper state!' I ought perhaps to add the entry of August 7, which is to this effect: 'George Hatton and bride called; Lady Charlotte is a sweet little perfection.'

'The Sherers' were the Rector of Godmersham and his wife. Mr. Sherer is often mentioned in my mother's diary, and seems to have been much liked. He died in 1825.

Evington, where 'the gentlemen' all dined one night, was and is the seat of the Honywood family, in the parish of Elmsted, some miles the other side of Wye from Godmersham. The Lady Honywood mentioned in these letters was the wife of Sir John Courtenay Honywood, and daughter of the Rev. Sir William Henry Cooper, Bart. The commendations which Jane bestows upon her in a later letter (No. 70), were well deserved, for even within my memory she was a graceful and charming woman, and must have been beautiful in her youth. I have always heard her spoken of as one of the most delightful people, and believe that she fully deserved the description.

I cannot unravel the 'Adlestrop Living business' at this distance of time, but it was a Leigh Living. The Rev. Thos. Leigh, younger son of William Leigh, of Adlestrop (who was eldest brother of Thomas Leigh, Rector of Harpsden, Henley-on-Thames, Mrs. George Austen's father), held this living in 1806, and in that year succeeded to Stoneleigh under a peculiar limitation in the will of Edward, fifth Lord Leigh, on the death of the latter's sister Mary. Mr. Leigh Perrot, his first cousin, claimed to be next in remainder, but sold his claim, and James Henry, son of James, eldest brother of the Rev. Thomas of Adlestrop, and grandfather of the present Lord Leigh, succeeded. I have no other clue to the matter, which is not of much importance, and has little to do with Jane Austen.

The 'Sackree' of whom such frequent mention is made in the letters from Godmersham was the old nurse of my grandfather's children, an excellent woman and a great favourite. I remember some of her stories to this day, especially one of a country girl who, on being engaged by the housekeeper of a certain family, inquired if she might 'sleep round.' 'Sleep round?' was the reply. 'Yes, of course; you may sleep round or square, whichever you please, for what *I* care!' However, after the lapse of a few days, the girl having been kept up for some work or other till ten o'clock, did not appear in the morning. After some delay, the housekeeper, fancying she must be ill, went up to her room about nine o'clock, and finding her fast asleep and snoring soundly, promptly woke her up, and began to scold her for an idle baggage. On this, the girl with an injured air, began to remonstrate, 'Why ma'am, you told me yourself I might *sleep round*, and as I wasn't in bed till ten o'clock last night, I a'nt a coming down till *ten this morning*.' Mrs. Sackree went by the familiar name of 'Caky,' the origin of which I have been unable to trace, but which was perhaps given to her in the Godmersham nursery by the little ones, who were doing their best to pronounce her real name. She lived on at Godmersham, saw and played with many of the children of her nurslings, and died in March, 1851, in her ninetieth year. Mrs. Sayce was her niece, and my mother's lady's-maid, of whom I know no more than that she occupied that honourable position for twelve years, married a German in 1822, and died at Stuttgard in 1844. Sackree succeeded her as housekeeper when she left Godmersham.

I have no further record of Jane's proceedings in September, save an entry of my mother's that 'Aunt Jane and I paid poor visits together,' and another that they 'called on the Reynolds' at Bilting,' which was a house belonging to the Godmersham property, about a mile from Godmersham, of which I suppose a family of that name were the tenants in 1813. I do not know who the Dr. Isham was who was so good as to say that he was 'sure that he should not like Madame D'Arblay's new novel half so well' as 'Pride and Prejudice' but I imagine that the vast majority of the readers of both books would have agreed with him; for the new novel referred to was 'The Wanderer,' of which I have already hinted my opinion that the falling off from the previous works of the fair authoress is so very manifest that it is difficult to suppose that it was written by the same hand to which we are indebted for 'Evelina', 'Cecilia' and 'Camilla'.

Mr. J. P. is Mr. John Pemberton Plumptre, grandson of the John Plumptre who married Margaretta Bridges in 1750. His father married a Pemberton, whence his second Christian name, and he himself married in 1818 Catherine Matilda Methuen, daughter of Paul Cobb Methuen, of Corsham House, Wilts; but, having only three daughters, Fredville came, on his decease in 1864, to Charles John, the son of his brother Charles. Mr. Plumptre represented East Kent for twenty years, from 1832 to 1852, having been returned as 'an unflinching Reformer,' but afterwards seeing reason to ally himself with the Conservative party. This caused much anger among his former political friends, and was the occasion of some amusing election squibs, one of which I remember. It was written in 1837, when Mr. Rider, whose property was in West Kent, contested Mr. Plumptre's seat in the Liberal interest. The squib was a parody on the song, 'Oh where, and oh where, is your Highland Laddie gone?' the words 'Jockey Rider' being substituted throughout for 'Highland Laddie';

and the verse, 'In what clothes, in what clothes, is your Highland Laddie clad?' was thus transformed – blue, it should be observed, being the Liberal colour in East Kent:–

> In what clothes, in what clothes, is your Jockey Rider clad?
> He's clad all o'er in Blue – but that Blue is *very bad*;
> For it's all *second-hand, being what J. P. Plumptre had!*

'Norton Court' was the residence of the Mr. Lushington, who came to Godmersham during this visit of Jane's, and who was afterwards, as the Right Hon. Stephen Rumbold Lushington, for some years Patronage Secretary of the Treasury, sat in several Parliaments for Canterbury, afterwards served as Governor of Madras, married the daughter of Lord Harris, and died at Norton Court in 1868, in his ninety-fourth year. He was a pleasant and agreeable man of the world, and I am not surprised to find that he made a favourable impression upon Jane. The most amusing thing I remember to tell about him is in connection with the celebrated East Kent election in 1852, when Sir E. Dering and Sir B. Bridges did battle for the seat vacated by Mr. Plumptre, and the latter won. Soon after the contest, I had a long talk with Mr. Lushington, who had very warmly espoused Sir E. Dering's cause, and who loudly declared that his defeat had been in a great measure owing to illegal expenditure on the part of Sir Brook, which he vehemently denounced, and expressed himself very strongly in favour of purity of election and as a hater of bribery of any sort. Presently, however, our conversation drifted into a talk about old times, and the days when he was Secretary of the Treasury before the Reform Bill of 1832. We talked of the Dering family, of their Borough of New Romney, which used to return two members, and of the present Sir Edward Dering's uncle, who managed the Surrenden estates during his long minority. Upon this subject our lover of purity of election waxed wroth. 'A confounded old screw he was!' he exclaimed. 'I was always ready, on the part of the Government, to give him a thousand for the seats, but the old fellow always insisted upon *two thousand guineas*, and I had to give him his price!' Whatever his views, however, upon such matters, he was certainly a favourite with the ladies, his musical talents being one of his recommendations, for I find an entry in my mother's pocket-book of one year 'Mr. Lushington sang. He has a lovely voice, and is quite delightful.' I gather from a similar source that he was generous with his 'franks,' another way to ladies' hearts of which unfortunate M.P.'s have been deprived by the progress of modern improvements. Mystole, to which allusion is made in the sixty-fifth and sixty-sixth letters, was, and is, the seat of the old Kentish family of Fagge. At the present moment it is let to Colonel Laurie, lately M.P. for Canterbury, but at the date of our letters it was occupied by the Rev. Sir John Fagge, rector of Chartham (in which parish Mystole is situate), who had, as the letters show, a wife (Miss Newman, of Canterbury, who survived her husband thirty-five years, and died in 1857), four sons and five daughters, all of the latter of whom Jane seems to have been lucky enough to find at home upon the occasion of her visit.

The Mr. Wigram who is introduced as the friend of Edward Bridges would have been mentioned more favourably by Jane if she had known him longer and better. I only knew him as a man somewhat advanced in years, who lived in Grosvenor Square, where I have had the honour of dining with him more than once. But, undoubtedly, he was a most kind-hearted and good man, a warm friend, of a generous and benevolent disposition, and quite agreeable enough to justify his parents in having called him Henry (see Letter 66).

'The good old original Brett and Toke' (Letter 66) refers to the heads of two very old Kentish families. 'Spring Grove' is about half-a-mile from 'Wye,' and was built in 1674, although Bretts had been buried in Wye some 150 years before. Mr. Toke was the owner of Godinton, near Ashford, which was and is a beautiful and interesting old house, standing in a pleasant and well-timbered park, which lies between the town of Ashford and the adjoining property of Hothfield Park, the seat of the Tufton family, the head of which is now Lord Hothfield. Hasted gives a somewhat lengthy description of the house at Godinton, and tells us that 'in the hall there is a series of fine family portraits, several of which are by Cornelius Johnson. The staircase is of very ancient carved work, in the windows of which are collected all the arms, quarterings, and matches – in painted glass – of the family. The drawing-room upstairs is curiously wainscotted with oak and carved; particularly along the upper part of it, all round the room, is a representation of the exercise and manoeuvres of the ancient militia, with the men habited and accoutred with their arms, in every attitude of marching, exercise, &c., which makes a very droll exhibition of them. There are several handsome chimney-pieces through the house, of Bethersden marble, well carved and ornamented with the arms of the family.' This was the house in which 'the Charles Cages' were staying, which brings me to an account of the two brothers of that name, who were both very cheery and popular visitors at many other houses besides hospitable Godinton.

Edward and Charles Cage were the younger brothers of Lewis, the husband of Fanny Bridges. They were both clergymen and both great sportsmen. Edward married a Welsh lady, who was very worthy but extremely small. My satirical relatives at Godmersham nicknamed her 'Penny Piece,' though I do not exactly know why, and all I can remember of her is that she hated butterflies and was terribly afraid of guns. Her husband was Rector of Eastling and kept harriers. I have been told that he had the names of his hounds upon his spoons and forks, and once observed to a visitor, 'If the Archbishop of Canterbury were to come here he would think it rather odd to see the names of my hounds upon my spoons and forks,' which was probably true, though in those days bishops might have sometimes seen even more extraordinary things in the houses of their clergy. Mr. E. Cage died in 1835, and his widow in 1848. Charles Cage had the livings of Bensted and Bredgar, and lived at Chrismill, near Milgate, but afterwards removed to Leybourne. He married Miss Graham, sister of Lady Knatchbull and Lady Oxenden, and of Charles Graham, rector of Barham, also referred to in our letters. She was much liked by the Godmersham family. She died in 1847, and he survived her little more than a year. There are many anecdotes of the two Cages, but I only recollect one of Charles – namely, that when one of his nieces was reading to him the 2nd Chapter of the Acts, he stopped her with a sigh at the mention of the 'Elamites,' and on being asked why, replied, 'It does so put me in mind of Brockman and his hounds in Elham Park!' (a noted fox covert in East Kent). I remember that he came to grief in a disagreeable manner during a visit to Hatch, which occurred in my boyish days. In one of the passages there are two doors precisely alike, one of which opens into a room and the other on to a back staircase. The worthy old gentleman, going along this passage, opened the latter under the impression that it was the former, marched boldly forward as if on level ground, and naturally enough tumbled downstairs. How he escaped serious injury I cannot imagine, but I believe he suffered no material inconvenience from the shock, unpleasant though it must have been.

The sixty-seventh letter possesses now a more melancholy interest to some who will read these pages than when I first discovered it among the rest. It will be seen to be a joint composition, the first part being written by Jane's niece, 'Lizzy,' afterwards Mrs. Rice, of Dane Court, who only died as these pages were being prepared for publication. Few women ever lived who possessed greater power of attracting the love of others, and few have ever been more fondly loved by those who had the good fortune to know her.

Milgate, mentioned in the sixty-ninth letter, was bought by Mr. R. Cage, a barrister, in 1624, and has been in the Cage family ever since; its present possessor being General (Lewis) Knight, only son of Henry and Sophia Cage.

The Mrs. Harrison mentioned in the sixty-ninth and seventieth letters must have been Mrs. Lefroy's sister, *née* Charlotte Brydges, who had first married Mr. Branfill, and, after his death in 1792 (leaving her with a son and daughter), Mr. John Harrison, of Denne Hill, who died in 1818 without issue. The madness is, of course, a pleasantry of the writer, since neither family was afflicted with more than the ordinary insanity which mankind enjoy, although both had plenty of that ability which sometimes appears like madness to those who do not happen to possess it.

The seventieth letter is the last from Godmersham, and begins by describing a dinner party at Chilham Castle. 'The Bretons' were Dr. Breton and his wife. He was a gentleman little in stature, somewhat odd in appearance, and eccentric in character. He married Mrs. Billington, and had the rectory of Kennington, between Godmersham and Ashford, where he lived and died. My mother chronicles this gathering as 'a better party than usual,' and by 'bits and scraps' of it Jane herself was 'very well entertained.' Then comes an amusing account of a concert at Canterbury to which she went, with my mother and Miss Clewes, and where the races of Bridges and Plumptre seem to have come in force from Goodnestone and Fredville, and to have had a pleasant time of it. My mother says of this concert that she had 'an enjoyable *cose* with sweet Mary Plumptre,' which corresponds with the account in the letter. The next letter – for I do not doubt there *was* a 'next' from Godmersham – would probably have given us an account of the Canterbury ball, which was to take place on the following Thursday, but unfortunately it is not forthcoming. All the same, however, the ball *did* take place, for the pocket-book informs me: 'We went to the Canty. Ball; good company, but no dancing; officers idle and scarcity of county Beaux. Sophia (Deedes) and I only danced the 2nd, and her partner was an officer, mine Wm. Hammond; white sarsnet and silver, silver in my hair.'

On Saturday, November 18, Jane left Godmersham, accompanying my grandfather and mother to Wrotham Rectory, on a visit to Mr. and Mrs. Moore, and on the 15th she went on to her brother Henry's house in Henrietta Street.

LXI

Sloane St.: Monday (May 24)

MY DEAREST CASSANDRA,

I am very much obliged to you for writing to me. You must have hated it after a worrying morning. Your letter came just in time to save my going to Remnant's, and fit me for Christian's, where I bought Fanny's dimity.

*I went the day before (Friday) to Layton's, as I proposed, and got my mother's gown – seven yards at 6*s. *6*d. *I then walked into No. 10 [Henrietta Street], which is all dirt and confusion, but in a very promising way, and after being present at the opening of a new account, to my great amusement, Henry and I went to the exhibition in Spring Gardens. It is not thought a good collection, but I was very well pleased, particularly (pray tell Fanny) with a small portrait of Mrs. Bingley, excessively like her.*

I went in hopes of seeing one of her sister, but there was no Mrs. Darcy.

Perhaps, however, I may find her in the great exhibition, which we shall go to if we have time. I have no chance of her in the collection of Sir Joshua Reynolds's paintings, which is now showing in Pall Mall, and which we are also to visit.

Mrs. Bingley's is exactly herself – size, shaped face, features, and sweetness; there never was a greater likeness. She is dressed in a white gown, with green ornaments, which convinces me of what I had always supposed, that green was a favourite colour with her. I dare say Mrs. D. will be in yellow.

Friday was our worst day as to weather. We were out in a very long and very heavy storm of hail, and there had been others before, but I heard no thunder. Saturday was a good deal better; dry and cold.

I gave 2s. 6d. *for the dimity. I do not boast of any bargains, but think both the sarsenet and dimity good of their sort.*

I have bought your locket, but was obliged to give 18s. *for it, which must be rather more than you intended. It is neat and plain, set in gold.*

We were to have gone to the Somerset House Exhibition on Saturday, but when I reached Henrietta Street Mr. Hampson [distant relation of the Austens] was wanted there, and Mr. Tilson and I were obliged to drive about town after him, and by the time we had done it was too late for anything but home. We never found him after all.

I have been interrupted by Mrs. Tilson. Poor woman! She is in danger of not being able to attend Lady Drummond Smith's party to night. Miss Burdett was to have taken her, and now Miss Burdett has a cough and will not go. My cousin Caroline *is her sole dependence.*

The events of yesterday were, our going to Belgrave Chapel in the morning, our being prevented by the rain from going to evening service at St. James, Mr. Hampson's calling, Messrs. Barlow and Phillips dining here, and Mr. and Mrs. Tilson's coming in the evening à l'ordinaire. She *drank tea with us both Thursday and Saturday;* he *dined out each day, and on Friday we were with them, and they wish us to go to them to-morrow evening, to meet Miss Burdett, but I do not know how it will end. Henry talks of a drive to Hampstead [where his late wife Eliza was buried], which may interfere with it.*

I should like to see Miss Burdett very well, but that I am rather frightened by hearing that she wishes to be introduced to me. *If I am a wild beast I cannot help it. It is not my own fault.*

There is no change in our plan of leaving London, but we shall not be with you before Tuesday. Henry thinks Monday would appear too early a day. There is no danger of our being induced to stay longer.

I have not quite determined how I shall manage about my clothes; perhaps there may be only my trunk to send by the coach, or there may be a band-box with it. I have taken your gentle hint, and written to Mrs. Hill.

The Hoblyns want us to dine with them, but we have refused. When Henry returns he will be dining out a great deal, I dare say; as he will then be alone, it will be more desirable; he will be more welcome at every table, and every invitation more welcome to him. He will not want either of us again till he is settled in Henrietta Street. This is my present persuasion. And he will not be settled there – really settled – till late in the autumn; 'he will not be come to bide' till after September.

There is a gentleman in treaty for this house. Gentleman himself is in the country, but gentleman's friend came to see it the other day, and seemed pleased on the whole. Gentleman would rather prefer an increased rent to parting with five hundred guineas at once, and if that is the only difficulty it will not be minded. Henry is indifferent as to the which.

Get us the best weather you can for Wednesday, Thursday, and Friday. We are to go to Windsor in our way to Henley, which will be a great delight. We shall be leaving Sloane Street about 12, two or three hours after Charles's party have begun their journey. You will miss them, but the comfort of getting back into your own room will be great. And then the tea and sugar!

I fear Miss Clewes is not better, or you would have mentioned it. I shall not write again unless I have any unexpected communication or opportunity to tempt me. I enclose Mr. Herington's bill and receipt.

I am very much obliged to Fanny for her letter; it made me laugh heartily, but I cannot pretend to answer it. Even had I more time, I should not feel at all sure of the sort of letter that Miss D. [1] would write. I hope Miss Benn is got well again, and will have a comfortable dinner with you to-day.

Monday Evening. – *We have been both to the exhibition and Sir J. Reynolds's, and I am disappointed, for there was nothing like Mrs. D. at either. I can only imagine that Mr. D. prizes any picture of her too much to like it should be exposed to the public eye. I can imagine he would have that sort of feeling – that mixture of love, pride, and delicacy.*

Setting aside this disappointment, I had great amusement among the pictures; and the driving about, the carriage being open, was very pleasant. I liked my solitary elegance very much, and was ready to laugh all the time at my being where I was. I could not but feel that I had naturally small right to be parading about London in a barouche.

Henry desires Edward may know that he has just bought three dozen of claret for him (cheap), and ordered it to be sent down to Chawton.

I should not wonder if we got no farther than Reading on Thursday evening, and so reach Steventon only to a reasonable dinner hour the next day; but whatever I may write or you may imagine we know it will be something different. I shall be quiet to-morrow morning; all my business is done, and I shall only call again upon Mrs. Hoblyn, &c.

Love to your much...party.

Yours affectionately,
J. AUSTEN.
May 2, 1813. From Sloane St.
Miss Austen, Chawton.
By favour of Messrs. Gray & Vincent.

1. Miss Darcy.

LXII

Henrietta St.: Wednesday (Sept. 15, 1/2 past 8).

Here I am, my dearest Cassandra, seated in the breakfast, dining, sitting-room, beginning with all my might. Fanny will join me as soon as she is dressed and begin her letter.

We had a very good journey, weather and roads excellent; the three first stages for 1s. 6d., and our only misadventure the being delayed about a quarter of an hour at Kingston for horses, and being obliged to put up with a pair belonging to a hackney coach and their coachman, which left no room on the barouche box for Lizzy, who was to have gone her last stage there as she did the first; consequently we were all four within, which was a little crowded.

We arrived at a quarter-past four, and were kindly welcomed by the coachman, and then by his master, and then by William, and then by Mrs. Pengird [this should read Perigord, servant of Henry Austen], who all met us before we reached the foot of the stairs. Mde. Bigion [housekeeper] was below dressing us a most comfortable dinner of soup, fish, bouillée, partridges, and an apple tart, which we sat down to soon after five, after cleaning and dressing ourselves and feeling that we were most commodiously disposed of. The little adjoining dressing-room to our apartment makes Fanny and myself very well off indeed, and as we have poor Eliza's [1] bed our space is ample every way.

Sace [lady's maid at Godmersham] arrived safely about half-past six. At seven we set off in a coach for the Lyceum; were at home again in about four hours and a half; had soup and wine and water, and then went to our holes.

Edward finds his quarters very snug and quiet. I must get a softer pen. This is harder. I am in agonies. I have not yet seen Mr. Crabbe [the poet, who was in London]. Martha's letter is gone to the post.

I am going to write nothing but short sentences. There shall be two full stops in every line. Layton and Shear's is *Bedford House. We mean to get there before breakfast if it's possible; for we feel more and more how much we have to do and how little time. This house looks very nice. It seems like Sloane Street moved here. I believe Henry is just rid of Sloane Street. Fanny does not come, but I have Edward seated by me beginning a letter, which looks natural.*

Henry has been suffering from the pain in the face which he has been subject to before. He caught cold at Matlock, and since his return has been paying a little for past pleasure. It is nearly removed now, but he looks thin in the face, either from the pain or the fatigues of his tour, which must have been great.

Lady Robert [Kerr] is delighted with P. and P. [2] and really was so, *as I understand, before she knew who wrote it, for, of course, she knows now. He told her with as much satisfaction as if it were my wish. He did not tell* me *this, but he told Fanny. And Mr. Hastings [Warren Hastings]! I am quite delighted with what such a man writes about it. Henry sent him the books after his return from Daylesford, but you will hear the letter too.*

Let me be rational, and return to my two full stops.

I talked to Henry at the play last night. We were in a private box – Mr. Spencer's – which made it much more pleasant. The box is directly on the stage. One is infinitely less fatigued than in the common way. But Henry's plans are not what one could wish. He does not mean to be at Chawton till the 29th. He must be in town again by Oct. 5. His plan is to get a couple of days of pheasant shooting and then return directly. His wish was to bring you back with him. I have told him your scruples. He wishes you to suit yourself as to time, and if you cannot come till later, will send for you at any time as far as Bagshot. He presumed you would not find difficulty in getting so far. I could not say you would. He proposed your going with him into Oxfordshire. It was his own thought at first. I could not but catch at it for you.

We have talked of it again this morning (for now we have breakfasted), and I am convinced that if you can make it suit in other respects you need not scruple on his account. If you cannot come back with him on the 3rd or 4th, therefore, I do hope you will contrive to go to Adlestrop. By not beginning your absence till about the middle of this month I think you may manage it very well. But you will think all this over. One could wish he had intended to come to you earlier, but it cannot be helped.

I said nothing to him of Mrs. H. [Heathcote] and Miss B. [Bigg], that he might not suppose difficulties. Shall not you put them *into our own room? This seems to me the best plan, and the maid will be most conveniently near.*

Oh, dear me! when I shall ever have done. We did *go to Layton and Shear's before breakfast. Very pretty English poplins at 4*s. *3*d.*; Irish, ditto at 6*s.*;* more *pretty, certainly – beautiful.*

Fanny and the two little girls are gone to take places for to-night at Covent Garden; 'Clandestine Marriage' and 'Midas.' The latter will be a fine show for L. and M. [3] They revelled last night in 'Don Juan,' whom we left in hell at half-past eleven. We had scaramouch and a ghost, and were delighted. I speak of them*;* my *delight was very tranquil, and the rest of us were sober-minded. 'Don Juan' was the last of three musical things. 'Five hours at*

Brighton,' in three acts – of which one was over before we arrived, none the worse – and the 'Beehive,' rather less flat and trumpery.

*I have this moment received 5*l. *from kind, beautiful Edward. Fanny has a similar gift. I shall save what I can of it for your better leisure in this place.* My *letter was from Miss Sharpe – nothing particular. A letter from Fanny Cage this morning.*

Four o'clock. – *We are just come back from doing Mrs. Tickars, Miss Hare, and Mr. Spence. Mr. Hall is here, and, while Fanny is under his hands, I will try to write a little more.*

Miss Hare had some pretty caps, and is to make me one like one of them, only white *satin instead of blue. It will be white satin and lace, and a little white flower perking out of the left ear, like Harriot Byron's feather. I have allowed her to go as far as* 1l. 16s. *My gown is to be trimmed everywhere with white ribbon plaited on somehow or other. She says it will look well. I am not sanguine. They trim with white very much.*

I learnt from Mrs. Tickars's young lady, to my high amusement, that the stays now are not made to force the bosom up at all; that *was a very unbecoming, unnatural fashion. I was really glad to hear that they are not to be so much off the shoulders as they were.*

Going to Mr. Spence's was a sad business and cost us many tears; unluckily we were obliged to go a second time before he could do more than just look. We went first at half-past twelve and afterwards at three; papa with us each time; and, alas! we are to go again to-morrow. Lizzy is not finished yet. There have been no teeth taken out, however, nor will be, I believe, but he finds hers *in a very bad state, and seems to think particularly ill of their durableness. They have been all cleaned,* hers *filed, and are to be filed again. There is a very sad hole between two of her front teeth.*

Thursday Morning, Half-past Seven. – *Up and dressed and downstairs in order to finish my letter in time for the parcel. At eight I have an appointment with Madame B., who wants to show me something downstairs. At nine we are to set off for Grafton House, and get that over before breakfast. Edward is so kind as to walk there with us. We are to be at Mr. Spence's again at 11 5; from that time shall be driving about I suppose till four o'clock at least. We are, if possible, to call on Mrs. Tilson.*

Mr. Hall was very punctual yesterday, and curled me out at a great rate. I thought it looked hideous, and longed for a snug cap instead, but my companions silenced me by their admiration. I had only a bit of velvet round my head. I did not catch cold, however. The weather is all in my favour. I have had no pain in my face since I left you.

We had very good places in the box next the stage-box, front and second row; the three old ones behind of course. I was particularly disappointed at seeing nothing of Mr. Crabbe. I felt sure of him when I saw that the boxes were fitted up with crimson velvet. The new Mr. Terry was Lord

Ogleby, and Henry thinks he may do; but there was no acting more than moderate, and I was as much amused by the remembrances connected with 'Midas' as with any part of it. The girls were very much delighted, but still prefer 'Don Juan'; and I must say that I have seen nobody on the stage who has been a more interesting character than that compound of cruelty and lust.

It was not possible for me to get the worsteds yesterday. I heard Edward last night pressing Henry to come to you, and I think Henry engaged to go there after his November collection [as Receiver General of Oxfordshire he had to make a personal collection of monies due]. Nothing has been done as to S. and S.[4] The books came to hand too late for him to have time for it before he went. Mr. Hastings never hinted *at Eliza in the smallest degree. Henry knew nothing of Mr. Trimmer's death. I tell you these things that you may not have to ask them over again.*

There is a new clerk sent down to Alton, a Mr. Edmund Williams, a young man whom Henry thinks most highly of, and he turns out to be a son of the luckless Williamses of Grosvenor Place.

I long to have you hear Mr. H.'s opinion of P. and P. His admiring my Elizabeth so much is particularly welcome to me.

Instead of saving my superfluous wealth for you to spend, I am going to treat myself with spending it myself. I hope, at least, that I shall find some poplin at Layton and Shear's that will tempt me to buy it. If I do, it shall be sent to Chawton, as half will be for you; for I depend upon your being so kind as to accept it, being the main point. It will be a great pleasure to me. Don't say a word. I only wish you could choose too. I shall send twenty yards.

Now for Bath. Poor F. [Fanny] Cage has suffered a good deal from her accident. The noise of the White Hart was terrible to her. They will keep her quiet, I dare say. She *is not so much delighted with the place as the rest of the party; probably, as she says herself, from having been less well, but she thinks she should like it better in the season. The streets are very empty now, and the shops not so gay as she expected. They are at No. 1 Henrietta Street, the corner of Laura Place, and have no acquaintance at present but the Bramstons.*

Lady Bridges drinks at the Cross Bath, her son at the Hot, and Louisa is going to bathe. Dr. Parry seems to be half starving Mr. Bridges, for he is restricted to much such a diet as James's bread, water and meat, and is never to eat so much of that as he wishes, and he is to walk a great deal – walk till he drops, I believe gout or no gout. It really is to that purpose. I have not exaggerated.

Charming weather for you and us, and the travellers, and everybody. You will take your walk this afternoon, and...
Henrietta St., the autumn of 1813.
Miss Austen, Chawton.
By favour of Mr. Gray.

1. Eliza, Henry Austen's first wife, who had died in the earlier part of this year.
2. 'Pride and Prejudice'.
3. Lizzie and Marianne.
4. 'Sense and Sensibility'.

LXIII

Henrietta St.: Thursday (Sept. 16, after dinner).

Thank you, my dearest Cassandra, for the nice long letter I sent off this morning. I hope you have had it by this time, and that it has found you all well, and my mother no more in need of leeches [for headaches]. Whether this will be delivered to you by Henry on Saturday evening, or by the postman on Sunday morning, I know not, as he has lately recollected something of an engagement for Saturday, which perhaps may delay his visit. He seems determined to come to you soon however.

I hope you will receive the gown to-morrow, and may be able with tolerable honesty to say that you like the colour. It was bought at Grafton House, where, by going very early, we got immediate attendance and went on very comfortably. I only forgot the one particular thing which I had always resolved to buy there – a white silk handkerchief – and was therefore obliged to give six shillings for one at Crook and Besford's; which reminds me to say that the worsteds ought also to be at Chawton to-morrow, and that I shall be very happy to hear they are approved. I had not much time for deliberation.

We are now all four of us young ladies sitting round the circular table in the inner room writing our letters, while the two brothers are having a comfortable coze in the room adjoining. It is to be a quiet evening, much to the satisfaction of four of the six. My eyes are quite tired of dust and lamps.

The letter you forwarded from Edward, junr., has been duly received. He has been shooting most prosperously at home, and dining at Chilham Castle and with Mr. Scudamore.

My cap is come home, and I like it very much. Fanny has one also; hers is white sarsenet and lace, of a different shape from mine, more fit for morning carriage wear, which is what it is intended for, and is in shape exceedingly like our own satin and lace of last winter; shaped round the face exactly like it, with pipes and more fulness, and a round crown inserted behind. My cap *has a peak in front. Large full bows of very narrow ribbon (old twopenny) are the thing. One over the right temple, perhaps, and another at the left ear.*

Henry is not quite well. His stomach is rather deranged. You must keep him in rhubarb, and give him plenty of port and water. He caught his cold farther back than I told you; before he got to Matlock, somewhere in his journey from the North, but the ill effects of that *I hope are nearly gone.*

We returned from Grafton House only just in time for breakfast, and had scarcely finished breakfast when the carriage came to the door. From 11 to half-past 3 we were hard at it; we did *contrive to get to Hans Place for ten minutes. Mrs. T. was as affectionate and pleasing as ever.*

After our return Mr. Tilson walked up from the Compting House and called upon us, and these have been all our visitings.

I have rejoiced more than once that I bought my writing-paper in the country; we have not had a quarter of an hour to spare.

*I enclose the eighteen-pence due to my mother. The rose colour was 6*s. *and the other 4*s. *per yard. There was but two yards and a quarter of the dark slate in the shop, but the man promised to match it and send it off correctly.*

*Fanny bought her Irish [linen] at Newton's in Leicester Square, and I took the opportunity of thinking about your Irish, and seeing one piece of the yard wide at 4*s.*, and it seemed to me very good, good enough for your purpose. It might at least be worth your while to go there, if you have no other engagements. Fanny is very much pleased with the stockings she has bought of Remmington, silk at 12*s.*, cotton at 4*s. 3d. *She thinks them great bargains, but I have not seen them yet, as my hair was dressing when the man and the stockings came.*

The poor girls and their teeth! I have not mentioned them yet, but we were a whole hour at Spence's, and Lizzy's were filed and lamented over again, and poor Marianne had two taken out after all, the two just beyond the eye teeth, to make room for those in front. When her doom was fixed, Fanny, Lizzy, and I walked into the next room, where we heard each of the two sharp and hasty screams.

The little girls' teeth I can suppose in a critical state, but I think he must be a lover of teeth and money and mischief, to parade about Fanny's. I would not have had him look at mine for a shilling a tooth and double it. It was a disagreeable hour.

We then went to Wedgwood's, where my brother and Fanny chose a dinner set. I believe the pattern is a small lozenge in purple, between lines of narrow gold, and it is to have the crest.

*We must have been three-quarters of an hour at Grafton House, Edward sitting by all the time with wonderful patience. There Fanny bought the net for Anna's gown, and a beautiful square veil for herself. The edging there is very cheap. I was tempted by some, and I bought some very nice plaiting lace at 3*s. 4d.

Fanny desires me to tell Martha, with her kind love, that Birchall assured her that there was no second set of Hook's Lessons for Beginners, and that, by my advice, she has therefore chosen her a set by another composer. I thought she would rather have something than not. It costs six shillings.

With love to you all, including Triggs [Godmersham gamekeeper], I remain.
Yours very affectionately,
J. AUSTEN.

Henrietta St., autumn of 1813.
Miss Austen, Chawton.
By favour of [blank]

LXIV

Godmersham Park: Thursday (Sept 23).
MY DEAREST CASSANDRA,

Thank you five hundred and forty times for the exquisite piece of workmanship which was brought into the room this morning, while we were at breakfast, with some very inferior works of art in the same way, and which I read with high glee, much delighted with everything it told, whether good or bad. It is so rich in striking intelligence that I hardly know what to reply to first. I believe finery must have it.

I am extremely glad that you like the poplin. I thought it would have my mother's approbation, but was not so confident of yours. Remember that it is a present. Do not refuse me. I am very rich.

Mrs. Clement [of Chawton] is very welcome to her little boy, and to my congratulations into the bargain, if ever you think of giving them. I hope she will do well. Her sister in Lucina [Lucina was the Roman goddess of childbirth], Mrs. H. Gipps, does too well, we think. Mary P.[Plumptre] wrote on Sunday that she had been three days on the sofa. Sackree does not approve it.

Well, there is some comfort in the Mrs. Hulbart's not coming to you, and I am happy to hear of the honey. I was thinking of it the other day. Let me know when you begin the new tea, and the new white wine. My present elegancies have not yet made me indifferent to such matters. I am still a cat if I see a mouse.

I am glad you like our caps, but Fanny is out of conceit with hers already; she finds that she has been buying a new cap without having a new pattern, which is true enough. She is rather out of luck to like neither her gown nor her cap, but I do not much mind it, because besides that I like them both myself, I consider it as a thing of course at her time of life – one of the sweet taxes of youth to choose in a hurry and make bad bargains.

I wrote to Charles yesterday, and Fanny has had a letter from him to-day, principally to make inquiries about the time of their visit here, to which mine was an answer beforehand; so he will probably write again soon to fix his week. I am best pleased that Cassy does not go to you.

Now, what have we been doing since I wrote last? The Mr. K.'s [1] came a little before dinner on Monday, and Edward went to the church with the two seniors, but there is no inscription [for a memorial to Mrs Knight in Godmersham Church] yet drawn up. They are very good-natured you know, and civil, and all that, but are not particularly superfine; however, they ate their dinner and drank their tea, and went away, leaving their lovely Wadham in our arms, and I wish you had seen Fanny and me running backwards and forwards with his breeches from the little chintz to the white room before we went to bed, in the greatest of frights lest he should come upon us before we had done it all. There had been a mistake in the housemaids' preparation, and they were gone to bed.

He seems a very harmless sort of young man, nothing to like or dislike in him – goes out shooting or hunting with the two others all the morning, and plays at whist and makes queer faces in the evening.

On Tuesday the carriage was taken to the painter's; at one time Fanny and I were to have gone in it, chiefly to call on Mrs. C. – Milles and Moy [2] – but we found that they were going for a few days to Sandling, and would not be at home; therefore my brother and Fanny went to Eastwell in the chair instead. While they were gone the Nackington Milles's called and left their cards. Nobody at home at Eastwell.

We hear a great deal of Geo. H.'s wretchedness. I suppose he has quick feelings, but I dare say they will not kill him. He is so much out of spirits, however, that his friend John Plumptre is gone over to comfort him, at Mr. Hatton's desire. He called here this morning in his way. A handsome young man certainly, with quiet, gentlemanlike manners. I set him down as sensible rather than brilliant. There is nobody brilliant nowadays. He talks of staying a week at Eastwell, and then comes to Chilham Castle for a day or two, and my brother invited him to come here afterwards, which he seemed very agreeable to.

''Tis night, and the landscape is lovely no more,' [quotation from a poem by James Beattie] but to make amends for that, our visit to the Tyldens is over. My brother, Fanny, Edwd., and I went; Geo. stayed at home with W. K. [Knatchbull]. There was nothing entertaining, or out of the common way. We met only Tyldens and double Tyldens. A whist-table for the gentlemen, a grown-up musical young lady to play backgammon with Fanny, and engravings of the Colleges at Cambridge for me. In the morning we returned Mrs. Sherer's visit. I like Mr. S. very much.

Well, I have not half done yet, I am not come up with myself. My brother drove Fanny to Nackington and Canty. yesterday, and while they were gone the Faggs paid their duty. Mary Oxenden is staying at Canty. with the Blairs, and Fanny's object was to see her.

The Deedes want us to come to Sandling for a few days, or at least a day and night. At present Edwd. does not seem well affected – he would rather not be asked to go anywhere – but I rather expect he will be persuaded to go for the one day and night.

I read him the chief of your letter; he was interested and pleased, as he ought, and will be happy to hear from you himself. Your finding so much comfort from his cows gave him evident pleasure. I wonder Henry did not go down on Saturday; he does not in general fall within a doubtful intention.

My face is very much as it was before I came away; for the first two or three days it was rather worse. I caught a small cold in my way down, and had some pain every evening, not to last long, but rather severer than it had been lately. This has worn off, however, and I have scarcely felt anything for the last two days.

Sackree is pretty well again, only weak. Much obliged to you for your message, &c.; it was very true that she blessed herself the whole time that the pain was not in her stomach. I read all the scraps I could of your letter to her. She seemed to like it, and says she shall always like to hear anything of Chawton now, and I am to make you Miss Clewes's assurance to the same effect, with thanks and best respects, &c.

The girls are much disturbed at Mary Stacey's [a Chawton villager] not admitting Dame L. Miss C. and I are sorry, but not angry; we acknowledge Mary Stacey's right, and can suppose her to have reason.

Oh! the church must have looked very forlorn. We all thought of the empty pew [because Edward Austen and his family had returned to Kent]. How Bentigh is grown! and the Canty. Hill Plantation! And the improvements within *are very great. I admire the chintz room very much. We live in the library except at meals, and have a fire every evening. The weather is set about changing; we shall have a settled wet season soon. I must go to bed.*

Friday. – *I am sorry to find that one of the nightcaps here belongs to you – sorry, because it must be in constant wear.*

Great doings again to-day. Fanny, Lizzy, and Marianne. are going to Goodnestone for the fair, which is to-morrow, and stay till Monday, and the gentlemen are all to dine at Evington. Edwd. has been repenting ever since he promised to go, and was hoping last night for a wet day, but the morning is fair. I shall dine with Miss Clewes, and I dare say find her very agreeable. The invitation to the fair was general. Edwd. positively declined his share of that, and I was very glad to do the same. It is likely to be a baddish fair – not much upon the stall, and neither Mary O. [3] nor Mary P. [4].

It is hoped that the portfolio may be in Canty. this morning. Sackree's sister found it at Croydon and took it to town with her, but unluckily did not send it down till she had directions. Fanny C. [Cage]'s screens can be done nothing with, but there are parts of workbags in the parcel, very important in their way. Three of the Deedes girls are to be at Goodnestone.

We shall not be much settled till this visit is over, settled as to employment I mean. Fanny and I are to go on with 'Modern Europe' together, but hitherto have advanced only twenty-five pages. Something or other has always happened to delay or curtail the reading hour.

I ought to have told you before of a purchase of Edward's in town; he desired you might hear of it – a thing *for measuring timber with, so that* you need not have the trouble of finding him in tapes any longer. He treated himself with this seven-shilling purchase, and bought a new watch and new gun for George. The new gun shoots very well.

Apples are scarce in this country – 1l. 5s. a sack. Miss Hinton should take Hannah Knight. Mrs. Driver [new housekeeper] has not yet appeared. J. Littleworth [Deane villager] and the grey pony reached Bath safely.

A letter from Mrs. Cooke: they have been at Brighton a fortnight; stay at least another, and Mary is already much better.

Poor Dr. Isham is obliged to admire P. and P. more, and to send me word that he is sure he shall not like Madame D'Arblay's new novel half so well. Mrs. C. invented it all, of course. He desires his compliments to you and my mother.

Of the Adlestrop living business, Mrs. C. says: 'It can be now no secret, as the papers for the necessary dispensations are going up to the Archbishop's Secretary. However, be it known that we all wish to have it understood that George takes this trust entirely to oblige Mr. Leigh, and never will be a shilling benefited by it. Had my consent been necessary, believe me, I should have withheld it, for I do think it on the part of the patron a very shabby piece of business. All these and other Scrapings from dear Mrs. E. L. are to accumulate no doubt to help Mr. Twisleton [Revd Thomas Twisleton, recipient of the living of Adlestrop, who was then working in Ceylon] to a secure admission again into England.' I would wish you, therefore, to make it known to my mother as if this were the first time of Mrs. Cooke's mentioning it to me.

I told Mrs. C. of my mother's late oppressions in her head. She says on that subject: 'Dear Mrs. Austen's is, I believe, an attack frequent at her age and mine. Last year I had for some time the sensation of a peck loaf resting on my head, and they talked of cupping me, but I came off with a dose or two of calomel, and have never heard of it since.'

The three Miss Knights and Mrs. Sayce are just off; the weather has got worse since the early morning, and whether Mrs. Clewes and I are to be tête-à-tête, or to have four gentlemen to admire us, is uncertain.

I am now alone in the library, mistress of all I survey; at least I may say so, and repeat the whole poem if I like it, without offence to anybody.

Martha will have wet races and catch a bad cold; in other respects I hope she will have much pleasure at them, and that she is free from ear-ache now. I am glad she likes my cap so well. I assure you my old one looked so smart yesterday that I was asked two or three times before I set off whether it was not my new one.

I have this moment seen Mrs. Driver driven up to the kitchen door. I cannot close with a grander circumstance or greater wit.

Yours affectionately,

J. A.

I am going to write to Steventon, so you need not send any news of me there.

Louisa's best love and a hundred thousand million kisses.

Miss Austen, Chawton, Alton, Hants.

1. Knatchbulls.
2. Mrs. C. Milles was the mother of Mr. R. Milles of Nackington and Elmham, Norfolk. 'Moy' means 'Molly' Milles – probably an imitation of her mother's way of pronouncing her name. She was sister to Mr. R. Milles, and 'the Nackington Milles' refers to his widow who lived there after his death
3. Mary Oxenden.
4. Mary Plumptre.

LXV

Godmersham Park: Monday (Oct 11).

(MY DEAREST AUNT CASS.,

I have just asked Aunt Jane to let me write a little in her letter, but she does not like it, so I won't. Good-bye!)

You will have Edward's letter to-morrow. He tells me that he did not send you any news to interfere with mine, but I do not think there is much for anybody to send at present.

We had our dinner party on Wednesday, with the addition of Mrs. and Miss Milles, who were under a promise of dining here in their return from Eastwell, whenever they paid their visit of duty there, and it happened to be paid on that day. Both mother and daughter are much as I have always found them. I like the mother – first, because she reminds me of Mrs. Birch; and, secondly, because she is cheerful and grateful for what she is at the age of ninety and upwards. The day was pleasant enough. I sat by Mr. Chisholme [rector of Eastwell], and we talked away at a great rate about nothing worth hearing.

It was a mistake as to the day of the Sherers going being fixed; they are *ready, but are waiting for Mr. Paget's answer.*

I inquired of Mrs. Milles after Jemima Brydges, and was quite grieved to hear that she was obliged to leave Canterbury some months ago on account of her debts, and is nobody knows where. What an unprosperous family!

On Saturday, soon after breakfast, Mr. J. P. [John Plumptre] left us for Norton Court. I like him very much. He gives me the idea of a very amiable young man, only too diffident to be so agreeable as he might be. He was out the chief of each morning with the other two, shooting and getting wet through. To-morrow we are to know whether he and a hundred young ladies will come here for the ball. I do not much expect any.

The Deedes cannot meet us; they have engagements at home. I will finish the Deedes by saying that they are not likely to come here till quite late in my stay – the very last week perhaps; and I do not expect to see the Moores at all. They are not solicited till after Edward's return from Hampshire.

Monday, November 15, is the day now fixed for our setting out.

Poor Basingstoke races! There seem to have been two particularly wretched days on purpose for them; and Weyhill week [a fair] does not begin much happier.

We were quite surprised by a letter from Anna at Tollard Royal [home of Henry and Lucy Rice], last Saturday; but perfectly approve her going, and only regret they should all go so far to stay so few days.

We had thunder and lightning here on Thursday morning, between five and seven; no very bad thunder, but a great deal of lightning. It has given the commencement of a season of wind and rain, and perhaps for the next six weeks we shall not have two dry days together.

Lizzy is very much obliged to you for your letter and will answer it soon, but has so many things to do that it may be four or five days before she can. This is quite her own message, spoken in rather a desponding tone. Your letter gave pleasure to all of us; we had all the reading of it of course, I three times, as I undertook, to the great relief of Lizzy, to read it to Sackree, and afterwards to Louisa.

Sackree does not at all approve of Mary Doe [maid at Chawton House] and her nuts – on the score of propriety rather than health. She saw some signs of going after her in George and Henry, and thinks if you could give the girl a check, by rather reproving her for taking anything seriously about nuts which they said to her, it might be of use. This, of course, is between our three discreet selves, a scene of triennial bliss.

Mrs. Breton called here on Saturday. I never saw her before. She is a large, ungenteel woman, with self-satisfied and would-be elegant manners.

We are certain of some visitors to-morrow. Edward Bridges comes for two nights in his way from Lenham to Ramsgate, and brings a friend – name unknown – but supposed to be a Mr. Harpur, a neighbouring clergyman; and Mr. R. Mascall is to shoot with the young men, which it is to be supposed will end in his staying dinner.

On Thursday, Mr. Lushington, M.P. for Canterbury, and manager of the Lodge Hounds, dines here, and stays the night. He is chiefly young Edward's acquaintance. If I can I will get a frank from him, and write to you all the sooner. I suppose the Ashford ball will furnish something.

As I wrote of my nephews with a little bitterness in my last, I think it particularly incumbent on me to do them justice now, and I have great pleasure in saying that they were both at the Sacrament yesterday. After having much praised or much blamed anybody, one is generally sensible of something just the reverse soon afterwards. Now these two boys who are out *with the foxhounds will come home and disgust me again by some habit of luxury or some proof of sporting mania, unless I keep it off by this prediction. They amuse themselves very comfortably in the evening by netting; they are each about a rabbit net, and sit as deedily to it, side by side, as any two Uncle Franks could do.*

I am looking over 'Self Control' again, and my opinion is confirmed of its being an excellently-meant, elegantly-written work, without anything of nature or probability in it. I declare I do not know whether Laura's passage down the American river is not the most natural, possible, everyday thing she ever does.

Tuesday.– *Dear me! what is to become of me? Such a long letter! Two-and-forty lines in the second page. Like Harriot Byron, I ask, what am I to do with my gratitude? I can do nothing but thank you and go on. A few of your inquiries, I think, are replied to* en avance.

The name of F. Cage's drawing-master is O'Neil. We are exceedingly amused with your Shalden news, and your self-reproach on the subject of Mrs. Stockwell made me laugh heartily. I rather wondered that Johncock, [1] the only person in the room, could help laughing too. I had not heard before of her having the measles. Mrs. H. [Heathcote] and Alethea's staying till Friday was quite new to me; a good plan however. I could not have settled it better myself, and am glad they found so much in the house to approve, and I hope they will ask Martha to visit them. I admire the sagacity and taste of Charlotte Williams. Those large dark eyes always judge well. I will compliment her by naming a heroine after her.

Edward has had all the particulars of the building, &c., read to him twice over, and seems very well satisfied. A narrow door to the pantry is the only subject of solicitude; it is certainly just the door which should not be narrow, on account of the trays; but, if a case of necessity, it must be borne.

I knew *there was sugar in the tin, but had no idea of there being enough to last through your company. All the better. You ought not to think this new loaf better than the other, because* that *was the first of five which all came together. Something of fancy, perhaps, and something of Imagination.*

Dear Mrs. Digweed! I cannot bear that she should not be foolishly happy after a ball. I hope Miss Yates and her companions were all well the day after their arrival. I am thoroughly rejoiced that Miss Benn has placed herself in lodgings, though I hope they may not be long necessary.

No letter from Charles yet.

Southey's 'Life of Nelson': I am tired of 'Lives of Nelson,' being that I never read any. I will read this, however, if Frank is mentioned in it.

Here am I in Kent, with one brother [Charles] in the same county and another brother's wife, and see nothing of them, which seems unnatural. It will not last so forever, I trust. I should like to have Mrs. F. A. and her children here for a week, but not a syllable of that nature is ever breathed. I wish her last visit had not been so long a one.

I wonder whether Mrs. Tilson has ever lain-in. Mention it if it ever comes to your knowledge, and we shall hear of it by the same post from Henry.

Mr. Rob. Mascall breakfasted here; he eats a great deal of butter. I dined upon goose yesterday, which, I hope, will secure a good sale of my second edition. Have you any tomatas? Fanny and I regale on them every day.

Disastrous letters from the Plumptres and Oxendens. Refusals everywhere – a blank partout *– and it is not quite certain whether we go or not; something may depend upon the disposition of Uncle Edward when he comes, and upon what we hear at Chilham Castle this morning, for we are going to pay visits. We are going to each house at Chilham and to Mystole. I shall like seeing the Faggs. I shall like it all, except that we are to set out so early that I have not time to write as I would wish.*

Edwd. Bridges's friend is a Mr. Hawker, I find, not Harpur. I would not have you sleep in such an error for the world.

My brother desires his best love and thanks for all your information. He hopes the roots of the old beech have been dug away enough to allow a proper covering of mould and turf. He is sorry for the necessity of building the new coin, but hopes they will contrive that the doorway should be of the usual width – if it must be contracted on one side, by widening it on the other. The appearance need not signify. And he desires me to say that your being at Chawton when he is will be quite necessary. You cannot think it more indispensable than he does. He is very much obliged to you for your attention to everything. Have you any idea of returning with him to Henrietta Street and finishing your visit then? Tell me your sweet little innocent ideas.

Everything of love and kindness, proper and improper, must now suffice.
Yours very affectionately,
J. AUSTEN.
Miss Austen, Chawton, Alton, Hants.

1. The butler at Godmersham.

LXVI

Godmersham Park: Thursday (Oct. 14).
MY DEAREST CASSANDRA,

Now I will prepare for Mr. Lushington, and as it will be wisest also to prepare for his not coming, or my not getting a frank, I shall write very close from the first, and even leave room for the seal in the proper place. When I have followed up my last with this I shall feel somewhat less unworthy of you than the state of our correspondence now requires.

I left off in a great hurry to prepare for our morning visits. Of course was ready a good deal the first, and need not have hurried so much. Fanny wore her new gown and cap. I was surprised to find Mystole [home of the Fagg family] so pretty.

The ladies were at home. I was in luck, and saw Lady Fagg and all her five daughters, with an old Mrs. Hamilton, from Canterbury, and Mrs. and Miss Chapman, from Margate, into the bargain. I never saw so plain a family – five sisters so very plain! They are as plain as the Foresters, or the Franfraddops, or the Seagraves, or the Rivers, excluding Sophy. Miss Sally Fagg has a pretty figure, and that comprises all the good looks of the family.

It was stupidish; Fanny did her part very well, but there was a lack of talk altogether, and the three friends in the house only sat by and looked at us. However, Miss Chapman's name is Laura, and she had a double flounce to her gown. You really must get some flounces. Are not some of your large stock of white morning gowns just in a happy state for a flounce – too short? Nobody at home at either house in Chilham.

Edward Bridges and his friend did not forget to arrive. The friend is a Mr. Wigram, one of the three-and-twenty children of a great rich mercantile, Sir Robert Wigram, an old acquaintance of the Footes, but very recently known to Edward B. The history of his coming here is, that, intending to go from Ramsgate to Brighton, Edw. B. persuaded him to take Lenham on his way, which gave him the convenience of Mr. W.'s gig, and the comfort of not being alone there; but, probably thinking a few days of Gm. would be the cheapest and pleasantest way of entertaining his friend and himself, offered a visit here, and here they stay till to-morrow.

Mr. W. is about five or six-and-twenty, not ill-looking, and not agreeable. He is certainly no addition. A sort of cool, gentlemanlike manner, but very silent. They say his name is Henry, a proof how unequally the gifts of fortune are bestowed. I have seen many a John and Thomas much more agreeable.

We have got rid of Mr. R. Mascall, however. I did not like him *either. He talks too much, and is conceited, besides having a vulgarly shaped mouth. He slept here on Tuesday, so that yesterday Fanny and I sat down to breakfast with six gentlemen to admire us.*

We did not go to the ball. It was left to her to decide, and at last she determined against it. She knew that it would be a sacrifice on the part of her father and brothers if they went, and I hope it will prove that she *has not sacrificed much. It is not likely that there should have been anybody there whom she would care for.* I *was very glad to be spared the trouble of dressing and going, and being weary before it was half over, so my gown and my cap are still unworn. It will appear at last, perhaps, that I might have done without either. I produced my brown bombazine yesterday, and it was very much admired indeed, and I like it better than ever.*

You have given many particulars of the state of Chawton House, but still we want more. Edward wants to be expressly told that all the round tower,

&c., is entirely down, and the door from the best room stopped up; he does not know enough of the appearance of things in that quarter.

He heard from Bath yesterday. Lady B. [Bridges] continues very well, and Dr. Parry's opinion is, that while the water agrees with her she ought to remain there, which throws their coming away at a greater uncertainty than we had supposed. It will end, perhaps, in a fit of the gout, which may prevent her coming away. Louisa thinks her mother's being so well may be quite as much owing to her being so much out of doors as to the water. Lady B. is going to try the hot pump, the Cross bath being about to be painted. Louisa is particularly well herself, and thinks the water has been of use to her. She mentioned our inquiries, &c., to Mr. and Mrs. Alex. Evelyn, and had their best compliments and thanks to give in return. Dr. Parry does not expect Mr. E. to last much longer.

Only think of Mrs. Holder's being dead! Poor woman, she has done the only thing in the world she could possibly do to make one cease to abuse her. Now, if you please, Hooper must have it in his power to do more by his uncle. Lucky for the little girl. An Anne Ekins can hardly be so unfit for the care of a child as a Mrs. Holder.

A letter from Wrotham yesterday offering an early visit here, and Mr. and Mrs. Moore and one child are to come on Monday for ten days. I hope Charles and Fanny may not fix the same time, but if they come at all in October they must. *What is the use of hoping? The two parties of children is the chief evil.*

To be sure, here we are; the very thing has happened, or rather worse – a letter from Charles this very morning, which gives us reason to suppose they may come here to-day. It depends upon the weather, and the weather now is very fine. No difficulties are made, however, and, indeed, there will be no want of room; but I wish there were no Wigrams and Lushingtons in the way to fill up the table and make us such a motley set. I cannot spare Mr. Lushington either, because of his frank, but Mr. Wigram does no good to anybody. I cannot imagine how a man can have the impudence to come into a family party for three days, where he is quite a stranger, unless he knows himself to be agreeable on undoubted authority. He and Edw. B. [Bridges] are going to ride to Eastwell, and as the boys are hunting, and my brother is gone to Canty., Fanny and I have a quiet morning before us.

Edward has driven off poor Mrs. Salkeld [housekeeper at Godmersham]. It was thought a good opportunity of doing something towards clearing the house. By her own desire Mrs. *Fanny [1] is to be put in the room next the nursery, her baby in a little bed by her; and as Cassy is to have the closet within, and Betsey William's little hole, they will be all very snug together. I shall be most happy to see dear Charles, and he will be as happy as he can with a cross child, or some such care, pressing on him at the time. I should be very happy in the idea of seeing little Cassy again, too, did not I fear she would disappoint me by some immediate disagreeableness.*

We had the good old original Brett and Toke calling here yesterday, separately. Mr. Toke I am always very fond of. He inquired after you and my mother, which adds esteem to passion. The Charles Cages are staying at Godington. I knew *they must be staying somewhere soon. Ed. Hussey is warned out of Pett [Place, Charing, Kent], and talks of fixing at Ramsgate. Bad taste! He is very fond of the sea, however. Some taste in that, and some judgment, too, in fixing on Ramsgate, as being by the sea.*

The comfort of the billiard-table here is very great; it draws all the gentlemen to it whenever they are within, especially after dinner, so that my brother, Fanny, and I have the library to ourselves in delightful quiet. There is no truth in the report of G. Hatton being to marry Miss Wemyss. He desires it may be contradicted.

Have you done anything about our present to Miss Benn? I suppose she must have a bed at my mother's whenever she dines there. How will they manage as to inviting her when you are gone? and if they invite, how will they continue to entertain her?

Let me know as many of your parting arrangements as you can, as to wine, &c. I wonder whether the ink-bottle has been filled. Does butcher's meat keep up at the same price, and is not bread lower than 2s. 6d.*? Mary's blue gown! My mother must be in agonies. I have a great mind to have* my *blue gown dyed some time or other. I proposed it once to you, and you made some objection, I forget what. It is the fashion of flounces that gives it particular expediency.*

Mrs. and Miss Wildman have just been here. Miss is very plain. I wish Lady B. may be returned before we leave Gm., that Fanny may spend the time of her father's absence at Goodnestone, which is what she would prefer.

Friday. – *They came last night at about seven. We had given them up, but* I still *expected them to come. Dessert was nearly over; a better time for arriving than an hour and a-half earlier. They were late because they did not set out earlier, and did not allow time enough. Charles did not* aim *at more than reaching Sittingbourne by three, which could not have brought them here by dinner time. They had a very rough passage; he would not have ventured if he had known how bad it would be.*

However, here they are, safe and well, just like their own nice selves, Fanny looking as neat and white this morning as possible, and dear Charles all affectionate, placid, quiet, cheerful, good humour. They are both looking very well, but poor little Cassy is grown extremely thin, and looks poorly. I hope a week's country air and exercise may do her good. I am sorry to say it can be but a week. The baby does not appear so large in proportion as she was, nor quite so pretty, but I have seen very little of her. Cassy was too tired and bewildered just at first to seem to know anybody. We met them in the hall – the women and girl part of us – but before we reached the library she kissed me very affectionately, and has since seemed to recollect me in the same way.

It was quite an evening of confusion, as you may suppose. At first we were all walking about from one part of the house to the other; then came a fresh dinner in the breakfast-room for Charles and his wife, which Fanny and I attended; then we moved into the library, were joined by the dining-room people, were introduced, and so forth; and then we had tea and coffee, which was not over till past 10. Billiards again drew all the odd ones away, and Edward, Charles, the two Fannies, and I sat snugly talking. I shall be glad to have our numbers a little reduced, and by the time you receive this we shall be only a family, though a large family, party. Mr. Lushington goes to-morrow.

Now I must speak of him, *and I like him very much. I am sure he is clever, and a man of taste. He got a volume of Milton last night, and spoke of it with warmth. He is quite an M.P., very smiling, with an exceeding good address and readiness of language. I am rather in love with him. I dare say he is ambitious and insincere. He puts me in mind of Mr. Dundas. He has a wide smiling mouth, and very good teeth, and something the same complexion and nose. He is a much shorter man, with Martha's leave. Does Martha never hear from Mrs. Craven? Is Mrs. Craven never at home?*

We breakfasted in the dining-room to-day, and are now all pretty well dispersed and quiet. Charles and George are gone out shooting together, to Winnigates and Seaton Wood. I asked on purpose to tell Henry. Mr. Lushington and Edwd. are gone some other way. I wish Charles may kill something, but this high wind is against their sport.

Lady Williams is living at the Rose at Sittingbourne; they called upon her yesterday; she cannot live at Sheerness, and as soon as she gets to Sittingbourne is quite well. In return for all your matches, I announce that her brother William is going to marry a Miss Austen, of a Wiltshire family, who say they are related to us.

I talk to Cassy about Chawton; she remembers much, but does not volunteer on the subject. Poor little love! I wish she were not so very Palmery, but it seems stronger than ever. I never knew a wife's family features have such undue influence.

Papa and mamma have not yet made up their mind as to parting with her or not; the chief, indeed the only, difficulty with mamma is a very reasonable one, the child's being very unwilling to leave them. When it was mentioned to her she did not like the idea of it at all. At the same time, she has been suffering so much lately from sea-sickness that her mamma cannot bear to have her much on board this winter. Charles is less inclined to part with her. I do not know how it will end, or what is to determine it. He desires his best love to you, and has not written because he has not been able to decide. They are both very sensible of your kindness on the occasion.

I have made Charles furnish me with something to say about young Kendall. He is going on very well. When he first joined the 'Namur' my brother did not find him forward enough to be what they call put in the office, and therefore placed him under the schoolmaster, but he is very much improved, and goes into the office now every afternoon, still attending school in the morning.

This cold weather comes very fortunately for Edward's nerves, with such a house full; it suits him exactly; he is all alive and cheerful. Poor James, on the contrary, must be running his toes into the fire. I find that Mary Jane Fowle was very near returning with her brother [Tom, also serving on the Namur*] and paying them a visit on board. I forget exactly what hindered her; I believe the Cheltenham scheme. I am glad something did. They are to go to Cheltenham on Monday se'nnight. I don't vouch for their going, you know; it only comes from one of the family.*

Now I think I have written you a good-sized letter, and may deserve whatever I can get in reply. Infinities of love. I must distinguish that of Fanny, senior, who particularly desires to be remembered to you all.

Yours very affectionately,

J. AUSTEN.

Faversham, Oct. 15, 1813.

Miss Austen, Chawton, Alton, Hunts.

Per S. R. Lushington.

[1] Mrs. Charles Austen, née Fanny Palmer.

LXVII

Godmersham Park (Oct. 18).

MY DEAR AUNT CASSANDRA,

I am very much obliged to you for your long letter and for the nice account of Chawton. We are all very glad to hear that the Adams are gone and hope Dame Libscombe will be more happy now with her deaffy child, as she calls it, but I am afraid there is not much chance of her remaining long sole mistress of her house.

I am sorry you had not any better news to send us of our hare, poor little thing! I thought it would not live long in that Pondy House*; I don't wonder that Mary Doe [maid] is very sorry it is dead, because we promised her that if it was alive when we came back to Chawton, we would reward her for her trouble.*

Papa is much obliged to you for ordering the scrubby firs to be cut down; I think he was rather frightened at first about the great oak. Fanny quite believed it, for she exclaimed: 'Dear me, what a pity, how could they be so stupid!' I hope by this time they have put up some hurdles for the sheep, or turned out the cart-horses from the lawn.

Pray tell grandmamma that we have begun getting seeds for her; I hope we shall be able to get her a nice collection, but I am afraid this wet weather is very much against them. How glad I am to hear she has had such good success with her chickens, but I wish there had been more bantams amongst them. I am very sorry to hear of poor Lizzie's fate.

I must now tell you something about our poor people. I believe you know old Mary Croucher, she gets maderer *and* maderer *every day. Aunt Jane has been to see her, but it was on one of her rational days. Poor Will Amos hopes your skewers are doing well; he has left his house in the poor Row, and lives in a barn at Builting. We asked him why he went away, and he said the fleas were so starved when he came back from Chawton that they all flew upon him and* eenermost *eat him up.*

How unlucky it is that the weather is so wet! Poor uncle Charles has come home half drowned every day.

I don't think little Fanny is quite so pretty as she was; one reason is because she wears short petticoats, I believe. I hope Cook is better; she was very unwell the day we went away. Papa has given me half-a-dozen new pencils, which are very good ones indeed; I draw every other day. I hope you go and whip Lucy Chalcraft every night.

Miss Clewes begs me to give her very best respects to you; she is very much obliged to you for your kind inquiries after her. Pray give my duty to grandmamma and love to Miss Floyd [Lloyd]. I remain, my dear Aunt Cassandra, your very affectionate niece,

ELIZTH. KNIGHT.

Thursday. – *I think Lizzy's letter will entertain you. Thank you for yours just received. To-morrow shall be fine if possible. You will be at Guildford before our party set off. They only go to Key Street, as Mr. Street the Purser lives there, and they have promised to dine and sleep with him.*

Cassy's looks are much mended. She agrees pretty well with her cousins, but is not quite happy among them; they are too many and too boisterous for her. I have given her your message, but she said nothing, and did not look as if the idea of going to Chawton again was a pleasant one. They have Edward's carriage to Ospringe.

I think I have just done a good deed – extracted Charles from his wife and children upstairs, and made him get ready to go out shooting, and not keep Mr. Moore waiting any longer.

Mr. and Mrs. Sherer and Joseph dined here yesterday very prettily. Edw. and Geo. were absent – gone for a night to Eastling. The two Fannies went to Canty. in the morning, and took Lou. and Cass. to try on new stays. Harriot and I had a comfortable walk together. She desires her best love to you and kind remembrance to Henry. Fanny's best love also. I fancy there is to be another party to Canty. to-morrow – Mr. and Mrs. Moore and me.

Edward thanks Henry for his letter. We are most happy to hear he is so much better. I depend upon you for letting me know what he wishes as to my staying with him or not; you will be able to find out, I dare say. I had intended to beg you would bring one of my nightcaps with you, in case of my staying, but forgot it when I wrote on Tuesday. Edward is much concerned about his pond: he cannot now doubt the fact of its running out, which he was resolved to do as long as possible.

I suppose my mother will like to have me write to her. I shall try at least.

No; I have never seen the death of Mrs. Crabbe. I have only just been making out from one of his prefaces that he probably was married. It is almost ridiculous. Poor woman! I will comfort him *as well as I can, but I do not undertake to be good to her children. She had better not leave any.*

Edw. and Geo. set off this day week for Oxford. Our party will then be very small, as the Moores will be going about the same time. To enliven us, Fanny proposes spending a few days soon afterwards at Fredville. It will really be a good opportunity, as her father will have a companion. We shall all three go to Wrotham, but Edwd. and I stay only a night perhaps. Love to Mr. Tilson.

Yours very affectionately,

J. A.

Miss Austen, 10 Henrietta St.,

Covent Garden, London.

LXVIII

Godmersham Park: Tuesday (Oct. 26).

MY DEAREST CASSANDRA,

You will have had such late accounts from this place as (I hope) to prevent your expecting a letter from me immediately, as I really do not think I have wherewithal to fabricate one to-day. I suspect this will be brought to you by our nephews; tell me if it is. It is a great pleasure to me to think of you with Henry. I am sure your time must pass most comfortably, and I trust you are seeing improvement in him every day. I shall be most happy to hear from you again. Your Saturday's letter, however, was quite as long and as particular as I could expect. I am not at all in a humour for writing; I must write on till I am.

I congratulate Mr. Tilson, and hope everything is going on well. Fanny and I depend upon knowing what the child's name is to be; as soon as you can tell us. I guess Caroline.

Our gentlemen are all gone to their Sittingbourne meeting, East and West Kent, in one barouche together – rather, West Kent driving East Kent. I believe that is not the usual way of the county. We breakfasted before nine, and do not dine till half-past six on the occasion, so I hope we three shall have a long morning enough.

Mr. Deedes and Sir Brook – I do not care for Sir Brook's being a baronet; I will put Mr. Deedes first because I like him a great deal the best. They arrived together yesterday, for the Bridges' are staying at Sandling, just before dinner; both gentlemen much as they used to be, only growing a little older. They leave us to-morrow.

You were clear of Guildford by half-an-hour, and were winding along the pleasant road to Ripley when the Charleses set off on Friday. I hope we shall have a visit from them at Chawton in the spring or early part of the summer. They seem well inclined. Cassy had recovered her looks almost entirely, and I find they do not consider the 'Namur' as disagreeing with her in general, only when the weather is so rough as to make her sick.

Our Canterbury scheme took place as proposed, and very pleasant it was – Harriot and I and little George within, my brother on the box with the master coachman. I was most happy to find my brother included in the party. It was a great improvement, and he and Harriot and I walked about together very happily, while Mr. Moore took his little boy with him to tailor's and hair-cutter's.

Our chief business was to call on Mrs. Milles, and we had, indeed, so little else to do that we were obliged to saunter about anywhere and go backwards and forwards as much as possible to make out the time and keep ourselves from having two hours to sit with the good lady – a most extraordinary circumstance in a Canterbury morning.

*Old Toke came in while we were paying our visit. I thought of Louisa. Miss Milles was queer as usual, and provided us with plenty to laugh at. She undertook in*three words *to give us the history of Mrs. Scudamore's reconciliation, and then talked on about it for half-an-hour, using such odd expressions, and so foolishly minute, that I could hardly keep my countenance. The death of Wyndham Knatchbull's son will rather supersede the Scudamores. I told her that he was to be buried at Hatch. She had heard, with military honours, at Portsmouth. We may guess how that point will be discussed evening after evening.*

Owing to a difference of clocks the coachman did not bring the carriage so soon as he ought by half-an-hour; anything like a breach of punctuality was a great offence, and Mr. Moore was very angry, which I was rather glad of. I wanted to see him angry; and, though he spoke to his servant in a very loud voice and with a good deal of heat, I was happy to perceive that he did not scold Harriot at all. Indeed, there is nothing to object to in his manners to her, and I do believe that he makes her – or she makes herself – very happy. They do not spoil their boy.

It seems now quite settled that we go to Wrotham on Saturday, the 13th, spend Sunday there, and proceed to London on Monday, as before intended.

I like the plan. I shall be glad to see Wrotham. Harriot is quite as pleasant as ever. We are very comfortable together, and talk over our nephews and nieces occasionally, as may be supposed, and with much unanimity; and I really like Mr. M. better than I expected – see less in him to dislike.

I begin to perceive that you will have this letter to-morrow. It is throwing a letter away to send it by a visitor; there is never convenient time for reading it, and visitor can tell most things as well. I had thought with delight of saving you the postage, but money is dirt. If you do not regret the loss of Oxfordshire and Gloucestershire I will not, though I certainly had wished for your going very much. 'Whatever is, is best.' [adaptation of Alexander Pope's line 'Whatever is, is right']. There has been one infallible Pope in the world.

George Hatton called yesterday, and I saw him, saw him for ten minutes; sat in the same room with him, heard him talk, saw him bow, and was not in raptures. I discerned nothing extraordinary. I should speak of him as a gentlemanlike young man – eh! bien tout est dit. We are expecting the ladies of the family this morning.

How do you like your flounce? We have seen only plain flounces. I hope you have not cut off the train of your bombazin. I cannot reconcile myself to giving them up as morning gowns; they are so very sweet by candlelight. I would rather sacrifice my blue one for that purpose; in short, I do not know and I do not care.

Thursday or Friday is now mentioned from Bath as the day of setting off. The Oxford scheme is given up. They will go directly to Harefield. Fanny does not go to Fredville, not yet at least.

She has had a letter of excuse from Mary Plumptre to-day. The death of Mr. Ripley, their uncle by marriage, and Mr. P.'s very old friend, prevents their receiving her. Poor blind Mrs. Ripley must be felt for, if there is any feeling to be had for love or money.

We have had another of Edward Bridges' Sunday visits. I think the pleasantest part of his married life must be the dinners, and breakfasts, and luncheons, and billiards that he gets in this way at Gm. Poor wretch! he is quite the dregs of the family as to luck.

I long to know whether you are buying stockings or what you are doing. Remember me most kindly to Mde. B. [Bigeon] and Mrs. Perigord. You will get acquainted with my friend, Mr. Philips, and hear him talk from books, and be sure to have something odd happen to you, see somebody that you do not expect, meet with some surprise or other, find some old friend sitting with Henry when you come into the room. Do something clever in that way. Edward and I settled that you went to St. Paul's, Covent Garden, on Sunday. Mrs. Hill will come and see you, or else she won't come and see you and will write instead.

I have had a late account from Steventon, and a baddish one, as far as Ben

[Lefroy] is concerned. He has declined a curacy (apparently highly eligible), which he might have secured against his taking orders; and, upon its being made rather a serious question, says he has not made up his mind as to taking orders so early, and that, if her father makes a point of it, he must give Anna up rather than do what he does not approve. They are going on again at present as before, but it cannot last. Mary says that Anna is very unwilling to go to Chawton and will get home again as soon as she can.

Good-bye. Accept this indifferent letter and think it long and good. Miss Clewes is better for some prescription of Mr. Scudamore's, and, indeed, seems tolerably stout now. I find time in the midst of port and Madeira to think of the fourteen bottles of mead very often.

Yours very affectionately,

J. A.

Lady Elizabeth, her second daughter, and the two Mrs. Finches have just left us; the two latter friendly, and talking, and pleasant as usual.

Harriot and Fanny's best love.

Miss Austen, 10 Henrietta St.,

Covent Garden, London.

LXIX

Godmersham Park: Wednesday (Nov. 3).

MY DEAREST CASSANDRA,

I will keep this celebrated birthday [probably of Princess Sophia] by writing to you, and as my pen seems inclined to write large, I will put my lines very close together. I had but just time to enjoy your letter yesterday before Edward and I set off in the chair for Canty., and I allowed him to hear the chief of it as we went along.

We rejoice sincerely in Henry's gaining ground as he does, and hope there will be weather for him to get out every day this week, as the likeliest way of making him equal to what he plans for the next. If he is tolerably well, the going into Oxfordshire will make him better, by making him happier.

Can it be, that I have not given you the minutiae of Edward's plans? See, here they are: To go to Wrotham on Saturday the 13th, spend Sunday there, and be in town on Monday to dinner, and, if agreeable to Henry, spend one whole day with him, which day is likely to be Tuesday, and so go down to Chawton on Wednesday.

But now I cannot be quite easy without staying a little while with Henry, unless he wishes it otherwise; his illness and the dull time of year together make me feel that it would be horrible of me not to offer to remain with him, and therefore unless you know of any objection, I wish you would tell him with my best love that I shall be most happy to spend ten days or a fortnight in Henrietta St., if he will accept me. I do not offer more than a fortnight, because I shall then have been some time from home; but it will be a great pleasure to be with him, as it always is. I have the less regret and scruple on your account, because I shall see you for a day and a-half, and because you will have Edward for at least a week. My scheme is to take Bookham in my way home for a few days, and my hope that Henry will be so good as to send me some part of the way thither. I have a most kind repetition of Mrs. Cooke's two or three dozen invitations, with the offer of meeting me anywhere in one of her airings.

Fanny's cold is much better. By dosing and keeping her room on Sunday, she got rid of the worst of it, but I am rather afraid of what this day may do for her; she is gone to Canty. with Miss Clewes, Liz., and Marianne., and it is but roughish weather for any one in a tender state. Miss Clewes has been going to Canty. ever since her return, and it is now just accomplishing.

Edward and I had a delightful morning for our drive there, *I enjoyed it thoroughly; but the day turned off before we were ready, and we came home in some rain and the apprehension of a great deal. It has not done us any harm, however. He went to inspect the gaol, as a visiting magistrate, and took me with him. I was gratified, and went through all the feelings which people must go through, I think, in visiting such a building. We paid no other visits, only walked about snugly together and shopped. I bought a concert ticket and a sprig of flowers for my old age.*

To vary the subject from gay to grave with inimitable address, I shall now tell you something of the Bath party – and still a Bath party they are, for a fit of the gout came on last week. The accounts of Lady B. are as good as can be under such a circumstance; Dr. P. says it appears a good sort of gout, and her spirits are better than usual, but as to her coming away, it is of course all uncertainty. I have very little doubt of Edward's going down to Bath, if they have not left it when he is in Hampshire; if he does, he will go on from Steventon, and then return direct to London, without coming back to Chawton. This detention does not suit his feelings. It may be rather a good thing, however, that Dr. P. should see Lady B. with the gout on her. Harriot was quite wishing for it.

The day seems to improve. I wish my pen would, too.

Sweet Mr. Ogle. I dare say he sees all the panoramas for nothing, has free admittance everywhere; he is so delightful! Now, you need not see anybody else.

I am glad to hear of our being likely to have a peep at Charles and Fanny at Christmas, but do not force poor Cass. to stay if she hates it. You have done very right as to Mrs. F. A. Your tidings of S. and S. give me pleasure. I have never seen it advertised.

Harriot, in a letter to Fanny to-day, inquires whether they sell cloths for pelisses at Bedford House, and, if they do, will be very much obliged to you to desire them to send her down patterns, with the width and prices; they may go from Charing Cross almost any day in the week, but if it is a ready money *house it will not do, for the* bru *of* feu *[1] the Archbishop says she cannot pay for it immediately. Fanny and I suspect they do not deal in the article.*

The Sherers, I believe, are now really going to go; Joseph has had a bed here the two last nights, and I do not know whether this is not the day of moving. Mrs. Sherer called yesterday to take leave. The weather looks worse again.

We dine at Chilham Castle to-morrow, and I expect to find some amusement, but more from the concert the next day, as I am sure of seeing several that I want to see. We are to meet a party from Goodnestone, Lady B. [wife of the 4th Sir Brook Bridges], Miss Hawley, and Lucy Foote, and I am to meet Mrs. Harrison [sister of Anne Lefroy and aunt of Ben], and we are to talk about Ben and Anna. 'My dear Mrs. Harrison,' I shall say, 'I am afraid the young man has some of your family madness, and though there often appears to be something of madness in Anna too, I think she inherits more of it from her mother's family than from ours.' That is what I shall say, and I think she will find it difficult to answer me.

I took up your letter again to refresh me, being somewhat tired and was struck with the prettiness of the hand: it is really a very pretty hand now and then – so small and so neat! I wish I could get as much into a sheet of paper. [2] Another time I will take two days to make a letter in: it is fatiguing to write a whole long one at once. I hope to hear from you again on Sunday and again on Friday, the day before we move. On Monday, I suppose, you will be going to Streatham, to see quiet Mr. Hill and eat very bad baker's bread.

A fall in bread by-the-bye. I hope my mother's bill next week will show it. I have had a very comfortable letter from her, one of her foolscap sheets quite full of little home news. Anna was there the first of the two days. An Anna sent away and an Anna fetched are different things. This will be an excellent time for Ben to pay his visit, now that we, the formidables, are absent.

I did not mean to eat, but Mr. Johncock [butler] has brought in the tray, so I must. I am all alone. Edward is gone into his woods. At this present time I have five tables, eight-and-twenty chairs, and two fires all to myself.

Miss Clewes is to be invited to go to the concert with us; there will be my brother's place and ticket for her, as he cannot go. He and the other connections of the Cages are to meet at Milgate that very day, to consult about a proposed alteration of the Maidstone road, in which the Cages are very much interested. Sir Brook comes here in the morning, and they are to be joined by Mr. Deedes at Ashford. The loss of the concert will be no great evil to the Squire. We shall be a party of three ladies therefore, and to meet three ladies.

What a convenient carriage Henry's is, to his friends in general! Who has it next? I am glad William's [Henry's manservant] going is voluntary, and on no worse grounds. An inclination for the country is a venial fault. He has more of Cowper than of Johnson in him – fonder of tame hares and blank verse than of the full tide of human existence at Charing Cross.

Oh! I have more of such sweet flattery from Miss Sharp. She is an excellent kind friend. I am read and admired in Ireland, too. There is a Mrs. Fletcher, the wife of a judge, an old lady, and very good and very clever, who is all curiosity to know about me – what I am like, and so forth. I am not known to her by name, *however. This comes through Mrs. Carrick, not through Mrs. Gore. You are quite out there.*

I do not despair of having my picture in the Exhibition at last – all white and red, with my head on one side; or perhaps I may marry young Mr. D'Arblay [Fanny Burney's son]. I suppose in the meantime I shall owe dear Henry a great deal of money for printing, &c.

I hope Mrs. Fletcher will indulge herself with S. and S. If I am *to stay in H. S. [Henrietta Street], and if you should be writing home soon, I wish you would be so good as to give a hint of it, for I am not likely to write there again these ten days, having written yesterday.*

Fanny has set her heart upon its being a Mr. Brett who is going to marry a Miss Dora Best, of this country. I dare say Henry has no objection. Pray, where did the boys sleep?

The Deedes come here on Monday to stay till Friday, so that we shall end with a flourish the last canto. They bring Isabella and one of the grown-ups, and will come in for a Canty. ball on Thursday. I shall be glad to see them. Mrs. Deedes and I must talk rationally together, I suppose.

Edward does not write to Henry, because of my writing so often. God bless you. I shall be so glad to see you again, and I wish you many happy returns of this day. Poor Lord Howard! How he does cry about it!

Yours very truly,

J. A.

Miss Austen, 10 Henrietta St.,

Covent Garden, London.

1. This expression completely puzzles me. It is clearly written 'Bru of feu' or 'face,' and may have been some joke in connection with the fact that 'Harriot' was the daughter-in-law of Archbishop Moore, but, if so, the joke is lost. [In French *bru* is 'daughter in law', while one of the many meanings of *feu* is 'deceased'.]

2. I cannot pass this paragraph over without remarking that it is hardly possible to imagine anything neater or prettier than Jane's own hand. Most of her letters are beautifully written, and the MS. of her 'Lady Susan' remarkably so.

LXX

Godmersham Park: Saturday (Nov. 6).

MY DEAR CASSANDRA,

Having half-an-hour before breakfast (very, snug, in my own room, lovely morning, excellent fire – fancy me!) I will give you some account of the last two days. And yet, what is there to be told? I shall get foolishly minute unless I cut the matter short.

We met only the Bretons at Chilham Castle, besides a Mr. and Mrs. Osborne and a Miss Lee staying in the house, and were only fourteen altogether. My brother and Fanny thought it the pleasantest party they had ever known there, and I was very well entertained by bits and scraps. I had long wanted to see Dr. Breton, and his wife amuses me very much with her affected refinement and elegance. Miss Lee I found very conversable; she admires Crabbe as she ought. She is at an age of reason, ten years older than myself at least. She was at the famous ball at Chilham Castle, so of course you remember her.

By-the-bye, as I must leave off being young, I find many douceurs *in being a sort of* chaperon, *for I am put on the sofa near the fire, and can drink as much wine as I like. We had music in the evening: Fanny and Miss Wildman played, and Mr. James Wildman sat close by and listened, or pretended to listen.*

Yesterday was a day of dissipation all through: first came Sir Brook to dissipate us before breakfast; then there was a call from Mr. Sherer, then a regular morning visit from Lady Honeywood in her way home from Eastwell; then Sir Brook and Edward set off; then we dined (five in number) at half-past four; then we had coffee; and at six Miss Clewes, Fanny, and I drove away. We had a beautiful night for our frisks. We were earlier than we need have been, but after a time Lady B. and her two companions appeared – we had kept places for them; and there we sat, all six in a row, under a side wall, I between Lucy Foote and Miss Clewes.

Lady B. was much what I expected; I could not determine whether she was rather handsome or very plain. I liked her for being in a hurry to have the concert over and get away, and for getting away at last with a great deal of decision and promptness, not waiting to compliment and dawdle and fuss about seeing dear Fanny, *who was half the evening in another part of the room with her friends the Plumptres. I am growing too minute, so I will go to breakfast.*

When the concert was over, Mrs. Harrison and I found each other out, and had a very comfortable little complimentary friendly chat. She is a sweet woman – still quite a sweet woman in herself, and so like her sister! I could almost have thought I was speaking to Mrs. Lefroy. She introduced me to her daughter, whom I think pretty, but most dutifully inferior to la Mère Beauté. *The Faggs and the Hammonds were there – Wm. Hammond the only young man of renown.* Miss *looked very handsome but I prefer her little smiling flirting sister Julia.*

I was just introduced at last to Mary Plumptre, but should hardly know her again. She was delighted with me, *however, good enthusiastic soul! And Lady B. found me handsomer than she expected, so you see I am not so very bad as you might think for.*

It was 12 before we reached home. We were all dog-tired, but pretty well to-day: Miss Clewes says she has not caught cold, and Fanny's does not seem worse. I was so tired that I began to wonder how I should get through the ball next Thursday, but there will be so much more variety then in walking about, and probably so much less heat, that perhaps I may not feel it more. My China crape is still kept for the ball. Enough of the concert.

I had a letter from Mary [Mrs James Austen] yesterday. They travelled down to Cheltenham last Monday very safely, and are certainly to be there a month. Bath is still Bath. The H. Bridges' must quit them early next week, and Louisa seems not quite to despair of their all moving together, but to those who see at a distance there appears no chance of it. Dr. Parry does not want to keep Lady B. at Bath when she can once move. That is lucky. You will see poor Mr. Evelyn's death.

Since I wrote last, my 2nd edit. has stared me in the face. Mary tells me that Eliza [Fowle] means to buy it. I wish she may. It can hardly depend upon any more Fyfield Estates [estates owned by the Fowle family which had been put up for sale]. I cannot help hoping that many *will feel themselves obliged to buy it. I shall not mind imagining it a disagreeable duty to them, so as they do it. Mary heard before she left home that it was very much admired at Cheltenham, and that it was given to Miss Hamilton. It is pleasant to have such a respectable writer named. I cannot tire* you, *I am sure, on this subject, or I would apologise.*

What weather, and what news [the gratitude shown by the Houses of Parliament to the Marquis of Wellington for the success of the battle of Vitoria]! We have enough to do to admire them both. I hope you derive your full share of enjoyment from each.

I have extended my lights and increased my acquaintance a good deal within these two days. Lady Honeywood you know; I did not sit near enough to be a perfect judge, but I thought her extremely pretty, and her manners have all the recommendations of ease and good humour and unaffectedness; and, going about with four horses and nicely dressed herself, she is altogether a perfect sort of woman.

Oh, and I saw Mr. Gipps last night – the useful Mr. Gipps, whose attentions came in as acceptably to us in handing us to the carriage, for want of a better man, as they did to Emma Plumptre. I thought him rather a good-looking little man.

I long for your letter to-morrow, particularly that I may know my fate as to London. My first wish is that Henry should really choose what he likes best; I shall certainly not be sorry if he does not want me. Morning church tomorrow; I shall come back with impatient feelings.

The Sherers are gone, but the Pagets [Revd William Paget and Mrs Paget] are not come; we shall therefore have Mr. S. again. Mr. Paget acts like an unsteady man. Dr. Mant, however, gives him a very good character; what is wrong is to be imputed to the lady. I dare say the house likes female government.

I have a nice long black and red letter from Charles, but not communicating much that I did not know. [Cross writing saved paper and postage. The writing across the letter was in red ink].

There is some chance of a good ball next week, as far as females go. Lady Bridges may perhaps be there with some Knatchbulls. Mrs. Harrison, perhaps, with Miss Oxenden and the Miss Papillons; and if Mrs. Harrison, then Lady Fagg will come.

The shades of evening are descending, and I resume my interesting narrative. Sir Brook and my brother came back about four, and Sir Brook almost immediately set forward again to Goodnestone. We are to have Edwd. B. tomorrow, to pay us another Sunday's visit – the last, for more reasons than one; they all come home on the same day that we go. The Deedes do not come till Tuesday; Sophia is to be the comer. She is a disputable beauty that I want much to see. Lady Eliz. Hatton and Annamaria called here this morning. Yes, they called; but I do not think I can say anything more about them. They came, and they sat, and they went.

Sunday. – *Dearest Henry! What a turn he has for being ill, and what a thing bile is! This attack has probably been brought on in part by his previous confinement and anxiety; but, however it came, I hope it is going fast, and that you will be able to send a very good account of him on Tuesday. As I hear on Wednesday, of course I shall not expect to hear again on Friday. Perhaps a letter to Wrotham would not have an ill effect.*

We are to be off on Saturday before the post comes in, as Edward takes his own horses all the way. He talks of 9 o'clock. We shall bait at Lenham.

Excellent sweetness of you to send me such a nice long letter; it made its appearance, with one from my mother, soon after I and my impatient feelings walked in. How glad I am that I did what I did! I was only afraid that you *might think the offer superfluous, but you have set my heart at ease. Tell Henry that I* will *stay with him, let it be ever so disagreeable to him.*

Oh, dear me! I have not time on paper for half that I want to say. There have been two letters from Oxford [Jane's nephews Edward and George were students at St John's College] – one from George yesterday. They got there very safely – Edwd. two hours behind the coach, having lost his way in leaving London. George writes cheerfully and quietly; hopes to have Utterson's rooms soon; went to lecture on Wednesday, states some of his expenses, and concludes with saying, 'I am afraid I shall be poor.' I am glad he thinks about it so soon. I believe there is no private tutor yet chosen, but my brother is to hear from Edwd. on the subject shortly.

You, and Mrs. H. [Heathcote], and Catherine, and Alethea going about together in Henry's carriage seeing sights – I am not used to the idea of it yet. All that you are to see of Streatham, seen already! Your Streatham and my Bookham may go hang. The prospect of being taken down to Chawton by Henry perfects the plan to me. I was in hopes of your seeing some illuminations, and you have *seen them. 'I thought you would come, and you* did *come.' I am sorry* he *[Frank] is not to* come *from the Baltic sooner. Poor Mary!*

My brother has a letter from Louisa to-day of an unwelcome nature; they are to spend the winter at Bath. It was just decided on. Dr. Parry wished it, not from thinking the water necessary to Lady B., but so that he might be better able to judge how far his treatment of her, which is totally different from anything she had been used to, is right; and I suppose he will not mind having a few more of her Ladyship's guineas. His system is a lowering one. He took twelve ounces of blood from her when the gout appeared, and forbids wine, &c. Hitherto, the plan agrees with her. She *is very well satisfied to stay, but it is a sore disappointment to Louisa and Fanny.*

The H. Bridges leave them on Tuesday, and they mean to move into a smaller house; you may guess how Edward feels. There can be no doubt of his going to Bath now; I should not wonder if he brought Fanny Cage back with him.

You shall hear from me once more, some day or other.

Yours very affectionately,

J. A.

We do not like Mr. Hampson's scheme.

Miss Austen, 10 Henrietta Street,
Covent Garden, London.

1814

I imagine that the sisters were but seldom separated in 1814, since I have but five letters belonging to that year. The first two are from Henrietta Street, Henry Austen's house, and were written in March. My mother had accompanied my grandfather to Chawton and Bath in February, where her grandmother, Lady Bridges, was staying for the benefit of the waters, and on their return home they paid Henry Austen a visit, arriving on Saturday, the 5th, and staying till Wednesday, the 9th of March. It was very cold weather, for in the winter and spring 1813–14 there were seventeen weeks of frost consecutively, and it was recorded as the hardest winter which had been known for twenty years. The weather, however, did not prevent the party in Henrietta Street from amusing themselves to the best of their ability. The visitors from Bath arrived shortly before five, and after dinner 'Aunt Jane' and her niece were escorted by Henry Austen to Drury Lane, to see Mr. Kean in 'Shylock.' Of this evening Aunt Jane says (Letter 71), 'We were quite satisfied with Kean,' whilst her younger companion notes in her diary, 'We were delighted.' In this same letter is the remark, 'Young Wyndham accepts the invitation. He is such a nice, gentleman-like, unaffected sort of young man that I think he may do for Fanny.' I think this must mean my uncle Dr. Knatchbull; the description does not agree with that which Mrs. Knight (Catherine Knatchbull) gives of her 'nephew Wyndham' in her letter to my father (see Appendix), and moreover, this son of 'old' Wyndham Knatchbull would seem to have died in 1813 (see Letter 68), unless there were two sons besides those two given in the Baronetage who survived their father's death in 1833.

This letter, continued on the two following days, tells us that on Sunday 'Fanny and I' drove in the park. I am happy to be able to narrate the fact, gathered from the pocketbooks, that they previously went to church at St. Paul's, Covent Garden. They 'could not stir in the carriage' on account of the snow, but somehow or other managed to get to Covent Garden Theatre on Monday night, of which the letter duly informs us, corroborated by the pocket-book, which says in addition that 'Miss Stephens' voice was delightful.'

In this letter is an allusion to a lawsuit in which my grandfather, Edward Austen, was involved, in consequence of a claim made upon his Chawton estates by a person of the name of Baverstoke. I do not know the exact circumstances, but believe the claim was founded upon the alleged insufficient barring of an entail. There is a curious story connected with this lawsuit, to the effect that an old, long since deceased Mr. Knight appeared twice or thrice in a dream to the claimant, and informed him that he was the rightful owner of Chawton. Whether this was the cause of the lawsuit or not, I cannot say, or whether the deceased gentleman took any further steps after the matter had been settled, but in any case it harassed Mr. Austen from 1814 (in the October of which year he was formally served with a writ of ejectment) to 1817, and he then compromised it by the payment of a certain sum of money, so that the 'opponent' could hardly have 'knocked under' in 1814, as 'Jane' supposed. On Tuesday was another night of theatrical dissipation, into which the party appear to have been led by Mr. John Pemberton Plumptre, who seems to have been much with them, and between whom and his niece Fanny Henry Austen thought he had discovered a 'decided attachment.' On Wednesday Edward Austen and his daughter betook themselves to Godmersham, and the next news I have of Jane is in my mother's diary for April, in which it appears that she went with her father and two eldest brothers, accompanied by Miss Clewes and her pupils, Louisa and Marianne, to Chawton Great House, on the 22nd, and that 'Aunt Cass. and Jane walked up in the evening.' 'The Cottage' and the 'Great House' lived on their usual intimate terms until June 20, when the Godmersham party went home. Every day the diary duly informs us that 'the Cottage dined here,' or 'papa and I dined at the Cottage,' 'Aunt Jane drank tea here,' 'Aunt Jane and I spent a bustling hour or two shopping in Alton'; but I can collect no more than that, as usual, the aunt and niece were much together; that the Bridges party, from Bath, came to spend a few days; that the illuminations for the peace took place at that time, and that 'Aunt Jane' seems to have taken part in all the proceedings of her relations. Her next letter (seventy-three) to her sister Cassandra was written during this visit of Godmersham to Chawton, under date June 13, Cassandra being with her brother Henry in Henrietta Street. There is nothing to require notice in this or the next letter, on June 20, and the last of 1814 is written on August 14, from Hans Place, when Jane had exchanged places with her sister. 'Tilson's Bank' was in Henrietta Street, which accounts for visits thereto on the part of Henry Austen being mentioned whilst he had a house elsewhere. But there must have been a dwelling-house attached to the bank, and it would seem as if he occupied this between his living in Sloane Street and moving to Hans Place.

LXXI

Henrietta Street: Saturday (March 5).
MY DEAR CASSANDRA,

Do not be angry with me for beginning another letter to you. I have read the 'Corsair,' mended my petticoat, and have nothing else to do. Getting out is impossible. It is a nasty day for everybody. Edward's spirits will be wanting sunshine, and here is nothing but thickness and sleet; and though these two rooms are delightfully warm, I fancy it is very cold abroad.

Young Wyndham [Knatchbull] accepts the invitation. He is such a nice, gentlemanlike, unaffected sort of young man, that I think he may do for Fanny; has a sensible, quiet look, which one likes. Our fate with Mrs. L. [Latouche] and Miss E. [East] is fixed for this day se'nnight. A civil note is come from Miss H. Moore [Harriet, Henry's friend], to apologise for not returning my visit to-day, and ask us to join a small party this evening. Thank ye, but we shall be better engaged.

I was speaking to Mde. B. this morning about a boiled loaf, when it appeared that her master has no raspberry jam; she *has some, which of course she is determined he shall have; but cannot you bring a pot when you come?*

Sunday. – *I find a little time before breakfast for writing. It was considerably past four when they arrived yesterday, the roads were so* very bad! As it was, they had four horses from Cranford Bridge. Fanny was miserably cold at first, but they both seem well.

No possibility of Edwd.'s writing. His opinion, however, inclines against a second prosecution; he thinks it would be a vindictive measure. He might think differently, perhaps, on the spot. But things must take their chance.[1]

We were quite satisfied with Kean. I cannot imagine better acting, but the part was too short; and, excepting him and Miss Smith, and she did not quite answer my expectation, the parts were ill filled and the play heavy. We were too much tired to stay for the whole of 'Illusion' ('Nour-jahad'), which has three acts; there is a great deal of finery and dancing in it, but I think little merit. Elliston was 'Nour-jahad,' but it is a solemn sort of part, not at all calculated for his powers. There was nothing of the best Elliston about him. I might not have known him but for his voice.

A grand thought has struck me as to our gowns. This six weeks' mourning [for the Queen's brother] makes so great a difference that I shall not go to Miss Hare till you can come and help choose yourself, unless you particularly wish the contrary. It may be hardly worth while perhaps to have the gowns so expensively made up. We may buy a cap or a veil instead; but we can talk more of this together.

Henry is just come down; he seems well, his cold does not increase. I expected to have found Edward seated at a table writing to Louisa, but I was first. Fanny I left fast asleep. She was doing about last night when I went to sleep, a little after one. I am most happy to find there were but five shirts. She thanks you for your note, and reproaches herself for not having written to you, but I assure her there was no occasion.

The accounts are not capital of Lady B. Upon the whole, I believe, Fanny liked Bath very well. They were only out three evenings, to one play and each of the rooms. Walked about a good deal, and saw a good deal of the Harrisons and Wildmans. All the Bridges are likely to come away together, and Louisa will probably turn off at Dartford to go to Harriot. Edward is quite [MS. torn].

Now we are come from church, and all going to write. Almost everybody was in mourning last night, but my brown gown did very well. Genl. Chowne was introduced to me; he has not much remains of Frederick. This young Wyndham does not come after all; a very long and very civil note of excuse is arrived. It makes one moralise upon the ups and downs of this life.

I have determined to trim my lilac sarsenet with black satin ribbon just as my China crape is, 6d. width at the bottom, 3d. or 4d., at top. Ribbon trimmings are all the fashion at Bath, and I dare say the fashions of the two places are alike enough in that point to content me. With this addition it will be a very useful gown, happy to go anywhere.

Henry has this moment said that he likes M.P. [Mansfield Park] better and better; he is in the third volume. I believe now he has changed his mind as to *foreseeing the end; he said yesterday, at least, that he defied anybody to say whether H. C. [Henry Crawford] would be reformed, or would forget Fanny in a fortnight.*

I shall like to see Kean again excessively, and to see him with you too. It appeared to me as if there were no fault in him anywhere; and in his scene with 'Tubal' there was exquisite acting.

Edward has had a correspondence with Mr. Wickham on the Baigent business [the case of a Chawton boy who was on trial at Winchester for stabbing another boy], and has been showing me some letters enclosed by Mr. W. from a friend of his, a lawyer, whom he had consulted about it, and whose opinion is for *the prosecution for assault, supposing the boy is acquitted on the first, which he rather expects. Excellent letters; and I am sure he must be an excellent man. They are such thinking, clear, considerate letters as Frank might have written. I long to know who he is, but the name is always torn off. He was consulted only as a friend. When Edwd. gave me* his *opinions against the second prosecution he had not read this letter, which was waiting for him here. Mr. W. is to be on the grand jury. This business must hasten an intimacy between his family and my brothers.*

Fanny cannot answer your question about button-holes till she gets home.

I have never told you, but soon after Henry and I began our journey he said, talking of yours, that he should desire you to come post at his expense, and added something of the carriage meeting you at Kingston. He has said nothing about it since.

Now I have just read Mr. Wickham's letter, by which it appears that the letters of his friend were sent to my brother quite confidentially, therefore don't tell. By his expression, this friend must be one of the judges.

A cold day, but bright and clear. I am afraid your planting can hardly have begun. I am sorry to hear that there has been a rise in tea. I do not mean to pay Twining till later in the day, when we may order a fresh supply. I long to know something of the mead, and how you are off for a cook.

Monday. – *Here's a day! The ground covered with snow! What is to become of us? We were to have walked out early to near shops, and had the carriage for the more distant. Mr. Richard Snow is dreadfully fond of us. I dare say he has stretched himself out at Chawton too.*

Fanny and I went into the park yesterday and drove about, and were very much entertained; and our dinner and evening went off very well. Messrs. J. Plumptre and J. Wildman called while we were out, and we had a glimpse of them both, and of G. Hatton too, in the park. I *could not produce a single acquaintance.*

By a little convenient listening, I now know that Henry wishes to go to Gm. for a few days before Easter, and has indeed promised to do it. This being the case, there can be no time for your remaining in London after your return from Adlestrop. You must not put off your coming therefore; and it occurs to me that, instead of my coming here again from Streatham, it will be better for you to join me there. It is a great comfort to have got at the truth. Henry finds he cannot set off for Oxfordshire before the Wednesday, which will be the 23rd; but we shall not have too many days together here previously. I shall write to Catherine [Hill] very soon.

Well, we have been out as far as Coventry St.; Edwd. escorted us there and back to Newton's, where he left us, and I brought Fanny safe home. It was snowing the whole time. We have given up all idea of the carriage. Edward and Fanny stay another day, and both seem very well pleased to do so. Our visit to the Spencers is, of course, put off.

Edwd. heard from Louisa this morning. Her mother does not get better, and Dr. Parry talks of her beginning the waters again; this will be keeping them longer in Bath, and of course is not palatable.

You cannot think how much my ermine tippet is admired both by father and daughter. It was a noble gift.

Perhaps you have not heard that Edward has a good chance of escaping his lawsuit. His opponent 'knocks under.' The terms of agreement are not quite settled.

We are to see 'The Devil to Pay' to-night. I expect to be very much amused. Excepting Miss Stephens, I daresay 'Artaxerxes' will be very tiresome.

A great many pretty caps in the windows of Cranbourn Alley. I hope when you come we shall both be tempted. I have been ruining myself in black satin ribbon with a proper pearl edge, and now I am trying to draw it up into kind of roses instead of putting it in plain double plaits.

Tuesday. – *My dearest Cassandra, – In ever so many hurries I acknowledge the receipt of your letter last night, just before we set off for Covent Garden. I have no mourning come, but it does not signify. This very moment has Richd. [servant] put it on the table. I have torn it open and read your note. Thank you, thank you, thank you.*

Edwd. is amazed at the sixty-four trees. He desires his love, and gives you notice of the arrival of a study table for himself. It ought to be at Chawton this week. He begs you to be so good as to have it inquired for and fetched by the cart, but wishes it not to be unpacked till he is on the spot himself. It may be put in the hall.

Well, Mr. Hampson dined here, and all that. I was very tired of 'Artaxerxes,' highly amused with the farce, and, in an inferior way, with the pantomime that followed. Mr. J. Plumptre joined in the latter part of the evening, walked home with us, ate some soup, and is very earnest for our going to Covent Garden again to-night to see Miss Stephens in the 'Farmer's Wife.' He is to try for a box. I do not particularly wish him to succeed. I have had enough for the present. Henry dines to-day with Mr. Spencer.

Yours very affectionately,

J. AUSTEN.
Miss Austen, Chawton.
By favour of Mr. Gray.

[1] There is no clue to the matter to which this refers.

LXXII

Henrietta St.: Wednesday (March 9).

Well, we went to the play again last night, and as we were out a great part of the morning too, shopping, and seeing the Indian jugglers, I am very glad to be quiet now till dressing time. We are to dine at the Tilsons', and to-morrow at Mr. Spencer's.

We had not done breakfast yesterday when Mr. J. Plumptre appeared to say that he had secured a box. Henry asked him to dine here, which I fancy he was very happy to do, and so at five o'clock we four sat down to table together while the master of the house was preparing for going out himself. The 'Farmer's Wife' is a musical thing in three acts, and, as Edward was steady in not staying for anything more, we were at home before ten.

Fanny and Mr. J. P. are delighted with Miss S. [Stephens], and her merit in singing is, I dare say, very great; that she gave me *no pleasure is no reflection upon her, nor, I hope, upon myself, being what Nature made me on that article. All that I am sensible of in Miss S. is a pleasing person and no skill in acting. We had Mathews, Liston, and Emery; of course, some amusement.*

Our friends were off before half-past eight this morning, and had the prospect of a heavy cold journey before them. I think they both liked their visit very much. I am sure Fanny did. Henry sees decided attachment between her and his new acquaintance.

I have a cold, too, as well as my mother and Martha. Let it be a generous emulation between us which can get rid of it first.

I wear my gauze gown to-day, long sleeves and all. I shall see how they succeed, but as yet I have no reason to suppose long sleeves are allowable. I have lowered the bosom, especially at the corners, and plaited black satin ribbon round the top. Such will be my costume of vine-leaves and paste.

Prepare for a play the very first evening, I rather think Covent Garden, to see Young, in 'Richard.' I have answered for your little companion's [Cassy, daughter of Charles Austen] being conveyed to Keppel St. immediately. I have never yet been able to get there myself, but hope I shall soon.

What cruel weather this is! and here is Lord Portsmouth married, too, to Miss Hanson. [1]

Henry has finished 'Mansfield Park' and his approbation has not lessened. He found the last half of the last volume extremely interesting.

I suppose my mother recollects that she gave me no money for paying Brecknell and Twining, and my *funds will not supply enough.*

We are home in such good time that I can finish my letter to-night, which will be better than getting up to do it to-morrow, especially as, on account of my cold, which has been very heavy in my head this evening, I rather think of lying in bed later than usual. I would not but be well enough to go to Hertford St. [where Henry's friends the Spencers lived] on any account.

We met only Genl. Chowne to-day, who has not much to say for himself. I was ready to laugh at the remembrance of Frederick, and such a different Frederick as we chose to fancy him to the real Christopher!

Mrs. Tilson had long sleeves, too, and she assured me that they are worn in the evening by many. I was glad to hear this. She dines here, I believe, next Tuesday.

On Friday we are to be snug with only Mr. Barlowe and an evening of business. I am so pleased that the mead is brewed. Love to all. I have written to Mrs. Hill, and care for nobody.

Yours affectionately,

J. AUSTEN.

Miss Austen, Chawton.

By favour of Mr. Gray.

1. His second wife. He died in 1853, and was succeeded by his brother, the father of the present earl.

LXXIII

Chawton: Tuesday (June 13).

MY DEAREST CASSANDRA,

Fanny takes my mother to Alton this morning, which gives me an opportunity of sending you a few lines without any other trouble than that of writing them.

This is a delightful day in the country, and I hope not much too hot for town. Well, you had a good journey, I trust, and all that, and not rain enough to spoil your bonnet. It appeared so likely to be a wet evening that I went up to the Gt. House between three and four, and dawdled away an hour very comfortably, though Edwd. was not very brisk. The air was clearer in the evening and he was better. We all five walked together into the kitchen garden and along the Gosport road, and they drank tea with us.

You will be glad to hear that G. Turner [farm labourer] has another situation, *something in the cow line, near Rumsey, and he wishes to move immediately, which is not likely to be inconvenient to anybody.*

The new nurseryman at Alton comes this morning to value the crops in the garden.

The only letter to-day is from Mrs. Cooke to me. They do not leave home till July, and want me to come to them, according to my promise. And, after considering everything, I have resolved on going. My companions promote it. I will not go, however, till after Edward is gone, that he may feel he has a somebody to give memorandums to, to the last. I must give up all help from his carriage, of course. And, at any rate, it must be such an excess of expense that I have quite made up my mind to it and do not mean to care.

I have been thinking of Triggs [game keeper at Chawton] and the chair, you may be sure, but I know it will end in posting. They will meet me at Guildford.

In addition to their standing claims on me they admire 'Mansfield Park' exceedingly. Mr. Cooke says 'it is the most sensible novel he ever read,' and the manner in which I treat the clergy delights them very much. Altogether, I must go, and I want you to join me there when your visit in Henrietta St. is over. Put this into your capacious head.

Take care of yourself, and do not be trampled to death in running after the Emperor [Alexander I of Russia]. The report in Alton yesterday was that they would certainly travel this road either to or from Portsmouth. I long to know what this bow of the Prince's will produce.

I saw Mrs. Andrews yesterday. Mrs. Browning had seen her before. She is very glad to send an Elizabeth.

Miss Benn continues the same. Mr. Curtis [apothecary], however, saw her yesterday and said her hand was going on as well as possible. Accept our best love.

Yours very affectionately,
J. AUSTEN.
Miss Austen, 10 Henrietta Street,
By favour of Mr. Gray.

LXXIV

Thursday (June 23).
DEAREST CASSANDRA,

I received your pretty letter while the children were drinking tea with us, as Mr. Louch [Henry Austen's banking partner] was so obliging as to walk over with it. Your good account of everybody made us very happy.

I heard yesterday from Frank. When he began his letter he hoped to be here on Monday, but before it was ended he had been told that the naval review would not take place till Friday, which would probably occasion him some delay, as he cannot get some necessary business of his own attended to while Portsmouth is in such a bustle. I hope Fanny has seen the Emperor, and then I may fairly wish them all away. I go to-morrow, and hope for some delays and adventures.

My mother's wood is brought in, but, by some mistake, no bavins [firewood]. She must therefore buy some.

Henry at White's [club in London]! Oh, what a Henry! I do not know what to wish as to Miss B., so I will hold my tongue and my wishes.

Sackree and the children set off yesterday, and have not been returned back upon us. They were all very well the evening before. We had handsome presents from the Gt. House yesterday – a ham and the four leeches. Sackree has left some shirts of her master's at the school, which, finished or unfinished, she begs to have sent by Henry and Wm. Mr. Hinton [who lived at Chawton Lodge] is expected home soon, which is a good thing for the shirts.

We have called upon Miss Dusantoy and Miss Papillon, and been very pretty. Miss D. has a great idea of being Fanny Price – she and her youngest sister together, who is named Fanny.

Miss Benn has drank tea with the Prowtings, and, I believe, comes to us this evening. She has still a swelling about the fore-finger and a little discharge, and does not seem to be on the point of a perfect cure, but her spirits are good, and she will be most happy, I believe, to accept any invitation. The Clements are gone to Petersfield to look.

Only think of the Marquis of Granby [the infant heir of the Duke of Rutland] being dead. I hope, if it please Heaven there should be another son, they will have better sponsors and less parade.

I certainly do not wish *that Henry should think again of getting me to town. I would rather return straight from Bookham; but, if he really does propose it, I cannot say No to what will be so kindly intended. It could be but for a few days, however, as my mother would be quite disappointed by my exceeding the fortnight which I now talk of as the outside – at least, we could not both remain longer away comfortably.*

The middle of July is Martha's time, as far as she has any time. She has left it to Mrs. Craven to fix the day. I wish she could get her money paid, for I fear her going at all depends upon that.

Instead of Bath the Deans Dundases have taken a house at Clifton – Richmond Terrace – and she is as glad of the change as even you and I should be, or almost. She will now be able to go on from Berks and visit them without any fears from heat.

This post has brought me a letter from Miss Sharpe. Poor thing! she has been suffering indeed, but is now in a comparative state of comfort. She is at Sir W. P.'s [William Pilkington], in Yorkshire, with the children, and there is no appearance of her quitting them. Of course we lose the pleasure of seeing her here. She writes highly of Sir Wm. I do so want him to marry her. There is a Dow. Lady P. presiding there to make it all right. The Man *is the same; but she does not mention what he is by profession or trade. She does not think Lady P. was privy to his scheme on her, but, on being in his power, yielded. Oh, Sir Wm.! Sir Wm.! how I will love you if you will love Miss Sharp!*

Mrs. Driver, &c., are off by Collier, but so near being too late that she had not time to call and leave the keys herself. I have them, however. I suppose one is the key of the linen-press, but I do not know what to guess the other.

The coach was stopped at the blacksmith's, and they came running down with Triggs and Browning [manservant], and trunks, and birdcages. Quite amusing.

My mother desires her love, and hopes to hear from you.

Yours very affectionately,

J. AUSTEN.

Frank and Mary are to have Mary Goodchild to help as Under *till they can get a cook.* She *is delighted to go.*

Best love at Streatham.

Miss Austen, Henrietta St.

By favour of Mr. Gray.

LXXV

23 Hans Place: Tuesday morning (August, 1814).

MY DEAR CASSANDRA,

I had a very good journey, not crowded, two of the three taken up at Bentley being children, the others of a reasonable size; and they were all very quiet and civil. We were late in London, from being a great load, and from changing coaches at Farnham; it was nearly four, I believe, when we reached Sloane Street. Henry himself met me, and as soon as my trunk and basket could be routed out from all the other trunks and baskets in the world, we were on our way to Hans Place in the luxury of a nice, large, cool, dirty hackney coach.

There were four in the kitchen part of Yalden, and I was told fifteen at top, among them Percy Benn. We met in the same room at Egham, but poor Percy was not in his usual spirits. He would be more chatty, I dare say, in his way from *Woolwich [he was a military cadet there]. We took up a young Gibson at Holybourn, and, in short, everybody either* did *come up by Yalden yesterday, or wanted to come up. It put me in mind of my own coach between Edinburgh and Stirling [a reference to her story* Love and Freindship*].*

Henry is very well, and has given me an account of the Canterbury races, which seem to have been as pleasant as one could wish. Everything went well. Fanny had good partners, Mr. — was her second on Thursday, but he did not dance with her any more.

This will content you for the present. I must just add, however, that there were no Lady Charlottes [Finch-Hatton], they were gone off to Kirby, and that Mary Oxenden, instead of dying, is going to marry Wm. Hammond.

No James and Edward yet. Our evening yesterday was perfectly quiet; we only talked a little to Mr. Tilson across the intermediate gardens; she *was gone out airing with Miss Burdett. It is a delightful place – more than answers my expectation. Having got rid of my unreasonable ideas, I find more space and comfort in the rooms than I had supposed, and the garden is quite a love. I am in the front attic, which is the bedchamber to be preferred.*

Henry wants you to see it all, and asked whether you would return with him from Hampshire; I encouraged him to think you would. He breakfasts here early, and then rides to Henrietta St. If it continues fine John [coachman] is to drive me there by-and-bye, and we shall take an airing together; and I do not mean to take any other exercise, for I feel a little tired after my long jumble. I live in his room downstairs; it is particularly pleasant from opening upon the garden. I go and refresh myself every now and then, and then come back to solitary coolness. There is one *maidservant only, a very creditable, clean-looking young woman. Richard remains for the present.*

Wednesday morning. – *My brother and Edwd. arrived last night. They could not get places the day before. Their business is about teeth and wigs, and they are going to breakfast to Scarman's and Tavistock St., and they are to return to go with me afterwards in the barouche. I hope to do some of my errands to-day.*

I got the willow yesterday, as Henry was not quite ready when I reached Hena. St. I saw Mr. Hampson there for a moment. He dines here to-morrow and proposed bringing his son; so I must submit to seeing George Hampson, though I had hoped to go through life without it. It was one of my vanities, like your not reading 'Patronage.'

After leaving H. St. we drove to Mrs. Latouche's; they *are always at home, and they are to dine here on Friday. We could do no more, as it began to rain.*

We dine at half-past four to-day, that our visitors may go to the play, and Henry and I are to spend the evening with the Tilsons, to meet Miss Burdett, who leaves town to-morrow. Mrs. T. called on me yesterday.

Is not this all that can have happened or been arranged? Not quite. Henry wants me to see more of his Hanwell favourite [Harriet Moore], and has written to invite her to spend a day or two here with me. His scheme is to fetch her on Saturday. I am more and more convinced that he will marry again soon, and like the idea of her *better than of anybody else at hand.*

Now, I have breakfasted and have the room to myself again. It is likely to be a fine day. How do you all do?

Henry talks of being at Chawton about *the 1st of Sept. He has once mentioned a scheme, which I should rather like – calling on the Birches and the Crutchleys in our way. It may never come to anything, but I must provide for the possibility by troubling you to send up my silk pelisse by Collier on Saturday. I feel it would be necessary on such an occasion; and be so good as to put up a clean dressing-gown which will come from the wash on Friday. You need not direct it to be left anywhere. It may take its chance.*

We are to call for Henry between three and four, and I must finish this and carry it with me, as he is not always there in the morning before the parcel is made up. And, before I set off, I must return Mrs. Tilson's visit. I hear nothing of the Hoblyns, and abstain from all enquiry.

I hope Mary Jane and Frank's gardens go on well. Give my love to them all – Nunna Hat's love to George [Frank Austen's son]. A great many people wanted to run up in the Poach as well as me. The wheat looked very well all the way, and James says the same of his *road.*

The same good account of Mrs. C.'s health continues, and her circumstances mend. She gets farther and farther from poverty. What a comfort! Good-bye to you.

Yours very truly and affectionately,

JANE.

All well at Steventon. I hear nothing particular of Ben [Lefroy], except that Edward is to get him some pencils.

Miss Austen, Chawton.

By favour of Mr. Gray.

1815

I glean no information concerning 'Aunt Jane' from my mother's pocket-books of the first nine months of the year 1815, save the record of various letters written to and received from her. In October Henry Austen was seized with a severe illness, in which Jane came to nurse him at his house in London, 23 Hans Place, and I find that on the 23rd of that month my mother writes: 'An express arrived from Aunt Jane Austen with a sad account of poor Uncle Henry. Papa set off for town directly.' Then follows a daily bulletin, and in about a week is chronicled the fact that the Godmersham household 'sent a basket of provisions to them, and wrote to Aunt Jane.' Godmersham provisions, aided possibly by London doctors, had their due effect. The patient rallied, gradually improved, was well enough for his brother to return home again in a week's time, and got so much better as time went on that on November 15 occurs the entry, 'Papa and I set off early, and reached Hans Place to dinner. Aunts Cass and Jane are here.' On the 20th Mr. Knight and Cassandra Austen went to Chawton, and on the 24th was written our first letter of this year (No. 76). Mr. Haden, I suppose, was one of Henry Austen's medical attendants, apparently an apothecary, by the playful manner in which Jane vehemently protests that he is no such thing. Whether apothecary or physician, however, the worthy man seems to have made a favourable impression upon both aunt and niece, for my mother records (November 20) that Mr. Haden, a delightful, clever, musical Haden, comes every evening, and is agreeable, and Jane, with the exception of a doubt as to the orthodoxy of the gentleman's opinion of the infallible wickedness of non-musical people, evidently shared this view of his character. During their stay in town my mother writes that 'Aunt Jane and I walk every day in the garden, but get no further.' 'Aunt Jane and I drove about shopping,' and similar entries, varied one evening as follows, 'Aunt Jane and I very snug,' which shows how thoroughly the two enjoyed and appreciated each other's society. Like all pleasant things, this visit came to an end, and the Godmersham party returned into Kent on December 8. Several letters are entered in the pocket-books as having been written and received before the end of the year, but none of these are to hand, and this is the more to be regretted because my mother was in the habit of keeping the letters of so many of her correspondents through life, that it is difficult to imagine how these came to be destroyed. The visit to Keppel Street (Letter 77) must have been to her brother Charles, whose first wife, Fanny Palmer, had just died, which accounts for 'Fanny' being 'very much affected by the sight of the children.' The celebrated Mr. Haden appears to have preferred 'Mansfield Park' to 'Pride and Prejudice' but perhaps he changed his opinion when he had read them both over again. The 'P. R.' mentioned in these 1815 letters must not be mistaken for the 'Prize Ring,' for which it sometimes stands, but with which our Jane had certainly nothing to do. The 'Prince Regent' is signified, who had been graciously pleased to express his approval of 'Mansfield Park' and directed his librarian, Mr. Clarke, to invite Jane to Carlton House, where she was informed that she might dedicate her forthcoming novel to His Royal Highness. Mr. Austen Leigh gives us a short correspondence between Jane and Mr. Clarke, which is so characteristic of her, that I venture to insert it in my Appendix. The Countess of Morley had also written a letter, which perhaps ought to appear in the same place, as Jane alludes to its receipt in the concluding paragraph of the seventy-seventh letter. The letter of 1816 is the latest I have. It was written on September 8th, just ten months before her death, when Cassandra was staying at Cheltenham. It will be observed that she refers to 'the pain in my back,' speaks of 'nursing myself into as beautiful a state as I can,' and shows some disinclination to 'company' in the house; but the letter is otherwise written in her usual cheerful style, and there are several amusing passages. I imagine that after Cassandra's return from Cheltenham the sisters were hardly separated again, so that this is in all probability one of the very last letters which passed between them.

One, and only one, more meeting took place between the aunt and niece who loved each other so well. I find from the pocket-books that on May 2, 1816, my mother accompanied her father to Chawton and remained until the 21st, when they returned to Kent. The usual meetings occurred between the 'Great House' and the 'Cottage,' but no special event is related, and one can only fancy how in after days my mother must have recalled this last time of confidential and loving intercourse with one who had become so very dear to her, and with whom she shared every secret of her heart. Jane was at this time in declining health, though no one anticipated that she was to be spared to her family only for one more short year. She wrote frequently to my mother after this visit, entered thoroughly into all her views and feelings, and in fact only ceased the correspondence when health and strength began rapidly to fail.

LXXVI

Hans Place: Friday (Nov 24).
MY DEAREST CASSANDRA,

I have the pleasure of sending you a much better account of my affairs, *which I know will be a great delight to you.*

I wrote to Mr. Murray [publisher] yesterday myself, and Henry wrote at the same time to Roworth [printer]. Before the notes were out of the house, I received three sheets and an apology from R. We sent the notes, however, and I had a most civil one in reply from Mr. M. He is so very polite, indeed, that it is quite overcoming. The printers have been waiting for paper – the blame is thrown upon the stationer; but he gives his word that I shall have no farther cause for dissatisfaction. He has lent us Miss Williams *and* Scott, *and says that any book of his will always be at* my *service. In short, I am soothed and complimented into tolerable comfort.*

We had a visit yesterday from Edwd. Knight, and Mr. Mascall joined him here; and this morning has brought Mr. Mascall's compliments and two pheasants. We have some hope of Edward's coming to dinner to-day; he will, if he can, I believe. He is looking extremely well.

To-morrow Mr. Haden is to dine with us. There is happiness! We really grow so fond of Mr. Haden that I do not know what to expect. He, and Mr. Tilson, and Mr. Philips made up our circle of wits last night; Fanny played, and he sat and listened and suggested improvements, till Richard came in to tell him that 'the doctor was waiting for him at Captn. Blake's'; and then he was off with a speed that you can imagine. He never does appear in the least above his profession, or out of humour with it, or I should think poor Captn. Blake, whoever he is, in a very bad way.

I must have misunderstood Henry when I told you that you *were to hear from him to-day. He read me what he wrote to Edward: part of it must have amused him, I am sure – one part, alas! cannot be very amusing to anybody. I wonder that with such business [his bank was failing] to worry him he can be getting better, but he certainly does gain strength, and if you and Edwd. were to see him now I feel sure that you would think him improved since Monday.*

He was out yesterday; it was a fine sunshiny day here *(in the country perhaps you might have clouds and fogs. Dare I say so? I shall not deceive you, if I do, as to my estimation of the climate of London), and he ventured first on the balcony and then as far as the greenhouse. He caught no cold, and therefore has done more to-day, with great delight and self-persuasion of improvement.*

He has been to see Mrs. Tilson and the Malings. By-the-bye, you may talk to Mr. T. of his wife's being better; I saw her yesterday, and was sensible of her having gained ground in the last two days.

Evening. – *We have had no Edward. Our circle is formed – only Mr. Tilson and Mr. Haden. We are not so happy as we were. A message came this afternoon from Mrs. Latouche and Miss East, offering themselves to drink tea with us to-morrow, and, as it was accepted, here is an end of our extreme felicity in our dinner guest. I am heartily sorry they are coming; it will be an evening spoilt to Fanny and me.*

Another little disappointment: Mr. H. advises Henry's not *venturing with us in the carriage to-morrow; if it were spring, he says, it would be a different thing. One would rather this had not been. He seems to think his going out today rather imprudent, though acknowledging at the same time that he is better than he was in the morning.*

Fanny has had a letter full of commissions from Goodnestone; we shall be busy about them and her own matters, I dare say, from 12 to 4. Nothing I trust will keep us from Keppel Street.

This day has brought a most friendly letter from Mr. Fowle, with a brace of pheasants. I did not know before that Henry had written to him a few days ago to ask for them. We shall live upon pheasants – no bad life!

I send you five one-pound notes, for fear you should be distressed for little money. Lizzy's work is charmingly done; shall you put it to your chintz? A sheet *came in this moment; 1st and 3rd vols. are now at 144; 2nd at 48. I am sure you will like particulars. We are not to have the trouble of returning the sheets to Mr. Murray's any longer, the printer's boys bring and carry.*

I hope Mary continues to get well fast, and I send my love to little Herbert [Frank and Mary Austen's new baby]. You will tell me more of Martha's plans, of course, when you write again. Remember me most kindly to everybody, and Miss Benn besides.

Yours very affectionately,

J. AUSTEN.

I have been listening to dreadful insanity. It is Mr. Haden's firm belief that a person not *musical is fit for every sort of wickedness. I ventured to assert a little on the other side, but wished the cause in abler hands.*

Miss Austen, Chawton.

LXXVII

Hans Place: Sunday (Nov. 26.).

MY DEAREST,

The parcel arrived safely, and I am much obliged to you for your trouble. It cost 2s. 10d., *but, as there is a certain saving of* 2s. 4 1/2d. *on the other side, I am sure it is well worth doing. I send four pair of silk stockings, but I do not want them washed at present. In the three neck-handkerchiefs I include the one sent down before. These things, perhaps, Edwd. may be able to bring, but even if he is not, I am extremely pleased with his returning to you from Steventon. It is much better; far preferable.*

I did *mention the P. R. [Prince Regent] in my note to Mr. Murray; it brought me a fine compliment in return. Whether it has done any good I do not know, but Henry thought it worth trying.*

The printers continue to supply me very well. I am advanced in Vol. III. to my arra-root, *upon which peculiar style of spelling there is a modest query in the margin. I will not forget Anna's arrowroot. I hope you have told Martha of my first resolution of letting nobody know that I* might *dedicate [*Emma *to the Prince Regent], &c., for fear of being obliged to do it, and that she is thoroughly convinced of my being influenced now by nothing but the most mercenary motives. I have paid nine shillings on her account to Miss Palmer; there was no more owing.*

Well, we were very busy all yesterday; from half-past 11 till 4 in the streets, working almost entirely for other people, driving from place to place after a parcel for Sandling, which we could never find, and encountering the miseries of Grafton House to get a purple frock for Eleanor Bridges. We got to Keppel St., however, which was all I cared for, and though we could stay only a quarter-of-an-hour, Fanny's calling gave great pleasure, and her sensibility still greater, for she was very much affected at the sight of the children [Charles Austen's children who had recently lost their mother]. Poor little F. [Fanny] looked heavy. We saw the whole party.

Aunt Harriet [Charles Austen's sister-in-law, later to become his second wife] hopes Cassy will not forget to make a pincushion for Mrs. Kelly, as she *has spoken of its being promised her several times. I hope we shall see Aunt H. and the dear little girls here on Thursday.*

So much for the morning. Then came the dinner and Mr. Haden, who brought good manners and clever conversation. From 7 to 8 the harp; at 8 Mrs. L. and Miss E. arrived, and for the rest of the evening the drawing-room was thus arranged: on the sofa side the two ladies, Henry, and myself, making the best of it; on the opposite side Fanny and Mr. Haden, in two chairs (I believe, *at least, they had* two *chairs), talking together uninterruptedly. Fancy the scene! And what is to be fancied next? Why, that Mr. H. dines here again to-morrow. Today we are to have Mr. Barlow. Mr. H. is reading 'Mansfield Park' for the first time, and prefers it to P. and P.*

A hare and four rabbits from Gm. yesterday, so that we are stocked for nearly a week. Poor Farmer Andrews! I am very sorry for him, and sincerely wish his recovery.

A better account of the sugar than I could have expected. I should like to help you break some more. I am glad you cannot wake early; I am sure you must have been under great arrears of rest.

Fanny and I have been to B. [Belgrave] Chapel, and walked back with Maria Cuthbert. We have been very little plagued with visitors this last week. I remember only Miss Herries, the aunt, but I am in terror for to-day, a fine bright Sunday; plenty of mortar, and nothing to do.

Henry gets out in his garden every day, but at present his inclination for doing more seems over, nor has he now any plan for leaving London before Dec. 18, when he thinks of going to Oxford for a few days; to-day, indeed, his feelings are for continuing where he is through the next two months.

One knows the uncertainty of all this, but, should it be so, we must think the best, and hope the best, and do the best; and my idea in that case is, that when he *goes to Oxford* I *should go home, and have nearly a week of* you *before you take my place. This is only a silent project, you know, to be gladly given up if better things occur. Henry calls himself stronger every day, and Mr. H. keeps on approving his pulse, which seems generally better than ever, but still they will not let him be well. Perhaps when Fanny is gone he will be allowed to recover faster.*

I am not disappointed: I never thought the little girl at Wyards [Anna and Ben Lefroy's new home] very pretty, but she will have a fine complexion and curly hair, and pass for a beauty. We are glad the mamma's cold has not been worse, and send her our love and good wishes by every convenient opportunity. Sweet, amiable Frank! why does he *have a cold too? Like Captain Mirvan to Mr. Duval, [1] 'I wish it well over with him.'*

Fanny has heard all that I have said to you about herself and Mr. H. Thank you very much for the sight of dearest Charles's letter to yourself. How pleasantly and how naturally he writes! and how perfect a picture of his disposition and feelings his style conveys! Poor dear fellow! Not a present! I have a great mind to send him all the twelve copies which were to have been dispersed among my near connections, beginning with the P. R. and ending with Countess Morley. Adieu.

Yours affectionately,

J. AUSTEN.

Give my love to Cassy and Mary Jane. Caroline will be gone when this reaches you.

Miss Austen.

1. Characters in Miss Burney's '*Evelina*.'

LXXVIII

Hans Place: Saturday (Dec. 2).

MY DEAR CASSANDRA,

Henry came back yesterday, and might have returned the day before if he had known as much in time. I had the pleasure of hearing from Mr. T. [Tilson] on Wednesday night that Mr. Seymour [Henry's friend and lawyer] thought there was not the least occasion for his absenting himself any longer.

I had also the comfort of a few lines on Wednesday morning from Henry himself, just after your letter was gone, giving so good an account of his feelings as made me perfectly easy. He met with the utmost care and attention at Hanwell, spent his two days there very quietly and pleasantly, and, being certainly in no respect the worse for going, we may believe that he must be better, as he is quite sure of being himself. To make his return a complete gala Mr. Haden was secured for dinner. I need not say that our evening was agreeable.

But you seem to be under a mistake as to Mr. H. You call him an apothecary. He is no apothecary; he has never been an apothecary; there is not an apothecary in this neighbourhood – the only inconvenience of the situation perhaps – but so it is; we have not a medical man within reach. He is a Haden, nothing but a Haden, a sort of wonderful nondescript creature on two legs, something between a man and an angel, but without the least spice of an apothecary. He is, perhaps, the only person not *an apothecary hereabouts. He has never sung to us. He will not sing without a pianoforte accompaniment.*

Mr. Meyers gives his three lessons a week, altering his days and his hours, however, just as he chooses, never very punctual, and never giving good measure. I have not Fanny's fondness for masters, and Mr. Meyers does not give me any longing after them. The truth is, I think, that they are all, at least music-masters, made of too much consequence and allowed to take too many liberties with their scholars' time.

We shall be delighted to see Edward on Monday, only sorry that you must be losing him. A turkey will be equally welcome with himself. He must prepare for his own proper bedchamber here, as Henry moved down to the one below last week; he found the other cold.

I am sorry my mother has been suffering, and am afraid this exquisite weather is too good to agree with her. I *enjoy it all over me, from top to toe, from right to left, longitudinally, perpendicularly, diagonally; and I cannot but selfishly hope we are to have it last till Christmas – nice, unwholesome, unseasonable, relaxing, close, muggy weather.*

Oh, thank you very much for your long letter; it did me a great deal of good. Henry accepts your offer of making his nine gallon of mead thankfully. The mistake of the dogs rather vexed him for a moment, but he has not thought of it since. To-day he makes a third attempt at his strengthening plaister [plaster], and, as I am sure he will now be getting out a great deal, it is to be wished that he may be able to keep it on. He sets off this morning by the Chelsea coach to sign bonds and visit Henrietta St., and I have no doubt will be going every day to Henrietta St.

Fanny and I were very snug by ourselves as soon as we were satisfied about our invalid's being safe at Hanwell. By manoeuvring and good luck we foiled all the Malings' attempts upon us. Happily I caught a little cold on Wednesday, the morning we were in town, which we made very useful, and we saw nobody but our precious [1] and Mr. Tilson.

This evening the Malings are allowed to drink tea with us. We are in hopes – that is, we wish *– Miss Palmer and the little girls [Charles Austen's daughters] may come this morning. You know, of course, that she could* not *come on Thursday, and she will not attempt to* name *any other day.*

God bless you. Excuse the shortness of this, but I must finish it now that I may save you 2d *[postage was paid by the recipient]. Best love.*

Yours affectionately,

J. A.

It strikes me that I have no business to give the P. R. [the Prince Regent's copy of Emma*] a binding, but we will take counsel upon the question.*

I am glad you have put the flounce on your chintz; I am sure it must look particularly well, and it is what I had thought of.

Miss Austen, Chawton, Alton, Hants.

1. Probably a playful allusion to Mr. Haden.

1816

LXXIX

Chawton: Sunday (Sept 8).

MY DEAREST CASSANDRA,

I have borne the arrival of your letter to-day extremely well; anybody might have thought it was giving me pleasure. I am very glad you find so much to be satisfied with at Cheltenham [Cassandra went to Cheltenham as company for her sister-in-law, who was taking the waters for a medical complaint]. While the waters agree, everything else is trifling.

A letter arrived for you from Charles last Thursday. They are all safe and pretty well in Keppel St., the children decidedly better for Broadstairs; and he writes principally to ask when it will be convenient to us to receive Miss P., the little girls, and himself. They would be ready to set off in ten days from the time of his writing, to pay their visits in Hampshire and Berkshire, and he would prefer coming to Chawton first.

I have answered him, and said that we hoped it might suit them to wait till the last *week in Septr., as we could not ask them sooner, either on your account or the want of room. I mentioned the 23rd as the probable day of your return. When you have once left Cheltenham I shall grudge every half-day wasted on the road. If there were but a coach from Hungerford to Chawton! I have desired him to let me hear again soon.*

He does not include a maid in the list to be accommodated, but if they bring one, as I suppose they will, we shall have no bed in the house even then for Charles himself – let alone Henry. But what can we do?

We shall have the Gt. House quite at our command; it is to be cleared of the Papillons' servants in a day or two. They themselves have been hurried off into Essex to take possession – not of a large estate left them by an uncle – but to scrape together all they can, I suppose, of the effects of a Mrs. Rawstorn, a rich old friend and cousin, suddenly deceased, to whom they are joint executors. So there is a happy end of the Kentish Papillons coming here.

No morning service to-day, wherefore I am writing between twelve and one o'clock. Mr. Benn [rector of Farringdon] in the afternoon, and likewise more rain again, by the look and the sound of things. You left us in doubt of Mrs. Benn's situation, but she has bespoke her nurse. Mrs. F. A. seldom either looks or appears quite well. Little Embryo is troublesome, I suppose. They dined with us yesterday, and had fine weather both for coming and going home, which has hardly ever happened to them before. She is still unprovided with a housemaid.

Our day at Alton was very pleasant, venison quite right, children well-behaved, and Mr. and Mrs. Digweed taking kindly to our charades and other games. I must also observe, for his mother's satisfaction, that Edward at my suggestion devoted himself very properly to the entertainment of Miss S. Gibson [a relation of Frank Austen's wife]. Nothing was wanting except Mr. Sweeney [a naval friend of Frank's], but he, alas! had been ordered away to London the day before. We had a beautiful walk home by moonlight.

Thank you, my back has given me scarcely any pain for many days. I have an idea that agitation does it as much harm as fatigue, and that I was ill at the time of your going from the very circumstance of your going. I am nursing myself up now into as beautiful a state as I can, because I hear that Dr. White means to call on me before he leaves the country.

Evening. – *Frank and Mary and the children visited us this morning. Mr. and Mrs. Gibson [Mary's parents] are to come on the 23rd, and there is too much reason to fear they will stay above a week. Little George could tell me where you were gone to, as well as what you were to bring him, when I asked him the other day.*

Sir Tho. Miller is dead. I treat you with a dead baronet in almost every letter.

So you have C. [Charlotte] Craven among you, as well as the Duke of

Orleans and Mr. Pocock. But it mortifies me that you have not added one to the stock of common acquaintance. Do pray meet with somebody belonging to yourself. I am quite weary of your knowing nobody.

Mrs. Digweed parts with both Hannah and old cook; the former will not give up her lover, who is a man of bad character; the latter is guilty only of being unequal to anything.

Miss Terry was to have spent this week with her sister, but as usual it is put off. My amiable friend knows the value of her company. I have not seen Anna since the day you left us; her father and brother visited her most days. Edward [Lefroy, Ben's brother] and Ben called here on Thursday. Edward was in his way to Selborne. We found him very agreeable. He is come back from France, thinking of the French as one could wish – disappointed in everything. He did not go beyond Paris.

I have a letter from Mrs. Perigord; she and her mother are in London again. She speaks of France as a scene of general poverty and misery: no money, no trade, nothing to be got but by the innkeepers, and as to her own present prospects she is not much less melancholy than before.

I have also a letter from Miss Sharp, quite one of her letters; she has been again obliged to exert herself more than ever, in a more distressing, more harassed state, and has met with another excellent old physician and his wife, with every virtue under heaven, who takes to her and cures her from pure love and benevolence. Dr. and Mrs. Storer are their Mrs. and Miss Palmer – for they are at Bridlington. I am happy to say, however, that the sum of the account is better than usual. Sir William is returned; from Bridlington they go to Chevet [the Pilkingtons' home], and she is to have a young governess under her.

I enjoyed Edward's [her nephew, son of James Austen] company very much, as I said before, and yet I was not sorry when Friday came. It had been a busy week, and I wanted a few days quiet and exemption from the thought and contrivancy which any sort of company gives. I often wonder how you can find time for what you do, in addition to the care of the house; and how good Mrs. West [the novelist Jane West] could have written such books and collected so many hard words, with all her family cares, is still more a matter of astonishment. Composition seems to me impossible with a head full of joints of mutton and doses of rhubarb.

Monday. – Here is a sad morning. I fear you may not have been able to get to the Pump. The two last days were very pleasant. I enjoyed them the more for your sake. But to-day it is really bad enough to make you all cross. I hope Mary will change her lodgings at the fortnight's end; I am sure, if you looked about well, you would find others in some odd corner to suit you better. Mrs. Potter charges for the name of the High St.

Success to the pianoforte! I trust it will drive you away. We hear now that there is to be no honey this year. Bad news for us. We must husband our *present stock of mead, and I am sorry to perceive that our twenty gallons is very nearly out. I cannot comprehend how the fourteen gallons could last so long.*

We do not much like Mr. Cooper's [Jane's cousin Revd. Edward Cooper had published two sermons] new sermons. They are fuller of regeneration and conversion than ever, with the addition of his zeal in the cause of the Bible Society.

Martha's love to Mary and Caroline, and she is extremely glad to find they like the pelisse. The Debarys are indeed odious! We are to see my brother to-morrow, but for only one night. I had no idea that he would care for the races without *Edward. Remember me to all.*

Yours very affectionately,

J. AUSTEN.

Miss Austen, Post Office, Cheltenham.

1814–1816

I confess to having entertained some doubts as to the publication of the five letters addressed by 'Aunt Jane' to my mother in 1814–16 – doubts not so much as to the propriety of their publication as to the possible dislike which some of my own family might feel at the dragging to light of items of private history which, seventy years ago, were no doubt secret and sacred to both the writer and the recipient of the letters which contain them. But two considerations have weighed with me above all others, and I trust they will be deemed sufficient, even if the lapse of time since the letters were written did not in itself remove every reasonable objection. The one consideration is that, as regards Jane herself, these five letters are peculiarly interesting, not only because in every line they are vividly characteristic of the writer, but because they differ from all the preceding letters in that they are written, not to an elder sister, but to a niece who constantly sought her advice and sympathy, and whom she addressed, of course, in a different manner, and from a different standpoint. The other and, naturally, to me a consideration even more important, is that, according to my humble judgment, these letters, whilst they illustrate the character of my great-aunt, cannot, when explained, do otherwise than reflect credit upon that of my beloved mother; whilst they prove the great and affectionate intimacy which existed between her and her aunt, and incidentally demonstrate the truth of a remark in one of Cassandra's letters that there were many points of similitude in the characters of the two. If my mother had preserved more of the thirty or forty letters which she received from 'Aunt Jane' during the years 1814–16, it might have been possible for me, if it seemed desirable, to eliminate the portions which related to her own 'love affairs,' and to still obtain the illustrations of Jane Austen's character which her letters to a niece specially afford when compared with her letters to a sister. I am not sure, however, that such an elimination would not have, to a great extent, spoiled, or at least diminished, the interest of the letters; and, when it became a question of omitting altogether these five letters, I thought that their interest was so great that I could not persuade myself to do so. After all, the story is very simple, and one which can offend or injure nobody by its relation. My mother was a handsome and agreeable young woman, fond of society, and endowed with a large portion of practical common sense. A friendship sprang up between her and a gentleman of about her own age, whose name it is unnecessary for me to mention. He was a man of high character, the two saw much of each other, and the friendship ripened into an attachment which very nearly became an engagement. There was, however, one point of difference which stood in the way, and prevented this result. The gentleman was of a very serious disposition, and eventually his religious views induced him to think dancing and other social amusements of the same sort things which ought to be eschewed and avoided by Christian people. My mother was of a different opinion. I do not suppose there ever was a woman more profoundly and really religious; throughout the whole of her life she attended assiduously to her religious duties, never a day passed that she did not devote some portion of it to the perusal of some pious author (which she called 'reading my goodness'), and no one ever strove more earnestly to do her duty and to follow the teaching of the Gospel. But she entertained a strong opinion that this might be done without a severance from the ordinary pursuits and amusements of other people; that a person might live 'in the world' without being 'of the world,' and that to perform the duties which came before her in life, and set a practical example of a Christian life in her everyday existence, was as likely to be acceptable to God as the withdrawal from pursuits in which everybody else indulged, as if a Christian's duty required that he should live apart from other people, by which means his influence over them for good must of necessity be diminished. From the entries in her diary, as well as from the letters before me, it is evident that about this time a struggle went on in my mother's mind upon these points. 'Plagued myself about Methodists all day,' and 'had a nice conversation with Mr. Sherer about Methodists,' are entries in the autumn of 1814, which evidently bear upon the matter, while other entries throughout this and the early part of the following year testify to the fact that she entertained a strong regard for the gentleman, but that she was in the position which many young women have been in before and since – namely, doubtful whether she cared enough for him to become his wife. This doubt became a certainty in 1815, and I find at the end of her pocket-book for that year, in her usual summary of the principal events of the year, that there were 'many serious discussions and vexatious circumstances on subjects tending nearly to dissolve the intimacy between — and myself.' I cannot more aptly illustrate my mother's real feelings upon these matters which she speaks of as 'serious' than by a quotation from a letter to her from my father before they were married, which appears to me to speak, in the stronger language of a man, that which was in her woman's heart. It so happened that immediately after they became engaged my father was summoned to Lincolnshire upon affairs arising out of the death of Sir Joseph Banks, and obliged to be away for more than a fortnight, during which time he wrote daily to my mother, who preserved all these letters – interesting mementoes to her children. In one of them, answering some remarks and inquiries of his correspondent, he writes as follows: – 'In all that I have had to undergo I have been supported by that Power from above without whose aid I must long ago have sunk; but, seriously as I have always regarded every occurrence of life, and attributing as I always do everything that happens to a superintending Power, I have never suffered these considerations to interfere with the duties or even the amusements of life. I have never felt that it could become me to find fault with the conduct of others, and dogmatically prescribe what course it is best to pursue. To act upon a steady and uniform principle, to adhere to what is right and to abstain from what is wrong, to afford the best example in my power, never to obtrude my opinions, but never upon proper occasions to be ashamed or afraid of avowing them – these have been the rules upon which I have acted, and I believe they will bring peace at the last. I dislike everything that savours of levity in matters of religion, and much more do I dislike that affected and presumptuous vanity which dares to censure the innocent amusements of life – which secludes people from the common enjoyments necessary to the comfort of society, and which, clothed in puritanical hypocrisy, affects a superiority to which it has no claim whatever. These are serious subjects; you first mentioned them to me, and I love you too well not to tell you without hesitation what I think and feel. Your own principles as expressed to me are right – grounded on humility, admitting how unequal we are to perform our duties, but resolutely and constantly persevering to the utmost of our ability to discharge them properly – thinking seriously of everything that happens, constantly mixing with the world, but enjoying it more or less according as we meet with similar feelings and kindred spirits, and always hoping that our example and principles will effect some good and receive the respect to which they are entitled.' It was necessary to the elucidation of these five letters that this insight into my mother's affairs should be given; her feelings may be gathered from 'Aunt Jane's' remarks upon them, and I might close these prefatory observations by saying that this difference upon 'serious subjects' *did* overcome my mother's regard for the gentleman in question, that the 'intimacy' *was* 'dissolved,' and within a couple of years he found his happiness elsewhere. I am unable, however, to avoid another quotation from one of my father's letters in 1820, which evidences the frank, fearless, open nature which, in common with 'Aunt Jane,' my mother possessed. He writes:

> I will now reply to that part of your letter which relates to Mr.—. Our meeting, my dearest Fanny, in the library at Godmersham on Friday fortnight we can neither of us ever forget – within ten minutes you mentioned to me the circumstances of this attachment. Of course I felt surprised till you told me all, and *then* I felt still more surprised, and happy beyond what I can declare, at having, as it were at once, developed to me a mind capable of expressing what I do not believe any other woman in the world would have had courage, or firmness, or candour, or sense enough to have mentioned. Let me say that my esteem for you is not of very recent date, but I hardly know of anything that has raised you higher in my opinion than your frank and sensible avowal in this instance. I would not say this if it were not true, and that you well know.

The meeting in the library at Godmersham was, of course, that at which my father and mother became engaged, and with the hatred of concealment which was a part of her character, she evidently told him at once and fully of the past, and by so doing confirmed and strengthened his confidence in herself for the future.

The first two of these letters were written in November, 1814, one from Chawton and the other from Hans Place; they speak for themselves and comment would only weaken their effect. The visit to Hendon (mentioned in the second letter was to 'Anna Lefroy,' née Austen, and the Mr. Hayter mentioned in the same letter was the same who was afterwards for many years Patronage Secretary of the Treasury in several Liberal Governments.

The third letter, written in February, 1816, may perhaps require a word of explanation. There are two gentlemen therein referred to, one whom Jane believes determined to marry her niece, the other (the hero of the former letters) for whom she suspects that 'sweet, perverse Fanny' has still some regard, which she no longer endeavours to rekindle and strengthen, but to lessen and extinguish. The first gentleman is again referred to in the next letter, before writing which Jane seems to have discovered that her niece's peril of matrimony was not so imminent as she had supposed: she considers upon the whole that Mr. — '*cannot* be in love with you, however he may try at it,' and exhorts her niece not to be 'in a hurry' – 'the right man is sure to come at last.' He did come, but unfortunately not until the grave had closed for three years over the aunt who took such a warm and lively interest in all that concerned her niece, and who would have sincerely and heartily rejoiced could she have seen her in the position which she so long and so worthily occupied.

LXXX

Chawton: Friday (Nov. 18, 1814).

I feel quite as doubtful as you could be, my dearest Fanny, as to when *my letter may be finished, for I can command very little quiet time at present; but yet I must begin, for I know you will be glad to hear as soon as possible, and I really am impatient myself to be writing something on so very interesting a subject, though I have no hope of writing anything to the purpose. I shall do very little more, I dare say, than say over again what you have said before.*

I was certainly a good deal surprised at first, *as I had no suspicion of any change in your feelings, and I have no scruple in saying that you cannot be in love. My dear Fanny, I am ready to laugh at the idea, and yet it is no laughing matter to have had you so mistaken as to your own feelings. And with all my heart I wish I had cautioned you on that point when first you spoke to me; but, though I did not think you then so* much *in love, I did consider you as being attached in a degree quite sufficiently for happiness, as I had no doubt it would increase with opportunity, and from the time of our being in London together I thought you really very much in love. But you certainly are not at all – there is no concealing it.*

What strange creatures we are! It seems as if your being secure of him had made you indifferent. There was a little disgust, I suspect, at the races, and I do not wonder at it. His expressions then would not do for one who had rather more acuteness, penetration, and taste, than love, which was your case. And yet, after all, I am *surprised that the change in your feelings should be so great. He is just what he ever was, only more evidently and uniformly devoted to* you. *This is all the difference. How shall we account for it?*

My dearest Fanny, I am writing what will not be of the smallest use to you. I am feeling differently every moment, and shall not be able to suggest a single thing that can assist your mind. I could lament in one sentence and laugh in the next, but as to opinion or counsel I am sure that none will be extracted worth having from this letter.

I read yours through the very evening I received it, getting away by myself. I could not bear to leave off when I had once begun. I was full of curiosity and concern. Luckily your At. C. dined at the other house; therefore I had not to manoeuvre away from her, *and as to anybody else, I do not care.*

Poor dear Mr. A.! Oh, dear Fanny! your mistake has been one that thousands of women fall into. He was the first *young man who attached himself to you. That was the charm, and most powerful it is. Among the multitudes, however, that make the same mistake with yourself, there can be few indeed who have so little reason to regret it;* his *character and* his *attachment leave you nothing to be ashamed of.*

Upon the whole, what is to be done? You have no inclination for any other person. His situation in life, family, friends, and, above all, his character, his uncommonly amiable mind, strict principles, just notions, good habits, all *that* you *know so well how to value,* all *that is really of the first importance, everything of this nature pleads his cause most strongly. You have no doubt of his having superior abilities, he has proved it at the University; he is, I dare say, such a scholar as your agreeable, idle brothers would ill bear a comparison with.*

Oh, my dear Fanny! the more I write about him, the warmer my feelings become – the more strongly I feel the sterling worth of such a young man and the desirableness of your growing in love with him again. I recommend this most thoroughly. There are *such beings in the world, perhaps one in a thousand, as the creature you and I should think perfection, where grace and spirit are united to worth, where the manners are equal to the heart and understanding, but such a person may not come in your way, or, if he does, he may not be the eldest son of a man of fortune, the near relation of your particular friend and belonging to your own county.*

Think of all this, Fanny. Mr. A. has advantages which do not often meet in one person. His only fault, indeed, seems modesty. If he were less modest he would be more agreeable, speak louder, and look impudenter; and is not it a fine character of which modesty is the only defect? I have no doubt he will get more lively and more like yourselves as he is more with you; he will catch your ways if he belongs to you. And, as to there being any objection from his goodness, *from the danger of his becoming even evangelical, I cannot admit* that. *I am by no means convinced that we ought not all to be evangelicals, and am at least persuaded that they who are so from reason and feeling must be happiest and safest. Do not be frightened from the connection by your brothers having most wit – wisdom is better than wit, and in the long run will certainly have the laugh on her side; and don't be frightened by the idea of his acting more strictly up to the precepts of the New Testament than others.*

And now, my dear Fanny, having written so much on one side of the question, I shall turn round and entreat you not to commit yourself farther, and not to think of accepting him unless you really do like him. Anything is to be preferred or endured rather than marrying without affection; and if his deficiences of manner, &c. &c., strike you more than all his good qualities, if you continue to think strongly of them, give him up at once. Things are now in such a state that you must resolve upon one or the other – either to allow him to go on as he has done, or whenever you are together behave with a coldness which may convince him that he has been deceiving himself. I have no doubt of his suffering a good deal for a time – a great deal when he feels that he must give you up; but it is no creed of mine, as you must be well aware, that such sort of disappointments kill anybody.

Your sending the music was an admirable device, it made everything easy, and I do not know how I could have accounted for the parcel otherwise; for though your dear papa most conscientiously hunted about till he found me alone in the dining-parlour, your Aunt C. had seen that he had *a parcel to deliver. As it was, however, I do not think anything was suspected.*

We have heard nothing fresh from Anna. I trust she is very comfortable in her new home. Her letters have been very sensible and satisfactory, with no parade *of happiness, which I liked them the better for. I have often known young married women write in a way I did not like in that respect.*

You will be glad to hear that the first edition of M.P. [1] is all sold. Your uncle Henry is rather wanting me to come to town to settle about a second edition, but as I could not very conveniently leave home now, I have written him my will and pleasure, and, unless he still urges it, shall not go. I am very greedy and want to make the most of it, but as you are much above caring about money I shall not plague you with any particulars. The pleasures of vanity are more within your comprehension, and you will enter into mine at receiving the praise *which every now and then comes to me through some channel or other.*

Saturday. – *Mr. Palmer spent yesterday with us, and is gone off with Cassy this morning. We have been expecting Miss Lloyd the last two days, and feel sure of her to-day. Mr. Knight and Mr. Edwd. Knight are to dine with us, and on Monday they are to dine with us again, accompanied by their respectable host and hostess [Frank and Mary Austen].*

...Sunday. – *Your papa had given me messages to you, but they are unnecessary, as he writes by this post to Aunt Louisa. We had a pleasant party yesterday, at least* we *found it so. It is delightful to see him so cheerful and confident. Aunt Cass. and I dine at the Great House today. We shall be a snug half-dozen. Miss Lloyd came, as we expected, yesterday, and desires her love. She is very happy to hear of your learning the harp. I do not mean to send you what I owe Miss Hare, because I think you would rather not be paid beforehand.*

Yours very affectionately,
JANE AUSTEN
Miss Knight, Goodnestone Farm,
Wingham, Kent.

1. 'Mansfield Park'.

LXXXI

23 Hans Place: Wednesday (Nov. 30, 1814).

I am very much obliged to you, my dear Fanny, for your letter, and I hope you will write again soon, that I may know you to be all safe and happy at home.

Our visit to Hendon [to see Anna and Ben Lefroy] will interest you, I am sure, but I need not enter into the particulars of it, as your papa will be able to answer almost *every question. I certainly* could *describe her bedroom, and her drawers, and her closet, better than he can, but I do not feel that I can stop to do it. I was rather sorry to hear that she* is *to have an instrument ; it seems throwing money away. They will wish the twenty-four guineas in the shape of sheets and towels six months hence; and as to her playing, it never can be anything.*

Her purple pelisse rather surprised me. I thought we had known all paraphernalia of that sort. I do not mean to blame her; it looked very well, and I dare say she wanted it. I suspect nothing worse than its being got in secret, and not owned to anybody. I received a very kind note from her yesterday, to ask me to come again and stay a night with them. I cannot do it, but I was pleased to find that she had the power *of doing so right a thing. My going was to give them* both *pleasure very properly.*

I just saw Mr. Hayter [a government minister] at the play, and think his face would please me on acquaintance. I was sorry he did not dine here. It seemed rather odd to me to be in the theatre with nobody to watch *for. I was quite composed myself, at leisure for all the agitated Isabella could raise.*

Now, my dearest Fanny, I will begin a subject which comes in very naturally. You frighten me out of my wits by your reference. Your affection gives me the highest pleasure, but indeed you must not let anything depend on my opinion; your own feelings, and none but your own, should determine such an important point. So far, however, as answering your question, I have no scruple. I am perfectly convinced that your present feelings, supposing you were to marry now, *would be sufficient for his happiness; but when I think how very, very far it is from a 'now,' and take everything that* may be *into consideration, I dare not say, 'Determine to accept him;' the risk is too great for* you, *unless your own sentiments prompt it.*

You will think me perverse perhaps; in my last letter I was urging everything in his favour, and now I am inclining the other way, but I cannot help it; I am at present more impressed with the possible evil that may arise to you *from engaging yourself to him – in word or mind – than with anything else. When I consider how few young men you have yet seen much of; how capable you are (yes, I do still think you* very *capable) of being really in love; and how full of temptation the next six or seven years of your life will probably be (it is the very period of life for the* strongest *attachments to be formed), – I cannot wish you, with your present very cool feelings, to devote yourself in honour to him. It is very true that you never may attach another man his equal altogether; but if that other man has the power of attaching you* more, *he will be in your eyes the most perfect.*

I shall be glad if you can *revive past feelings, and from your unbiassed self resolve to go on as you have done, but this I do not expect; and without it I cannot wish you to be fettered. I should not be afraid of your* marrying *him; with all his worth you would soon love him enough for the happiness of both; but I should dread the continuance of this sort of tacit engagement, with such an uncertainty as there is of* when *it may be completed. Years may pass before he is independent; you like him well enough to marry, but not well enough to wait; the unpleasantness of appearing fickle is certainly great; but if you think you want punishment for past illusions, there it is, and nothing can be compared to the misery of being bound* without *love – bound to one, and preferring another;* that *is a punishment which you* do not *deserve.*

I know you did not meet, or rather will not meet, to-day, as he called here yesterday; and I am glad of it. It does not seem very likely, at least, that he should be in time for a dinner visit sixty miles off. We did not see him, only found his card when we came home at four. Your Uncle H. merely observed that he was a day after 'the fair.' *He asked your brother on Monday (when Mr. Hayter was talked of) why he did not invite* him *too; saying, 'I know he is in town, for I met him the other day in Bond St.' Edward answered that he did not know where he was to be found. 'Don't you know his chambers?' 'No.'*

I shall be most glad to hear from you again, my dearest Fanny, but it must not be later than Saturday, as we shall be off on Monday long before the letters are delivered; and write something *that may do to be read or told. I am to take the Miss Moores back on Saturday, and when I return I shall hope to find your pleasant little flowing scrawl on the table. It will be a relief to me after playing at ma'ams, for though I like Miss H. M. as much as one can at my time of life after a day's acquaintance, it is uphill work to be talking to those whom one knows so little.*

Only one *comes back with me to-morrow, probably Miss Eliza, and I rather dread it. We shall not have two ideas in common. She is young, pretty, chattering, and thinking chiefly, I presume, of dress, company, and admiration. Mr. Sanford [friend and business associate of Henry] is to join us at dinner, which will be a comfort, and in the evening, while your uncle and Miss Eliza play chess, he shall tell me comical things and I will laugh at them, which will be a pleasure to both.*

I called in Keppel Street and saw them all, including dear Uncle Charles, who is to come and dine with us quietly to-day. Little Harriot sat in my lap, and seemed as gentle and affectionate as ever, and as pretty, except not being quite well. Fanny is a fine stout girl, talking incessantly, with an interesting degree of lisp and indistinctness, and very likely may be the handsomest in time. Cassy did not show more pleasure in seeing me than her sisters, but I expected no better. She does not shine in the tender feelings. She will never be a Miss O'Neil, more in the Mrs. Siddons line.

Thank you, but it is not settled yet whether I do *hazard a second edition. We are to see Egerton [publisher] to-day, when it will probably be determined. People are more ready to borrow and praise than to buy, which I cannot wonder at; but though I like praise as well as anybody, I like what Edward calls '*Pewter,*' too. I hope he continues careful of his eyes and finds the good effect of it. I cannot suppose we differ in our ideas of the Christian religion. You have given an excellent description of it. We only affix a different meaning to the word* evangelical.
Yours most affectionately,
J. AUSTEN.
Miss Knight, Godmersham Park,
Faversham, Kent.

LXXXII

[The following three letters were actually written in 1817.]
Chawton: (Feb. 20, 1816).
MY DEAREST FANNY,

You are inimitable, irresistible. You are the delight of my life. Such letters, such entertaining letters, as you have lately sent! such a description of your queer little heart! such a lovely display of what imagination does. You are worth your weight in gold, or even in the new silver coinage. I cannot express to you what I have felt in reading your history of yourself – how full of pity and concern, and admiration and amusement, I have been! You are the paragon of all that is silly and sensible, common-place and eccentric, sad and lively, provoking and interesting. Who can keep pace with the fluctuations of your fancy, the capprizios of your taste, the contradictions of your feelings? You are so odd, and all the time so perfectly natural! – so peculiar in yourself, and yet so like everybody else!

It is very, very gratifying to me to know you so intimately. You can hardly think what a pleasure it is to me to have such thorough pictures of your heart. Oh, what a loss it will be when you are married! You are too agreeable in your single state – too agreeable as a niece. I shall hate you when your delicious play of mind is all settled down in conjugal and maternal affections.

Mr. B— frightens me. He will have you. I see you at the altar. I have some *faith in Mrs. C. Cage's observation, and still more in Lizzy's; and, besides, I know it* must *be so. He must be wishing to attach you. It would be too stupid and too shameful in him to be otherwise; and all the family are seeking your acquaintance.*

Do not imagine that I have any real objection; I have rather taken a fancy to him than not, and I like the house for you. I only do not like you should marry anybody. And yet I do wish you to marry very much, because I know you will never be happy till you are; but the loss of a Fanny Knight will be never made up to me. My 'affec. niece F. C. B – ' will be but a poor substitute. I do not like your being nervous, and so apt to cry – it is a sign you are not quite well; but I hope Mr. Scud [Mr Scudamore, Fanny's doctor] – as you always write his name (your Mr. Scuds amuse me very much) – will do you good.

What a comfort that Cassandra should be so recovered! It was more than we had expected. I can easily believe she was very patient and very good. I always loved Cassandra, for her fine dark eyes and sweet temper. I am almost entirely cured of my rheumatism – just a little pain in my knee now and then, to make me remember what it was, and keep on flannel. Aunt Cassandra nursed me so beautifully.

I enjoy your visit to Goodnestone, it must be a great pleasure to you; you have not seen Fanny Cage in comfort so long. I hope she represents and remonstrates and reasons with you properly. Why should you be living in dread of his marrying somebody else? (Yet, how natural!) You did not choose to have him yourself, why not allow him to take comfort where he can? In your conscience you know *that he could not bear a companion with a more animated character. You cannot forget how you felt under the idea of its having been possible that he might have dined in Hans Place.*

My dearest Fanny, I cannot bear you should be unhappy about him. Think of his principles; think of his father's objection, of want of money, &c. &c. But I am doing no good; no, all that I urge against him will rather make you take his part more, sweet, perverse Fanny.

And now I will tell you that we like your Henry [Fanny's brother] to the utmost, to the very top of the glass, quite brimful. He is a very pleasing young man. I do not see how he could be mended. He does really bid fair to be everything his father and sister could wish; and William [Fanny's brother] I love very much indeed, and so we do all; he is quite our own William. In short, we are very comfortable together; that is, we can answer for ourselves.

*Mrs. Deedes is as welcome as May to all our benevolence to her son; we only lamented that we could not do more, and that the 50*l. *note we slipped into his hand at parting was necessarily the limit of our offering. Good Mrs. Deedes! Scandal and gossip; yes, I dare say you are well stocked, but I am very fond of Mrs. — for reasons good. Thank you for mentioning her praise of 'Emma' &c.*

I have contributed the marking to Uncle H.'s shirts, and now they are a complete memorial of the tender regard of many.

Friday. *– I had no idea when I began this yesterday of sending it before your brother went back, but I have written away my foolish thoughts at such a rate that I will not keep them many hours longer to stare me in the face.*

Much obliged for the quadrilles, which I am grown to think pretty enough, though of course they are very inferior to the cotillions of my own day.

Ben and Anna walked here last Sunday to hear Uncle Henry [recently ordained], and she looked so pretty, it was quite a pleasure to see her, so young and so blooming, and so innocent, as if she had never had a wicked thought in her life, which yet one has some reason to suppose she must have had, if we believe the doctrine of original sin. I hope Lizzy will have her play very kindly arranged for her. Henry is generally thought very good-looking, but not so handsome as Edward. I think I prefer his face. Wm. is in excellent looks, has a fine appetite, and seems perfectly well. You will have a great break up at Godmersham in the spring. You must *feel their all going. It is very right, however! Poor Miss C. [Clewes]! I shall pity her when she begins to understand herself.*

Your objection to the quadrilles delighted me exceedingly. Pretty well, for a lady irrecoverably attached to one *person! Sweet Fanny, believe no such thing of yourself, spread no such malicious slander upon your understanding, within the precincts of your imagination. Do not speak ill of your sense merely for the gratification of your fancy; yours is sense which deserves more honourable treatment. You are* not *in love with him; you never* have *been really in love with him.*

Yours very affectionately,

J. AUSTEN.

Miss Knight, Godmersham Park

Faversham, Kent.

LXXXIII

Chawton: Thursday (March 13).

As to making any adequate return for such a letter as yours, my dearest Fanny, it is absolutely impossible. If I were to labour at it all the rest of my life, and live to the age of Methuselah, I could never accomplish anything so long and so perfect; but I cannot let William go without a few lines of acknowledgment and reply.

I have pretty well done with Mr. —. By your description, he cannot *be in love with you, however he may try at it; and I could not wish the match unless there were a great deal of love on his side. I do not know what to do about Jemima Branfill. What does her dancing away with so much spirit mean? That she does not care for* him, *or only wishes to* appear *not to care for him? Who can understand a young lady?*

Poor Mrs. C. Milles, that she should die on the wrong day at last, after being about it so long! It was unlucky that the Goodnestone party could not meet you, and I hope her friendly, obliging, social spirit, which delighted in drawing people together, was not conscious of the division and disappointment she was occasioning. I am sorry and surprised that you speak of her as having little to leave, and must feel for Miss Milles, though she is *Molly, if a material loss of income is to attend her other loss. Single women have a dreadful propensity for being poor, which is one very strong argument in favour of matrimony, but I need not dwell on such arguments with* you, *pretty dear.*

To you I shall say, as I have often said before, Do not be in a hurry, the right man will come at last; you will in the course of the next two or three years meet with somebody more generally unexceptionable than anyone you have yet known, who will love you as warmly as possible, and who will so completely attach you that you will feel you never really loved before.

Do none of the A.'s [Plumptres] ever come to balls now? You have never mentioned them as being at any. And what do you hear of the Gipps, or of Fanny and her husband?

Aunt Cassandra walked to Wyards yesterday with Mrs. Digweed. Anna has had a bad cold, and looks pale. She has just weaned Julia.

I *have also heard lately from your Aunt Harriot, and cannot understand their plans in parting with Miss S., whom she seems very much to value now that Harriot and Eleanor are both of an age for a governess to be so useful to, especially as, when Caroline was sent to school some years, Miss* Bell *was still retained, though the others even then were nursery children. They have some good reason, I dare say, though I cannot penetrate it, and till I know what it is I shall invent a bad one, and amuse myself with accounting for the difference of measures by supposing Miss S. to be a superior sort of woman, who has never stooped to recommend herself to the master of the family by flattery, as Miss Bell did.*

I will *answer your kind questions more than you expect. 'Miss Catherine' [later published as* Northanger Abbey*] is put upon the shelf for the present, and I do not know that she will ever come out; but I have a something ready for publication, which may, perhaps, appear about a twelvemonth hence. It is short – about the length of 'Catherine.' This is for yourself alone. Neither Mr. Salusbury [Fanny's friend] nor Mr. Wildman [the Mr B. of the previous letter] is to know of it.*

I am got tolerably well again, quite equal to walking about and enjoying the air, and by sitting down and resting a good while between my walks, I get exercise enough. I have a scheme, however, for accomplishing more, as the weather grows spring-like. I mean to take to riding the donkey; it will be more independent and less troublesome than the use of the carriage, and I shall be able to go about with Aunt Cassandra in her walks to Alton and Wyards.

I hope you will think Wm. [Fanny's brother] looking well; he was bilious the other day, and At. Cass. supplied him with a dose at his own request. I am sure *you would have approved it. Wm. and I are the best of friends. I love him very much. Everything is so* natural *about him – his affections, his manners, and his drollery. He entertains and interests us extremely.*

Mat. Hammond and A. M. Shaw [Godmersham neighbours who were soon to marry] are people whom I cannot care for, in themselves, but I enter into their situation, and am glad they are so happy. If I were the Duchess of Richmond, I should be very miserable about my son's choice.

Our fears increase for poor little Harriot; the latest account is that Sir Ev. Home is confirmed in his opinion of there being water on the brain. I hope Heaven, in its mercy, will take her soon. Her poor father will be quite worn out by his feelings for her; he cannot spare Cassy at present, she is an occupation and a comfort to him.

Yours very affectionately,

J. Austen

LXXXIV

Chawton: Sunday (March 23).

I am very much obliged to you, my dearest Fanny, for sending me Mr. W.'s [Wildman] conversation; I had great amusement in reading it, and I hope I am not affronted, and do not think the worse of him for having a brain so very different from mine; but my strongest sensation of all is astonishment *at your being able to press him on the subject so perseveringly [Fanny had been seeking Mr Wildman's opinion on Jane's books without telling him that she was the author]; and I agree with your papa, that it was not fair. When he knows the truth he will be uncomfortable.*

You are the oddest creature! Nervous enough in some respects, but in others perfectly without nerves! Quite unrepulsable, hardened, and impudent. Do not oblige him to read any more. Have mercy on him, tell him the truth, and make him an apology. He and I should not in the least agree, of course, in our ideas of novels and heroines. Pictures of perfection, as you know, make me sick and wicked; but there is some very good sense in what he says, and I particularly respect him for wishing to think well of all young ladies; it shows an amiable and a delicate mind. And he deserves better treatment than to be obliged to read any more of my works.

*Do not be surprised at finding Uncle Henry acquainted with my having another ready for publication [*Persuasion*]. I could not say No when he asked me, but he knows nothing more of it. You will not like it, so you need not be impatient. You may* perhaps *like the heroine, as she is almost too good for me.*

Many thanks for your kind care for my health; I certainly have not been well for many weeks, and about a week ago I was very poorly. I have had a good deal of fever at times, and indifferent nights; but I am considerably better now and am recovering my looks a little, which have been bad enough – black and white, and every wrong colour. I must not depend upon being ever very blooming again. Sickness is a dangerous indulgence at my time of life. Thank you for everything you tell me. I do not feel worthy of it by anything that I can say in return, but I assure you my pleasure in your letters is quite as great as ever, and I am interested and amused just as you could wish me. If there is a Miss Marsden, I perceive whom she will marry.

Evening. – *I was languid and dull and very bad company when I wrote the above; I am better now, to my own feelings at least, and wish I may be more agreeable. We are going to have rain, and after that very pleasant genial weather, which will exactly do for me, as my saddle will then be completed, and air and exercise is what I want. Indeed, I shall be very glad when the event at Scarlets is over [James Leigh Perrot was dying], the expectation of it keeps us in a worry, your grandmamma especially; she sits brooding over evils which cannot be remedied, and conduct impossible to be understood.*

Now the reports from Keppel St. are rather better; little Harriot's headaches are abated, and Sir Evd. is satisfied with the effect of the mercury, and does not despair of a cure. The complaint I find is not considered incurable nowadays, provided the patient be young enough not to have the head hardened. The water in that case may be drawn off by mercury. But though this is a new idea to us, perhaps it may have been long familiar to you through your friend Mr. Scud. I hope his high renown is sustained by driving away William's cough.

Tell Wm. that Triggs [gamekeeper on the Chawton estate] is as beautiful and condescending as ever, and was so good as to dine with us to-day and tell him that I often play at nines *and think of him.*

The Papillons [rector of Chawton and his sister] came back on Friday night, but I have not seen them yet, as I do not venture to church. I cannot hear, however, but that they are the same Mr. P. and his sister they used to be. She has engaged a new maidservant in Mrs. Calker's room, whom she means to make also housekeeper under herself.

Old Philmore was buried yesterday, and I, by way of saying something to Triggs, observed that it had been a very handsome funeral; but his manner of reply made me suppose that it was not generally esteemed so. I can only be sure of one *part being very handsome – Triggs himself, walking behind in his green coat. Mrs. Philmore attended as chief mourner, in bombazine, made very short, and flounced with crape.*

Tuesday. – *I have had various plans as to this letter, but at last I have determined that Uncle Henry shall forward it from London. I want to see how Canterbury looks in the direction. When once Uncle H. has left* us *I shall wish him with* you. *London has become a hateful place to him [following his bankruptcy], and he is always depressed by the idea of it. I hope he will be in time for your sick. I am sure he must do that part of his duty as excellently as all the rest. He returned yesterday from Steventon, and was with us by breakfast, bringing Edward with him, only that Edwd. stayed to breakfast at Wyards. We had a pleasant family day, for the Altons [Frank and Mary Austen, now approaching the end of another pregnancy] dined with us, the last visit of the kind probably which* she *will be able to pay us for many a month.*

I hope your own Henry is in France, and that you have heard from him; the passage once over, he will feel all happiness. I took my first ride yesterday, and liked it very much. I went up Mounter's Lane and round by where the new cottages are to be, and found the exercise and everything very pleasant; and I had the advantage of agreeable companions, as At. Cass. and Edward walked by my side. At. Cass. is such an excellent nurse, so assiduous and unwearied! But you know all that already.

Very affectionately yours,

J. AUSTEN.

Miss Knight, Godmersham Park,

Canterbury.

The following letters have been given me by one of Mrs. B. Lefroy's daughters, and are interesting as showing the sympathy which Jane had for a young authoress, and the care and minuteness with which she looked into every detail of composition. 'Anna Austen' was engaged to Mr. Lefroy in 1814, and was occupied at the same time in writing a novel which she submitted to the valuable criticism of 'Aunt Jane.' The first letter has no date, but from the context must have been written in May or June.

LXXXV

MY DEAR ANNA,

I am very much obliged to you for sending your MS. It has entertained me extremely; indeed all of us. I read it aloud to your Grandmama and Aunt Cass., and we were all very much pleased. The spirit does not droop at all. Sir Thos., Lady Helen and St. Julian are very well done, and Cecilia continues to be interesting in spite of her being so amiable. It was very fit you should advance her age. I like the beginning of Devereux Forester very much, a great deal better than if he had been very good or very bad. A few verbal corrections are all that I felt tempted to make; the principal of them is a speech of St. Julian to Lady Helen, which you see I have presumed to alter. As Lady H. is Cecilia's superior, it would not be correct to talk of her being introduced. It is Cecilia who must be introduced. And I do not like a lover speaking in the 3rd person; it is too much like the part of Lord Overtley, and I *think it not natural. If* you *think differently, however, you need not mind me. I am impatient for more, and only wait for a safe conveyance to return this.*

Yours affectionately,

J. A.

LXXXVI

August 10, 1814.

MY DEAR ANNA,

I am quite ashamed to find that I have never answered some question of yours in a former note. I kept it on purpose to refer to it at a proper time and then forgot it. I like the name 'Which is the Heroine' very well, and I daresay shall grow to like it very much in time; but 'Enthusiasm' was something so very superior that my common title must appear to disadvantage. I am not sensible of any blunders about Dawlish; the library was pitiful and wretched twelve years ago and not likely to have anybody's publications. There is no such title as Desborough either among dukes, marquises, earls, viscounts, or barons. These were your inquiries. I will now thank you for your envelope received this morning. Your Aunt Cass is as well pleased with St. Julian as ever, and I am delighted with the idea of seeing Progillian again.

Wednesday *17. – We have now just finished the first of the three books I had the pleasure of receiving yesterday. I read it aloud and we are all very much amused, and like the work quite as well as ever. I depend on getting through another book before dinner, but there is really a good deal of respectable reading in your forty-eight pages. I have no doubt six would make a very good-sized volume. You must have been quite pleased to have accomplished so much. I like Lord Portman [1] and his brother very much. I am only afraid that Lord P.'s good nature will make most people like him better than he deserves. The whole family are very good, and Lady Anne, who was your great dread, you have succeeded particularly well with. Bell Griffin is just what she should be. My corrections have not been more important than before; here and there we have thought the sense could be expressed in fewer words, and I have scratched out Sir Thos. from walking with the others to the stables, &c. the very day after breaking his arm; for, though I find your papa did walk out immediately after his arm was set, I think it can be so little usual as to appear unnatural in a book. Lynn will not do. Lynn is towards forty miles from Dawlish and would not be talked of there. I have put Starcross instead. If you prefer Easton that must be always safe.*

I have also scratched out the introduction between Lord Portman and his brother and Mr. Griffin. A country surgeon (don't tell Mr. C. Lyford) would not be introduced to men of their rank, and when Mr. P. is first brought in, he would not be introduced as the Honourable. That distinction is never mentioned at such times, at least I believe not. Now we have finished the second book, or rather the fifth. I do *think you had better omit Lady Helena's postscript. To those that are acquainted with 'Pride and Prejudice' it will seem an imitation. And your Aunt C. and I both recommend your making a little alteration in the last scene between Devereux F. and Lady Clanmurray and her daughter. We think they press him too much, more than sensible or well-bred women would do; Lady C., at least, should have discretion enough to be sooner satisfied with his determination of not going with them. I am very much pleased with Egerton as yet. I did not expect to like him, but I do, and Susan is a very nice little animated creature; but St. Julian is the delight of our lives. He is quite interesting. The whole of his break off with Lady Helena is very well done. Yes; Russell Square is a very proper distance from Berkeley Square. We are reading the last book. They must be two days going from Dawlish to Bath. They are nearly 100 miles apart. [2]*

Thursday. – *We finished it last night after our return from drinking tea at the Great House. The last chapter does not please us quite so well; we do not thoroughly like the play, perhaps from having had too much of plays in that way lately (vide 'Mansfield Park'), and we think you had better not leave England. Let the Portmans go to Ireland; but as you know nothing of the manners there, you had better not go with them. You will be in danger of giving false representations. Stick to Bath and the Foresters. There you will be quite at home.*

Your Aunt C. does not like desultory novels, and is rather afraid yours will be too much so, that there will be too frequently a change from one set of people to another, and that circumstances will be introduced of apparent consequence which will lead to nothing. It will not be so great an objection to me if it does. I allow much more latitude than she does, and think nature and spirit cover many sins of a wandering story, and people in general do not care so much about it, for your comfort.

I should like to have had more of Devereux. I do not feel enough acquainted with him. You were afraid of meddling with him I dare say. I like your sketch of Lord Clanmurray, and your picture of the two young girls' enjoyment is very good. I have not noticed St. Julian's serious conversation with Cecilia, but I like it exceedingly. What he says about the madness of otherwise sensible women on the subject of their daughters coming out is worth its weight in gold.

I do not perceive that the language sinks. Pray go on.

1. It must be remembered that there was no 'Lord Portman' in 1814, the creation of that title having been in 1837.
2. Our modern race of travellers would hardly be satisfied with this rate of progress. We have somewhat accelerated our speed since Jane's day, and when inclined to grumble because a train is ten minutes late, should do well to remember what advantages we enjoy over our respected predecessors.

LXXXVII

Chawton: (Sept. 9).

MY DEAR ANNA,

We have been very much amused by your three books, but I have a good many criticisms to make, more than you will like. We are not satisfied with Mrs. Forester settling herself as tenant and near neighbour to such a man as Sir Thomas, without having some other inducement to go there. She ought to have some friend living thereabouts to tempt her. A woman going with two girls just growing up into a neighbourhood where she knows nobody but one man of not very good character, is an awkwardness which so prudent a woman as Mrs. F. would not be likely to fall into. Remember she is very prudent. You must not let her act inconsistently. Give her a friend, and let that friend be invited by Sir Thomas H. to meet her, and we shall have no objection to her dining at the Priory as she does; but otherwise a woman in her situation would hardly go there before she had been visited by other families. I like the scene itself, the Miss Leslie, Lady Anne, and the music very much. Leslie is a noble name. Sir Thomas H. you always do very well. I have only taken the liberty of expunging one phrase of his which would not be allowable – 'Bless my heart!' It is too familiar and inelegant. Your grandmother is more disturbed at Mrs. Forester's not returning the Egertons' visit sooner than by anything else. They ought to have called at the Parsonage before Sunday. You describe a sweet place, but your descriptions are often more minute than will be liked. You give too many particulars of right hand and left. Mrs. Forester is not careful enough of Susan's health. Susan ought not to be walking out so soon after heavy rains, taking long walks in the dirt. An anxious mother would not suffer it. I like your Susan very much, she is a sweet creature, her playfulness of fancy is very delightful. I like her as she is now exceedingly, but I am not quite so well satisfied with her behaviour to George R. At first she seems all over attachment and feeling, and afterwards to have none at all; she is so extremely confused at the ball and so well satisfied apparently with Mr. Morgan. She seems to have changed her character.

You are now collecting your people delightfully, getting them exactly into such a spot as is the delight of my life. Three or four families in a country village is the very thing to work on, and I hope you will do a great deal more, and make full use of them while they are so very favourably arranged.

You are but now coming to the heart and beauty of your story. Until the heroine grows up the fun must be imperfect, but I expect a great deal of entertainment from the next three or four books, and I hope you will not resent these remarks by sending me no more. We like the Egertons very well. We see no blue pantaloons or cocks or hens. There is nothing to enchant one certainly in Mr. L. L., but we make no objection to him, and his inclination to like Susan is pleasing. The sister is a good contrast, but the name of Rachel is as much I can bear. They are not so much like the Papillons as I expected. Your last chapter is very entertaining, the conversation on genius, &c.; Mr.

St. Julian and Susan both talk in character, and very well. In some former parts, Cecilia is perhaps a little too solemn and good, but upon the whole her disposition is very well opposed to Susan's, her want of imagination is very natural. I wish you could make Mrs. Forester talk more; but she must be difficult to manage and make entertaining, because there is so much good sense and propriety about her that nothing can be made very broad. Her economy and her ambition must not be staring. The papers left by Mrs. Fisher are very good. Of course one guesses something. I hope when you have written a great deal more, you will be equal to scratching out some of the past. The scene with Mrs. Mellish I should condemn; it is prosy and nothing to the purpose; and indeed the more you can find in your heart to curtail between Dawlish and Newton Priors, the better I think it will be – one does not care for girls until they are grown up. Your Aunt C. quite understands the exquisiteness of that name – Newton Priors is really a nonpareil. Milton would have given his eyes to have thought of it. Is not the cottage taken from 'Tollard Royal'? [1]

Sunday. – *I am very glad, dear Anna, that I wrote as I did before this sad event occurred. I have only to add that your Grandmama does not seem the worse now for the shock.*

I shall be very happy to receive more of your work if more is ready; and you write so fast that I have great hopes Mr. Digweed will come back freighted with such a cargo as not all his hops or his sheep could equal the value of.

Your grandmama desires me to say that she will have finished your shoes to-morrow, and thinks they will look very well. And that she depends upon seeing you as you promise before you quit the country, and hopes you will give her more than a day.

Yours affectionately,
J. AUSTEN.

1. Thus far the letter was written on the ninth, but before it was finished news arrived at Chawton of the death of Mrs. Charles Austen. She died in her confinement and the baby died also. She left three little girls – Cassie, Harriet and Fanny. It was not until the 18th that Jane resumed her letter.

Jane was quite right in her expectation of more. A considerable packet was transmitted by the next opportunity. In these days, a bride expectant has all the time she can spare from her lover occupied by writing innumerable notes of thanks for innumerable presents and good wishes, to say nothing of those concerning the expensive and enormous trousseau now thought necessary. Of such business Miss Anna Austen had very little, and therefore she had ample leisure for her story.

LXXXVIII

Chawton: Wednesday (Sept. 28).

MY DEAR ANNA,

I hope you do not depend on having your book again immediately. I kept it that your grandmama may hear it, for it has not been possible yet to have any public reading. I have read it to your Aunt Cassandra, however, in our own room at night, while we undressed, and with a great deal of pleasure. We like the first chapter extremely, with only a little doubt whether Lady Helena is not almost too foolish. The matrimonial dialogue is very good certainly. I like Susan as well as ever, and begin now not to care at all about Cecilia; she may stay at Easton Court as long as she likes. Henry Mellish will be, I am afraid, too much in the common novel style – a handsome, amiable, unexceptionable young man (such as do not much abound in real life), desperately in love and all in vain. But I have no business to judge him so early. Jane Egerton is a very natural comprehensible girl, and the whole of her acquaintance with Susan and Susan's letter to Cecilia are very pleasing and quite in character. But Miss Egerton does not entirely satisfy us. She is too formal and solemn, we think, in her advice to her brother not to fall in love; and it is hardly like a sensible woman – it is putting it into his head. We should like a few hints from her better. We feel really obliged to you for introducing a Lady Kenrick; it will remove the greatest fault in the work, and I give you credit for considerable forbearance as an author in adopting so much of our opinion. I expect high fun about Mrs. Fisher and Sir Thomas. You have been perfectly right in telling Ben Lefroy of your work, and I am very glad to hear how much he likes it. His encouragement and approbation must be 'quite beyond everything.' [1] I do not at all wonder at his not expecting to like anybody so well as Cecilia at first, but I shall be surprised if he does not become a Susanite in time. Devereux Forester's being ruined by his vanity is extremely good, but I wish you would not let him plunge into a 'vortex of dissipation.' I do not object to the thing, but I cannot bear the expression; it is such thorough novel slang, and so old that I daresay Adam met with it in the first novel he opened. Indeed, I did very much like to know Ben's opinion. I hope he will continue to be pleased with it, and I think he must, but I cannot flatter him with there being much incident. We have no great right to wonder at his not valueing the name of Progillian. That is a source of delight which even he *can hardly be quite competent to.*

Walter Scott has no business to write novels, especially good ones. It is not fair. He has fame and profit enough as a poet, and should not be taking the bread out of the mouths of other people.

I do not like him, and do not mean to like 'Waverley' if I can help it, but fear I must.

I am quite determined, however, not to be pleased with Mrs. West's 'Alicia De Lacy,' should I ever meet with it, which I hope I shall not. I think I can be stout against anything written by Mrs. West. I have made up my mind to like no novels really but Miss Edgeworth's, yours, and my own.

What can you do with Egerton to increase the interest for him? I wish you could contrive something, some family occurrence to bring out his good qualities more. Some distress among brothers and sisters to relieve by the sale of his curacy! Something to carry him mysteriously away, and then be heard of at York or Edinburgh in an old great coat. I would not seriously recommend anything improbable, but if you could invent something spirited for him it would have a good effect. He might lend all his money to Captain Morris, but then he would be a great fool if he did. Cannot the Morrises quarrel and he reconcile them? Excuse the liberty I take in these suggestions.

Your Aunt Frank's nursemaid has just given her warning, but whether she is worth your having, or would take your place, I know not. She was Mrs. Webb's maid before she went to the Great House. She leaves your aunt because she cannot agree with the other servants. She is in love with the man and her head seems rather turned. He returns her affection, but she fancies every one else is wanting him and envying her. Her previous service must have fitted her for such a place as yours, and she is very active and cleanly. The Webbs [Chawton villagers] are really gone! When I saw the wagons at the door, and thought of all the trouble they must have in moving, I began to reproach myself for not having liked them better, but since the wagons have disappeared my conscience has been closed again, and I am excessively glad they are gone.

I am very fond of Sherlock's sermons and prefer them to almost any.

Your affectionate Aunt,

J. AUSTEN.

If you wish me to speak to the maid, let me know.

1. A phrase always in the mouth of one of the Chawton neighbours, Mrs. H. Digweed.

In October, Jane's correspondent paid her last visit to Chawton as Anna Austen. Very soon after her return, she wrote to tell them her wedding day was fixed. On November 8 she was married in the parish church of Steventon. Mr. B. Lefroy did not take holy orders until about three years after the marriage, and the first home of the young couple was at Hendon, to which place the following letter was addressed:

LXXXIX

Chawton: (Nov. 21, 1814).

MY DEAR ANNA,

I met Harriet Benn yesterday. She gave me her congratulations and desired they might be forwarded to you, and there they are. The chief news from this country is the death of old Mrs. Dormer. Mrs. Clement walks about in a new black velvet pelisse lined with yellow, and a white bobbin net veil, and looks remarkably well in them.

I think I understand the country about Hendon from your description. It must be very pretty in summer. Should you know from the atmosphere that you were within a dozen miles of London? Make everybody at Hendon admire 'Mansfield Park.'

Your affectionate Aunt,

J. A.

The next letter is written from Hans Place, where Jane was staying with her brother Henry, and from which they had recently driven down to see the newly-married couple at Hendon.

XC

Hans Place (Nov. 28, 1814).

MY DEAR ANNA,

I assure you we all came away very much pleased with our visit. We talked of you for about a mile and a half with great satisfaction; and I have been just sending a very good report of you to Miss Benn, with a full account of your dress for Susan and Maria.

We were all at the play last night to see Miss O'Neil in 'Isabella.' I do not think she was quite equal to my expectations. I fancy I want something more than can be. I took two pocket-handkerchiefs, but had very little occasion for either. She is an elegant creature, however, and hugs Mr. Young delightfully. I am going this morning to see the girls in Keppel Street. Cassy was excessively interested about your marriage when she heard of it, which was not until she was to drink your health on the wedding day.

She asked a thousand questions in her usual manner, what he said to you and what you said to him. If your uncle were at home he would send his best love, but I will not impose any base fictitious remembrances on you, mine I can honestly give, and remain

Your affectionate Aunt,

J. AUSTEN.

Marriage did not immediately stop Mrs. Lefroy's story-writing, and early in December she sent her aunt another packet, which elicited the following letter:–

XCI

Hans Place (Wednesday).

MY DEAR ANNA,

I have been very far from finding your book an evil, I assure you. I read it immediately, and with great pleasure. I think you are going on very well. The description of Dr. Griffin and Lady Helena's unhappiness is very good, and just what was likely to be. I am curious to know what the end of them will be. The name of Newton Priors is really invaluable; I never met with anything superior to it. It is delightful, and one could live on the name of Newton Priors for a twelvemonth. Indeed, I think you get on very fast. I only wish other people of my acquaintance could compose as rapidly. I am pleased with the dog scene and with the whole of George and Susan's love, but am more particularly struck with your serious conversations. They are very good throughout. St. Julian's history was quite a surprise to me. You had not very long known it yourself I suspect; but I have no objection to make to the circumstance, and it is very well told. His having been in love with the aunt gives Cecilia an additional interest with him. I like the idea – a very proper compliment to an aunt! I rather imagine indeed that nieces are seldom chosen but out of compliment to some aunt or another. I daresay Ben was in love with me once, and would never have thought of you if he had not supposed me dead of scarlet fever. Yes, I was in a mistake as to the number of books. I thought I had read three before the three at Chawton, but fewer than six will not do. I want to see dear Bell Griffin again; and had you not better give some hint of St. Julian's early history in the beginning of the story?

We shall see nothing of Streatham while we are in town, as Mrs. Hill is to lye in of a daughter. Mrs. Blackstone is to be with her. Mrs. Heathcote and Miss Bigg [1] are just leaving her. The latter writes me word that Miss Blackford is married, but I have never seen it in the papers, and one may as well be single if the wedding is not to be in print.

Your affectionate Aunt,

J. A.

1. Sisters to Mrs. Hill.

In August, 1815, Mr. and Mrs. B. Lefroy moved from Hendon, and took a small house called Wyards, near Alton and within a walk of Chawton. Wyards is more than once mentioned in our letters. In the autumn of 1815, Jane went up to Hans Place (as has been already stated) to visit her brother Henry, and to superintend the publishing of 'Emma' and at that time the following letter was written.

XCII

Chawton: Friday (Sept. 29).

MY DEAR ANNA,

We told Mr. B. Lefroy that if the weather did not prevent us we should certainly come and see you to-morrow and bring Cassy, trusting to your being good enough to give her a dinner about one o'clock, that we might be able to be with you the earlier and stay the longer. But on giving Cassy her choice between the Fair or Wyards, it must be confessed that she has preferred the former, which we trust will not greatly affront you; if it does, you may hope that some little Anna hereafter may revenge the insult by a similar preference of an Alton Fair to her Cousin Cassy. In the meanwhile we have determined to put off our visit to you until Monday, which we hope will be not less convenient. I wish the weather may not resolve on another put off. I must come to you before Wednesday if it be possible, for on that day I am going to London for a week or two with your Uncle Henry, who is expected here on Sunday. If Monday should appear too dirty for walking, and Mr. Lefroy would be so kind as to come and fetch me, I should be much obliged to him. Cassy might be of the party, and your Aunt Cassandra will take another opportunity.

Yours very affectionately, my dear Anna,

J. AUSTEN.

But before the week or two to which she had limited her visit in Hans Place was at an end, her brother fell ill, and on October 22 he was in such danger that she wrote to Steventon to summon her [Anna's] father to town. The letter was two days on the road, and reached him on Sunday the 24th. Even then he did not start immediately. In the evening he and his wife rode to Chawton, and it was not until the next day that he and Cassandra arrived in Hans Place. The malady from which Henry Austen was suffering was low fever, and he was for some days at death's door; but he rallied soon after his brother and sisters arrived, and recovered so quickly that the former was able to leave him at the end of the week. The great anxiety and fatigue which Jane underwent at this time was supposed by some of her family to have broken down her health. She was in a very feeble and exhausted condition when the bank in which her brother Henry was a partner broke, and he not only lost all that he possessed, but most of his relations suffered severely also. Jane was well enough to pay several visits with her sister in the summer of 1816, including one to Steventon – the last she ever paid to that home of her childhood. The last note which Mrs. Lefroy had preserved is dated.

XCIII

June 23, 1816.

MY DEAR ANNA,

Cassy desires her best thanks for the book. She was quite delighted to see it. I do not know when I have seen her so much struck by anybody's kindness as on this occasion. Her sensibility seems to be opening to the perception of great actions. These gloves having appeared on the pianoforte ever since you were here on Friday, we imagine they must be yours. Mrs. Digweed returned yesterday through all the afternoon's rain, and was of course wet through, but in speaking of it she never once said 'it was beyond everything,' which I am sure it must have been. Your Mama means to ride to Speen Hill to-morrow to see the Mrs. Hulberts, who are both very indifferent. By all accounts they really are breaking now – not so stout as the old jackass.

Yours affectionately,

J.A.

Chawton: Sunday, June 23.

Uncle Charles's birthday.

I insert here a letter of Jane Austen's written *backwards,* addressed to her niece 'Cassy,' daughter of Captain Charles Austen (afterwards Admiral) when a little girl.

XCIV

YM RAED YSSAC,

I hsiw uoy a yppah wen raey. Ruoy xis snisuoc emac ereh yadretsey, dna dah hcae a eceip fo ekac. Siht si elttil Yssac's yadhtrib, dna ehs si eerht sraey dlo. Knarf sah nugeb gninrael Nital ew deef eht Nibor yreve gninrom. Yllas netfo seriuqne retfa uoy. Yllas Mahneb sah tog a wen neerg nwog. Teirrah Thgink semoc yreve yad ot daer nwog. Teirrah Thgink semoc yreve yad ot daer ot Tnua Ardnassac. Doog eyb ym raed Yssac.

Tnua Ardnassac sdnes reh tseb evol, dna os ew od lla.

Ruoy etanoitceffa Tnua, ENAJ NETSUA.

Notwahc: Naj. 8.

In January 1817 she wrote of herself as better and able to walk into Alton, and hoped in the summer she should be able to walk back. In April her father in a note to Mrs. Lefroy says, 'I was happy to have a good account of herself written by her own hand, in a letter from your Aunt Jane; but all who love, that is all who know her, must be anxious on her account.' We all know how well grounded that anxiety was, and how soon her relations had to lament over the loss of the dearest and brightest member of their family.

And now I come to the saddest letters of all, those which tell us of the end of that bright life, cut short just at the time when the world might have hoped that unabated intellectual vigour, supplemented by the experience brought by maturer years, would have produced works if possible even more fascinating than those with which she had already embellished the literature of her country. But it was not to be. The fiat had gone forth – the ties which bound that sweet spirit to earth were to be severed, and a blank left, never to be filled, in the family which her loved and loving presence had blessed, and where she had been so well and fondly appreciated. In the early spring of 1817 the unfavourable symptoms increased, and the failure of her health was too visible to be neglected. Still, no apprehensions of immediate danger were entertained, and it is probable that when she left Chawton for Winchester in May, she did not recognize the fact that she was bidding a last farewell to 'Home.' Happy for her if it was so, for there are few things more melancholy than to look upon any beloved place or person with the knowledge that it is for '*the last time*.' In all probability this grief was spared to Jane, for even after her arrival at Winchester she spoke and wrote as if recovery was hopeful; and I fancy that her relations were by no means aware that the end was so near.

I find from my mother's pocket-books that she received at least four letters from 'Aunt Jane' in 1817, the date of the last being March 26, but of these I have found none. She wrote to her Aunt several times in June (as Cassandra's letters imply), and as late as July 9, 10, and 15, the last letter of which must either be the one specially alluded to in Letter 95, or must have arrived after her death. The entries in my mother's pocket-books at this time show how much her heart was with her relations at Winchester.

June 14. – 'A sad account of my poor dear Aunt Jane.'

June 18. – 'Another hopeless account from Winchester.'

June 29. – 'Much the same account of dear Aunt Jane.'

Then comes (July 20) 'A letter from Papa announcing my poor dear Aunt Jane Austen's death at four on Friday morn,' and further on are allusions to the letters which follow.

July 22. – 'A long letter from dear Aunt Cass., with many affecting particulars.' 'Wrote great part of a letter to Aunt Cass. and was miserable.' My mother always summarized the 'principal events of the year' at the end of each pocket-book, and at the head of her summary of those in 1817 comes: 'I had the misery of losing my dear Aunt Jane after a lingering illness.' So terminated the friendship of two natures, which in many respects singularly harmonized, and each of which, whilst on earth, contributed in a remarkable degree to the happiness of those among whom its lot was cast.

Cassandra's letters tell the tale of the event in words that require no addition from me. They are simple and affecting – the words of one who had been stricken by a great grief, but whose religion stood her in good stead, and enabled her to bear it with fortitiude. The firm and loving bond of union which had ever united the Austen family, naturally intensified their sorrow at the loss of one of their number, and that the one of whom they had been so proud as well as so fond. They laid her within the walls of the old cathedral which she had loved so much, and went sorrowfully back to their homes, with the feeling that nothing could replace to them the treasure they had lost. And most heavily of all must the blow have fallen upon the only sister, the correspondent, the companion, the other self of Jane, who had to return alone to the desolate home, and to the mother to whose comforts the two had hitherto ministered together, but who would henceforward have her alone on whom to rely. The return must have been sad indeed; every moment the surrounding associations must have awakened old memories and kept alive her heart-grief, and nothing could have rendered the misery endurable save that hope so earnestly expressed in her letters, that she and her sister would be re-united hereafter. They are indeed sad letters, but they form the proper conclusion to the series which I give to the world. The lock of Jane's hair, mentioned at the end of the last letter, was set in an oval brooch, bearing simply the inscription of her name and the date of her death. I have it now in my possession.

Letters from Miss Cassandra Austen to her niece Miss Knight, after the death of her sister Jane, July 18, 1817.

XCV

Winchester: Sunday.

MY DEAREST FANNY,

Doubly dear to me now for her dear sake whom we have lost. She did love you most sincerely, and never shall I forget the proofs of love you gave her during her illness in writing those kind, amusing letters at a time when I know your feelings would have dictated so different a style. Take the only reward I can give you in the assurance that your benevolent purpose was *answered; you* did *contribute to her enjoyment.*

Even your last letter afforded pleasure. I merely cut the seal and gave it to her; she opened it and read it herself, afterwards she gave it to me to read, and then talked to me a little and not uncheerfully of its contents, but there was then a languor about her which prevented her taking the same interest in anything she had been used to do.

Since Tuesday evening, when her complaint returned, there was a visible change, she slept more and much more comfortably; indeed, during the last eight-and-forty hours she was more asleep than awake. Her looks altered and she fell away, but I perceived no material diminution of strength, and, though I was then hopeless of a recovery, I had no suspicion how rapidly my loss was approaching.

I have *lost a treasure, such a sister, such a friend as never can have been surpassed. She was the sun of my life, the gilder of every pleasure, the soother of every sorrow; I had not a thought concealed from her, and it is as if I had lost a part of myself. I loved her only too well – not better than she deserved, but I am conscious that my affection for her made me sometimes unjust to and negligent of others; and I can acknowledge, more than as a general principle, the justice of the Hand which has struck this blow.*

You know me too well to be at all afraid that I should suffer materially from my feelings; I am perfectly conscious of the extent of my irreparable loss, but I am not at all overpowered and very little indisposed, nothing but what a short time, with rest and change of air, will remove. I thank God that I was enabled to attend her to the last, and amongst my many causes of self-reproach I have not to add any wilful neglect of her comfort.

She felt herself to be dying about half-an-hour before she became tranquil and apparently unconscious. During that half-hour was her struggle, poor soul! She said she could not tell us what she suffered, though she complained of little fixed pain. When I asked her if there was anything she wanted, her answer was she wanted nothing but death, and some of her words were: 'God grant me patience, pray for me, oh, pray for me!' Her voice was affected, but as long as she spoke she was intelligible.

I hope I do not break your heart, my dearest Fanny, by these particulars; I mean to afford you gratification whilst I am relieving my own feelings. I could not write so to anybody else; indeed you are the only person I have written to at all, excepting your grandmamma – it was to her, not your Uncle Charles, I wrote on Friday.

Immediately after dinner on Thursday I went into the town to do an errand which your dear aunt was anxious about. I returned about a quarter before six and found her recovering from faintness and oppression; she got so well as to be able to give me a minute account of her seizure, and when the clock struck six she was talking quietly to me.

I cannot say how soon afterwards she was seized again with the same faintness, which was followed by the sufferings she could not describe; but Mr. Lyford had been sent for, had applied something to give her ease, and she was in a state of quiet insensibility by seven o'clock at the latest. From that time till half-past four, when she ceased to breathe, she scarcely moved a limb, so that we have every reason to think, with gratitude to the Almighty, that her sufferings were over. A slight motion of the head with every breath remained till almost the last. I sat close to her with a pillow in my lap to assist in supporting her head, which was almost off the bed, for six hours; fatigue made me then resign my place to Mrs. J. A. for two hours and a-half, when I took it again, and in about an hour more she breathed her last.

I was able to close her eyes myself, and it was a great gratification to me to render her those last services. There was nothing convulsed which gave the idea of pain in her look; on the contrary, but for the continual motion of the head she gave one the idea of a beautiful statue, and even now, in her coffin, there is such a sweet, serene air over her countenance as is quite pleasant to contemplate.

This day, my dearest Fanny, you have had the melancholy intelligence, and I know you suffer severely, but I likewise know that you will apply to the fountain-head for consolation, and that our merciful God is never deaf to such prayers as you will offer.

The last sad ceremony is to take place on Thursday morning; her dear remains are to be deposited in the cathedral. It is a satisfaction to me to think that they are to lie in a building she admired so much; her precious soul, I presume to hope, reposes in a far superior mansion. May mine one day be re-united to it!

Your dear papa, your Uncle Henry, and Frank and Edwd. Austen, instead of his father, will attend. I hope they will none of them suffer lastingly from their pious exertions. The ceremony must be over before ten o'clock, as the cathedral service begins at that hour, so that we shall be at home early in the day, for there will be nothing to keep us here afterwards.

Your Uncle James came to us yesterday, and is gone home to-day. Uncle H. goes to Chawton to-morrow morning; he has given every necessary direction here, and I think his company there will do good. He returns to us again on Tuesday evening.

I did not think to have written a long letter when I began, but I have found the employment draw me on, and I hope I shall have been giving you more pleasure than pain. Remember me kindly to Mrs. J. Bridges (I am so glad she is with you now), and give my best love to Lizzie and all the others.

I am, my dearest Fanny,

Most affectionately yours,

CASS. ELIZ. AUSTEN.

I have said nothing about those at Chawton, because I am sure you hear from your papa.

XCVI

Chawton: Tuesday (July 29, 1817).

MY DEAREST FANNY,

I have just read your letter for the third time, and thank you most sincerely for every kind expression to myself, and still more warmly for your praises of her who I believe was better known to you than to any human being besides myself. Nothing of the sort could have been more gratifying to me than the manner in which you write of her, and if the dear angel is conscious of what passes here, and is not above all earthly feelings, she may perhaps receive pleasure in being so mourned. Had she *been the survivor I can fancy her speaking of* you *in almost the same terms. There are certainly many points of strong resemblance in your characters; in your intimate acquaintance with each other, and your mutual strong affection, you were counterparts.*

Thursday was not so dreadful a day to me as you imagined. There was so much necessary to be done that there was no time for additional misery. Everything was conducted with the greatest tranquillity, and but that I was determined I would see the last, and therefore was upon the listen, I should not have known when they left the house. I watched the little mournful procession the length of the street; and when it turned from my sight, and I had lost her for ever, even then I was not overpowered, nor so much agitated as I am now in writing of it. Never was human being more sincerely mourned by those who attended her remains than was this dear creature. May the sorrow with which she is parted with on earth be a prognostic of the joy with which she is hailed in heaven!

I continue very tolerably well – much better than any one could have supposed possible, because I certainly have had considerable fatigue of body as well as anguish of mind for months back; but I really am well, and I hope I am properly grateful to the Almighty for having been so supported. Your grandmamma, too, is much better than when I came home.

I did not think your dear papa appeared well, and I understand that he seemed much more comfortable after his return from Winchester than he had done before. I need not tell you that he was a great comfort to me; indeed, I can never say enough of the kindness I have received from him and from every other friend.

I get out of doors a good deal and am able to employ myself. Of course those employments suit me best which leave me most at leisure to think of her I have lost, and I do think of her in every variety of circumstance. In our happy hours of confidential intercourse, in the cheerful family party which she so ornamented, in her sick room, on her death-bed, and as (I hope) an inhabitant of heaven. Oh, if I may one day be re-united to her there! I know the time must come when my mind will be less engrossed by her idea, but I do not like to think of it. If I think of her less as on earth, God grant that I may never cease to reflect on her as inhabiting heaven, and never cease my humble endeavours (when it shall please God) to join her there.

In looking at a few of the precious papers which are now my property I have found some memorandums, amongst which she desires that one of her gold chains may be given to her god-daughter Louisa, and a lock of her hair be set for you. You can need no assurance, my dearest Fanny, that every request of your beloved aunt will be sacred with me. Be so good as to say whether you prefer a brooch or ring. God bless you, my dearest Fanny. Believe me, most affectionately yours,

CASS. ELIZTH. AUSTEN.

Miss Knight, Godmersham Park

Canterbury.

Enclosed in one of the Letters of 1807.

Verses to rhyme with 'Rose.'

1. Mrs. Austen
This morning I woke from a quiet repose,
I first rubb'd my eyes, and I next blew my nose;
With my stockings and shoes I then covered my toes,
And proceeded to put on the rest of my clothes.
This was finished in less than an hour, I suppose.
I employ'd myself next in repairing my hose.
T'was a work of necessity, not what I chose;
Of my sock I'd much rather have knit twenty rows
My work being done, I look'd through the windows,
And with pleasure beheld all the bucks and the does,
The cows and the bullocks, the wethers and ewes.
To the library each morning the family goes,
So I went with the rest, though I felt rather froze.
My flesh is much warmer, my blood freer flows,
When I work in the garden with rakes and with hoes.
And now I believe I must come to a close,
For I find I grow stupid e'en while I compose.
If I write any longer my verse will be prose.

2. Miss Austen (Cassandra).
Love, they say, is like a rose;
I'm sure t'is like the wind that blows,
For not a human creature knows
How it comes or where it goes.
It is the cause of many woes:
It swells the eyes and reds the nose,
And very often changes those
Who once were friends to bitter foes.
But let us now the scene transpose
And think no more of tears and throes.
Why may we not as well suppose
A smiling face the urchin shows?
And when with joy the bosom glows,
And when the heart has full repose,
'Tis mutual love the gift bestows.

3. Miss Jane Austen
Happy the lab'rer in his Sunday clothes!

In light-drab coat, smart waistcoat, well darn'd hose,
And hat upon his head, to church he goes;
As oft, with conscious pride, he downward throws
A glance upon the ample cabbage rose
Which stuck in button-hole, regales his nose,
He envies not the gayest London beaux.
In church he takes his seat among the rows,
Pays to the place the reverence he owes,
Likes best the prayers whose meaning least he knows,
Lists to the sermon in a softening doze,
And rises joyous at the welcome close.

4. Mrs. Elizabeth Austen.
Never before did I quarrel with a rose,
Till now, that I am told some lines to compose,
Of which I have little idea, God knows;
But since that the task is assigned me by those
To whom love, affection, and gratitude owes
A ready compliance, I feign *would dispose*
And call to befriend me the muse who bestows
The gift of poetry both on friends and foes.
My warmest acknowledgements are due to those
Who watched near my bed and soothed me to repose,
Who pitied my sufferings and shared in my woes,
And, by their simpathy, *relieved my sorrows.*
May I as long as the blood in my veins flows
Feel the warmth of love which now in my breast glows,
And may I sink into a refreshing doze
When I lie my head on my welcome pillows.

In Jane Austen's handwriting, enclosed in the same Letter of 1807.

ON SIR HOME POPHAM'S SENTENCE, APRIL 1807
Of a Ministry pitiful, angry, mean,
A gallant commander the victim is seen.
For promptitude, vigour, success, does he stand
Condemn'd to receive a severe reprimand!
To his foes I could wish a resemblance in fate:
That they, too, may suffer themselves, soon or late,
The injustice they warrant. But vain is my spite,
They *cannot so suffer who never do right.*

[Rear Admiral Home Riggs Popham was court martialled in 1807 for leaving his station]

TO MISS BIGG, PREVIOUS TO HER MARRIAGE, WITH SOME POCKETHANDKERCHIEFS I HAD HEMMED FOR HER.
Cambrick! With grateful blessings would I pay
The pleasure given me in sweet employ.
Long may'st thou serve my friend without decay,
And have no tears to wipe but tears of joy.

ON THE SAME OCCASION, BUT NOT SENT.
Cambrick! thou'st been to me a good,
And I would bless thee if I could.
Go, serve thy mistress with delight,
Be small in compass, soft and white;
Enjoy thy fortune, honour'd much
To bear her name and feel her touch;
And that thy worth may last for years,
Slight be her colds and few her tears.

Appendices

1.
The notice taken by the Prince Regent of Jane Austen's novels cannot be better described than in the words of Mr. Austen-Leigh in the following passage, which I venture to transcribe from his book:–

'It was not till towards the close of her life, when the last of the works that she saw published was in the press, that she received the only mark of distinction ever bestowed on her; and that was remarkable for the high quarter whence it emanated rather than for any actual increase of fame that it conferred. It happened thus. In the autumn of 1815 she nursed her brother Henry through a dangerous fever and slow convalescence at his house in Hans Place. He was attended by one of the Prince Regent's physicians. All attempts to keep her name secret had at this time ceased, and though it had never appeared on a title-page, all who cared to know might easily learn it: and the friendly physician was aware that his patient's nurse was the author of 'Pride and Prejudice.' Accordingly he informed her one day that the prince was a great admirer of her novels; that he read them often, and kept a set in every one of his residences; that he himself therefore had thought it right to inform his Royal Highness that Miss Austen was staying in London, and that the Prince had desired Mr. Clarke, the librarian of Carlton House, to wait upon her. The next day Mr. Clarke made his appearance, and invited her to Carlton House, saying that he had the Prince's instructions to show her the library and other apartments, and to pay her every possible attention. The invitation was of course accepted, and during the visit to Carlton House Mr. Clarke declared himself commissioned to say that if Miss Austen had any other novel forthcoming she was at liberty to dedicate it to the Prince. Accordingly such a dedication was immediately prefixed to 'Emma,' which was at that time in the press.

'Mr. Clarke was the brother of Dr. Clarke, the traveller and mineralogist, whose life has been written by Bishop Otter. Jane found in him not only a very courteous gentleman, but also a warm admirer of her talents: though it will be seen by his letters that he did not clearly apprehend the limits of her powers, or the proper field for their exercise. The following correspondence took place between them.

'Feeling some apprehension lest she should make a mistake in acting on the verbal permission which she had received from the Prince, Jane addressed the following letter to Mr. Clarke:–

NOV. 15, 1815.
SIR, – I must take the liberty of asking you a question. Among the many flattering attentions which I received from you at Carlton House on Monday last was the information of my being at liberty to dedicate any future work to His Royal Highness the Prince Regent, without the necessity of any solicitation on my part. Such, at least, I believed to be your words; but as I am very anxious to be quite certain of what was intended, I entreat you to have the goodness to inform me how such a permission is to be understood, and whether it is incumbent on me to show my sense of the honour by inscribing the work now in the press to His Royal Highness; I should be equally concerned to appear either presumptuous or ungrateful.

'The following gracious answer was returned by Mr. Clarke, together with a suggestion which must have been received with some surprise:–

Carlton House: (Nov. 16, 1815).

DEAR MADAM, – It is certainly not incumbent *on you to dedicate your work now in the press to His Royal Highness; but if you wish to do the Regent that honour either now or at any future period I am happy to send you that permission, which need not require any more trouble or solicitation on your part.*

Your late works, Madam, and in particular 'Mansfield Park,' reflect the highest honour on your genius and your principles. In every new work your mind seems to increase its energy and power of discrimination. The Regent has read and admired all your publications.

Accept my best thanks for the pleasure your volumes have given me. In the perusal of them I felt a great inclination to write and say so. And I also, dear Madam, wished to be allowed to ask you to delineate in some future work the habits of life, and character, and enthusiasm of a clergyman, who should pass his time between the metropolis and the country, who should be something like Beattie's Minstrel –

Silent when glad, affectionate tho' shy,
And in his looks was most demurely sad;
And now he laughed aloud, yet none knew why.

Neither Goldsmith, nor La Fontaine in his 'Tableau de Famille,' have in mind quite delineated an English clergyman, at least of the present day, fond of and entirely engaged in literature, no man's enemy but his own. Pray, dear Madam, think of these things.

Believe me at all times with sincerity and respect, your faithful and obliged servant,

J. S. Clarke, Librarian.

'The following letter, written in reply, will show how unequal the author of "Pride and Prejudice" felt herself to delineating an enthusiastic clergyman of the present day, who should resemble Beattie's Minsrel:–

Dec. 11

DEAR SIR, – My 'Emma' is now so near publication that I feel it right to assure you of my not having forgotten your kind recommendation of an early copy for Carlton House, and that I have Mr. Murray's promise of its being sent to His Royal Highness, under cover to you, three days previous to the work being really out. I must make use of this opportunity to thank you, dear Sir, for the very high praise you bestow on my other novels. I am too vain to wish to convince you that you have praised them beyond their merits. My greatest anxiety at present is that this fourth work should not disgrace what was good in the others. But on this point I will do myself the justice to declare that, whatever may be my wishes for its success, I am strongly haunted with the idea that to those readers who have preferred 'Pride and Prejudice' it will appear inferior in wit, and to those who have preferred 'Mansfield Park' inferior in good sense. Such as it is, however, I hope you will do me the favour of accepting a copy. Mr. Murray will have directions for sending one. I am quite honoured by your thinking me capable of drawing such a clergyman as you gave the sketch of in your note of Nov. 16th. But I assure you I am not. The comic part of the character I might be equal to, but not the good, the enthusiastic, the literary. Such a man's conversations must at times be on subjects of science and philosophy, of which I know nothing; or at least be occasionally abundant in quotations and allusions which a woman who, like me, knows only her own mother-tongue, and has read little in that, would

be totally without the power of giving. A classical education, or at any rate a very extensive acquaintance with English literature, ancient and modern, appears to me quite indispensable for the person who would do any justice to your clergyman; and I think I may boast myself to be, with all possible vanity, the most unlearned and uninformed female who ever dared to be an authoress.
Believe me, dear Sir,
Your obliged and faithful hum^{bl} serv^{t}
JANE AUSTEN. [1]

'Mr. Clarke, however, was not to be discouraged from proposing another subject. He had recently been appointed chaplain and private secretary to Prince Leopold, who was then about to be united to the Princess Charlotte; and when he again wrote to express the gracious thanks of the Prince Regent for the copy of "Emma" which had been presented, he suggests that "an historical romance illustrative of the august House of Cobourg would just now be very interesting," and might very properly be dedicated to Prince Leopold. This was much as if Sir William Ross [portrait painter] had been set to paint a great battle-piece; and it is amusing to see with what grave civility she declined a proposal which must have struck her as ludicrous, in the following letter;

MY DEAR SIR, – I am honoured by the Prince's thanks and very much obliged to yourself for the kind manner in which you mention the work. I have also to acknowledge a former letter forwarded to me from Hans Place. I assure you I felt very grateful for the friendly tenor of it, and hope my silence will have been considered, as it was truly meant, to proceed only from an unwillingness to tax your time with idle thanks. Under every interesting circumstance which your own talents and literary labours have placed you in, or the favour of the Regent bestowed, you have my best wishes. Your recent appointments I hope are a step to something still better. In my opinion, the service of a court can hardly be too well paid, for immense must be the sacrifice and feeling required by it.

You are very kind in your hints as to the sort of composition which might recommend me at present, and I am fully sensible that an historical romance, founded on the House of Saxe-Cobourg, might be much more to the purpose of profit or popularity than such pictures of domestic life in country villages as I deal in. But I could no more write a romance than an epic poem. I could not sit seriously down to write a serious romance under any other motive than to save my life; and if it were indispensable for me to keep it up and never relax into laughing at myself or at other people, I am sure I should be hung before I had finished the first chapter. No. I must keep to my own style

and go on in my own way; and though I may never succeed again in that, I am convinced that I should totally fail in any other.
I remain, my dear Sir,
Your very much obliged, and sincere friend,
J. AUSTEN.
Chawton, near Alton, April 1, 1816

1. It was her pleasure to boast of greater ignorance than she had any just claim to. She knew more than her mother-tongue, for she knew a good deal of French and a little of Italian.

I append, also, Lady Morley's letter to which Jane refers in one of her own, and also her reply:–

Saltram: (December 27, 1815).
MADAM, – I have been most anxiously awaiting for an introduction to 'Emma,' and am infinitely obliged to you for your kind recollection of me, which will procure me the pleasure of her acquaintance some days sooner than I should otherwise have had it. I am already become intimate with the Woodhouse family, and feel that they will not amuse and interest me less than the Bennetts, Bertrams, Norrises, and all their admirable predecessors. I can give them no higher praise.
I am, Madam, your much obliged
F. MORLEY.

Miss J Austen to the Countess of Morley.
MADAM, – Accept my thanks for the honour of your note, and for your kind disposition in favour of 'Emma.' In my present state of doubt as to her reception in the world, it is particularly gratifying to me to receive so early an assurance of your Ladyship's approbation. It encourages me to depend on the same share of general good opinion which 'Emma's' predecessors have experienced, and to believe that I have not yet, as almost every writer of fancy does sooner or later, overwritten myself.
I am, Madam,
Your obliged and faithful servt
J. AUSTEN.
December 31, 1815.

Letters from Fanny Fowler, Lady Bridges, announcing the engagement of her three daughters, Elizabeth, Fanny, and Sophia.
Goodnestone: (March 2, 1791)
MY DEAR MRS. FIELDING,
I cannot leave to my Daurs the pleasure of informing you of an event

that gives us the greatest satisfaction. We had for some time observed a great attachment between Mr. Austin (Mr. Knight's Relation) and our dear Eliz[th] *; and Mr. Knight has, in the handsomest manner, declared his entire approbation of it; but as they are both very young, he wis'd it not to take place immediately, and as it will not suit him to give up much at present, their Income will be small, and they must be contented to live in the Country, which I think will be no hardship to either party, as they have no high Ideas, and it is a greater satisfaction to us than if she was to be thrown upon the world in a higher sphere, young and inexperienced as she is. He is a very sensible and amiable young man, and I trust and hope there is every prospect of Happiness to all parties in their union. This Affair has very much agitated Sir B., and he has not been quite so well for some days past as he had been for a month before; but now it is decided he will, I make no doubt, be better again in a few days, but I have long observed that when his mind has been agitated he has had a return of cough and oppression. He has sent his case to Bath, and if he is encouraged to go there, we shall set out according to the time pointed out from thence, as he has desired to know when the Waters have most efficacy. [1] Fatty is so good (as) to stay with my Girls during our absence, or I should be much distress'd at leaving them so long. She has been pretty well, upon the whole, ever since she has been here, and in remarkable good Looks and Spirits.*

Adieu, my dearest Mrs. Fielding. All here unite with me in kindest love and compts: as due. My Dau[rs] *desire their duty to you. Believe me ever yours affectionately,*

F.B.

To Mrs. Fielding, St. James's Palace, London.

1. Sir Brook died before his daughters were married. 'Fatty' was Isabella, sister of Mrs. C. Fielding's husband, and daughter of 'Anne Palmer,' by her second husband Col. Fielding. She seems to have been a popular person, known all her life as 'Fatty Fielding,' and often at Goodnestone and Godmersham. She was godmother to one of Mr. E. Knight's children (Marianne), and died unmarried in 1812.

Goodnestone: (March 28,1791)

MY DEAR MRS. FIELDING,

I flatter myself you are so truly interested in the welfare of my dearest children, that I am not afraid of being troublesome in writing again so soon, but must infrom you that my dearest Fanny has received an offer of Marriage from Mr. Lewis Cage, a Gentlemen of this County of an unexceptionable good character. His proposal has our entire approbation. As you was so kind as to express a wish to be acquainted with Mr. Austin, I inform'd him of it, in consequence of which he call'd at St. James's, and was very much

disappointed he was not so fortunate to find you at home, as his Time would not permit him to make a Second Attempt; indeed, I should be quite happy that your two future Nephews should be known to you, and I hope it will not be long before they have an opportunity of being introduced. My Daughters are going tomorrow to Godmersham for a Week; I do not accompany them, as Mr. Bridges is here. Sir Brook continues charmingly well, and is in good spirits. I hope we shall get a glimpse of you as we pass through town to Bath the middle of next month, tho' our stay will be very short. How is Miss Finch? [1] I hope much recovered since she left Margate. I am quite delighted to hear such good accounts of Augusta, [2] and hope she feels no remains of her severe Illness, but that she and all the rest of your Family are well. All here unite with me in kindest Love to you all.
Believe me, ever yours affectionately,
F.B.

1. 'Miss Finch' must mean one of Mrs. C. Fielding's three sisters, who all died unmarried.
2. 'Augusta Sophia' was the youngest daughter of Mrs. C. Fielding; she married Mr. Geo. Hicks in 1813, and lived to a good old age.

Brock St., Bath: (July 10, 1791)
MY DEAR MRS. FIELDING,

After having wrote to you so lately you will be no doubt surprised at hearing again so soon, and not less so to find that the Cause of my addressing myself to you is to inform you that we have received proposals of Marriage from Mr. William Deedes for your God-daughter, our dear Sophia. He is a young Man of a very Amiable Disposition and universally beloved, and his father has been so kind to approve his Choice. I hope it will meet with your approbation, and think she bids as fair to be happy with her Connection as her sisters with theirs. It is certainly a very singular instance of good fortune in One Family, that 3 Girls, almost unknown, should have attach'd to themselves three Young Men of such unexceptionable Characters, and I pray to God that their future conduct will ever do credit to their Choice. Mr. William Deedes is gone with Mr. Knight on the Scotch Tour; he had been long engaged to accompany them, but did not choose to set out on so long an excursion till he had explain'd himself. As I have many letters to write I will not obtain *you longer than to beg our best Love and good wishes to you and all your dear Family, and kind Compliments to Lady Charlotte and Miss Finch.*
Believe me, ever affectionately yours,
F.B.

Mrs. Knight to Mr. Knatchbull.

Saturday.

Indeed, my dear Edward, I am very glad your wife gave you a scold: as I did not know that another sore finger prevented her holding a Pen,I was quite surprised at not hearing from her – her constant attention has spoiled me and made me unreasonable. Yesterday, however, a kind present from Col. *Knatchbull satisfied me that* you *were alive, whatever might have happened to your wife and children. It was very good of you to think of me; I am very fond of smelts, and enjoyed them exceedingly, but you should not have sent half the number, for I was obliged to let a neighbour help me to consume them. I was soon awakened from the dream of happiness in which Lady Honywood found me, for the next day, which was not cold, I was almost as ill as at any time, and I have since that had many painful Days, and am quite desponding again. People talk of the fine weather – the hot sun I do not feel, but the cold N.E. wind penetrates to my fireside, and I am always very cold.*

I am glad I shall get a peep at dear Belle on the 15th. I hope you will both contrive to dine here *with Charlie and his wife. The first day of their arrival I always provide for them. I do not much like the accounts they send me of my nephew Wyndham; he seems a most indolent young man, and I heartily wish he had gone into a Regiment of the Line. The sight of the Installations he pronounced a bore, and rejected a ticket. His father then kindly sent a chaise for Wadham, but Dr. Butler had refused permission to some other boys to go, and therefore could not grant it to him. I wonder whether you have seen your new neighbours yet. What an elegant way they fixed on to pass part of their wedding Day! An Ostler and Housemaid at an Inn, who had a* chay *lent them by their master for the Day, would probably have spent it in the same manner. Indeed, my dear Edward, I hope* Lord Burleigh *will not make his appearance in my Room at the same time with his son again; I have hardly recovered it yet. As the christening is to be on Tuesday, I suppose the whole Party will soon adjourn to Hatch; by that time, perhaps, he will be obliged to begin his canvass, and some puzzling questions he will have to answer in the course of it.*

Miss Toke is much the same. Their sea Plan is now fixed, and a good House in Nelson's Crescent is engaged for them, from the 1st July for 2 months, at 80 guineas. The expense seems to be a dreadful burthen *upon* all *their minds; but as it will only cause Mr. T.'s putting a 100l. instead of a 1,000l in the stocks, I cannot pity them. You will be glad to resign the correspondence to your wife, if you are to be plagued with such long letters. I expect you will put this into her hand before you have got half through it.*

Adieu, dear Edward. My best love to Belle, and believe me, affectionately yours,

C.K.[1]

1. This letter must have been written in 1808 or 1809. 'Dear Belle' was Mrs. Knatchbull, my father's first wife, Annabella-Christiana Honywood, who married in 1806, and died in1814. 'My nephew Wyndham' must mean a son of her brother Wyndham, who died during his father's lifetime, although I cannot find his name in any family pedigree. 'Lord Burleigh' was her nickname for her cousin, my grandfather, Sir Edward Knatchbull. My father, by the kindness of Sir Joseph and Lady Banks (his aunt), had been placed in a position not so dependent upon his father as would otherwise have been the case and was eventually very gratefully benefited from the same sources. My grandfather, having married three times, and having many younger children, some differences upon pecuniary matters occurred between him and his son, during which they seem to have accidentally met at 'Whitefriars' to which Mrs. Knight here alludes. I do not know what were 'the puzzling questions' which my grandfather would have to answer; the fact of his third wife being Roman Catholic had given offence to the hot Protestants of Kent; but they had had their revenge in 1802, when he was defeated at the general election, and the reference to my father's first wife shows that this letter was written several years later.

Talking of elections, the three famous contests of 1796, 1802, and 1806 furnished the text for some verses which I may as well insert here, although they have no more to do with Jane Austen than with the man in the moon, but may amuse those who take an interest in matters of the sort. The facts are briefly these – Knatchbull and Honywood – Tory and Whig – were the great contending powers, whilst Geary was the moderate politician of neutral tint, who was happy to receive support from both, and had, moreover, as a popluar and good man of business, a number of personal friends. In 1796, Knatchbull, by throwing his second votes to Geary, brought him in at Honywood's expense. In 1802, when he tried to do the same thing, various causes had contributed to strengthen Honywood, who was able to turn the tables and throw Knatchbull out by splitting votes with Geary. In 1806 both had grown wary, each polled all the 'plumpers' he could, and Geary, getting scarcely any second votes from the other two, had to retire discomfited. Hence the following verses in 1806:–

Some ten years ago, three men of great fame,
Filmer, Honywood, Knatchbull, and Geary by name,
To the County of Kent did their service propose
As Parliament men, with a view to be chose.
The Freeholders then did most wisely decree
That Knatchbull and Geary were the best of the three.
Six years had elapsed when the very same men

To the County did offer their service again;
The Freeholders then did as wisely decide
To take t'other two and set Knatchbull aside;
Four years after this came another election
When Geary in turn underwent his rejection.
Let no one from hence most rashly insist on't
That the County of Kent is not truly consistent
Most consistent to all she appears, without doubt,
By putting *all* 'in' and by turning *all* 'out'!

Mrs Knight to Miss Knight, afterwards Lady Knatchbull.

Oct. 26, 1809

I was quite delighted with your letter, my dearest Fanny, but you have got yourself into a scrape by your kind attention to my wishes, for you sent me just such an account as I like to receive, and I shall therefore be the more desirous of hearing from you again. I have also heard from your uncle Henry, so that I believe I am almost as much acquainted with all your proceedings as if I had been one of your Party. As I now do nothing, or go anywhere, it will not be in my Power to reward you for your trouble by an amusing letter in return, but as you are a reasonable, good girl, I know you will be satisfied with what I can tell you. Our *jubilee went off with great éclat; above 600*l *were subscribed, and about as many persons were regaled with meat, Bread and Beer, and every private House, I believe, presented a scene of festivity and happiness. Mary Fox and Daniel* assisted *at a Bowl of Punch &c.&c. at the Friars, and I was glad to hear from them a good account of the little ones at Godmersham. Mr. Honywood sent a Jubilee donation of 100*l *to the Hospital, with a very handsome letter to Mr. Toke. Of the grand Ball I hope to give you an account which my Friends promised to bring me this morning. I hear the gowns &c. for the Goodnestone Party were got ready, but to be sure it was a little in the usual dilatory style of the Bridges's to put off all preparations till the preceding Monday. Pray tell me whether you ever saw your intended Aunt. It is a pity she cannot change her Christian, with her other name, for* Dolly, my dear, *will not sound well. I know something of her and have heard more, and as Sir Brook makes a second match I think the Family are very lucky in the Person he has fixed upon. I had a letter from dear Harriet, but she did not then know what was going forward. I am sorry to hear from herself, as well as others, that she is* very *thin, without any cause for it. She tells me she has had her hair cut off, and there are various opinions as to the effect. Her Husband, however, thinks it an improvement, and that is sufficient for a good wife. I heard of the Chawton Party looking very comfortable at Breakfast, from a gentleman who was travelling by their door in a Post-chaise about ten days ago. Your account of the whole family gives me the sincerest*

Pleasure, and I beg you will assure them all how much I feel interested in their happiness. I think, my dearest Fanny, that your poor little watch always seemed in an uncomfortable state. If you like to have a new one, I shall have great pleasure in providing you with one,and as I suppose you will be in Sloane Street a day or two in your return, it would be a good opportunity to make your choice. A watch and chain will certainly not cost less than 20 guineas, and you may be assured I shall not grudge 5 or 10 more to please my dear God-daughter. Draw upon your Uncle Henry, therefore, for what you require. By a letter from Miss Cuthbert, I find I am in your Papa's debt.

The Ball was full, but the harmony of the evening was destroyed by the folly of Lady C. Nelson, who made a select *Supper Party, and disobliged all the rest. When she and her Party returned to the Ball-room, the* other *set would not join in her dance, the music was stopped, and in short there was a grand Row. The Dinner had passed off better. No Toast was drank with more enthusiasm than Mr. Milles, who represented Canterbury at the time of the Kings accession. He bow'd and bow'd again, and was cheer'd and cheer'd again. Mrs. Palmer was at the Ball.*

Adieu, my dear. Affectionately yours,

C.K.[1]

1. The 'intended aunt' – 'Dolly, my dear' – was Dorothy Hawley, Sir Brook's second wife.

7

An Updated Family Record

In the early twentieth century the family memoirs of Jane Austen were updated by the next generation of the family. Jane Austen, Her Life and Letters, A Family Record *was written by William Austen-Leigh, the son of James Edward Austen-Leigh, and William's nephew Richard Arthur Austen-Leigh. They were helped by Mary Augusta Austen-Leigh, William's sister.*

The decision to update the family record was made because new sources of knowledge had become available since the Memoir *was first published in 1869. The most important source was the letters published by Lord Brabourne. New information had also appeared in* Jane Austen's Sailor Brothers, *written by descendants of Francis Austen, which was published in 1906, and several biographies by authors outside the family, such as Oscar Fay Adams and Constance Hill.*

William and Richard Arthur Austen-Leigh stated that it was not their intention to supersede the Memoir *but to supplement it using new material and to provide a new perspective on Jane Austen's life made possible by the passage of time. They also wanted to remove some misconceptions which had arisen about her.*

Jane Austen, Her Life and Letters, A Family Record, *was published by E. P. Dutton and Company in 1913.*

This chapter contains information, extracts, and letters from this work which do not appear in previous chapters.

Jane Austen, Her Life and Letters, A Family Record William and Richard Arthur Austen-Leigh

One important episode in Jane's life, which occurred in 1802, was only briefly mentioned by James Edward Austen-Leigh in his Memoir *but was described in detail by William and Richard Austen-Leigh.*

In November 1802 Jane and Cassandra Austen travelled from Bath to Steventon Rectory, their childhood home, to visit their brother James and his wife Mary. While at Steventon they spent a few days with their old friends Catherine and Alethea Bigg at Manydown House. On the evening of 2 December Harris Bigg-Wither, the younger brother of her friends, made Jane an offer of marriage which she accepted. However, Jane changed her mind overnight and hastily retracted her acceptance the following morning. The Austen sisters were so embarrassed and distressed by this that they hurried back to Steventon Rectory and insisted that their brother accompany them home to Bath, much to his inconvenience. Many years later Caroline Austen made the following observations on the reason for her aunt's behaviour:

> I conjecture that the advantages he could offer, and her gratitude for his love, and her long friendship with his family, induced my aunt to decide that she would marry him when he should ask her, but that having accepted him she found she was miserable. To be sure, she should not have said "yes" overnight; but I have always respected her for her courage in cancelling that "yes" the next morning; all worldly advantages would have been to her, and she was of an age to know this quite well (she was nearly twenty-seven). My aunts had very small fortunes; and on their father's death they and their mother would be, they were aware, but poorly off. I believe most women so circumstanced would have gone on trusting to love after marriage.

The updated family record also provided information about Jane's attempt to get her novel Susan *published. In 1803 Jane sold the manuscript of this novel to Messrs. Crosby and Son of London. They did not publish the novel, however, and in 1809 Jane wrote the following letter to the publisher using a pseudonym.*

Wednesday 5th April 1809
Gentlemen,

In the Spring of 1803 a Ms. Novel in 2 vol. entitled Susan *was sold to you by a gentleman of the name of Seymour, & the purchase money £10. recd. at the same time. Six years have since passed, & this work of which I avow myself the Authoress, has never to the best of my knowledge, appeared in print, tho' an early publication was stipulated for at the time of the Sale. I can only account for such an extraordinary circumstance by supposing the MS by some carelessness to have been lost; & if that was the case, am willing to supply You with another Copy if you are disposed to avail yourselves of it, & will engage for no farther delay when it comes into your hands. – It will not be in my power from particular circumstances to command this Copy before the Month of August, but then, if you accept my proposal, you may depend on receiving it. Be so good as to send me a Line in answer, as soon as possible, as my stay in this place will not exceed a few days. Should no notice be taken of this address, I shall feel myself at liberty to secure the publication of my work, by applying elsewhere. I am Gentlemen &C &C*

M.A.D.
Direct to Mrs Ashton Dennis
Post Office, Southampton

Jane received the following disappointing reply to her letter.

Saturday 8th April 1809

Madam,

We have to acknowledge the receipt of your letter of the 5th inst. It is true that at the time mentioned we purchased of Mr Seymour a MS. novel entitled Susan *and paid him for it the sum of 10£ for which we have his stamped receipt as a full consideration, but there was not any time stipulated for its publication, neither are we bound to publish it. Should you or anyone else we shall take proceedings to stop the sale. The MS. shall be yours for the same as we paid for it.*

For R. Crosby &Co
I am yours etc.
Richard Crosby

Jane could not afford to buy back her manuscript so no further action was taken. The manuscript was recovered by her brother Henry in 1816 and was published after Jane's death as Northanger Abbey.

The Austen-Leighs, like all the family authors, described the exceptionally close relationship between Jane Austen and her sister Cassandra. The final information taken from their updated family memoir is this paragraph describing the different temperaments of the sisters:

> Their attachment was never interrupted or weakened; they lived in the same home, and shared the same bedroom, till separated by death. They were not exactly alike. Cassandra's was the colder and calmer

disposition; she was always prudent and well-judging, but with less outward demonstration of feeling and less sunniness of temper than Jane possessed. It was remarked in the family that 'Cassandra had the merit of having a temper always under command, but that Jane had the happiness of a temper which never required to be commanded'.

Letters

The following extract from the updated family memoir contains paragraphs from letters sent by Jane's parents, George and Cassandra Austen, to Mr and Mrs Walter, their relatives in Kent. These give an idea of the happy and peaceful life at Steventon Rectory in the early years of their marriage. The only blight on their happiness was the health of their second son George. It was during these years that the Austen children were born and Mr Austen tutored a few sons of the local gentry and aristocracy. The last of Mrs Austen's letters was written in August 1775, when she was expecting Jane.

Extract

On July 8 1770, George writes from Steventon of his wife's journey to London to be present at the birth of her sister's child, and adds:

My James and his brother are both well, and what will surprise you, bear their mother's absence with great philosophy, as I doubt not they would mine, and turn all their little affections towards those who were about them and good to them; this may not be a pleasing reflection to a fond parent, but is certainly wisely designed by Providence for the happiness of the child.

A month or so later Cassandra is back again, and writing:

I was not so happy as to see my nephew Weaver – suppose he was hurried in time, as I think everyone is in town; t'is a sad place, I would not live in it on any account, one has not time to do one's duty either to God or man. What luck we shall have with those sort of cows I can't say. My little Alderney one turns out tolerably well, and makes more butter than we use, and I have just bought another of the same sort, but as her calf is but just gone, cannot say what she will be good for yet.

December 9, 1770. – My poor little George is come to see me today, he seems pretty well, tho' he had a fit lately; it was near a twelve-month since he had one before, so was in hopes they had left him, but must not flatter myself so now.

In June 1771, the Austen's fourth child, Henry, was born, and Mrs Austen writes on November 8, 1772:

My little boy is come home from nurse, and a fine, stout little fellow he is, and can run anywhere, so now I have all four at home, and some time in January I expect a fifth, so you see it will not be in my power to take any journeys for one while. I believe my sister Hancock will be so good as to come and nurse me again.

Unfortunately, poor little George never recovered sufficiently to take his place in the family, and we hear no more of him, though he lived on as late as 1827 [in fact he lived until 1838].

The fifth child, Cassandra, was born in January 1773, and on June 6, 1773, Mrs Austen writes:

We will not give up the hopes of seeing you both (and as many of your young people as you can conveniently bring) at Steventon before the summer is over. Mr. Austen wants to show his brother his lands and his cattle and many other matters; and I want to show you my Henry and my Cassy, who are both reckoned fine children. Jemmy and Neddy are very happy in a new playfellow, Lord Lymington, whom Mr. Austen has lately taken the charge of; he is between five and six years old, very backward of his age, but good-tempered and orderly. He is the eldest son of Lord Portsmouth, who lives about ten miles from hence, I have got a nice dairy fitted up, and am now worth a bull and six cows, and you would laugh to see them; for they are not much bigger than Jack-asses – and here I have got duckies and ducks and chickens for Phyllis's amusement. In short you must come,and, like Hezekiah, I will show you all my riches.

December 12, 1773:

I thank God we are all quite well and my little girl is almost ready to run away. Our new pupil, Master Vanderstegen, has been with us about a month, he is near fourteen years old, and is very good tempered and well disposed. Lord Lymington has left us, his mamma began to be alarmed at the hesitation in his speech, which certainly grew worse, and is going to take him to London in hopes a Mr. Angier (who undertakes to cure the disorder) may be of service to him.

A sixth child, Francis William, was born in April 1774.

August 20, 1775:

We are all, I thank God, in good health, and I am more nimble and active than I was last time, expect to be confined some time in November. My last boy is very stout, and has run alone these two months, and is not yet sixteen months old. My little girl talks all day long, and in my opinion is a very entertaining companion. Henry has been in breeches some months, and thinks himself near as good a man as his brother Neddy. Indeed no one would judge by their looks that there was above three years and a half difference in their ages, one is so little and the other so great. Master Van. is got very well again, and has been with us again these three months; he is gone home this morning for a few holidays.

The new infant, however, did not appear quite so soon as was expected, and the last letter of the series is written by George Austen on December 17, 1775:

Steventon: December17, 1775.
DEAR SISTER, You have doubtless been for some time in expectation of hearing from Hampshire, and perhaps wondered a little we were in our old age grown such bad reckoners, but so it was, for Cassy certainly expected to have been brought to bed a month ago; however, last night the time came, and without a great deal of warning, everything was soon happily over. We have now another girl, a present plaything for her sister Cassy, and a future companion. She is to be Jenny, and seems to me as if she would be as like Harry as Cassy is to Neddy. Your sister, thank God, is pure well after it.

The following paragraph from a letter, written by Jane's cousin Philadelphia in July 1788, gives an interesting description of Jane at the age of twelve:

Yesterday I began an acquaintance with my two female cousins, Austens. My uncle, aunt, Cassandra, and Jane arrived at Mr. F. Austen's the day before. We dined with them there. As it's pure nature to love ourselves, I may be allowed to give the preference to the eldest, who is generally reckoned a most striking resemblance of me in features, complexion, and manners. I never found myself so much disposed to be vain, as I can't help thinking her very pretty, but fancied I could discover she was not so well pleased with the comparison, which reflection abated a great deal of the vanity so likely to arise and so proper to be suppres't. The youngest, Jane, is very like her brother Henry, not at all pretty and very prim, unlike a girl of twelve; but it is hasty judgment which you will scold me for. My aunt has lost several fore-teeth, which makes her look old; my uncle is quite white-haired, but looks vastly well; all in high spirits and disposed to be pleased with each other.

The following letters were all sent by Jane to her sister Cassandra. The first was written when Jane was staying with Martha Lloyd at Ibthorp House in Hurstbourne Tarrant, Hampshire.
Ibthorp: Sunday [November 30, 1800].

MY DEAR CASSANDRA,—shall you expect to hear from me on wednesday or not? i think you will, or I should not write, as the three days and half which have passed since my last letter have not produced many materials towards filling another sheet of paper. But, like Mr. Hastings, 'I do not despair,' and you perhaps, like the faithful Maria, may feel still more certain of the happy event. I have been here ever since a quarter after three on Thursday last, by the Shrewsbury clock, which I am fortunately enabled absolutely to ascertain because Mrs. Stent [who lived with the Lloyds] once lived at Shrewsbury, or at least at Tewksbury. I have the pleasure of thinking myself a very welcome guest, and the pleasure of spending my time very pleasantly. Martha looks well, and wants me to find out that she grows fat; but I cannot carry my complaisance farther than to believe whatever she asserts on the subject. Mrs. Stent gives us quite as much of her company as we wish for, and rather more than she used to do; but perhaps not more than is to our advantage in the end, because it is too dirty even for such desperate walkers as Martha and I to get out of doors, and we are therefore confined to each other's society from morning till night, with very little variety of books or gowns. Three of the Miss Debaries called here the morning after my arrival, but I have not yet been able to return their civility. You know it is not an uncommon circumstance in this parish to have the road from Ibthorp to the Parsonage much dirtier and more impracticable for walking than the road from the Parsonage to Ibthorp. I left my Mother very well when I came away, and left her with strict orders to continue so.

The endless Debaries are of course very well acquainted with the lady who is to marry Sir Thomas, and all her family. I pardon them, however, as their description of her is favourable. Mrs. Wapshire is a widow, with several sons and daughters, a good fortune, and a house in Salisbury; where Miss Wapshire has been for many years a distinguished beauty. She is now seven or eight and twenty, and tho' still handsome, less handsome than she has been. This promises better than the bloom of seventeen, and in addition to this they say that she has always been remarkable for the propriety of her behaviour distinguishing her far above the general classes of town misses, and rendering her of course very unpopular among them.

Martha has promised to return with me, and our plan is to have a nice black frost for walking to Whitchurch, and throw ourselves into a post chaise, one upon the other, our heads hanging out of one door and our feet at the opposite one. If you have never heard that Miss Dawes has been married these two months, I will mention it in my next. Pray do not forget to go to the Canterbury Ball; I shall despise you all most insufferably if you do.

I have charged my myrmidons to send me an account of the Basingstoke Ball; I have placed my spies at different places that they may collect the more; and by so doing, by sending Miss Bigg to the Town-hall itself, and posting my

mother at Steventon I hope to derive from their various observations a good general idea of the whole.
Yours ever,
J.A.
Miss Austen, Godmersham Park, Faversham, Kent.

The next extract is from a letter sent to Cassandra in February 1801, when she was staying with Henry Austen and his wife in London.

I should not have thought it necessary to write to you so soon, but for the arrival of a letter from Charles to myself. It was written last Saturday from off the Start, and conveyed to Popham Lane by Captain Boyle, on his way to Midgham. He came from Lisbon in the Endymion. I will copy Charles's account of his conjectures about Frank: 'He has not seen my brother lately, nor does he expect to find him arrived, as he met Captain Inglis at Rhodes, going up to take command of the Peterel as he was coming down; but supposes he will arrive in less than a fortnight from this time, in some ship which is expected to reach England about that time with despatches from Sir Ralph Abercrombie.' The event must show what sort of a conjuror Captain Boyle is. The Endymion has not been plagued with any more prizes. Charles spent three pleasant days in Lisbon.
They were very well satisfied with their royal passenger [the Duke of Sussex] whom they found jolly, fat, and affable, who talks of Lady Augusta as his wife, and seems much attached to her.
When this letter was written the Endymion was becalmed, but Charles hoped to reach Portsmouth by Monday or Tuesday. He received my letter, communicating our plans, before he left England, was much surprised, of course, but is quite reconciled to them, and means to come to Steventon once more while Steventon is ours.

The following letter was written soon after the Austens moved to Bath. Cassandra was paying another visit to the Lloyds at Ibthorp House.

Paragon: Tuesday [May 26, 1801].
The Endymion *came into Portsmouth on Sunday and I have sent Charles a short letter by this day's post. My adventures since I wrote you three days ago have been such as the time would easily contain. I walked yesterday morning with Mrs. Chamberlayne to Lyncombe and Widcombe, and in the evening I drank tea with the Holders. Mrs. Chamberlayne's pace was not quite so magnificent on this second trial as on the first: it was nothing more than I could keep up with, without effort, and for many many yards together on a raised narrow footpath I led the way. The walk was very beautiful, as my companion agreed whenever I made the observation. And so ends*

our friendship, for the Chamberlaynes leave Bath in a day or two. Prepare likewise for the loss of Lady Fust, as you will lose before you find her. My evening visit was by no means disagreeable. Mrs. Lillingston came to engage Mrs. Holder's conversation, and Miss Holder and I adjourned after tea to the inner drawing-room to look over prints and talk pathetically. She is very unreserved and very fond of talking of her deceased brother and sister, whose memories she cherishes with an enthusiasm which, though perhaps a little affected, is not unpleasing. She has an idea of your being remarkably lively, therefore get ready the proper selection of adverbs and due scraps of Italian and French. I must now pause to make some observation on Mrs. Heathcote's [their friend Elizabeth] having got a little boy. I wish her well to wear it out—and shall proceed. Frank writes me word that he is to be in London to-morrow: some money negotiation, from which he hopes to derive advantage, hastens him from Kent and will detain him a few days behind my father in town. I have seen the Miss Mapletons this morning. Marianne was buried yesterday, and I called without expecting to be let in to enquire after them all. On the servant's invitation, however, I sent in my name, and Jane and Christiana, who were walking in the garden, came to me immediately, and I sat with them about ten minutes. They looked pale and dejected but were more composed than I had thought probable. When I mentioned your coming here on Monday they said they should be very glad to see you.

We drink tea to-night with Mrs. Lysons: now this, says my Master, will be mighty dull.

I assure you in spite of what I might choose to insinuate in a former letter, that I have seen very little of Mr. Evelyn since my coming here; I met him this morning for only the fourth time, and as to my anecdote about Sydney Gardens, I made the most of the story because it came into advantage, but in fact he only asked me whether I were to be in Sydney Gardens in the evening or not. There is now something like an engagement between us and the Phaeton, which to confess my frailty I have a great desire to go out in; but whether it will come to anything must remain with him. I really believe he is very harmless; people do not seem afraid of him here, and he gets groundsel for his birds and all that.

Yours affectionately,

J. A.

Wednesday.—*I am just returned from my airing in the very bewitching Phaeton and four for which I was prepared by a note from Mr. E., soon after breakfast. We went to the top of Kingsdown, and had a very pleasant drive. One pleasure succeeds another rapidly. On my return I found your letter, and a letter from Charles, on the table. The contents of yours I suppose I need not repeat to you; to thank you for it will be enough. I give Charles great credit for remembering my uncle's direction, and he seems rather surprised at it himself. He has received £30 for his share of the privateer, and expects*

£10 more, but of what avail is it to take prizes if he lays out the produce in presents to his sisters? He has been buying gold chains and topaze crosses for us—he must be well scolded. The Endymion *has already received orders for taking troops to Egypt—which I should not like at all if I did not trust to Charles being removed from her somehow or other before she sails. He knows nothing of his own destination he says—but desires me to write directly—as the* Endymion *will probably sail in three or four days. He will receive my yesterday's letter to-day, and I shall write again by this post to thank and reproach him. We shall be unbearably fine.*

The next letter was written shortly before the Austens left Bath. Cassandra was once again staying at Ibthorp House with Martha Lloyd, whose mother was dying.

25 Gay Street: Monday (April 8, 1805).
MY DEAR CASSANDRA, – Here is a day for you! Did Bath or Ibthorp ever see a finer 8th of April? It is March and April together, the glare of one and the warmth of the other. We do nothing but walk about. As far as your means will admit, I hope you profit by such weather too. I dare say you are already the better for change of place. We were out again last night. Miss Irvine invited us, when I met her in the Crescent, to drink tea with them, but I rather declined it, having no idea that my mother would be disposed for another evening visit there so soon; but when I gave her the message, I found her very well inclined to go; and accordingly, on leaving Chapel, we walked to Lansdown. This morning we have been to see Miss Chamberlayne look hot on horseback. Seven years and four months ago we went to the same riding-house to see Miss [Lucy] Lefroy's performance! What a different set are we now moving in! But seven years, I suppose, are enough to change every pore of one's skin and every feeling of one's mind. We did not walk long in the Crescent yesterday. It was hot and not crowded enough; so we went into the field, and passed close by S. T. and Miss S. again. I have not yet seen her face, but neither her dress nor air have anything of the dash or stylishness which the Browns talked of; quite the contrary; indeed, her dress is not even smart, and her appearance very quiet. Miss Irvine says she is never speaking a word. Poor wretch; I am afraid she is en pénitence. *Here has been that excellent Mrs. Coulthart calling, while my mother was out, and I was believed to be so. I always respected her, as a good-hearted friendly woman. And the Brownes have been here; I find their affidavits on the table. The* Ambuscade *reached Gibraltar on the 9th of March, and found all well; so say the papers. We have had no letters from anybody, but we expect to hear from Edward to-morrow, and from you soon afterwards. How happy they are at Godmersham now! I shall be very glad of a letter from Ibthorp, that I may know how you all are, but particularly yourself. This is nice weather for Mrs. J. Austen's going to*

Speen, and I hope she will have a pleasant visit there. I expect a prodigious account of the christening dinner; perhaps it brought you at last into the company of Miss Dundas again.

Tuesday. – *I received your letter last night, and wish it may be soon followed by another to say that all is over; but I cannot help thinking that nature will struggle again, and produce a revival. Poor woman! May her end be peaceful and easy as the exit we have witnessed! And I dare say it will. If there is no revival, suffering must be all over; even the consciousness of existence, I suppose, was gone when you wrote. The nonsense I have been writing in this and in my last letter seems out of place at such a time, but I will not mind it; it will do you no harm, and nobody else will be attacked by it. I am heartily glad that you can speak so comfortably of your own health and looks, though I can scarcely comprehend the latter being really approved. Could travelling fifty miles produce such an immediate change? You were looking very poorly here, and everybody seemed sensible of it. Is there a charm in a hack post-chaise? But if there were, Mrs. Craven's carriage might have undone it all. I am much obliged to you for the time and trouble you have bestowed on Mary's cap, and am glad it pleases her; but it will prove a useless gift at present, I suppose. Will not she leave Ibthorp on her mother's death? As a companion you are all that Martha can be supposed to want, and in that light, under these circumstances, your visit will indeed have been well timed.*

The Cookes want us to drink tea with them to-night, but I do not know whether my mother will have nerves for it. We are engaged to-morrow evening—what request we are in! Mrs. Chamberlayne expressed to her niece her wish of being intimate enough with us to ask us to drink tea with her in a quiet way. We have therefore offered her ourselves and our quietness through the same medium. Our tea and sugar will last a great while. I think we are just the kind of people and party to be treated about among our relations; we cannot be supposed to be very rich.

Thursday. – *I was not able to go on yesterday; all my wit and leisure were bestowed on letters to Charles and Henry. To the former I wrote in consequence of my mother's having seen in the papers that the* Urania *was waiting at Portsmouth for the convoy for Halifax. This is nice, as it is only three weeks ago that you wrote by the* Camilla. *I wrote to Henry because I had a letter from him in which he desired to hear from me very soon. His to me was most affectionate and kind, as well as entertaining; there is no merit to him in* that; *he cannot help being amusing. He offers to meet us on the sea coast, if the plan of which Edward gave him some hint takes place. Will not this be making the execution of such a plan more desirable and delightful than ever? He talks of the rambles we took together last summer with pleasing affection.*

Yours ever,

J. A.

In the next letter and extract from another Jane informed her brother Frank of the death of their father. The second letter was sent because the first had gone to the wrong address.

Green Park Buildings:
Tuesday evening, January 22, 1805

MY DEAREST FRANK, – I wrote to you yesterday, but your letter to Cassandra this morning, by which we learn the probability of your being by this time at Portsmouth, obliges me to write to you again, having unfortunately a communication as necessary as painful to make to you. Your affectionate heart will be greatly wounded, and I wish the shock could have been lessened by a better preparation; but the event has been sudden and so must be the information of it. We have lost an excellent father. An illness of only eight and forty hours carried him off yesterday morning between ten and eleven. He was seized on Saturday with a return of the feverish complaint which he had been subject to for the last three years. A physician was called in yesterday morning, but he was at that time past all possibility of cure; and Dr. Gibbs and Mr. Bowen had scarcely left his room before he sunk into a sleep from which he never woke.

It has been very sudden. Within twenty-four hours of his death he was walking about with only the help of a stick – was even reading.

We had, however, some hours of preparation, and when we understood his recovery to be hopeless, most fervently did we pray for the speedy release which ensued. To have seen him languishing long, struggling for hours, would have been dreadful, and, thank God, we were all spared from it.

Except the restlessness and confusion of high fever, he did not suffer, and he was mercifully spared from knowing that he was about to quit objects so beloved, and so fondly cherished as his wife and children ever were. His tenderness as a father, who can do justice to?

The funeral is to be on Saturday at Walcot Church. The serenity of the corpse is most delightful. It preserves the sweet benevolent smile which always distinguished him. They kindly press my mother to remove to Steventon as soon as it is all over, but I do not believe she will leave Bath at present. We must have this house for three months longer, and here we shall probably stay till the end of that time. We all unite in love, and I am
Affectionately yours,
J. A.

Heavy as is the blow, we can already feel that a thousand comforts remain to us to soften it. Next to that of the consciousness of his worth and constant preparation for another world, is the remembrance of his having suffered, comparatively speaking, nothing. Being quite insensible of his own state, he was spared all pain of separation, and he went off almost in his sleep. My mother bears the shock as well as possible; she was quite prepared for it and feels all the blessing of his being spared a long illness. My uncle and aunt have been with us and show us every imaginable kindness.

Adieu, my dearest Frank. The loss of such a parent must be felt, or we should be brutes. I wish I could give you a better preparation, but it has been impossible.

Yours ever affectionately,

J. A

The following letters were written by Jane in 1813. The first is a long extract from a letter to Cassandra when she was staying with her brother James at Steventon Rectory.

Chawton: Sunday evening, January 24, 1813.

MY DEAR CASSANDRA, – This is exactly the weather we could wish for, if you are but well enough to enjoy it. I shall be glad to hear that you are not confined to the house by an increase of cold.

We quite run over with books. My mother has got Sir John Carr's Travels in Spain from Miss B. and I am reading a Society [Chawton Book Society] octavo, An Essay on the Military Police and Institutions of the British Empire by Capt. Pasley of the Engineers: a book which I protested against at first, but which upon trial I find delightfully written and highly entertaining. I am as much in love with the author as ever I was with Clarkson or Buchanan, or even the two Mr. Smiths of the City – the first soldier I ever sighed for – but he does write with extraordinary force and spirit. Yesterday, moreover, brought us Mrs. Grant's Letters with Mr. White's compliments; but I have disposed of them, compliments and all, for the first fortnight to Miss Papillon, and among so many readers or retainers of books as we have in Chawton I dare say there will be no difficulty in getting rid of them for another fortnight if necessary. I learn from Sir J. Carr that there is no Government House at Gibraltar; I must alter it to the Commissioner's [a reference to Mansfield Park].

Our party on Wednesday was not unagreeable. We were eleven altogether, as you will find on computation, adding Miss Benn and two strange gentlemen, a Mr. Twyford, curate of Great Worldham, who is living in Alton, and his friend Mr. Wilkes. I don't know that Mr. T. is anything except very dark-complexioned, but Mr. W. was a useful addition, being an easy, talking, pleasantish young man – a very young man, hardly twenty, perhaps. He is of St. John's, Cambridge, and spoke very highly of H. Walter [grandson of Revd. George Austen's half-brother] as a scholar. He said he was considered as the best classic in the University. How such a report would have interested my father!

Upon Mrs. D.'s mentioning that she had sent the Rejected Addresses to Mr. H., I began talking to her a little about them, and expressed my hope of their having amused her. Her answer was 'Oh dear, yes, very much, very droll indeed – the opening of the House and the striking up of the fiddles!' What she meant, poor woman, who shall say? I sought no farther. The P.'s [Papillons] have now got the book, and like it very much; their niece Eleanor has recommended it most warmly to them. She looks like a rejected addresser. As soon as a whist party was formed, and a round table threatened, I made my mother an excuse and came away, leaving just as many for their round table as there were at Mrs. Grant's. I wish they might be as agreeable a set.

The Miss Sibleys want to establish a Book Society in their side of the country like ours. What can be a stronger proof of that superiority in ours over the Manydown and Steventon society, which I have always foreseen and felt? No emulation of the kind was ever inspired by their proceedings; no such wish of the Miss Sibleys was ever heard in the course of the many years of that Society's existence. And what are their Biglands and their Barrows, their Macartneys and Mackenzies to Captain Pasley's Essay on the Military Police of the British Empire and the Rejected Addresses?

I have walked once to Alton, and yesterday Miss Papillon and I walked together to call on the Garnets. I had a very agreeable walk, and if she had not, more shame for her, for I was quite as entertaining as she was. Dame G. is pretty well, and we found her surrounded by her well-behaved healthy, large-eyed children. I took her an old shift, and promised her a set of our linen, and my companion left some of her Bank Stock with her.

Tell Martha that I hunt away the rogues every night from under her bed; they feel the difference of her being gone.

Chawton: July 3, 1813.

MY DEAREST FRANK, – Behold me going to write you as handsome a letter as I can! Wish me good luck. We have had the pleasure of hearing from you lately through Mary, who sent us some of the particulars of yours of June 18 (I think), written off Rugen, and we enter into the delight of your having so good a pilot. Why are you like Queen Elizabeth? Because you know how to chuse wise ministers. Does not this prove you as great a Captain as she was a Queen? This may serve as a riddle for you to put forth among your officers, by way of increasing your proper consequence. It must be a real enjoyment to you, since you are obliged to leave England, to be where you are, seeing something of a new country and one which has been so distinguished as Sweden. You must have great pleasure in it. I hope you may have gone to Carlscroon. Your profession has its douceurs to recompense for some of its privations; to an enquiring and observing mind like yours such douceurs must be considerable. Gustavus Vasa, and Charles XII., and Cristina and Linneus. Do their ghosts rise up before you? I have a great respect for former Sweden, so zealous as it was for Protestantism. And I have always fancied it more like England than other countries; and, according to the map, many of the names have a strong resemblance to the English.

July begins unpleasantly with us, cold and showery, but it is often a baddish month. We had some fine dry weather preceding it, which was very acceptable to the Holders of Hay, and the Masters of Meadows. In general it must have been a good hay-making season. Edward has got in all his in excellent order; I speak only of Chawton, but here he has better luck than Mr. Middleton ever had in the five years that he was tenant. Good encouragement for him to come again, and I really hope he will do so another year. The pleasure to us of having them here is so great that if we were not the best creatures in the world we should not deserve it. We go on in the most comfortable way, very frequently dining together, and always meeting in some part of every day. Edward is very well, and enjoys himself as thoroughly as any Hampshire-born Austen can desire. Chawton is not thrown away upon him.

He will soon have all his children about him. Edward, George and Charles are collected already, and another week brings Henry and William.

We are in hopes of another visit from our true lawful Henry very soon; he is to be our guest this time. He is quite well, I am happy to say, and does not leave it to my pen, I am sure, to communicate to you the joyful news of his being Deputy Receiver no longer. It is a promotion which he thoroughly enjoys, as well he may; the work of his own mind. He sends you all his own plans of course. The scheme for Scotland we think an excellent one both for himself and his nephew. Upon the whole his spirits are very much recovered. If I may so express myself his mind is not a mind for affliction; he is too busy, too active, too sanguine. Sincerely as he was attached to poor Eliza moreover, and excellently as he behaved to her, he was always so used to be away from her at times, that her loss is not felt as that of many a beloved wife might be especially when all the circumstances of her long and dreadful illness are taken into the account. He very long knew that she must die, and it was indeed a release at last. Our mourning for her is not over, or we should be putting it on again for Mr. Thomas Leigh, who has just closed a good life at the age of seventy-nine.

Poor Mrs. L. P. [Leigh Perrot] would now have been mistress of Stoneleigh had there been none of the vile compromise, which in good truth has never been allowed to be of much use to them. It will be a hard trial.

You will be glad to hear that every copy of S. and S. is sold, and that it has brought me £140 besides the copyright, if that should ever be of any value. I have now, therefore, written myself into £250, which only makes me long for more I have something in hand which I hope the credit of P. and P. will sell well, though not half so entertaining, and by the bye shall you object to my mentioning the Elephant *in it, and two or three other old ships? I have done it, but it shall not stay to make you angry. They are only just mentioned.*

I hope you continue well and brush your hair, but not all off.

Yours very affectionately,
J. A.
Godmersham Park, September 25, 1813.

MY DEAREST FRANK, – The 11th of this month brought me your letter, and I assure you I thought it very well worth its two and three-pence [the cost she had to pay for postage]. I am very much obliged to you for filling me so long a sheet of paper; you are a good one to traffic with in that way, you pay most liberally; my letter was a scratch of a note compared to yours, and then you write so even, so clear, both in style and penmanship, so much to the point, and give so much intelligence, that it is enough to kill one. I am sorry Sweden is so poor, and my riddle so bad. The idea of a fashionable bathing-place in Mecklenberg! How can people pretend to be fashionable or to bathe out of England? Rostock market makes one's mouth water; our cheapest butcher's meat is double the price of theirs; nothing under nine-pence all this summer, and I believe upon recollection nothing under ten-pence. Bread has sunk and is likely to sink more, which we hope may make meat sink too. But I have no occasion to think of the price of bread or of meat where I am now; let me shake off vulgar cares and conform to the happy indifference of East Kent wealth. I wonder whether you and the King of Sweden knew that I was come to Godmersham with my brother. Yes, I suppose you have received due notice of it by some means or other. I have not been here these four years, so I am sure the event deserves to be talked of before and behind, as well as in the middle. We left Chawton on the 14th, spent two entire days in town, and arrived here on the 17th. My brother, Fanny, Lizzie, Marianne and I composed this division of the family, and filled his carriage inside and out. Two post-chaises, under the escort of George, conveyed eight more across the country, the chair brought two, two others came on horseback, and the rest by coach, and so by one means or another, we all are removed. It puts me in remind of St. Paul's shipwreck, when all are said, by different means, to reach the shore in safety. I left my mother, Cassandra, and Martha well, and have had good accounts of them since. At present they are quite alone, but they are going to be visited by Mrs. Heathcote and Miss Bigg, and to have a few days of Henry's company likewise.

Of our three evenings in town, one was spent at the Lyceum, and another at Covent Garden. The Clandestine Marriage *was the most respectable of the performances, the rest were sing-song and trumpery; but it did very well for Lizzie and Marianne, who were indeed delighted, but I wanted better acting. There was no actor worth naming. I believe the theatres are thought at a very low ebb at present. Henry has probably sent you his own account of his visit in Scotland. I wish he had had more time, and could have gone further north, and deviated to the lakes on his way back; but what he was able to do seems to have afforded him great enjoyment, and he met with scenes of higher beauty in Roxburghshire than I had supposed the South of Scotland possessed. Our nephew's gratification was less keen than our brother's. Edward is no enthusiast in the beauties of nature. His enthusiasm is for the sports of the field only. He is a very promising and pleasing young man, however, behaves with great propriety to his father, and great kindness to his brothers and sisters, and we must forgive his thinking more of grouse and partridges than lakes and mountains.*

In this house there is a constant succession of small events, somebody is always going or coming; this morning we had Edward Bridges unexpectedly to breakfast with us, on his way from Ramsgate, where is his wife, to Lenham, where is his church, and to-morrow he dines and sleeps here on his return. They have been all the summer at Ramsgate for her health; she is a poor honey – the sort of woman who gives me the idea of being determined never to be well and who likes her spasms and nervousness, and the consequence they give her, better than anything else. This is an ill-natured statement to send all over the Baltic. The Mr. Knatchbulls, dear Mrs. Knight's brothers, dined here the other day. They came from the Friars, which is still on their hands. The elder made many inquiries after you. Mr. Sherer is quite a new Mr. Sherer to me; I heard him for the first time last Sunday, and he gave us an excellent sermon, a little too eager sometimes in his delivery, but that is to me a better extreme than the want of animation especially when it evidently comes from the heart, as in him. The clerk is as much like you as ever. I am always glad to see him on that account. But the Sherers are going away. He has a bad curate at Westwell, whom he can eject only by residing there himself. He goes nominally for three years, and a Mr. Paget is to have the curacy of Godmersham; a married man, with a very musical wife, which I hope may make her a desirable acquaintance to Fanny.

I thank you very warmly for your kind consent to my application [for permission to use the names of his ships in Mansfield Park*], and the kind hint which followed it. I was previously aware of what I should be laying myself open to; but the truth is that the secret [of her authorship] has spread so far as to be scarcely the shadow of a secret now, and that, I believe, whenever the third appears, I shall not even attempt to tell lies about it. I shall rather try to make all the money than all the mystery I can of it. People shall pay for their knowledge if I can make them. Henry heard P. and P. warmly praised in Scotland by Lady Robert Kerr and another lady; and what does he do, in the warmth of his brotherly vanity and love, but immediately tell them who wrote it? A thing once set going in that way – one knows how it spreads, and he, dear creature, has set it going so much more than once. I know it is all done from affection and partiality, but at the same time let me here again express to you and Mary my sense of the superior kindness which you have shown on the occasion in doing what I wished. I am trying to harden myself. After all, what a trifle it is,*

in all its bearings, to the really important points of one's existence, even in this world.
Your very affectionate sister,
J. A.
There is to be a second edition of S. and S. Egerton advises it.

The next series of letters was written by Jane to her young niece Caroline Austen, who enjoyed writing stories which she sent to her aunt for her opinion. They show how good Jane was at addressing a child and her close relationship with her young niece. The last two letters were written when Jane's health was deteriorating.

December 6 [1814].
MY DEAR CAROLINE, – I wish I could finish stories as fast as you can. I am much obliged to you for the sight of Olivia, *and think you have done for her very well; but the good-for-nothing father, who was the real author of all her faults and sufferings, should not escape unpunished. I hope he hung himself, or took the surname of Bone or underwent some direful penance or other.*
Yours affectionately,
J. AUSTEN.

Chawton: Monday, July 15 [1814]
MY DEAR CAROLINE, – I have followed your directions and find your handwriting admirable. If you continue to improve as much as you have done, perhaps I may not be obliged to shut my eyes at all half a year hence. I have been very much entertained by your story of Carolina and her aged father; it made me laugh heartily, and I am particularly glad to find you so much alive upon any topic of such absurdity, as the usual description of a heroine's father. You have done it full justice, or, if anything be wanting, it is the information of the venerable old man's having married when only twenty-one, and being a father at twenty-two.

I had an early opportunity of conveying your letter to Mary Jane, having only to throw it out of the window at her as she was romping with your brother in the Back Court. She thanks you for it, and answers your questions through me. I am to tell you that she has passed her time at Chawton very pleasantly indeed, that she does not miss Cassy so much as she expected, and that as to Diana Temple, *she is ashamed to say it has never been worked at since you went away.*

Edward's visit has been a great pleasure to us. He has not lost one good quality or good look, and is only altered in being improved by being some months older than when we saw him last. He is getting very near our own age, for we do not grow older of course.

Yours affectionately,
J. AUSTEN.

Chawton: Wednesday, March 13 [1815].

MY DEAR CAROLINE, – I am very glad to have an opportunity of answering your agreeable little letter. You seem to be quite my own niece in your feelings towards Mme. de Genlis. I do not think I could even now, at my sedate time of life, read Olympe et Theophile *without being in a rage. It really is too bad! Not allowing them to be happy together when they are married. Don't talk of it, pray. I have just lent your Aunt Frank the first volume of* Les Veillees du Chateau, *for Mary Jane to read. It will be some time before she comes to the horror of Olympe.*

I had a very nice letter from your brother not long ago, and I am quite happy to see how much his hand is improving. I am convinced that it will end in a very gentlemanlike hand, much above par.

We have had a great deal of fun lately with post-chaises stopping at the door; three times within a few days we had a couple of agreeable visitors turn in unexpectedly – your Uncle Henry and Mr. Tilson, Mrs. Heathcote and Miss Bigg, your Uncle Henry and Mr. Seymour. Take notice it was the same Uncle Henry each time.
I remain, my dear Caroline,
Your affectionate Aunt,
J. AUSTEN.

Hans Place: Monday night October 30, 1815.

MY DEAR CAROLINE, – I have not felt quite equal to taking up your Manuscript, but think I shall soon, and I hope my detaining it so long will be no inconvenience. It gives us great pleasure that you should be at Chawton. I am sure Cassy must be delighted to have you. You will practise your music of course, and I trust to you for taking care of my instrument and not letting it be ill-used in any respect. Do not allow anything to be put on it but what is very light. I hope you will try to make out some other tune besides the Hermit.

I am sorry you got wet in your ride; now that you are become an Aunt you are a person of some consequence and must excite great interest whatever you do. I have always maintained the importance of Aunts as much as possible, and I am sure of your doing the same now.
Believe me, my dear Sister-Aunt,
Yours affectionately,
J. AUSTEN.

January 23, 1817.

MY DEAR CAROLINE, – I am always very much obliged to you for writing to me, and have now I believe two or three notes to thank you for; but whatever may be their number, I mean to have this letter accepted as a handsome return for all, for you see I have taken a complete, whole sheet of paper, which is to entitle me to consider it as a very long letter whether I write much or little.

We were quite happy to see Edward, it was an unexpected pleasure, and he makes himself as agreeable as ever, sitting in such a quiet comfortable way making his delightful little sketches. He is generally thought grown since he was here last, and rather thinner, but in very good looks. He read his two chapters to us the first evening – both good, but especially the last in our opinion. We think it has more of the spirit and entertainment of the early part of his work.

I feel myself getting stronger than I was half a year ago, and can so perfectly well walk to Alton, or back again, without the slightest fatigue that I hope to be able to do both when summer comes. I spent two or three days with your Uncle and Aunt lately, and though the children are sometimes very noisy and not under such order as they ought and easily might, I cannot help liking them and even loving them, which I hope may be not wholly inexcusable in their and your affectionate Aunt,

J. AUSTEN.

The Pianoforte often talks of you; in various keys, tunes, and expressions, I allow – but be it Lesson or Country Dance, Sonata or Waltz, you are really its constant theme. I wish you could come and see us, as easily as Edward can.

J. A.

Wednesday night. 1817.

You send me great news indeed, my dear Caroline, about Mr. Digweed, Mr. Trimmer, and a Grand Pianoforte. I wish it had been a small one, as then you might have pretended that Mr. D.'s rooms were too damp to be fit for it, and offered to take charge of it at the Parsonage.

I look forward to the four new chapters with pleasure. – But how can you like Frederick better than Edgar? You have some eccentric tastes however, I know, as to Heroes and Heroines. Goodbye.

Yours affectionately,

J. AUSTEN.

Chawton: Wednesday, March 26, 1817.

MY DEAR CAROLINE, – Pray make no apologies for writing to me often, I am always very happy to hear from you.

I think you very much improved in your writing, and in the way to write a very pretty hand. I wish you could practise your fingering oftener. Would not it be a good plan for you to go and live entirely at Mr. Wm. Digweed's?

He could not desire any other remuneration than the pleasure of hearing you practise.

I like Frederick and Caroline better than I did, but must still prefer Edgar and Julia. Julia is a warm-hearted, ingenuous, natural girl, which I like her for; but I know the word natural is no recommendation to you.

How very well Edward is looking! You can have nobody in your neighbourhood to vie with him at all, except Mr. Portal. I have taken one ride on the donkey and like it very much – and you must try to get me quiet, mild days, that I may be able to go out pretty constantly. A great deal of wind does not suit me, as I have still a tendency to rheumatism. In short I am a poor honey at present. I will be better when you can come and see us.

Yours affectionately,

J. AUSTEN.

The following extract is from a letter to Jane written by her brother Charles, who was in Italy. It shows how Jane's fame had begun to spread during her lifetime:

Books became the subject of conversation, and I praised Waverley highly, when a young man present observed that nothing had come out for years to be compared with Pride and Prejudice, Sense and Sensibility, &c. As I am sure you must be anxious to know the name of a person of so much taste, I shall tell you it is Fox, a nephew of the late Charles James Fox. That you may not be too much elated at this morsel of praise, I shall add that he did not appear to like Mansfield Park so well as the two first, in which, however, I believe he is singular.

The final letter taken from the updated family memoir was sent by James Austen to his son Edward when it was obvious that Jane did not have long to live.

Steventon: Thursday.

MY DEAR EDWARD, – I grieve to write what you will grieve to read; but I must tell you that we can no longer flatter ourselves with the least hope of having your dear valuable Aunt Jane restored to us. The symptoms which returned after the first four or five days at Winchester, have never subsided, and Mr. Lyford has candidly told us that her case is desperate. I need not say what a melancholy gloom this has cast over us all. Your Grandmamma has suffered much, but her affliction can be nothing to Cassandra's. She will indeed be to be pitied. It is some consolation to know that our poor invalid has hitherto felt no very severe pain – which is rather an extraordinary circumstance in her complaint. I saw her on Tuesday and found her much altered, but composed and cheerful. She is well aware of her situation. Your

Mother has been there ever since Friday and returns not till all is over – how soon that may be we cannot say – Lyford said he saw no signs of immediate dissolution, but added that with such a pulse it was impossible for any person to last long, and indeed no one can wish it – an easy departure from this to a better world is all that we can pray for. I am going to Winchester again to-morrow; you may depend upon early information, when any change takes place, and should then prepare yourself for what the next letter may announce.

Mrs. Heathcote is the greatest possible comfort to them all.

We all join in love.

Your affectionate Father,
J. AUSTEN.

Edward's young sister Caroline (aged twelve) added a few unhappy lines about her aunt, saying, 'I now feel as if I had never loved and valued her enough.'

8

A Great-Niece's Biography

Mary Augusta Austen-Leigh was the daughter of James Edward Austen-Leigh and, therefore, the great-niece of Jane Austen. She helped her brother William Austen-Leigh and her nephew Richard Arthur Austen-Leigh to prepare the updated family record which was published in 1913.

Over the next few years Miss Austen-Leigh realised that a number of myths and misconceptions about Jane Austen still persisted, despite the biographical material published by her family, and that new ones had arisen. In order to correct these mistaken ideas she wrote Personal Aspects of Jane Austen *which was published in 1920.*

Among the beliefs which this book sets out to dispel was that Jane Austen was unemotional, unsentimental, passionless, unpatriotic, that she lacked sympathy with the poor and that she did not like children. Miss Austen-Leigh also disproved some outrageous myths about Jane Austen's education and her family. This book included new material about Jane's early life, an analysis of the novels and a number of charades written by members of the Austen family.

PERSONAL ASPECTS OF JANE AUSTEN
MARY AUGUSTA AUSTEN LEIGH

Chapter I – Introduction

Jane Austen was born at Steventon Rectory in Hampshire on Saturday, December 16, 1775, and died in Mrs. David's lodgings, College Street, Winchester, on Friday, July 18, 1817, in her forty-second year.

Little was known by the world in general either of herself or of her surroundings for many years after the latter date. She had named her brother Henry as her literary executor, and in six months' time he published the two novels she had left in manuscript, 'Northanger Abbey' and 'Persuasion' (to which he himself gave these titles), prefixing to the former a short sketch of their author, called a 'Biographical Notice of Jane Austen'.

The same 'Notice', enlarged by a few additional paragraphs, appeared again in 1833, when Mr. R. Bentley, who had acquired the copyright of all her works, brought out a complete edition of the novels, no other edition being published during the first sixty-four years that elapsed after her death. The smallness of the print employed, ill-suited to any but young and strong eyes, may in part account for the slowness with which her fame grew during that period. But though a slow it was a sure growth, and with an increase in the number of her readers came an increased desire to know more details concerning herself.

As curiosity on these points became stronger, while the family remained silent, it was not unnatural that in the absence of definite information certain erroneous ideas should be entertained, and some mistaken statements made respecting herself, her home, and her position and opportunities in life. Reviewers were inclined to assume that her outlook upon the world at large must have been narrow and restricted to a small circle, though chiefly, as it would seem, because they themselves knew little about her beyond the facts that she had been a daughter of the Rector of Steventon, that she had lived in the country, had never mixed in literary circles, and had died almost before reaching middle age. Surprise would sometimes be expressed as to how, under these disadvantageous circumstances, it should have been possible for her to paint the varied pictures of human nature and give the accurate descriptions of contemporary manners with which her books were filled. Again, conjectures were made that these dealt with one class of life only, that of the English gentry, not from choice but from necessity, because she had no knowledge of anything beyond it. It was also reported that 'Jane Austen was not fond of children' – it was left to a modern foreign critic to add that 'She was not fond of animals.'

To some degree, though not entirely, these mistaken ideas were dispelled when, in 1869, the first 'Memoir of Jane Austen' was published by her nephew, the Rev. J. E. Austen-Leigh. He had been the youngest of the mourners at her funeral fifty years earlier, and many friends, knowing how well fitted he was to write a memoir of his aunt, had in after years often begged him to undertake this labour of love which he for long declined on the score that he had so little to relate. In saying this he was referring to his own recollections of the aunt who died when he himself had hardly reached manhood, and to the scantiness of the records he possessed concerning her. At last, however, he consented to make an attempt, and, being much assisted by the excellent memories of his two sisters, Mrs. Lefroy and Miss Austen, he found it possible to complete a

Memoir of Jane Austen. This work must always hold a unique position as containing the testimony of those who well knew its subject and of being absolutely authentic and faithful so far as the biographer's memory, which was admirable, and those of his sisters could ensure its perfect accuracy. It could not relate that which none of them knew, respecting the details of her earlier life, nor could it describe many facts given in letters not then before him, to which later writers have had access.

The book was rightfully named a 'Memoir,' as his chief object was to record that which he himself remembered. Readers would on their side do well to bear in mind that his recollections ranged only from childhood to very early manhood, and that his Aunt Jane could never have appeared to him as a young person. When, therefore, he speaks of her life as 'domestic' or 'uneventful', his thoughts were going back only to the quiet years she spent towards its close in her home at Chawton. Of her earlier and gayer experiences, he probably knew nothing, and still less likely was it that, in spite of their strong mutual affection, he should have any knowledge of the intimate and private feelings of an aunt whose years, at the time of her death, numbered more than twice his own.

It is, perhaps, not surprising that contemporary reviewers of the 'Memoir' should, without sufficiently considering these circumstances, have caught up some of his expressions and dwelt upon them, as though they described the whole of her lifetime and not the latter part only. These writers speak of her life as being 'uniform' and the circle of her experience as 'narrow'. They say 'her lifeworld presented a limited experience'. 'It was a simple and uneventful, monotonous life', while one critic also gives it as his opinion that 'the range of her sympathies was narrow.' 'Miss Austen lacks the breadth and depth of feeling which distinguished her great successor, George Eliot.' Another says, 'a neat, natty, little artist was Jane Austen,'and yet another, 'When we compare her to George Eliot the reader will see at once the eminence on which we place her.'

Such were some of the judgments passed on Jane Austen half a century ago.

But a considerable amount of additional information concerning her earlier life and its surroundings has now been acquired, of which later biographers were able to avail themselves. First in order came the 'Letters of Jane Austen,' published in 1884 by Lord Brabourne. The existence of these letters was known to the writer of the 'Memoir' but he could not examine them, as their owner, his cousin, was then too infirm to undertake the labour of looking through them and, without having done so, she did not wish to place them in any other hands.

They had been written by Jane to Cassandra, and though of high value in supplying a biographer with many facts, are yet a peculiarly restricted selection, which should never be taken as a specimen of her general correspondence, having been spared by Cassandra only in the full belief that they contained nothing sufficiently interesting to induce any future generation to give them to the world. Since the publication of these letters by Lord Brabourne, other letters, written by more distant branches of the Austen family, have been recovered, which bear upon the life at Steventon Rectory in old days, and consequently upon that of Jane herself.

Another book, giving some authentic details of the same, dealing principally with the careers of her sailor brothers, was published in 1916 by a great nephew and niece. [1] All the fresh knowledge thus acquired has been embodied in the latest 'Life of Jane Austen' which was published in 1913 by a great nephew and a great, great nephew. [2]

So much fresh information having been given to the world respecting Jane Austen's youthful years since the publication of the original 'Memoir' which dealt almost wholly with her later life, it certainly occasions some surprise to find critics of the present day apparently disregarding these later biographies and reverting to the standpoint of those writers who knew only the earliest. Yet so it is. In a recently published book we again hear of her 'narrow experience' and are told that she 'lived aside from the world,' also that 'concerning her personal character and private interests we know remarkably little' and that 'her life provided even less variety of incident than she discovered at Longbourn or Uppercross', while the same writer states, in spite of all evidence to the contrary, that 'her father was not very much better educated and scarcely more strenuous than his neighbours nor were there granted to her any of the consolations of culture.'

Since it is still possible for an earnest and acute student of her works to offer, as ascertained facts, views of his own concerning their writer which contain so many misapprehensions, it may be well once more to record a few simple truths about Jane Austen's position in life, her education, and her choice of subjects as an author.

1. *Jane Austen's Sailor Brothers*, by J. H. Hubback and Edith C. Hubback.
2. *Life and Letters of Jane Austen*, by W. Austen-Leigh and R. A. Austen-Leigh.

Chapter II – Position

That Jane Austen should take as her field of work one which, though far from being narrow, was certainly definite, the life, namely, of the English gentry, was so natural as hardly to require either remark or explanation. It was the class to which her ancestors had for some centuries belonged and with which she had always associated. The Austens of Steventon Rectory were descended from many generations of Kentish Austens who, arising like other county families from the powerful clan of Clothiers, known in the Middle Ages as the 'Gray coats of Kent', were, in the sixteenth century, settled as landowners in two small and picturesque old manor houses, Grovehurst and Broadford, which still form part of the Austen property, though the heads of the family removed long ago to larger habitations and increased possessions in the parish of Horsmonden, near Sevenoaks, a neighbourhood where the name of Austen has long been known and held in honour. They were a purely English family. No admixture of Scottish, Irish, or foreign blood appears in the pedigree of the Austens of Broadford, which runs back to the close of the sixteenth century.

They were also a race accustomed to prize both religion and education. On the tomb of the wife of the first John Austen, of Broadford (Joan Berry), in Horsmonden Church, dated A.D. 1604, it is recorded that she met her death 'often utteringe these speeches, "Let neither husband nor children nor lands nor goods separate me from my God." A hundred years later another Mrs. John Austen existed, whose name (Elizabeth Weller) deserves to be held in perpetual respect and esteem by her descendants. In her portrait, taken when she was a blooming young woman, she appears in brocade and pearls, suitable to the wife of the heir to the estate, and future Lady of the Manor. But the latter position she never held, as her husband died before his father, who, like 'the old Gentleman' in 'Sense and Sensibility' showed an exclusive care for his eldest grandson and heir, and, soon dying himself, left to his daughter-in-law the task of bringing up on small means her remaining five sons and a daughter. Without repining at her want of fortune, she quickly set to work to give them that which she thought would best supply its absence, namely, learning, and that they might receive a sound classical education, she removed to Sevenoaks, to send them as day-boys to its old Grammar School, and to take some of its masters as lodgers into her own house as an assistance towards defraying the expenses of her large family. She had her reward in living to see her daughter married and all her sons established in different professions. This brave woman was Jane Austen's great grandmother, as her fourth son, William, a surgeon in Tonbridge, became the father of George Austen – he being the first of the race to leave his native county and make a home in Hampshire.

When he was settled at Steventon, regular communications with the relations he had quitted in Kent were kept up. The Kentish Austens had, naturally, formed many connections by marriage with families in their own county, and when Jane, at the age of twelve, had for the first time the delight of going with her parents and her sister into Kent, she would make acquaintance with a number of relations hitherto unknown to her excepting by name – an epoch in life to a girl of that age, gifted with strong family instincts and quick power of observation. It is due to the correspondence maintained between the Hampshire and the Kentish cousins that various facts relating to the period of Jane Austen's girlhood were not long ago discovered by one of the authors of 'Life and Letters'.

None of these early letters were written by Jane herself, but in later life it was her custom to write many to relations at a distance, thus acting up to a remark she once made to a niece, 'I like cousins to be cousins, and interested in one another.'

This hereditary interest was also felt to the full towards the maternal side of the house, where the young George Austen's descent was of an interesting and varied character. Mrs. George Austen had been Cassandra Leigh, one of the Leighs of Addlestrop in Gloucestershire, an elder branch of the Leighs of Stoneleigh in Warwickshire, to which property they succeeded when the junior line died out. All came from the family of Leighs, who were settled at Highleigh in Cheshire from the date of the Norman Conquest. Early in the reign of Henry VIII one of these, Thomas Leigh, came when a lad to seek his fortune in London. In this quest he was highly successful and was knighted by Queen Elizabeth, being Lord Mayor of London in the year of her accession, 1557. As such he had the honour of receiving her and preceding her, carrying the sceptre before her Grace when she first entered the City to take up her residence at the Tower. He also bore a leading part in the ceremonies of her Coronation in the following year. Romantic incidents and stirring events belong to the history of Sir Thomas Leigh's descendants, who must have possessed much determination, strength of character, and keen sense of humour. They were also noted for inflexible loyalty to the House of Stuart through every change of fortune that befell its monarchs. When Charles I was on his march to Nottingham, there to set up the Royal Standard, he found on reaching Coventry that the gates of that city were closed against him by order of the Mayor. On this he rode off to Stoneleigh Abbey, where he and his escort were hospitably received by the reigning Sir Thomas Leigh, a grandson of the original Sir Thomas. Again, in 1745 apartments were prepared in the Abbey which, it was hoped, that Charles Edward would occupy for at least one night; but he was not destined to enjoy such comfortable quarters in England, and very fortunate beyond a doubt was it for the Leighs that he retreated without reaching the midland counties. To Jane Austen, who was, as will be shown further on, a most worthy descendant of the 'loyal Leighs' every story or relic connected with these historic memories of the Stuarts must have been deeply interesting, when she spent some time at Stoneleigh Abbey in August 1804 [it was, in fact, in August 1806 that this visit took place]; and greatly indeed would her delight have been increased could she have beheld a remarkable family treasure which the house then contained, the very existence of which was at that time unknown, and so remained for another twenty years. It was in 1827 that Sir George Beaumont, well known as a connoisseur in art, when examining a flower- piece in oils at

Stoneleigh Abbey, detected what appeared to be a human eye looking at him from amongst the flowers. On further examination it was ascertained that these had been thinly painted over another picture, and when they were removed a fine portrait of Charles I by Vandyke came to light. This method of concealment, adopted no doubt to save the picture from the thrust of some Parliamentary pikestaff, had proved so effectual that not even a tradition of the portrait had survived. It must have lain hidden for nearly two centuries until chance, as in the case of 'The Bride of the Mistletoe Bough' [a legend in which a bride remains hidden for two centuries] revealed the long-kept secret, and the fine painting, happier in fortune than the ill-fated bride, emerged again in all its pristine beauty. Stuart monarchs have been accused of ingratitude towards their followers, but here, on the contrary, it is a pleasant, as well as a probable, theory that the portrait was sent to Sir Thomas Leigh in token of the gratitude felt by a King who had been sheltered by him in a time of need.

It was through her Leigh relations that Jane became, while still young, well acquainted with Bath. Cassandra Austen's brother, James Leigh (Perrot), himself a man of good fortune, had married a well-endowed lady, Miss Cholmeley, from Lincolnshire. They possessed a country home in Berkshire, and had also, as a winter residence, a house in Bath at No 1 Paragon, commanding a lovely and extensive view. There they lived as people of fashion and fortune in the later years of the eighteenth century, and parts of beautiful old costumes worn by them still exist to show how brilliant must have been the scenes then presented by the gay world of Bath. The Leigh Perrots, who were childless, received their Steventon relations as visitors, and the eldest of Cassandra's sons was generally looked upon as his uncle's natural heir.

Through circumstances which befell her next brother, Edward (Knight), Jane had again a fresh and a wide view of English society opened to her observation. Edward had been adopted, while still a young boy, by another childless couple, Mr. and Mrs. Thomas Knight, who were cousins on the Austen side of the house, and possessors of large properties both in Hampshire and in East Kent. It was in the latter neighbourhood that Edward married and settled, at first in a home of his own, whence he removed after Mr. Knight's death to the large house and beautiful estate of Godmersham Park, near Canterbury, and in East Kent, Jane, as a young woman, began to visit her brother Edward and his family. Visits, like the journeys that led to them, were in those days long affairs, and hers must have afforded ample time as well as opportunity to mix in the society of that neighbourhood, where she could observe English county life from a fresh point of view, and could compare it with the corresponding class of society she already knew well in Hampshire around Steventon. The share taken in the latter by the George Austens has been thus described by the author of the original 'Memoir.' He says:

> Their situation had some peculiar advantages beyond those of ordinary rectories. Steventon was a family living. Mr. Knight, the patron, was also proprietor of nearly the whole parish. He never resided there and, consequently, the rector and his children came to be regarded in the neighbourhood as a kind of representatives of the family. They shared with the principal tenant the command of an excellent manor and enjoyed, in this reflected way, some of the consideration usually awarded to landed proprietors. They were not rich, but, aided by Mr. Austen's powers of teaching, they had enough to afford a good education to their sons and daughters, to mix in the best society in the neighbourhood, and to exercise a liberal hospitality to their own relations and friends. A carriage and pair of horses were kept. The horses probably, like Mr. Bennet's, were often employed in farm work.

From the foregoing account it will be evident that to place, as has been done by a recent critic, Jane Austen and Charlotte Bronte together in one sentence, as both 'living aside from the world' is entirely wide of the mark. Beyond the facts that their fathers were clergymen and that both lived in the country, no resemblance whatever can be discovered in their situations, which were as unlike as were their several characters. No counterpart to the isolation and sadness of Haworth Rectory could be found in the happy and sociable atmosphere of the Rectory at Steventon. Her nephew, who well knew those of whom he wrote, says in his original 'Memoir' – 'There can be no doubt that the general colouring of Jane Austen's early life was bright. She lived with indulgent parents in a cheerful home, which afforded an agreeable variety of society.' Jane, like most young girls, thoroughly enjoyed the gaieties of the neighbourhood around her, of which dancing formed a great feature. Her brother Henry says: 'She was fond of dancing and excelled in it.' It may be remembered that nearly all her heroines shared in this taste – even the timid Fanny feeling that a ball 'was indeed delightful'. That Jane Austen was in every way well fitted to write of the lives and feelings of English gentle-people is not to be questioned, nor that this would be a determining factor in directing her imagination towards such a field of work. It is not, however, a proof, as may be shown later, that there was none other at her command had she thought well to choose it.

Chapter III – Education I

Cassandra and Jane Austen, while still children, must have had a larger acquaintance with the world than can usually fall to the lot of such young girls. Space was probably needed within their own home for the reception of George Austen's pupils, and his little daughters, at the ages of nine and six, were sent to be educated elsewhere, not, as we are told, because it was supposed that Jane at six years old required very much education, but because it would have broken her heart to be separated from Cassandra. The sisters, therefore, went together to Oxford, there to be placed under the care of Mrs. Cawley, who was a connection of their mother and the widow of a Principal of Brasenose College; a lady of whom no record remains beyond the fact that she was a stiff-mannered person. Mrs. Cawley removed after a time to Southampton, and by so doing very nearly put an end to Jane's short existence, for in that town both she and Cassandra fell very ill of what was then called 'putrid fever', and Jane's life was at one time despaired of. Mrs. Cawley would not at first write word of this illness to Steventon Rectory, but Jane Cooper, the little girls' cousin, who was one of the party, thought it right to do so, an action which was probably instrumental in saving the life of Jane. Mrs. Austen at once set off for Southampton together with her sister, Mrs. Cooper, and they brought with them a remedy, to the use of which Jane's recovery was ascribed. But a heavy price had to be paid for this blessing. Poor Mrs. Cooper took the infection herself and died at Bath, whither she went on quitting Southampton. Such a tragical time must have remained fixed in any child's memory, and in the delirium and distress of Marianne Dashwood, when lying dangerously ill at Cleveland, also of a 'putrid fever', and also awaiting the arrival of a mother, we probably hear an echo of poor little Jane's delirious entreaties for her own mother, when lying equally ill in the strange world of Southampton.

The next experience of the sisters was of a happier nature. They and their cousin, Jane Cooper, spent two years in the kindly Abbey School at Reading, with its beautiful garden and picturesque old buildings. From all accounts, discipline here was not of a rigid order, for when their brother and cousin, Edward Austen and Edward Cooper, were passing through Reading Cassandra and the two Janes were allowed to dine with them at an inn in the town. [1] When, therefore, these early adventures in search of education came to an end and the sisters returned to continue their lessons at home, it must have been with imaginations already enriched by some acquaintance with the three old towns of Oxford, Southampton, and Reading.

At Steventon they would not suffer from any want of competent teachers. Basingstoke was near enough to furnish whatever occasional instructions might be needed from masters, such as Elizabeth Bennet told Lady Catherine could always be had at Longbourn for those who desired them. But the most valuable and solid part of their mental training they must have received in their own home, where they would find excellent opportunities for studying English literature and language under their father, who ceased by degrees to take private pupils into his house, and would, therefore, have sufficient leisure for teaching his own children. The recent critic who spoke of him as being probably 'not very much better educated, and scarcely more strenuous than his neighbours' makes an entire mistake. George Austen had won an open scholarship and fellowship at St. John's College, Oxford, and had been for a time a master at his own former school, Tonbridge, before returning again to reside at St. John's as an Oxford Don. In later life he prepared two of his sons for matriculation at the same College, and one of these has thus written of him, with especial reference to the, 'education he gave to Jane'. 'Being not only a profound Scholar, but possessing an exquisite taste in every species of Literature, it is not wonderful that his daughter Jane should at a very early age have become sensible of the charms of style and enthusiastic in the cultivation of her own language.' We may, perhaps, allow for a little filial exaggeration here, but we should also remember that it is first-hand evidence, coming from one of George Austen's own pupils. That he would be a kind and welcome instructor is certain from the way in which Jane afterwards recalls his strong affection for his family, his 'indescribable tenderness as a father', and 'the sweet, benevolent smile which always distinguished him'. To learn of such a teacher must have been a constant pleasure, and she had another assistant at hand in her eldest brother James, himself a classical scholar and a cultivated man, of whom his son, the author of the original 'Memoir', thus writes: 'He was well read in English literature, had a correct taste, and wrote readily and happily both in prose and verse. He was more than ten years older than Jane and had, I believe, a large share in directing her reading and forming her taste.' He was also a good French scholar, spending some months in France to perfect himself in the language. Perhaps Jane remembered this brother's assistance when she made Edmund Bertram perform the same kind offices for his little cousin, Fanny Price.

One glimpse of Jane at her lessons has been spared to us by time and may be found in her own handwriting in an old copy of Oliver Goldsmith's 'History of England'. From internal evidence, she must have been reading it for the first time, with an excited interest that would recall Marianne Dashwood's enthusiastic soul rather than Catherine Morland's indifference to history, where she found 'the men all so bad, and hardly any women at all'. Jane's age can only be guessed at, but from the nature of the remarks she inscribes on the margin of this work, twelve or thirteen years seems a probable time of life for her to have then reached. It was the 'History of the Rebellion' that stirred her loyal soul to its depths. At first she contents herself with these short interjections on the behaviour of Cromwell's party – '*Oh! Oh! The Wretches*' but she grows eloquent when Goldsmith delivers his verdict against the whole family of Stuart, and cries out in answer – '*A family who were always ill-used, BETRAYED OR NEGLECTED, whose virtues are seldom allowed, while their errors are never forgotten.*'

It is perhaps fortunate – in case some destructive critic should arise in the future to declare the improbability of Jane Austen having written any such words – that a postscript has been added to this note by a sympathetic young nephew, into whose possession the book afterwards passed: 'Bravo, Aunt Jane! Just my opinion of the case.'

At the conclusion of Walpole's speech her remark is slightly ironical – '*Nobly said! Spoken like a Tory.*' And, again, when Goldsmith refers to the King as a Master unworthy of faithful followers, come these words – '*Unworthy, because he was a Stuart, I suppose – unhappy family.*'

Lord Balmerino's execution in 1745 is thus lamented – '*Dear Balmerino! I cannot express what I feel for you!*'

On the subsequent change in the dress of the Highlanders she writes – '*I do not like this. Every ancient custom ought to be Sacred, unless it is prejudicial to Happiness.*'

Next comes a very sapient announcement. Goldsmith having condemned those who were 'Stunning mankind with a cry of Freedom', Jane thus addresses him – '*My Dear Mr. G—, I have lived long enough in the world to know that it is always so.*'

Here she was probably thinking of the French Revolution, in which all at Steventon had a special reason for taking very deep interest.

She did not approve of Anne leaving her father's cause to side with her brother-in-law, and, being unwilling to blame any Stuart, finds her own way out of the dilemma – '*Anne should not have done so, indeed I do not believe she did.*'

In writing of James II's obstinate adherence to his own policy, Goldsmith refers it to this King's conviction that 'nothing could injure schemes calculated to promote the cause of heaven' on which Jane observes – '*Since he acted upon such motives he ought not to be blamed.*'

It must be left to those critics who have described Jane Austen's disposition as 'calm', as 'unemotional', 'unsentimental', 'passionless' to reconcile such epithets with these eager outpourings, which are given here for the benefit of all who may care to form some truer conception of the real Jane than the tame and colourless personality, devoid of all enthusiasm and ardour, which has at times been set before the public as hers, though something better than this might, one would think, have been divined from the characters of her favourite heroines, Emma Woodhouse and Elizabeth Bennet, neither of whom can well be decried as wanting in high spirit or liveliness of nature.

Of Jane's accomplishments in music and drawing we know little more than can be found in her brother's notice. He says:

> She had not only an excellent taste for drawing, but in her earlier days evinced great power of hand in the management of the pencil. She was a

> warm and judicious admirer of landscape, both in nature and on canvas. At a very early age she was enamoured of Gilpin on the Picturesque [William Gilpin, originator of the idea of the picturesque], and she seldom changed her opinion either on books or men.

None of her efforts in drawing have survived, though a few of Cassandra's slight water-colour portraits still exist, and also some pencil sketches taken by others of the family, showing that a general love of drawing existed amongst them, in which Jane very probably shared. Her delight in beautiful scenery was so great that she thought it must hereafter form one of the joys of heaven. As regards music, her brother says she 'held her own musical attainments extremely cheap'. They were, of course, not remarkable, but she was the most musical of an unmusical family, and a niece, when writing of her, says she had a natural taste for music. A manuscript music book of hers is still preserved at Chawton, containing, in exquisitely fine writing, some of the songs she used to sing.

How large a share Mrs. Austen may have taken in the intellectual part of her daughters' education we do not know, but she may no doubt be credited with the charge of two important departments – writing and needlework. She herself wrote an admirable hand, both powerful and interesting, rivalling, though not much resembling, that of her daughter Jane, the beauty of whose writing many of her readers know. Jane herself looked upon good handwriting as an art to be carefully cultivated. She alludes to it more than once in her notes to a little niece, Caroline Austen, and of her nephew Edward Austen's writing she says: 'I am quite happy to see how his hand is improving. I am convinced that it will end in a very gentlemanlike hand, much above Par.' Good writing was general in Jane's home, and those who study calligraphy as a key to character might be interested by finding signs of imagination, grace of mind, and other pleasant qualities repeated in the various scripts.

Good needlework was in their time an accomplishment of great importance in every household, and this their mother would certainly teach them, for she was herself a proficient in it even to the close of a very long life, and her daughters were her imitators. The only time Jane ever bestows serious praise upon a performance of her own is when she writes word from Rowling, her brother Edward's first home in Kent, that they are 'all very busy making shirts, and I am proud to say that I am the neatest worker of the party.' No one who has seen the specimens of her needlework which still exist can doubt that the praise was well deserved. One of these, which looks as if it were fashioned by fairy fingers, is a tiny housewife containing needles an inch in length, made for a friend [Mary Lloyd] by Jane at the age of seventeen. Another, belonging to later years, is a scarf of Indian muslin, two and a half yards long embroidered throughout in white satin stitch, its delicate beauty being unmarred by a single fault. [2] Equally industrious was she in humbler tasks. Her niece Anna has written of her aunts as constantly sitting together, making clothes for the poor, and varying their occupation by here and there teaching a boy or girl to read, Jane very probably instructing a god-daughter of her own, whose father was coachman to her brother James Austen.

Let those who have done the same declare whether this shows any interest in their poorer neighbours or not! Yet a foreign admirer of her works has not hesitated to charge her with indifference to the needs of the poor, with visiting them as seldom as possible, and with never doubting that they had been created in order that they might serve and respect 'their betters',adding, 'Grief and poverty shock her, as offensive to her taste, things which she forgets as quickly as possible' and 'she always turns away from suffering, sadness, and ugliness.' Of such a character could it ever have been said that 'to know her was to love her?' The only train of thought, in this critic's mind appears to be, 'She did not write of the poor, and therefore she did not care for them'. Jane has, however, left an unconscious contradiction of such imputations on the margin of her Goldsmith, who in one place has described the extreme destitution of the poorer classes after the Revolution, in consequence of which a man and his wife committed suicide. On this her comment is ready – '*How much are the poor to be pitied, and the Rich to be Blamed!*'

The baseless accusation that she always turned away from whatever was sad, unpleasant, or painful, cannot be allowed to pass unnoticed. One simple instance to the contrary (among many) is described in a family letter. During their residence at Chawton Cottage a general outbreak of measles took place among the Frank Austens, who were at the time inhabiting the Great House. As some relief to the overworked nurses at the House, Miss Gibson, a sister of Mrs. Frank Austen, who was one of the party, was invited over to the Cottage to have *her* attack of measles there, and Mrs. Austen, in a letter to her grand-daughter Anna, that sums up the result: 'She wanted a great deal of good nursing, and a great deal of good nursing she had,' the nurses being Cassandra, Jane, and their friend Martha Lloyd. Anna, when recording this incident merely adds: 'It was their quiet way of doing great kindnesses.' Jane's powers as a nurse were more severely tried some years later when for many weeks she attended on her brother Henry in an illness in London of which he nearly died.

In returning to the question of early education, it must be pointed out that in the acquisition of foreign languages the daughters of Steventon Rectory were unusually fortunate, often having an excellent teacher of the same resident for long periods together under its hospitable roof. This was their own first cousin on the paternal side, the Comtesse de Feuillide, Elizabeth Hancock by birth, who in later life became their sister-in-law.

She was greatly attached to the family at Steventon, especially to her Uncle George, and she with her mother spent much time at the Rectory before she was taken by the latter to finish her education in Paris, where in 1781 she married a French nobleman, Jean Capotte, Comte de Feuillide. She was a lovely and accomplished young woman, who went out much into gay and high society both in Paris and in London. Her husband's estates were situated in the south of France, and thither she at one time travelled, making in the course of the summer an expedition across the Pyrenees to take part in the gaieties of the beautiful watering place, Bagneres de Bigorre, on their further side. The affectionate and regular correspondence she maintained with her English relations does not seem to have been diminished by these foreign experiences, and when political thunderclouds gathered over France the Comte dispatched her, with her infant son, to England, to find a safe refuge in Steventon Rectory, where she frequently resided in the dark days that were to follow, both before and after the unfortunate Comte perished on the scaffold in February, 1794.

It was probably in part to Elizabeth that her younger cousins owed their easy familiarity with the French language, and also some knowledge of Italian; as much, we may suppose, as Anne Elliot owns to in 'Persuasion'. Whatever the amount may have been, Jane was tolerably certain, like Anne, to have decried, as far as possible, her own personal share in it. But when she describes herself, long afterwards, to Mr. Clarke, the Regent's Librarian, as one who 'knows only her mother tongue and has read little in that', and as 'the most unlearned and uninformed female who ever dared to be an authoress', she is indulging in a flight of fancy and self-depreciation unusual even for her. It may have formed the foundation for a strange statement made by a modern critic that 'if she was fond of reading, she knew nothing about literature. Her letters do not suggest the uneasiness attached to the possession of a soul as we moderns understand it.' The connection of these sentences is not very easy to follow, as a large number of persons who certainly know nothing of literature still believe themselves to possess 'a soul' as that word is usually understood. But the 'modern soul' appears to belong to some distinct order of its own, and thankful may we be that Jane Austen did not possess its 'uneasiness' for had she done so, we could never have possessed works such as those she has left to the world. Once more, respecting her knowledge of literature, neither here, nor on any similar occasion, is she to be taken at her own valuation. Not only was this honestly a low one, but it suited her playful turn of mind to describe her attainments (excepting in needlework) as even lower than she believed them to be. Thus, when assuring Mr. Clarke of her inability to produce a romance on the whole House of Coburg, the spirit of nonsense evidently rose up within her at the idea, making her add that if, on pain of death, she were forbidden to laugh at herself or other people, she would certainly be hung before she had finished the first chapter. Mr. Clarke may or may not have been capable of a smile here – it must remain doubtful – for there have evidently been other persons of a later date quite unable to perceive when the writer is indulging in the welcome luxury of a pleasant little jest against herself. Her brother's account is altogether different. He says: 'Her reading was very extensive in history and belles-lettres, and her memory extremely tenacious. Her favourite moral writers were Johnson in prose, and Cowper in verse. It is difficult to say at what age she was not intimately acquainted with the merits and defects of the best essays and novels in the English language.'

The predominance given to Crabbe amongst Jane Austen's favourite writers by various annotators is rather singular. It has been due to her joke against herself, preserved by family tradition, and mentioned in the original 'Memoir' that 'she thought she could fancy marrying Mr. Crabbe,' and on the certain knowledge that she enjoyed his works. But this was no exclusive enjoyment, and he has no place among the poets, passages from whose works appear in connection with her own heroines. Of these there are a considerable number. Cowper was read by Marianne Dashwood and Fanny Price, the former declaring that his 'beautiful lines have frequently driven me almost mad'. Anne Elliot studied and discussed Scott and Byron, and in the laughing choice of passages from the poets supposed to have assisted in developing Catherine Morland's mind, Pope, Gray, Thomson, and Shakespeare have a place. 'Hamlet' was read aloud in Mrs. Dashwood's drawing-room, and Henry Crawford assumes that a knowledge of Shakespeare is instinctively imbibed from the atmosphere of every educated household. A fairly wide acquaintance with English poets is thus incidentally shown by her writings, but of Crabbe we only hear that his 'Tales' lay among the books on Fanny Price's table.

A pleasant picture of the home circle to which Jane belonged while still a child, as it appeared to a visitor in the house, exists in a family manuscript, written by a Mrs. Thomas Leigh, who speaks of her cousin Cassandra as being the wife of 'the truly respectable Mr. Austen' and says:

> With his sons (all promising to make figures in life) Mr. Austen educates a few youths of chosen friends and acquaintances. When among this Liberal Society, the simplicity, hospitality, and taste which commonly prevail in different families among the delightful valleys of Switzerland ever occurs to my memory.

1. A charming fancy drawing of this happy young party has been made by Miss Ellen Hill [in Constance Hill's *Jane Austen, Her Life and Her Friends*].

2. The pattern of this scarf has been produced on the covers of Miss Hill's book and also been carved on the oaken margin surrounding the tablet which was erected through their exertions on the wall of Chawton Cottage, in 1917 to commemorate the centenary of Jane Austen's death.

Chapter IV – Education II

The general love of literature that prevailed in Steventon Rectory is a sufficient security that Jane could not suffer from any intellectual poverty in her home. In the broader aspects of the word 'education' she was also fortunately placed. The thoughts of her family were bounded by no narrow horizon. They had private as well as public reasons for taking a deep interest in important matters then agitating the nation at large. While Jane was still quite young the elders of the family could not, if they would, have refrained from following with close attention the great political drama being played out at that time in another hemisphere. The then very far off land of India was brought near to them, and they were familiarised with many details of Indian life through the marriage of George Austen's only surviving sister, Philadelphia, to Saul Tysoe Hancock. Mr. Hancock had been a companion and early friend of Warren Hastings before his own marriage took place at Calcutta, and after that event he and Philadelphia lived on terms of close intimacy with Hastings, who became god-father to their only child, Elizabeth. His own only child had been placed with the George Austens, and to their great grief had died as a young boy when still under their care. Intercourse between Steventon and Calcutta remained, nevertheless, unbroken; the trial of Warren Hastings was followed with the deepest interest at the Rectory, and when the impeachment of the latter (begun in 1788) was concluded by an acquittal in 1795, great were the joy and exultation felt by his friends in Hampshire.

Of the letters that must have passed on the occasion only one is extant, coming from the fluent pen of young Henry Austen, who addresses Hastings with respectful devotion and celebrates the great event in many magnificent phrases. Jane, who was twenty years old in December, 1795, would have heard much of Warren Hastings all her life, and cannot have failed to take a part in the excitement and enthusiasm felt by the whole family. Neither was India the only foreign land with which the George Austens were personally concerned. The troubles already arising in distracted France must have claimed an even greater share of their anxious attention, since they so closely affected their own nearest relations. Many must have been the stories, both gay and grievous, told by the young Comtesse and her mother on their return to Steventon, of life in the

French capital at that thrilling crisis, mixed with descriptions of French chateau life in the south, and accounts of the gaieties of the fashionable world of Paris at the court of Louis XVI. Another view of foreign society would also reach the George Austens through their son, Edward, who, having been when a young man entirely adopted by the Thomas Knights, was sent by them, not to a University, but to make the then fashionable 'Grand Tour of Europe.' In his case this included a year spent in Dresden, where he was kindly received at the Saxon court. Many years afterwards, when his two eldest sons had spent some time in that city and had, like their father, received marks of attention from the Royal Family, there was a pleasant exchange of letters and presents between Prince Maximilian of Saxony and 'Edward Knight, *ci-devant* Austen.' The educational tour of the latter was afterwards extended to Rome. Its date was probably 1786–88, and it comprehended a view of that old Europe soon to be changed by the convulsion of wars and revolutions. Edward, on his return home, would have much to relate of deep interest at Godmersham and Steventon; Jane being at this period twelve or thirteen years old.

Nor should it be forgotten that while every intelligent and patriotic Englishman must have been following the events in the British fleet with unbroken interest, the Steventon party had a double reason for so doing, since two of George Austen's sons were beginning their careers and hazarding their lives in those naval actions upon the success of which the safety of the whole nation depended.

We see, then, that at Steventon Rectory an ample supply of food for the mind, the heart, and the imagination was furnished both by public events and by private interests, and some expressions used by Jane in later years show that the girl of twelve or thirteen, whose comments on the course of English history, occurring a century or more before her own birth, we have been reading, remained to the end of her life a firm patriot and a strong believer in the superiority in the ways and the merits of her native country over those of other lands. In a letter written to an old friend a few months before her death, she says: 'I hope your letters from abroad are satisfactory. They would not be satisfactory to me I confess, unless they breathed a strong spirit of regret for not being in England.' Yet critics have arisen, ready to accuse her of possessing only narrow sympathies and little patriotism, on the sole ground that no discussions on public affairs, or on the war with France, appear in her private, intimate correspondence with her sister Cassandra. Here we have once more the old cry 'She did not write of them, therefore she did not care for them'. The falseness of such an argument, when it attacks a belief in the kindness of Jane Austen's heart has, it is hoped, been already shown but the second charge, if somewhat less offensive, stands on no securer foundation than the first. Why should she write of public affairs unless their sailor brothers' personal histories were at the moment affected by them? Then indeed her pen is always active; but on public issues let us judge her by ourselves. Our war of five years' duration is just over; how many sisters, when a lapse of two or three years had familiarised them with the thought of its existence would have discussed it, in its public bearings, in letters to each other devoted to home details? Yet might they not justly resent an imputation that the absence of such discussions proved any want of ardent patriotism on their own parts? But to Jane Austen, war, if far from being a new and unheard of horror, was an almost normal state of things. Her England had during a large portion of her short life been constantly at war. The gravity of the situation could never be forgotten, but the recent excitement of our own country, fed as it has been by telegrams and journalists, did not exist a hundred years earlier, when intelligence of great battles was often long in reaching England. Such news might take weeks on its journey, and private information was still longer on the passage home. Francis Austen was made a post captain in consequence of gallantry shewn in a naval action in the Mediterranean, but he did not hear of his promotion until six months after the action had been fought, the necessary details having taken three months to travel home to England, while another period of three months was required to bring news of such promotion back to himself.

Nor is it accurate to say that Jane makes no mention of the war to Cassandra; it is referred to more than once, even in the few fragments of her letters that we possess. One passage may be cited, and also interpreted, to exculpate the writer from any apparent want of feeling on account of the words she employs: 'May 21, 1811. How horrible to have so many people killed! And what a blessing that one cares for none of them!' The action here alluded to is no doubt Albuera, a very bloody battle, and among the regiments which suffered most was that of the 'Buffs' from East Kent. It is probable that this contained some Godmersham friends and that the object of her remark was to express satisfaction that none of them were among the dead.

Considerations such as these may, perhaps, have some weight in causing critics to hesitate before accusing Jane Austen, on negative evidence only, of narrow sympathies, or any other deficiency. There is also a further reflection which might have checked any writer in drawing conclusions from such of her letters as have been published, but it is one from which the bulk of her commentators turn away, being apparently reluctant to accept the plain account given by a member of her own family, to whom all the attendant circumstances of the occurrence he relates were perfectly well known. Once more let a most important fact, already referred to in a previous chapter, be stated; this being, not merely that the great mass of Jane's letters were destroyed by Cassandra, but that she kept only those which she considered so totally devoid of general interest that it was impossible anyone should, at any time, contemplate their publication. These she bequeathed to her niece, Lady Knatchbull, whose attachment to her Aunt Jane had, she knew, been so intense that letters however trifling would be loved by her even for the sake of the handwriting alone. Not only, therefore, in quantity, but which is far more important – in quality, these letters are entirely unworthy specimens of her correspondence in general. They are but 'a gleaning of grapes when the vintage is done' – when all that was precious had been safely gathered up, and garnered in Cassandra's faithful memory, and nothing had been left behind excepting that which even she deemed to be altogether negligible. How vain, then, must be any attempt to extract from this unvalued remainder that wine of the spirit with which all the spontaneous and uncensored works of Jane Austen's imaginative soul are richly filled!

The mistake already referred to made by a recent writer, relating rather to her family than herself, must be once more noticed, as it concerns the subject of her education. Being, as it would seem, unaware of the considerable amount of learning possessed by Jane's father, and passed on by him to his children, he pities her for a want of 'culture' in her own home, together with the lack of opportunities by which she might have 'sought for its consolations' in some larger sphere. He asserts without hesitation that her life must have been 'in a measure isolated, from superiority. She gave more than she received. Nor can we believe her entirely unconscious of what life might have yielded her in more equal companionship.' That 'the highest mounted minds' are compelled to fulfil their separate missions in noble solitude, is no doubt true. Eminent pioneers of abstract intellectual effort must necessarily be in advance of other minds – 'Voyaging through strange seas of thought. Alone for ever.'

So is it also in the world of imagination. Every possessor of true creative genius, having received his separate inspiration, must as an artist dwell alone with his work, in which no other human being can claim a share. But this is a totally distinct thing from the isolation here declared to have been experienced by Jane Austen in daily life, because she had an unavoidable sense of mental superiority to all her companions. Nothing can be more opposed to every family record and all inherited knowledge than such a conjecture as this. Far from deeming herself to be the intellectual superior of those around her, she sincerely believed to the end of her days that her sister was much wiser and better informed than herself. Her brother Henry writes: 'She had an invincible distrust of her own judgment.' 'She shrank from notoriety.' 'No accumulation of fame would have induced her had she lived to affix her name to any productions of her pen.'

To imagine Jane Austen appearing as an authoress in any literary circle, 'in search of the consolations of culture' is indeed a strange idea, as unimaginable to later generations of her family as it would have been to her own. To live quietly at home and remain unknown as a writer of fiction, was her great wish, and the secret was carefully kept by all her relations until it was at length revealed by the irrepressible Henry himself. Her thoughts and words on this occurrence are already recorded, and they are like herself. So also are the only regrets she ever expressed regarding shortcomings in education to be found in her home, these being directed entirely against herself, and not at all against other people. She wished she had 'written less and read more before the age of sixteen'. Her father's library must have contained books amply sufficient for the purpose, as, when quitting Steventon, he left five hundred volumes to be sold, in addition to those he may have taken away with him. Jane also had to dispose of her own modest collection of books, which was sold for eleven pounds. In respect to her own characteristic self-criticism, we may remember that book-learning does not form the whole of education, and that the facility for writing clear English, which by a constant use of the pen she acquired very early in life, together with the formation of a humorous style, were to prove in her case invaluable attainments. All the family could write light, amusing trifles in verse, some of which had considerable merit, and Jane's childish absurdities with their solemn dedications to one or other of the party would, no doubt, be well received as the kind of productions naturally to be expected from a droll and merry little sister. When the character of her writings changed with advancing years, and they became secrets not lightly to be revealed to critics downstairs, she was equally fortunate in the possession of one favourite and favoured listener. A genial atmosphere of warm and encouraging sympathy is much needed to foster the developing shoots of romantic authorship, and of this she was secure in the companionship of Cassandra, who, while able to form and maintain opinions of her own, felt the strongest possible admiration and enthusiasm for her sister's works.

One of their nieces, writing in 1856, speaks of having met 'a most ardent and enthusiastic lover of Aunt Jane's novels' and adds: 'Aunt Cassandra herself would be satisfied at her appreciation of them; nothing ever like them, before or since.' This niece's brother, the first Lord Brabourne, who was sixteen when Cassandra Austen died in 1845, has thus written of her: 'From my recollections of "Great Aunt Cassandra", in her latter days, she must have been a very sensible, charming, and agreeable person.' Had she been less than this she could hardly have filled Jane's sisterly heart with such absolute satisfaction, respect, and admiration as we know to have been the case, and if further testimony to the strength and beauty of Cassandras character is needed, it may be found in the letters written by Cassandra herself, immediately after Jane's death, to their niece, Fanny Knight.

No sense of isolation or unfulfilled longings can have troubled Jane's soul when she had Cassandra beside her, and another and an older friend for whom she felt intense love and reverence was also constantly at hand. This was Mrs. Lefroy, of Ashe Rectory, always known in Ashe parish, which bordered on that of Steventon and Deane, as 'Madam Lefroy'. The author of the original 'Memoir' thus describes her:

> She was a remarkable person. Her rare endowments of goodness, talents, graceful person, and engaging manners were sufficient to secure her a prominent place in any society into which she was thrown; while her enthusiastic eagerness of disposition rendered her especially attractive to a clever and lively girl.

The notice and encouragement which Mrs. Lefroy bestowed upon Jane from her childhood shows her to have possessed quick powers of discernment, and great was Jane's grief when this beloved friend died suddenly, in consequence of a fall from her horse, in 1804. With so perfect an example of good breeding always before her eyes, and living continually in the midst of a family whose manners and bearing towards each other always struck the next generation as particularly pleasant and harmonious, with the addition moreover of any information the Comtesse might occasionally impart concerning what Sir William Lucas would have termed 'the manners of the great.' Jane could have no difficulty in learning how to observe and appreciate in the world at large those various shades of good breeding, or of its opposite, which appear again and again in characters scattered throughout her books.

In one of the most sympathetic and correct of the shorter works dealing with Jane Austen that have been published in recent years, the author has inserted all the correspondence that passed between Mrs. Thomas Knight and young Edward Austen who was to succeed her late husband at Godmersham Park. A portion of this appears in 'Life and Letters' Chap. VI, while the whole of it is of so charming a character that every letter would repay perusal. [1]

On these letters Mr. Pollock makes the following remarks:

> Comment has often been made, and most justly made, on the perfect breeding and manners of those people in Miss Austen's novels who are supposed and intended to be well bred. The object in quoting these letters is to show in what a perfect atmosphere of dignity and good feeling Miss Austen passed her life. There is surely something singularly touching in the sincere affection and the delightful courtesy of this correspondence, and it is certainly most characteristic of the race to which Miss Austen belonged.

The writer, as a resident at Chawton, had enjoyed the friendship of the late owner of Chawton House, Montagu George Knight, Squire of Chawton Manor, and no one who was so happy as to know him can ever have doubted that in courtesy, in charm of personality and manner, combined with an unfailing kindness of heart, he might well have served as a model for the highest ideals of his great aunt, Jane Austen.

In returning to the subject of Jane's education, and taking that word in an extended sense, one characteristic of the family life around her ought not to be overlooked, namely, the strong hereditary love of sport to be found among its members. George Austen must have received it from his Kentish ancestors, for he certainly transmitted it to his descendants, even of a third and fourth generation. All his own boys hunted at an early age on anything they could get hold of, and Jane when five or six must often have gazed with admiring, if not envious, eyes at her next oldest brother, Frank, setting off for the hunting field at the ripe age of seven, on his bright chestnut pony Squirrel (bought by himself for a guinea and a half), dressed in the suit of scarlet cloth made for him from a riding habit which had formed part of his mother's wedding outfit. Such early remembrances would be of real advantage to a future novelist, and in the cursory references to sport occurring in her books we feel that she is perfectly at home in all branches of the subject, and could readily enter into the feelings of Sir John Middleton and Charles Musgrove towards the precious fox or the pernicious rat. Nor is it impossible that she was indulging in a secret smile, born of remembrance, when Mrs. Jennings exclaims, 'Tis a sad thing for sportsmen to lose a day's pleasure, poor souls! I always pity them when they do – they seem to take it so much to heart.'

When the foregoing statements as to Jane Austen's home, education, and intercourse with society are considered, they will, it is hoped, put an end to any surprise that she was so well able to paint the lives of the English gentry, as well as to every surmise that she took this class for her subject because she had no knowledge of anything beyond it. So far as varied reading, first-hand evidence, and strong personal interest can teach us, she was probably better acquainted with other interesting phases of life than many young English women of the same period, age, and station. That any surprise at her choice, of this, for her, most natural field of work should be felt, is itself the surprising thing. No one wonders that Miss Edgeworth wrote of Ireland, or Sir Walter Scott of Scotland. Jane Austen was intensely English, by birth and by sympathies. England she loved and of England she wrote; finding her happiness and interest in the lives of those around her. She might, no doubt, have indulged in romantic flights of fancy with India or France for a background, and filled them with fictitious delights such as were to be found in the fairy tales with which she enchanted her little nieces during their happy visits to

Chawton Cottage, but this would have been play work – and her books were to be solid pieces of real work, carefully designed and constructed, polished also with the utmost skill and patience before they could reach the high standard of original invention joined to entire accuracy in minute particulars, which she appears always to have set before herself. In no foreign field of work could she have exhibited that intimate acquaintance with every aspect and detail which her own scrupulous judgment demanded. Vagueness of method, or inaccuracy in particulars, her taste would have condemned as destructive of the true object to be aimed at in fiction. Never having left England herself, she never attempts to convey her characters across the sea, and in one of her letters she warns a young niece who was beginning to compose stories against committing this mistake. Her standard as to the right method by which to captivate the reader's attention and transport him to another world, at once imaginary and real, remains firmly fixed, and the manner in which she attained it affords, as has been well said in another connection, 'an instance of that patient elaboration to which the highest effects in art are due.' Such results can only be obtained where a complete knowledge of the actual goes hand-in-hand with a clear vision of the ideal. Nothing less than first-hand, personal knowledge could satisfy the thoroughness of Jane Austen's nature, or enable her to fulfil, to the utmost of her ability, the imperative requirements of her creative art.

Another highly valuable, and only too rare gift, which she possessed must not be left unmentioned, as it was one in which education bore a share, for 'Nature and Art both joined' to make her a delightful and accomplished reader aloud. Her brother Henry writes:

> Her voice was extremely sweet. She read aloud with very great taste and effect. Her own works were probably never heard to so much advantage as from her own mouth, for she partook largely in all the best gifts of the comic muse.

It may be remembered that when her mother began to read 'Pride and Prejudice' aloud on its first arrival from London, Jane could not repress a secret regret that she read it too fast, and did not always make the characters 'speak as they should do'. But her own aspirations were high, for as regarded the stage itself she owns, 'Acting seldom satisfies me. I think I want something more than can be.'

Her nephew and first biographer often formed part of the family party to whom she would read her novels aloud, and as he also was endowed with a charming voice and excellent taste, the few survivors among the many of those who in former years listened to his reading can still believe that they have, through him, heard the tones and the manner in which

Jane Austen was accustomed to make her characters 'speak as they should do'. Nor did she read from her own writings alone. One of her hearers wrote, as an old man in 1870:

> She was a very sweet reader. I last heard her when she was on a visit to Steventon. She had finished the first canto of 'Marmion' and had begun the second, when a visitor was announced. It was like the interruption of some pleasing dream, the illusions of which suddenly vanished.

Nothing has hitherto been said concerning the most important part of the education Jane Austen received in her home – her moral and religious training. It will be found that this is dealt with in the course of the following chapter.

1.'Jane Austen: Her Contemporaries and Herself' Walter Herries Pollock.

Chapter V – Morality

'Was Jane Austen a Moralist? 'No!' many of her fervent admirers will exclaim – 'Thank Heaven that she was *not*!' Her mission was to amuse, to delight, to refresh us – but neither to reprove nor to condemn us! Those who want 'Moral Tales' must seek them elsewhere; they are not to be found among Jane Austen's writings! They are not, indeed, if to be moral is to be dull, and if no one can instruct without growing tedious. Far, far away from such odious reproaches must those pages for ever shine to which we turn again and again, as beguilers of trouble and companions in mirth, equally welcome in society or solitude, in sickness or health, in early life or in advancing years. They even seem to grow with our growth and strengthen with our strength, for old though we may be, and wise as we may think ourselves, we never outgrow their freshness or their wisdom. Such is the creed of Jane Austen's earnest adherents. Nor is this all. In addition to the unflagging interest taken in her books by successive generations of readers, a separate interest has grown up in the hearts of many. For them to know her books – in some cases almost by heart – is much, but it is not enough. They desire to know herself also, they seek after a more intimate acquaintance with their unseen lifelong friend, Jane Austen, who, more than one hundred years ago, was laid to rest, early on a summer morning, within the walls of Winchester Cathedral.

The existence of such a feeling came to light as soon as the original 'Memoir of Jane Austen' already mentioned, was published in 1869 by her nephew, the Rev. J. E. Austen-Leigh. When this book appeared, a singular change took place. It not only brought into being a large number of articles, notices, and reviews concerning its subject and her works, but it also brought to himself a variety of interesting letters from unknown correspondents, both English and American, describing the effect that its perusal had produced upon the writers' minds. These letters afforded him much pleasure and not a little surprise. Until that period he had not realised to how large a number of readers, and in what a high degree, the Aunt to whom he as a boy and young man had been so warmly attached, had also become a living, though an unseen, friend.

An extract from one of the letters may be given to serve as a specimen of many others:

> Your Memoir has but one drawback – it leaves us with a sad craving for more ... much as we loved and honoured her before, we love and honour her the more for what you have told us of her, and in the name of my Grandfather, Father, Uncles and Aunts, Cousins and Children, I thank you for your book.

Words such as these showed that it was not only as an author but as a woman that Jane Austen had made her way into the affections of many readers. Entreaties also arrived that any stories, or fragments of stories, left by her in manuscript might be published, one correspondent urging that 'Every line from the pen of Jane Austen is precious'. In response to these warmhearted applications, the writer of the 'Memoir' could do little beyond attending to the last-mentioned request. Having obtained the necessary permission from those members of his family to whom the original manuscripts had been bequeathed by Jane's sister, Cassandra, he included in the second edition of his 'Memoir' 'Lady Susan', 'The Watsons', the alternative ending of 'Persuasion' and some of her childish writings. The reasons why it was impossible for him at the time to do more than this have been already stated – and mention has been made of books subsequently put forth by other members of Jane Austen's family, containing fresh information regarding the external aspects of her history which may in some degree have fulfilled the wishes of the eagerly enquiring readers of the original 'Memoir.'

But though gratified, they may not be wholly satisfied. They may still desire a more intimate acquaintance with her inner self, with those hidden recesses of feeling concerning which a delicate reserve impelled her to keep a very sacred silence. They long for a sight of the vanished not from idle curiosity, but that, in the words already recorded, 'Much as they loved and honoured her before, they might learn to love and honour her still more.' A natural but a vain wish! The letters perished long ago – sacrificed by Cassandra as an offering of love and reverence to the memory of a sister unspeakably dear to herself.

Yet though in this way we can learn nothing, there is another path, hitherto, we believe, untrodden, by the help of which we may attain a point of view affording us some fresh knowledge respecting those inner convictions Jane Austen was always slow in revealing to the public gaze, and which will at the same time offer a reason for the question at the beginning of this chapter. To accomplish such an object we must turn to her books and reverse our usual attitude of mind towards them by considering each story, not as a separate creation, but as part of a general whole. From an artistic standpoint there is nothing that can tempt us to act in this manner. Every novel is complete in itself, possessing its own plot, characters, and distinctive atmosphere in a remarkable degree. We find scarcely any repetition of ideas among the six, and this may induce the belief that while comparison is easy, combination is impossible, as they possess no similarity among themselves apart from the creative, dramatic, humorous qualities common to all. This is our first, and not unnatural, conclusion. Nevertheless it will be seen on reflection that there is one feature which declares their family likeness. There is one line of thought, one grace, or quality, or necessity, whichever title we like to know it by, apparent in all her works. Its name is – Repentance.

It will be found on examination that this incident recurs in all her novels, neither being dragged in as a moral nor dwelt upon as a duty, but quietly taking its place as a natural and indispensable part of the plot – as an inevitable incident in the formation and development of each successive child of her imagination. Every one, gayer or graver as the case may be, has its own testimony to give on this question, while all display the skill with which the author knew how to handle the subject according to the varying needs of place, character, and surroundings. We shall find that it could not be dispensed with, even in her very early and most lighthearted story, 'Northanger Abbey'. Here the young heroine, under the excitement of wild and captivating romances, allows herself to believe that the man in whose house she is a guest had, not long before, desired, perhaps connived at, the death of his own excellent and charming wife, or, at the very least, is keeping her immured in some dungeon on the premises. Such delusions could not be suffered to go unpunished. Nor were they, but having arisen from nothing worse than wonderful folly, the penalty inflicted is mercifully abridged. Still, the offender has to undergo a period of sharp anguish, brought upon her by a not unreasonable remonstrance on the part of the hero, a son of the supposed villain. Its effect was immediate. 'Catherine,' we read, 'was completely awakened. Most grievously was she humbled. Most bitterly did she cry. She hated herself more than she could express.' But Jane Austen, we are very sure, would never break a butterfly upon the wheel, consequently we learn with no surprise that, after forming a resolution of 'always judging and acting in the future with the greatest good sense' and being assisted by Henry Tilney's 'astonishing generosity and nobleness of character in never alluding to what had passed' Catherine is ready to be consoled by 'the lenient hand of time' which 'did much for her by insensible gradations in the course of another day' and that she has nothing to do but to 'forgive herself and be happier than ever'. Nevertheless, so effectually has the work of penitence been performed that when General Tilney, not long afterwards, turns her out of his house at a few hours' notice, she magnanimously abstains from reverting to her previous suspicions that he has at an earlier period either poisoned or shut up his wife.

Passing from these playful pages to those of her latest and most pathetic work, 'Persuasion', we find the same chord struck, but in a minor key and with a softer tone. Nothing glaringly wrong could become a character of whom her own creator wrote beforehand to a niece, 'You may perhaps like the heroine, as she is almost too good for me.' Anne Elliot's error was want of judgment, of too meek a submission to the direction of an older friend, an error that 'leaned to virtue's side' and which was embraced by her unselfish spirit the more readily because, though destructive of her own happiness, she was persuaded to believe that it would promote the future good of a man whom she devotedly loved. Want of mental balance and some youthful weakness of character are the worst charges that can be brought against this almost perfect being, yet for these she has to suffer long and to learn, through suffering, the nature of the mistake she had made. Repentance, in the form of deep regret, overtook her as years passed on. 'She felt' we are told, that were any young person in similar circumstances to apply to her for counsel they would never receive any of such certain immediate wretchedness – such uncertain future good.

Captain Wentworth had on his side a worse fault to repent of. 'I was proud' he cried, 'too proud to understand or to do you justice – too proud to ask you again. This is a recollection which ought to make me forgive everyone sooner than myself.' Readers can only agree with both speakers and rejoice in the sequel that closes these confessions.

Much graver instances of misconduct and its subsequent results will be found in the four remaining novels. Even in the story written when Jane Austen was quite a young girl, called first 'Elinor and Marianne' and afterwards 'Sense and Sensibility', the plot is made to hinge upon the evils inflicted by the heroine upon herself and her family through too violent indulgence in a romantic passion. This renders her indifferent to the needs and the claims of other people, and blind to the sorrow of her sister, who is also suffering in silence from an unfortunate attachment. It is not until Marianne is herself in the depths of disappointed affection that her eyes are opened to the truths around her. Then 'Oh Elinor' she cries, 'you have made me hate myself for ever. How barbarous have I been to you! you, who have been my only comfort, who have borne with me in all my misery, who have seemed to be only suffering for me!' Such is her first burst of penitence, to be strengthened by time and a severe illness, after which she speaks once more: 'I considered the past. I saw in my own behaviour nothing but a series of imprudence towards myself and want of kindness to others. I saw that my own feelings had prepared my sufferings, and that my want of fortitude under them had almost led me to the grave. Had I died, it would have been self- destruction.' The enthusiasm of her self- reproving spirit flows on – to be checked only by resolutions of future amendment, for though as yet unable to believe that her remembrance of Willoughby will ever be weakened by time, she can still add, 'But it shall be regulated, it shall be checked by religion, by reason, by constant employment' – a resolution sincerely made and faithfully kept.

Repentance in a double form comes before us in the next novel. Nowhere in any of her other writings does it play so conspicuous a part as in 'Pride and Prejudice.' The whole scheme of the book depends upon its being felt, in a very high degree, by the two principal characters, upon its influencing their actions during the last half of the book and leading steadily up to its closing scenes. The late Professor W. Courthope has left a striking analysis of the manner in which this feeling affected the hero of the book and the consequent changes it wrought within him [1]. For this, as for the whole work, he expresses the warmest possible admiration, comparing it, on account of the manner in which 'under a commonplace surface a great artist has revealed a most dramatic conflict of universal human emotions', to the structure of some grand Greek play. By no other writer can Jane Austen's genius have been dwelt upon with more eloquence or more sympathetic recognition; but even this appreciation is incomplete, for it contains no reference to the corresponding work of repentance effected in the heroine by the words and actions of the hero. Yet had this been lacking, the perfectly proportioned plot, to which he accords unqualified praise, could never have been constructed and developed. Elizabeth's self-reproach, so soon as she recognises the truth, is not less severe than Darcy's. 'She grew absolutely ashamed of herself – of neither Darcy nor Wickham could she think without feeling that she had been blind, partial, prejudiced, absurd.' 'How despicably have I acted,' she cried, 'I who have valued myself on my abilities ... how humiliating is this discovery! Yet how just a humiliation! I have courted prepossession and ignorance and have driven reason away, where either were concerned. Till this moment I never knew myself.' Again, in a confession to her sister she admits 'I was very uncomfortable, I may say, unhappy, and with no one to speak to of what I felt, no Jane to comfort me and say I had not been so very weak and vain and nonsensical as I knew I had! Oh! how I wanted you!' Time, by disclosing more of Darcy's real character, could only deepen such regrets and make her grieve over 'every ungracious sensation she had ever encouraged, every saucy speech she had ever directed towards him. For herself she was humbled, but she was proud of him. Proud that in a cause of compassion and honour he had been able to get the better of himself. Darcy's self-condemnation was equally strong. 'My behaviour towards you' he assures her, merited the severest reproof. It was unpardonable. I cannot think of it without abhorrence. The recollection of what I said, of my conduct, my manners, my expressions, is now, and has been for many months, inexpressibly painful to me. I have been a selfish being all my life ... what do I not owe you! You taught me a lesson hard indeed at first, but most advantageous. By you I was properly humbled.

Such reciprocal repentance and confession could not fail to bring reciprocal forgiveness, and the title of the book ceases to be appropriate before the last page is turned.

Reciprocity in error and penitence were not destined to console the remaining heroine, who falls, entirely through her own fault, into deep distress. Emma Woodhouse, having erred alone, has to endure her burden of remorse in solitude. Every reader will admit that Emma went through vanity further astray than Elizabeth Bennet through prejudice, a verdict foreseen by the author, who, while declaring that how she would be able to 'tolerate those who do not like Elizabeth she does not know,' frankly admits that in Emma she is going to take a heroine 'whom no one will like but herself.' She did take her, however, to endow her with that 'nature and spirit' which were dear to her own heart, and drawing a being, full of faults, and yet, as Emma's lover believes at the end, 'faultless in spite of them.' But justice could not allow this conclusion to be reached until great vicissitudes of feeling had been endured. Emma's faults had inflicted much pain and distress upon other persons, consequently, at the proper moment, they had to bring corresponding wretchedness upon herself. 'Her feelings' we are told, after Mr. Knightley's expostulation on Box Hill, were combined of anger against herself, mortification, and deep concern. The truth of his representation there was no denying. She felt it at her heart. How could she have been so brutal, so cruel to Miss Bates!

Far heavier retribution, however, is still awaiting her when she, with horror, finds herself obliged to listen to Harriet Smith's outpourings of hopes and expectations respecting Mr. Knightley. Then she saw her own conduct with a clearness which had never blessed her before. What blindness, what madness, had led her on! It struck her with dreadful force, and she was ready to give it every bad name in the world.

With insufferable vanity had she believed herself to be in the secret of everybody's feelings; with unpardonable arrogance proposed to arrange everybody's destiny. She was proved to have been universally mistaken; and she had not quite done nothing for she had done mischief.
'What' in conclusion, could be increasing Emma's wretchedness but the reflection, never far distant from her mind, that it had been all her own work? The only source whence anything like consolation or composure could be drawn was in the resolution of her own better conduct and in the hope that every future winter of her life would find her more rational, more acquainted with herself, and leave her less to regret when it were gone.

Satisfied with such genuine repentance, the author can now permit herself to make this favourite heroine once more happy.

Can we avoid perceiving that these five pictures of life resemble each other in so far that every one of them gives a description, closely interwoven with the structure of the story and concerned with its principal characters, of error committed, conviction following, and improvement effected, all of which may be summed up in the word 'Repentance'? If so, do we not also through this perception gain more knowledge as to the habitual bent of that mind in which these successive creations arose? Does not Jane Austen's outlook upon life grow clearer to us when we learn that it was not merely by the 'follies and nonsense, whims and inconsistencies' (as she makes Elizabeth Bennet call them) ever visible on the surface of society, that her quick eyes were caught, but that her penetrating gaze went down to the hidden springs of action, prompting her to reflect upon the race that all human beings have to run in this world, upon the various courses they pursue, and upon the necessity of powerful influences being exercised over them, in order to bring about that improvement of character which is the final purpose of it all? Can we fail to see how, in dealing with these heroines, she desired to leave them, not only happier, but better, than she found them; wiser, stronger, humbler, and more charitable, richer in self-control, and in that self-knowledge on which she always places a high value? If we have seen all this, we have seen also something of her hidden self.

There is still another book, standing in some respects apart from the rest, through which we acquire even more information on this subject. 'Mansfield Park' is the gravest novel Jane Austen ever wrote. It was composed after a long interval of silence, and may be called a 'Second First'. It was the result of a wider experience of mankind, together with that of various personal trials which she had to undergo during eight years passed in large towns after quitting Steventon in 1801. She herself when writing this book declared 'it was not half so entertaining as "Pride and Prejudice",' an opinion with which her readers may or may not agree. In its pages humour, insight into character, creative genius, and power of description shine as brightly as ever, but in addition, to these we are aware of a deeper seriousness and a more searching enquiry into the ultimate issues of conduct than had as yet appeared in her works. The author of the original 'Memoir' was informed that a number of well-known literary men who happened to meet at a country house agreed to write down the title of their favourite novel. The only name which appeared more than once was 'Mansfield Park' and this had been chosen by three or four of the company, while all united in admiring the book. Such a power of attracting powerful minds may be due to the union of brilliant writing with serious reflection which its pages contain, and it is interesting to recall the circumstances under which this novel, the first important original work taken in hand by her for ten years, was written.

The lapse of ten years, beginning in early womanhood, can hardly pass over any head without producing sensible differences. To Jane Austen they had brought many changes, as enumerated in 'Life and Letters'. Sorrow had touched her closely. She had lost through sudden death, and almost simultaneously, her father and her much-loved friend, Mrs. Lefroy of Ashe. The same cause had brought to an end her own personal romance, inflicting a wound which was, as we know, not the less but the more likely to have been deeply felt, on account of the silence preserved by Cassandra on this subject for many years after her sister's death, and the guarded manner in which she at length alluded to it. Other trials and troubles had come upon the Austen family in recent years, one being of a most unusual nature, threatening to overwhelm some of them in irretrievable disaster, and to bring lasting distress upon their whole circle. [The false accusation and trial of Mrs Leigh Perrot]. That such practical acquaintance with some of life's heaviest afflictions should for a time stop all flow of fancy on Jane Austen's part is not surprising, nor that the only new work she began during this period should have been broken off at the end of the twelfth chapter, apparently because the author ceased to feel any interest in its contents.

One more loss, this time neither sudden nor unusual, must be added to those already mentioned. She had lost her youth. At the age of twenty-five, while still a young woman, she had left her native place, her earliest friends, and every well-loved scene associated with the first overflowings of her happy girlish fancies. It was the birthplace, not of herself alone, but of many creations, born to a far longer existence than hers was destined to be upon earth – all those characters that live and move for us throughout the pages of her first three novels. Eight years were to pass before a return to Hampshire would take place, and her own words have described how much such a period can include. 'Eight years

... what might not eight years do? Events of every description, changes, alienations, removals, all, all must be comprised in it.'

The varied events which this passage of time had held for herself can hardly have been absent from her thoughts when she placed such a reflection in the mind of Anne Elliot, rejoicing no doubt that it was in her power to restore to that heroine a happiness which her own heart might never now know. It is certain that on beginning a country life at Chawton she and Cassandra were satisfied to assume to themselves, too readily as some of their relations considered, the position of middle-aged women. It is impossible, however, not to rejoice at any decision that ensured to her a larger amount of quiet leisure for composition, and now it was, after the revision of two earlier works had renewed the habit of writing, that 'Mansfield Park' was begun in February, 1811, to be finished in June, 1813.

Here we find the theme, never absent from her works, displayed again, and in an acuter form, for in this book we meet with the chief and saddest example of repentance that her pen ever drew – the saddest because, in a sense, the most unavailing. There can be no comparison between any of the cases already mentioned and that of an unhappy father whose 'anguish arising from the conviction of his own errors in the education of his daughters was never to be entirely done away'. Such are Sir Thomas Bertram's feelings as he contemplates a domestic tragedy for which he believes these errors to have been the primary cause. It is not with folly and thoughtlessness that 'Mansfield Park' deals, but with vice and sin, with misery and degradation; subjects the writer herself describes as 'odious,' which she touches as distantly and dismisses as rapidly as possible. That she forced herself to write of them at all tends to show that some of the phases of the fashionable life she had been observing around her had impressed themselves so deeply on her soul that her spirit could not rest until she had entered a protest, through the medium of her own dramatic art, against these forms of evil. A record remains which shows that in her opinion this was the only proper method for a writer of fiction to employ. Soon after the publication of the original 'Memoir' its writer received a letter from a well-known clergyman, who stated that he had been intimately acquainted with a lady who had known Jane Austen well, and from whom he had heard much about her. He spoke of 'the tribute of my old friend to the real and true spring of a religion which was always present though never obtruded.' 'Miss Austen' she used to say, 'had on all the subjects of enduring religious feeling the deepest and strongest convictions, but a contact with loud and noisy exponents of the then popular religious phase made her reticent almost to a fault.' She had something to suffer in the way of reproach from those who believed she might have used her genius to greater effect, 'but' (her old friend used to say)

> I think I see her now, defending what she thought was the real province of a delineator of life and manners and declaring her belief that example, and not 'direct preaching', was all that a novelist could afford properly to exhibit. [1]

Means such as these when employed by herself are so powerful and speak so plainly that it is difficult to see how to any author the title of 'Moralist' can be more justly given. Those who object to it in her case, as necessarily implying a double point of view in a writer's mind, destructive of that simplicity of aim which ought to be the inspiring motive of any true work of art, should consider whether there is in 'Mansfield Park' any evidence that the design of the artist has been cramped by the mind of the moralist. There are, again, others who would disapprove of the terms 'Morality', 'Moral Precepts' as falling short of the highest ideals, and implying something that may be only cold and formal, based upon a theory that correct conduct should be maintained because it is in the long run the most likely method of obtaining success and comfort in this world. If so, then 'Mansfield Park' may again be quoted to refute, in its author's opinion, any such theory, for it contains a strong protest against worldliness and the ideals that worldliness upholds, whether in education, marriage, or general society. In this book she plainly declares her belief that moral conduct must spring from a deeper source and cherish a higher aim than this.

She had seen, and would describe, how little dependence can be placed upon well-bred decorum and outward propriety unless they are inspired by religious principles. The veil of habitual reticence employed by her on these subjects is here drawn further back, and the language used is more explicit than in any of her other books. Sir Thomas Bertram's self-reproach is addressed to this very point. He came to feel, we are told, that 'Something must have been wanting within.' He feared that principle, active principle had been wanting; that his daughters had never been taught to govern their inclinations and tempers properly by that sense of duty which alone can suffice. They had been instructed theoretically in their religion, but never required to bring it into daily practice. To be distinguished for elegance and accomplishments, the authorised object of their youth, could have had no useful influence that way, no moral effect on 'the mind of the necessity of self-denial and humility he feared they had never heard from any lips that could profit them.' Again, the term 'Sin' is given to express flagrant evil. Edmund employs it in his last interview with Mary Crawford, and of her brother we are told that 'though too little accustomed to serious reflection to know good principles by their proper name, yet in his highest praises of Fanny he expressed what was inspired by the knowledge of her being well principled and religious.'

We learn here more of Jane Austen's deep feelings on moral questions than she has expressed elsewhere, but every allusion to them in her other works is in complete harmony with the teachings set forth in the latter chapters of 'Mansfield Park'. When, therefore, we find in the sister volumes the not infrequent words 'principles' and 'duty' we should remember how much they imply, and that we have, as already stated, evidence proving her general reticence on these important points to be intentional and not accidental. 'Still waters run deep' and the uniform though restrained teaching in these books assures us of the steadfastness of conviction respecting the highest subjects on the part of her to whom we owe their existence.

The virtues she loves to cultivate in her characters she would certainly seek after for herself; the 'self-knowledge' she prizes so highly as a means of improvement she would personally desire for the same reason, nor was there in her that want of humility which prevents some souls from ever acquiring it. All her life she looked up to Cassandra as her superior in wisdom and goodness, and to its very close she esteemed others as better than herself, for on her deathbed she wrote to a nephew,

> God bless you, my dear Edward. If ever you are ill, may you be as tenderly nursed as I have been. May the same blessed alleviations of anxious sympathising friends be yours; and may you possess, as I daresay you will, the greatest blessing of all in the consciousness of not being unworthy of their love. I could not feel this.

That she had reflected silently on solemn questions some expressions in her letters show us, and one of her elder nieces has written: 'When Aunt Jane was grave she was very grave, graver I think even than Aunt Cassandra.' Such thoughts on her part, and such an attitude of mind will not appear improbable when we recall her ancestry and education. Her father on one side, her grandfather on the other, had been excellent and active parish priests. By precept and by example she had received both from her stricter mother and her gentler father the firm religious principles which governed her throughout life. Mrs. George Austen writes, on returning from a visit to London, that in it 'everyone seems in a hurry' adding 'Tis a sad place, I would not live in it on any account, one has not time to do one's duty either to God or Man' – a verdict that may provoke a smile, but which serves to show the speaker's conviction as regards the great object of human life. George Austen's instructions to his sons express, as might be expected, the same belief. In a long letter of advice, written to the elder of his two sailor sons, Francis, when the latter first went to sea, 'attention to religious duties' is given the primary place, and never were they forgotten by him or by his brothers to the close of their long and honourable careers. Round these twin poles, therefore, 'Duty to God and duty to Man' had Jane Austen been taught that life should revolve, and this it is that she always presupposes would be accepted in a like manner by the heroes and heroines in all her books. Not that she considers them to be 'already perfect'. 'Pictures of perfection,' she owns, 'make me sick and wicked.' No wonder! She knew human nature too well for it to be possible that she should accept them as faithful portraits, but this is what she wishes to make her own favourite creations aspire towards throughout the course of their several histories.

To some, perhaps to many, it may appear hardly necessary to insist upon all this. 'We have long known,' they would say, 'the moral tendency of her books, and have believed in the firmly religious convictions of the mind that produced them. Why, then, spend so much time on gilding gold or painting the lily white? 'Two reasons may be given in answer to this question, the first and obvious one being that what is evident to certain minds is not therefore so to all, and that among the latter class there may be those who sincerely desire a closer intimacy with Jane Austen's inner self, and who may, by taking the novels as a whole, find that they can come nearer to comprehending something fresh and fundamental respecting the nature and soul of their author. But there is a second reason, and not a slight one. Jane Austen has now more than one public. Her novels are read, appreciated, and reviewed in other countries besides our own.

In France they have recently been again brought forward in a work of great ability, by a writer who describes her as 'une romanciere que l'Angleterre compte parmi ses plus parfaits artistes de lettres et que l'originalite aussi bien que le merite de son ceuvre font qualifier d'incomparable.' [One of England's most perfect authors whose work's originality and value make her incomparable]. Mlle. Villard gave further proof of her admiration for Jane Austen's novels by choosing them as the subject of her thesis when standing for the Doctorial degree lately bestowed upon her by the Sorbonne. Her knowledge and enthusiasm could hardly be surpassed, while the insight and talent with which her long and important book is filled can scarcely be overpraised. But though the merit of the book is great, this makes it only the more regrettable that the view taken by its writer of Jane Austen's character is so mistaken as to be in some respects exactly the reverse of the truth. This is especially the case when dealing with its religious aspect. Mlle. Villard first asserts that the Church of England was in the eighteenth century destitute of all religious fervour, which, in her own words, 'a disparu pour faire place a l'indifference', [has disappeared to make way for indifference] and then passes from the general to the particular by assuming that the same must therefore be true of Jane Austen's writings, and that, for the characters she depicts, religion is merely 'une fait de meme ordre que celui d'observer les regles de la bienseance mondaine' [a fact of the same realm as respecting proper decorum when in someone else's company]. In proof of this statement a remark of Archbishop Seeker, divorced from its context, is given, no reference being made to any evidence leaning the other way furnished by English divines, or, above all, by those who employed the natural voice of strong emotion, poetry – though of these there were a considerable number, including such as belonged to the school of religious mystics. Of one of these latter – Norris – Sir F. Palgrave writes that in 1730 his poems had passed through ten editions, 'one proof out of many,' he adds, 'how exaggerated is that criticism which describes that period as devoid of inner life and spiritual aspiration.' It is thus spoken of in ' La Vie,' where it is called cold, formal, concerned with externals only, and destitute of any 'elan vers un au-dela' [momentum towards an after life].

Having passed this judgment upon the Church to which Jane Austen belonged, similar conclusions are come to regarding herself. Sermons, it is said, were wearisome to her; but a love of sermons, as St. Louis told our Henry III long ago, is not an indispensable element in the religious life. Moreover, Jane Austen herself says: 'I am very fond of Sherlock's Sermons, and prefer them to almost any.'

It is also asserted that she took no interest in anything outside 'a series of traditional rites', as the services of her Church are called, and that she as a writer 'eloigne de son observation la souffrance, la tristesse et la laideur', [distances herself from suffering, sadness and ugliness] proving that, as a woman, she cared nothing for the sorrows and wants of the poor. Other entire misapprehensions of her nature are also evident, but being concerned with points of comparatively minor importance these need not be entered upon here. The sum total, however, represents a narrow nature, with a heart cold towards God and unsympathetic towards man, somewhat contemptuous of the needy and ignorant and caring little for any fellow creatures beyond those of her immediate family circle. Easy indeed is it to prove the contrary, both from her own letters and from the writings of her relations, and to show how completely such a conclusion misrepresents her attitude of mind towards the highest questions. But all serious students of her biography may be left to discover this for themselves. They can weigh the assertions made in 'La Vie' against the testimony given by those who knew her intimately as to her faith, unselfishness, humility, and the 'piety which ruled her in life and supported her in death'. Above all, they will examine the records of that closing scene, when face to face with a comparatively early death, 'neither her love of God nor her fellow creatures flagged for a moment,' and will consider whether such faith, courage, and entire submission to the Divine will could have been felt by one to whom religion was 'merely a matter of externals'.

Mlle. Villard's book is, as a literary criticism, so exhaustive and valuable that it will probably be accepted in France as a standard work on Jane Austen and her novels. It may have already served to increase the number of readers in that country, and this number is likely to become larger, for at the present time, when a strong desire is felt that the bonds between our nearest Ally and ourselves should be drawn closer, those formed by a mutual study of each other's literature can hardly be neglected. As it must be desirable that correct ideas of the writer of any English classic should be offered to the French nation, those who are the most nearly concerned in seeing that justice is done to the personal character of Jane Austen, and who are best able to speak of it from authentic and unimpeachable testimony, could hardly be excused if they failed to offer a protest against the estimate regarding it put forth in 'La Vie' as being utterly unworthy of her and entirely misleading in respect of a vital part of her nature. It is well to recall that this was comprehended and rightly described by a juster and more discriminating judge nearly one hundred years ago, when Archbishop Whately, in the Quarterly Review [January 1821] thus summed up his estimate of herself and her works;

> Miss Austen introduces very little of what is technically called religion into her books, yet that must be a blinded soul which does not recognise the vital essence, everywhere present in her pages, of a deep and enlightened piety.

Note. – The present writer is happy to state that she has received an assurance from Mlle. Villard that the misapprehensions relating to Jane Austen's character objected to in this chapter shall be revised and amended in any future edition of 'La Vie'.

1. This lady used to add, 'Anne Elliott was herself, her enthusiasm for the navy and her perfect unselfishness reflect her completely.'

Chapter VI – 'Lady Susan'

When 'Lady Susan' first appeared in print, this title being prefixed to the second edition of Mr. Austen Leigh's original 'Memoir', it was remarked by more than one critic that so short a story should hardly have been allowed to give a name to a whole volume. With this observation the editor entirely agreed. He knew it had been arranged that the tale itself should be placed after the 'Memoir', together with other unpublished writings of the author, and, therefore, when the second edition of his work appeared, bearing the title of 'Lady Susan', he felt both surprise and regret. He foresaw the disappointment of its readers when they should discover the nature and brevity of the story, and still more did he feel that to put forward, as though on a par with her other works, a character sketch which she never intended to give to the world, would not appear on his own part to be showing due respect to the memory and judgment of his aunt. So scrupulous was he on this point that even in writing the short notice prepared for it, when he had no expectation that the title would be affixed to the whole volume, he said, 'If it should be judged unworthy of the publicity now given to it, the censure must fall on him who has put it forth and not on her who kept it locked up in her desk.'

The exact date of its composition is uncertain, but there are several reasons for preferring an early one. It was written in letters, the form used in some of the novels known to Jane Austen almost from childhood and employed by her when she was very young in (a) an unpublished fragment, (b) the first version of 'Sense and Sensibility', called 'Elinor and Marianne', and again (c) in 'Lady Susan' which seems to place the latter in the category of early compositions. This, it is true, would not be a sufficient proof if taken alone. The author may have thought that the most forcible way of dealing with Lady Susan would be by leaving her to speak for herself, and might therefore have chosen to narrate the history in the form of letters. Critics have observed, not unnaturally, that this remarkable analysis of a vicious woman's nature seems a strange subject for a young girl either to have attempted or to have succeeded in, and such a conviction has made it the more difficult for them to imagine what date should be assigned to the work. There is, we believe, but one solution to this puzzle, one that was discerned by a correspondent of the present writer, whose position had enabled him to observe human nature closely, and who, though knowing Jane Austen's six novels well, had recently read 'Lady Susan' for the first time. He says in his letter concerning the book, 'I find it very clever. It is, of course, more bitter and worldly than her other works, but it shows a tremendous insight into shams. I feel quite sure the character is drawn from life.' How far the last remark is justified by facts may be decided after the reader has perused the following true history taken from a family MS.

> About two hundred years ago, Mr. and Mrs. —, well-connected people, were living on their property in the Midlands, with a family of one son and five daughters. The daughters had but a rough life. Their mother, a beautiful woman and most courteous and fascinating in society, was

of a stern, tyrannical temper. They were brought up in fear, not in love. They were sometimes not allowed proper food, but were required to eat what was loathsome to them, and were often relieved from hunger by the maids privately bringing them up bread and cheese after they were in bed. Perhaps some of the traditions of their mother's personal cruelty to her children as endangering their lives went beyond the truth, but there could be no doubt that she was a very unkind and severe mother. When making long visits from home it was her custom to take one daughter with her to act, it was said, as her maid. On one occasion, all her daughters being then young women, and one of them being married, she did so – taking one daughter with her, and leaving three at home. Her absence lasted for several months. Their father, so far as is known, was likewise absent. Two of the three daughters took this opportunity of marrying, but not in their own condition of life. One married the son of a neighbouring yeoman, and the other, a friend of her new brother-in-law, a horse-dealer. The first marriage turned out not so very bad, but the second was deplorable. The remaining sister, knowing how much her mother would resent these mis-alliances, and foreseeing nothing but increased severity in the house, could not resolve to face her anger. She also left her home before Mrs. — could get back to it. All the sisters had £500 a-piece, left to them by an uncle and on the interest of this little sum she resolved to try and live. The further history of the last daughter was brighter. Friends and relations assisted her, and she finally made a suitable marriage in her own rank in life.

Mrs. —, when afterwards left a widow, married a gentleman of good property, with whom she had long been well acquainted. The descendants of the last-named daughter always spoke of her as 'the cruel Mrs. —.'

Among these, Jane, as a young girl, had intimate friends [the Lloyd sisters], and the whole tale would naturally become known to her. That it was so is also shown by a passage in one of her letters, perfectly comprehensible to those who are acquainted with the names and details belonging to the foregoing history.

This being certain, and it being also certain that she wrote 'Lady Susan' there is no room for doubt that the two facts are closely related to each other, and that she could not have depicted an inhuman, repulsive mother, carrying on her barbarities beneath a mask of charm and beauty, without having constantly before her thoughts the prototype of this exceptional character, of whose actual existence she was well aware. Why this knowledge caused her to write such a sketch not for publication may claim a moment's thought. To strongly imaginative and sensitive souls, 'wax to receive, and marble to retain', revelations of beauty and glory, or of darkness and horror, come with a force beyond that which others can know, leaving an impression, amounting to a possession of the soul, not to be flung off until relief has been found through some outward and concrete act. When Byron died, and all the Tennyson family mourned him, it was Alfred who, as a boy, rushed out and endeavoured to express his sense of England's unspeakable loss by carving on a rock of sandstone, 'Byron is dead'. He may have felt that in this way he and nature could mourn together, and that he had at least done something to record the despair of his heart in the face of this great calamity. A similar intensity of feeling, though this time of horrified indignation, may have seized upon Jane Austen's soul when the story of an unnatural and brutal mother was made known to her, overpowering her fancy to so great a degree that she was at last impelled to seek relief in gibbeting this repulsive being by setting down her character in writing, thus to express the depth of her disgust through the medium of her own peculiar Art.

So far as we know, it is the only 'Study from Life' that she ever made, nor was it now accomplished in order that it might appear again in any of her longer works. She once said that 'it was her desire to create, not to reproduce', and there is nothing in the novels which calls 'Lady Susan' to mind, unless some hint of her unblushing worldliness can be found in Mary Crawford's letter to Fanny or of her maternal harshness in Mrs. Ferrars' behaviour to her eldest son. We are, therefore, compelled to believe that the horror which oppressed her imagination, when reflecting on this picture of outward beauty and secret barbarity, could not be relieved without giving expression to her sense of its enormity by placing it upon paper. Had she never heard the tale, her youth might have saved her from conceiving the possibility of so evil a being, but having heard it, that same youth would intensify the repulsion and disgust it must create within her. That the sketch was not meant to meet the public eye is clear, partly because, in 1803, she attempted to publish a novel in two volumes, then called 'Susan', later 'Catherine', and finally 'Northanger Abbey' and she would not have wished to give the same name to two published works, and yet more so because the strong resemblance between the character of 'Lady Susan' and that of her friends' ancestress would render such a thought impossible to her scrupulous sense of honour. The structure of the story itself confirms this view. Incident and plot are neglected throughout its course, in which there is little attempt to elaborate any character in such a way as to arouse the interest of the reader. The book is a figurepiece, with a cruel, heartless woman for its single subject. In comparison with this central object, the rest of the dramatis personae are but shadowy beings. Of one of these the author writes at the close that 'it must already have been evident that Mr. Vernon existed only to do whatever might be required of him,' and the same remark may be applied with a slight expansion in its meaning to the whole of the company, who exist merely to bring out the various vices united in one woman, a creature entirely devoid of conscience, and without a single redeeming quality.

That such unnatural mothers can be found is unhappily certain, a fact proved by the existence of a modern society for 'Prevention of Cruelty to Children' – generally from the cruelty of their own parents – but that they are on the whole rare is also happily true, and so great a monster is not to be met with anywhere in the six published novels. In this the author shows her usual wisdom. An artist, speaking of landscape painting, has observed that 'Nature employs only small spots of deep dark' and the same may be said of that field of Nature in which Jane Austen painted – human nature. She did not commit the mistake of taking exceptions for rules, nor of thinking the world must be villainous as a whole because some villains can be found in it. She avoids the use of 'deep darks' and employs but seldom the lighter shades of evil, coarseness, and vulgarity, being, as it would seem, unwilling to blacken her canvas more than might be found necessary in order to provide some contrast to the brighter and purer tints of her picture. That she had either kind at command, should she choose to make use of them, is proved by the introduction, in their proper places, of Mr. Price and Nancy Steele, and, above all, by the more lately revealed character, 'Lady Susan', who is drawn with an unsparing hand, showing that 'tremendous insight into shams' already mentioned. This inborn gift must have been greatly quickened by hearing the history of Mrs. —. It would teach her to look below the surface, even in the case of parents and children, and would serve to assure her, whenever in the future she was describing parental harshness or tyranny, that she was still keeping well within the mark.

Although 'Lady Susan' must be placed in a totally different category from the other novels, it should not be neglected by anyone who wishes to form a just estimate of Jane Austen's varied powers as a writer, or of herself as a woman. That she drew such a portrait once enlarges our conception of her genius; that she never drew such another increases our value for her as a woman. She chose wholesome, sane, cheerful subjects, 'things of good report', for her own imagination and that of her readers to dwell upon, describing evil as little as possible and never with a needless detail. This consideration will, it is thought, give additional force to what has been already said respecting the silent strength of her moral character. We can thus learn how to appreciate the self-control with which she resists any temptation to the use of extravagant language in describing emotions and situations, such as has earned for later writers the title of 'intense', deeming it to be beneath the dignity both of true art and of that which is highest and best in human nature.

The words of an American writer, Mr. W. L. Phelps, well deserve to be quoted here: 'Let no one believe,' he says, that Jane Austen's men and women are deficient in passion because they behave with decency; to those who have the power to see and interpret there is a depth of passion in her characters that far surpasses the emotional power displayed in many novels where the lovers seem to forget the meaning of such words as honour, virtue, and fidelity.

These words Jane Austen certainly never forgot, either as an author or a woman. Several passages in her personal history show her to have been possessed of keen sensibility and deep attachments, but we know that her own sensations never made her indifferent to the claims of those with whom she lived, nor caused her to forget the call of 'Self-reverence, self-honour, self-control.' Tennyson's words she could not know, but the spirit that inspired them was akin to her own. Neither is there any evidence that she was acquainted with Wordsworth's poems, though the earliest of these were published twenty-four years before her own death. She probably never saw 'Laodamia', written three years prior to that event, but if Wordsworth knew her writings and had wished to give a voice to her consistent utterances concerning the strongest of all human emotions, he could not have done so more fittingly than in Protesilaus' well-known lines:

> Be taught, O faithful Consort, to control
> Rebellious passion: for the Gods approve
> The depth, and not the tumult, of the soul;
> A fervent, not ungovernable, love.

Chapter VII – Parents and Children

Mention has already been made of various mistaken rumours spread abroad concerning Jane Austen during the first half-century that followed her death, one of these being that 'she did not like children'. No supposition could have been further from the truth. On no point is the family testimony more unanimous than on the unfailing love and kindness she bestowed upon them, together with the warm love they felt for her in return. She was quickly provided with such objects of affection, as four of her five brothers had families, and two nieces were born before she was herself grown up, both of whom lived to become, as young women, her close and intimate friends. Another younger niece [Caroline Austen] has written:

> My visits to Chawton were frequent. I cannot tell when they began.

> They were very pleasant to me and Aunt Jane was the great charm. As a very little girl I was always creeping up to her and following her whenever I could, in the house and out of it. Her charm to children was great sweetness of manner; she seemed to love you, and you loved her naturally in return. This was what I felt in my earliest days, before I was old enough to be amused by her cleverness. But soon came the delight of her playful talk. Everything she could make amusing to a child. Then, as I got older and cousins came to share the entertainment, she would tell us the most delightful stories, chiefly of Fairyland, and her Fairies had all characters of their own. The tale was invented, I am sure, on the spur of the moment, and was sometimes continued for two or three days if occasion served. I believe we were, all of us, according to our different ages and natures very fond of our Aunt Jane, and that we ever retain a strong impression of the pleasantness of Chawton life. One of my cousins, after he was grown up, used occasionally to go and see Aunt Cassandra, then left the sole inmate of the old house, and he told me that his visits were always a disappointment to him, for that he could not help expecting to feel particularly happy at Chawton, and never, till he got there, could he realise to himself how all its peculiar pleasures were gone.

Similar testimony on these points has been given by another niece – the little Anna who, when three years old, was placed by her widowed father, James Austen, at Steventon Rectory, to be 'mothered' by his two sisters. Anna composed stories of her own long before she was old enough to write them down, and had always a vivid recollection of the way in which her kind Aunt Jane performed that office for her. On reaching the age of seven she dictated to her aunt a drama founded on 'Sir Charles Grandison', [the novel by Samuel Richardson] which still exists in Jane Austen's handwriting. Anna's half brother and sister, Edward and Caroline, had the same love of inventing stories, and all brought their compositions to be read and reviewed by their Aunt Jane – Anna continuing the practice as a young woman when she had embarked on what was intended to be a serious novel. For an author to be ready at any time to put aside her own writing – and such writings – in order to interest herself in these very young performances shows that entire unselfishness of nature and ready sympathy with the wants of childhood which was always ascribed to Jane Austen by those who truly knew her.

Her pen was often at their service when they were apart, for she wrote them charming notes, with many playful turns, containing now and then a little good advice as well. Her niece Caroline has truly said that 'in addressing a child she was perfect.' She lived indeed in a circle of childhood, and when we look at her books we see how steady and consistent a place children take in them – without uttering a word! The old-fashioned maxim that, when in company, children should always be seen and not heard, was no doubt one on which Jane had herself been brought up, and she observes the same rule as regards the children of her fancy; the reader is not troubled with any of their remarks. Even the elder among them are not allowed to say much. The author advised her niece Anna to remember that, in novel writing, 'girls are not interesting until they are grown up,' consequently of the speeches of little Fanny Price and her cousins only enough are given to show in few words their relative conditions and characters, to bring out the kindness of Edmund and the negligence of his sisters. Margaret Dashwood, as a half-grown girl, utters a few remarks equally malapropos in themselves, and apropos to the conduct of the story. But the younger ones are all silent, yet not the less valuable on that account. They provide motives for action and conversation on the part of their elders, and are even allowed on one occasion to take a small share in carrying on the drama of the plot. No fewer than twenty children, known to us by number or by name, and generally by the latter, appear in the course of the six novels, without counting the vaguer groups of little Harvilles at Lyme, and happily occupied little Perrys at Highbury. However slight the sketch may be, we can always recognise in it the sure touch of one who herself moved about childhood's realm as a constant visitor and a ready sympathiser. If we try to imagine Jane Austen's novels deprived of their children, we shall see that in some cases they could hardly be carried on at all, while in every instance that sense of simple truthfulness, of warmth, and of life which they now possess would be greatly lessened or altogether wanting. Just as in the figure-pieces of early Italian masters the charm is enhanced and the general effect is completed by those miniature hills, rivers, and houses in the background, which provide a fitting setting for the central objects upon which they are never suffered unduly to intrude, so do Jane Austen's little people fill up, furnish, and decorate in a suitable manner the more distant portions of her scenes. Though at no time allowed to put themselves forward, they are, in their proper places and angles, highly useful by imparting a constant feeling of reality and by supplying a due sense of perspective, atmosphere, colouring, and space.

What is there, then, to be found in these books that could have led anyone to suppose their author did not like children? The idea must have rested on the fact that she did not like spoilt children, or, rather, that she strongly objected to the spoiling of children – a subject on which it is evident she bestowed a good deal of thought. But that this showed no want of interest in the children themselves may be read in a letter, written towards the close of her life to a niece, after she had been spending some days in a house filled with younger cousins of the latter. She says:

> Though the children are sometimes very noisy and not under such order as they ought and easily might [be], I cannot help liking them or even loving them, which I hope may be not wholly inexcusable in their, and your, affectionate Aunt Jane Austen.

Here we see at once, not only a natural quickness of vision towards children, but also the even balance of her judgment when reviewing the whole case, 'the children might, and should [have been] kept in better order.'

It was towards the middle of the last century that a striking tale appeared, named 'A School for Fathers', in which a charming young hero is forced into a duel, against his own inclination, by parental pride, and falls in consequence fatally wounded. Jane Austen's novels may be not unjustly entitled 'A School for Parents', and this not merely with reference to the young children to be found in them, who are over-indulged by mothers until they become an annoyance to everyone. Her outlook goes much further than this. Our language, unfortunately, contains no word expressive of the connection between parents and their sons and daughters, after the latter have ceased to be 'children' – properly speaking – and are becoming, or have become, men and women. But it is in these later stages of life that we find Jane Austen exhibiting to us the results of early training or of its absence. We do not learn this only in the case of such spoilt children as the little Middletons and Betsy Price, for older examples are as plainly dealt with, and their parents' faults are indicated with equal clearness. Mr. Allen, who is 'a sensible man' soon discovers that 'Mrs. Thorpe is, without doubt, too indulgent to her daughters' and we have Isabella in consequence. Mrs. Dashwood tells Marianne to ascribe her misfortunes to 'her mother's imprudence' a remark with which the reader will easily agree – while of Mrs. Bennet it is enough to say that she was exactly fitted to be the mother of Lydia. Irreproachable parents – mothers especially – are indeed greatly in the way of any novelist, who has to get them out of the way as handsomely as may be.

This truth was discerned very early in her own literary career by Jane Austen, one of her girlish fragments, called 'Kitty, or The Bower', beginning with these words: 'Kitty' (afterwards changed to Catherine) 'had the misfortune, as many heroines have had before her, of losing both her parents while she was still quite young.' But even when the maternal parent has been disposed of by death or by distance, the daughter must, none the less, be brought up or brought out by someone, who may contrive to go as far wrong in the process as any mother herself could do. Mrs. Weston, charming and sensible though she was, had been ruled for many years by her own charge, Emma; Edmund and Fanny agree in ascribing Mary Crawford's want of principle to deficiencies in the education she had received from her aunt, together with the bad example set by her uncle;

and the one error into which Anne Elliot falls is spoken of as having been due to the mistaken advice of an older friend, who has over her almost the influence of a mother. Nor are the fathers spared. Mrs. Ferrars is the only instance of unfeeling harshness among the mothers, while both General Tilney and Sir Walter Elliot are absolutely unpardonable fathers, and there is also a good deal requiring forgiveness in Mr. Woodhouse, Sir Thomas Bertram, and – not least – in Mr. Bennet, one of the author's most surprising creations. She had, as we have seen, gained a knowledge when still quite young, through a history belonging to past days, of the depths to which parental cruelty can descend, and we have also seen how this knowledge very probably quickened her insight respecting lighter shades of the same evil visible around her, the evil, it may be, 'that is wrought from want of thought, and not from want of heart.'

Shortcomings on the side of parents are not shown to us merely by Jane Austen herself, speaking from her position as author, since she frequently points out that they were clearly apprehended by a daughter of their own. Some time later, a school of fiction arose, intended to a great extent for the young, in which it would have been held highly disrespectful for daughters to comment adversely, even to themselves, upon any action on the part of their parents, while to utter a remonstrance to either father or mother on their neglect of a parent's duties, would have been looked upon as an unpardonable liberty. Jane Austen, however, takes a different view, and never blames her heroines for possessing some acquaintance with the characters of those by whom they had been brought up, being, as it would seem, of opinion that they could not become rational and thinking beings without acquiring such a perception, which she has no hesitation in attributing to some of the best among them. Poor Eleanor Tilney, when compelled to turn Catherine Morland out of the house, can only exclaim, 'Alas! for my feelings as a daughter. He is certainly greatly, very greatly, discomposed. I have seldom seen him more so.' Anne Elliot, who 'often wished her knowledge of her father's character were less', could not but be aware of the weak vanity that laid him open to Mrs. Clay's insidious designs, while the most striking example of filial insight and resolution in character in all the novels is to be found in Elizabeth Bennet's remonstrance with her father on his neglect of responsibility as a parent. It must have been a hard task, but when it was over she 'felt confident of having performed her duty', a reflection that can only do her honour in the mind of the reader, and, coupled with Mr. Bennet's most characteristic reference to it after Lydia's elopement had taken place, shows that it had done her honour in his judgment also. Though distrust of a parent's wisdom was the compelling cause of the action taken by Elizabeth and by Anne, there was no lack of filial respect in their manner of performing it. This is at no time wanting on the part of the heroines, even towards those for whom it was impossible that love should be felt. Where this did exist, parental shortcomings were never suffered to check it. Marianne Dashwood ardently loved her mother, imprudent though she had shown herself to be, and Emma Woodhouse, when engaged to the man of her heart, at once formed a solemn resolution never to quit her father, and 'even wept over the idea of it, as a sin of thought.'

We must, then, come to the conclusion that Jane Austen's quick intuition had deeply impressed upon her the extreme importance of parental duties being well performed and of the evils sure to follow if these were neglected. Dogmatic she never was, but her own light and delicate touches, joined in the working out of various incidents in her plots, sufficiently indicate the views she held on this point and give us some cause to suspect that, if things went wrong between the two parties, her sympathies would be mostly found on the side of the children, even when over-indulged and, consequently, troublesome. For these she was unwilling to abandon hope, and here Mr. Knightley is deputed to speak her mind. When Emma looks forward to Mrs. Weston's educating her infant daughter in a perfect manner, since she had had the advantage of practising first upon herself –

> 'That is,' replied Mr. Knightley, 'she will indulge her even more than she did you, and believe that she does not indulge her at all. It will be the only difference.'
>
> 'Poor child!' cried Emma, 'at that rate what will become of her?'
>
> 'Nothing very bad – the fate of thousands. She will be disagreeable in infancy and correct herself as she grows older. I am losing all my bitterness against spoilt children, my dearest Emma. I, who am owing all my happiness to *you*, would it not be horrible ingratitude in me to be severe on them?'

Jane Austen could also admit the existence of other influences likely to affect the ultimate fate of children. She could take into consideration the child's own character and the power of surrounding circumstances. The young Prices, not through parental good training, but in spite of its absence, prospered when aided by Sir Thomas Bertram, on account of 'The advantages of early hardships and discipline', and 'The consciousness of being born to struggle and endure.' Such a consciousness, meeting with a like success, their efforts being in this instance encouraged by their own parents, Jane may have often rejoiced over when reflecting upon the careers of her two sailor brothers.

'Persuasion' supplies us with a very different type of sailor, whose ill-doing is ascribed to his own perverse character and not to any neglect on the part of his parents. Many readers have objected to the terms in which the unlucky Dick Musgrove's history and his mother's lamentations over him are described; they have been thought hard and unworthy of Jane Austen's kind heart and delicate taste. One reply alone can be made to this charge. Though she wrote this passage, she did not publish it. On March 13, 1817, four months before her own death, she tells her niece, Fanny Knight, 'I have a something ready for publication, which may perhaps come out in a twelvemonth's time.' And again on March 23,

> Do not be surprised at finding Uncle Henry acquainted with my having another ready for publication. I could not say No when he asked me, but he knows nothing more of it. You will not like it, so you need not be impatient. You will, perhaps, like the heroine, as she is almost too good for me.

Why Fanny was not to like it does not appear, but the tone of these remarks, coupled with the author's intention of keeping it laid by for a whole year, points clearly in the direction of an intended revision when a considerable length of time should have elapsed. Her brother Henry's testimony confirms the belief that such was her usual custom. He says:

> Though in composition she was equally rapid and correct, yet an invincible distrust of her own judgment induced her to withhold her works from the public till time and many perusals had satisfied her that the charm of recent composition was dissolved.

A possible allusion to this practice may be found in the advice she offered to her niece Anna, when the latter was composing a novel: 'I hope when you have written a great deal more you will feel equal to scratching out some of the past.'

The book, though called 'ready for publication', in the sense, perhaps, that its final page had been written, does not seem to have been ready for perusal, nor as yet for announcement to her frequent confidant, Henry, to whom, even after his persistent enquiries had forced her to confess its existence, it was not to be shown at present. In another way it was certainly unfinished; it had received no name. Younger generations of the family learnt subsequently, through their Aunt Cassandra, that this question had been a good deal discussed between Jane and herself, and that among several possible titles, the one seemed most likely to be chosen was 'The Elliots'. Nothing, however, was finally settled, and Henry Austen, to whose care in had been bequeathed, brought it out under the name of 'Persuasion', re-naming at the same time her other work left in MS. which she had called 'Catherine', but which he published as 'Northanger Abbey'.

Though it is possible to object to both titles, as overweighting either book by referring to one incident or one division, rather than to the entire work, criticism must give way to thankfulness that we possess them, even in a slightly imperfect condition, and what the fate of one might have been had its author lived longer is rendered a little questionable by her words to Fanny Knight in March, 1817: 'Miss Catherine is put upon the shelf for the present, and I do not know that she will ever come out.' Had she never done so, much delight must have been lost to many readers, and not a few terraces and streets in Bath would have been the poorer in associations for all those who now love to imagine they are treading in the steps of Morlands, Thorpes, and Tilneys, while 'Persuasion' has so captured some hearts that their owners feel inclined to assign it to the highest place of all. Nevertheless, when judgment is passed upon the position that Jane Austen's books have won as English classics, it should be remembered that 'Emma' is the last novel put forth by her as a completely finished work of art; while it is open to anyone to believe that changes might, and probably would, have been made in her later and unpublished story had she herself survived to the close of the twelve months which she had allotted to it as a term of silent retirement.

There is still one theory, advanced by a reviewer, that must be mentioned before quitting the subject dealt with in this chapter, as it concerns Jane Austen's personal experience of the relations subsisting between parents and children. He takes up a position that these, in Steventon Rectory, were not pleasant, and that the family circle did not contain enough union and sympathy among its members for Jane to have felt or witnessed much domestic happiness beneath her father's roof, and that on this account she hardly ever gives in her books any description of a happy and affectionate family party. A most extraordinary theory indeed! It leads us to enquire how far its inventor has closely studied either her books or her biographies. Did he altogether forget Mrs. Dashwood and her daughters – their grief at parting and their eagerness for a reunion? Or the household of the John Knightleys, with its master's 'strong domestic habits and all sufficiency of home to himself'? Or the return of Catherine Morland to Fullerton, where, in spite of her woes as a heroine, she was welcomed with such affectionate eagerness that 'in the embrace of each she found herself soothed, surrounded, caressed – even happy'? Or the Crofts – never satisfied if apart – or the Westons, the Harvilles in quitting whose house 'Anne thought she left great happiness behind her' – or the Gardiners, and the 'fine family piece' of the Christmas party at Uppercross, alive with boys and girls, Mr. Musgrove with children clamouring on his knees and Mrs. Musgrove glancing happily round the room and observing that 'After all she had gone through nothing was so likely to do her good as a little quiet cheerfulness at home'?

Whether we examine her writings or her memoirs we are equally led to believe that no one knew better than Jane Austen, both by observation and experience, the meaning of the word 'home' in its fullest and best sense. So baseless is the conjecture mentioned above that we may rather say the conditions of life to be found in her father's house would quicken her perception of the contrast afforded to them by some other families, through an absence of peace and harmony in the latter between parents and children, brothers and sisters. To assume that these were lacking in Steventon Rectory is a most unwarrantable conclusion, and one that is absolutely opposed to the truth. Evidence on this point is, happily, equally abundant and convincing. Mrs. George Austen, writing in 1796 to Mary Lloyd, soon to become her daughter-in-law, speaks of her own and her husband's heartfelt satisfaction in the prospect of 'adding you to the number of our very good children'. In a letter written more than twenty years later she explains to her sister-in-law, Mrs. Leigh Perrot, the particulars of her income, she dwells upon the eagerness all her sons had shown, when she had been left a widow in 1805, to make it a comfortable one. Of her two eldest she says:

> Mr. Knight (the second son) has a most active mind, a clear head, and a sound judgment; he is quite a man of business. That my dear James was not. Classical knowledge, literary taste, and the power of elegant composition he possessed in the highest degree. To these Mr. Knight makes no pretensions. *Both* equally good, amiable, and sweet-tempered.

The feelings and the conduct of all her sons on the death of their father are shown in letters written to the one then absent on naval duty (Captain Frank Austen) by his brothers at home. Henry laments the loss of 'the best of Fathers and of Men', adding 'Language is so inadequate to what we feel on such a subject that you will know why I prefer silence to imperfect praise. The survivors are now what we must all think of.' The letters that then passed between the brothers on the question of making a comfortable provision for their mother are equally remarkable for the generosity they display towards herself and for the courtesy and affection they exhibit towards each other. When the result was finally made known to Mrs. Austen she exclaimed that 'Never were children so good as hers', at the same time declining to accept the whole of the income which they offered her.

The author of the original 'Memoir' has indicated that if there were a family fault, it lay in exactly the opposite direction from that suggested by this critic. He says: 'There was so much that was agreeable in this family party that its members may be excused if they were inclined to live somewhat too exclusively within it. They might see in each other much to love and esteem and something to admire.' To this may be added, from family tradition, that of all the party, Jane was the one chiefly conscious of this family tendency, and most alive to the duty of struggling against it. To this another testimony may be added, that of the last-named writer's sister, Caroline Austen, who, as a child and young girl, was often at Chawton Cottage both before and after her Aunt Jane's death; nor could any more fitting words be found than hers with which to close these 'Personal Aspects of Jane Austen' –

> In the time of my childhood, it was a cheerful house, my uncles, one or another, requently coming for a few days, and they were all pleasant in their own families; I have thought since, after seeing more of other households, *wonderfully* so. The family talk had such spirit and vivacity, and it was never troubled by disagreement, as it was not their habit to argue with one another. There was always perfect harmony amongst the brothers and sisters, with firm family union, never broken but by death, and over my Grandmother's door might have been inscribed the text: 'Behold how good and joyful a thing it is, Brethen, to dwell together in unity.'

Appendix

Some additional information respecting Jane Austen and the family party immediately surrounding her may be acceptable to that inner circle of her readers who are willing to bear with a little repetition of facts in order to glean, from original documents, a few particulars not yet fully known to them. It is to such readers that the following extracts and remarks are offered.

The original 'Memoir,' after giving the account of her funeral, closes with these words:

> Her brothers went back sorrowing to their several homes. They were very fond and very proud of her...and each loved afterwards to fancy a resemblance in some niece or daughter of his own to the dear sister Jane, whose perfect equal they yet never expected to see.'

Of these nieces, many were at that time so young that such a resemblance could develop at a later period only. The three of whom she had seen most were, Fanny Knight, her brother Edward's eldest daughter; Anna Austen, her brother James's eldest daughter, who, prior to her Aunt Jane's death, had married Benjamin Lefroy of Ashe (son of Madam Lefroy, Jane Austen's beloved friend); and Anna's half-sister Caroline Austen. It was of the latter that their father wrote in April 1819: 'Caroline has that playfulness of mind, united with an affectionate heart, which so peculiarly marked our lamented Jane.' Fatherly partiality did not mislead him in his high estimate of this daughter. Like her Aunt Jane, she had gifts both of humour and pathos, which combined with a similar originality and independence of mind, made her in later years a delightful companion and a charming converser. Like her, also, she, in her turn, became a perfect aunt to whom nephews and nieces are indebted for many kindnesses, one of these being the manner in which she related, both by word of mouth and in writing, family history and personal reminiscences. One of these gives an account of her sister's wedding. This was deeply interesting to her grandmother, and to her aunts, Cassandra and Jane, the first-named sending good wishes to the bride, both in prose and verse. Nevertheless all three stayed quietly at home, making no attempt to attend the ceremony, though Steventon and Chawton are but sixteen miles apart. It is true that sixteen miles of indifferent road then formed a considerable barrier in wintry weather for ladies who possessed no carriage and horses, but their absence from the wedding is a fresh proof of the customary simplicity of procedure on these occasions, such as we meet with in 'Mansfield Park' and in 'Emma', which strongly characterised Anna Austen's wedding day.

Caroline Austen writes:

> On the 8th November, 1814, my sister was married to Benjamin Lefroy Esq. He had not then taken orders, although of the full age that was necessary. Weddings were then usually very quiet. The old fashion of festivity and publicity had quite gone by, and was universally condemned as showing the bad taste of former generations. But it revived again, and no protest is now ever heard against it. My Sister's wedding was certainly in the extreme of quietness; yet not so as to be in any way remarked upon, or censured, and this was the order of the day: The Bridegroom came from Ashe Rectory, where he had hitherto lived with his Brother; and Mr. and Mrs. Lefroy (his Brother and Sister-in-law) came with him, as well as another brother, Mr. Edward Lefroy. Anne Lefroy, the eldest little girl, was one of the Bridesmaids and I was the other. My Brother came from Winchester that morning, but was to stay only a few hours. We in the house had a slight early breakfast upstairs; and between nine and ten the Bride, my Mother, Mrs. Lefroy, Anne and myself, were taken to Church in our carriage; all the gentlemen walked. The weather was dull and cloudy but it did not actually rain. The season of the year, the unfrequented road of half a mile to the lonely old Church, the grey light within of a November morning, making its way through the narrow windows, no stove to give warmth, no flowers to give colour and brightness,no friends, high or low, to offer their

> good wishes – and so to claim some interest in the great event of the day – all these circumstances and deficiencies must, I think, have given a gloomy air to our Wedding. Mr. Lefroy read the service. My father gave his daughter away. The Clerk, of course, was there, though I do not particularly remember him, but I am quite sure there was no one else in the Church. Nor was anyone asked to the Breakfast, to which we sat down as soon as we got back. I do not think this idea of sadness struck me at the time. The bustle in the house and all the preparations had excited me, and it seemed to me a festivity from beginning to end.
>
> The Breakfast was such as best Breakfasts then were. Some variety of bread, hot rolls, buttered toast, tongue or ham, and eggs. The addition of Chocolate at one end of the table and the Wedding Cake in the middle marked *the* speciality of the day. I and Anne Lefroy, nine and six years old, wore white frocks and had white ribband on our straw bonnets, which I suppose were new for the occasion. Soon after breakfast the Bride and Bridegroom departed. They had a long day's journey before them to Hendon. The other Lefroys went home, and in the afternoon my Mother and I went to Chawton to stay at the Great House, then occupied by my Uncle Captain (Francis) Austen and his large family. My Father stayed behind for a few days and then joined us. The servants had cake and wine in the evening, and Mr. Digweed walked down to keep my father company. Such were the Wedding fesitivities of Steventon in 1814!

The dress of the bride has been recorded by one of her own daughters.

> She wore a dress of fine white muslin, and over it a soft silk shawl, white, shot with primrose, with embossed white satin flowers and very handsome fringe, and on her head a small cap to match trimmed with lace, and the delicate yellow tints must have been most becoming to her bright brown hair, hazel eyes, and sunny clear complexion.

The bride was then twenty-one, and was considered to be the prettiest girl in the neighbourhood, the most striking feature of her face being the widely-opened large dark eyes, which retained their brilliant beauty to the close of a long life. It was necessary for the bridal pair to start early that Bagshot Heath, a resort of highwaymen, should be passed over in daylight. Jane Austen went to her brother Henry's house in London a few days later, and had then the satisfaction of driving out to Hendon to visit her niece as a bride. Anna and her husband afterwards returned from Hampstead to live in a house called 'Wyards', within a walk of Chawton Village, and frequent communication with her relations in that place could thus be easily maintained.

Caroline Austen on the Life at Chawton Cottage Written in 1867

I have been told the house had formerly been an Inn, and it was well placed for such a purpose, just where the road from Winchester comes into the London and Gosport road. The front door opened on the road; a very narrow enclosure on each side protected the house from possible shock of any runaway vehicle. A good-sized entrance and two parlours, called dining and drawing-room, made up the length of the house, all intended originally to look on the road, but the large drawing-room window was blocked up and turned into a bookcase when Mrs. Austen took possession, and another was opened at the side which gave to view only turf and trees. A high wooden fence shut out the road (to Winchester) all the length of the little domain, and trees were planted inside to form a shrubbery walk which, carried round the enclosure, gave a very sufficient space for exercise. You did not feel cramped for room, and there was a pleasant irregular mixture of hedgerow and grass and gravel walk, and long grass for mowing, and Orchard, which I imagine arose from two or three little enclosures having been thrown together and arranged as best might be for ladies' occupation. There was, besides, a good kitchen garden; large and many out buildings, not much occupied. All this affluence of space was very delightful to children and I have no doubt added considerably to the pleasure of a visit.

Everything, indoors and out, was well kept, the house was well furnished, and it was altogether a comfortable and ladylike establishment, though I believe the means which supported it were but small.

The house was quite as good as the generality of Parsonage Houses then were, and much in the same old style, the ceilings low and roughly finished, some bedrooms very small, none very large, but in number sufficient to accommodate the inmates and several guests.

The dining-room could not be made to look anywhere but on the road, and there my Grandmother often sat for an hour or two in the morning, with her work [needlework] or her writing, cheered by its sunny aspect and by the stirring scene it afforded.

I believe the close vicinity of the road was no more an evil to her than it was to her grandchildren. Collyer's daily coach with six horses was a sight to see! – and most delightful was it to a child to have the awful stillness of the night frequently broken by the noise of passing carriages, which seemed sometimes even to shake the bed.

The village of Chawton has, of course, long since been tranqillised; it is no more a great thoroughfare …

As to my Aunt Jane's personal, appearance, hers was the first face that I can remember thinking pretty, not that I used that word to myself but

I know I looked at her with admiration. Her face was rather round than long; she had a bright, but not a pink, colour, a clear, brown complexion, and very good hazel eyes. She was not, I believe, an absolute beauty, but before she left Steventon she was established as a very pretty girl in the opinion of most of her neighbours, as I learnt afterwards from some of those who still remained. Her hair, a darkish brown, curled naturally in short curls round her face (for then ringlets were not.) She always wore a cap. Such was the custom with ladies who were not quite young – at least of a morning – but I never saw her without one. My Aunts were particularly neat; they held all untidy ways in great dis-esteem ...

Aunt Jane began the day with music, for which I conclude she had a natural taste, as she thus kept it up, though she had no-one to teach, and was never induced (as I have heard) to play in Company, and none of her family cared much for it. I suppose that she might not trouble them she chose her practising time before breakfast, when she could have the room to herself. She practised regularly every morning. She played very pretty tunes, I thought, and I liked to stand by her and listen to her. Much that she played was from Manuscript copies written out by herself...

At 9 o'clock she made breakfast – that was her part of the household work. The tea and sugar stores were under her charge – and the wine. Aunt Cassandra did all the rest, for my Grandmother had suffered herself to be superseded by her daughters *before* I can remember, and soon *after* she ceased even to sit at the head of the table.

I don't believe Aunt Jane observed any particular method in parcelling out her day, but I think she generally sat in the drawing- room till luncheon, when visitors were there, chiefly at work. She was fond of work, and was a great adept at overcast and satin-stitch – the peculiar delight of that day. She was wonderfully successful with cup and ball, and found a resource sometimes in that simple game when she was suffering from weak eyes and could not work or read for long together.

After luncheon my Aunts generally walked out; sometimes they went to Alton for shopping, often, one or the other of them to the 'Great House', as it was then called, in order, when a brother was inhabiting it, to make a visit; or, if the house were standing empty, they liked to stroll about the grounds, sometimes to Chawton Park, a noble beechwood, just within a walk, and sometimes – but that was rarely – to call on a neighbour. They had no carriage and their visitings did not extend far. There were a few families living in the village, but no great intimacy was kept up with any of them; they were on friendly, but rather distant, terms with all. Yet I am sure my Aunt Jane had a regard for her neighbours and felt a kindly interest in their proceedings. She liked immensely to hear all about them. They sometimes served for her amusement, but it was her own nonsense which gave zest to the gossip. She never turned *them* into ridicule; she was as far as possible from being censorious or satirical; she never abused them or 'quizzed' them. That was the word of the day – an ugly one, now obsolete – and the ugly practice which it bespoke is far less prevalent now, under any name, than it was then. The laugh she occasionally raised was by imagining for her neighbours impossible contingencies by relating in prose or verse some trifling incident, coloured to her own fancy, or in writing a history of what they had said or done, that *could* deceive nobody ...

My Aunt must have spent much time in writing. Her desk lived in the drawing-room; I often saw her writing letters on it, and I believe she wrote much of her novels in the same way, sitting with her family when they were quite alone, but I never saw any manuscript of that sort in progress (Caroline may, however, have done so without knowing it, as it was her Aunt's habit to write them on note paper, the better to be able to cover them with blotting paper if a visitor were shown in). She wrote very fully to her brothers when they were at sea, and she corresponded with many others of the family.

There is nothing in these letters which I have seen that would be acceptable to the public. They were very well expressed, and they must have been very interesting to those who received them, but they detailed chiefly home and family events and she seldom committed herself even to any opinion, so that to strangers there could be no transcript of her mind; they would not feel that they knew her any the better for having read them. They were rather overcautious for excellence. Her letters to Aunt Cassandra were, I daresay, open and confidential. My Aunt looked them over and burnt the greater part as she told me three or four years before her own death. She left or gave some as legacies to the nieces, but of those that I have seen several had portions cut out. (The 'Brabourne Letters' did not appear during this writer's life-time).

When staying at Chawton, if my two cousins, Mary Jane and Cassy Austen, were there, we often had amusements in which my Aunt was very helpful. She was the one to whom we always looked for help. She would furnish us with what we wanted from her wardrobe and she would often be the entertaining visitor in our make-believe house. She amused us in various ways, once, I remember, in giving a conversation, as between myself and my two cousins, supposed to be grown up, the day after a Ball.

She was considered to read aloud remarkably well. I did not often hear her, but once I knew her take up a volume of 'Evelina' [by Fanny Burney] and read a few pages of 'Mr. Smith and the Brangtons', and I thought it was like a play. She had a very good speaking voice. This was the opinion of her contemporaries and though I did not *then* think of it as a perfection, or even hear it observed upon, yet its tones have never been forgotten. I can recall them even now, and I know they *were* very pleasant.

Aunt Jane was a very affectionate sister to all her brothers. One of them in particular (Henry) was her especial pride and delight, but of all her family her nearest and dearest throughout her whole life was her only sister, Cassandra. Aunt Cassandra was the elder by three or four years, and the habit of looking up to her, begun in childhood, seemed always to continue. When I was a little girl, Aunt Jane would frequently say to me, if opportunity offered, that Aunt Cassandra could teach everything much better than she could – Aunt Cassandra knew more – Aunt Cassandra could tell me better whatever I wanted to know – all of which I received in respectful silence. Perhaps she thought my mind wanted a bias in that direction, but I truly believe that she did always really think of her sister as the superior to herself. The most perfect confidence and affection ever subsisted between them, and great and lasting was the sorrow of the survivor when the final separation was made.'

(The testimony given by Caroline's elder sister Anna is entirely to the same effect.) Aunt Cassandra's loss in her sister was great indeed, and most truly a loss never to be repaired. They were everything to each other. They seemed to lead a life to themselves within the general family life which was shared only by each other. I will not say their true, but their *full,* feelings and opinions were known only to themselves. They alone fully understood what each had suffered and felt and thought. Yet they had such a gift of reticence that the secrets of their respective friends were never betrayed to each other. They were thoroughly trustworthy, and the young niece who brought her troubles to Aunt Jane for advice and sympathy knew she could depend absolutely on her silence, even to her sister.

When writing to her brother, Capt. Frank Austen, then stationed in the Baltic, in September, 1813, Jane refers to the fact of her authorship of 'Sense and Sensibility' and 'Pride and Prejudice' having been revealed by their brother Henry, and says:

> I know it is all done from affection and partiality, but at the same time let me here again express to you and Mary my sense of the superior kindness which you have shown on the occasion in doing what I wished. I am trying to harden myself. After all, what a trifle it is, in all its bearings, to the really important points of one's existence – even in this world.

She must have had an equally keen sense of gratitude to her eldest brother James and his wife (another Mary) for the strictly honourable silence they had preserved on the subject, in spite of what must have been a strong temptation to act otherwise. Their son Edward, then a boy at Winchester, had read both these books with great delight, but had never been told that his Aunt Jane had written them. Now, however further silence was needless, and he has left a record of his feelings, on hearing the great news, in the following lines. Though written by a boy not yet quite fifteen years old, they are worth reading, if only to show the happy and intimate terms on which he and his Aunt Jane stood towards each other: –

To Miss J. AUSTEN

No words can express, my dear Aunt, my surprise
Or make you conceive how I opened my eyes,
Like a pig Butcher Pile has just struck with his knife,
When I heard for the very first time in my life
That I had the honour to have a relation
Whose works were dispersed through the whole of the nation -
I assure you, however, I'm terribly glad;
Oh dear! Just to think (and the thought drives me mad)
That dear Mrs. Jenning's good-natured strain
Was really the produce of your witty brain,
That you made the Middletons, Dashwoods, and all,
And that you (not young Ferrars) found out that a ball
May be given in cottages, never so small.
And though Mr. Collins, so grateful for all,
Will Lady de Bourgh his dear Patroness call,
'Tis to your ingenuity really he owed
His living, his wife, and his humble abode.
Now if you will take your poor nephew's advice,
Your works to Sir William pray send in a trice,
If he'll undertake to some grandees to show it,
By whose means at last the Prince Regent might know it,
For I'm sure If he did, in reward for your tale,
He'd make you a countess at least, without fail,
And indeed if the Princess should lose her dear life
You might have a good chance of becoming his wife.

Oh! Journal. Oh! Journal,
Thou torment diurnal,
No Hydra so hopeless to slay!
I demolish one head
Before going to bed,
And another starts up the next day!

These lines, composed about ninety years ago recurred involuntarily to the mind of the present writer before this book was finished. One reason for undertaking the work was a desire to put an end if possible to various mis-statements made by commentators respecting Jane Austen and her surroundings. To members of her own family some of these mistakes seem hardly excusable, but in the conviction that they were not 'set down in malice', but only in haste, or in an unconscious desire to support some pre-conceived theory, it was hoped that by drawing together in a connected whole a variety of facts scattered throughout Jane Austen's biographies, all serious misrepresentations of her home, her family, and her own nature would be avoided in the future. But quite suddenly a new and strange tale respecting her has started up. It appears in an interesting book, recently published, and as it may be widely read, such a story cannot be left unnoticed. Miss Ethel Smyth, the authoress, who had a bachelor great uncle, Wm. Smyth, Master of Peterhouse, Cambridge, says: My father used to tell an odd little story about his uncle and Jane Austen, who were close friends. It appears that the authoress, wishing to get at his real opinion of one of her novels, put on a friend to pump him, concealing herself meanwhile behind a curtain. The verdict was luckily all that could be desired till the Professor remarked he was not quite certain as to her orthodoxy, having detected slight Unitarian leanings in her later works, upon which Jane Austen burst forth from her hiding place, indignantly crying : 'That's not true!' One may question whether any degree of intimacy condones such a stratagem, but no doubt she knew her man.

Miss Smyth describes this as 'a curious sidelight on an elusive personality'.

For more than one reason this story cannot be accepted as accurate. That Dr. Smyth should discover in either of her 'later works', 'Mansfield Park' and 'Emma', Unitarian leanings, may surprise us, but it would be far more surprising could we believe that Jane Austen, with her high sense of honour, had chosen to imitate some of her least worthy characters, the two Miss Steeles, by concealing herself in order to overhear anything concerning herself which she believed the speaker would have desired she should not hear. Elinor Dashwood's displeasure when she finds that Nancy Steele has been behaving in this way, cannot be forgotten by the readers of 'Sense and Sensibility'. Dr Smyth may have been well acquainted with Jane Austen, though, as his name never appears in any extant letters, it must be uncertain whether he could have been 'a close friend' of one who did not easily make such friends. But however well she may have known him, nothing would in her eyes have excused such conduct, nor will the hasty action and language here imputed to her appear, to those who have studied her books and her character, to bear any resemblance to her own.

There are also other reasons for declining to accept the story as it now stands. 'Emma' was published in December, 1815, and in the same month Jane Austen returned from London to her home at Chawton, which she finally quitted for her last journey to Winchester, May 23. 1817. The intervening seventeen months brought severe trial and distress to all the

George Austens. Henry was declared a bankrupt in March, 1816, having only just recovered, in January, 1815, from a three months' illness, in the course of which his life had been despaired of. Jane had nursed him all the time, at the expense, as her relations afterwards believed, of her own health and strength. These began to fail her, and she consulted a physician in London before returning home, not yet as an avowed, but as an incipient, invalid, who was depending more and more exclusively upon her immediate family for society.[1]

She scarcely left her home after this return, but she once paid a visit to old friends in Berkshire (who noticed with concern that a change had taken place in her health and bearing), and she once went to Cheltenham in the vain hope of deriving benefit from its waters. Cheltenham is the only place where she might have fallen in with Dr. Smyth after 'Emma' was published; but if such a meeting occurred her state of depression and weakness makes it doubly unlikely she would lay a trap for a friend such as she had denounced many years before in one of earliest books. We can only conclude that whoever may have attempted to deceive Dr. Smyth in this way it could not at any time, and least of all at that time, have been Jane Austen, who never had anything in common with the tricks of the Miss Steeles or the hoydenish mannersof Lydia Bennet. Collecting the opinions of those who read her novels was a great entertainment to her, and there is a long list of such verdicts, both good and bad, on 'Emma' given in her biography. [2] In this list Dr. Smyth's name does not appear. It is, however, possible that an attempt to obtain his opinion in the manner described above, was made by some common friend, so intimately acquainted with Dr. Smyth as to make the artifice appear permissible, since it it would relate to a third person only.

At the close of the original 'Memoir' its author; after correcting a complete mistake made by Miss Mitford respecting Jane Austen which she had given on her mother's authority, adds these words which may very well be quoted here: 'All persons who undertake to narrate from hearsay things which are supposed to have taken place before they were born, are liable to error and are apt to call in imagination to the aid of memory : and hence it arises that many a fancy piece has been substituted for genuine history.'

1. *Jane Austen, Her Life and Letters, a Family Record,* William and Richard Arthur Leigh, Chapter XX.
2. Ibid, Chapter XVIII.

Charades – Written a Hundred Years Ago by Jane Austen and Her Family

It is hoped that these old-fashioned charades and conundrums possess a degree of merit sufficient to afford entertainment to any persons inclined to take pleasure in this kind of amusement, and, more especially, that they may interest that inner circle of readers who love the name of Jane Austen.

It is not as a celebrated writer that she appears in these pages, but as one of a family group gathered round the fireside at Steventon Rectory, Chawton Manor House, or Godmersham Park, to enliven the long evenings of a hundred years ago by merry verses and happy, careless inventions of the moment, such as flowed without difficulty from the lively minds and ready pens of those amongst whom she lived.

Three of these charades are by Jane herself, and even if her name did not appear beneath them their authorship might possibly have been apparent to those already acquainted with the playful exaggerations and sparkling nonsense in which she sometimes loved to indulge when writing with perfect unrestraint to her sister and other relations. In all work intended for the public eye these had to be kept within bounds; we find nothing but the soberest decorum in the charade laid long ago upon the table at Hartfield, and transcribed by Emma into that thin quarto of hot-pressed paper in which Harriet was making 'her only mental provision for the evening of life'.

The habit of writing charades seems to have been general in the Austen family. Only one by her father survives, but there are several by her mother, Cassandra Leigh by birth, who was well gifted with – to use a term of her own – 'sprack wit'. Cassandra's brother, James Leigh, who inherited the estate of North Leigh in Oxfordshire from the Perrots, and added their name to his own, was noted in the family as a writer of good charades, and four of his lead the way in this little collection. They may have been composed by him in his young days in Bath, in which gay and fashionable resort he and his wife were often to be found, or at his country home, Scarlets, in Berkshire, where as an older man he passed most of his time.

All the other charades come from the pens of three generations of Austens, and are inserted according to the ages of the writers. Next in order to the charades by Jane's parents come those of her eldest brother, James, who on his father's death succeeded to the family living of Steventon, Hants; then one by her brother Henry, a brilliant, versatile member of the family party. The next is by her sister, her second self, Cassandra; and the succeeding one by Francis, the elder of her two sailor brothers, who survived all the rest of his generation and died as Sir Francis Austen, Admiral of the Fleet, in 1865, aged ninety-two. Jane's own charades follow next in order. Two of her brothers are not represented here, Edward Austen, afterwards Edward Knight, and Charles, the youngest of the family. The last two charades are by a nephew, who, being nearly nineteen at the time of her death in July, 1817, and well able to use his pen before that time, can claim a place among the Steventon writers, even though his charades may possibly date from the comparatively modern period of only seventy or eighty years ago.

The key to No. 5, the only one of her father's we possess, was long lost, and many accomplished charade-guessers tried in vain to recover the meaning, which he had hidden with much graceful subtilty (sic). It was at last discovered not very long ago by his great-great-grandson, the late William Chambers Lefroy, Esq., of Goldings, Basingstoke.

I

Two brothers, wisely kept apart,
Together are employed.
Though to one purpose both are bent,
Each takes a different side.
To us nor heads nor mouths belong,
Yet plain our tongues appear,
With them we never speak a word,
Without them useless are.
In blood and wounds we deal,
Yet good in temper we are proved;
We are from passion always free,
Yet oft in anger moved.
We travel much, yet prisoners are,
And close confined to boot,
Can with the swiftest horse keep pace,
Yet always go on foot.
[James Leigh Perrot]

II

A head and mouth I have, but – what's the wonder –
My head and mouth are very far asunder.
In at my mouth each day what I receive,
Without emetics, back again I give.
Eyes I have none, yet never miss my way;
I have no legs, yet quickly run away.
With one hint more enough will sure be said,
I always travel, always keep my bed.
[James Leigh Perrot]

III

In confinement I'm chained every day,
Yet my enemies need not be crowing,
To my chain I have always a key,
And no prison can keep me from going.
Small and weak are my hands I allow,
Yet for striking my character's great.
Though ruined by one fatal blow,
My strokes, if hard pressed, I repeat.
I have neither mouth, eye, nor ear,
Yet I always keep time as I sing,
Change of season I never need fear,
Though my being depends on the spring.
Would you wish, if these hints were too few,
One glimpse of my figure to catch?
Look round! I shall soon be in view
If you have but your eyes on the watch.
[James Leigh Perrot]

IV

Though low is my station
The Chief in the Nation
On me for support oft depend;
Young and old, strong and weak,
My assistance all seek,
Yet all turn their backs on their friend.
At the first rout in town
Every Duchess will own my company not a disgrace;
Yet at each rout you'll find
I am still left behind,
And to everyone forced to give place.
Without bribe or treat,
I have always a seat
In the Chapel so famed of St. Stephen;
There I lean to no side,
With no party divide,
But keep myself steady and even.
Each debate I attend
From beginning to end,
Yet I seem neither weary nor weaker;
In the house every day
Not a word do I say,
Yet in me you behold a good speaker.
[James Leigh Perrot]

V
Without me, divided, fair ladies, I ween,
At a ball or a concert you'll never be seen,
You must do me together, or safely I'd swear,
Whatever your carriage, you'll never get there.
[George Austen]

VI
Sometimes I am bright, sometimes covered with soot,
I'm of very great use at a feast;
I am often applied to the right or left foot;
I'm a Fish, I'm a Boy, I'm a Beast.
[Cassandra Austen Senior]

VII
My first, when good, may claim another;
My second water cannot smother;
My whole stands in the way before ye,
And puts a stop to speed and hurry.
[Cassandra Austen Senior]

VIII
My first implies mirth, and my second reflection.
If my whole you divide in a proper direction,
It will tell you your fortune and answer your question.
[Cassandra Austen Senior]

IX
Singly to possess my charms,
Soldiers, fearless, rush to arms;
Lawyers to their briefs apply,
Politicians scheme and lie;
Disregarding toil and scars,
And when they've gained me – bless their stars
But when joined with any other,
Though it be a very brother,
All our glory's banished quite,
We are then kept out of sight.
Modest ladies scarce will name us,
Though we made one lady famous,
Yet guess for once our name aright,
And when you find us, keep us tight.
[James Austen]

X
In my first, that he may not be tardy and late
My second to do, and make nobody wait,
A curate oft crosses the plain;
But if to my whole he should ever advance,
To me it appears an improbable chance
That he'll ever do either again.
[James Austen]

XI
By all prudent folk he a rash man is reckoned
Who, before he has gotten my first, takes my second,
Yet my first will afford him but little delight
To the name of my whole if my second's no right.
[James Austen]

XII
Divided, of an ancient house am I
A long, and dark, and sometimes useless story;
United, I declare the station high
Of those who best support old England's glory.
[James Austen]

XIII
My first a horseman's dire disgrace would tell
If it were only longer by an ell;
My next, if strong enough and not too short,
Will always prove old age's best support;
But much I doubt if any living wight
Could well support my whole for one short night.
[James Austen]

XIV
If there be truths in proverbs old, my first,
Though best of servants, is of masters worst;
Ruin unlimited my second brings;
Then, flushed with triumph, knaves exult o'er kings;
My whole a different scene, more welcome, gave,
Saw kings victorious, and a vanquished knave.
[James Austen]

XV
I with a footboy once was curst,
Whose name when shortened made my first.
He an unruly rogue was reckoned
And in the house oft raised my second.
My whole stands high in lists of fame,
Exalting e'en great Chatham's name.
[Henry Austen]

XVI
Should you chance to suffer thirst
Turn my second to my first;
My whole is in the garden dug,
And may be fairly called a drug.
[Cassandra Elizabeth Austen]

XVII
By my first you may travel with safety and speed,
Though many dislike the conveyance indeed;
My second no woman can well be.
My whole takes a change several times in a year
Hot and cold, wet and dry, benignant, severe,
What am I, fair lady, pray tell me?
[Francis William Austen]

XVIII
When my first is a task to a young girl of spirit,
And my second confines her to finish the piece,
How hard is her fate but how great is her merit
If by taking my whole she effect her release!
[Jane Austen]

XIX

Divided, I'm a gentleman
In public deeds and powers;
United, I'm a monster, who
That gentleman devours.
[Jane Austen]

XX

You may lie on my first by the side of a stream.
And my second compose to the nymph you adore,
But if, when you've none of my whole, her esteem
And affection diminish-think of her no more!
[Jane Austen]

XXI

Shake my first, and to you in return it will give
A good shake, perhaps rather too rough.
If you suffer my second a twelvemonth to live
You will find it grown quite big enough.
My whole stands all day with its back to the wall,
A sad gossip as ever you'll meet,
Knows the first of each robbery, concert, or ball,
And tells every soul in the street.
[James Edward Austen (Leigh)]

XXII

My first to aid the works of man
From heaven a present came.
And yet this gift, do what you can,
He cannot catch nor tame.
For now t'is on the mountain's brow,
And now t'is on the wave,
Now sighs in Beauty's bower, and now
Howls o'er the maniac's grave.
My second, like my first, I'm sure
From heaven its essence drew
As soft, as fragrant, and as pure;
Say not, as changeful too!
My whole explores earth's deepest stores,
And draws exhaustless up
The purest draught that e'er is quaffed
From mortal's varying cup.
[James Edward Austen (Leigh)]

KEY

I. Pair of Spurs. II. River. III. Repeating Watch. IV. Chair. V. A Light. VI. Jack. VII. Turnpike. VIII. Merry-thought. IX. Garter(s). X. Canterbury. XI. Housewife. XII. Aloft. XIII. Falstaff. XIV. Waterloo. (in the game of Loo, Knaves are reckoned above Kings. One form of the game is called 'Unlimited Loo'. XV. Patriot. XVI. Liquorice. XVII. Season. XVIII. Hemlock. XIX. Agent. XX. Bank Note. XXI. Handbill. XXII. Windlass

9
A Niece's Diary

Jane Austen enjoyed a particularly close and affectionate relationship with her niece Fanny, the eldest daughter of her brother Edward Austen (later Knight) and his wife Elizabeth. Jane was seventeen when her niece was born.

Jane saw Fanny regularly on her visits to Godmersham House and also when Edward and his family stayed at Chawton House, his Hampshire property. As Fanny grew older she began to keep in touch with her aunt by letter (very little of this correspondence has survived, unfortunately). They became so close that Jane described Fanny as 'almost another sister.' After the death in October 1808 of Fanny's mother, Jane became her niece's trusted confidante and advisor, especially with regard to her romantic attachments.

From the age of eleven Fanny kept a diary, or 'pocket book,' which provides an interesting source of information on Jane from 1805 until her death. Fanny used her diary to record daily happenings, including the many visits of family and friends to Godmersham House as well as trivia such as details of the weather. She continued to keep a diary for the rest of her long life.

The following extracts from the diary provide a glimpse of Jane enjoying the pleasures of family life and reveal the ordinary person behind the great novelist. This is a picture which Jane, who never courted fame, would have liked her readers to see.

Fanny Knight's Diary – Extracts from 1805–1817

1805

June:– Jane, her mother, sister and niece Anna were at Godmersham House for a long stay.

Tuesday 25 – We had a whole holiday [from lessons]. Aunts & G(rand) mama played at school with us. Aunt C. was Miss Teachum, the Governess, Aunt Jane was Miss Popham, the teacher, Aunt Harriot, Sally the Housemaid, Miss Sharpe, the Dancing Master, the Apothecary and the Sergeant, G(rand)mama, Betty Jones the Pie Woman & Mama the Bathing Woman. They dressed in character & we had a most delightful day – After dessert we acted a Play called Virtue Rewarded. Anna was Duchess St. Albans, I was the Fairy Serena & Fanny Cage a shepherdess Mona. We had a Bowl of Syllabub in the evening.

July

Tuesday 30 – Aunts C. and Jane, Anna, Edward, George, Henry, William & myself acted The Spoilt Child & Innocence Rewarded, afterwards we danced & had a most delightful evening.

September: – Jane, her mother, sister and Martha Lloyd went to Sussex with Edward and his family.

Tuesday 16 – Papa, Mama, Aunts C. & Jane & I set off from Godmersham for Battel [*sic*], where we arrived about 4, & finding no accommodation, we proceeded to Horsebridge where we slept. We saw the abbey at Battel.

Wednesday 17 – We proceeded for Worthing, spent 2 or 3 hours at Brighton & arrived there at 5. We walked on the Sands in the evening.

Friday 19 – We dined at 4 & went to a Raffle in the evening, which Aunt Jane won & it amounted to 17s.

Sunday 22 – Morning church. Miss Lloyd and G(rand)mama & Aunt Jane went to church.

1807

September: – Edward Austen and his family visited his mother and sisters in Southampton.

Sunday 13 – We all went to church and afterwards walked to the Polygon [an area of the city].

Monday 14 – In the evening Papa, Aunts C. and J., W(illia)m & I went to the play. They performed The Way to Keep Them.

Tuesday 15 – We went in a hired boat to call on Mrs. Palmer [Charles Austen's mother-in-law] who called on us the day before. Mama, to everybody's astonishment, was of the party, and not at all sick. In the evening Uncle Henry A. came. Aunts C. & J. walked in the High Street till late.

Wednesday 16 – We all, excepting Mama, took a boat and went to Netley Abbey, the ruins of which are beautiful. We eat there of some biscuits we had taken and returned quite delighted. Aunt Jane and I walked in the High Street till late.

1813

April:– Fanny and her family spent four months at Chawton House. She saw Jane regularly as there were lots of visits between Chawton House and Chawton Cottage.

June

Thursday 24 – Aunt Jane and I had a delicious morn(in)g together.

Friday 25 – A holiday. A(unt)s C and J came to read before b(reak)fast, & the latter and I b(reak)fasted here. We drank tea at the Cottage.

Saturday 26 – The cottage dined here. Sweet weather now. Aunt Jane and I walked to Alton.

July

Monday 5 – Aunt Jane and I rode out with Papa to Chawton Farm. We drank tea at the Cottage.

***1817:** – Fanny recorded the death of her beloved aunt in her diary two days after it happened (due to the inevitable delay in the news reaching Kent from Hampshire.)*

July

Sunday 20 – Evening Church – I did not go in consequence of a letter from Papa announcing my dear Aunt Jane Austen's death at 4 on Friday morning.

In the late 1860s Edward Austen Leigh asked Fanny if she would like to contribute her memories of their aunt to his biography but she declined to do so. At around the same time Fanny made the following unkind and disparaging remarks about Jane in a letter to her sister:–

Yes my love it is very true that Aunt Jane from various circumstances was not so refined *as she ought to have been from her* talent, *& if she had lived 50 years later she would have been in many respects more suitable to our more refined tastes. They were not rich & the people around with whom they chiefly mixed, were not at all high bred, or in short anything more than* mediocre & they *of course tho' superior in* mental powers & cultivation *were on the same level as far as refinement goes – but I think in later life their intercourse with Mrs. Knight (who was very fond of and kind to them) improved them both & Aunt Jane was too clever not to put aside all possible signs of "common-ness" (if such an expression is allowable) & teach herself to be more refined, at least in intercourse with people in general. Both the Aunts (Cassandra and Jane) were brought up in the most complete ignorance of the World & its ways (I mean as to fashion &c) & if it had not been for Papa's marriage which* *brought them into Kent, & the kindness of Mrs. Knight, who used often to have one or the other of the sisters staying with her, they would have been, tho' not less clever and agreeable in themselves, very much below par as to good Society & its ways. If you hate all this I beg yr. pardon, but I felt it at my* pen's end, *& it chose to come along and speak its truth.*

These remarks are difficult to understand considering how close Fanny had once been to her aunt, and they make a rather sad footnote to the story of Jane Austen. However, it should perhaps be taken into account that Fanny, who was in the early stages of senility, was looking back as an old lady, with Victorian attitudes and sensibilities, on a different age long past.

10
Enduring Fame

Following the publication of the books written by the later generations of the Austen family, Jane's reputation and fame continued to flourish. The authors would have been delighted to know that the popularity of her novels, which were originally written to amuse herself and her family, has never waned.

The next wave of books about Jane Austen began in 1926 when Dr R. W. Chapman published a new edition of James Edward Austen-Leigh's Memoir, *using the text of 1871, with additional notes of his own. Six years later he published a collection of all the extant letters of Jane Austen. Some of these letters had previously been published only in part or with omissions and names suppressed. Dr Chapman published all the letters in full with additional brief notes. This book included a copy of a sketch of Jane by her sister, illustrations of significant places and plans of Steventon and Bath. It was republished in 1952 with the inclusion of five hitherto unpublished letters.*

In 1938 Elizabeth Jenkins published a biography of Jane Austen written with the aid of Dr Chapman's book and other unpublished family papers. Jenkins' very readable, highly illustrated work included literary criticism of the novels. It was acclaimed at the time as a 'classic biography' with the emphasis on Jane Austen as a woman of her time and revealing what is was like to be a parson's daughter in the late eighteenth and early nineteenth centuries.

In 1942 Austen Papers 1704–1856 *was published privately by Richard Arthur Austen-Leigh. This brought together all the letters and papers he had collected over a number of years, including correspondence between Revd George Austen and his relatives in Kent. Mr Austen-Leigh had apparently intended to use this material to revise and extend the 1913 book* Jane Austen, Her Life and Letters, A Family Record. *He did not complete this project but it was undertaken many years later by Deirdre Le Faye.* Jane Austen, A Family Record *was published in 1989 and filled in many of the remaining gaps in the knowledge of Jane Austen's life.*

A new edition of Jane Austen's letters, written using updated research, was published by Deirdre Le Faye in 1984. This incorporated fragments of letters which had come to light in the previous thirty years. This book, which includes extensive notes, biographical and topographical indices, is an excellent resource for students and authors.

Of the many biographies written in recent years Claire Tomalin's Jane Austen, A Life, *published in 1997, stands out. Tomalin portrays a very different person to the gentle, retiring, perfect creature of the early family memoirs. The tough worldly woman she describes had a far from ideal life, from which she sought escape in writing.*

In 2002 a new edition of the first biography of Jane Austen was published. J. E. Austen-Leigh, A Memoir of Jane Austen and Other Family Recollections, *introduced and edited by Kathryn Sutherland, also contains the recollections of Henry Austen, Anna Lefroy and Caroline Austen. This comprehensive work includes extensive, in-depth explanatory notes which are particularly useful for the academic reader.*

The interest in Jane Austen continues unabated in the twenty-first century. Despite the outpouring of books about her our knowledge is not complete. Very little is known, for example, about Jane's movements between May 1801 and September 1804 due to a gap in her surviving letters. It was during these years that Jane had a brief holiday romance in Devon. Cassandra Austen believed that her sister would have married the man concerned but, tragically, they heard of his dearth shortly after they returned home. The picture of Jane's life would be enhanced by more information about these lost years and particularly the tragic romance.

As long as Jane Austen's novels continue to be widely read the interest in her life will carry on. While this interest remains there will always be a market for books about her, a fact which would have astonished and amused the lady herself.

11
Jane Austen's Family and Friends

George Austen (father)

Born in 1731, George was the son of William Austen, a surgeon, and his wife Rebecca. When he was orphaned at the age of nine, George was provided for by his wealthy uncle Francis Austen, a successful lawyer, of Sevenoaks in Kent.

George went to Tonbridge School where he won an open scholarship to St. John's College, Oxford. He gained B.A. and M.A. degrees and was ordained in 1754.

In 1764 George married Cassandra Leigh at Walcot Church in Bath. The Austens set up home in Deane, Hampshire and George became rector of the neighbouring village of Steventon. This living was given to him by a wealthy distant cousin Thomas Knight. The Austen family moved to Steventon Rectory in 1768. In 1773 George's uncle Francis bought him the living of Deane.

George supplemented his stipend and income from glebe lands by teaching a few sons of the local aristocracy and gentry. He also educated his own sons and tutored his daughters after their formal education ended. He encouraged Jane in her writing and attempted to get the first version of *Pride and Prejudice* published.

George Austen retired to Bath with his wife and daughters in 1801 and died there at the age of seventy-four. He is buried in Walcot Church, Bath.

Cassandra Austen (mother)

Born in 1737, Cassandra was the daughter of Revd Thomas Leigh and his wife Jane. Thomas Leigh was descended from an old, illustrious family and was related to the Leighs of Stoneleigh Abbey in Warwickshire. He was a former fellow of All Souls College, Oxford and was vicar of Harpsden in Oxfordshire.

Cassandra married George Austen in 1764. As well as bringing up a large family Mrs Austen looked after her husband's pupils who boarded at Steventon Rectory. She taught her daughters all the traditional female accomplishments, including sewing and handwriting. Mrs Austen enjoyed writing charades and poetry. Her family believed that Jane inherited her mother's writing talent and wit.

After her husband's death in Bath in 1805 Mrs Austen, her daughters and Martha Lloyd, who had joined their household, moved a number of times. They eventually settled in Chawton, Hampshire in a cottage which belonged to Edward Austen.

Mrs Austen survived Jane by ten years, despite regular bouts of ill-health throughout her life. She died in Chawton in 1827 at the age of eighty-seven. She is buried there in the churchyard of St Nicholas Church.

James Austen (brother)

Born in 1765, James was the eldest child of George and Cassandra Austen. He was educated by his father before going to St John's College, Oxford in 1779 on a Founder's Kin Scholarship. He was awarded B.A. and M.A. degrees and became a Fellow of St John's College.

James was an able writer who founded a weekly periodical at Oxford called The Loiterer. He helped his father in educating his sisters after their formal education ended.

In 1787 James was ordained and began his clerical career as curate of Overton in Hampshire. In 1792 he married Anne Mathew, daughter of General Edward Mathew of Overton, and became his father's curate at Deane. Anne died in 1795 when their only child Anna was two years old.

In 1797 James married Mary Lloyd, a friend of his sisters. James and Mary had two children, James Edward born in 1798 and Caroline born in 1805. In 1801, when his father retired, James took over as rector of Steventon and Deane.

Despite his own ill-health, James visited Jane in her final weeks but was too unwell to attend her funeral. He died in 1819, having outlived his sister by only two and a half years. He is buried in the churchyard of St

Nicholas Church, Steventon and the church contains a commemorative tablet to him erected by his son.

George Austen (brother)

Born in 1766, George was the second child of George and Cassandra Austen.

George suffered from epilepsy and learning disabilities and was probably deaf as well. He was looked after by a family in their home in the village of Monk Sherborne, Hampshire. Although the Austens made financial provision for George and visited him, he was never really a part of their lives. He remained in the care of others for the rest of his life and died in 1838, at the age of seventy-two. George is buried in an unmarked grave in the churchyard of All Saints Church, Monk Sherborne.

Edward Austen (later Knight) (brother)

Born in 1767, Edward was the third child of George and Cassandra Austen. He was educated by his father until the age of sixteen when he was adopted by Thomas Knight II, a wealthy kinsman of his father, and his wife Catherine. The Knights, who were childless, had grown fond of Edward and wanted to make him their heir. He was sent on a Grand Tour of Europe as part of his preparation for his future role as a country gentleman.

In 1791 Edward married Elizabeth Bridges, daughter of Sir Brook Bridges of Goodnestone Park, near Wingham, Kent. He inherited the Knight estates in Kent and Hampshire in 1797. As well as running his estates he took on the roles of Justice of the Peace, High Sheriff and leader of the local militia during the Napoleonic Wars. Jane Austen enjoyed many visits to Godmersham House, Edward's home in Kent, and used this first-hand experience of country house life in her novels.

After the premature death of his wife, following the birth of her eleventh child, Edward carried on with his work supported by his daughter Fanny. In 1812, on the death of his adoptive mother, Edward and his children took the name of Knight, a condition of his inheritance.

Edward provided his mother and sisters with a home in Chawton, Hampshire. He died in 1852 at the age of eighty-five and is buried beside his wife in the Knight family vault in Godmersham Church.

Henry Austen (brother)

Born in 1771, Henry was the fourth child of George and Cassandra Austen. He was particularly close to Jane and was described as her 'favourite brother'.

Henry was educated by his father, who regarded him as the most promising of his sons. He followed his brother James to St John's College, Oxford in 1788. He was awarded B.A. and M.A. degrees.

Despite his early promise, Henry turned out to be the least stable of the Austen brothers and changed his occupation a number of times. He married his widowed cousin Eliza de Feuillide in 1797. He supported Jane in her writing and acted as her representative in negotiations with publishers.

Henry's wife died in 1813 and at the end of 1815 he suffered a life-threatening illness himself. Jane helped to nurse him through this illness and it is believed that the strain this caused her contributed to the decline in her own health. Following the failure of Henry's banking business in 1816 he took holy orders. He became curate of Chawton and acquired a reputation as an earnest Evangelical preacher.

Following Jane's death Henry acted as her literary executor. He wrote the first biographical information of his sister which was published with her posthumous novels in 1818.

In 1820 Henry married Eleanor Jackson and succeeded his brother as rector of Steventon. He later held other clerical positions and worked as a schoolmaster. Henry died at Tunbridge Wells, Kent in 1850, at the age of seventy-eight. He is buried at Woodbury Park Cemetery in Tunbridge Wells.

Cassandra Austen (sister)

Born in 1773, Cassandra was the fifth child of George and Cassandra Austen. Cassandra was very close to her sister, who adored her from early childhood, and always looked up to her as 'wiser and better' than herself. They became inseparable.

In 1783 Cassandra went to Oxford with her cousin Jane Cooper to be tutored by a Mrs Cawley. Jane, despite her tender years, went with them as she would have been heartbroken at being separated from her sister. This period away from home ended when the Austen sisters caught putrid fever and Jane nearly died.

Cassandra, Jane and their cousin went to the Abbey School in Reading in 1785 where they were taught female accomplishments. Formal education ended for the Austen sisters in 1787 when they returned home and their father took over their education.

In 1792 Cassandra became engaged to Tom Fowle, a former pupil of her father. Tom went abroad in 1796 as chaplain to a regiment bound for the West Indies, with the intention of saving money on which to get married. He died there of yellow fever just before he was due to return home. Cassandra remained unmarried.

The Austen sisters lived together throughout their adult lives. Cassandra nursed Jane through her final illness and accompanied her to Winchester to seek the help of an eminent doctor. She was with Jane when she died on 18 July 1817.

Cassandra survived Jane by twenty-eight years. She lived at Chawton Cottage for the rest of her life, devoting her time to her family and charity work. She died in 1845, at the age of seventy-two, and is buried beside her mother in the churchyard of St Nicholas Church, Chawton.

Francis Austen (brother)

Born in 1774, Francis (known as Frank) was the sixth child of George and Cassandra Austen. He was educated by his father until the age of twelve when he entered the Royal Naval Academy in Portsmouth. Frank rose rapidly through the ranks of the navy and was described by Nelson as 'an excellent young man'. He was disappointed not to have taken part in the Battle of Trafalgar as he was engaged in duties elsewhere.

In 1806 Frank married Mary Gibson. He and his wife shared a home in Southampton with his mother, sisters and Martha Lloyd from 1806 to 1809. He wrote regularly to his mother and sisters while he was away at sea and lived near them when they were in Chawton. Frank's wife died in 1823 during the birth of their eleventh child. Five years later he married his sisters' friend Martha Lloyd.

Frank finished his illustrious career in the navy as Admiral of the Fleet. He outlived Jane by forty-eight years and survived all his siblings and his second wife. He died in 1865 at the age of ninety-one and is buried in the churchyard of Wymering Church, Sussex.

Charles Austen (brother)

Born in 1779, Charles was the eighth and youngest child of George and Cassandra Austen. He was educated by his father until the age of twelve when he entered the Royal Naval Academy in Portsmouth, following in the footsteps of his brother Frank. Charles rose through the ranks of the navy and became a commander in 1804. While he was at sea he wrote regularly to his mother and sisters. The latter referred to him as 'our own particular little brother'.

In 1807 Charles married Fanny Palmer, who died seven years later following the birth of their fourth child. In 1820 Charles married Harriet Palmer, the sister of his first wife, with whom he had four more children.

Charles ended his naval career in the post of Commander-in-Chief in the East Indies. He died of cholera on board H.M.S Pluto off Prome, Burma in 1852, at the age of seventy-three, having outlived Jane by thirty-five years. He is buried at Trimcomalee, Ceylon.

Mary Austen (sister-in-law)

Born in 1771, Mary was the youngest daughter of Revd Noyes Lloyd and his wife Martha. She became a friend of Cassandra and Jane Austen after moving into Deane Parsonage in 1789. In 1797 Mary married the widowed James Austen. Mary and James had two children – (James) Edward born in 1798 and Caroline born in 1805.

Mary helped Cassandra to nurse Jane in the final weeks of her life.

On the death of her husband in 1819 Mary and Caroline left Steventon Rectory and moved to Newtown, Berkshire. They later moved to a house in Speen, Berkshire which Edward bought for them after he inherited the Leigh estate.

Mary died at Speen in 1843 and is buried beside her husband in the churchyard of St Nicholas Church, Steventon.

Elizabeth Austen (sister-in-law)

Born in 1773, Elizabeth was the daughter of Sir Brook Bridges and his wife Fanny, of Goodnestone Park, near Wingham, Kent. She married Edward Austen in 1791 and moved with him to Godmersham House, near Canterbury, Kent when he in took over the Knight estates in 1797.

As mistress of Godmersham House, Elizabeth played an important role in helping her husband to run their grand country house and estates, and supported him in his roles in the local community. She was also involved in philanthropic work.

Elizabeth died at the age of thirty-four shortly after the birth of her eleventh child. She is buried beside her husband in the Knight vaults in Godmersham church.

Elizabeth Austen (sister-in-law)

Born in India in 1761, Elizabeth (known as Eliza) was the daughter of Revd George Austen's sister Philadelphia and her husband Tysoe Saul Hancock. She was educated in Paris.

In 1781 Eliza married a French nobleman Jean Capotte, Comte de Feuillide, with whom she had one son. She was sent by her husband to England to escape the French Revolution and took refuge with the Austen family at Steventon Rectory. Eliza developed a close friendship with her cousin Jane.

Eliza was widowed in 1794 when her husband lost his life during the Reign of Terror in France. Three years later she married her cousin Henry Austen. They lived in London, where Jane frequently visited them and enjoyed the pleasures of the capital and London society with them.

Jane helped her brother to nurse Eliza through a long terminal illness. Eliza died in 1813 and is buried in Hampstead parish churchyard in London.

Mary Austen (sister-in-law)

Born in 1785, Mary was the daughter of John Gibson of Ramsgate, Kent. She married Frank Austen in 1806 and became one of the best-loved of Jane Austen's sisters-in law.

Mary shared a home with her mother-in-law, sisters-in-law and Martha Lloyd in Southampton from 1806 to 1809. She later lived at Alton near Jane's home in Chawton.

Mary died in 1823 during the birth of her eleventh child.

Frances Austen (sister-in-law)

Born in 1790, Frances (known as Fanny) was the daughter of John Grove Palmer, the former Attorney General of Bermuda. She married Charles Austen in 1807. Fanny died in 1814 following the birth of their fourth child.

Fanny Austen (*later* Knight) (niece)

Born in 1793, Fanny was the eldest child of Edward and Elizabeth Austen. From childhood she enjoyed a close relationship with her Aunt Jane, who described her in 1808 as 'almost another sister'.

When her mother died suddenly in 1808 Fanny took over the heavy burden of running Godmersham House, caring for her siblings and supporting her father. Jane became a confidante and advisor to her motherless niece.

In 1820 Fanny married, as his second wife, Sir Edward Knatchbull of Merstham-le-Hatch, Kent, who was M.P. for the county for twenty-six years.

Later in life Fanny, probably due to her status in society as a politician's wife, became embarrassed about the humble origins of her Austen forebears and made disparaging remarks about her aunts. When asked by her cousin to contribute her memories to his biography of Jane Austen Fanny was not very forthcoming. In her final years she devoted herself to her family and charity work.

Fanny died in 1882 and is buried in the chapel of the church of St Peter and St Paul, Lymsted, Kent.

Anna Austen (*later* Lefroy) (niece)

Born in 1793, Jane Anna Elizabeth (known as Anna) was the only child of James Austen and his first wife Anne. Anna's mother died when she was two years old and her father sent her to Steventon Rectory to be comforted and cared for by her grandparents and aunts. Anna's closeness to Jane dated from this time. Jane was very supportive of Anna as she grew up and encouraged her in her attempts to write novels. She became her trusted confidante and advisor.

In 1814 Anna married Ben Lefroy, the son of Jane's late friend Anne Lefroy. In 1815 Anna and Ben moved to Alton, Hampshire, near Jane's home in Chawton. They had seven children.

After the death of her husband in 1829 Anna's life became a hard struggle against poverty and ill-health. She helped her half-brother Edward to gather material for his biography of their aunt. Anna died in 1872.

James Edward Austen (*later* Austen-Leigh) (nephew)

Born in 1798, James Edward (known as Edward) was the son of James Austen and his second wife Mary. He was educated at Winchester School and Exeter College, Oxford. Edward enjoyed a close relationship with his Aunt Jane who encouraged him in his attempt to write a novel. He was the youngest mourner at her funeral.

Edward was ordained in 1820. In 1823 he married Emma Smith and was appointed curate of the church in Tring, Hertfordshire. Edward and Emma had ten children.

In 1836 Edward inherited the Berkshire estate of his great-aunt Jane Leigh Perrot and added the name of Leigh to his own. He became vicar of Bray in Berkshire in 1852. In the 1860s Edward began to gather material for a biography of his aunt. Profits from the sale of the biography were used to pay for a memorial brass tablet to be placed beside Jane's grave in Winchester Cathedral. Edward died at Bray in 1874.

Caroline Austen (niece)

Born in 1805, Caroline was the daughter of James Austen and his second wife Mary. Caroline had a close relationship with Jane and remembered her as a kind, affectionate and playful aunt who helped her to write stories as a child.

Caroline had an excellent memory and made a considerable contribution to her brother's biography of their aunt. Her memories were published by the Jane Austen Society in 1952, as My Aunt Jane Austen, A Memoir.

After her father's death in 1819 Caroline and her mother left Steventon Rectory and moved to Newtown in Berkshire. They later moved to a house in Speen in Berkshire bought for them by Edward after he inherited the Leigh estates.

Caroline did not marry but, like her aunt, she acquired numerous nephews and nieces. Towards the end of her life Caroline moved to Sussex to keep house for two unmarried nephews. She died in 1880.

Francis Austen (great-uncle)

Born in 1698, Francis was the uncle and benefactor of Revd George Austen. He was a successful solicitor in Sevenoaks, Kent. In 1793 Francis purchased the living of Deane for his nephew. Jane visited her great-uncle on her first trip to Kent in 1788.

Francis Austen died in 1791.

Philadelphia Hancock (aunt)

Born in 1730,Philadelphia was the sister of Revd George Austen. Little is known about her until she went to India in 1752, presumably in search of a husband. She met and married Tysoe Saul Hancock, who worked for the East India Company, and spent her early married life in India. The Hancocks had one daughter Eliza, who was born in 1761.

Philadelphia and Eliza moved to France for Eliza to be educated and then to England. They frequently stayed with the Austen family at Steventon Rectory. Philadelphia helped to bring up her grandson. She died in London in 1792.

Jane Cooper (aunt)

Born in 1736, Jane Cooper was the sister of Mrs Cassandra Austen and the wife of Edward Cooper, an Anglican clergyman.

It is likely that Jane acquired her early knowledge of Bath during her visits to the Coopers at their home there. The Coopers had two children, Edward who was born in 1770 and Jane who was born in 1771.

Jane Cooper died in 1783 from putrid fever which she caught from her nieces Cassandra and Jane.

Jane Cooper (*later* Williams) (cousin)

Born in 1771, Jane was the daughter of Jane and Edward Cooper. She became close to the Austen sisters from the time she accompanied them to Oxford to be tutored. It was a letter from Jane to Mrs Austen, relaying news of her cousins' illness, which saved Jane Austen from dying of putrid fever.

Jane married Thomas Williams, a captain in the Royal Navy, in 1792. Her tragic early death in 1798, as a result of a carriage accident, greatly grieved Jane Austen.

Samuel Cooke (godfather)

Samuel Cooke, Jane Austen's godfather, was the husband of Cassandra (née Leigh), a cousin of Jane Austen's mother. He was the rector of Great Bookham in Surrey.

Jane's knowledge of the Surrey countryside, which she used for the setting of Emma, was acquired on visits to her godfather and his family.

Thomas and Catherine Knight (adoptive parents of Edward Austen)

Thomas Knight was the son of Thomas Knight I, the wealthy kinsman of Revd George Austen, who presented him with the living of Steventon.

In 1793 the Knights, who were childless, adopted Edward Austen and made him their heir. Three years after her husband's death in 1794 Mrs Knight handed over the extensive Knight properties and estates to Edward Austen.

Catherine Knight was very fond of Jane Austen and helped her with gifts of money as well as taking an interest in her writing. She died in 1812.

James and Jane Leigh-Perrot (uncle and aunt)

Born in 1735, James was the brother of Mrs Cassandra Austen. He and his wife Jane had homes in Bath and Berkshire.

In 1799 Jane Leigh-Perrot was falsely accused of theft and committed to jail awaiting trial. Mrs Austen offered for one or both of her daughters to stay with Mrs Leigh-Perrot during her imprisonment – an offer which was declined. Mrs Leigh-Perrot was later acquitted.

On first moving to Bath in 1801, the Austens lived with the Leigh-Perrots. Jane was close to her uncle and accompanied him on his daily walks to the Pump Room to take the waters.

When the wealthy James Leigh-Perrot died in 1817 Mrs Austen was distressed to discover that no immediate provision had been made for her or her children in his will. This was particularly upsetting in view of her straitened circumstances.

Jane Leigh-Perrot died in 1836 leaving her estate to her husband's great-nephew Edward Austen.

Martha Lloyd (friend)

Born in 1765, Martha was the daughter of the Revd Noyes Lloyd and his wife Martha. She became a friend of the Austen sisters after moving into Deane Parsonage in 1789 with her widowed mother and sister Mary. In 1792 the Lloyds moved to Ibthorp near Hurstbourne Tarrant in Hampshire.

Following her mother's death in 1805 Martha joined Mrs Austen's household in Bath and moved with them to Southampton and then to Chawton in Hampshire.

In 1828 Martha married the widowed Frank Austen and moved with him to Portsmouth. She died in 1843.

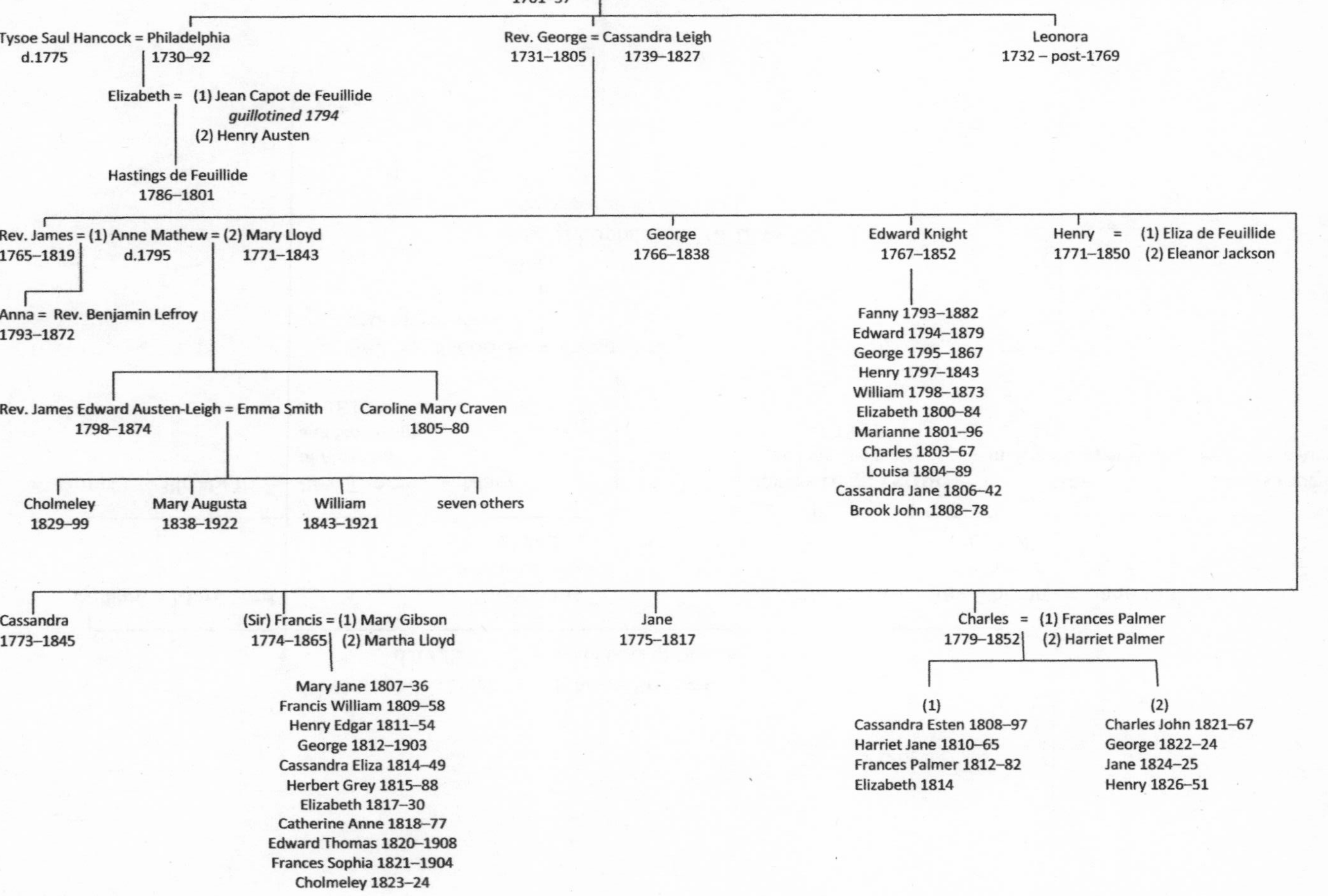
1701–37
Tysoe Saul Hancock = Philadelphia
d.1775 1730–92
Rev. George = Cassandra Leigh
1731–1805 1739–1827
Leonora
1732 – post-1769
Elizabeth = (1) Jean Capot de Feuillide
guillotined 1794
(2) Henry Austen
Hastings de Feuillide
1786–1801
Rev. James = (1) Anne Mathew = (2) Mary Lloyd
1765–1819 d.1795 1771–1843
Anna = Rev. Benjamin Lefroy
1793–1872
Rev. James Edward Austen-Leigh = Emma Smith
1798–1874
Caroline Mary Craven
1805–80
Cholmeley
1829–99
Mary Augusta
1838–1922
William
1843–1921
seven others
George
1766–1838
Edward Knight
1767–1852
Fanny 1793–1882
Edward 1794–1879
George 1795–1867
Henry 1797–1843
William 1798–1873
Elizabeth 1800–84
Marianne 1801–96
Charles 1803–67
Louisa 1804–89
Cassandra Jane 1806–42
Brook John 1808–78
Henry = (1) Eliza de Feuillide
1771–1850 (2) Eleanor Jackson
Cassandra
1773–1845
(Sir) Francis = (1) Mary Gibson
1774–1865 (2) Martha Lloyd
Mary Jane 1807–36
Francis William 1809–58
Henry Edgar 1811–54
George 1812–1903
Cassandra Eliza 1814–49
Herbert Grey 1815–88
Elizabeth 1817–30
Catherine Anne 1818–77
Edward Thomas 1820–1908
Frances Sophia 1821–1904
Cholmeley 1823–24
Jane
1775–1817
Charles = (1) Frances Palmer
1779–1852 (2) Harriet Palmer
(1)
Cassandra Esten 1808–97
Harriet Jane 1810–65
Frances Palmer 1812–82
Elizabeth 1814
(2)
Charles John 1821–67
George 1822–24
Jane 1824–25
Henry 1826–51

Austen Family Tree

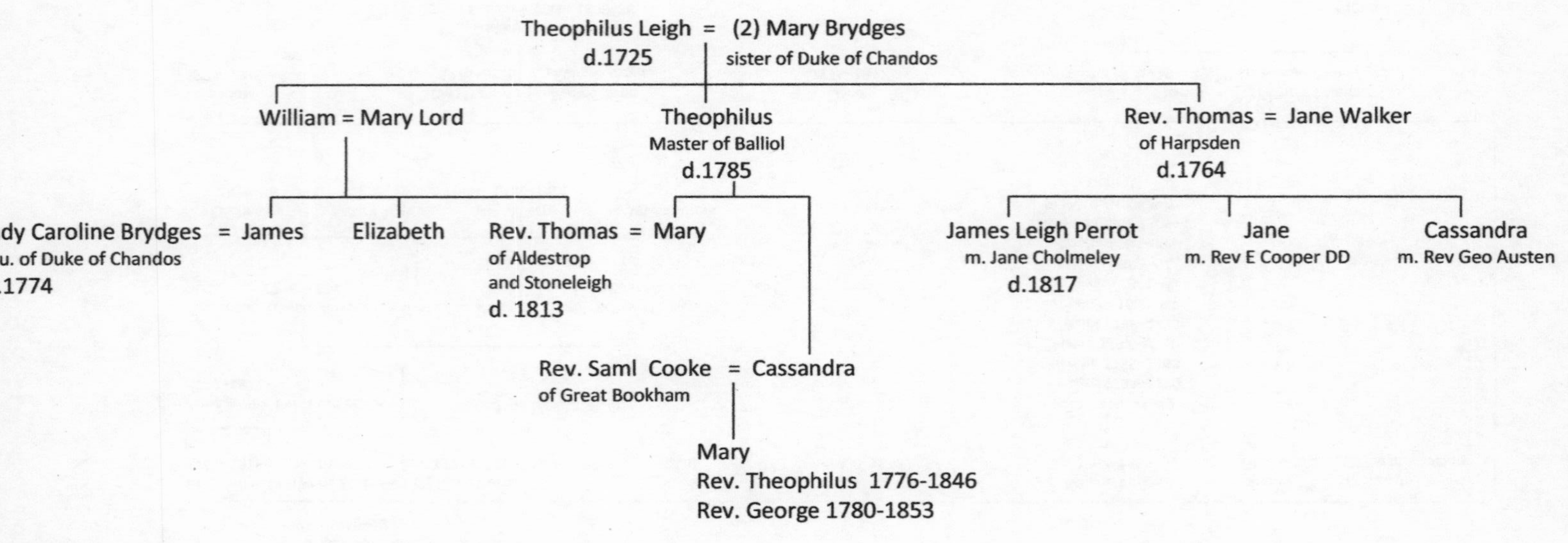

Leigh Family Tree

Bibliography

Amy, Helen, Jane Austen *(Amberley Publishing, 2013)*

Austen-Leigh, William, Austen-Leigh, Richard Arthur, Le Faye, Deirdre, Jane Austen, A Family Record *(The British Library, 1989)*

Chapman. R. W. (Editor), Jane Austen, Selected Letters, *1796-1817 (Oxford University Press, 1985)*

Le Faye, Deirdre (Editor), Jane Austen's Letters *(Oxford University Press, 1995)*

Sutherland, Kathryn (Editor), J. E. Austen-Leigh, A Memoir of Jane Austen and Other Family Recollections *(Oxford University Press, 2002)*

Tomalin, Claire, Jane Austen, A Life *(Viking, 1997)*

Acknowledgements

The author would like to thank the following:
The Jane Austen Society for permission to reprint *My Aunt Jane Austen, A Memoir* by Caroline Austen.
The owners of Anna Lefroy's letter to James Edward Austen Leigh dated December 1864 for permission to publish it.
The staff of the Hampshire County Record Office for their assistance.
The staff of the Kent History and Library Centre for their assistance and for permission to publish extracts from *Fanny Knight's Diary*.